Information Age Economy

Information Age Economy

F. Rose
The Economics, Concept, and Design
of Information Intermediaries
1999, ISBN 3-7908-1168-8

S. Weber
Information Technology in Supplier Network
2001, ISBN 3-7908-1395-8

K. Geihs, W. König and F. von Westarp (Eds.)
Networks
2002, ISBN 3-7908-1449-0

F. von Westarp
Modeling Software Markets
2003, ISBN 3-7908-0009-0

D. Kundisch
New Strategies for Financial Services Firms
2003, ISBN 3-7908-0066-X

T. Weitzel
Economics of Standards
in Information Networks
2004, ISBN 3-7908-0076-7

Jens Dibbern

The Sourcing of Application Software Services

Empirical Evidence of Cultural, Industry and Functional Differences

With 21 Figures
and 27 Tables

Physica-Verlag
A Springer-Verlag Company

Dr. Jens Dibbern
Universität Mannheim
Lehrstuhl für Wirtschaftsinformatik I
Schloss S 135
68131 Mannheim
Germany
dibbern@uni-mannheim.de

ISBN 3-7908-0217-4 Physica-Verlag Heidelberg New York

Zugl. Diss., Univ. Bayreuth, 2003

Cataloging-in-Publication Data applied for
A catalog record for this book is available from the Library of Congress.
Bibliographic information published by Die Deutsche Bibliothek
Die Deutsche Bibliothek lists this publication in the Deutsche Nationalbibliografie; detailed bibliographic data is available in the Internet at *http://dnb.ddb.de*.

Physica-Verlag is a part of Springer Science+Business Media

springeronline.com

Printed in Germany

Softcover Design: Erich Kirchner, Heidelberg

SPIN 10998564 88/3130 – 5 4 3 2 1 0 – Printed on acid-free paper

To my Parents

Preface

Outsourcing has been one of the most controversially discussed topics in the information systems (IS) management field within the last decade. While some organizations have been quick to adopt outsourcing, others have been slow to consider this sourcing option. Still others have evaluated outsourcing but adopted insourcing instead. In other words, organizations appear to behave totally different in the sourcing of their IS tasks. There are no generally accepted practices, e.g., outsourcing certain types of IS services while keeping others in-house. The sourcing decision appears to be highly dependent on the specific situation of each organization.

Recognizing the unique context of each organization, this book presents an empirically tested model that can be used to analyze the options of IS insourcing versus outsourcing of every organization. The model takes into account the unique IS requirements and the differences between insourcing and outsourcing at both the individual (i.e., worker) and the organizational level.

The development of the model is guided by the following question: *Why do some organizations wholly or partially outsource particular IS functions while others keep them in-house*? This research question, is closely related to one of the most fundamental questions in economics and business administration: The question of *why firms exist at all*, i.e. why not all of the multitude of tasks that are required to produce certain products and services are performed by individual companies (or persons) who deal with each other based on contractual arrangements – as it was proposed by Adam Smith in his 'Wealth of Nations' in 1776.

Obviously, there are certain situations where economic actors find it useful or advantageous to organize themselves under one common umbrella, called organization (e.g., a company with an independent legal form), rather than building a net of contractual relationships between each other. In searching for such a general *theory of the* (existence of the) *firm*, it soon became apparent that there are various different explanatory approaches in the literature and that none of them appears to satisfactorily and exclusively explain why organizations exist at all.

It is therefore of little surprise that research on IS outsourcing turned out to be very fragmented as well. Many different theoretical lenses have been applied to address the factors and processes that explain why firms outsource IS functions. This, accompanied with a number of issues that make the context even more complex, like the fact that particular theories were applied differently, that different research approaches were used to examine sourcing decisions and relationships, that the unit of analysis (i.e., the IS function) was treated very differently, and that the phenomenon was studied in various organizational settings (e.g., different countries and business types, such as industries and public versus private organizations) has lead to a lack of generally agreed upon knowledge about the IS outsourcing phenomenon.

Accordingly, it is no wonder that practitioners are faced with a high level of uncertainty about the sourcing of IS functions and its wider implications.

I therefore felt that the time was ripe to integrate existing research on the theory of the firm, on IS outsourcing, and on general decision making, and to come up with a comprehensive model. This model addresses the needs of two *practitioner* groups. First, it helps client organizations to make better IS sourcing decisions. Second, it shows vendors what they need to do in order to influence the evaluative appraisal of potential and existing customers towards outsourcing particular IS functions.

Readers should recognize, however, that this model on IS sourcing is specifically developed to explain under which circumstances *application services,* including both the *development and maintenance* of software applications, are outsourced. In other words, the model would need to be adjusted if using it to explain why other IS functions, like systems operations, the design and maintenance of the network infrastructure, or even non-IS business functions, may be outsourced. In particular, readers need to recognize the *service nature* of the application development and maintenance work which often requires collaborative efforts between various stakeholders including users, different groups of IS professionals as well as IS and non-IS managers. Recognizing the focus of this study is particularly important when considering the empirical findings about the validity of the IS sourcing model.

The IS sourcing model is empirically tested across two countries (Germany *versus* USA), two industries (Finance *versus* Machinery), and, as already indicated, two IS functions (Application Development *versus* Maintenance). Altogether, data about the sourcing behavior of 180 companies was gathered via a mailed questionnaire survey and systematically analyzed.

Some of the lessons learned from the model testing appear to be generally applicable, no matter what country, what industry, and what particular application service is looked at. Others are valid only for Germany or the US, for the Machinery or Finance Industry, and for the development or maintenance of software applications. This means that the sourcing context has a profound impact on the IS sourcing decision – an issue wildly ignored in previous contributions on IS outsourcing.

I hope that both researchers and practitioners will benefit from the theoretical and empirical insights on the IS sourcing phenomenon provided in this book, and I wish you happy reading!

Acknowledgment

I would like to acknowledge with great appreciation the contributions and assistance of many individuals that supported me in the research process that finally resulted in this book. First and foremost, I would like to thank my academic advisor Prof. Dr. Armin Heinzl. During my interaction with him as a student, I discovered my enjoyment in doing research and it was Armin Heinzl who motivated me to continue my research with the creation of a dissertation at his department. From then on, he thoughtfully guided my research efforts, encouraged me to write a proposal at the *Deutsche Forschungsgemeinschaft (DFG)* and to submit papers to conferences and journals. Moreover, he enabled my visiting scholarship at the University of Houston, Texas, which gave me the opportunity to get to know two outstanding U.S. academics that turned out to become highly influential on my research. They are Prof. Rudy Hirschheim, who recently moved on to Louisiana State University and Prof. Wynne Chin from UH. My conversations with Rudy have broadened my research perspective considerably. Although Rudy never told me that I should try alternative empirical research methods beside the quantitative approach, reading his research articles and talking to him nevertheless motivated me to study the IS sourcing decision from a different perspective: that of a participant observer that tries to understand IS sourcing by conducting interviews with decision makers in twelve German companies. Today, I can say that the knowledge that I gained through this qualitative assessment was so valuable that I would never approach an empirical research project without spending a significant amount of time in the field. On the other hand, no person had a greater influence on my understanding of causal model building and testing than Wynne Chin. He was able to explain to me how theorizing, measurement, and statistical data analysis techniques relate to each other – an issue that I could not find in any text book. A forth academic who deserves special mentioning is Prof. Dr. Kühlmann, whose dedicated comments on my questionnaire helped me to improve my measurement instruments. Beside Armin Heinzl and Wynne Chin, he also took the burden to serve at my dissertation committee and to review my work. I greatly acknowledge the extra effort that this has caused for the three of them.

Beyond these credits to my academic advisors, I would like to express my gratitude to a number of people that also supported me during my "dissertation time". First, I thank my colleagues Birte Autzen, Franz Rothlauf, Frederick Loos, Tobias Grosche, and Torsten Paulussen as well as my former colleagues Christof Göbel, Lars Brehm, Jürgen Gerstacker, Michael Zapf, Sigrid Mandel, Stefan Hocke, Thomas Schoberth, and Wolfgang Güttler for not only being helpful and supportive in all matters of daily work life, but also in establishing a social environment that has made my time in Bayreuth and Mannheim very enjoyable. Second, I thank all of the students that worked for and with me. In supporting me in organizing the *2nd International Con-*

ference on Outsourcing of Information Services, held in Bayreuth in 2001, I am particularly grateful to Andreas Gaube, Jan Herzhoff, Stephan Löffler, and Katharina Pfeuffer. In the process of gathering the data for my dissertation, I am much obliged to Bastian Popp, Katrin Mullahy, Nicole Oemus, Stefan Wittenbeck, and Timo Berger. Third, I would like to thank Alexander Georgius, Anja Schumann, Silvia Leibbrandt and Christian Neuner for greatly illuminating my research. In this realm, I am also grateful to Jens Arndt, and Jessica Winkler for being conscientious and creative editors of part of my work. Fourth, I would like to thank the team at the Institute for Small and Medium Sized Firms at the University of Bayreuth (BF/M) for their support. Fifth, I highly appreciate the discussions that I had with Peter Glänzel, the former CIO from Heidelberger Druck, and his efforts in reactivating his network of relationships with other IT managers to stimulate my survey response rate.

The price that my partner Sabine paid for this book was high. Nevertheless, she always exercised patience and supported me wherever she could. Her pragmatic advise often saved me from loosing time and space. This is just one of the reasons that make life with her so wonderful.

Finally, I would like to express my gratitude and indebtedness to my parents. The book is dedicated to them.

Mannheim, February 2004 Jens Dibbern

Table of Contents

1 Introduction

1.1 Problem Statement

When in the 60s some organizations began to outsource their information systems (IS) function to external service providers, academics and practitioners hardly paid attention.[1] This is of little surprise as the awareness of the importance of IS was generally quite low at that time. The role of IS within organizations was mostly limited to the processing of mass data in administrative business functions, like accounting or payroll (Heinzl, 1996).

However, with an increasing need for information and the arrival of more advanced informations technologies (IT), organizations were faced with a growing complexity of their IS tasks. They began to realize that they could also use the advantages of IT in other business functions that go beyond standardized administrative processes. To meet the increased IS requirements, one of the logical responses was to divide the overall IS task into partial tasks and to delegate them to specialized subunits, teams, or individual workers. Accordingly, partial IS functions have emerged, like (1) the development and maintenance of application software, (2) the design and maintenance of telecommunication systems and networks, (3) the operation of data centers, (4) the provision of user support services, and (4) the overall IS planning and management (Mertens and Knolmayer, 1998; Teng, et al., 1995).

Paralleling this trend towards an increasing division of labour in the IS field, the importance of IS has increased significantly. In most organizations, IS has been established as an independent business function. Moreover, in the 80s, the message has spread out that IS can help organizations to realize competitive advantages (Ives and Learmonth, 1984; McFarlan and McKenney, 1983; Mertens and Plattflaut, 1986). In this phase, organizational issues were mostly limited to the internal situation, e.g., whether to centralize or to decentralize IS functions (King, 1983). Hardly any organization thought about handing over its IS functions to third parties.

It therefore created quite a stir in the IS community, when in 1989 Eastman Kodak announced that it was outsourcing its IS function to IBM, DEC and Businessland. Never before had such a well-known organization, where IS was considered to be a strategic asset, turned the IS function over to third party providers (Applegate and Montealegre, 1991). While this first "mega deal" (500 billion US$) served as a starting signal for additional several billion dollar outsourcing deals in the USA, other countries like Germany still stay reluctant in signing outsourcing contracts in comparable dimensions. Certainly, the trend of IS outsourcing has been growing in Germany at rates between 10% and 20% within the last ten years as well (IDC, 1998),

---

1 One remarkable exception is the study by Heinrich (1969).

however, the direct comparison shows: recognizing the economic ratio of both countries and their expenditures for IT, the USA is spending three times more money on IS outsourcing than Germany (IDC, 1999; OECD, 2000).

These significant differences in overall IS outsourcing, however, do not allow any general conclusion about the outsourcing behavior in both countries. Not only the degree of outsourcing differs from organization to organization – within countries and particular industries – but also the area. Today, most organizations that decide to outsource seem to prefer a selective approach, where only particular IS functions are transferred wholly or partially to legally independent service providers (Apte, et al., 1997; Barthélemy and Geyer, 2001; Dibbern and Heinzl, 2001; Lacity and Hirschheim, 1993a; Lacity, et al., 1996; Teng, et al., 1995). Recognizing this phenomenon, first comparative descriptive studies between Japan, Finland and the USA (Apte, et al., 1997), as well as between Germany and France (Barthélemy and Geyer, 2001) have shown that countries tend to differ in the amount of money that they spend on the outsourcing of particular IS functions, too. Hence, it is very likely that similar functional differences do exist between Germany and the USA.

In summarizing these observations, two conclusions may be drawn. First, the totally heterogeneous behavior of organizations *within* countries and industries indicates that an organization's sourcing (insourcing versus outsourcing) behavior highly depends on its individual situation and how it responds to its environment. Second, the differences *between* nations suggest that country specific factors may impact an organization's decision to insource or outsource its IS functions.

Both arguments, however, seem to be in partial contradiction to each other. Why should country specific factors play an important role in IS sourcing, when organizations within countries behave totally different? There need to be factors that differ both between countries and between organizations. Legal and institutional surroundings do not necessarily meet these requirements, since they are equal for all organizations within countries and therefore fail to explain heterogeneous behavior within countries.[2]

More promising are country specific factors that represent overall behavioral patterns and attitudes of employees and managers of organizations. Cross-cultural studies have found empirical support for these cultural dimensions to differ across countries. For example, different studies indicate that employees of US organizations show highly individual behavioral patterns and attitudes, while Germany tends to be more collectivist (Hofstede, 1983b; Kuchinke, 1999; Trompenaars and Hamden-Turner, 1994). It has to be considered, however, that those cultural indices are based on statistical averages. Therefore, the particular instances of the cultural dimensions generally vary among organizations within countries. Although organizational culture has been suggested to be treated separately from national culture (Hofstede, et al., 1990), the dimensions used to study both cultural groups partially

2 In Germany special labor rules may serve as an example (Koffka, 1997).

overlap. Accordingly, cultural differences in the behavior of employees from organizations could contribute both to explain differences between countries and between organizations.

While the potential influence of cultural issues on IS sourcing has largely been ignored in previous outsourcing studies, research at the organizational level has already reached a very advanced state. During the last ten years, a number of research studies have been undertaken to explore the reasons for IS outsourcing. They have primarily been originated in the Anglo-American speech area and show a considerable methodological and theoretical range and depth. Especially conspicuous are the preponderance of empirical studies and the large number of reference theories that have been applied to explain why organizations outsource IS functions (Dibbern, et al., 2001; Klein, 2002). This indicates that focusing only on particular factors and one-sided streams of reasoning, e.g., economic or strategic, may not be appropriate to deal with the complexity of the sourcing decision. As a consequence, some works have started to systematically select (Dibbern, et al., 2001) and integrate complementary theories (Dibbern, et al., 2001; Poppo and Zenger, 1998). In addition, some studies try to consider the aspect of selective outsourcing more strongly. They either use several IS functions as levels of analysis, that together reflect the whole IS function of organizations (Dibbern and Heinzl, 2001; Poppo and Zenger, 1998), or concentrate on single or few areas (Beath and Walker, 1998; Loh, 1994). Finally, literature synopses are emerging that seek to synthesize the already existing knowledge on the IS sourcing decision (Dibbern, et al., 2004; Goo, et al., 2000).

In spite of the maturing field in research on the determinants of IS outsourcing, however, *three main gaps* soon become apparent. *First* and foremost, there is a lack of a comprehensive model that integrates multiple reference theories in a way that recognizes the existing body of knowledge. *Second*, it has been shown that the consideration of the individual and group level – as represented by cultural dimensions – could further the understanding of both the heterogeneous outsourcing behavior of organizations within and across countries. The importance of considering the individual level becomes even more apparent when looking at research on success factors of IS outsourcing. It is telling that factors derived from social exchange theory were found to have a profound impact on a successful outsourcing relationship (Goles, 2001; Lee and Kim, 1999). Their importance is essentially attributed to the nature of the IS function as a service, which requires – to varying degrees – the participation of the customers (i.e. users) in the IS production process. The work from Ang and Slaughter (1998) indicates the importance of considering the individual level in explaining IS sourcing. Their empirical study brings to light that performance differences between internal and external IS professionals are associated with differences in the psychological profiles between both groups.

The consideration of the soft attributes of the human workforce could also contribute to close a *third* gap: there is few, if any, knowledge on functional differences in the IS sourcing decision. While there is some evidence that the reasons for outsourcing differ, depending on what IS function is taken as a unit of analysis (Dibbern and

Heinzl, 1999; 2002; Teng, et al., 1995), there are hardly any explanations for such differences.

In accordance to these research gaps, practitioners seem to lack a solid foundation when it comes to an IS sourcing decision. Often the emphasis is on reducing production costs or focusing on core competencies. The wider implications of such a one-sided decision process often appear much later during the life of the contact, when organizations realize that other factors should have been taken into account. The results are costly attempts to renegotiate the contract, increased efforts in managing the relationship with the vendor, or even the decision to backsource. These problems are often rooted in an uninformed sourcing decision and this then provides an additional, more immediate motivation for this work.

1.2 Research Focus and Objectives

Consequently, this study has two broad goals. First, the scientific objective of this study is to examine the overall pattern that explains the totally heterogeneous IS sourcing behavior of organizations in practice. The research seeks to develop a comprehensive model which helps to understand a firm's IS sourcing behavior. The desired theoretical enhancements dovetail nicely with a second, more normative objective of this work. On the one hand, it is intended to provide guidance for a sophisticated sourcing decision at the customer side. On the other hand, service providers shall be demonstrated how to arrange their supply to be an attractive alternative for meeting the IS needs of organizations. To reach these research objectives, three more specific goals are addressed:

1) Ascertain the determinants of selective IS outsourcing

A first step is to identify those factors that explain an organization's IS sourcing behavior, i.e. the extent to which particular IS functions are outsourced to external service providers (from totally in-house to totally outsourced). These determinants are primarily deduced from selected reference theories, since they provide the reasoning for their impact. In addition, the results from prior studies on IS outsourcing are considered to get a feeling for the importance of individual factors and to critically reflect on the main stream reasoning of the reference theories. One big challenge will be to bring order into the diverse factors and to integrate different theoretical lenses into a coherent whole.

There is, however, one problem that needs to be addressed carefully before starting the process of theorizing. There is some evidence from prior research that the determinants of IS outsourcing are not consistent among IS functions. For example, the issue of data security seems to be far more critical when it comes to decide upon the outsourcing of the data center function as compared to the user support or help desk function.

This means, the higher the generalizabilty of a model on selective IS outsourcing, the less it is possible to elaborate on the individual characteristics of particular IS functions. One strategy to overcome the resulting limited explanatory power of such a global model would be to develop supplementary individual models for each IS function. This, however, would far exceed the capacity of a single empirical research project.

To reduce the complexity of the problem statement, but still enable focused model building, this study will concentrate on two IS functions: (1) the development ("Gestalten") of application software and (2) the maintenance of application software. Both functions are distinct from each other, in that the output of the development – the implemented application software – serves as an input for the maintenance work. Within the software life cycle, both are distinctive in their work processes, as illustrated by the application of different tools and techniques (Banker, et al., 1998). Consequently, some organizations have found it advantageous to divide both tasks and to delegate them to different units or teams (Swanson and Beath, 1989; 1990). Multi-national surveys reveal that the separate organizational treatment is being reflected by varying degrees of outsourcing of both functions (Apte, et al., 1997; Barthélemy, 2001). This indicates that the issue of selective outsourcing is of high relevance for both functions.

What makes it especially interesting to focus on application development and maintenance, however, is that both functions deal with the same component of an IS: the application software. This means that, while both functions require the completion of different tasks, they can – to the most part – still be described and evaluated using the same factors. This opens the way to develop a global model for both functions, without ignoring their individual features.

2) *Elaborate on the impact of selected cultural dimensions on selective IS outsourcing*

Current research on IS outsourcing mostly takes IS functions as anonymous entities that may be governed either internally or externally. The attributes of the actual workers that perform the particular IS functions and the fact that those attributes may significantly differ between in-house an outsourced personnel have rarely been considered. Cultural dimensions provide fruitful insights into the personal attributes of individuals and groups. They can not only vary between organizations but also – on an aggregated level – between countries.

Although the main focus is to explain the IS sourcing behavior of companies in general, it seems worth to contrast German behavior against that of the USA. Most of the prior scientific knowledge on IS outsourcing stems from the USA, and it is not clear whether this knowledge is universally applicable. In order to elaborate on the impact of cultural dimensions, it seems reasonable to concentrate on those factors that were found to differ between both countries in former cross-cultural studies. A next step would then be to integrate these cultural dimensions into the overall model on selective IS sourcing.

3) Explore functional, industry and country differences in IS outsourcing

The first two objectives aim to develop a comprehensive model on selective outsourcing. The explanatory power of the model depends on its consistency in different contexts. In this study, the context will be changed on three different levels: (1) the IS function (Application Development versus Maintenance), (2) the industry (Finance versus Machinery), and (2) the country (USA versus Germany).

As soon as the explanatory content varies within one of these levels, it would appear that additional factors need to be integrated into the model. Uncovering those differences – if indeed they exist – provides a differentiated picture of the sourcing behavior in practice and allows for manifold practical and theoretical interpretations.

1.3 Overview of Research Methodology

As outlined in the problem statement, research into the determinants has already reached an advanced state. A variety of exploratory studies and a few studies that rigorously test hypotheses do exist already. Therefore, it is not seen critical to explore totally new concepts. Instead, the focus is on integrating existing theories and systematically evaluating the resulting comprehensive model. Accordingly, a confirmatory empirical approach is preferred in this research study. A survey based methodology is utilized to rigorously examine the relationships hypothesized in the research model. The design of the survey instrument follows the special requirements of the statistical method of "Structural Equation Modeling", which will be utilized to analyze the data. This method perfectly corresponds with the confirmatory nature of the study, as it allows both testing multiple hypotheses simultaneously and testing the quality of the survey instrument.

1.4 Study Organization

The study is divided into five chapters. Chapter 1 has provided an overview of the research problem, the study objectives, and the methodology. In Chapter 2, a theoretical framework will be developed. It begins with explaining why and how the sourcing decision may be framed into a variance theory. This is followed by a literature review that aims to identify both promising patterns in explaining IS outsourcing and avenues to improve the existing body of knowledge. Then a pool of reference theories will be examined closely. From those with the highest explanatory power, determinants are deduced and hypotheses about their impact on the sourcing of IS functions will be built. The resulting basic framework will then be extended by incorporating cultural dimensions that represent the individual or group level. In Chapter 3, the hypotheses will be tested in an empirical study. This requires the transformation of the framework into a model. That is, the determinants are operationalized considering the special requirements of the survey-based research method. Subsequently, the survey is actually conducted. That is, the survey procedure is introduced, the data is analyzed, and the findings are presented. In Chapter 4, the model findings are discussed and interpreted. This includes a discussion of the commonalities and differences between the model testing across countries, industries and IS functions as well as the presentation of the major theoretical and practical implications. Moreover, the limitations of this study will be addressed and an outlook into future research opportunities will be given. Finally, in Chapter 5, the study will be summarized.

2 Theoretical Framework on Information Systems Sourcing

The building of a *theoretical framework* may be viewed as a preliminary state of model building. It comprises statements about relations among broadly defined concepts within a set of boundary assumptions and constraints. The *model* building refines the theoretical framework and puts it into concrete terms, so that it can be examined empirically. Together they form what may be called a well structured theory (Bacharach, 1989; Kirsch, 1981).

The objective of building a *theory* is to understand the systematic reasons for a particular occurrence or non-occurrence (Sutton and Staw, 1995). It "(...) tries to make sense out of the observable world by ordering the relationships among elements that constitute the theorist's focus of attention in the real world" (Dubin, 1976, p. 26). In this study, the goal of theorizing is to explain why organizations behave totally different with regard to the sourcing of IS functions – in particular the development of application software and the maintenance of application software. The different sourcing behavior of organizations is reflected by different degrees of outsourcing of both IS functions, on a continuum from totally in-house to totally outsourced. Consequently, the *central phenomenon* to be explained is the varying degree of outsourcing (i.e. the extent to which outsourcing occurs on the level of a particular IS function). This raises the question for the *explanatory factors* that determine the degree of outsourcing and – more importantly – the reasons for their influence.

In order to identify these determinants, a threefold procedure will be undertaken. First, the core concepts will be defined and a realistic impression will be formed of the process that leads to an organization's IS sourcing situation. This process is generally regarded as a *decision process*, which has substantial implications for the process of theorizing. It provides evidence for the main structural elements of a theory on IS sourcing, implies important boundary assumptions about the role of time within and between those elements, and implicitly leads to assumptions about the values of those about whom the theory poses its relationships. Second, the literature will be reviewed in order to identify those theoretical lenses that are appropriate to explain heterogeneous behavior in IS sourcing. Third, hypotheses will be deduced from the selected theories and complementary cultural dimensions.

2.1 The Nature of the Information Systems Sourcing Decision

2.1.1 Definition of Core Concepts

Before starting to theorize about the nature of IS sourcing, it will be useful to define the object of analysis more closely. It includes a combination of "IS function" and "sourcing".

2.1.1.1 Information Systems Function

The terms "IS" and "function" need some clarification. They are used so frequently and unreflectively that it is worth to recall what exactly they mean. In particular, it appears to be necessary to distinguish information technology (IT) from information systems (IS), and to differentiate the term "function" from other terms like "task" and "service". Based on the conceptualization of the broader notion of "IS function", the two partial IS functions, "application development" and "application maintenance", will be defined. They are of particular interest in this study.

Information Systems have been defined in various ways:

> "(...) an information system consists of at least one person of a certain psychological type who faces a problem within some organizational context for which he needs evidence to arrive at a solution (i.e. to select some course of action) and that the evidence is made available to him through some mode of presentation (Mason and Mitroff, 1973)."
>
> "(...) information system is interpreted here as a computer [technology]-supported system which provides a set of people (users) with information on specified topics of interest in a certain organizational context" (Iivari and Hirschheim, 1996, p. 552).
>
> "(...) information systems (...) may be thought of as marking the organizational need to manage the use of IT in relation to an organization's activities and intentions" (Checkland and Holwell, 1998, p. 9).
>
> "(...) information systems is an instantiation of information technology, where the same information technology can be *instantiated* in many ways" (Lee, 1999a, p. 7), (...) people in organizational contexts can use, manage and maintain (or, in short, 'instantiate') information technology" (Lee, 1999a, p. 9).
>
> "(...) if information systems are broken down on an abstract level, the following components will result:
>
> - the task carriers in organizations (human beings);
> - the organizational task (task);
> - the information and communication technology (ICT).
>
> Therefore, information systems are (...) in short: human/task/technology systems (Heinrich, 1996, p. 14 – translated from German).

In trying to find a common ground between these definitions, it soon becomes apparent that the term "information technology" is part of the definitions of IS in all of the more recent definitions. All of them tend to emphasize that IT *per se* does not make up an IS. The decisive factor tends to be the deployment and application of the IT within the organizational context. Taken separately, IT has been defined as follows:

> "(...) IT refers to a technology, one which might be taken to refer mainly to the hardware of computers and telecommunication equipment. But 'technology' is often interpreted in a broader sense; for example queuing theory is often taken to be part of the 'technology' of management science. This is the case here. IT, without being sharply defined is usually regarded as a collection of both practices, techniques and devices concerned with collecting, storing, processing and distributing data or information (though these two terms are frequently confused as well as we shall see)" (Checkland and Holwell, 1998, p. 9).

> "(...) IT describes the entirety of the applicable and actually applied technical procedures of work, development, production and implementation. Often it includes both the 'Technik' [in sense of technical device] and the technique. Technology is the broad term, "Technik" the more narrow term" (Heinrich, 1998, p. 196).

Drawing on these definitions, IT refers to a collection of instruments that enable the collecting, storing, processing, analyzing, and distributing of information and/or data.[3] Moreover, Lee (1999a, p. 8) has empathized the special character of IT as opposed to other technologies:

> "(...) information technologies being an *intellectual* technology, as opposed to an industrial technology (...). The latter, like a drill press or steam engine, typically has a set of fixed functionalities. The former, however, has functionalities, that are not fixed at the outset, but can be innovated endlessly, depending on its interaction with the intellect of the human beings that use and implement it."

The development of IT has created an own industry – generally referred to as the IT Industry (Primary Industry). As a corresponding academic discipline, computer science (or "Informatik" in Germany) has been established. Both provide IT either for free or against payment for individuals or organizations, which generally are referred to as client or user organizations (Secondary Industries) (Friedewald, et al., 2001).

In general, a user organization acquires IT with a certain objective that is closely linked to the context of its application (Andelfinger, 1997, p. 13) – although situations are known "(...) in which organizations have purchased computers or off-the-shelf systems and only then asked themselves what they are going to use them for" (Checkland, 1999).

Making IT usable and beneficial within the organizational context has become an

---

3 For an overview of the evolution of "data processing" in corporations, see Heinzl (1996, pp. 315-322).

organizational task in its own. The actual workers, that carry out the task, take over a particular function. Accordingly, *IS functions* refer to IS tasks that are allocated to particular persons or groups (based on Kosiol, 1959, p. 29). *IS services* refer to the manner in which IS functions are performed. They reflect the notion that information systems exist to serve, help or support people taking action in the real world (Checkland and Scholes, 1990, Chapter 2).

Moreover, the IS function is characterized by a division of labour. Partial tasks have emerged that are allocated to specialized units or teams. Broadly speaking, one may distinguish between the development, the maintenance, the operation, the planning and management, and the more immediate support of the IS users. However, an IS may also be split into its constituent parts, such as the application software, the telecommunication and network infrastructure, central (e.g., data and application servers) and decentral computers (e.g., desktops). Accordingly, research has differentiated between various IS functions: e.g., application development and application maintenance; systems / data center operations; design and maintenance of networks and telecommunication centers; user support and training; as well as planning and management (Grover, et al., 1994a; Heinzl and Stoffel, 1991; Mertens and Knolmayer, 1998).

As outlined in the introduction, the focus of this research will be on two of these IS functions: The development of application software and the maintenance of application software, whereby the application software carries the logic or functionality that the users require to do their job using an IS.

Both functions are distinct from each other, in that the output of the development – the implemented application software – serves as an input of the maintenance work (Banker, et al., 1998). Within the software life cycle, both are distinctive in their work processes. *Application development* is generally understood to refer to the definition, design, and implementation of customized software (Balzert, 2001). In recent years, however, the traditional work procedures during the development process have begun to change. The IT Industry more and more anticipates the basic information requirements of certain groups of organizations, e.g., industries or business types, and produces standard software packages (Mertens and Lohmann, 2000; Sprott, 2000). These packages remain to be tailored according to an organization's individual requirements and need to be integrated into the overall IS architecture (Bansler and Havn, 1994). They constitute "(...) a design process in its own right" (Bansler and Havn, 1994, p. 710). In organizations that substitute their customized applications by standard software products, the original activities of definition and design become a new meaning. The definition now serves as a basis to select the right product, and the design is limited to the tailoring of the software (i.e. its configuration and possible modification) (Bansler and Havn, 1994; Markus and Tanis, 2000).

These changes in the development activities are not without consequences for the maintenance activities (Brehm, et al., 2001). *Application maintenance* may be defined as to include all corrective, adaptive, and perfective (i.e. optimizing) modifications of application software, without including major functional enhancements (Swanson, 1976; Swanson and Beath, 1989). If an organization makes use of standard software products, the maintenance resides to the correction of failures in the tailoring and implementation phase. Fundamental bucks in the software, however, can often only be corrected by the company from which the software has been purchased (Brehm, 2001).

Notwithstanding these changes due to the increasing diffusion of standard software packages in certain industries, the fundamental concepts used to understand the nature of the development and maintenance work have mostly stayed constant. Both functions are labour intensive tasks. They require different kinds of knowledge in order to provide application software that matches the organizational and social needs of the workplace. These knowledge types include categories such as *technical knowledge* (i.e. knowledge about the methods and techniques required to actually create, configure and modify software products); *organizational knowledge* (i.e. knowledge about the social and economic processes in the organizational context, in particular, the work processes that are to be supported and reflected by the software); and *application knowledge* (i.e. knowledge about the structure, functionality and use of the application software) (Iivari, et al., 2001). In general, different kinds of knowledge are distributed asymmetrically among stakeholders of an organization and require various types of knowledge exchange. In this realm, the notions of user participation and social interaction have especially been emphasized in the IS development process (Hirschheim, et al., 1991; Hirschheim, et al., 1996; Newman and Robey, 1992; Nygaard, 1986; Robey and Newman, 1996).

2.1.1.2 Sourcing

The term "IS sourcing" has two different meanings: it may be viewed as a current state (static) or as a decision process (dynamic).

(1) *Static view of sourcing.* First, it may be viewed as a pure description of the current organizational arrangement of an organization's IS functions. *Organizational arrangement* refers to the formal structure of the responsibility and allocation of tasks within the IS function. This could be handled either internally (in-house, insourcing) or externally (outsourcing) (Heinzl and Stoffel, 1991; Heinzl and Uhrig, 1991; Lacity and Hirschheim, 1993a; Loh and Venkatraman, 1992a).

In-house provision refers to the portion of the tasks and activities necessary for the provision of an IS function that is performed by an organization's own employees. *Outsourcing* refers to the extent to which the tasks and activities necessary for the provision of an IS function are carried out by one or more external service providers. The term "external service provider" refers to a company or corporation that represents an independent legal entity, e.g., an incorporation (Inc.) in the USA or a "GmbH" in Germany. External service providers can occasionally represent legal entities that an organization is connected by capital (e.g., joint-ventures or spin-offs). In case of a *spin-off,* the former in-house IS unit is transferred into a legally independent company, which may either be newly founded or already be existing, e.g., an established IS service provider. This means that an IS unit may be *totally outsourced,* in terms of contracting out one or more of its IS functions to a legally independent service provider, but its assets *still be owned* by the parent company through a 100% capital share (Heinzl, 1992; 1993a). In case of a *joint-venture*, the former in-house IS department may be transferred into a newly founded, legally independent company that is jointly owned through capital shares by the client and the vendor. Alternatively, the client may own part of an existing company through capital sharing, or the vendor my acquire capital shares of the client organization (Heinzl and Weber, 1993). Moreover, all kind of IS outsourcing deals can include the transfer of people and assets from the client organization to the external service provider.

(2) *Dynamic view of sourcing.* In addition to its descriptive character, however, a *second,* more procedural meaning can be attributed to the term "sourcing". It may be taken as a *management action* that includes the *choice* between alternative organizational arrangements. That is, it implies a *decision process* on whether to perform an IS function in-house or externally, or – to put it another way – it implies a decision whether to stay with the current organizational arrangement or to change it.

In combining both the static and the dynamic meaning of "sourcing", it is obvious that a sourcing decision always results in a particular sourcing situation. However, it may not easily be taken for granted that each sourcing situation is based on a former decision process.

Prior research on IS outsourcing has either implicitly assumed that the sourcing situation stems from a decision process (e.g., Ang and Straub, 1998; Dibbern and Heinzl, 2001; Teng, et al., 1995) or has specifically examined cases where organizations actually went through a decision process (e.g., Beath and Walker, 1998; Clark, et al., 1995; Currie, 1998; DiRomualdo and Gurbaxani, 1998; Fowler and Jeffs, 1998; Lacity and Willcocks, 1995; McLellan, et al., 1995). Most of the latter have investigated cases of organizations that outsourced one or more IS functions. They sought to identify the reasons for these decisions. It is just recently that insourcing decisions have explicitly been investigated as well (Hirschheim and Lacity, 2000). These include cases where organizations either evaluated the option of IS outsourcing but decided to stay in-house, or they experienced IS outsourcing and decided to bring the IS function(s) back in-house (backsourcing). These cases indicate that organizations with an in-house provision of IS do not generally ignore the option of IS outsourcing.

While outsourcing may have been a fairly new and unknown administrative innovation or management technique in the early 90s (Loh and Venkatraman, 1992b), it is now widely recognized as a serious alternative organizational arrangement to provide IS services. Organizations are confronted with IS outsourcing on a continuous basis, through various communication channels, e.g., media, peer organizations, offensive vendor offers, or consultants. Accordingly, it seems reasonable to assume that even organizations that have not yet experienced IS outsourcing themselves, are still well aware of this option and have – at least implicitly – undertaken a sourcing decision process.

The emerging cases of backsourcing further illustrate the maturing domain of IS outsourcing (Hirschheim, 1998). Organizations begin to build a more realistic picture of the positive and negative implications of IS outsourcing, which results in more sophisticated sourcing decisions (Poppo and Lacity, 2002). But how does such a decision process generally look like? What are the main activities included in a sourcing decision and how do they hang together?

2.1.2 Main Components of Sourcing Decision

Interestingly, the actual decision process has rarely been explored systematically up to now. Although it has never been questioned that outsourcing is an important management decision, it has not been investigated using a structured approach, as provided by general decision-process models (i.e. phase-theorems). In the following, the phase-theorem will be introduced and then applied to identify the main components of an IS sourcing decision.

2.1.2.1 The Phase-theorem

Decision process models are part of decision theory and may be characterized as stage-, step- or phase-models (Witte, 1990). They have primarily been developed in the American management literature (for an overview see Witte, 1968, p. 626; 1972, p. 164). One of the well known decision models that is often referred to as a foundation for the development of decision support systems in the field of IS (Davis and Olson, 1985), is that of Simon (1960, pp. 54ff.).

The model provides a good basis to describe the decision-making process and consists of three phases: the intelligence, the design and the choice phase. The phases are thought to build on each other, however, at each phase there may be a return to a previous one. *Intelligence* relates to the identification of the problem that needs to be solved. This requires the individual problem solver to gather information about the area under scrutiny, e.g., controlling the current state or searching for new opportunities in the environment. *Design* refers to generating and analyzing alternative solutions that the individual problem solver avails himself of to solve the identified problem. This stage often requires obtaining additional information beyond what was collected during the intelligence stage. *Choice* consists of evaluating and choosing among the various alternative solutions identified in the design stage. This stage may also require obtaining additional information beyond what was collected during the intelligence and design stages. While Simon's model ends with the choice phase, extended models like that of Rubenstein and Haberstroh (1965) also include *implementation* and *feedback from the results* of the decision (Davis and Olson, 1985, pp. 165ff.). They round up the whole process and lead to five different phases.

Empirical studies that actually have tested the phase-theorem are rare and limited to decisions other than IS outsourcing. One of the most comprehensive studies is that from Witte (1968; 1972). Based on the examination of 275 decision processes of organizations in Germany that initially acquired a data processing system, he tested the validity of the decision process model from Brim et al. (1962), which includes five phases from problem recognition to gathering information to developing alternatives to evaluating alternatives and to choice. His results reveal that it is more than often that the activities do not follow a sequence of stages as predicted in the model. Rather they were found to spread uniformly across the whole decision making process and to include a variety of sub-decisions.

In another study, Mintzberg et al. (1976) examined 25 strategic decision processes in US organizations based on Simon's three-stage model and found support for Witte's findings, "The framework used in this paper agrees with Witte's basic conclusions. We find logic for delineating distinct phases of the strategic decision process, but not in postulating a simple sequential relationship between them" (p. 252).

It can be concluded that, while the particular phases may not occur in the order as predicted by the phase theorem, they still provide a valuable tool to analyze, understand and critically reflect on decision processes in reality. For that reason, the phase theorem will be used to analyze the main activities of the IS sourcing decision.

2.1.2.2 Applying the Phase-theorem

Although no empirical study on IS sourcing has explicitly examined the decision process based on any type of phase-theorem, some case studies still provide evidence on the processes and activities that lead to an organization's sourcing decision. They allow to reflect on the phase theorem by matching the activities and their relationships, as they emerged from the literature, with the logic of the phase-theorem. In the following, Simon's three-stage model, supplemented by the phases of implementation and feedback (Rubenstein and Haberstroh, 1965), will be used as a basis of reference.

The review of the literature reveals that the decision process often starts when certain stakeholders of a sourcing arrangement realize some sort of dissatisfaction with the current state. The stakeholders of an IS sourcing arrangement may be split into two groups: the providers of IS services (i.e. those that perform the main work in an IS function) and the clients of the service – notwithstanding the fact that both parties often have to work together in order to reach the desired output. If the IS function is performed *in-house*, the clients are represented by senior management, the management of the business units, and the individual users in the business units; while the provider is personated by the internal IS management and the IS personnel in each of the IS functions (Hirschheim and Lacity, 2000). In case of IS *outsourcing*, the provider changes to an external provider represented by its managers and the actual workers, while the client representatives remain the same – with one exception: often IS management or key IS persons remain at the client site or are newly hired. They manage the external provider(s) and serve as intermediaries between the other client stakeholders and the vendor(s) (Heinzl and Uhrig, 1991).

Each stakeholder group has its own expectations and desires. Whenever the expectations and desires of one of the parties are not met for any reason, they become dissatisfied with the current sourcing arrangement and begin to search for solutions (i.e. initiate design activities). If no solution can be found, or an identified solution not be implemented within the current sourcing arrangement, external solutions are taken into consideration. This process from intelligence to design is nicely illustrated in the study of IS insourcing by Hirschheim and Lacity (2002). In six out of 14 cases, the following pattern emerged from their data analysis:

> "It begins when external pressures threaten the organization causing senior management to search for ways to reduce costs, including IT costs. Under this scrutiny, senior executives question the value of rising IT expenditures and mandate that IT managers cut costs. IT managers counter that costs are high because users resist their cost reduction tactics. Senior management despairs at the gridlock and formally invites outsourcing vendors to submit bids. IT manager rally, requesting they be allowed to compete with vendor bits." (p. 100)

The longitudinal study from Reponen (1993), who examined six cases of organizations in Finland that opted for outsourcing, may be taken as an additional example:

> "Business managers expressed considerable doubts as to the efficiency and effectiveness of data processing departments. Their opinion was that even small changes took a long time, though, expectations were high due to the promise of easy-to-use, high benefit IT by pundits in journals and at seminars. As a result, there was a wide gap between vision and reality." (p. 105)

Quite often, however, dissatisfaction with the current state is paired with the awareness of alternative sourcing options. In this case, intelligence and design are mutually conditional on each other. They seem to occur at same time. Currie and Willcocks (1998) summarize their findings from four outsourcing cases in the U.K. as follows:

> "In many cases, client organizations become dissatisfied with in-house IT service provision and are encouraged by supplier rhetoric offering a streamlined service at lower cost" (pp. 140f.).

Here, an alternative sourcing arrangement is associated with the perception of certain benefits or advantages, which may increase the level of expectations and desires regarding an IS function. If the level of expectations increases, the likelihood of dissatisfaction with the current sourcing arrangement likely rises as well.

It may indeed happen that the design – in form of generating alternatives – takes place even before an organization becomes aware of a severe problem in the current IS sourcing arrangement, e.g., if an external vendor offensively offers his services without being asked for a bit.

> "In the mid 1980s, PETRO1, one of the world's largest petroleum companies, suffered severe financial difficulties that forced senior management to find ways to cut costs. An outsourcing vendor, cognizant of the situation, called the CEO and offered to purchase his IT assets, hire his IT staff, and reduce his current IT costs while still maintaining service levels" (Hirschheim and Lacity, 2000, p. 102).

In this case, the design, which according to Simon's model includes the "(...) inventing, developing and analyzing possible courses of action" (Simon, 1960, p. 2), enfolds before problem identification (intelligence). In other words the necessity to analyze may not always result from a self-contained process of finding alternative solutions to a given problem.

Notwithstanding these different causes for analyzing alternative sourcing options, the actual analysis appears to follow a certain pattern. First, in order to analyze, the unit of analysis has to be identified. The analysis may start on the level of a particular IS function and then be extended to include other IS functions, or, it may begin on a very global level leading to a subsequent disaggregation into particular IS subfunctions and subproblems. This requires a break down of IS into its separate elements, as described in the case study about the outsourcing decision from Continental (Huber, 1993). Moreover, Willcocks et al. (1996) conclude based on their multiple case analysis, "(...) treating IT as a portfolio helps to identify outsourcing candidates by analyzing an IT activity's contribution not only to competitive strategy but also to business operations" (p. 20). Similarly, Palvia (1995) reports on the use of extensive spreadsheets to document and analyze all IS activities and their requirements.

In general, it may be concluded that, while the intelligence is more concerned with why to change the current sourcing arrangement at all, the design phase deals with the question on what IS functions to outsource or insource and to what extent. One of the more elaborated strategies to analyze particular sourcing options is to estimate their outcomes. There seems to be widespread agreement in the literature that IS outsourcing bears a number of risks (Aubert, et al., 1998; Buhl and Wirth, 1995; Duncan, 1998; Earl, 1996; Jurison, 1995). Risk may be defined as the probability of a negative outcome associated with choosing an alternative sourcing arrangement (Aubert, et al., 1998).

The analysis of alternative sourcing arrangements serves as a precondition for the final *choice*, where the options are *evaluated* and *compared* with each other using certain (decision) criteria. For example, in case of risk analysis, the risks of both insourcing and outsourcing need to be assessed and then compared with each other. Moreover, the decision criteria are closely linked to the initial problems that started the process and those identified in the course of finding and analyzing solutions.

Some studies, however, reject the general assumption that "(...) decision makers select an outcome only after analyzing alternatives" (Lacity and Willcocks, 1995, p. 233). They show cases where the decision was made early on and that the rest of the process was merely an exercise in *justification* (De Looff, 1995; Lacity and Willcocks, 1995; Palvia, 1995). The justification is often driven by interests of particular stakeholder groups. Such groups could be opponents or advocates of a change in the current sourcing arrangement. Both groups may instrumentalize the decision process to reach their objectives. The case where opponents of IS outsourcing instrumentalize the decision process to push their interests is illustrated by Hirschheim and Lacity (2000) in four out of 14 cases of IS insourcing:

> "IT Managers took charge of the evaluation for a number of political reasons, such as proving efficiency, justifying new resources, or trying to enhance their reputation as a business person. They used the outsourcing evaluations to confirm to senior management the legitimacy of continued sourcing through the internal IT departments" (Hirschheim and Lacity, 2000, p. 102).

After the decision is made, it needs to be *implemented*. In case of IS outsourcing, this means that one or more appropriate vendors have to be selected – if vendor selection has not indeed been part of the decision in order to enable a sound comparison between the vendor bit and the in-house option (Lacity, et al., 1996). Moreover, the contract has to be settled and the relationship be managed during the life of the contract. During the relationship and after the end of the contract, the outcome (i.e. success or failure) needs to be determined. This *feedback* could eventually lead to the identification of new problems, which could initiate another sourcing decision process. For example, companies that formerly decided to outsource may be dissatisfied with the outcome of the outsourcing arrangement and consider to bring IS back in-house. This scenario is illustrated by Hirschheim and Lacity (2002, p. 101):

> "Due to poorly negotiated contracts, however, IT costs rose and service levels dropped. The senior IT managers assembled a case to terminate the outsourcing contract."

In summary, the empirical evidence on IS sourcing decisions suggests that the decision process does not follow a single pattern of sequential stages. The events that start the process, the activities undertaken during the process, the length of the process, the effort made in generating, analyzing, and evaluating alternatives, the motives for these activities, and the stakeholders involved in the process tend to be very different from organization to organization.

This then rises the question on how to build a theory that explains the IS outsourcing behavior in a way that is general enough to be meaningful for all organizations, but still applies to the idiosyncratic decision process of particular organizations. In answering this question, the more general problem on how to construct theories at all is being addressed. This is taken up next in order to motivate the basic structure and nature of the theoretical framework that is thought to be appropriate to reach the research objectives of this study.

2.1.3 Framing the Sourcing Decision into a Variance Theory

2.1.3.1 Variance versus Process Theory

Every theory poses some kind of *logical structure* to explain a phenomenon. In general, two kinds of logical structure may be differentiated in social sciences: variance theories and process theories (Markus and Robey, 1988; Mohr, 1982).

Both types primarily differ on three dimensions: (1) the conceptualization of the phenomenon (i.e. the outcome or behavior that is sought to be explained); (2) the conceptualization of the factors that explain the phenomenon, and the nature of the link between these explanatory factors and the phenomenon that is sought to be explained; and (3) the role of time among the explanatory factors.

(1) What is explained? In variance theories the outcome to be explained is treated as a dependent variable that can take at least two different instances, e.g., total insourcing versus total outsourcing. Process theories are concerned with how an outcome changes over time. The final outcome that is sought to be explained is treated as a particular event or state (Mohr, 1982, p. 54), e.g., backsourcing may be viewed as an event that reflects a change from the state of IS outsourcing to the state of in-house provision of IS. The way, the outcome is conceptualized, is decisive for the character of its precursors.

(2) How is explained? In variance theories the explanatory factors are treated as independent variables that serve as necessary and sufficient conditions to explain the variance in the dependent variable. For example, it may be argued that an organization will prefer to outsource rather than to insource an IS function if the costs of in-house provision are thought to be higher than in case of outsourcing (Ang and Straub, 1998). Process theories are different in that the precursors take the form of events or states in accordance to the conceptualization of the outcome.

> "The predominant flavour of a process model is that of a series of occurrences of events rather than a set of relations among variables" (Mohr, 1982, p. 54).

These events serve as necessary but not sufficient conditions for the outcome to occur. The theoretical core of process theories lies in explaining and predicting the way in which one state changes to another state. Phase, stage or step models *per se* are regarded as "(...) incomplete process models because they generally lack specification of the mechanism by which subsequent stages come about" (Markus and Robey, 1988, p. 592, in referring to Mohr, 1982).

(3) Role of time? The objective of variance theories is to explain and predict a particular instance of an outcome at any point of time. Accordingly, the predictors or explanatory factors are independent of time.

> "In variance theory the time ordering among the contributory (independent) variables is immaterial to the outcome, (...) the independent variables within the precursor are considered from the viewpoint of the outcome, as though they all happened at once. Variance theory is state oriented (Simon, 1969, pp. 111-112); it deals in snapshots rather than movies. The functional relation among the independent causes is important (for example it may be linear or nonlinear), but the time ordering among those causes is unimportant because each contributor has an independent effect. Each cause is always sufficient with the others held constant, to produce a given impact on Y" (Mohr, 1982, p. 43).

This is in contrast to process theory, where the time ordering plays a fundamental role.

> "Loosely a process theory is one that tells a little story about how something comes about, but in order to qualify as theoretical explanation of recurrent behavior, the manner of the storytelling must conform to narrow specifications" (Mohr, 1982, p. 44).

The storytelling begins at some point in time and ends at another point. The objective is to identify a general pattern on how the change from one state to another occurs. One of the rare examples where process theory is applied in IS outsourcing research are studies on the diffusion of IS outsourcing within a social system, e.g., within the US economy (Hu, et al., 1997; Loh and Venkatraman, 1992b). IS outsourcing events are identified within a certain time span. The objective is to identify certain patterns in these time series that may be explained by certain factors, such as the communication behavior among the entities of the social system. Another example is the study from Heisekanen (1996), who provides insight into the dynamics of IS sourcing by interpreting cases where organizations changed from one particular sourcing arrangement to another.

For the purpose of this study, it is necessary to decide whether to go with a process theory or with a variance theory and to be clear about the implications of this choice.

The objective of this study – and this will be treated as the decisive factor – is to explain the heterogeneous behavior of organizations in IS sourcing. As a consequence, variance theory would be most appropriate. Treating the phenomenon as a dependent variable allows to capture a whole continuum of sourcing options, whereas process theory generally focuses on just one specific event, e.g., insourcing *or* outsourcing.

When looking at the power of the explanatory factors, however, process theory clearly has its merits as it correspondents more faithfully with the actual decision process that leads to an organization's sourcing arrangement.

Although this would call for a combination of elements from process and variance theory, such a mixture has generally been rejected by theorists because the conceptualizations of the respective explanatory factors and outcome(s) simply do not match (Mohr, 1982, pp. 65ff.). Variance theory has to remain variance theory linking variables with variables. Nevertheless, it seems reasonable, and indeed fruitful, to construct a variance theory that recognizes some of the logic that may be learned from the process perspective. More specifically, the analysis of the decision process, as illustrated in the previous section, may be informative for the general structure of a variance theory.

2.1.3.2 Structural Elements of a Variance Theory

In reflecting the activities within the phases of the IS sourcing decision process, there seems to be at least some common ground. Each sourcing decision involves some kind of evaluation of and comparison between alternatives. From a process perspective this would mean that alternatives need to be generated and evaluative criteria be found to analyze the options. For example, costs may be used as one criteria to evaluate the options of insourcing and outsourcing a particular IS function. In order to evaluate, however, each organization has to perform some kind of analysis to determine the instances of the criteria. As soon as the instances are known, the options can be compared with each other. For example, the costs of the in-house option and the outsourcing option have to be determined in order to compare them.

All these activities may occur at different time intervals and may be repeated until the final choice, or, in order to justify a choice that was made early on. This *process structure* is illustrated in the upper box of Figure 2-1.

In variance theory, the time order within the precursors is irrelevant. For a variance theory, what matters are the criteria that are used for the evaluation and comparison. Each of these criteria may be treated as an independent variable that reflects the perceptions of an organization's main decision makers regarding the comparative advantages of insourcing versus outsourcing particular IS functions. Accordingly, one step in building a theoretical framework would be to identify those evaluative criteria that are used to compare the options of insourcing versus outsourcing particular IS functions. Each of these variables can take at least two different instances. For example, the costs of performing a particular IS function may be higher or lower in case of outsourcing as opposed to in-house provision. The theoretical impact of a particular variable on the degree of IS outsourcing may be positive (+) or negative (–). As an example, one may argue that the higher the costs of in-house provision as opposed to IS outsourcing, the more an IS function will be outsourced (positive impact) (*cf.* Ang and Straub, 1998).

In parallel to the process perspective, however, where the instances of the decision criteria have to be determined through certain types of analysis, the instances of the comparative variables would need to be determined as well. For example, it would be of interest to know under which circumstances in-house costs for a particular IS function are regarded to be higher as in case of outsourcing. Consequently, the comparative variables themselves become dependent variables, whereby the variance of which may be explained by a second level of independent variables.

The general structure of a variance theory to explain heterogeneous behavior in IS sourcing is illustrated in the lower box of Figure 2-1. It shows the relationship between the two types of independent variables (LEVEL 1 and 2) with the central dependent variable – the degree of IS outsourcing.

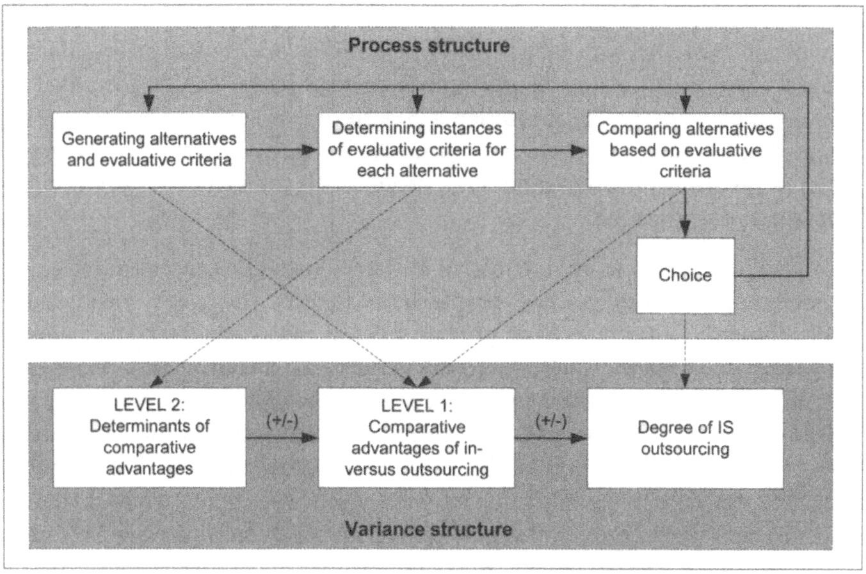

Figure 2-1: Structural Elements of Variance versus Process Theory

The variance structure as illustrated in Figure 2-1, however, is nothing more than a lifeless body or "skeleton". It needs to filled with life. That is, the particular variables and the logic of their relationships need to be identified. This may be viewed as the core of theorizing.

2.2 Analysis and Selection of Theoretical Lenses

One of the principles in building a theoretical framework is to understand "(...) how a given theory fits in the other preexisting and apparently related theories" (Bacharach, 1989, p. 511). Similarly, Spinner (1974) argues that theorizing may be viewed as a dynamic process or indeed a heuristic where "(...) theories are only created *from theories* and *through theories*" (p. 177, translated from German). Accordingly, the next step in theorizing will be to identify those pre-existing theories that are apparently related to the variance theory on selective IS outsourcing that is intended to be built (see Figure 2-1, p. 23). In order to reach this objective, it is obvious to start with reviewing the pre-existing research on the reasons for IS outsourcing for their theoretical foundation. This is taken up next.

2.2.1 Literature Review

2.2.1.1 Theoretical and Methodological Diversity

In reviewing the literature, a considerable diversity can be noted. It soon becomes apparent that instead of generating totally new theories to explain IS outsourcing behavior, most research with a theoretical base relied on one or more pre-existing reference theories. In total, nine different theoretical lenses can be identified. To simplify this diversity, the structuring approach of Lee et al. (2000) (who in turn adopted the Cheon et al. (1995) approach) will initially be adapted combining the alternate reference theories into three categories: (I) economic, (II) strategic, and (III) social/organizational.

Economic theories focus on some sort of efficiency criteria to coordinate and govern economic agents. They include (1) transaction cost theory, (2) agency theory and (3) other economic lenses that cover production economies, labor market economics, and more general considerations of costs and financial indices. *Strategic* theories focus on how firms develop and implement strategies to achieve an organization's objectives. Reference theories of this type include: (4) resource-based theory/view and (5) lenses on overall organizational strategies and strategic analysis.[4] *Social/behavioral* theories take an entirely different focus. Eschewing rigidly rational views of organizations, these theories concentrate on relationships and dependencies that exist between individuals or groups. Reference theories of this type include: (6) innovation diffusion theory, (7) power/politics theory, (8) resource-dependence theory, and (9) institutional theory. An overview of the reference theories used by the particular research studies is given in Table 2-1.

Together 49 research papers published in major business and IS Journals as well as international conference proceedings are included in the synopsis. An overview of the included publication outlets is given in Appendix A. As can be inferred from Table 2-1, the number of papers using one or more reference theories (29) exceeds the number of papers without a well-defined theoretical foundation (20).

There is about an equal split between the number of papers using multiple theoretical perspectives (15) and those with a single theoretical focus (14). Early research mainly was confined to one, and occasionally two, theoretical perspectives. Over time, however, the use of two or more theoretical lenses in a single paper became more common, with some papers embracing as many as four theories. This may be seen as a response to the complex and continually evolving nature of outsourcing.

---

4 Resource-dependence theory has been categorized as strategic by Lee et al. (2000), because it was applied in a strategic sense in the IS outsourcing literature, however, it is more rooted in the social/behavioral perspective as will be shown subsequently.

Table 2-1: Diversity of Research on the Determinants of IS Outsourcing

Study			Methodology					Reference Theories									
Year	Author(s)	Publication Outlet	Empirical			Non empirical		Economic			Strategic		Social				
			Interpretive	Descriptive	Positivist	Conceptual	Mathematical	Trans. Cost	Agency	Other	Res. Based	Firm Strategy	Innov. Diffus.	Power-Politics	Res. Depend.	Institutional	Non
1991	Heinzl / Stoffel	IM				X											X
1992	Heinzl	IM		X													X
	Loh / Venkatraman	ISR			X								X				
	Loh / Venkatraman	JMIS			X					X							
	Picot / Maier	IM				X		X				X					
1993	Huber	HBR		X													X
	Reponen	ICIS	X														X
1994	Arnett / Jones	I&M		X													X
	Grover et al.	EJIS			X						X	X					
	Knolmayer	IM				X											X
	Knolmayer	BFuP					X			X							
	Loh	ICIS			X			X	X								
	Quinn / Hilmer	SMR				X						X					
1995	Cheon, et al.	JIT				X		X	X		X				X		
	Clark, et al.	JIT		X													X
	Cronk / Sharp	JIT				X											X
	Cross	HBR		X													X
	Jurison	JIT				X		X									
	Lacity / Willcocks	AMIT	X					X									
	Lacity, et al.	HBR	X														X
	Loh / Venkatraman	ICIS			X			X		X							
	McFarlan / Nolan	SMR		X								X					
	McLellan, et al.	JIT			X												X
	Sobol / Apte	JIT		X													X
	Teng, et al.	DS			X						X	X			X		
1996	Aubert, et al.	I&M			X			X									
	Earl	SMR				X											X
	Heisekanen, et al.	ICIS	X					X									
	Nam, et al.	CACM			X			X				X		X			
	Nelson, et al.	CACM			X			X	X								
	Slaughter / Ang	CACM			X					X							
1997	Ang / Cummings	OS			X			X								X	
	Apte, et al.	JIT		X													X
	Hu, et al.	ISR			X								X				
	Lacity / Willcocks	ISJ	X														X
	Wang, et al.	MS					X		X								
1998	Ang / Straub	MISQ			X			X		X							
	Beath / Walker	HICSS	X								X						
	Currie / Willcocks	ISJ	X														X
	DiRomualdo / Gurbaxani	SMR	X									X					
	Duncan	HICSS				X		X			X						
	Fowler / Jeffs	JIT	X														X
	Hirschheim / Lacity	HICSS	X														X
	Poppo / Zenger	SMJ			X			X	X		X						
	Smith, et al.	JMIS			X												X
1999	Hancox / Hackney	HICSS			X			X	X			X					
2000	Hirschheim / Lacity	CACM	X														X
2001	Dibbern, et al.	ZfB				X		X			X	X					
	Dibbern / Heinzl	WI			X			X			X	X		X			
	TOTAL 2001	49	11	8	18	[illegible]	2	17	6	5	8	10	2	2	2	1	20
	Ranking		**2nd**		**1st**			**2nd**				**3rd**					**1st**

The use of reference theories is closely linked to the applied methodology. In particular, (I) *empirical* approaches that may be split into the categories (1) positivist, (2) descriptive, and (3) interpretive, and (II) *non-empirical* approaches, including (4) conceptual and (5) mathematical approaches were found in the literature (see Table 2-1). The meaning of theses methodologies is described in Appendix B.

Research that referred to one or more reference theories is – to the most part – positivist empirical or conceptual in nature. By contrast, descriptive and the majority of interpretive empirical studies did not refer to any reference theory. The theoretical contribution of interpretivist studies may be viewed as theory emergent. In a few cases they contribute to a process perspective. In the majority of cases, however, variance theoretic arguments emerge from their data analysis. They often reflect the logic as provided by the applied reference theories. Therefore, it may be concluded that as far as variance theoretic arguments are concerned, most of the empirical logic can be traced back to reference theories (Dibbern et al., 2004).

2.2.1.2 Theoretical Challenges

One item of note, however, in cases where multiple theories are used, is the varying treatment of *inter-theoretical* relationships; that is, the linkages, tensions, inconsistencies, and contradictions between theories (Van De Ven, 1989). For example, Loh (1994) deduced a variety of theoretical constructs from agency and transaction cost theory without thoroughly exploring any linkages between these constructs. Similarly, Cheon et al. (1992) developed a theoretical framework based on four different theories without fully delving into their connections and contradictions. On the other hand, Poppo and Zenger (2002) tested competing chains of causality, derived from transaction cost and resource-based theories; Jurison (1995) incorporated the concept of risk into transaction cost economics; and Duncan (1998) focused on the different risk perspectives in transaction cost theory and resource-based theory. Similarly, the treatment of theoretical constructs varies in studies using only one reference theory. For example, Lacity and Willcocks (1995) scrupulously deal with contradictions within one theoretical framework by offering different interpretations of findings based on pro and con views of transaction cost theory.

Another point that needs to be considered, when applying multiple reference theories, is the reasoning behind the selection of particular theories. The higher the maturity in a particular stream of research, the greater the necessity to clearly outline the pool of theories from which the selection is made and the criteria used to distinguish and evaluate the theories.

- *Selection criteria.* The main criteria for selecting reference theories should be the phenomenon that is sought to be explained (e.g., Seth and Thomas, 1994, p. 187). As outlined in the problem statement, the objective of this study is to explain the varying degree of outsourcing the IS functions of application development and application maintenance. The logical structure from which to start in explaining this variance has been outlined in the previous section (see Figure 2-1, p. 23). In particular, the selected theories should pose some kind of rationality that may serve as a criteria on whether to insource or outsource IS functions, and provide some background information on how the instances of these criteria may be affected.
- *Base for selection.* Following an inductive approach, the nine different reference theories identified in prior IS outsourcing research may serve as a basis for selection. However, on the one hand, it is not clear if they provide a sufficient pool from which to select. There may indeed be additional theoretical lenses that have been neglected in prior research, but are fruitful for the purpose of this research project. On the other hand, it is not obvious how those theories hang together. What do they have in common and how can they be distinguished? In searching for answers to these questions, the "theory of the firm" emerged as a promising overall umbrella that covers most of the reference theories identified in the literature review, plus a view additional lenses (Dibbern, et al., 2001). In fact, only innovation diffusion theory cannot be regarded as a theory of the firm. It will be analyzed separately.

Analyzing reference theories from the perspective of the theory of the firm, allows to understand their historical background, the original intentions associated with their development, and potential linkages between them.

2.2.2 The Theory of the Firm

The "theory of the firm" may be viewed as a generic term that covers a number of theoretical contributions that are all concerned with the *function* of the firm (i.e. company, enterprise, corporation or profit organization). They all differ more or less strongly on four dimensions: (1) the main explanatory objective associated with the firm, (2) the way the firm is conceptualized, (3) the assumptions about the behavior of the firm's stakeholders – in particular the management, and (4) the assumptions about the relationship between the firm and its environment.

In limiting the resulting diversity, four broad categories may be differentiated: (I) Neoclassics, Industrial Economics, and Gutenberg's General Theory of the Firm, (II) Behavioralism, (III) Institutional Economics, and (IV) Dynamic Theories. Neoclassics and Industrial Economics are less concerned with the function of the firm itself, but more with the firm as being part of the market system. The firm is treated as an anonymous entity. Contrastingly, the focus of Gutenberg's General Theory of the Firm and the other three main streams has shifted more to the actual firm and its function in relation to the market system or indeed opposed to the market. Gutenberg's General Theory of the Firm is the only German based approach. It takes an intermediate role between neoclassics and industrial economics on the one side, and the other three main steams, that may also be called "new theories of the firm", on the other side (Schmidt, 2000). An overview of the theories of the firm, that are considered for the analysis, is given in Table 2-2. The structure of the synopsis has been informed by the works from Seth and Thomas (1994) and Knudsen (1995).

Some authors have argued that the major characteristic of the theory of the firm is its effort to answer questions like "Why do firms exist? What factors determine the scope and size of the firm? What is the function of the firm and its managers?" (Seth and Thomas, 1994, 1994, p. 166; see also Holmstrom and Tirole, 1989, p. 65). If theories of the firm do indeed cope with these challenging questions, then it may be argued that they should also offer answers to the question "Why do particular functions of a firm exist?" and, more specifically, "Why does the in-house IS function exist?". One notable contribution in the IS outsourcing context that has recognized the parallel between the objectives of the theory of the firm and the issue of sourcing is that from Duncan (1998). She noted, "(...) we find that theory [the theory of the firm] helps us answer not 'which resources should be outsourced', but rather, 'which ones should *not*?' " (p. 675 – italics original).

Consequently, the selection of theories of the firm will be done according to the following procedure: *First*, the core of each theory will be presented briefly based on the four dimensions introduced earlier. *Second*, whenever a particular theory has already been used in the context of IS outsourcing, its application will briefly be summarized. *Third*, the particular theory will be evaluated for its usefulness in contributing to explain the variance of IS outsourcing as illustrated in Figure 2-1, p. 23.

Table 2-2: Synopsis of Theories of the Firm (Page 1 from 2)

Theories of the Firm		Selected Represen-tatives	Central Explanatory Objective	Concept of the Firm	Behavioral Assumption	Assumption towards Environment
Neoclassical Economics		Marshall (1890); Cournot (1938)	Market behavior, determination of market prices	Production function; "black-box"	Rational actor; profit maximizing	Certain, symmetrically distributed knowledge
Industrial Organization	**Tradi-tional**	Bain (1956; 1968; 1972); Mason (1959); *newer*: Porter (1980)	Market structure-conduct-performance paradigm; strategic positioning	Part of the competitive industry structure; "black-box"	Rational actor; profit maximizing	Certain, symmetrically distributed knowledge; adapt to homogenous external environment
	Modern/ Game	Nash (1950; 1953); Spence (1976); Kreps, Willson, Milgrom, Roberts (1982)	Industry structure, strategic behavior of actors	Part of a game; strategic player; "black-box"	Strategically rational actor; profit maximizing	Symmetrically distributed knowledge; uncertainty regarding actions of others
General ("Àllgemeine Betriebswirt-schaftslehre")		Gutenberg (1969/1980, 1955/1984, 1951/1983)	Functionalities of firm production, sales/distri-bution, and finance	System of inter-dependent functions	Rational actor; profit maximizing	Certain, symmetrically distributed knowledge; firm autonomy
Behavioralism	**Behavior-al**	Simon (1957; 1959); Cyert and March (1963)	Empirical, observable organizational behavior and decision making	Political coalition	Boundedly rational actor; 'satisficing animal'	Active adaptation to uncertain environment via learning process
	Power / Politics	Weber (1947); Pfeffer and Salancik (1974); Tushman (1977); Pfeffer (1981)	Development and exercise of intra-organizational power in order to affect decision making and execution	Organized, structured social system	Rational actor; enabling and enforcing self interests on group or individual level	Environment may force decisions that require the skill to develop power and the willingness to employ it.
	Resource Depen-dence	Hickson et al. (1971); Pfeffer and Salancik (1978)	Intra- and inter-organizational dependencies	Open social systems	Rational actor; active choice behavior	Active adaptation or resistance to visible environmental pressures

Table 2-2: Synopsis of Theories of the Firm (Page 2 from 2)

Theories of the Firm		Selected Represen-tatives	Central Explanatory Objective	Concept of the Firm	Behavioral Assumption	Assumption towards Environment
Behavioralism	**Institutio-nal**	Meyer and Rowan (1977); DiMaggio and Powell (1983)	Relationship between environment and organizational structures and actions	Part of a social network	Conformity to institutiona-lized beliefs, values, and practices;	Passive conformity to invisible environmental pressures
New Institutional Economics	**Transac-tion Costs**	Coase (1937); Williamson (1975; 1985)	Internal or external governance, hierarchy vs. market	Hierarchical, authoritarian structure	Boundedly rational actor; opportunistic behavior	Adaptation to uncertain environment
	Agency	Berle and Means (1932); Jensen and Meckling (1976)	Optimal contractual relationships	Nexus of contracts	Rational actor; minimizing of risk; self interest	Uncertainty; asymmetrically distributed information
	Property Rights	*earlier*: Commons (1931); *newer*: Demsetz (1967), Alchian and Demsetz (1972);	Creation, transfer of property rights; Creation of contracts for property rights	Nexus of contracts	Rational actor; maximizing of utility function; prevention of shirking	Reduction of uncertainty via contracts; passive adaptation to environment
	Incom-plete Contracts	Grossmann and Hart (1986); Hart and More (1990)	Allocation of ownership over assets	Set of assets under common ownership	Rational actor; self interest	Certain environment
Dynamic	**Evolutio-nary**	Schumpeter (1934), Nelson and Winter (1982), Rumelt (1991)	Evolution and competition	Pool of routines, experiences	Entrepreneur; searching for opportunities and learning from past behavior	Uncertain and unpredictable environment
	Resource-based	Penrose (1959), Wernerfelt (1984) Barney (1991)	Competitive advantage via resources	Pool of resources	Experience based rationality; strategic decision maker	Reduction of uncertainty via learning process

2.2.2.1 Neoclassics, Industrial Economics and Gutenberg

Neoclassics. The conceptual origin of the term "theory of the firm" may be traced back to neoclassical microeconomics, which were heavily influenced by Marshall (1890), Cournot (1938) and others (for an overview see Schneider, 1995, pp. 19f.; Schneider, 1997, p. 249). The objective of this stream of research is to explain market prices. The firm is merely treated as a pure production function. Its objective is to transfer inputs into outputs in a profit maximizing way. Preferences of customers and the underlying technology are assumed to be constant. In referring to Nelson (1991b), Knudsen (1995, p. 185) has appropriately called the latter assumption as a "cookbook metaphor" illustrating that all companies have access to the same production techniques ("recipes") without additional costs. Firms are perceived as homogenous entities. The size of the firm is not treated as a dependent variable that is sought to be explained, but rather as an independent variable that determines market prices and industry size. Only diseconomies of scale, due to increasing bureaucracy and limited capacity for decision makers, may limit the growth of firms, which has been criticized as to be in contradiction to the underlying modelling assumptions of perfect and free information (Demsetz, 1991). In spite of its market focus, however, traditional price theory has established such important concepts like "economies of scale" (due to specialization of the work force, learning curve effects, digression of fixed costs, savings in batch sizes, or centralized storage of reserves) and "economies of scope" (due to sharing of assets) (Baumol, et al., 1988). These concepts have stimulated Operations Research to study the efficiency of a firm's production system using different kinds of engineering production functions. The causal agencies of the production functions serve as a basis, or indeed input, to determine the production costs in Accounting. Especially, determining the influencing factors of total costs has been of paramount interest. It should be noted, however, that studying the actual production function of firms, in order to help firms optimize and control their production system, resides within the modelling assumptions of microeconomics (Albach, 1999). That is, factor and product markets are assumed to be homogenous. This means that, by definition, heterogeneous behavior between firms – as it is the case in IS sourcing – cannot be explained by traditional production economics. Neoclassical economics simply do not and never were intended to provide any plausible explanation for *why* production costs may differ between organizations independent of scale and scope.

Paradoxically, however, neoclassical concepts such as "economies of scale" and "economies of scope" are widely used arguments in favour of IS outsourcing as opposed to the in-house provision of IS. Indeed, Ang and Straub (1998) have explicitly referred to neoclassical economics to explain the variance in the degree of IS outsourcing in the Banking Industry based on differences in production costs between in-house and outsourced provision of data processing facilities.

Opposed to micro economics, however, here the production techniques, i.e., the actual way the IS services are performed by a particular organization, are not assumed to be homogeneous across all organizations. The production functions may differ independent from size and scope. Therefore, it may be concluded that production costs are indeed an important factor when it comes to an IS sourcing decision, however, only if the neoclassical assumption of firms being homogenous entities is being relaxed.

Traditional Industrial Organization (IO) Economics. The origins of traditional IO may be traced back to Bain's entry-barrier model (Bain, 1956). Its earlier versions were primarily concerned with explaining how *industry structure* (e.g., the degree of concentration and product differentiation, stages of production, barriers to entry, relationship between fixed and variable costs) influences *firm conduct* (e.g., pricing, supply), which in turn determines *firm performance* (e.g., firm profitability in relation to average industry) (Conner, 1991; Knudsen, 1995; Schneider, 1997; Seth and Thomas, 1994). There is, however, nothing in the theory that would explain why firms may react (conduct) differently to a homogenous industry, which is defined through its structural elements. Similar to neoclassics, the firm itself remains a "black-box" (Knudsen, 1995, p. 187; Seth and Thomas, 1994, p. 169). Accordingly, heterogeneous behavior, such as selective IS outsourcing, can hardly be explained by this lens.

The exclusive focus on the industry has been somewhat relaxed in later contributions by Porter (1980). He developed the well known frameworks of the "Five Competitive Forces" and the "Value Chain". These concepts allow to analyze the industry structure and to identify generic types of strategic positioning (e.g., cost leadership or differentiation) of firms within the market. Based on and illuminated by these theoretical insights, Porter (1985) himself, and his colleagues in the MIS community (Ives and Learmonth, 1984; McFarlan and Nolan, 1995; Parsons, 1984), began to analyze how IT/IS can alter industry structures and hence the strategic positioning of firms within industries. Although these analyses have significantly influenced the awareness of the strategic role of IT/IS, they do not satisfactorily explain the sources of a sustained competitive advantage through the use of IT/IS (Sambamurthy, 2000, p. 248). Accordingly, they do not provide sufficient insights into the wider implications of IS insourcing or outsourcing on the strategic role of IS, and, for that reason, fail to provide a rationale for the IS sourcing decision.

New Industrial Economics (i.e. Game Theory) (Nash, 1950; Nash, 1953) is quite similar to traditional IO regarding its assumption of homogenous firms. However, it is different, in that it is less concerned with empirical relationships between firm and market, but more with formal analytical game theoretic models (Schneider, 1997; Seth and Thomas, 1994). Game theory attempts to provide guidelines for the strategic behavior of players or actors (e.g., companies) in particular game situations. These situations are characterized by specific assumptions concerning the production function of a company, the environment, and informational structures. It is assumed that all players work under the same conditions and make rational and intelligent decisions to maximize their profits. The only determinant for these decisions is the perception of the expected actions of the antagonist (i.e. other player).

In general, it is possible to have 2-player games or n-player games. Newer, i.e., dynamic game theory (Kreps, et al., 1982; Spence, 1976), as opposed to traditional mathematical game theory, incorporates the assumption of incomplete information into its analytical models (Fudenberg and Tirole, 1990). In IS outsourcing research, mathematical game theoretic models have been applied in the context of contract structuring in software development projects (Whang, 1992). By incorporating certain incentive issues into the model, a mathematical structure is developed that results in an equilibrium state between outsourced and in-house software development efforts. Elitzur and Wensley (1997), in a theoretical essay, use game theory to examine and explain certain characteristics of IS outsourcing, including asset transfer, risk sharing, technology upgrading, contract duration, relationship management, and fee determination. They focus on the role of incentives and fees as tools to help shape the structure of outsourcing arrangements. Overall, it may be concluded that, while game theory provides insights into contractual issues of IS outsourcing, it does not provide any rationality on whether to insource or outsource IS.

Gutenberg's General Theory of the Firm. In the field of business management ("Betriebswirtschaftslehre"), Gutenberg (1951/1983; 1955/1984; 1969/1980) has laid down the foundations for a "General Theory of the Firm" ("Allgemeine Betriebswirtschaftslehre") in Germany, which covers the fundamental principles of an organization's major business functions including production, sales/distribution, and finance. Gutenberg's General Theory of the Firm takes a systems view of the firm which recognizes the interdependency and complementarity between its constituent parts (Albach, 1988a; Schmidt, 2000).

> Viewed thus, one can describe the enterprise as a complex of qualities whose relationship to one another is that of interdependence (they are linked by virtue of reciprocal functionalities)" (Gutenberg, 1929, p. 42; translated and cited by Schmidt, 2000, p. 11).

Gutenberg's main theoretical arguments, however, are not directly applicable for building empirically testable theories. They are mostly explicated in a formal manner, showing a strong microeconomic foundation. Moreover, Gutenberg has always been concerned with addressing and solving problems of real firms (Albach, 2000b, p. 59). At the time of Gutenberg's 'productive phase', however, phenomena like "multinational enterprise, outsourcing and market strategies" had not been on the 'radar screen' of Gutenberg and therefore had not been addressed explicitly (Schmidt, 2000, p. 4).

2.2.2.2 Behavioralism

Behavioralism in its *original* form is primarily based on the works from Simon (1947; 1957) and Cyert and March (1963). Its main focus is to explain decision making processes within organizations. In contrast to neoclassics and IO, Simon holds that a firm's decision makers are "boundedly rational", that is, they are "intendedly rational but only limited so" (Simon, 1965, p. XXIV). Accordingly, a decision maker may not be a "maximizing" but a "satisficing animal" (Simon, 1959, p. 277). The firm is treated as a political coalition that consists of a sum of individual decision makers that all have their own objectives (Cyert and March, 1963). The theory has been applied to analyze decision processes in depth (see Section 2.1.2). It has also served as a conceptual basis to build tools that simulate and support decisions (Todd and Benbasat, 2000). However, the theory does not provide any logic or rationale for why and how a particular decision should actually be made. It does not provide insight into potential criteria used within a decision and therefore does not provide any rationale for why a firm may selectively outsource some functions.

Power / Politics Theory explicitly focuses on the role of power and politics in organizational decision making. Power can be defined as a party's potential to influence the behavior of another party in certain situations, whereas politics is the manner in which power is exercised (Pfeffer, 1981, p. 7; Tushman, 1977, p. 207). The theory does not provide any concrete criteria that may be used to compare alternative sourcing options. It should be noted, however, that it still provides valuable insight into the process of IS outsourcing decision making, as illustrated by Lacity and Hirschheim (1993a). It has also been argued that the higher the power of an in-house IS unit, the less likely it will be outsourced. However, little support was found for this view (Dibbern and Heinzl, 2001; 2002; Nam, et al., 1996). Moreover, the concept of power has mostly been studied at the overall IS level. There is little knowledge about power differences on the level of partial IS functions.

Resource-dependence Theory is closely linked to power theory. The notion of control over resources has been used as one indicator to determine the power of a group or coalition, e.g., a subunit within a firm (Emerson, 1962). What makes the theory distinctive, is its focus on the firm's dependence on external resources. According to Oliver (1991, p. 148), the theory "(...) focuses on a wide range of active choice behaviors that organizations can exercise to manipulate external dependencies or exert influence over the allocation or source of critical resources" (based on Pfeffer and Salancik, 1978, and others). On the one hand, the theory is concerned with the role of resource dependencies in already existing inter-organizational relationships. In this realm, it is closely related to social exchange theory (Blau, 1964), which has been used in IS outsourcing research in order to study the relationship between vendor and client (Klepper, 1995; Willcocks and Kern, 1998) and its impact on outsourcing success (Goles, 2001; Lee and Kim, 1999). The theory may also provide an useful frame to analyze the situational factors that lead to decisions about the allocation of critical resources. However, it does not provide any rationale for why a company should acquire resources on a contractual basis from external suppliers. Questions like "Is it good or bad to use the external market?", or "Does a firm increase environmental uncertainly or lower it when using external suppliers?" remain unanswered. Nevertheless, Teng et al. (1995) have used this lens in parallel to resource-based theory in order to explain the variance in IS outsourcing. They argue that resource dependence theory "(...) would suggest outsourcing as a strategy to fill gaps when performance of internal resources and capabilities falls short of expectations" (p. 81). It should be noted, however, that the internal view is absent in resource dependence theory. For that reason, this lens can, at best, be used complementary to an internal perspective when it comes to explain the IS sourcing decision.

Institutional theory is similar to resource-dependence theory in emphasizing the role of the external environment as to shape the behavior of organizations. However, opposed to the dependence perspective, that concedes the organization an active role in responding to market pressures, institutional theory holds that organizations passively adapt to its environment. The firm is viewed as part of a social network. It strives for conformity in order to match the norms, rules, and regulations of the institutionalized environment, in which it is embedded. Ang and Cummings (1997) provide a rare and valuable example on how to apply this perspective in the IS outsourcing context of the US Banking Industry. They investigated institutional pressures of banks towards outsourcing their data processing facilities. Their results indicate that banks outsource, to a limited extent, in response to the sourcing behavior of other (peer) banks and to a somewhat higher extent to pressures from bank regulators, like the Federal Reserve Bank. More importantly, however, Ang and Cummings (1997) show that firms do not unreflectively respond to conformity pressures. In accordance to critics of pure institutional theory, like Oliver (1991), they find support for the notion that "(...) banks may enact different strategic responses to institutional pressures for IS sourcing" (p. 237). The strategic responses reflect determinants on the firm level. They primarily represent situational variables and comparative decision criteria derived from economic lenses.

It may be concluded that the primary objective of institutional theory is to explain homogenous behavior of organizations. This is in contradiction to observations in practice which suggest that firms behave very heterogeneous in IS sourcing. Nevertheless, the study of Ang and Cummings (1997) has shown that external influences can indeed contribute to explain the variance in IS outsourcing, if treated as a variable that can take different instances. In this case, organizations can decide whether they feel pressured or not. This means that the variance of IS outsourcing may partially be explained by factors that go beyond those illustrated in Figure 2-1, p. 23. The nature of these factors will be examined more closely in Section 2.2.3, p. 41. There is a close link between institutional theory and the innovation adoption perspective which is worth to be examined more intensively.

2.2.2.3 New Institutional Economics

In congruence to behavioralism, new institutional economics have been developed in response to the restrictive assumptions of neoclassics, in which the firm is treated as a "black box". The focus is on the function of the firm as opposed to the market system. The term "new institutional economics" may be traced back to Oliver E. Williamson, who initially used it as a synonym for his transaction cost economics (Richter and Bindseil, 1995). Accordingly, it may be appropriate to start with an outline of transaction cost theory and then proceed with analyzing agency, property rights, and incomplete contracts theory.

Transaction Cost Theory. Although Williamson has been established as the main contributor to transaction cost theory, his ideas have heavily been illuminated by Coase's (1937) essay on the "Nature of the Firm" and to a certain extent by Common's (1931) introduction of the transaction as the basic unit of economic analysis (Williamson, 1981). Ronald Coase raised the question on why firms exist at all, as opposed to the market, and gave a simple, but still revolutionary, answer (Schmidt, 2000, p. 15), "(...) there is a cost of using the price mechanism", i.e., the market (Coase, 1937, p. 390).

Williamson (1975; 1981; 1985) elaborated on Coase's argument that using the market is costly and developed the core of transaction cost theory. In particular, he extended Coase's explanation on five levels. First, he substituted market costs by transaction costs, which he defined as "(...) comparative costs of planning, adapting, and monitoring task completion under alternative governance structures" (Williamson, 1981, p. 552f.).[5] According to this definition, transaction costs can occur both when using the market and when using the firm. Second, while Coase remained vague on what makes up the firm, Williamson defined it as a hierarchical or authority system. Third, he explicated the conditions under which the firm is more transaction cost efficient than the market. Fourth, beside transaction costs (which include market costs), he considered production costs as a second comparative criteria to distinguish the market form the hierarchy. Fifth, he laid down the behavioral foundations about the individuals, i.e., economic actors that work under alternative governance structures (of which firms and markets are the leading alternatives). In this realm, he relied on Simon's concept of bounded rationality and the view that some economic actors tend to behave opportunistic.

Overall, it is the most often applied lens in explaining IS outsourcing (see Table 2-1, p. 25).[6] The theory is highly relevant in explaining selective IS outsourcing as it provides both economic criteria to decide whether to insource or outsource particular IS functions and insights into the determinants that impact the instances of these criteria.

Agency Theory is based on the conceptualization of the firm as "(...) a nexus of a set of contracting relationships (...)" between principals and agents (Jensen and Meckling, 1976, p. 310). This means that the firm is not defined as an individual entity,

5 This goes back to Arrow (1969, p. 48) who stated, "(...) market failure is not absolute; it is better to consider a broader category, that of transaction costs, which, in general, impede and in particular case block the formation of markets" (cited by Williamson, 1981b, p. 676).

6 Prior to outsourcing research it has been used to study vertical integration and make-or-buy choices (for an overview see the reviews from Rindfleisch and Heide, 1997 as well as Shelanski and Klein, 1995).

but through its inside and outside relationships. Accordingly, the main focus of the theory is not to explain why and when to enter into relationships with other stakeholders, e.g., external suppliers, but how to design the resulting contractual relationships in an efficient way. The efficiency criteria are called agency costs. They emerge when the principal allocates decision rights to the agent. Assuming that the agent has information advantages over the principal, the principal sets incentives in order to assure that the agent behaves in her/his interest. When calculating the magnitude of these incentives, the anticipated agency costs are considered. They are the sum of monitoring and bonding costs, including issues such as residual loss (Jensen and Meckling, 1976, p. 308). Building on these basic ideas, positive and normative agency theory may be distinguished (Richter and Bindseil, 1995, p. 134). *Normative* agency theory is mathematical in nature. It is build on neoclassical restrictive modelling assumptions, like a certain environment. The objective is to optimize contractual design activities in a way that maximizes the utility functions of the principal and the agent. By contrast, *positive* agency theory is more concerned with the verbal description of principal-agent relationships and the identification of the methods used to design and monitor contracts. Both types are primarily concerned with already existing relationships. They do not provide a rationale for why firms exist (Demsetz, 1991, p. 168). Nevertheless, some outsourcing researchers have found it useful to refer to normative agency theory in explaining the variance in IS outsourcing. In particular, they use concepts from agency theory such as measurement difficulty (Poppo and Zenger, 1998) and different types of costs that emerge in client(principal)-vendor(agent) relationships (Loh, 1994). Normative agency theory has only been applied to outsourcing in general. Sridhar and Balachandran (1997) developed a model that is concerned with whether two different types of tasks, characterized as downstream (associated with the final stage of the production process) and upstream (intermediate state), should be assigned internal to the firm or outsourced. Chalos and Sung (1998) design an agency model, which deals with the question of why a firm cannot replicate market incentives for cost reduction internally. Overall, it may be concluded that agency theory may at best be used complementary to transaction cost theory in order to explain the phenomenon of selective IS outsourcing.

Property Rights. The conceptualization of the firm as a nexus of contracts is rooted in the work from Alchian and Demsetz (1972), who developed the core of property rights theory. The theory is – in many ways – complementary to transaction cost economics, but still fundamentally different in its conceptualization of the firm. In congruence to TCE, it seeks to identify those situations under which the firm is more efficient than the market. In particular, Alchian and Demsetz (1972) argue that in situations where joint input, i.e., team production, is necessary, the costs of preventing "shirking" ("free-rider" problem) of the team members, are lower within the firm as opposed to the market (Alchian and Demsetz, 1972, p. 783, 794). In contrast to TCE, however, which holds that opportunistic behavior can better be reduced within the firm due the authority system, Alchian and Demsetz (1972) argue that the firm "(...) has no power or fiat, no authority, no disciplinary action any different in the slightest degree from ordinary market contracting between any two people" (p. 777). The firm is treated as a contractual system, in which it is indifferent whether the contacting partners are own employees or external vendors. Paradoxically, however, the alternative explanation for why a firm may prevent shirking more efficiently than the market is still – even though indirectly – related to the authority concept. Alchian and Demsetz intimate that it is the ownership over the input factors which gives the owner the "(...) right to renegotiate any input's contract independently of contracts with other input owners (...)" and "(...) the right to sell his central contractual residual status" (p.783). Overall, however, the rationale for why a firm exists has not been outlined explicitly (Foss, 1993, p. 130; Knudsen, 1995, p. 168; Schneider, 1995, p. 260). Moreover, the fact that employment contracts are treated as to equal market contracts is somewhat out of reality (Holmstrom and Roberts, 1998; Schmidt, 2000, p. 17).

Incomplete Contracts. Oliver Hart and his colleagues (Grossmann and Hart, 1986; Hart, 1996; Hart and Moore, 1990) have taken up the idea of ownership to explain the existence of the firm and developed what may be called the incomplete contracts theory (Foss, 2000; Holmstrom, 1999). Hart and Moore (1990, p. 1149) conclude, "(...) we have developed a theory of the optimal alignment of assets and used it to understand the boundaries of the firm."

The theory poses that in a world of incomplete contracts, ex-post bargaining matters greatly. That is, a party that undertakes a specific investment has to make sure that the other party performs as well. In order to safeguard against non-performance, it needs a base of power to exercise authority. More importantly, the exercise of authority has to serve as an incentive for the other party to perform. According to incomplete contracts theory *only* ownership of those non-human assets, that are necessary within the production process, provides this type of authority. It gives the owner the residual right to exclude the other party from using the assets, e.g., to dissolve the contract with individual employees rather than with a whole firm.

In the IS outsourcing context, the issue of ownership has gained momentum with the arrival of special ownership deals, in which the client holds a certain amount of the vendor's capital. Some researchers have focused on explaining the existence of particular ownership arrangements in IS outsourcing. For example, Heinzl (1992; 1993b) has explicitly addressed the issue of ownership, studying the reasons for and wider implications of spin-off arrangements in Germany, other European countries, and the USA. Similarly, Reponen (1993) has undertaken a longitudinal study on spin-off arrangements in Finland. In a few studies, the ownership issue is addressed more implicitly, in that different clusters of outsourcing arrangements are linked to different motivations and strategic intents. For example, selective outsourcing and multi-supplier outsourcing (non-ownership) were found to be associated with different motivations than joint-ventures (partial ownership) and strategic alliances, which in turn differ from spin-offs or cases of insourcing (total ownership) (Currie, 1998; DiRomualdo and Gurbaxani, 1998). Overall, the empirical results of these studies are consistent with the general conclusion from Holmstrom that, "(...) ownership boundaries serve many purposes [other than backing up authority] and investment incentives are provided in many ways" (Holmstrom and Roberts, 1998. p. 92).

The objective of this research project is not to explain the existence of different ownership structures. Ownership is not treated as a dependent variable that is sought to be explained. In other words, the boundaries of the firm are not defined by ownership, but by legal forms that manifest the economic autonomy ("Eigenverantwortlichkeit") of a firm. Nevertheless, it may be promising to treat ownership as an independent variable that impacts client attitudes towards IS outsourcing. In this realm, ownership may be viewed as an instrument to safeguard against opportunistic behavior of vendor personnel. If viewed in this sense, incomplete contracts theory may provide valuable insight into the sources of authority and therefore may serve as an important complementary lens to transaction cost theory, in which the firm is conceptualized as a authority system.

2.2.2.4 Dynamic Theories

Dynamic theories comprise evolutionary theory and resource-based theory. Both may be viewed as to provide a micro foundation of Schumpetarian dynamic theory of competition (Knudsen, 1995, p. 205). Schumpeter (1934) furnished the view of market competition as a dynamic process that enfolds by chance. Economic actors (i.e. firms) are characterized as entrepreneurs that constantly search for new opportunities to innovate, e.g., by setting up new production functions that outperform its predecessors (Schumpeter, 1939).[7] As a consequence, firms do not only survive in the market due to economies of scale in using a given homogenous production function, but rather due to their ability to constantly improve their production process.

Evolutionary Theory. Nelson and Winter (1982) have taken over the dynamic view of market competition. In particular, they integrated the concepts of tacit knowledge (Polanyi, 1966) and routines to Schumpetarian competition (Rumelt, et al., 1991, p. 16).[8] The firm is conceptualized as a bundle of routines and as a historical entity whose productive knowledge is the result of an experience-based learning process. Since all firms go through different learning processes, they are able to develop distinctive capabilities and identities. This view is fundamentally different from Neoclassics and IO Economics, where the firm is merely treated as a homogenous entity without a past (Knudsen, 1995).

However, evolutionary theory also clashes with institutional economics, as it rigorously denies that selection processes of organizations are rational or at least boundedly rational, and that they result in efficient solutions (Knudsen, 1995). According

---

7 In this realm, it may be noted that Hayek (1945) has been the more radical and consistent proponent of this view.

8 In addition, Nelson and Winter's work has been illuminated by Penrose (1959), Simon (1957), and Cyert and March (1963).

to Winter, a firm's selection mechanism will "(...) produce progress, but (...) not (...) an 'answer' to any well-specified question or list of questions about how activities should be organized" (Winter, 1988. p. 177; cited by Knudsen, 1995, p. 204). Accordingly, evolutionary theory does not provide any rationale for why a firm should insource or outsource IS functions.

Resource-based Theory. While Nelson and Winter still rely on a market or industry perspective, closely tied to Schumpeter's original contribution, resource-based theory is more concerned with the individual firm and its growth process. Edith Penrose (1959) has conceptualized the firm as a collection of productive resources. She questions the practicability of the neoclassical search for equilibrium states. The main reasons against such a "state of rest" are grounded in the nature of the resources – in particular, in their "indivisibility"; the fact that they can be "used differently" and in a "specialized manner"; and due to the fact that "(...) in the ordinary process of operation and expansion [i.e. within the process of using the resources] new productive services are constantly being created" (Penrose, 1959, p. 68).

Based on Penrose's ground work, representatives of the resource-based theory/view, on the one hand, have focused on the identification and differentiation of firm resources. On the other hand, they elaborated on the characteristics of resources that furnish a sustained competitive advantage of the firm (Amit and Schoemaker, 1993; Barney, 1991; Collis and Montgomery, 1996; Dierickx, et al., 1989; Grant, 1991; Wernerfelt, 1984). They are concerned with the internal sources of competitive advantage as opposed to external forces that have been in the center of traditional IO research.

In IS outsourcing research, the resource-based theory has been used in two different ways. On the one hand, it is argued that the evaluation of a firm's IS resources influences the IS outsourcing decision, either by indentifying internal resource gaps (Teng, et al., 1995) or comparative resource deficits against the market (Dibbern and Heinzl, 2001; 2002). On the other hand, it is proposed that those IS resources that provide a competitive advantage for a firm should not be outsourced (Dibbern and Heinzl, 2001; 2002; Loh, 1994). Empirical support for the strategic argument, however, has been quite inconsistent. In fact, it does not seem uncommon that companies outsource IS functions even though IS is rated as a strategic asset (McLellan, et al., 1995). In spite of these contradictions – whose sources need to be investigated more deeply – it may be concluded that the resource-based theory is predestined to explain heterogeneous firm behavior. Rather than transaction cost theory, that focuses solely on cost efficiency, it recognizes the fact that the resources themselves and the benefits that may result from their deployment may vary in alternative sourcing arrangements.

2.2.3 From Innovation Diffusion to Attitude-Behavior Approaches

One theory that does not fit under the overall umbrella of the theory of the firm, but still has been applied in order to study the reasons for IS outsourcing, is the innovation diffusion theory. Two important concepts in innovation theories are adoption and diffusion (Rogers, 1983). While adoption is the decision to use the innovation, diffusion is the process by which an innovation spreads out into social systems (e.g., in organizations, industries, countries).

In IS outsourcing research, only the diffusion perspective has been applied (Hu, et al., 1997; Loh and Venkatraman, 1992b). In this realm, IS outsourcing is viewed as an administrative innovation, arguing that it amounts to adopting new arrangements for governing the IS infrastructure. Rather than studying IS outsourcing from the perspective of an individual firm, the focus is on investigating how IS outsourcing has spread out within the USA. It provides a rare example of a process perspective, where longitudinal data is used to explore alternative diffusion patterns.

Both the level of analysis (social system) and the logical structure (process theory), incorporated in innovation diffusion theory, do not match with the firm level variance theoretic logic that will be used in this research. However, the theoretical arguments used to explain the diffusion may still be of relevance in explaining the variance in IS outsourcing at the individual firm level.

The two studies on innovation diffusion (Hu, et al., 1997; Loh and Venkatraman, 1992b) tested competing diffusion models that best matched the observed distribution of outsourcing events in a particular time period. The diffusion models are based on the argument that the diffusion reflects an imitation process. The differences in the models are due to different sources of influence of the imitation, which reflect different communication channels. Loh and Venkatraman (1992b) found evidence for internal sources of influence (outsourcing behavior of other organizations) being better predictors for the observed distribution of outsourcing events than external sources (mass media reports and vendor sales figures) or mixed sources of influence (both external and internal). They noted that the tendency to outsource in response to other organizations (internal) was stronger after the Kodak announcement – the so-called "Kodak effect". By Contrast, Hu et al. (1997) did not find any evidence for the Kodak effect, but did find support that a mixture of internal and external communication channels drove outsourcing decisions.

From a methodological point of view, it may appear somewhat stylized to link certain patterns of distribution to socializing actions, which are assumed to be reflected by different communication channels. However, the idea that IS outsourcing may result from a simple imitation process has been supported in an alternative research setting as well (Lacity and Hirschheim, 1993b). It therefore deserves closer examination.

The one theory of the firm, that comes close to this kind of reasoning, is institutional theory. Indeed, Ang and Cummings (1997, p. 237) explicitly referred to the work from Loh and Venkatraman (1992b) in motivating the consideration of external institutional influences on IS sourcing in the Banking Industry. Opposed to innovation diffusion theory, however, they take a variance theoretic perspective. That is, they want to explain heterogeneous sourcing behavior of banks rather than homogenous behavior. Accordingly, external pressures are treated as variables. It is assumed that organizations may perceive external influences differently. Some may feel strongly pressured and conform to such pressures, while others may not feel pressured at all. This view comes close to the notion of adoption (i.e. whether to adopt IS outsourcing or not). It should be noted that *adoption* may be viewed as a choice among alternatives, including non-adoption, partial adoption, or full adoption. The rate of adoption can be treated as a continuos variable. This means that the degree of IS outsourcing may be viewed as a level of adoption, where non-adoption means insourcing.

Roger's classic innovation theory is concerned with both explaining adoption and diffusion behavior. Its empirical support for the adoption perspective, however, is quite inconsistent (Dowes and Mohr, 1979). One reason for these inconsistencies may be traced back to the fact that it lacks a solid theoretical foundation. It has been developed inductively from a synthesis of over 3000 literature sources spanning five decades of innovation research in multiple disciplines. They range from anthropology and agricultural studies to psychology and business administration. In a review of various applications of Roger's model in the IS context, Fichman (1992) concludes that the explanatory power of the model is mostly limited to the adoption behavior of individual persons regarding homogenous IT products. Overall, innovation diffusion theory appears to be too specific as to provide a general frame for adoption behavior, while at the same time it is too general to explain specific adoption behavior. From an extensive review of innovation adoption research, Fichman (2000, p. 107f.) concludes, "The absence of a general theory of innovation suggests that researchers should develop theories of the middle range – that is, theories tailored to specific classes of technologies and/or to a particular adoption context."

There is, however, one theory that is concerned with predicting and explaining individual behavior, and that appears to provide a promising *general framework* that can guide the formation of specific adoption theories. It is the *theory of reasoned action* (Ajzen and Fishbein, 1980; Fishbein and Ajzen, 1975) and its extended successor, the *theory of planned behavior* (Ajzen, 1985). They are rooted in social psychology research.

The *theory of reasoned action* has been viewed as "(...) the dominant theoretical framework in the attitude-behavior literature" (Olson and Zana, 1993, p. 131). Its objective is to predict and understand motivational influences on individual behavior, where "(...) behavior involves a choice among two or more alternatives" (Ajzen and Fishbein, 1980, p. 79). The actual behavior of a person is assumed to be influenced by her/his intention to behave in a certain direction. The intentions, again, are driven by the person's own attitudes toward the behavior and the influential opinions of others regarding the behavior (subjective norm). The *theory of planned behavior* adds the degree of control over the behavior as a third variable that influences intentions and the actual behavior. Moreover, behavioral beliefs are postulated to be the underlying influence on an individual's attitude towards performing a particular behavior. Corresponding types of beliefs impact subjective norm and perceived behavioral control (Ajzen, 1985; Madden, et al., 1992). Overall, the logical structure is of a variance type. All constructs are treated as variables that can take different instances.

Although the theory of planned behavior has nearly exclusively been used to explain the behavior of individuals, it may fruitfully be applied to the organizational context (see, e.g., Cordano and Frieze Hanson, 2000). As already outlined (Section 2.1.2), IS sourcing may be viewed as a major organizational decision. Organizations are represented by individuals that make decisions as agents of the organization. That is, decisions in organizations are made either by individuals or by groups of individuals. It, therefore, may be concluded that the general variance theoretic structure of the theory of planned behavior may illuminate the prediction and understanding of the sourcing decision. In particular, the two dimensions "subjective norm" and "perceived behavioral control" may be used as complementary explanatory factors to the variance theoretic structure that has been identified previously (see Figure 2-1, p. 23).

"Subjective norm" correspondents with the notion of institutional theory that external others influence an organization's actions. "Perceived behavioral control" adds to the notion that there may be other organizational impediments that limit the ability of organizational decision makers to act strictly rational or intendedly rational.

2.2.4 Summary of Selection Process

The objective of the previous review was to identify those theoretical lenses that can fruitfully be applied to explain the variance in IS outsourcing. Altogether 14 different theoretical lenses have been analyzed. They include 12 theories of the firm, the innovation diffusion and adoption perspective, and the attitude-behavior view from social psychology. The selection process has been guided by the variance structure, as illustrated in Figure 2-1, p. 23. In particular, potential reference theories should provide criteria to compare the alternatives of IS insourcing and outsourcing.

From the theories considered, *transaction cost theory* and *resource-based theory* best matched theses requirements. They provide two complementary rationales for IS outsourcing. Transaction cost theory focuses on cost efficiency as the ultimate criterion for the sourcing decision. Resource-based theory takes into consideration that the resources, required to provide an IS function, and the benefits, resulting from the effective deployment of these resources, may differ between organizations.

Both lenses are based on the view that organizational decision makers act strictly rational or at least intendedly rational. That is, they analyze, evaluate and compare alternative (strategic) options based on some sort of criteria that reflect the overall objectives of the firm.

Such a view implies strong assumptions about the actual behavior of economic actors. For example, transaction cost theory is based on the assumption that some humans behave opportunistic and that the internal authority system provides more efficient safeguards against such behavior than formal authority through market contracts – especially if the expected negative consequences of such behavior are especially high. Such a view has motivated others to either find reasons that back up these assumptions or to find alternative explanations. Both are worth to be considered complementary to TCT and RBT.

One theory that remains within the rationalist chain of causality is the *incomplete contracts theory*. It provides insights into the role of ownership as to back up a firm's authority over those that do the work.

By contrast, institutional theory may provide an alternative explanation to the notion that an organization's IS sourcing situation results from an active choice of alternatives. It holds that organizations passively adapt to external pressures. However, the theory remains silent on how exactly such an adaptation process takes place. Organizations are treated as if they have an own identity. In reality, however, they are represented by individuals. These individuals act and react to the environment on behalf of the organization, for which they work.

Such an individual level view is consistent with the notion that IS outsourcing results from a decision made by individuals. Accordingly, it seems worth to consider a theoretical perspective that explicitly addresses the behavior of individuals. The *theory of planned behavior* provides a general framework that explains and predicts individual behavior. It fruitfully combines the rational actor view of behavior with social dimensions of decision making. Thereby, it goes beyond the variance theoretic structure, presented in Figure 2-1, p. 23, and complements the reasoning from transaction cost theory, resource-based theory, and incomplete contracts theory.

2.3 Hypotheses from Selected Theoretical Lenses

From the four theoretical lenses, selected in the previous section, hypotheses will be deduced to understand and predict why firms behave different regarding the sourcing of their IS functions – in particular application development and maintenance. The hypotheses represent cause-effect relationships between variables. They reflect the chain of causality that each theory contributes to explain heterogeneous behavior in IS sourcing. Moreover, "(...) they serve as crucial bridges to link the theory with data" (Sutton and Staw, 1995, p. 376). That is, they specify the theoretical relationships that are to be tested empirically. The building of hypotheses begins with transaction cost theory and precedes with resource-based theory, incomplete contracts theory, and the theory of planned behavior. Each theory has its own set of variables. However, some variables may overlap between theories, some linkages between variables may be the same between theories, while others may be in contradiction to each other (Spinner, 1974, p. 173). These inter-theoretical relationships will be highlighted during the sequential process of applying each theory. Finally, the hypotheses will be synthesized into a comprehensive framework, that serves as a basis to theorize about the impact of cultural dimensions.

2.3.1 Transaction Cost Theory

According to transaction cost theory, a firm's current sourcing option for a particular IS function may be explained from a cost comparison between the in-house option and the market option. While the primary focus is on transaction costs, Williamson (1981a; 1985; 1990) notes that production costs need to be considered as well. In fact, he argues that it is decisive to consider the sum of production and transaction cost differences between the firm and the market.

The core of the theory provides insight into the conditions under which both types of costs – with a clear emphasis on transaction costs – differ under alternative governance modes.

In the context of this study, these conditions may be called determinants of comparative cost advantages of insourcing versus outsourcing (see Figure 2-1, p. 23). These determinants are of a contextual character. They describe the features of the sourcing object (i.e. the particular IS functions) using certain variables.

In the following, the two types of costs will first be defined in the IS context. They have to be clearly divided. Then, the determinants will be introduced and analyzed. The relevant constructs will be defined and their impacts on the sourcing decision will be deduced. The resulting transaction cost theoretic framework is graphically depicted in Figure 2-4, p. 62.

2.3.1.1 Production and Transaction Costs

Transaction Costs. Williamson (1981, p. 552f.) defined transaction costs as "(...) comparative costs of planning, adapting, and monitoring task completion under alternative governance structures." This definition is grounded on Common's (1931) conceptualization of the term "transaction" as the transfer of property rights. Accordingly, transaction costs have also broadly been defined as the costs that arise in defining, transferring, and enforcing property rights (Tietzel, 1981, p. 1981; cited by Picot and Dietl, 1990, p. 178).

Based on Picot (1982, p. 270), transactions within an economic exchange relationship may be decomposed into four phases: (1) *Initiation*, e.g., searching for and gathering information about the exchange partner(s); (2) *Agreement*, e.g., negotiating and specifying the terms of the exchange relationship(s) regarding timing, quality, quantity, price, security, secrecy, and other factors; (3) *Control*, e.g., ensuring compliance to the agreed terms; and (4) *Adaptation*, e.g., changing agreements over time (see also Windsperger, 1983, p. 896). As a fifth phase, (5) *Cancellation* may be added, which refers to the dissolution of the exchange relationship, with all its associated legal consequences and residual obligations (Albach, 1988b, p. 1160).

These activities are necessary to varying degrees and may take different forms when delegating IS tasks to internal or external agents. For example, the tasks are usually specified in a written contract with an external vendor, while the specification of tasks with employees may be manifested in work descriptions, that are not necessarily part of the employment contract. In summarizing all these activities, *transaction costs* may broadly be *defined* as all costs in terms of time, effort, and money spent, that arise when delegating tasks of an IS function to one or more agents.[9]

Basic Behavioral Assumptions for the Existence of Transaction Costs. Two fundamental assumptions back up the existence of transaction costs. First, it is assumed that economic actors are *boundedly rational* (based on Simon, 1957). Accordingly, they tend to be satisfied with second best rather than optimal solutions. That is, principals search for cost efficient solutions and strive to settle perfect contracts, but often they have to realize that many contracts can only be settled incompletely (Williamson, 1981a, p. 554). The incompleteness of contracts would not matter if the contractual partners were completely trustworthy ("stewardship behavior," Williamson, 1975, p. 26). This, however, is neglected by a second assumption. It is assumed that some actors behave *opportunistic*, which means that they cunningly take advantage of opportunities at the expense of others – also referred to as "(...) self-interest seeking with guile" (Williamson, 1981, p. 554). It is assumed that it is hard, or indeed impossible to anticipate an other's attitude towards opportunism, which likely leads to opportunistic behavior (Williamson, 1985, p. 64).[10] Accordingly, transaction costs arise in order to safeguard against the potential opportunistic behavior of an exchange partner.

Production Costs. By contrast, production costs (or service costs) are independent of specific behavioral assumptions. They include all costs that arise for performing the actual activities necessary to complete the tasks associated with the provision of

---

9 That is, transaction costs do not only include direct costs, but also opportunity costs "(...) in form of time and effort that is taken away from alternative value creating usage" (Kaas, 1992, p. 10 – translated from German; similar by Rindfleisch and Heide, 1997, p. 47; both cited by Jensen, 2001, p. 20).

10 The difference between opportunistic behavior and attitudes towards opportunism has been explicated by Ghoshal and Moran (1996).

an IS function. More specifically, they comprise the costs for all input factors that are needed in order to reach a desired output (Albach, 1981). Within the process of developing and maintaining software applications, the input factors, to the most part, are made up by the human work forces (Prosser, 1997, p. 155). They mainly refer to the money spent for the combined working hours of all individuals involved in the process of developing and maintaining applications (Boehm, 1987; De Marco and Lister, 1987; Sneed, 1987). The actual means of production, e.g., the required hardware and software tools, play a subordinate role. (This is in contrast to systems operations, where hardware and software make up a significant part of overall costs.) The actual productivity process is often characterized by information and knowledge exchange relationships between various stakeholders (see also Section 2.1.1.1, p. 10).

2.3.1.2 Comparative Cost Advantages

According to Williamson (1979; 1981a), three basic constructs can be distinguished that serve as determinants of cost differences between alternative IS sourcing arrangements. These are (1) frequency, (2) asset specificity, and (3) uncertainty. Williamson has called these three factors "attributes" of transactions, as may be seen from the following statement,

> "The main hypothesis out of which transaction cost economics works is this: *Firms seek to align transactions, which differ in their attributes, with governance structures, which differ in their costs and competencies, in a discriminating (mainly transaction costs economizing) way*" (Williamson, 1991, p. 79, italics original).

It can be shown, however, that treating frequency, asset specificity and uncertainty as attributes of transactions likely leads to misunderstandings. Recalling that transactions equal such actions like planning, adapting and monitoring task completion – as it may be concluded from Williamson's definition of transaction costs – attributes would be associated with planning, adapting, and monitoring. For example, *frequency* – if treated as an attribute of transactions – would refer to the frequency of planning, adapting and monitoring task completion. At the same time, however, frequency is meant to be a determinant of transaction costs, which refer to the costs for activities like contracting, monitoring or contract adaptation. This, however, would bring 'frequency' close to a *tautological* concept, as it seems inevitable that a high frequency of performing transactions leads to higher transaction costs.

Therefore, it may be concluded that the term "transactions" would need to be substituted by *"tasks"* or *"business functions"* in Williamson's definition. Not transactions are organized in alternative governance modes, but certain tasks or business functions. If viewed in this vein, the attributes become a different meaning. They may be treated as (1) the *frequency* with which a task is carried out, (2) the *specificity of the assets* that are required for task completion, and (3) *uncertainty* associated with the task. Most of the empirical studies have implicitly treated the three constructs in this sense. Williamson's own examples on how to apply transaction cost theory appear to support this semantic correction. In the following, the three concepts are treated as attributes or characteristics of IS functions. Frequency will be addressed later on. The focus will be on asset specificity and uncertainty, first.

Williamson (1990, p. 142) defined asset specificity as follows, "(...) Asset specificity has reference to the degree to which an asset can be redeployed to alternative uses and by alternative users without sacrifice of productive value." In other words, the *specificity of assets* refers to the degree to which the assets necessary to perform an IS function are unique by being especially tailored to the requirements of the user organization. The more tailored they are to a particular exchange relationship, the less they are of value in alternative exchange settings. This means that both parties to the exchange are locked into the relationship (Williamson, 1981a, p. 555). The user organization (principal) can not easily switch to another provider (internal or external agents) and the provider cannot use the assets in an alternative user context.

In particular, three types of asset specificity can be distinguished: (1) physical asset specificity, (2) human asset specificity, and (3) site specificity.

In this study, *physical assets* refer to the special hardware products and software tools necessary to build and maintain application software. In general, they can be purchased from the market as standard products. That is, they are *not specifically* build or customized to develop or maintain application software as part of an IS. They usually remain unchanged and can easily be deployed in alternative uses, e.g., in building and maintaining other software applications within a different organizational context.

Human assets refer to special characteristics of the actual workers that are involved in developing and maintaining software applications. In particular, they refer to different kinds of knowledge sets that are required to perform each IS function. According to Williamson (1981a, p. 563), it is the nature of knowledge that matters in order to differentiate between highly and less specific human assets. In exemplifying situations in which knowledge may be characterized as specific, Williamson (1981a, p. 242) refers to "(...) Polanyi's discussion of personal knowledge". Polanyi (1966) distinguishes two types of knowledge: (1) explicit knowledge and (2) tacit knowledge.

(1) Explicit knowledge refers to knowledge that is transmittable in formal, systematic language. Not only can it be acquired outside a particular organizational setting, it may also be used in alternative exchange relationships. Therefore, explicit knowledge is, by definition, not firm specific. However, not all knowledge can be acquired and usefully be deployed independent of the context of its use.

(2) Tacit knowledge is distinctive from explicit knowledge both regarding its attributes and the process through which it is being acquired. One of its main *attributes* refers to the difficulty in articulating and documenting tacit knowledge. According to Polanyi (1966, p. 4), "(...) we can know more than we can tell". On the other hand, Nonaka (1994, p. 16) describes the *process* by which tacit knowledge is

being built, "Tacit knowledge is deeply rooted in action, commitment and involvement in a specific context." The transfer of tacit knowledge requires socialization action between individuals as a basis to share experiences (Nonaka, 1994, p. 19).

Accordingly, it may be concluded that both the attributes and the process characteristics of tacit knowledge amount to understand why human asset specificity may differ. Before applying the concepts to the IS context, however, it is necessary to examine the notion of IS knowledge more closely.

IS Knowledge Types. In the IS context, a number of researchers have categorized IS knowledge in terms of "knowledge about what" (Iivari, et al., 2001; Nelson, 1991a; Vitalari, 1985). In application development and maintenance the "what" may include such issues as (a) the *technology*, in particular the methods and techniques (e.g., programming languages, methods for requirement analysis or design, and maintenance tools) required to actually create, configure and modify software products, (b) the *organizational context* that is reflected by the social and economic processes, in particular, the work processes that are to be supported and reflected by the software, and (c) the *software application* itself, e.g., its structure, functionality, underlying operational procedure, and use (Iivari, et al., 2001).

(a) Technology/technical knowledge is mostly of an explicit nature. It can be learned within an educational program, e.g., in university, through special training programs, or, idiosyncratically, from text books or other external media.

(b) By contrast, *organizational knowledge* can be highly tacit (i.e. specific). Beath and Walker (1998) differentiate between standard and unique organizational processes. Standard processes are "best practice" within industries and business types. For example, some accounting procedures are highly standardized. By contrast, a unique process "(...) is one that is distinctive in some important way, as compared to other firms in the industry, (...) by design (...) or by accident" (p. 668f.). Unique processes often bear a high amount of tacit knowledge of those people that are involved in the process. As far as application software is sought to reflect and support the unique processes of organizations, the persons that develop and maintain the software have to gain a solid understanding of these unique processes. Accordingly, one attribute of human asset specificity is the extent to which unique organizational knowledge is required to perform an IS function.

(c) Application software knowledge. On the other hand, if unique process knowledge flows into the development and maintenance process of a firm's application software, then the software itself can become a unique product. If associated with poor documentation, applications may become so individually tailored to an organization's needs that only view people actually understand its functionality and structure. Accordingly, a second attribute of human asset specificity is the extent to which unique application knowledge is required to perform an IS function.

Acquiring specific IS knowledge. Human asset specificity, however, can also be characterized by the process in which unique organizational and application knowledge is being acquired. This process may be characterized by knowledge exchange and socializing action between various stakeholders (Hirschheim, et al., 1991; Hirschheim, et al., 1996; Newman and Robey, 1992; Nygaard, 1986; Robey and Newman, 1996). The process activities may be termed *socializing collaboration,* defined as the extent to which the work within an IS function requires close interpersonal relations and communication between individuals. Two groups of persons that are involved in the process of developing and maintaining software applications are the users (i.e, clients) and the IS workers (e.g., analysts, programmers, designers). Considering that user participation is often necessary but not sufficient for developing and maintaining IS, two process characteristics of human asset specificity are the extent to which performing an IS function requires intensive social collaboration (1) between IS workers and users, as well as (2) within the group of IS workers.

Overall, human asset specificity may be decomposed into four sub-constructs as illustrated in Figure 2-2.

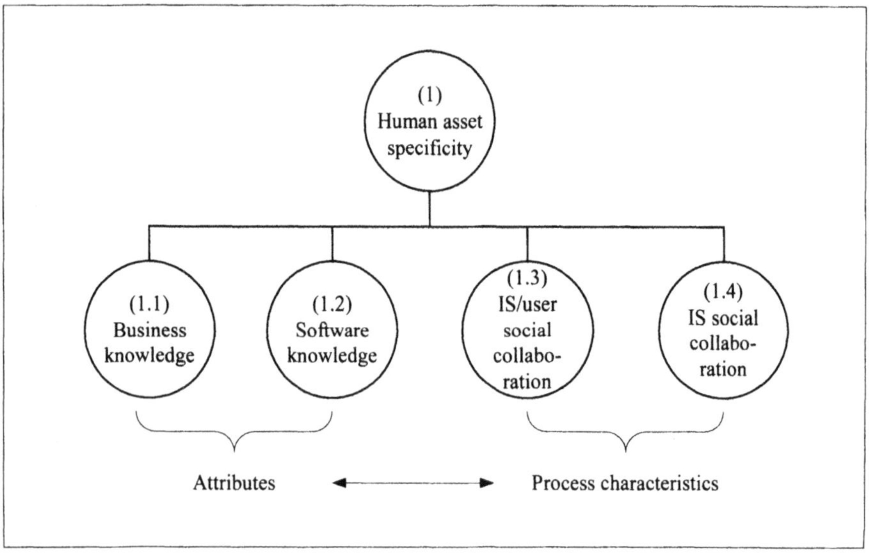

Figure 2-2: Decomposition of Human Asset Specificity

Site specificity. The concept of socializing collaboration is related to Williamson's third type of specificity, which is site specificity. It refers to situations in which the assets, necessary to complete a task, have to be located at the client site. It may be argued that collaborative IS work, which requires face-to-face interaction between users and IS workers, usually is being carried out at the client site. This assumption is in accordance with the service character of both functions. Marshall (1949, p. 471) has noted years ago:

> "(...) when a person sells his services, he has to present himself where they are delivered. It matters nothing to the seller of bricks whether they are to be used in building a palace or a sewer: but it matters a great deal to the seller of labor."

This view may still be true in today's business, as certain problems that cannot be easily articulated or written down (tacit) are best discussed and solved in face-to-face interaction. New communication technologies partially serve as substitutes for face-to-face collaboration (e.g., video conferences), however, they hardly provide a medium to exchange tacit knowledge, as this requires more immediate social interaction. Accordingly, site specificity – as far as it is still of relevance – is being incorporated in the concept of social collaboration.

Overall, it may be concluded that from the assets involved in the development and maintenance of application software, human assets can significantly differ in their specificity between organizations. However, what are the wider implications of human asset specificity for the sourcing of both functions?

According to Williamson, asset specificity has a profound impact on both transaction cost differences (ΔTC) and production cost differences (ΔPC) between the firm and the market. In turn, the sum of cost differences $(\Delta PC + \Delta TC)$ determines whether an IS function should be performed in-house or outsourced to an external service provider. These dependencies can be depicted graphically in a simplified model (see Figure 2-3). It takes sourcing as a dichotomous choice between the in-house and outsourcing option. Cost differences between both options are a taken as a function of human asset specificity.

If the degree of human asset specificity is low, both types of costs may be lower if the IS function is outsourced to an external service provider. This may be the case if a company has purchased standard software products, that marginally need to be adjusted to the company's needs, e.g., if the software supports standard processes. External suppliers may easily build up the knowledge to configure the software and use that knowledge with a broad range of customers (Beath and Walker, 1998).

At the same time, transaction costs are likely higher internally. The right employees have to be found, they need to be integrated into the company, be motivated, the tasks have to be specified, and it may be quite difficult to dismiss employees, when no longer needed. On the other hand, outside transaction costs may be quite low. The coordination, motivation, and monitoring of the IS staff can fully or partially be transferred to the responsibility of the external vendor. If problems arise, the vendor can easily be exchanged, since there usually are many vendors available with the required standard skill sets.

By contrast, external transaction costs may supersede internal transaction costs (right hand from A_1), when human asset specificity increases. It then becomes more difficult to specify ex ante the terms of the contract. Bilateral negotiations become increasingly important. This is especially true if software has to be newly developed or standard software be tailored to unique business processes. In this case, vendors need to be carefully selected. Soft skills become more meaningful. Tasks can only loosely be specified, and the total costs involved only roughly be estimated. This increases the danger of opportunistic behavior. Vendors may bit low to be hired, knowing that the customer is unable to correctly estimate total costs. During the life of the contract, the vendor may try to renegotiate or may perform at lower quality than expected, in order to realize his profit margin (see also Hill, 1990, p. 500, 501). This forces the customer to constantly monitor the vendor. By contrast, in-house transaction costs may be significantly lower if one assumes that opportunistic behavior can more effectively be prevented through internal authority.

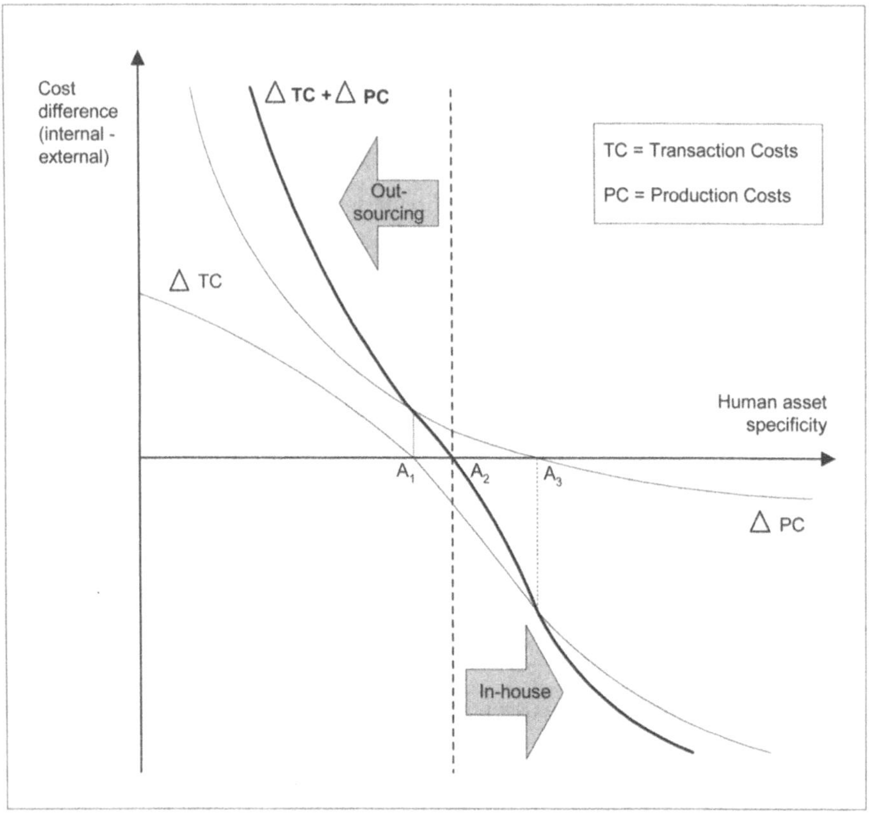

Figure 2-3: Impact of Human Asset Specificity on Cost Differences
(based on Williamson 1981, p. 560, the same 1985, p. 93, the same 1990, p. 153; see also Dibbern et al. 2001, p. 684)

The function of the sum of production and transaction cost differences ($\Delta PC + \Delta TC$) shows that up to a certain degree of human asset specificity (A_2), the production cost advantages of an external vendor may still supersede associated transaction cost disadvantages. However, with increasing specificity (right hand of A_2), the transaction cost disadvantages become predominate and in-house performance becomes superior. In parallel, the production cost advantages of external vendors diminish. There may actually be a point (A_3), when in-house production costs are lower than external ones. If a high degree of unique client business understanding is required to build and maintain software applications, the vendor's set up costs for adapting this knowledge are likely higher than those of in-house IS workers. In-house workers may already be familiar with the special requirements of the users, based on past experiences. Moreover, they may have advantages in social interaction with key client stakeholders as they are more familiar with the client's language as well as with the norms and regulations of the organization they serve. In summarizing the preceding relationships, the following hypotheses may be deduced:

Hypothesis 1a: The more *specific* the human assets required to perform an IS function are, the higher the comparative *transaction cost* advantage of insourcing as opposed to outsourcing an IS function.

Hypothesis 1b: The more *specific* the human assets required to perform an IS function are, the higher the comparative *production cost* advantage of insourcing as opposed to outsourcing an IS function.

Hypothesis 2a: The higher the comparative *transaction cost* advantage of insourcing as opposed to outsourcing an IS function, the less it will be *outsourced.*

Hypothesis 3a: The higher the comparative *production cost* advantage of insourcing as opposed to outsourcing an IS function, the less it will be *outsourced.*

Uncertainty. The second construct that may explain cost differences between IS insourcing and outsourcing is uncertainty. Similar to asset specificity, uncertainty is a multi-faceted construct (Sutcliffe and Zaheer, 1998). In particular, environmental and behavioral uncertainty may be distinguished (Williamson, 1985). In the IS context, the *environment* may refer both to the intra firm context, which is reflected by the business functions that are served by an IS, and forces endogenous to the firm, which are manifested in the IT Industry. Both types of environments exert a significant influence on an organization's IS functions. The business functions reflect the 'What is to be served?' by an IS. If processes within the business functions change, information requirements likely change as well. This may force adaptations of the IS. The IT reflects the "means with which it is being served". If new innovative IT is developed in the market, the existing IT, as part of an IS, becomes challenged. IS workers have to understand the requirements and opportunities that arise from these environmental changes. This requires a learning process, which takes time and effort. Accordingly, two types of environmental uncertainty may be distinguished (see also Willcocks, et al., 1995a, p. 63): The first, *business driven uncertainty,* refers to the extent to which the required business skill sets for the completion of tasks within an IS function constantly change. The second, *technology driven uncertainty,* captures the extent to which the required technical skill sets for the completion of tasks within an IS function constantly change due to the technological environment.

IS managers have to decide how to best cope with these changing requirements in skill sets. As outlined previously, skill sets are among the most important input factors in application development and maintenance. When it comes to delegating tasks to IS agents, it is important to have a good estimate of the required skill sets and time needed to acquire them. If, however, skill sets constantly change due to dynamics in the IS environment, it becomes nearly impossible to make any realistic forecast. This, again, increases the danger of opportunistic behavior leading to transaction costs. The costs incurred may be lower internally, because internal authority can safeguard against opportunistic behavior, whereas similar safeguards would cause significantly higher transaction costs in case of outsourcing. Accordingly, the following hypotheses may be deduced:

Hypothesis 4a: The higher the *technology driven uncertainty* associated with the provision of an IS function, the higher the comparative *transaction cost* advantage of insourcing as opposed to outsourcing an IS function.

Hypothesis 5a: The higher the *business driven uncertainty* associated with the provision of an IS function, the higher the comparative *transaction cost* advantage of insourcing as opposed to outsourcing an IS function.

In addition, environmental uncertainty may impact production costs. External suppliers may be more efficient in coping with a high level of technological uncertainty. They often have higher budgets to constantly test innovative IT. Moreover, they can permanently learn from a large pool of customers on how new IT can be used effectively in different organizational settings. Accordingly, they may have lower set up costs in adapting innovative IT knowledge from the market, which leads to the following hypotheses:

Hypothesis 4b: The higher the *technology driven uncertainty* associated with the provision of an IS function, the lower the comparative *production cost* advantage of insourcing as opposed to outsourcing an IS function.

By contrast, an internal IS unit may have production cost advantages, when it comes to adapting to constantly changing business processes. Internal IS workers usually can better anticipate and understand such changes as they are more experienced with the business context.

Hypothesis 5b: The higher the *business driven uncertainty* associated with the provision of an IS function, the higher the comparative *production cost* advantage of insourcing as opposed to outsourcing an IS function.

On the other hand, internal employees may have production cost disadvantages, if the actual *work load* in an IS function shows high deviations during a year. In this case, it may not be worth employing own IS people, because they are not working at full capacity over the year (Picot and Maier, 1992). It may then be more efficient to switch from fixed salary costs to variable contractual costs with an external vendor, e.g., through a pay per use agreement (Currie and Willcocks, 1998; Huber, 1993; Knolmayer, 1994a). In this sense, the concept of work load variations is related to *frequency* of performing activities necessary to provide an IS function (Picot and Maier, 1992, p. 22). The following hypotheses may be deduced:

Hypothesis 6: The higher the *work load variations* associated with the provision of an IS function, the lower the comparative *production cost* advantage of insourcing as opposed to outsourcing an IS function.

While environmental uncertainty and work load variations indirectly influence human assets, behavioral uncertainty is more directly related to the IS workers. According to Williamson (1981a, p. 564), "(...) human assets can (...) be described in terms of (1) the degree to which they are firm-specific and (2) the ease with which productivity can be metered." The metering problem goes back to property rights theory (Alchian and Demsetz, 1972). It has widely been used as an equivalent of behavioral uncertainty. Rindfleisch and Heide (1997, p. 43) conclude from a review of studies on transaction cost theory, "Most of the studies in our review conceptualize behavioral uncertainty as the degree of difficulty associated with assessing the performance of the transaction partners."

In the IS context, *measurement difficulty* may be defined as the extent to which it is difficult to evaluate and determine the performance of those who do the work within an IS function (Poppo and Zenger, 1998). For example, it is difficult to evaluate the performance of individual IS workers if the software product that arises from the development or maintenance work results from a team effort. This raises the difficulty in specifying the tasks of individuals, which in turn may increase the need to safeguard against opportunistic behavior. Based on the assumption that such negative behavior can be prevented at lower costs in-house, due to the authority principle, the following hypothesis may be deduced:

Hypothesis 7b:[11] The higher the *difficulty in measuring the performance* of those that do the work in an IS function, the higher the comparative *transaction cost* advantages of insourcing as opposed to outsourcing an IS function.

---

[11] Hypotheses 7a follows subsequently.

More recently, however, some researchers have begun to relate behavioral uncertainty directly to the assumption of opportunistic behavior. For example, Sutcliffe and Zaheer (1998, p. 4) state, "Behavioral uncertainty arises from the possibility of *ex ante* or *ex post* opportunism on the part of the exchange partner." As a consequence, opportunistic behavior is no longer treated as an externally given assumption. According to Rindfleisch and Heide (1997, p.48), "(...) the current TCE literature explicitly acknowledges that opportunism is an endogenous variable rather than a invariable fixed condition." One of the questions surrounding opportunism are the implications of deviations from opportunism (Rindfleisch and Heide, 1997, p. 48). More specifically, the question arises, "What kind of behavioral attitudes and actual behaviors may replace opportunism, if the behavioral threats that result from hidden attitudes towards opportunism no longer dominate an exchange relationship?" Or, in other words, "What are the *behavioral antipodes* of opportunism and how do they impact the more traditional reasoning within the frame of transaction cost theory?" Answering these questions is taken up next.

2.3.1.3 Integrating Behavioral Antipodes of Opportunism

Trustworthiness. A number of authors have suggested that *trust* may serve as an antipode of opportunism (e.g., Chiles and McMackin, 1996; Ghoshal and Moran, 1996; Joshi and Stump, 1999; Noorderhaven, 1996). Chiles and McMackin (1996, p. 88) conclude that the "(...) inclusion of the social-context variable of trust in the TCE framework will yield a model with greater predictive validity."

Trust is a multidisciplinary phenomenon (Noorderhaven, 1996). It goes far beyond this contribution to list all its different definitions. One useful overview of its various treatments and aspects has been given by Blois (1999). In addition, Noorderhaven's (1996) analysis of the role of trust in transaction cost economics is very illuminating. According to the latter, trust – in relation to opportunism – is especially be represented by "character trust", which he defines as the "(...) belief in the other party's inherent trustworthiness, that is, his or her disposition to live up to explicit and implicit commitments (Noorderhaven, 1996, p. 111).

For the purpose of this study, trust will be treated as *trust in IS workers*. It equals *trustworthiness of IS workers* and refers to the combined emotional feeling and cognitive belief that those that perform an IS function will act predictably, will fulfill their obligations, and will behave fairly in performing an IS function, even when the possibility for opportunism is present (based on Zaheer and Venkatraman, 1994). It has to be noted that this type of trust is different from blanked trust, in that it provides "(...) an answer not just to the question, Whom do you trust? but to the question, *What* do you trust to them?" (Baier, 1986, p. 236; cited by Blois, 1999, p. 200). Here the "*What*" refers to the particular IS function (application development or maintenance) that is delegated to another party.

In accordance to opportunism, trust may be treated as a variable that can take different instances. That is, some economic actors can be trusted while others cannot. As noted earlier, the assumption of opportunism serves as a precondition for the existence of transaction costs. The inverse conclusion is that in the absence of opportunism transaction costs are negligible in an exchange relationship. This means that as far as the risk of opportunistic behavior decreases in the presence of trust, transaction costs are lowered as well. At the same time, however, this implies that trust only becomes meaningful if the danger of opportunistic behavior were conceivably high (Chiles and McMackin, 1996). In other words, trust becomes meaningful in situations where transaction costs, that arise in order to safeguard against opportunistic behavior, are potentially high. As outlined previously, transaction costs, associated with the provision of an IS function, are especially high in case of high human asset specificity.

With regard to asset specificity, Noorderhaven (1996, p. 108) has explicated the influential role of trust on transaction cost economic reasoning as follows, "If differential trustworthiness is assumed, trust can be hypothesized to be an intervening variable between asset specificity and safeguards."

The concept of trust would, however, still be meaningless for the IS sourcing decision, if the level of trust were independent from the sourcing arrangement. Assuming that both in-house agents and external agents are totally trustworthy, both in-house and outsourcing transaction costs would tend to become zero. On the other hand, if both parties cannot be trusted at all, then this would equal the assumption of opportunism. Overall, no matter what level of trust one may assume, the absolute difference between in-house and outsourcing transaction costs remains unaffected (and hence the degree of outsourcing), as long as the level of trust is assumed to be independent of the sourcing arrangement. Accordingly, trust only becomes meaningful for the sourcing decision, if its magnitude differs between alternative sourcing arrangements.

If the trustworthiness of IS workers is assumed to be higher in-house compared to an outsourcing relationship, the necessity to safeguard against opportunistic behavior of internal employees decreases. The consequences are lower in-house transaction costs. Hence, trust may be viewed as an alternative explanation for lower in-house transaction costs in situations where the necessity to safeguard against opportunistic behavior is especially high. Both internal *authority* and *internal trust advantages* partially substitute the need for costly safeguards against opportunism. Similarly, the role of trust, as an alternative explanation for the cost efficiency of organizations, has been recognized by Ouchi (1980, p. 134) some time ago:

> "(...) the bureaucratic organization can create an atmosphere of trust between employees much more readily than a market can between the parties of the exchange. Because members of an organization assume some commonality of purpose, because they learn that long-term relationships will reward good performance and punish poor performance, they develop some goal congruence. This reduces their opportunistic tendencies and thus the need to monitor their performance."

Empirical studies on the differential role of trust, however, are rare. In the IS context, Ang and Slaughter (1998; 2001) intensively studied the sourcing arrangement of one case company, taking different software development projects as a unit of analysis. In each of the projects, they compared employees with outsourced workers on a number of dimensions. Their findings support the notion that outsourced workers are less trustworthy and at the same time perform at a lower level than in-house workers. Currie and Willcocks (1998) found cases were the decision to insource was partially driven by a lack of trust about supplier motivation.

Nevertheless, the findings that in-house IS employees are more trustworthy than external vendor staff may not be generalizable. The arrival of an increasing number of partnership style IS outsourcing relationships and so called strategic alliances partially contradict this view (Currie and Willcocks, 1998; DiRomualdo and Gurbaxani, 1998). A number of studies found support for the notion that organizations recognize the importance of trust for the success of an outsourcing relationship (Goles, 2001; Grover, et al., 1996; Kern, 1997; Lee and Kim, 1999; Sabherwal, 1999). Especially, in situations were contracts cannot be fully specified, trust is suggested to be critical for the success of an outsourcing relationship (Sabherwal, 1999). Therefore, it is not surprising that trust in external vendors can also promote IS outsourcing decisions. Drawing on their analysis of seven outsourcing cases in the Banking Industry, McLellan et al. (1995, p. 311) note that "(...) executives emphasized the importance of trust as a precursor to outsource their IT function."

Moreover, it is important to recognize that trust develops over time. The perception of trust towards another party is significantly rooted in past experience. In the same way as good experiences with an exchange partner can lead to a higher level of trust, bad experiences can severely damage trust for a long time (Chiles and McMackin, 1996, p. 95). This is true for both in-house and outsourcing relationships. If an organization has constantly made bad experiences with in-house provision of an IS function and somewhat better experiences with outsourcing, it may indeed tend to trust external personnel more than internal employees.

Accordingly, it seems reasonable to take trust as a comparative construct, where *comparative trust advantage* is the extent to which the trust associated with providing an IS function within the organization is higher than using a service provider. The above analysis thus suggests the following moderator effect of comparative trust advantages:

Hypothesis 8a: The higher the *trustworthiness of* in-house as opposed to outsourced IS workers, the higher is the impact of human asset specificity *(H1a)* on in-house transaction cost advantages in performing an IS function.

In addition, however, it may be argued that highly trusted IS worker perform at a higher level, and hence work more efficient than less trusted personnel. Conversely, IS workers may know that the best way to signal their trustworthiness is to show a high level of efficiency in their work. Accordingly, the following hypothesis may be put forth:

Hypothesis 8b: The higher the *trustworthiness* of in-house as opposed to outsourced IS workers in providing an IS function, the higher is the *production cost advantage* of the in-house as opposed to outsourced provision of an IS function.

Intrinsic Motivation. Up to now, however, it has been taken for granted that the interests of others are extrinsically motivated. It is believed that an agent behaves in a certain direction, only because s/he can expect some sort of externally provided compensation for her/his behavior (e.g., money, praise), or because s/he wants to avoid negative sanctions (e.g., penalties or criticism). The flip side is that principals are thought to be able to manipulate agents through setting incentives that extrinsically motivate the agent. Motivation is treated as a means to an end (Frey and Osterloh, 1997).

According to Osterloh and Frey (2000, p. 539) the assumption of "(...) opportunism is a strong form of extrinsic motivation." More precisely opportunism contains assumptions about the *means* through which an individual would try to reach her/his extrinsically motivated objectives. This becomes clear in recalling how Williamson (1985, p. 47) defined opportunism, "More generally, opportunism refers to the incomplete or distorted disclosure of information, especially to calculated efforts to mislead, distort, disguise, obfuscate, or otherwise confuse." It may be argued that the term "calculated" implies the assumption of extrinsic motivation. This means that a principal can possibly satisfy the calculus of an agent by extrinsically motivating him, e.g., through monetary incentives. However, s/he can never directly impact an agent's attitude towards opportunism.

The inclusion of trustworthiness, as opposed to opportunism, does not *per se* change the fact that human beings are thought to be extrinsically motivated. As stated by Blois (1999, p. 202), "(...) trusting another makes an assumption about their interests." In other words, it is assumed that IS workers do not behave trustworthy on their own free will. They may only do so because they believe that signalling trustworthiness increases the discounted cash flow resulting from the relationship with the principal, e.g., the employer or client. An internal employee may want to secure or improve her/his current position by signaling his trustworthiness. An external vendor may want to signal his trustworthiness in order to maintain or improve his reputation and to be considered for future services.

There may, however, be situations where IS workers are not solely motivated by externally provided incentives. They may partially be *intrinsically motivated.* Intrinsic motivation "(...) is valued for its own sake and appears to be self sustained" (Calder and Staw, 1975, p. 599 – cited by Osterloh and Frey, 2000, p. 539). This would mean that IS workers are motivated through the development and maintenance work itself, e.g., because they feel competent in what they are doing or because they enjoy the actual work (Schuster, et al., 1997). Steinmann (1997, p. 589) rates an individual as intrinsically motivated if "(...) action results from her/his autonomous realization and acceptance of the correctness and sense of [her/his] objectives, aims and operating procedures" (translated from German). This would result in agents "(...) acting off their own bat" (translated from German).

If those objectives, aims and operating procedures match with the preferences of the principal, then extrinsic motivation partially becomes obsolete. Under certain conditions, extrinsic motivation may even be counterproductive, in that it undermines intrinsic motivation and therefore may actually lower the overall motivation of an agent. The empirical support for these "crowding effects" (Osterloh and Frey, 2000, p. 541), however, is not consistent. The empirical findings mostly stem from experiments in social psychology and have been discussed controversially (see the meta-analyses from Deci, et al., 1999; Eisenberger and Cameron, 1996). Accordingly, they will not be examined more deeply. The focus will be on the wider implications of the presence of intrinsic motivation.

It may be argued that intrinsically motivated IS workers are less fixed on calculus based motivation. As soon, however, as their extrinsic motivation decreases, the "(...) calculated efforts to mislead, distort, disguise, obfuscate, or otherwise confuse", i.e., the tendency to behave opportunistically will decrease as well. Consequently, transaction costs will be lowered in the presence of intrinsic motivation of agents (as indicated by Osterloh and Frey, 2000).

This again raises the question if there may be differences in intrinsic motivation between in-house employees and external vendors. In analyzing this question, it is useful to recall the nature of the application development and maintenance work. Both IS functions are service functions and require a certain amount of interaction between IS and non-IS stakeholders. If these interactions constantly create misunderstandings, conflicts and eager, then it is very likely that the intrinsic motivation of an IS worker is negatively effected. By contrast, if the relationship with other stakeholders is characterized by friendly interaction, it may positively impact intrinsic motivation. While there may be many different sources of intrinsic motivation, it becomes clear that it can significantly differ depending on the organizational surroundings. Especially environments that enable and encourage socializing action may be predestined to promote intrinsic motivation. For example, Ouchi (1980, p. 132) has stressed the beneficial role of socialization:

> "Thus, industrial organization can, in some instances, rely to a great extent on socialization as the principal mechanism of mediation or control, and this 'clan' form (...) can be very efficient in mediating transactions between interdependent individuals.

Although Ouchi (1980) and others (Frey and Osterloh, 1997; Osterloh and Frey, 2000) tend to argue that socializing action and intrinsic motivation are special attributes of firms rather than markets, empirical support for this view has yet to be provided. The arrival of partnership style outsourcing relationships and strategic alliances may again contradict this view.

Accordingly, intrinsic motivation will be treated as a comparative construct. For reasons of simplification, intrinsic motivation will be substituted by "non-monetary incentives". In the IS context, non-monetary incentives may be defined as all factors that encourage the willingness of the IS workers to do quality work without resulting in a direct monetary benefit for them. Although this neglects the fact that non-monetary incentives may also include instruments of informal extrinsic motivation, e.g., praise (Güth and Kliemt, 1997), it is believed that this construct will be sufficient to serve as an antipode of opportunism. Based on the preceding arguments, the following hypothesis may be deduced:

Hypothesis 9a: The higher the level of *non-monetary incentives* of in-house as opposed to outsourced IS workers, the higher is the impact of human asset specificity *(H1a)* on in-house transaction cost advantages in performing an IS function.

In addition, however, it may be argued that highly motivated IS worker perform at a higher level, and hence work more efficient than less motivated personnel (Kubitschek and Meckl, 2000, p. 752). In particular, IS workers may be more willing to exchange knowledge as part of their work if they are intrinsically rather than extrinsically motivated. Employees that are only extrinsically motivated may even have an incentive to hide, i.e. lock in their knowledge, because they see it as a competitive advantage against others, which guarantees their future income stream. Accordingly, the following hypothesis may be put forth:

Hypothesis 9b: The higher the *non-monetary incentives* of in-house as opposed to outsourced IS workers in providing an IS function, the higher is the *production cost advantage* of the in-house as opposed to outsourced provision of an IS function.

2.3.1.4 Overview

An overview of the constructs and relationships deduced from transaction cost theory is presented in Figure 2-4. The graph may be viewed as both a decomposition and an extension of Figure 2-1, p. 23. It shows that comparative cost advantages of insourcing as opposed to outsourcing an IS function will lead to a lower level of IS outsourcing of this function. The cost differences are dependent on an organization's IS characteristics. Moreover, the behavioral perceptions associated with insourcing as opposed to outsourcing an IS function may moderate the impact of asset specificity on the perceived cost differences.

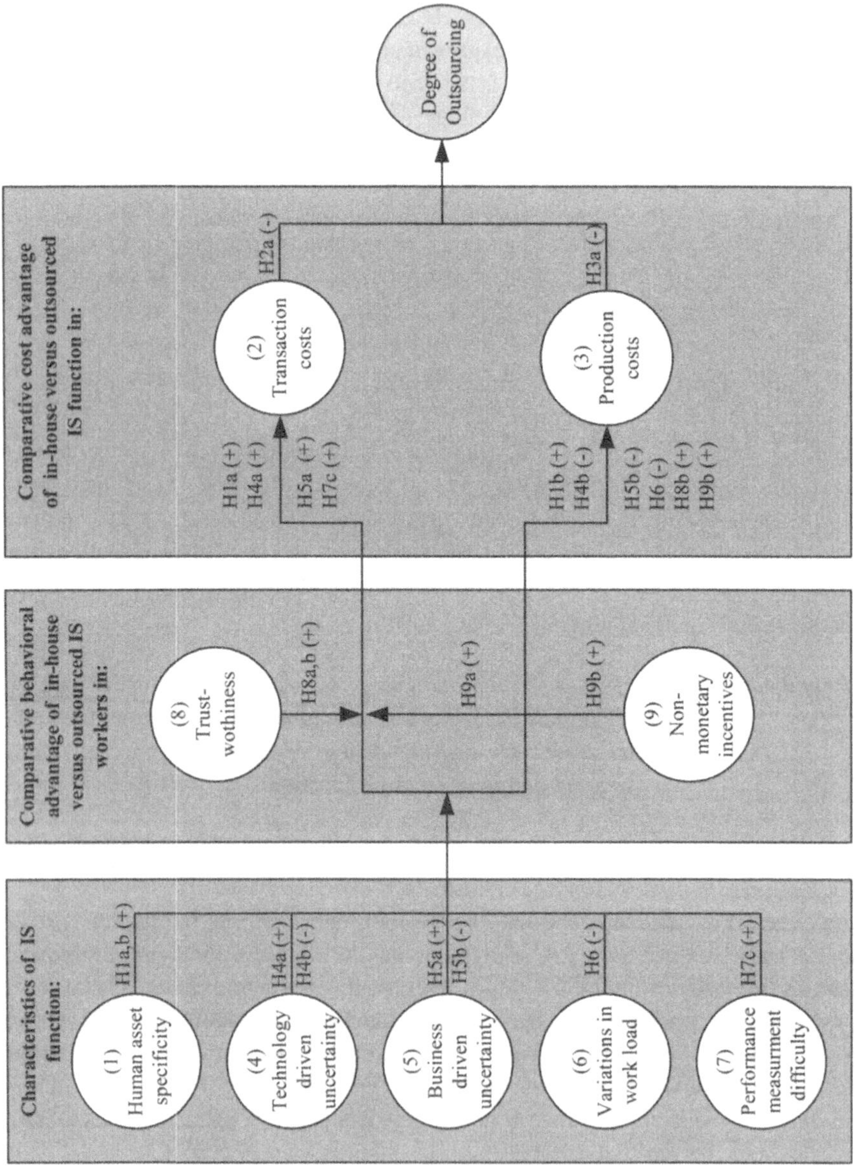

Figure 2-4: Hypotheses from Transaction Cost Theory

2.3.2 Resource-based Theory

It can be argued that the reasoning of resource-based theory begins where transaction cost theory has its limits and vice-versa. In focusing solely on cost differences between alternative governance modes, transaction cost theory neglects that organizations can differ on other dimensions than costs. A pure cost comparison of alternative sourcing options implies that an IS function can be provided in the same manner and at the same quality, no matter whether it is performed in-house or externally. It is assumed that the firm and the market have access to the same input factors and can create the same outputs (Conner, 1991, p. 142; Demsetz, 1988, p. 147). Williamson (1992, p. 339) has made his point clear in arguing that all actions taken within the firm could equally be performed by an external vendor.

By contrast, resource-based theory holds that organizations generally differ in their resources and capabilities (Penrose, 1959). Both the input factors required to perform an IS function as well as the outputs and organizational impacts produced by an IS function may differ between organizations. These differences may serve as additional criteria to evaluate and compare alternative sourcing options.

On the other hand, resource-based theory neglects transaction costs and insufficiently discusses the behavioral assumptions on which some of its main arguments are based. It can be shown that opportunism and its antipodes, *trust and non-monetary incentives*, that complemented transaction cost theory, can also have a profound impact on some of the reasoning of resource-based theory.

In the following, four potential differences – other than cost differences – in providing an IS function will first be introduced. In particular, three types of impacts of an IS function, and the heterogeneity of resources themselves, may be distinguished. The three potential impacts, are (1) the *strategic contribution* of an IS function, (2) the *operational contribution* of an IS function, and (3) the *systemic impact* of an IS function. Moreover, the (4) *base of resources* required to perform an IS function may differ between a client organization and external vendors. An overview of these four dimensions is presented in Figure 2-5.

Following the definition of each of these four concepts, their impact on IS sourcing will be analyzed. Hypotheses will be deduced about the theoretical linkages. The resulting sub-model is illustrated in Figure 2-8, p. 85.

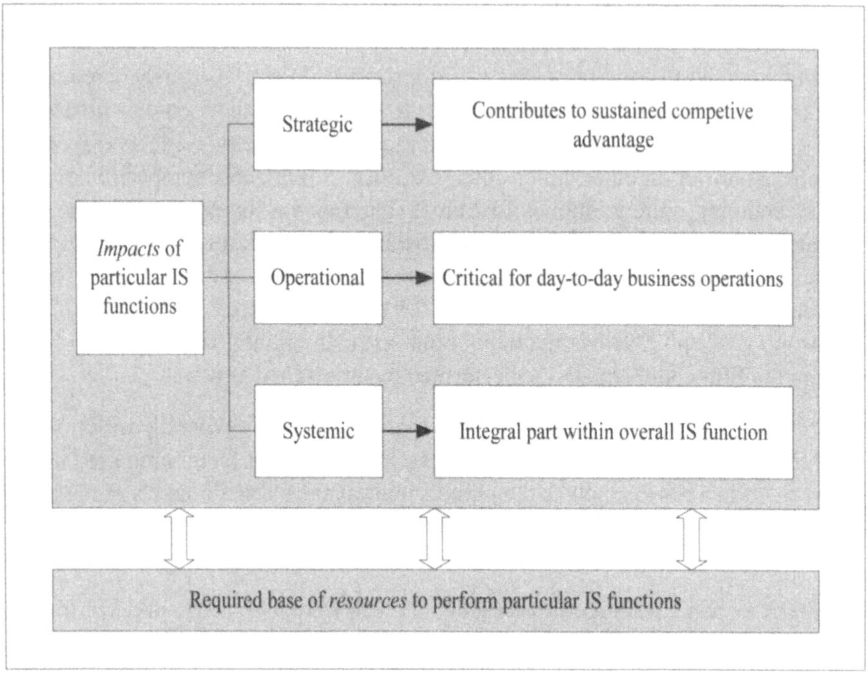

Figure 2-5: Resource Base and Impacts of IS Functions

2.3.2.1 Information Systems Resources and Impacts

(1) *Strategic contribution*. Firms deploy different *strategies* in order to defend and expand their benefits against current and potential competitors in the market. In general, benefits may be defined as the positive difference between the revenue that a firm creates through selling its products and/or services and the costs incurred by generating revenue. Firms that succeed in the market are said to have some type of a *sustained competitive advantage*. According to Barney, "(...) A firm is said to have a sustained competitive advantage when it is implementing a value creating strategy not simultaneously being implemented by any current or potential competitors and when these other firms are unable to duplicate the benefits of this strategy" (Barney, 1991, p. 102).

With regards to "value creating strategy", Porter (1980; 1985) has identifies two generic types that a firm may choose to follow in determining its course of competitive action. These are overall cost leadership and differentiation. Similarly, Conner (1991, p. 132) stated, "In a resource-based view, obtaining (...) returns requires either that (a) the firm's product be distinctive in the eyes of the buyers (...) or (b) that the firm selling a identical product in comparison to competitors must have a low-cost position."

In the early 80s, researchers began to conceptually analyze how IT/IS can impact the competitive position of firm's (Sambamurthy, 2000). Most of these conceptual pieces underline their arguments using a view illustrative case examples. Porter and Millar (1985) have been among the first, who argued that the deployment of IT would enable firms to both lower costs and enhance differentiation. McFarlan (1985) used Porter's (1980) five competitive forces model to analyze the organizational impact of IS. Ives and Learmonth (1984) argued that IS can serve to build and maintain the loyalty of a firm's customer base (see also Mertens and Plattflaut, 1986, for examples in Germany).

More recently, researchers tend to emphasize the *complementary* role of IS in generating a sustained competitive advantage (Clemons and Row, 1991; Henderson and Venkatraman, 1993; Powell and Dent-Micallef, 1997). According to Powell (1997, p. 378), the (...) notion that ITs *per se* do not generate sustainable performance advantages has received increasing support in recent IT research, and has produced a perspective known as the strategic necessity hypothesis to which most IT researchers now adhere." He further suggests that "(...) if IT per se do not provide distinctive advantages, then firms must use them to leverage or exploit firm specific, intangible resources such as organizational leadership, culture and business processes (Powell and Dent-Micallef, 1997, p. 378). Similarly, Clemons (1991, p. 289) concludes that the "(...) benefits resulting from an innovative application of the information technology can be more readily defended if the system exploits unique resources of the innovating firm so that competitors do not fully benefit from imitation."

Two conclusions can be drawn from these insights. First, user-organizations can hardly create a sustained competitive advantage through developing new innovative IT. Developing and selling IT is not their business. Second, however, they can use, deploy and manage IT in an innovative way through continuously building and maintaining IS in accordance to their particular organizational context (see the difference between IT and IS in Section 2.1.1.1, p. 10 f.). For example, IS can lower the costs of intra- and inter-organizational business processes. In this realm, IS can *contribute* rather than directly create a sustained competitive advantage, by leveraging the benefits attained from those non-IT business processes that are distinctive from their competitors.

The exception from this indirect strategic contribution are profit center arrangements, in which client organizations try to generate revenue by offering IS services to external clients (Venkatraman, 1997). These arrangement, however, are more an exception to the rule. Companies that want to generate revenue through their IS department often spin-off this unit, which results in a special ownership outsourcing arrangement (Heinzl, 1993a).

In reviewing the literature on the strategic importance of IS, however, another issue soon becomes apparent. The discussion about the strategic impact of IS/IT mostly takes place on an aggregated level rather than on the level of particular IS sub-functions. One exception is the strategic grid by McFarlan and McKinney (1983). While the one dimension of the strategic grid refers to the strategic impact of existing *systems*, the other dimension refers to the strategic impact of a firm's *application development* portfolio. This easy to understand framework has been widely used among practitioners and researchers (Raghunathan, et al., 1999). It indicates that the evaluation of the strategic significance of IS may be broken down to the level of individual components of an IS, e.g., the application software. Accordingly, the strategic significance of particular IS functions may be assessed separately from the strategic importance of the overall IS function. This view is supported by studies in the IS outsourcing context. From their multiple case study, McLellan et al. conclude, "At the organizational level, executives considered IS to be core, but recognized that at micro or individual IT-activity level, some different aspects may not be core (McLellan, et al., 1995, p. 310). Hancox and Hackney (1999, p. 6) find similar results in their case studies in the U.K. private and public sector.

Accordingly, *strategic significance* will broadly be defined as the degree to which a partial IS function contributes to generate a sustained competitive advantage (e.g., through reducing costs, adding new features to differentiate existing products or services, or improving customer service).

(2) *Operational contribution.* Paradoxically, however, IS are often treated as strategic systems, although they do not clearly contribute to generate benefits or even a sustained competitive advantage (Lacity, et al., 1995, p. 87; Nelson, et al., 1996, p. 34).

This phenomenon may partially be attributed to the difficulty or indeed impossibility to prove the "indirect" impact of IS to contribute to a firm's benefits. IS may be viewed as a *coupling product*. The output of IS, the information, serves as an input for various organizational work processes. However, its impact is mostly invisible in the final products or services. Accordingly, the contribution of IS to sales and cost savings often can only vaguely be estimated. The perceived misfit between the investment into IT and the received benefits has been named the "productivity paradox" (Brynjolfsson, 1993), and it has become an enduring challenge for both researchers and practitioners to proof the value created by IS (see e.g., Bharadwaj, 2000). In a recent review of the IT productivity debate, Willcocks and Lester (2000, p. 551) conclude that "(...) an important part, but by no means all, of the uncertainty about the IT payoff relates to weaknesses in measurement and evaluation practice."[12]

Accordingly, it is not surprising, that opposed to the benefits attained from IS, failures in performing IS functions are more directly felt by IS users and clients because they immediately affect their day-to-day work processes. Many organizational business processes are highly dependent on the functionality of IS. Consequently, any

[12] The increasing diffusion of internet applications, which support customer interaction paired by more advanced data mining tools may be viewed as a promising starting point to improve the transparency of the influential role of IS on sales.

breakdown, mistakes or bad performance of an organization's IS can severely threaten business operations. In a recent empirical assessment of the two dimensions of the strategic grid (McFarlan and McKenney, 1983), the strategic importance of an organization's current systems portfolio has implicitly been treated as operational significance (Raghunathan, et al., 1999). The authors state, "The items comprising the current portfolio capture the importance of existing systems to the achievement of an organization's basic operating objectives" (Raghunathan, et al., 1999, p. 351). One example of these items reads as follows, "IS breakdown for extended periods will affect organizational activity severely" (p. 354).

The responsibility for IS breakdown is generally attributed to those that provide the IS functions (i.e. those that develop, operate and maintain IS). While IS breakdown is the extreme form of operating failure, there are less dramatic, but still important failures that negatively effect day-to day operations. These are especially based on the dynamic nature of information systems. The IS function is constantly challenged by changing business needs and technological innovations. For example, the compatibility of IS between organizations has become increasingly important. It happens to be that suppliers are forced to constantly adjust their IS to the systems requirements of their main customers. If the IS development and maintenance work is not performed properly, e.g., if new systems functionalities are not provided in time, the day-to-day inter-organizational business processes can be effected severely. In a literature survey on IS failure research, Lyytinen and Hirschheim (1987; cited by Sauer, 1999, p. 286) call these types of failures, process failures. They refer to negative outcomes of the IS production process, e.g., project abandonment, budget blowouts and schedule overruns. IS process failures may refer to the overall IS function or to partial IS functions. Indeed, it may be argued that many overall IS failures are based on failures in one or more partial IS functions, e.g., failures in application development or maintenance.

In accordance, *operational significance* will be introduced as to reflect the critical role of a partial IS function for an organization's business operations. In contrast to strategic significance, it captures the degree to which an organization's day-to-day business operations critically depend on the performance of an IS function.

(3) *Systemic Impact.* Up to now, the potential impact of a particular IS function has been analyzed with regard to its overall strategic and operational contribution. Most empirical and conceptual works about these organizational level impacts, however, have been undertaken at the level of the overall IS function rather than on the level of particular IS sub-functions. Although there appear to be good reasons for these higher level analyses, they have rarely been explicated.

One of the major reasons may be attributed to the fact that the organizational impacts of an IS – in particular their potential to integrate and coordinate work processes of organizations – result from the *interplay* of its sub-components. As outlined previously, the application software makes up just one component of an IS (see Section 2.1.1.1, p. 10ff.). Other components are the systems software, the telecommunications and network infrastructure, as well as central (e.g., data and application servers) and decentral computers (e.g., desktops). This means that IS services, other than application development and maintenance, contribute to the overall performance of an IS, and hence to its organizational impacts. For example, the application software *per se* is of little use, if not based on a reliable and secure operating system, or if not dynamically connected to other source or target applications via powerful networks in order to enable a meaningful identification, gathering, processing, and transfer of information. In other words, the added value of the individual components of an IS *per se* is lower than the value of the whole IS. Accordingly, the combined outcome of each particular IS function is lower than the outcome produced by the meaningful combination, coordination, and integration of all functions together.

This view agrees with one of the basic ideas of systems theory, which emphasizes the difference between the whole and its parts (Krieger, 1996; Luhmann, 1994, pp. 20ff.; Rapoport, 1988; Stünzner, 1996).

Therefore, it may be argued that the more immediate impact of the development or maintenance of applications is reflected by their *systemic impact*, defined as the extent to which a particular IS function is an integral part within the overall IS function.

(4) The *resources,* on which an organization is based, have been classified in various ways. For example, Barney (1991, p. 101) distinguishes between physical resources, human resources, and organizational resources. Under a wider umbrella resources may also include such issues like capital equipment, patents, or brand names (Grant, 1991).

There is a close relationship between resources and assets. Some proponents of resource-based theory speak of assets rather than resources (see also Amit and Schoemaker, 1993; Dierickx, et al., 1989). Wernerfelt (1984, p. 172) defined resources as "(...) those (tangible and intangible) assets which are tied semi permanently to the firm." Likewise, studies in the IS context, that explicitly refer to resource-based theory, tend to treat resources and assets equally. For example, Ross et al. (1996) distinguish between three types of IT assets rather than resources: (1) human assets, which refer to technical skills, the business understanding, and the problem-solving orientation of a firm's IT staff, (2) technical assets, including such issues like the technical architecture and standards, and (3) relationship assets, which refer to the attitudes and behaviors between IT and business unit management. Others speak of IT resources (Clemons and Row, 1991; Powell and Dent-Micallef, 1997) or of IT attributes (Mata, et al., 1995). In the following, assets and resources will be treated interchangeable. To avoid redundancy, the classification of IS assets into "human" and "physical" as elaborated in Section 2.3.1.2 (p. 47ff.) will be adopted.

One note of caution, however, refers to the term "capabilities", in relation to resources or assets. A view researchers have stressed the distinction between resources and capabilities. For example, Grant (1991, p. 119) states, "A capability is the capacity for a team of resources to perform some task or activity." Similarly, Amit and Schumacker (1993, p. 35 – italics original) hold, "*Capabilities*, by contrast, refer to a firm's capacity to deploy *Resources*, usually in combination, using organizational processes, to effect a desired end." In the IS context, capabilities may refer to applied knowledge at the individual, group, or firm level that is directed to reach the objectives or desired impacts associated with performing an IS function.

More recently, research tends to recognize the increasing importance of human rather than physical assets within an organization's base of resources (Boisot, 1998). Consequently, the term *"intellectual capital"* has emerged as to combine the closely related issues of knowledge, skills, experiences, and capabilities into a coherent concept (Keen, 1999; Nahapiet and Ghoshal, 1998). For example, Nahapiet and Ghoshal (1998, p. 245) argue:

> (...) we use the term 'intellectual capital' to refer to the knowledge and knowing capability of a social collectivity, such as an organization, intellectual community, or professional practice. We have elected to adopt this terminology because of its clear parallel with the concept of human capital, which embraces the acquiring knowledge, skills, and capabilities that enable persons to act in new ways (Coleman, 1988)."

In the following, the concept of "intellectual capital" will be used as a substitute for human IS assets. It differs from the concept "other resources" which includes objective quantities, like the staffing level, the financial resources, and the technical equipment, required to perform an IS function.

Having laid down the conceptual foundations to understand what is meant by an IS function's base of resources, its strategic contribution, operational contribution, and its systemic impact, the next step is to analyze how these dimensions may influence the sourcing decision. Due to the central position that is attributed to the concept "strategic significance" in resource-based theory in general, and outsourcing research in particular, its impact on IS sourcing will be analyzed first.

2.3.2.2 Comparative Advantage in Strategic Contribution

Following the traditional stream of arguments, strategic IS functions, that belong to the core competencies of an organization, are difficult or indeed impossible to contract out. Hence, it is recommended to keep them in-house (Bühner and Tuschke, 1997; Chatterjee and Wernerfelt, 1991; Montgomery, 1994; Picot and Maier, 1992). The reasons for resistance against outsourcing strategic IS functions appear to be convincing at the first view. It may be argued that organizations will loose the strategic potential of their IS functions in case of outsourcing, because the sources of a sustained competitive advantage can neither be maintained nor extended (Dibbern, et al., 2001; Dibbern and Heinzl, 2001; 2002).

According to resource-based theory, the *sources* of a sustained competitive advantage are inevitably linked to an organization's base of resources (Amit and Schoemaker, 1993; Barney, 1991; Collis and Montgomery, 1996; Dierickx, et al., 1989; Grant, 1991; Rumelt, 1984; Wernerfelt, 1984). An organization can only differentiate itself from current and potential competitors if some of its resources are non-tradable, non-imitable, and non-substitutable (Dierickx, et al., 1989). These conditions are fulfilled, in particular, if the resources are firm specific (Amit and Schoemaker, 1993, p. 39; Dierickx, et al., 1989, p. 1505; Hall, 1993; Silverman, 1999).

There is a close link between specific resources and specific assets, as defined in transaction cost theory (Dibbern, et al., 2001; Foss, et al., 1995; Langlois, 1995; Poppo and Zenger, 1998; Tsang, 2000). Foss et al. (1995) have argued that the notion of asset specificity could amount to integrate resource-based theory and transaction cost theory:

> "(...) it seems evident that transaction costs are relevant to evolutionary and resource approaches, and therefore to their integration. For example, there are rather direct correlations between rent earning resources and specific assets" (p. 14).

Paradoxically, Williamson (1990, p. 142) has recognized that specific assets cannot "(...) be redeployed to alternative users and by alternative uses without sacrifice of productive value." However, he has never considered these differences in productive value as separate criteria for the choice among alternative governance modes. His focus has solely been on transaction and production cost differences between the firm and the market.

In this realm, it is notable that the impact of asset specificity on comparative production cost advantages between insourcing and outsourcing can be equally deduced from transaction cost theory and resource-based theory. There are only differences in wording. While resource-based theory always speaks of in-house production cost advantages based on specific assets, transaction cost theory emphasizes production cost disadvantages of the market (market failure) (Conner, 1991, p. 139). Overall, however, a production cost comparison comes to the same result in both theoretic lenses (Dibbern, et al., 2001; Langlois, 1995). Therefore, hypothesis H3a (–) (see p. 53), and its supporting arguments, could be attributed to both transaction cost theory and resource-based theory. However, since Williamson has made that argument first, it will primarily be attributed to transaction costs.

What gives resource-based theory a distinctive character, is the consideration of the rent generating potential of specific assets in alternative governance modes.

In Section 2.3.1.2 (p. 47ff.), it has been shown that especially human assets required to develop and maintain software applications may differ in their specificity. On the one hand, they refer to business and application knowledge that is uniquely tight to the context of an organization. On the other hand, they refer to the process of social collaboration necessary to acquire firm specific knowledge. Firm specific knowledge required to perform an IS function cannot be traded. It has to be developed in a long-term learning-by doing process within the context of an organization. Competitors can hardly imitate or substitute this tacit type of knowledge, simply because they may not even understand what is to be imitated or substituted. Specific human assets amount to constantly build and maintain application software that matches the unique social and procedural requirements of an organization. Assuming that the work processes supported by the functionality of the resulting application software create benefits for an organization, the sustainability of the benefits is being leveraged by the unique IS resources.

If competitors cannot replicate value creating specific IS functions of an organization, this, however, does not automatically mean that external suppliers can not do so either. An external supplier may take over the personnel of the client – if indeed former in-house employees are willing to work for an IS service provider. This means that the vendor may eventually get immediate access to the client's unique knowledge resources required to perform an IS function.

The decisive question, however, is whether the vendor is interested in developing and maintaining application software that is specifically tailored to the requirements of one customer. Even if the vendor is taking over the client's personnel, keeping this personnel at the client site will result in a specific investment for him. The specific investment has to pay off for the vendor. It will pay off if the price that the client is charged outweighs the vendor's costs. Assuming that the price, that the vendor can charge, is limited through the contractual agreement, then the vendor can only increase its profit margin by reducing the costs for each customer account. In application development and maintenance, the variable costs are inevitable linked to personnel costs (Prosser, 1997, p. 155). This means that the vendor could increase his profit margin if part of the work can be charged at more than one client. In other words, if the work required to serve different customers partly overlaps, the vendor can increase his profit margin. Unfortunately, however, the likelihood that work processes overlap between different customers is quite small if the knowledge required to develop and maintain application software is uniquely tight to each of the clients. In this case, the vendor has to build up and cultivate the required knowledge for each client separately and will be unable to increase his profit margin by leveraging his knowledge assets over a broad range of customers.

Based on the preceding arguments, it becomes clear that outsourcing strategically significant IS functions is associated with the risk that the vendor will focus on increasing his own profit margin rather than acting in accordance with the strategic objectives of the client. A number of authors have also stressed the strategic risk of loosing innovative IS capabilities and control over the strategic direction of IS internally (Beyah and Gallivan, 2001; Dibbern and Heinzl, 2001; Dibbern and Heinzl, 2002; Duncan, 1998; Earl, 1996; McFarlan and Nolan, 1995; Quinn and Hilmer, 1994). Based on field research in Europe and the USA, Willcocks et al. (1995b, p. 61) conclude, "With IT in the hands of a vendor, future opportunities for identifying IT as a source of competitive advantage and competitive differentiation for the organization can become cut off."

The loss of own strategic resources, however, would be meaningless, as long as the vendor fully compensates that loss through his specific investments. Therefore, strategic risks of IS outsourcing are inevitably linked to the threat of opportunistic behavior of an agent, which plays a central role in transaction cost theory. The distinctive character of resource-based theory, however, is grounded on the *consequences* that are attributed to opportunistic behavior. While in transaction cost theory, a principal could generally safeguard against opportunistic behavior through respective costly transactions, resource-based reasoning takes a different view. According to the latter, strategic assets, by definition, can neither be imitated nor substituted. The "receipt" that creates a sustained competitive advantage cannot be articulated or written down, because it involves a high amount of tacit knowledge. Consequently, even if the client would wish to safeguard against opportunistic behavior, s/he may hardly be able to do so, as it is impossible to specify and control the specific investment of the vendor. A client cannot specify the way in which a vendor has to perform a strategic IS function. Moreover, it makes little sense to specify the expected outcome, unless the client fully understands the sources of the sustained competitive advantage through an IS function. If the expected benefits are not achieved, e.g., cost savings in a business process, it is the client that has to proof the vendor's failure, which again may be impossible for the client.

As a result from the inability to effectively safeguard against opportunistic behavior, transaction costs may become less important as a criteria for the sourcing decision. It becomes more critical, whether the potential strategic contribution of an IS function is threatened if changing from one sourcing mode to another. Considering that an external service provider could generally provide a strategic IS function – if only it would be willing to make the respective specific investments – the concept of strategic contribution needs to be treated as a comparative construct. The *comparative advantage in strategic contribution* may be defined as the extent to which the strategic contribution of an IS function is weakened if provided by an external vendor rather than in-house.

As outlined previously, the strategic contribution of the IS functions of application development and maintenance is especially dependent on the degree of human asset specificity. Assuming that an external vendor is more inclined to behave opportunistic than the client's own employees, the strategic risks are higher in case of outsourcing as opposed to insourcing. Assuming further that clients are risk averse and that they cannot effectively safeguard against strategic risks, the following two hypotheses may be deduced:

Hypothesis 1c: The more *specific* the human assets required to perform an IS function are, the higher is the advantage of insourcing as opposed to outsourcing in providing a *strategically significant* IS function.

Hypothesis 10a: The higher the advantage of insourcing as opposed to outsourcing in providing a *strategically significant* IS function, the less it will be *outsourced.*

Hypotheses 10, however, is also based on the assumption that an organization would actually consider the strategic potential of an IS function in a sourcing decision. This is especially likely if an IS function is in fact rated as strategically significant. If it is not strategic at all, the comparison of alternative sourcing options will likely be based on other criteria. Accordingly, the additional two hypotheses are put forth:

Hypothesis 1d: The more *specific* the human assets required to perform an IS function are, the higher is the *strategic significance* of an IS function.

Hypothesis 11a: The higher the level of the *strategic contribution* of an IS function, the higher is the impact of comparative advantages in providing a strategically significant IS function on the degree of IS outsourcing *(H10a).*

In accordance with transaction cost theory, however, the preceding arguments are based on strong assumptions about the behavior of in-house versus outsourced personnel. For that reason, it seems worth to critically reflect on these behavioral assumptions and to analyze how the reasoning will be affected if these assumptions are relaxed or substituted.

2.3.2.3 Influence of Behavioral Factors

In transaction cost theory, it has been shown that the inclusion of trust and non-monetary incentives, as antipodes of the assumption of opportunism, can increase the explanatory power of this stream of reasoning (see Section 2.3.1.3, p. 56ff). In reviewing previous studies on how the consideration of strategic factors may impact the IS sourcing decision, it soon becomes apparent that the behavioral mechanisms that lower transaction costs, may also effectively safeguard against strategic vulnerability. Their explicit consideration could increase the explanatory power of resource-based theory as well.

First of all, the empirical support for the traditional notion that strategic functions are less outsourced is quite inconsistent. While a few surveys have actually confirmed the thesis that strategic IS functions are less outsourced (Loh, 1994; Teng, et al., 1995), others do not find any relationship between the strategic role of IS functions and the extend to which they are outsourced (Dibbern and Heinzl, 2001; 2002; Nelson, et al., 1996). Although these inconsistencies may partly be attributed to different operationalizations of the term "strategic" and to different levels of analysis (particular IS functions versus overall IS), qualitative empirical research that intensively studied the outsourcing decision of particular companies gives raise for an alternative explanation.

They find evidence for some organizations outsourcing IS functions, although, or indeed because they are rated as strategic or core. Drawing on multiple case studies in the Banking Industry, McLellan et al. (1995) argue that contrary to conventional strategic management thinking, outsourcing was undertaken when at the organizational level IS was rated as a core activity, defined as providing the competitive capabilities that lead to competitive advantage. They conclude, "Outsourcing offers an opportunity to use resources beyond those contained in the bank to increase competitive capabilities within the IS function (McLellan, et al., 1995, p. 310). Likewise, Saunders et al. (1997, p. 71) conclude from their multiple case analysis that "(...) outsourcing (...) helps firms successfully make the transition to new technologies, deal with seasonal business, and realize strategic advantage." DiRomualdo and Gurbaxani (1998) identify various strategic reasons for why firms choose to outsource IS functions. Three generic types of strategic intents emerge from their multiple case study analysis. In particular, firms were found to outsource in order to (1) improve their IS, (2) leverage their IS business impact, and for (3) commercial exploitation.

Obviously, many clients belief that they can increase the strategic benefits attained from an IS function through outsourcing. However, what about the strategic risks associated with the external provision of IS services?

A closer examination of the empirical findings reveals that the strategic intentions, associated with outsourcing IS functions, are consistently linked with certain types of relationships between client and vendor. The appropriate relationships, implemented to leverage the strategic objectives, are often called partnerships, cooperations, or strategic alliances (Currie and Willcocks, 1998; DiRomualdo and Gurbaxani, 1998; Heinzl and Sinß, 1993; McLellan, et al., 1995). Based on their case analysis of banks that outsourced strategic IS functions, McLellan et al. (1995, p. 311) conclude:

> "Effective utilization of these vendor resources is only possible if there is a governance structure in place that allows the bank sufficient leverage and control over the resources. The contracts, the trust, the working relationship with account executives, and the alliance nature of outsourcing relationships (...) provide such a governance structure (...)."

Obviously, client organizations are well aware of their strategic vulnerability through IS outsourcing. However, they belief that the strategic risks, resulting from opportunistic behavior, can be alleviated through effectively implementing the outsourcing relationship. The implementation includes the processes of selecting the appropriate vendor, configuring the relationship – including the written contract and verbal agreements – and managing the relationship with the vendor during the life of the contract (Dibbern, et al., 2003a). Within each of these processes, the vendor has the opportunity to signal his trustworthiness. A recent comparative study of the client-vendor relationship has shown that, beside other factors, commitment and trust have a profound impact on the quality of an IS outsourcing relationship, which in turn increases the benefits attained from the outsourcing arrangement (Goles, 2001). The study further has shown that vendors appear to be even more sensitive to relationship issues than clients, which highlights the vendors' willingness to behave trustworthy rather than opportunistic. On the other hand, relationship studies show that clients are receptive to the signals of the vendor (Goles, 2001; Grover, et al., 1996; Kern, 1997; Lee and Kim, 1999; Sabherwal, 1999). The more convincing and enduring these signals are, the more a client may trust a vendor to perform a strategically significant IS function.

The above analysis of the recent empirical literature, together with conceptual underpinnings from resource-based theory, has provided strong indications that the trustworthiness of another party lowers the perception of strategic vulnerability. Therefore, the fundamental question, when deciding upon the sourcing of a strategic IS function, is, "Whom can be trusted more in performing an IS function – own employees or the personnel of the vendor?" Considering that the strategic contribution of an IS function, and hence the strategic risks, depend on the degree of human asset specificity required to perform the function, the following hypotheses may be put forth:

Hypothesis 8c: The higher the *trustworthiness* of in-house as opposed to outsourced IS workers in providing an IS function, the higher is the impact of human asset specificity on in-house advantages in providing a strategically significant IS function *(H1c)*.

In accordance to transaction cost theory, however, it may be argued that the signalling of trustworthiness is extrinsically motivated (see Section 2.3.1.3, p. 56ff.). In other words, a vendor may behave trustworthy, only because the benefits from being trusted are expected to be higher than the costs associated with signalling trustworthiness.

An IS manager, however, may realize that providing an IS function in a way that outperforms similar efforts of competitors, requires work forces whose motivation goes beyond pure extrinsic motivation. The highest level of motivation may result from a combination of both extrinsic and intrinsic motivation (Frey and Osterloh, 1997).

Managers usually are well aware of the real motivations of the work forces. They realize whether IS workers are enthusiastically doing their job or if they act routinely in order to meet the agreed performance or service levels. As outlined previously, specific investments require IS workers to build up unique business and applications knowledge. Acquiring these types of knowledge often requires social collaboration with others, e.g., a team effort between systems analysts and users, or within the team of IS workers, e.g., between systems analysts and programmers. According to Osterloh and Frey (2000, p. 547), contributing (...) one's tacit knowledge in a team hinges on intrinsic motivation."

Therefore, it may be argued that IS functions that require IS workers to make firm specific investments, will even more contribute to create a sustained competitive advantage for an organization, if the IS work forces are intrinsically motivated. Thus, another vital question in order to provide a strategic IS function is, whether in-house employees or external personnel are more intrinsically motivated to perform an IS function that requires to build up specific knowledge assets. In accordance with transaction cost theory, intrinsic motivation may be captured by non-monetary incentives of IS workers leading to the following hypothesis:

Hypothesis 9c: The higher the level of *non-monetary incentives* of in-house as opposed to outsourced IS workers, the higher is the impact of human asset specificity on in-house advantages in providing a strategically significant IS function *(H1a)*.

2.3.2.4 Comparative Advantage in Operational Contribution

As outlined previously, a second dimension, that reflects the organizational impact of an IS function is its operational contribution. From an analysis of nearly 150 interviews with business executives, who initiated outsourcing evaluations, Lacity et al. (1995, p. 87) conclude, "An IT system could be critical but not strategic. That is, a system could be crucially important without differentiating Energen [a fictitious organization] from its competitors."

On the other hand, it may be argued that an IS function may contribute to gain a sustained competitive advantage, while also being an absolute necessity for an organization's day-to-day business operations. This means that the consideration of the operational significance of an IS function may become an evaluative criteria on its own. It is important to be considered within the sourcing decision because an organization can become highly dependent on the provision of an operationally significant IS function. However, what factors determine if the in-house option or outsourcing is superior to perform an operationally significant IS function?

Other than the strategic contribution, the operational significance of an IS function is not necessarily dependent on the specificity of human assets. IS functions may be critical for the day-to-day operations of an organization, although they do no require specific investments of IS workers.

It may be argued, however, that trust plays a major role when delegating the provision of an operationally significant IS function to an agent. Any bad performance of such an IS function could lead to severe losses for an organization. The best monitoring and contractual arrangements may be of little use for an organization if bad performance in an IS function leads to irreparable damages. This means that a party that performs an operationally significant IS function needs to be fully trusted by the principal. Moreover, it can be argued that highly motivated IS workers are more inclined to consider the operational significance of an IS function in doing their work.

Accordingly, the following hypotheses may be put forth:

Hypothesis 8d: The higher the *trustworthiness* of in-house as opposed to outsourced IS workers in providing an IS function, the higher is the perceived advantage of providing an *operationally significant* IS function internally rather than outsourcing it to an external service provider.

Hypothesis 9d: The higher the *non-monetary incentives* of in-house as opposed to outsourced IS workers in providing an IS function, the higher is the perceived advantage of providing an *operationally significant* IS function internally rather than outsourcing it to an external service provider.

Hypothesis 12a: The higher the advantage of insourcing as opposed to outsourcing in providing a *operationally significant* IS function, the less it will be *outsourced.*

Again, it may be argued, however, that Hypothesis 12 is heavily based on the assumption that an organization would actually consider the operational contribution of an IS function in a sourcing decision. This is especially likely if an IS function is, in fact, rated as operationally significant. If it is not of operative importance at all, the comparison of alternative sourcing options will likely be based on other criteria. Accordingly, the following hypothesis is put forth:

Hypothesis 13a: The higher the level of *operational contribution of an* IS function, the higher is the impact of comparative advantages in providing a strategically significant IS function on the degree of IS outsourcing *(H12a).*

2.3.2.5 Comparative Advantage in Sustained Systemic Impact

The third impact of an IS function, that is worth to be considered when it comes to a sourcing decision, is the systemic impact. As outlined previously, organizational impacts (strategic and operational) of a particular IS function often result from its meaningful combination and integration with other IS functions. Together, they form a coherent whole, whose outcome is of higher value than that of each particular IS function separately.

To build such a coherent whole, however, it requires a certain level of interaction and cooperation between each of the specialized IS functions. The possible net of interactions is illustrated in Figure 2-6. For reasons of simplification, five clusters of IS activities are distinguished (see also Section 2.1.1.1, p. 10ff), with the functions of application development and maintenance being one of them.

The interconnection between IS functions becomes especially obvious if one of the components of an IS is significantly altered. For example, the introduction of an ERP standard software package, that is sought to replace a heterogeneous landscape of customized applications, has a profound impact on various components of the overall IS (Dibbern, et al., 2002). Although the most radical change occurs within the function of application development itself, other functions may be severely affected as well. Vast network planning and implementation efforts may be required to provide a client-server-based infrastructure on which ERP systems are usually based. Moreover, the overall planning and management gets challenged, as the ERP subsystem may need to be connected to satellite systems and integrated into the overall systems architecture. In addition, data center operations have to be adjusted to the required systems software and operating procedures of the ERP package. Often the data structures of the old systems need to be converted to fit into the centralized ERP data base. Furthermore, training sessions must be provided for users, and the help desk must be prepared for the new line of inquiry from users.

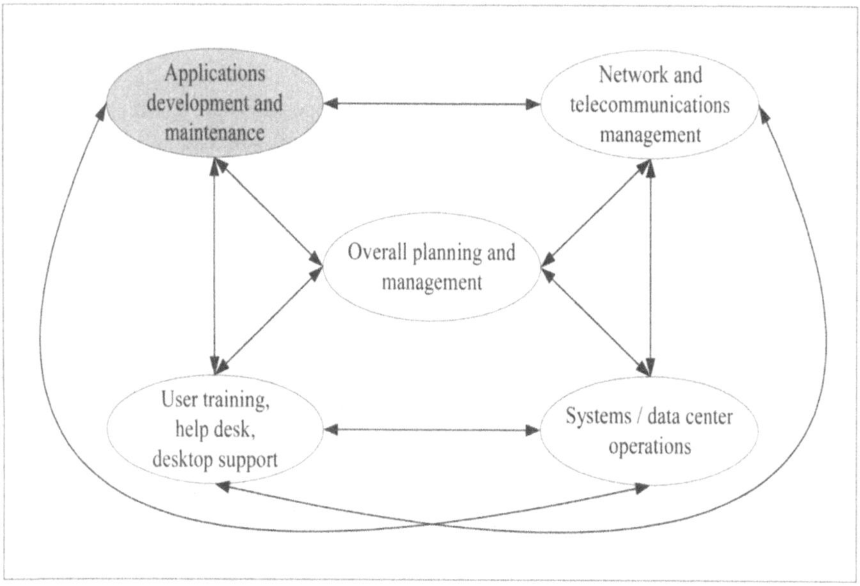

Figure 2-6: Net of Interactions between IS Functions

Overall, the ERP example illustrates how the work processes in one IS function can significantly influence other functions. In order to reach the best available performance of an IS, interdependencies between particular IS functions need to be managed effectively.

In general, *interdependence* is the extent to which each party completes behaviors, acts, or goals that the other party is dependent on for completion of their own behaviors, acts, or goals (Pfeffer and Salancik, 1978). According to Thompson (1967), greater interdependence between organizational units requires greater cooperation efforts. Thompson further argues that the degree of interdependence between tasks should be recognized in organizing these tasks (see also Kilmann, 1983). Highly interdependent tasks should be organized under one common umbrella to furnish the smooth cooperation between task carries. If interdependent tasks are separated from each other, their combined output may be weakened.

Certainly, the highest interdependence occurs within each of the IS functions. However, as outlined previously, there may still exist various lower bound interdependencies between IS functions, that can significantly differ from organization to organization. This raises the question on how to organize interdependent specialized IS functions. Does it matter whether or not one of these functions is selectively outsourced? What happens if all the IS functions are outsourced and how does this compare with the option of total insourcing?

In the previous literature on IS sourcing, there are only view indications how interdependencies between IS functions may influence the sourcing decision. For example, Lacity et al. (1995) argue, based on their extensive case analysis, "Most IT systems require data from or feed data to other systems and therefore cannot be successfully isolated and handed over to an outside provider." Furthermore, Willcocks and Fitzgerald (1993) identified the degree of systems interconnectedness and complexity as one out of six factors that need to be considered as a conceptual base to study the outsourcing decision of organizations. They argue, "Some IT/IS activities may have simple interfaces with the rest of the organization's systems (...) and so be easy to isolate and contract out. Others may have complex and extensive interactions with a wide range of other systems, implying that there will be high switching costs involved." Unfortunately, however, they do not provide any empirical evidence about the importance of this dimension within the sourcing decision. Their case study analysis focuses solely on the strategy dimension.

Lacity and Willcocks (1995) discuss the appropriate unit of analysis for studying IS sourcing decisions, based on 61 sourcing decisions in U.K. and US organizations. In referring to related work from Milgrom and Robertsm (1990; 1995) on *complementary* activities in manufacturing, they argue that similar phenomena do exist in the field of information systems.

> "An example of complementary transactions in the informations systems field is building an information network in conjunction with implementing new application software. As standalone transactions, the network and software add little value...it is the combined benefits of building both that add value" (Lacity and Willcocks, 1995, p. 240).

For that reason, they suggest a multi-level analysis to understand IS sourcing decisions, in which complementary activities between IS functions are taken into account.

Although the empirical evidence about the relationship between the systemic impact of an IS function and the sourcing decision is quite limited, there appears to be agreement that interdependent IS functions should not be governed in different sourcing arrangements. They may either be kept totally in-house, or totally outsourced to a single vendor. Both solutions are single sourcing options. Consequently, the advantage of insourcing as opposed to outsourcing partly depends on the sourcing of other IS functions. In addition, the coordinating capabilities within alternative sourcing arrangements may be critical.

Therefore, *systemic impact,* again, may be treated as a *comparative advantage* construct, defined as the degree to which the systemic impact of an IS function is threatened if it is outsourced rather than provided in-house. Accordingly, the following hypotheses may be put forth:

Hypothesis 14a: The higher the advantage of insourcing as opposed to outsourcing in recognizing the *systemic impact* of an IS function, the less it will be *outsourced.*

Within the current state of research, it may be sufficient to only test the impact of this comparative dimension on IS sourcing, without further elaborating on the sources of differences in systemic impact between alternative sourcing options. However, one variable may nevertheless be considered as a potential predictor. In accordance to the notion of operational significance, it may be argued that the realization of the systemic impact of an IS function critically depends on the motivation of IS workers. Non-motivated IS workers may not care about how their work affects other related work. Therefore, the following hypotheses may be put forth:

Hypothesis 9e: The higher the *non-monetary incentives* of in-house as opposed to outsourced IS workers in providing an IS function, the higher is the perceived in-house advantage in recognizing the *systemic impact* of an IS function.

2.3.2.6 Comparative Advantage in Resources

The purpose of the previous sections has been to demonstrate, how the impacts produced by IS functions can influence the sourcing decision. In particular, three types of impacts have been distinguished. They differ in their content and in their *evaluative radius* (see Figure 2-7). The evaluative radius reflects the *reach* of the considered impacts of an IS function – in terms of different levels of intra and inter-organizational boundaries.

The *strategic contribution* of an IS function represents the most far-reaching evaluative radius that a decision maker may take. It captures the impacts of an IS function on the overall organization and its competitive environment. The *operational contribution* of an IS function represents the second far-reaching evaluative radius. It is limited to more immediate organizational level consequences. Third, the *systemic impact* recognizes the influential role of a particular IS function on the overall IS function.

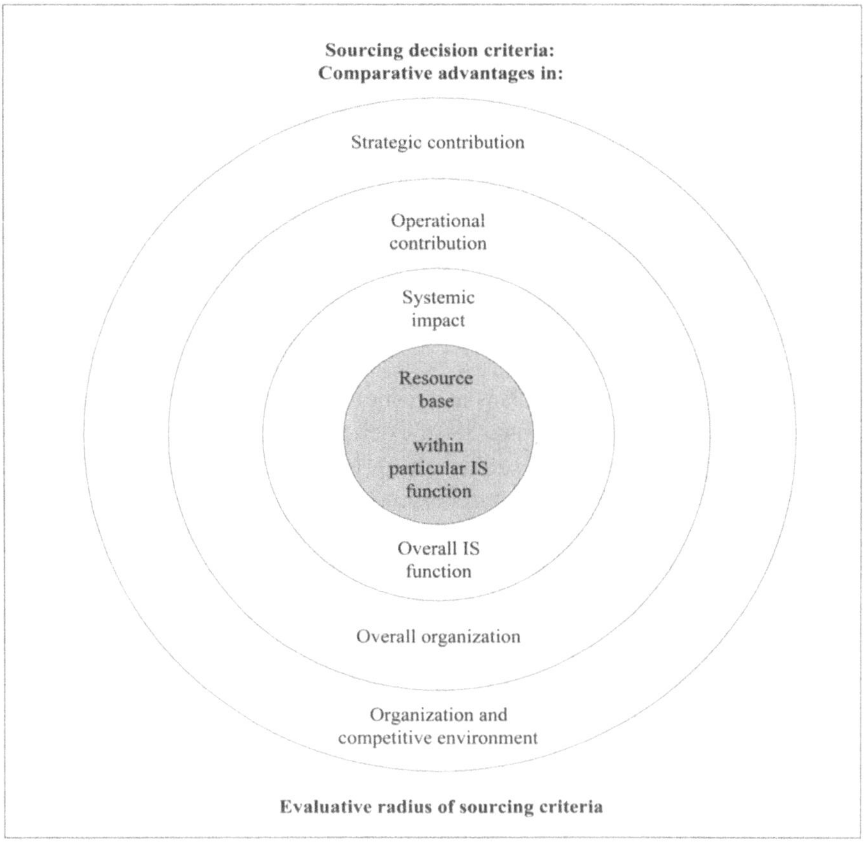

Figure 2-7: Radius of Information Systems Evaluation Perspective

For the sourcing decision, it is important to determine whether these impacts can better be achieved in-house or by one ore more external vendors. In order to create any type of impact, however, an IS function has to be performed adequately. Performing an IS function in a way that recognizes the potential impacts of an IS function, requires an appropriate base of resources. The resources are the limiting factor for reaching the objectives associated with performing an IS function. At the same time, resources may be seen as the enablers of setting objectives (Grant, 1991). The higher the quality and potential of an organizations's base of resources, the more an organization is able to aim for more advanced objectives. For example, an organization with a very limited IS budget and marginal investments in IT, compared to the average industry, will hardly treat its IS function as a competitive weapon (Dibbern, et al., 2003b).

Whenever an organization finds that it does not posses the required resources to reach its current or future objectives, it either has to correct its objectives or it has to close its resource gaps (Grant, 1991).

In general, there are three options to gain access to missing resources (see also Barney, 1999, p.140). First, an organization could try to improve its own base of resources by taking actions internally, e.g., training employees, re-engineering work processes, etc. Second, an organization could acquire the resources externally and integrate them into the organization – provided that the missing resources are indeed available in the market place, e.g., hire new employees or buy more advanced technical equipment and tools to support the development and maintenance of application software. Third, it could contract out the respective IS function to an external service provider, that brings in the required resources.

While the first two options may be treated as in-house solutions, the third includes an outsourcing arrangement. This means that both insourcing and outsourcing are viable options to close resource gaps in performing IS functions. In order to become influential for the sourcing decision, an organization's base of resources needs to be compared with the available resources of external vendors. Accordingly, *resource base advantages* are the extent to which the resources necessary in providing an IS function are better within the organization compared to those of an external service provider. The importance of considering the differences in the base of resources in explaining IS sourcing decisions is widely supported by previous empirical studies.

Teng, et al. (1995) have even found support for the notion that internal deficits *per se* may encourage firms to outsource IS functions. In particular, discrepancies between the desired and actual level of support and staff quality were found to be positively related to the degree of IS outsourcing.

The majority of studies, however, takes a more comparative view. The study of Dibbern and Heinzl (2002; 2001) confirms the hypothesis that small and mid-sized firms in Germany increasingly outsource IS functions when facing resource deficits compared to an external vendor, in closing current performance gaps and coping with future knowledge requirements. There is also a series of studies that present similar arguments, although they do not explicitly refer to resource-based theory. For example, Loh (1994) supports the hypotheses that firms increasingly outsource IS functions if IS outsourcing provides an advantage through getting access to new technology, expert knowledge, and the promotion of innovative use of IS (technological imperative). Further indications for the fact that companies outsource IS functions in order to get access to state of the art skill sets and technological know-how can be found in the exploratory works by Clark et al. (1995), DiRomualdo and Gurbaxani (1998), Lacity and Hirschheim (1993a), McLellan et al. (1995), and Fowler and Jeffs (1998).

Overall, the empirical findings reveal that especially *intellectual capital*, including skill sets, knowledge, and capabilities, may differ between the in-house and outsourced provision of IS services. What is less clear, are the circumstances under which vendors may posses superior intellectual capital. A number of studies suggest that external vendors are superior in technological knowledge, i.e., knowledge about new IT products, like standard software packages and best practice knowledge on how to effectively deploy these technologies (e.g., Beath and Walker, 1998).

The findings of the work from Poppo and Zenger (1998) confirms the view that companies will outsource IS functions if the demands for personnel with extensive knowledge and skills are particularly high. Nelson et al. (1996) show that software development projects, which are based on specific technology and advanced development environments, are more likely to be outsourced. Nam et al. (1996) show that strong systems heterogeneity is associated with a higher degree of outsourcing IS functions.

By contrast, in-house IS departments are said to have advantages in knowledge about unique business processes of the organization and knowledge about customized applications that have been tailored according to unique organizational requirements (Beath and Walker, 1998; Dibbern, et al., 2003b). Moreover, there is some evidence that in-house IS departments – especially those of larger organizations – do not necessarily lack behind external vendors in terms of technical skill sets (Dibbern, et al., 2003b; Hirschheim and Lacity, 2000). This is especially true when companies that outsourced find themselves supported by the same personnel as before (Fowler and Jeffs, 1998, p. 121).

Based on these empirical insights, two conclusions may be drawn. First, resources have to be treated as a comparative advantage construct. Second, while there is no evidence that technical IS components may differ between insourcing and outsourcing, human assets may significantly differ. In particular, the in-house base of intellectual capital may be superior if the provision of an IS function requires a high level of firm specific knowledge that can only be acquired through a long-term learning process within the boundaries of a firm. Therefore, the following two hypotheses may be put forth:

Hypothesis 1e: The higher the *human asset specificity* required to perform an IS function, the higher is the advantage of an organization's in-house *base of intellectual capital* as compared to that of an external vendor.

Hypothesis 15a: The higher the in-house advantages compared to an external vendor in the *base of intellectual capital* required to perform an IS function, the less the IS function will be *outsourced.*

Moreover, there are other types of resources that may differ between insourcing and outsourcing arrangements. These resources represent more objective measures of an organization's IS service capacity. They comprise such issues as the staffing level, the financial resources, and the technical equipment, summarized as *other resources*. Accordingly, the following additional hypothesis may be stated:

Hypothesis 16a: The higher the in-house advantages compared to an external vendor in the *base of other* (than intellectual) res*ources* required to perform an IS function, the less the IS function will be *outsourced.*

Finally, there is one variable from transaction cost theory that may play a different role in resource-based theory. It is the *difficulty in measuring the performance* of an IS function. There is some evidence in the literature that organizations outsource IS functions in order to increase the control over that function (Fowler and Jeffs, 1998; Heinzl, 1993; Huber, 1993; Reponen, 1993). It appears as if organizations believe that they could get rid of the metering problem, by transferring it to an external vendor. Such an argument would be in line with the reasoning from resource-based theory. It may be argued that measurement difficulties are perceived as *gaps* that can be closed through outsourcing (Teng et al., 1996). Therefore, resource-based theory would lead to the following hypothesis:

Hypothesis 7a: The higher the *difficulty in measuring the performance* of an IS function, the more likely it will be outsourced to an external vendor.

It has to be noted, however, that outsourcing an IS functions that the client organization is unable to evaluate is not without risks. Indeed, such practices have heavily been criticized by researchers, because they can lead to significant ex post bargaining costs (Lacity et al., 1995; Willcocks et al., 1996). This shows the darker side of resource-based theory. It usually neglects the risks associated with solely focusing on resource allocation issues.

2.3.2.7 Overview

An overview of the constructs and relationships deduced from resource-based theory is presented in Figure 2-8. The graph may be viewed as both a decomposition and an extension of Figure 2-1, p. 23. Again, different types of comparative advantages of insourcing as opposed to outsourcing serve as direct predictors of an IS function's degree of outsourcing. In particular, organizations will not tend to outsource an IS function if its strategic and operational contribution as well as its systemic impact is significantly threatened through outsourcing. Moreover, in-house advantages in the intellectual capital and other types of resources are proposed to be damage the extent to which the development and maintenance work is outsourced. The graph also shows that perceived in-house advantages in the strategic contribution of an IS function and the intellectual capital required to do the work, are more likely if the development and maintenance of software applications requires highly specific human assets. In addition, in-house advantages in the operational contribution of an IS function are more likely if in-house IS workers are more trustworthy and more motivated by non-monetary incentives.

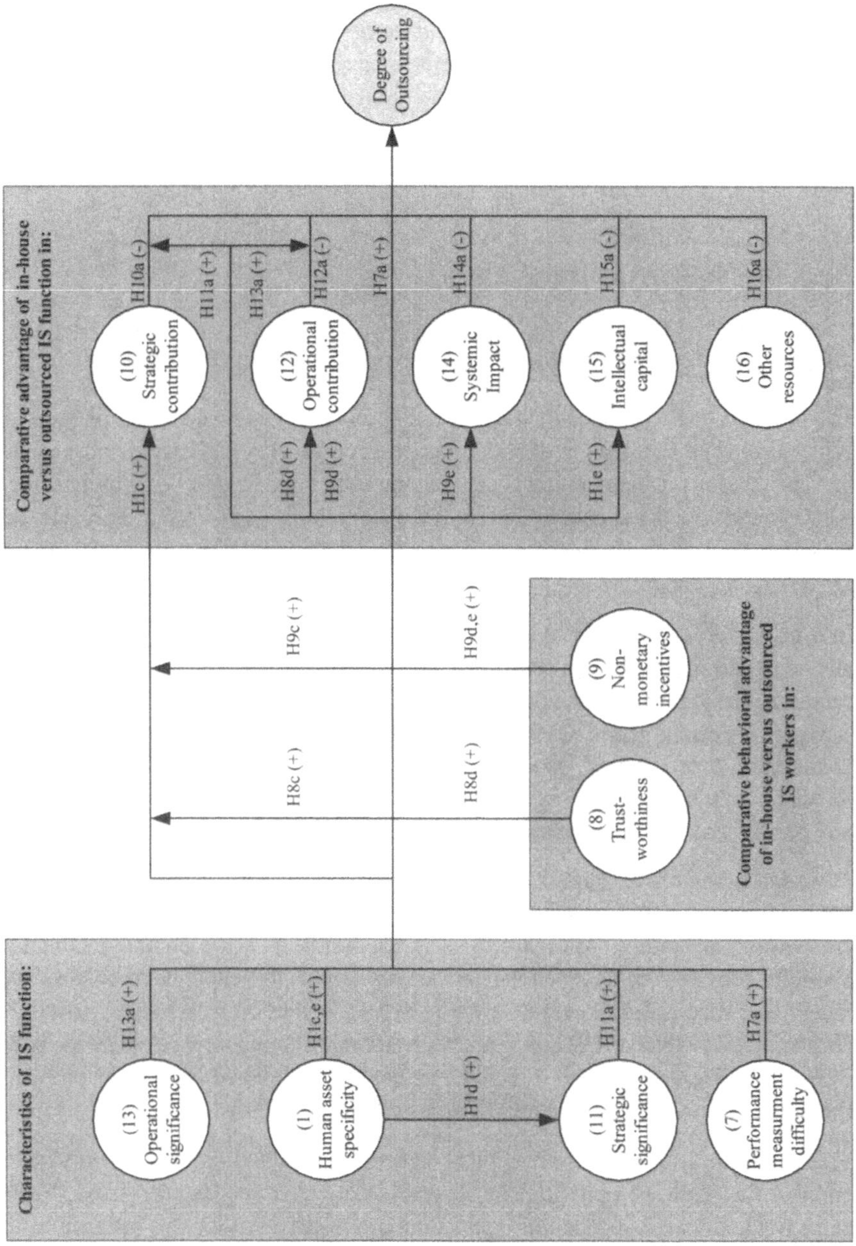

Figure 2-8: Hypotheses from Resource-based Theory

Moreover, comparative systemic impact advantages are influenced by differences in the motivation of in-house versus outsourced IS workers. Finally, there are two types of *moderator* effects. First, the extent to which an IS function is being less outsourced due to in-house advantages in the strategic and operational contribution of an IS function, is proposed to be higher, if indeed the IS function is strategic (i.e. operationally significant). Second, comparative behavioral advantages in trust and non-monetary incentives are proposed to increase the impact of human asset specificity on comparative in-house advantages in strategic contribution.

2.3.3 Incomplete Contracts Theory

2.3.3.1 Cost-Benefit Dilemma of Compensating Incomplete Contracts

The previous analysis has shown that the notion of incomplete contracts plays a significant role in the reasoning of both transaction cost theory and resource-based theory. In situations, where contracts can only be settled incompletely, an organization faces the risk that the agents make use of the contractual gaps. That is, they may behave opportunistic by increasing their own benefits rather than those of the organization that they serve.

In *transaction cost theory* it is argued that the inability to settle complete contracts, and hence the threat of opportunistic behavior, is especially high if (1) the assets required to perform an IS function are highly firm specific, if (2) the task environment is highly uncertain, and if (3) the performance of those that do the work is difficult to measure. It is assumed, however, that opportunistic behavior can be alleviated through costly transactions, e.g., through carefully selecting and testing the contractual partner and through permanent monitoring.

Resource-based theory takes a different view. It argues that firm specific assets can not be traded, imitated, or substituted. They provide the basis for a firm's sustained competitive advantage. Accordingly, it is impossible to settle complete contracts about the provision of IS functions that heavily rely on these unique resources. This means that incomplete contracts are a necessary condition to achieve a sustained competitive advantage. The opportunities resulting from incomplete contracts, however, are severely threatened if the contractual partner behaves opportunistic by rationally underinvesting in the relationship (holdup problem).

This means that the benefits resulting from firm specific investments can only be secured if the threat of opportunistic behavior can effectively be alleviated. At the same time, however, safeguards against opportunistic behavior can increase transaction costs, which may offset the benefits. The resulting trade-off may be called the *"cost-benefit dilemma"* of specific investments. Obviously, any mechanisms that help solve this cost-benefit dilemma of specific investments will optimize the provision of an IS function.

In this realm, *trust and non-monetary incentives* have been identified as two antipodes of opportunism. They do not only lower the influence of human asset specificity on increased transaction costs, but also leverage the effect of specific investments on the strategic contribution of an IS function. However, no conclusive evidence could be identified that supports the notion that the trustworthiness or the non-monetary incentives of IS workers should be higher in case of insourcing as opposed to outsourcing. Accordingly, both constructs were treated as comparative constructs. That is, in situations in which the danger of opportunistic behavior of the contractual partner is especially high, e.g., if the provision of an IS function requires a high level of specific investments, it is decisive whether the trustworthiness and the non-monetary incentives of IS worker are perceived to be higher or lower in case of insourcing as opposed to outsourcing.

In spite of these two comparative behavioral mechanisms, traditional transaction cost theory has provided another more *normative* solution to the problem. It assumes that in situations, in which no complete contracts can be settled, the *internal authority system* of an organization generally provides a more efficient frame to govern these tasks than any relationship with external vendors.

This strong assumption has been heavily criticized by representatives of property rights theory and provided the very basis for the theory of incomplete contracts. Incomplete contracts theory seeks to answer two fundamental questions that remain unanswered in transaction cost theory:

(1) *What* backs up authority and

(2) *how* can authority solve the holdup problem?

According to Grossmann, Hart and Moore, *ownership* over non-human assets provides the ultimate source of authority. It gives the owner *residual control rights* over the use of the assets (Hart and Moore, 1990, p. 1120) and provides bargaining power to decide upon the distribution of the ex post surplus resulting from specific investments in human assets (Grossmann and Hart, 1986, p. 696f., 716f.; Hart, 1996, p. 379; Hart and Moore, 1990, p. 1122). The following statements from the main proponents of incomplete contracts theory illustrate their basic arguments:

> "In contrast to transaction-cost theory, however, the property rights approach stresses the role of asset ownership and residual control rights as a way of overcoming contractual incompleteness" (Hart, 1996, p. 372).
>
> (...) residual control rights are important because they explain how authority is sustained, i.e. what ensures that someone with authority can actually exercise it (Hart, 1996, p. 376).
>
> "(...) ownership confers residual rights of control over the firm's assets: the right to decide how these assets are to be used except to the extent that particular usages have been specified in an initial contract" (Hart and Moore, 1990, p. 1120).

> "(...) an employer's authority is represented not by the ability to force an employee to do what s/he wants, but rather by the ability to obtain a substantial share of the *ex post* surplus from the relationship through the control of non-human assets" (Hart, 1996, p. 379).

Based on these general arguments that illustrate the nexus between ownership and authority, Hart and Moore (1990) have developed a formal model that allows to logically deduce the optimal allocation of ownership in situations, where two parties consider to enter into an exchange relationship. In order to proof their propositions, Hart and Moore (1990) have chosen a *formal mathematical approach*[13]. Like all mathematical models, however, they rely on a number of simplifying assumptions. This means that the model is *not directly applicable* to empirically examine real world phenomena, like IS outsourcing. In fact, there are few, if any, empirical studies that have examined the relationship between incomplete contracts, ownership and firm boundaries (Holmstrom, 1999). In the following, the model will be applied less formally and more closely related to its verbal interpretations (see Foss, 2000; Hart, 1996; Holmstrom, 1999).

2.3.3.2 Institutional Safeguards through Ownership

As already outlined previously, the ownership dimension has gained momentum in the IS outsourcing arena with the arrival of special ownership arrangements between client and vendor. These ownership arrangements include spin-offs and joint-ventures, in which the client holds all or part of the vendor's capital. A number of authors found evidence for the notion that the motivation to enter into these special ownership deals is closely related to the motivations and expectations associated with IS outsourcing (Heinzl, 1993a). For example, strategic objectives tend to be allied with ownership arrangements (Currie and Willcocks, 1998; DiRomualdo and Gurbaxani, 1998). However, no study has explicitly outlined why ownership arrangements are more appropriate than non-ownership relationships in situations where outsourcing contracts can only be settled incompletely. This explanatory gap may be filled by the reasoning of incomplete contracts theory.

There is, however, one note of caution that needs to be addressed before starting to theorize about the role of ownership in IS outsourcing. It refers to the *level of analysis* on which the formal models developed in incomplete contracts theory are usually based. Holmstrom (1999, p. 87) has critically argued:

> "The problem is that the theory as presented, really is a theory about asset ownership by individuals rather than by firms, at least if one interprets it literally."

Indeed, the model as presented by Hart and Moore is largely based on the assumption that the parties that enter into an exchange relationship are individuals. That is, the agents that perform the work are assumed to be identical with the owners of the

---

[13] A preliminary model has been developed by Grossmann and Hart, 1986.

non-human assets required to do the work. In a large number of profit organizations, however, there is a separation between the owners, i.e., the shareholders of a firm, and those that do the work. It may be assumed, however, that a firm's top management acts in behalf of the shareholders' interests. This is consistent with the argument from Hart (1996, p. 382):

> "(...) authority rests with the owner (or owners) of the asset, or someone to whom the owner has delegated residual rights of control (a board of directory or management)".

The residual control rights, resulting from ownership, are in the hands of a firm's top management. They decide upon the investment of the shareholders' capital and upon the use of non-human assets.

Moreover, the residual control rights, resulting from ownership, give the management the legal right to exclude employees from the use of assets (Hart and Moore, 1990, p. 1120). Using an organization's assets means to provide IS services for an organization and to get paid for these services. In other words, exclusion from the use of assets equals the right to selectively dismiss IS workers (Hart and Moore, 1990, p. 1121) (which may be more or less difficult due to internal or external employment regulations).

Accordingly, an IS employee has an incentive to work in the employers best interest, because otherwise s/he may loose her/his job. This means that s/he is extrinsically motivated to make an investment in non-alienable firm specific assets, e.g., build up firm specific knowledge. Moreover, an employee may realize that her/his specific investments will contribute to build and maintain application software that significantly improves the work of the users, which in turn may positively influence the firm's benefits or even give the firm a sustained competitive advantage. Provided that an employee is aware of these consequences and that s/he recognizes the inevitable link between her/his income and the distribution of the return on investment generated by the firm, her/his extrinsic motivation may even increase.

However, how do a number of employment relationships differ from a relationship with an external vendor?

Of course the employer or owner can cancel the contract with an external IS vendor as well. However, in this case, the vendor staff may not automatically loose their job. They normally stay with the vendor and take over another job – potentially using the assets of another client. (This may slightly change if the vendor is a single person, i.e., a freelancer (Knolmayer, 2002) that is not managed by an intermediary company). Consequently, the client's ability to exercise authority over IS workers is severely limited if they are employed by a legally independent external organization. Moreover, external personnel may have an incentive to work in the best interest of the vendor rather than client. This may lead to conflicts, provided that the objectives of the client do not necessarily match with the profit motive of the vendor. Accordingly, the danger of holdup is higher in case of non-ownership.

While this would suggest that the clients own the IS assets of an IS function, if it requires specific investments by the IS workers, it does not mean that those workers need to be employees of the client organization. Instead of integrating the IS function into the organizational structure of the client, the function could be outsourced, but still owned by the client through capital shares with the vendor. As Holmstrom (1999, p. 88) has stated, "If I own 10% of a firm, I own 10% of all its assets." This means that a client organization can keep residual rights of control over an IS function through capital shares.

In the following, the *degree of ownership in external service provider(s),* therefore, refers to the average percentage share of capital that an organization has with external vendor(s) that provide part or all of an IS function.

For example, the former in-house IS department may be spun off into a legally independent corporation. This means that IS workers are no longer employed by the client organization but by an affiliated independent legal corporation that provides IS services. This may positively affect the motivation of IS employees. First, the return on investment achieved from IS services directly shows up in the balance sheet of the spin-off. This allows employees to better understand how their performance affects the benefits of the organization for which they work. Second, the customer focus of the IS workers, and hence their motivation to satisfy the users, may be sharpened as soon as they realize that the profits of their organization critically depend on the value that they create for their customers. It should be considered, however, that the motivation to make specific investments into the owner company, for which they formerly worked, may eventually decline over time if more and more external vendors become customers of the newly founded spin-off (Heinzl, 1993a).

Nevertheless, partial or full ownership of an external service provider can help to solve the holdup problem. The legal sources of internal authority can partially or fully be substituted by partial or total ownership of external service providers. This means that ownership in external service providers can help solve the cost-benefit dilemma introduced earlier. The increasing risks of high transaction costs and strategic vulnerability, resulting from outsourcing highly specific IS functions, may be lowered through special ownership arrangements with external vendors. Accordingly, the following two hypotheses may be put forth:

Hypothesis 17a: The higher the degree of ownership in the external service provider(s), the less will an increasing degree of human asset specificity lead to lower in-house as opposed to outsourcing transaction costs in performing an IS function *(H1a).*

Hypothesis 17b: The higher the degree of ownership in the external service provider(s), the less will an increasing degree of human asset specificity lead to in-house advantages in providing a strategically significant IS function *(H1c).*

The moderating impact of the degree of capital shares with external service provider(s) on the relationship between asset specificity and comparative advantages in transaction costs and strategic contribution is illustrated in Figure 2-9.

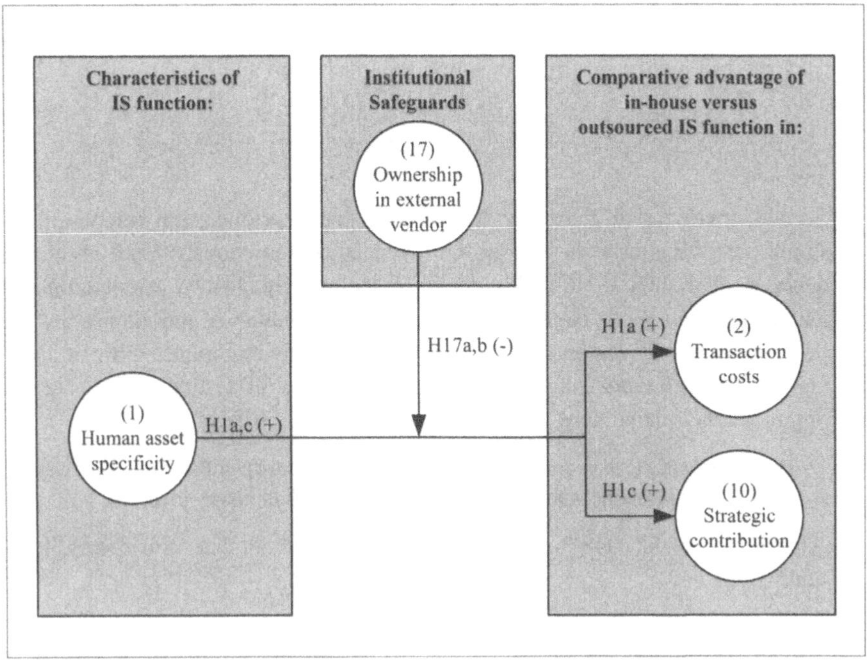

Figure 2-9: Hypotheses from Incomplete Contracts Theory

2.3.4 Theory of Planned Behavior

2.3.4.1 Nexus between Individual and Organizational Behavior

The theory of planned behavior is fundamentally different from any of the previous three theories of the firm. Rather than explaining organizational behavior, it provides a general frame to understand individual behavior. At the first view, this appears to be an invincible conflict in the level of analysis. How can a theory that is concerned with explaining the behavior of individual persons, contribute to explain organizational level phenomena such as IS outsourcing?

In answering this question, a second view on the relationship between the explanation of individual and organizational behavior reveals the following insights:

- First, IS sourcing is a major management decision made by individuals rather than organizations. Empirical studies have supported the view that the final decision over the sourcing of IS functions is mostly made by an organization's highest ranking IS executives (Apte, et al., 1997; Sobol and Apte, 1995). Moreover, the sourcing decision process is most often initiated by either top management or IS management (Lacity and Willcocks, 1995; Willcocks, et al., 1996). Of course, the decision makers are influenced by their social environment. This becomes especially obvious during the process of evaluating alternative sourcing options. These activities tend to be under the control of IS management, but supported by internal staff and/or external consultants (Hirschheim and Lacity, 2000; Palvia, 1995). Thus, in general, IS executives are the primary decision makers. However, they are influenced by their social environment – either deliberately or unintendedly.

- Second, the focus on the individual is consistent with the main behavioral assumptions of the three theories of the firm analyzed previously. Each of them is deeply rooted in the notion of "methodological individualism", which maintains that social phenomena can be traced back to the behavior of individuals, i.e. rational or boundedly rational actors (Arrow, 1994). The importance of the individual becomes obvious no later than in the course of testing theories about organizational phenomena, as emphasized by Arrow (1994, p. 3),

  > "It is a salutary check on any theory of the economy or any other part of society that the explanations make sense on the basis of the individuals involved."

  Similarly, Hayek (1948, p. 135) made up his mind about what constitutes "true" individualism,

  > "(...) its basic contention is (...) that there is no other way toward an understanding of social phenomena but through our understanding of individual actions directed toward other people and guided by their expected behavior."

  Unfortunately, however, theories of the firm rarely address the cognitive process that leads to an individual's behavior. They merely treat decision making as a "black box". This means that the "salutary check", as described by Arrow, could be improved by adding more information about the more immediate drivers of individual decision making.

- Third, the perspective of management, acting rational or at least boundedly rational, implies that the behavior of individuals always results from a process of evaluating and comparing alternatives based on certain criteria. This perspective ignores that the cognitive process that guides decision making behavior may be influenced or constrained by the individual's perceptions of her/his social environment. In addressing limitations of transaction cost theory, Hodgson (1996, p. 250) has stated:

  > „Methodological individualism starts with the rational being sovereign over his or her choices. A problem of the methodological individualism is the constitutive and mutually reinforcing feedback mechanisms between individuals, such as imitation and conformism, and the way in which individuals and institutions mutually condition and constitute each other."

> The theory of planned behavior tends to broaden the rational actor perspective by recognizing the potential influences of the social environment on an individual's choice behavior.

Overall, it may be concluded that a better understanding of the general nexus of cognitive influences that drive the behavior of individuals can enhance the explanatory and predictive power of any theory that seeks to explain the outcome of major management decisions. IS sourcing is such a management decision and therefore appears to be a promising object to look at from the perspective of the theory of planned behavior. In the following, the main concepts and relationships of this theory will be introduced and applied in the IS outsourcing context. The individual perspective is analyzed from the view of the highest ranking IS executive of an organization.

2.3.4.2 Attitudes, Subjective Norm and Behavioral Control

The theory of planned behavior aims to predict and explain the *behavior* of individuals. According to Ajzen (1980, p. 41), "(...) all behavior involves a choice, be it a choice between performing or not performing a given action or a choice between several qualitatively and quantitatively different action alternatives." More specifically, behavior may be characterized by "(...) behavioral criteria (...) comprised of four elements: the action, the target at which the action is directed, the context in which it occurs, and the time at which it is performed" (Ajzen and Fishbein, 1980, p. 39). Applied to this study, the *action* is the insourcing or outsourcing directed at the *target* of both the development and maintenance of software applications within the *context* of user organizations. Moreover, it is supposed that the action has already taken place, reflected by an organization's current (*time*) degree of outsourcing both IS functions.

According to the theory of planned behavior, the choice is determined by an individual's intention to perform a certain behavior (see Figure 2-10). This means that the current degree of outsourcing would critically depend on *past intentions* of IS executives to insource or outsource an IS function. The intentions, again, are influenced by three main factors: (1) the attitude towards the behavior, (2) the subjective norm, and (3) the perceived behavioral control. Each of theses concepts is influenced by corresponding types of beliefs (see Figure 2-10).

In general, *attitude* "(...) refers to the degree to which a person has a favorable or unfavorable evaluation or appraisal of the behavior in question" (Ajzen, 1991, p. 188). In the IS sourcing context, the concept of *attitude towards outsourcing* may be introduced, defined as the overall evaluative appraisal of an IS executive towards having an IS function provided by an external vendor. The attitudes are influenced by more specific salient beliefs about the decision object. In describing the nature of these salient beliefs, Ajzen (1991, p. 191) has stated:

"In case of attitudes towards a behavior, each believe links the behavior to a certain outcome, or to some other attribute such as the cost incurred by performing the behavior. (...) In this fashion, we learn to favour behaviors we believe have largely desirable consequences and we form unfavorable attitudes towards behaviors we associate with mostly unfavorable consequences."

The major beliefs associated with the choice of insourcing versus outsourcing IS functions have already been identified. They have been deduced from transaction cost theory and resource-based theory and comprise the perceived comparative advantages of insourcing versus outsourcing an IS function, including relative advantages in transaction costs, production costs, strategic contribution, operational contribution, systemic impact, intellectual capital, and other resources.

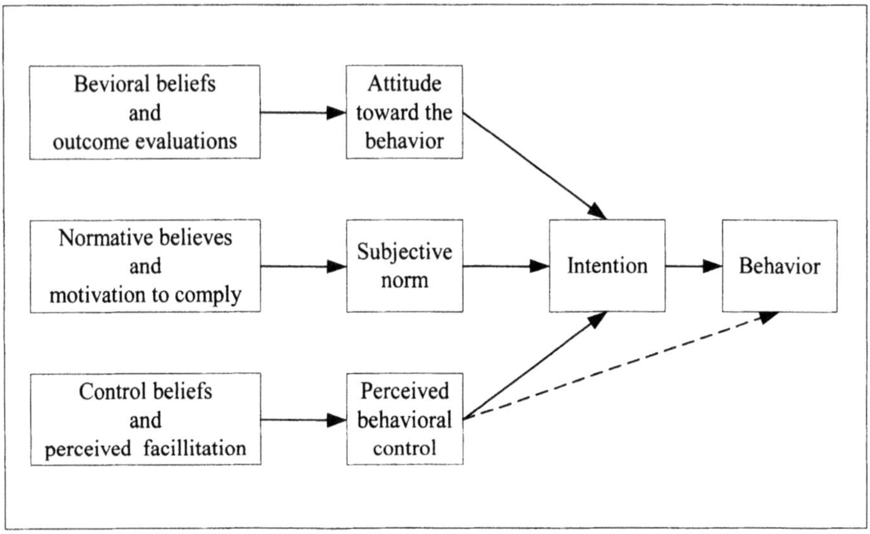

Figure 2-10: Theory of Planned Behavior (Ajzen, 1989, p. 252)

These factors were proposed to be direct predictors of the current degree of IS outsourcing. According to the theory of planned behavior, however, their impact is *mediated* by the attitude construct. Moreover, the influence of attitude on behavior is *mediated* by intentions towards the behavior. Ajzen (1980, p. 80) has stressed:

"Our argument that behavior is ultimately determined by beliefs should not mean that there is a direct link between beliefs and behavior."

In most of the applications of the theory of reasoned action and the theory of planned behavior in the IS field, however, researchers did not fully examine the chain of causality from beliefs to attitudes to intentions and to behavior. Most studies are concerned with explaining IT adoption behavior. The pioneering work can be traced back to Davis (1989). He developed and tested the technology acceptance model (TAM) in order to predict and explain the extent to which individuals make use of information systems components, e.g., electronic mail or a file editor as part of an IS. According to the TAM, current system usage critically depends on two salient beliefs – the *ease of use* and the *usefulness* of the technology in question (see also Adams, et al., 1992; Chin and Todd, 1995; Segars and Grover, 1993; Straub, et al., 1995). Others have followed suite and extended the TAM by adding predictors of ease of use and usefulness (Igbaria, et al., 1995), by including additional beliefs from innovation theories and testing their impact on both current use and future intentions (Agarwal and Prasad, 1997), by testing the impact of ease of use and usefulness on attitudes and intentions rather than current usage (Mathieson, 1991), by including subjective norm and behavioral control derived from the theory of planned behavior, decomposing them together with attitude beliefs into multidimensional belief constructs, and testing their impact on intentions and actual behavior (Taylor and Todd, 1995), or only on intentions (Harrison, et al., 1997). Overall, the following conclusions may be drawn from the insights provided by the IT adoption studies:

- First, beliefs can directly influence current behavior without being mediated by attitude and intentions. Accordingly, it appears to be a reasonable practice to directly link the various comparative advantages of insourcing versus outsourcing (beliefs), as derived from transaction cost theory and resource-based theory, to the current degree of IS outsourcing. Moreover, if attitudes are included in the analysis, their role as full mediators of beliefs has been questioned by some research (Agarwal, 2000, p. 94). Therefore, it appears to be possible or indeed useful to test the direct impact of beliefs on current IS sourcing behavior *together* with their mediated affect through attitudes.
- Second, IS research has either tested the impact of beliefs on current behavior *or* on intentions, but rarely has included both intentions and future behavior within the same model (with a notable exception by Taylor and Todd, 1995). The reason for this limitation appears to be straight forward. If the objective is to explain current behavior, it makes little sense to include past intentions in the analysis, because they can hardly be determined *ex post* within an empirical test. By contrast, if current intentions are included in the analysis, future behavior rather than current behavior would have to be included in the analysis. This would require a longitudinal research design, which is very demanding given the difficulty to observe the sourcing behavior of a large number of organizations over multiple periods. Indeed, the test of the full model is mostly limited to phenomena that can be studied in experimental designs, where the researcher has control over the research setting and is able to directly observe time dependent cause-effect relationships, like those between intentions and future behavior (e.g., Bhattacherjee, 1996).

As the primary objective of this study is to explain the current heterogeneous IS sourcing behavior of organizations, the relationship between beliefs, attitudes and current sourcing behavior is of primary concern. Accordingly, the following hypotheses may be put forth (see also Figure 2-11, p. 102):

Hypothesis 2b: The higher the perceived comparative *transaction cost* advantage of insourcing as opposed to outsourcing an IS function, the more negative is an IS executive's *attitude* towards outsourcing this IS function.

Hypothesis 3b: The higher the perceived comparative *production cost* advantage of insourcing as opposed to outsourcing an IS function, the more negative is an IS executive's *attitude* towards outsourcing this IS function.

Hypothesis 10b: The higher the perceived comparative advantage of insourcing as opposed to outsourcing in providing a *strategically significant* IS function, the more negative is an IS executive's *attitude* towards outsourcing this IS function.

Hypothesis 12b: The higher the perceived comparative advantage of insourcing as opposed to outsourcing in providing an *operationally significant* IS function, the more negative is an IS executive's *attitude* towards outsourcing this IS function.

Hypothesis 14b: The higher the perceived comparative advantage of insourcing as opposed to outsourcing in keeping up the *systemic impact* of an IS function, the more negative is an IS executive's *attitude* towards outsourcing this IS function.

Hypothesis 15b: The higher the perceived in-house advantages compared to an external vendor in the *base of intellectual capital* required to perform an IS function, the more negative is an IS executive's *attitude* towards outsourcing this IS function.

Hypothesis 16b: The higher the perceived in-house advantages compared to an external vendor in the *base of other* (than intellectual) *resources* required to perform an IS function, the more negative is an IS executive's *attitude* towards outsourcing this IS function.

Moreover, the following two moderator effects from resource-based theory can be put forth accordingly:

Hypothesis 11b: The higher the level of the *strategic contribution* of an IS function, the higher is the impact of comparative advantages in providing a strategically significant IS function on the *attitude* towards outsourcing this IS function (H10b).

Hypothesis 13b: The higher the level of *operational contribution of an* IS function, the higher is the impact of comparative advantages in providing a strategically significant IS function on the degree of IS outsourcing *(H12a)*.

The aggregate of all the beliefs about the comparative advantages of insourcing versus outsourcing is supposed to determine an IS executive's overall evaluative appraisal of IS outsourcing. It is an empirical question, which of the individual beliefs most strongly (negatively) influence the overall attitude towards outsourcing. Moreover, it is an empirical question, to what extent these overall attitudes towards IS outsourcing explain the current degree of IS outsourcing. In particular, three conditions would have to be fulfilled for a strong predictive power of attitude. First, an IS executive would have to make her/his sourcing decision based on a careful evaluation and comparison of alternative sourcing options. Second, an IS executive would need to immediately react to any changes in her/his attitude towards IS outsourcing and adjusts the degree of IS outsourcing in accordance with these changes. Third, an IS executive would need to have full control over the sourcing decision and should not be influenced by any other factors. Assuming that all these conditions apply, the following hypothesis can be put forth:

Hypothesis 18a: The more negative the overall *attitudes* towards outsourcing an IS function are, the less it will be *outsourced.*

Of course, the assumption that IS executives act fully rational may not always be true in reality. The potential limitations of such a view have been recognized by the theory of planned behavior. It adds two additional explanations for individual behavior.

The first is reflected by the construct *subjective norm*, which "(...) refers to the perceived social pressure to perform or not perform the behavior. It is influenced by normative beliefs which are concerned with the likelihood that important referent individuals or groups approve or disapprove of performing a given behavior" (Ajzen, 1991, p. 195).

Previous research on IS outsourcing indicates that an organization's sourcing decision may not always result from an evaluation and comparison of alternative sourcing options (see also Section 2.1.2.2, p. 16ff). For example, there are indications of a "bandwagon-effect" (Lacity and Hirschheim, 1993b; 1995). That is, organizations outsource IS functions, because other organizations have done so. On the other hand, they may not outsource because influential others have reported bad experiences from IS outsourcing. Tests of innovation diffusion theory have found support for the notion that the diffusion of IS outsourcing events is influenced by various communication channels that enhance imitative behavior (Hu, et al., 1997; Loh and Venkatraman, 1992b). Overall, the empirical findings support the view that the opinion of others could have a profound impact on the sourcing decision of organizations. Applied to the IS context, *subjective norm* will therefore broadly be defined as the degree to which most people, who are important to an organization, think that the organization should outsource an IS function rather than keeping it in-house. In particular, the opinion of others may influence the sourcing decision in two ways.

On the one hand, subjective norm could have a direct impact on the degree of IS outsourcing – independent of an IS executive's attitude towards outsourcing an IS function. For example, organizations may unreflectively imitate the sourcing behavior of other organizations or be heavily influenced by peer individuals or groups, without thoroughly evaluating the sourcing options based on criteria such as IS costs, resources or impacts. On the other hand, and contrary to the theory of planned behavior, subjective norm may also impact an IS executive's evaluative appraisal of IS outsourcing. This is especially likely if influential others participate in the process of evaluating and comparing alternative sourcing options, e.g., if they are members of an evaluation committee (Huber, 1993; Lacity and Willcocks, 1997; Palvia, 1995). The notion of participative decision making may be an important difference between individual and organizational behavior. This is considered by the following two hypotheses:

Hypothesis 19a: The more negative the opinion of influential others (*subjective norm*) towards outsourcing an IS function, the less it will be *outsourced.*

Hypothesis 19b: The more negative the opinion of influential others (*subjective norm*) towards outsourcing an IS function, the more negative is the overall *attitude* towards outsourcing this IS function.

Of course, the explanatory power of the notion of subjective norm may be increased by adding more specific normative believes as predictors of subjective norm, e.g., by differentiating between the beliefs of various influential stakeholder groups. However, for the purpose of this study, the overall concept of subjective norm is deemed to be sufficient in achieving a first confirmatory cut about its influence on IS sourcing.

The second concept, which complements the rational actor view of behavior, is an individual's *perceived behavioral control* over the behavior in question. It "(...) refers to the perceived ease or difficulty of performing the behavior and it is assumed to reflect past experience as well as anticipated impediments and obstacles" (Ajzen, 1991, p. 188).

Past research has reported a number of difficulties associated with both insourcing and outsourcing IS functions. In particular, politics, i.e., the exercise of power by other stakeholder groups, tend to limit the ability of the main decision makers to act strictly rationally (Lacity and Hirschheim, 1993a; Lacity, et al., 1994; Lacity and Willcocks, 1997; Palvia, 1995). Within organizations, power is usually exercised by certain political coalitions, that have some sort of common interest (Pfeffer, 1981).

Changes in an organization's IS sourcing arrangement can severely affect the interests of IS workers. For example, IS outsourcing can threaten the work place of IS employees or alter the nature of the working environment. These changes can lead to restrictive or supportive behaviors by IS employees (Lacity and Hirschheim, 1993a).

In Germany, the protection of employee interests is codified in law. On the one hand, there is a special law (§ 613 BGB) that regulates the transfer of organizational units to legally independent organizations (*"Betriebsübergang"*), including the outsourcing of IS subunits to external service providers (Koffka, 1997, p. 124ff.). This law determines that the external vendor is obliged to take over former in-house employees to the same conditions as before outsourcing. Moreover, it gives employees the right to protest against being taken over by an external vendor. Both protective rights may become obsolete, however, if the work performed by former in-house IS employees is no longer needed due to major operative changes in an IS function. In this case, the employer – either the client organization or the potential external vendor – is given the right to dismiss employees because of operative reasons (*"betriebsbedingte Kündigung"*) (Koffka, 1997, p. 131ff., 139). On the other hand, employee interests are legally supported by the works constitution act (*"Betriebsverfassungsgesetz – BetrVG"*). This law guarantees the right of employee participation and codetermination (*"Mitbestimmung"*) in social, economic, and personnel affairs (Richardi, 1990, p. 1282).

The right of *participation* is institutionalized through the works council *("Betriebsrat")* (Chmielewicz, 1990, p. 425). The works council is an organizational institution, represented by a limited number of employees, that are elected to protect the interests of an organizations's work forces – either on a part or full time basis. It is legally authorized to be heard, e.g., in the case of dismissals, and has the right to be consulted, when it comes to management decisions that severely affect operational procedures (Richardi, 1990, p. 1282). If an IS outsourcing decision causes the transfer of an essential part of an IS function to an external vendor (more than 5% of the function's personnel), the works council has to be consulted in order to work out a social plan and generate a balance of interests between the affected employees, the client organization and the external vendor (Koffka, 1997, p. 142f.). On this occasion, it is important that the respective IS function can be defined as an independent organizational unit that contributes to reach the objectives of the company.

Codetermination provides employees the legal right to participate in organizational decisions that impact their personal disposition or the disposition of the group that they belong to. It recognizes the interests of employees in relation to an organization's shareholders and top management (Chmielewicz, 1990, p. 414). In particular, it gives employees the right to be involved in the selection and control of management through thc membership of employee representatives in the supervisory board (the *"Aufsichtsrat"* in case of stock corporations). In Germany, management control is characterized by a two tier-system (Albach, 2000a, p. 285; Witt, 2002). That is, management and control are separated. The former is represented by an organization's highest ranking executives (board of inside-directors), while the latter is made up by external stakeholders and employees (outside-directors). In case of stock corporations ("*Aktiengesellschaften*"), the number of employee representatives depends on an organizations's overall number of employees. They may either make up one third (<2000) or fifty percent (49.5% of the votes) of the head count of the supervisory board (Albach, 2000a; Schmidt and Seger, 1998). In most of the cases, employee representatives are members of the works council, who again are often affiliated with trade unions. With regard to the influence of unions, Argyres and Liebeskind (1999, p. 59) have argued that "(...) some countries, such as Germany and France, accord greater bargaining power to labor unions than do other countries. This greater power of unions will tend to engender a greater degree of governance inseparability than where union bargaining power is weaker."

Overall, it may be concluded that large scale IS outsourcing decisions could potentially be influenced by the supervisory board and hence by employee representatives. Accordingly, the ability of management to act unrestrictedly, when it comes to an IS sourcing decision, may be limited.

> "Work councils can narrow the scope for action of a company as far as personnel and social matters are concerned" (Chmielewicz, 1990, p. 415).

Both the legal and legitimized institutional constraints are particularly important in Continental Europe. This does not mean, however, that institutional forces cannot limit management actions in the US as well. In the US, employee interests may be enforced less formally, but may still be effectively deployed if employees act together. For example, if an IS outsourcing arrangement critically depends on IS employees being transferred to the external vendor in order to maintain specific knowledge resources, the bargaining power of the employees increases significantly. Provided that employees are aware of their base of power and that they bundle their interests, they may severely limit the flexibility of management to change organizational arrangements.

Overall, it may be concluded that an organization's behavioral control over the process of IS outsourcing can be severely limited in both German and US companies. In the context of this study, *perceived behavioral control* is defined as the extent to which an organization has unlimited power of direction over all necessary activities associated with outsourcing an IS function to an external service provider. An IS executive's perceived behavior control over outsourcing an IS function may influence both the current degree of IS outsourcing and her/his attitude towards outsourcing a particular IS function:

Hypothesis 20a: The lower the *perceived behavioral control* over the outsourcing of an IS function, the less it will be *outsourced.*

Hypothesis 20b: The lower the *perceived behavioral control* over IS outsourcing, the more negative is the *attitude* towards outsourcing.

In addition to perceived behavioral control, however, a fourth variable may be introduced. As outlined previously, the theory of planned behavior proposes a direct link from attitudes to *intentions* rather than current behavior. This recognizes the fact that current attitudes may not be fully reflected by current behavior. The attitudes of IS executives may change over time and these changes may not immediately be reflected by changes in the current sourcing arrangement. This may lead to a *misfit* between current attitudes towards outsourcing and the current degree of outsourcing. Therefore, it would be interesting to compare the strength of the impact of attitudes towards outsourcing on the current degree of outsourcing with the *ideal degree* of outsourcing. If the strength of both impacts deviates considerably, then this would indicate a certain level of mismatch between the preferences of IS executives and the sourcing practices of their organization. This again could be interpreted as an indicator for an IS executive's power of decision making and implementation. Therefore, the following hypothesis is put forth:

Hypothesis 18b: The more negative the overall *attitudes* towards outsourcing an IS function are, the lower is the perceived *ideal* degree of *outsourcing.*

2.3.4.3 Overview

The hypotheses derived from the theory of planned behavior are illustrated in Figure 2-11. The believes are represented by the comparative advantages derived from transaction cost theory and resource-based theory. All the hypotheses, linking the comparative advantage box with attitudes, are consistent with the causal agencies of both theories of the firm. The inclusion of the attitude construct has two functions. First, it serves as an aggregate of all the salient believes about the advantages of insourcing versus outsourcing an IS function. Second, it mediates the impact of the salient beliefs in order to better understand the cognitive process that may lead to an organization's sourcing decision. It is an empirical question, to what extent an IS executive's attitude toward outsourcing is reflected by an organization's current degree of IS outsourcing.

Moreover, the power of IS executives to act unrestrictedly and strictly rational may be limited by other influences. These potential external impacts are reflected by the concepts of behavioral control and subjective norm. Moreover, the influence of attitudes on the ideal rather than current degree of IS outsourcing has been added. Overall, the inclusion of the major concepts from the theory of planned behavior allows for a more complete assessment of the cognitive process that leads to an organization's IS sourcing behavior. In fact, it allows to critically reflect upon the rational actor view of organizational behavior.

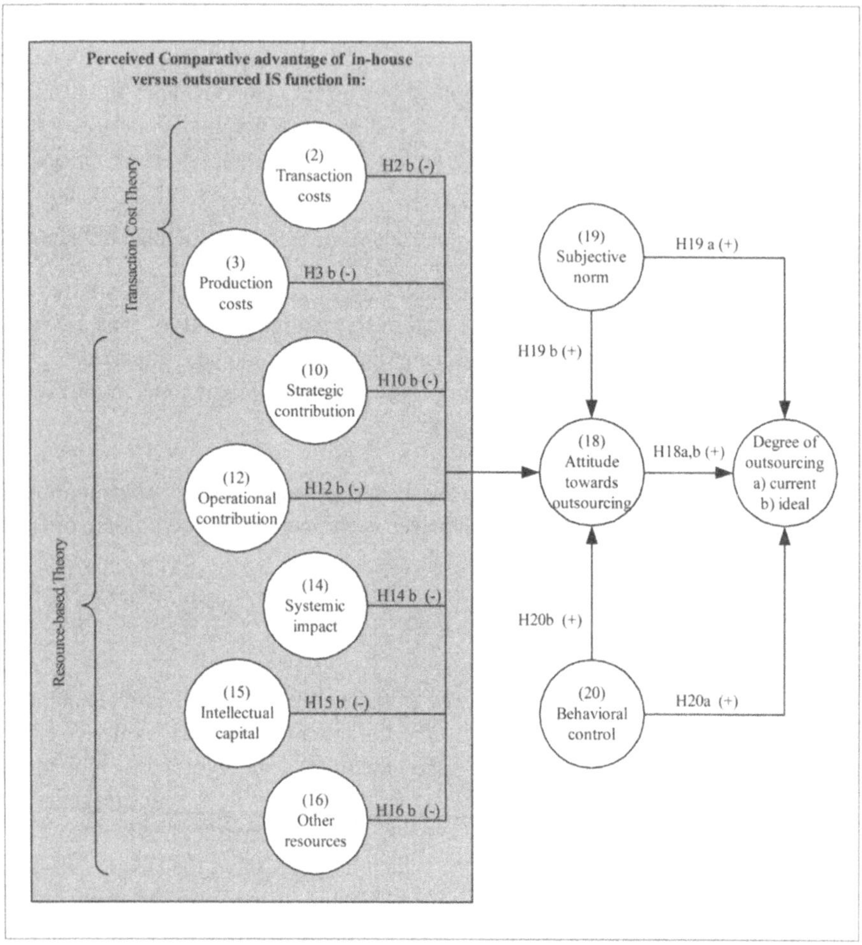

Figure 2-11: Hypotheses from the Theory of Planned Behavior

2.3.5 Synthesis of Theoretical Concepts

The previous application of four different theoretical lenses occurred in a sequential process of theorizing. This is consistent with the idea of *theoretical pluralism* (Spinner, 1974). The remaining task is to combine the four partial frameworks into a coherent whole. The resulting integrative framework is illustrated in Figure 2-12 (p. 105). It may be viewed as a "mid-range theoretical framework of IS sourcing".

In the course of integrating the four theoretical lenses, four types of intertheoretical linkages have emerged:

- Overlaps in the independent *or* dependent variables, leading to *complementary* causal agencies (hypotheses);
- overlaps in the independent *and* dependent variables *as well as* in the directional link between them, leading to *agreement* in causal agencies;
- overlaps in the independent *and* dependent variables, *but* opposing directional links between them, leading to *contradictions* in causal agencies; and
- newly founded *linkages* between variables from different theories, leading to *truly integrated* causal agencies between different theories.

Complementarity. One necessary, but not sufficient condition for the *complementarity* of different theories are overlaps between their theoretical constructs. The most obvious case of construct overlap may be seen in the concept "human asset specificity". It plays an important role in both transaction cost theory (TCT) and resource-based theory (RBT). Contrary to RBT, however, TCT holds that human asset specificity will lead to in-house transaction cost advantages, while resource-based theory argues that it will lead to in-house advantages in the strategic contribution of an IS function and in the base of resources required to perform an IS function. This does not mean that both theories are in contradiction to each other. They only differ in the reasons *why* human asset specificity will lower the tendency to outsource IS functions. Moreover, they are not intended to substitute each other. Instead, the different hypotheses derived from both theoretical lenses are *complementary explanatory* in nature.

Moreover, both theories partially overlap in the behavioral assumptions, on which some of their main arguments are based. In particular, the assumption of opportunistic behavior plays an important role in both theories. Consequently, the inclusion of the two behavioral antipodes of opportunism – *trust* and *non-monetary incentives* – has a profound impact on both the reasoning of TCT and RBT. On the one hand, both constructs moderate the impact of human asset specificity on comparative transaction cost advantages (TCT). On the other hand, they moderate the impact of human asset specificity on comparative advantages in the strategic contribution of an IS function (RBT). Again, both types of impacts are *complementary explanatory* in nature, since different consequences are attributed to the meaning of the behavioral antipodes.

In this realm, it may be noted that those comparative advantage constructs that differ between TCT and RBT are *complementary predictive* in relation to the attitude construct and to the degree of IS outsourcing. Indeed, all relationships between independent variables derived from different theories, that are linked to the same dependent variable, are complementary predictive in nature. As another example, the concepts of behavioral control and subjective norm from the TPB are complementary predictors to the comparative advantage constructs derived from transaction cost theory and resource-based theory, since they all directly influence the degree of IS outsourcing.

Agreement. There is one example for agreement between TCT and RBT. From the perspective of both lenses it can be argued that a higher level of an IS function's human asset specificity will lead to increased in-house production cost advantages, which are proposed to lower the level of outsourcing, and to negatively affect the attitude toward outsourcing (see Section 2.3.1.2).

Contradiction. Moreover, there is one example for contradictory causal agencies between theories. From the perspective of transaction cost theory it may be argued that a higher level of *measurement difficulty* will increase in-house transaction cost advantages and hence lead to a lower level of outsourcing. By contrast, according to resource-based theory, it can be argued that measurement problems are perceived as resource deficits and hence will lead to a higher level of outsourcing.

In addition, there are two examples of competing chains of causality *within the same theoretical lens*. In transaction cost theory a high level of environmental uncertainty on the one hand is proposed to lead to in-house transaction cost advantages. On the other hand, it is expected to decrease in-house production cost advantages. This implies a trade-off between transaction cost advantages and production costs disadvantages in case of high environmental uncertainty. It is an empirical question which of these effects dominates.

Truly Integrative Linkages. Linkages between constructs from different theories can be found in two cases. First, the concept of *ownership*, derived from the theory of incomplete contracts (ICT), moderates both the relationship between human asset specificity and comparative transaction cost advantages (TCT) and the relationship between human asset specificity and comparative advantages in the strategic contribution of an IS function (RBT). More precisely, this is an example of a construct of one theory (ICT) influencing the theoretical linkages between two concepts of another theory (both from TCT and RBT). This intertheoretical relationship is truly integrative, because the ownership dimension increases the explanatory power of two other theoretical lenses rather than adding alternative chains of causality.

A second, more obvious example of construct linkages from different theories refers to the impacts of the *comparative advantage constructs*, derived from TCT and RBT, on the *attitude* construct, derived from the theory of planned behavior (TPB). The comparative constructs take over the role of salient beliefs in the TPB. The attitude construct serves as an aggregate of all the comparative advantage constructs and as a mediator between these salient beliefs and the degree of IS outsourcing. Again, the attitude construct increases the explanatory power of TCT and RBT, because it brings in a new dependent variable that has been neglected previously.

Overall, the four theories are highly complementary in nature. Concertedly, they increase the ability to explain and predict the heterogeneous IS sourcing behavior of organizations.

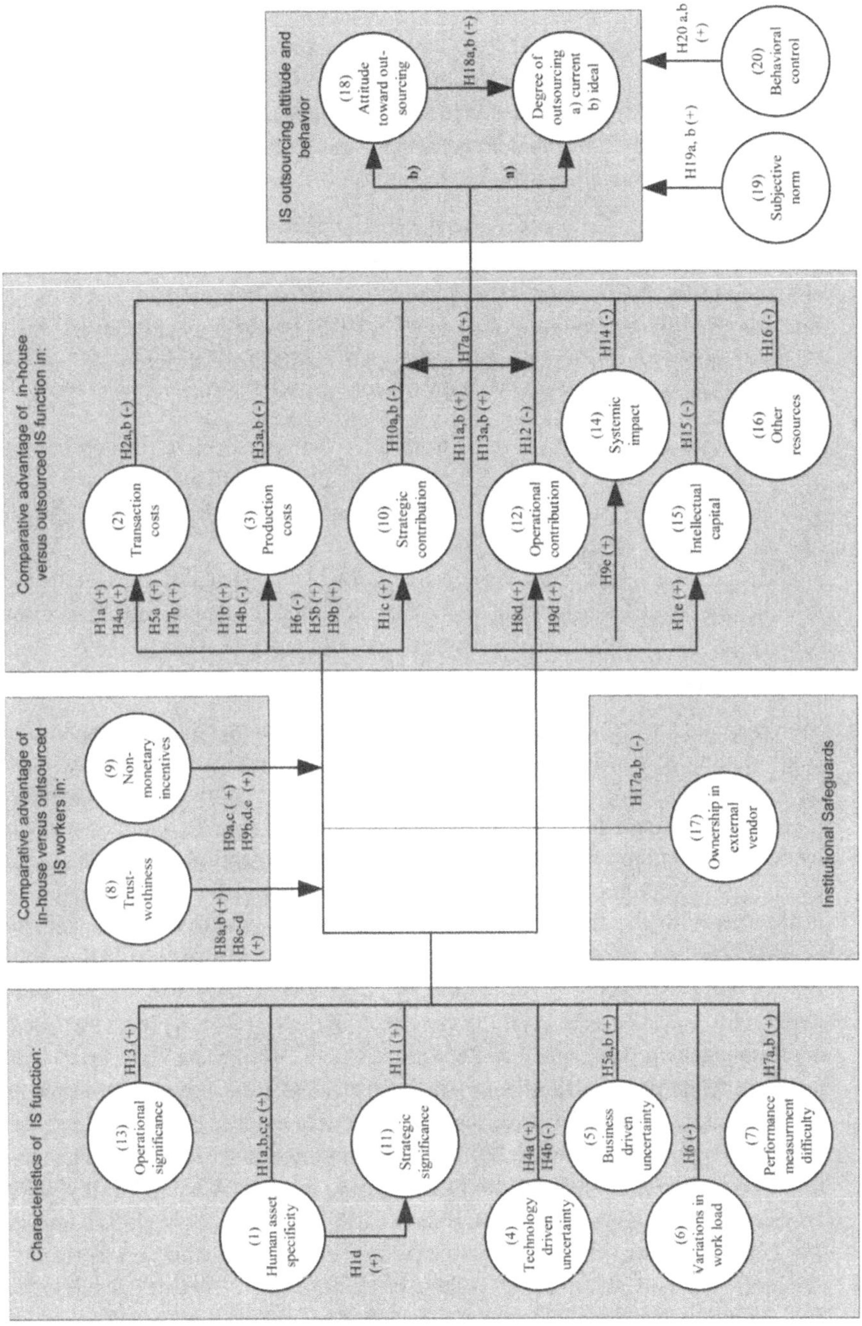

Figure 2-12: Mid-range Theoretical Framework of IS Sourcing

2.4 Complementary Hypotheses from Selected Cultural Dimensions

The objective of the previous section has been to develop a generally applicable framework that helps to explain why firms behave different in IS sourcing. The resulting framework may be characterized as a mid-range theory of IS sourcing. There are, however, a number of indications that cultural factors could fruitfully be integrated into the mid-range theory.

- The first indication that gives rise to the supposition that cultural factors may influence the IS sourcing decision refers to the observation of significant differences in the amount of money that is spent for the outsourcing of particular IS functions in different countries (Apte, et al., 1997; Barthélemy and Geyer, 2001). There appear to be hidden behavioral and/or institutional differences between countries that account for these macro level differences.

- Second, since this research is done from a German perspective, it soon became apparent that most of the scientific knowledge, produced to answer questions on why and how firms outsource, stems from Anglo-American researchers. In particular, *empirical* studies on IS sourcing were primarily conducted in Anglo-American regions. In Germany, there are hardly any empirical studies on the topic – neither on IS outsourcing nor on outsourcing in general (Matiaske and Mellewigt, 2002) – with a few exceptions (Dibbern and Heinzl, 2001; 2002; Heinzl, 1993a; Schott, 1997).

- Moreover, the theoretical lenses used to study the phenomenon mostly stem from Anglo-american researchers. This is not to say that German speaking countries have not established an own research tradition in business management and economics. In the field of economics, the Austrian school of Economics with the works from Schumpeter (1934; 1939), Hayek (1945) and others, have significantly influenced modern economic thinking and illuminated new developments in the theory of the firm, e.g., resource-based theory and dynamic theory (see Section 2.2.2.4). Moreover, the "General theory of the firm" ("Allgemeine Betriebswirtschaftslehre"), furnished by Gutenberg (1951/1983; 1955/1984; 1969/1980), may be seen as an independent German way of approaching business management problems (see Section 2.2.2.1). Notwithstanding these independent developments, the theory of the firm – as it has been established by Anglo-American and also furnished by Scandinavian researchers – has been widely recognized in Germany. For example, transaction cost theory has been introduced in Germany early on and finds ongoing interest (Albach, 1988b; 2000a; Brockhoff, 1992; Burr, 2003; Hammes and Poser, 1992; Picot, 1981; Prosser, 1997; Windsperger, 1983) – albeit not without critical reflections on its role as a "general" theory of the firm (Schneider, 1985; Schneider, 1991). There are, however, very few empirical investigations about the applicability of theories of the firm to explain organizational phenomena in Germany.

A number of researchers, that have personally studied cross-cultural issues, have begun to question the universality of management and organizational behavior theories that have been developed in particular countries (Cheng, et al., 2001; England, 1983; Hofstede, 1993; 1994; 1983c; Triandis, 1982). Most of the theories (of the firm) that address organizational issues, are based on particular views of human nature that may not be generalizable across different countries. In order to overcome the resulting limitations, it appears to be useful to re-evaluate the behavioral assumptions, on which these theories are based, and to incorporate cultural aspects in the analysis. For example, Triandis (1982, p. 139) has stated,

> "Culture is the human-made part of the environment (...). Its significance for organizational behavior is that it operates at such a deep level that people are not aware of its influences. It results in unexplained patterns of thought that seem so natural that most theorists of social behavior fail to take them into account. As a result, many aspects of organizational theories produced in one culture may be inadequate in other cultures."

Overall, the observation of (1) heterogeneous practices in IS outsourcing across countries, (2) the dominant Anglo-American perspective in both the underlying reference theories and the empirical evidence provided on IS sourcing, as well as (3) the general doubt about the universality of organizational and management theories across countries, suggest the explicit consideration of *culture* in the analysis.

Before starting to examine the role of culture to explain IS sourcing behavior, however, it appears to be necessary to define what is meant by the concept "culture" and to outline the general approach taken to examine the influence of culture.

2.4.1 Definition of Culture

Research on cultural differences has a long history. Especially research in anthropology, sociology, and psychology has enhanced the understanding of what constitutes culture and how it may be conceptualized (Kroeber and Kluckhohn, 1963, p. 11). In 1952, Kroeber and Kluckhohn have undertaken a review of the origins and various definitions of the culture concept. Even at that point of time, they found 164 different definitions (Kroeber and Kluckhohn, 1963, p. 291) and about 100 additional assessments of the concept (Keller, 1982, p. 114). In synthesizing the various aspects, they elaborated the following central idea of culture:

> "Culture consists of patterns, explicit and implicit, of and for behavior acquired and transmitted by symbols, constituting the distinctive achievement of human groups, including their embodiments in artifacts; the essential core of culture consists of traditional (i.e. historically derived and selected) ideas and especially their attached values; culture systems may, on the one hand, be considered as products of action, on the other as conditioning elements of future action" (Kroeber and Kluckhohn, 1963, p. 357).

Kroeber and Kluckhohn consciously speak of "central idea" rather than definition of culture since there are many different aspects that help to understand the concept of culture. These aspects are especially reflected by the answers to the following questions:[14] (1) Who creates culture?; (2) What constitutes culture?; (3) How is culture created and transmitted?; (4) What is the impact, i.e. effect of culture?

The answers to these questions help to better understand the concept and to identify those aspects of culture that are especially important for this research project.

- *Who creates culture?* First and foremost, culture is created by *human beings*.
- *What constitutes culture?* A common element of culture is a presumption of a shared understanding and adherence as a prerequisite for belonging to a social group. Culture becomes manifested in collectively shared characteristics of a social group.

  On the one hand, these characteristics include all *visible* products and expressions created by the members of a social group. These *objective* elements may comprise physical products (e.g., literature, music, items of everyday use, buildings), traditions (e.g., customs, rites) and social institutions and organizations that regulate and enable the living within a social group (e.g., legislation and educational systems). Hence, culture is to a certain extent codified in the *artifacts* that are created by a social group.

  On the other hand, they refer to implicit behavioral values, norms, believes, and attitudes, that are collectively shared by the members of a social group. These *subjective* elements appear to be the most distinctive and important properties of cultures (Kroeber and Kluckhohn, 1963, p. 338). They are reflected by a wide variety of dimensions (or syndromes) of cultural variation. These *cultural dimensions* have been defined as "(...) cognitive structures that help one organize and interpret the world by focusing attention on certain patterns or themes in the subjective elements of the environment, such as values, norms, beliefs, and assumptions" (Roberts and Wasti, 2002, p. 545).

  In order to help separate the forrest from the trees, so to speak, some researchers have attempted to classify these dimensions. Triandis (1982) has build three classes of dimensions that group human beings into homogenous cultural clusters according to their (1) perceptual differentiations, (2) their utilization and evaluation of information, and (3) their patterns of action. Likewise, Lytle et al. (1995) classified cultural dimensions based on the following labels: (1) definitions of self and others, (2) motivational orientation, (3) relationship between societal members, (4) patterns of communication, (5) orientation toward time,

---

[14] The idea of structuring the concepts by asking different questions has been illuminated by the work from Kroeber and Kluckhohn (1963, p. 311ff.), who elaborated six major features of culture, and by Keller (1982, p. 144ff.), who identified eight characteristics of culture.

change, and uncertainty or risk, and (6) patterns of institutions and social systems.

Moreover, the term culture is often used in an *institutional* sense (Keller, 1982, p. 119). That is, the boundaries of a social group are defined through institutional characteristics, such as nationality, religion, or different types of formal and informal organizations. Whenever one cultural group is part of another cultural group, one speaks of sub-cultures. For example, the culture of an organization within a particular country may be treated as a sub-culture of national culture, or the culture of a particular unit or department within an organization may present an organizational sub-culture. In general, the treatment of a social group as a culture or sub-culture depends on the perspective and the objectives of the observer or researcher (Keller, 1982, p. 120).

More recently, researchers suggested that different types of these "real world" social groups could be described using the same set of cultural dimensions. For example, organizational culture could be described using dimensions that have primarily been used to study national cultures (Earley and Gibson, 1998, p. 279; for an example see Roberts and Wasti, 2002). Moreover, cultural dimensions have successfully been used to describe individual differences rather than differences between social groups (Triandis, 1995; Wagner, 1995). Accordingly, cultural dimensions appear to be useful to study behavioral patterns at any level of analysis (Earley and Gibson, 1998, p. 270). They are not limited to study country differences.

- *How is culture created and transmitted?* Culture is created through the *actions* of a group or collective of people over a long-term process. In contrast to inherited biological dispositions, i.e genetics, the elements that constitute a cultural whole have to be experienced and learned. Culture may also be seen as the social inheritance of a society (Keller, 1982). In this realm, language plays a critical role as to enable social exchange relationships that are necessary in order to transfer the norms and values that constitute the implicit elements of culture from one generation to another (Keller, 1982, p. 115, p.116). The transformational process, however, also enables cultural changes, e.g., if members from different cultural groups enter into social exchange relationships. The exchange relationships may lead to cultural clashes until a new cultural stability has been established. For example, increased globalization has been said to partially diminish cultural boundaries between nations. That is, cultures are adaptable over time (Keller, 1982, p. 118).
- *What is the impact, i.e., effect, of culture?* The shared norms and values of a social group serve as generally accepted patterns of behavior and hence influence the behavior of the members of a social group (Keller, 1982, p. 117). They provide general guidelines on how to behave in certain situations.

For the purpose of this research, two of the four perspectives on the concept of culture appear to especially relevant. These are the *characteristics* that constitute culture and the *behavioral influences* of culture on members of a social group. It is neither of direct interest how cultural patterns, that can currently be observed within a social group, have been created nor how they may be transmitted.

The deciding question is, how and why culture may influence the IS sourcing decision. More specifically, the question is, how and why particular cultural dimensions may influence the mid-range theoretical framework on IS sourcing developed previously.

Based on an extensive literature review of cross-cultural research, Lytle et al. (1995) laid down a *paradigmatic approach* on how to examine cultural influences on mid-range theories about organizational phenomena. Their approach appears to be especially helpful in positivist research settings that seek to develop and test variance type theories. Accordingly, they speak of *confirmatory cross-cultural research* and elaborate five steps for accomplishing this type of research. First, a mid-range theory that explains the phenomenon of interest has to be identified, whereas it "(...) is not necessary for the mid-range theory or model to have been previously tested" (p. 177). Second, cultural dimensions need to be identified that are expected to influence the mid-range theory. Third, the cultural groups need to be selected. Fourth, hypotheses need to be deduced about how and why the selected cultural dimensions affect the mid-range theory. Fifth, the cross-cultural study needs to be designed in accordance with the previous steps taken.

Two of these steps have already been accomplished. On the one hand, a mid-range theoretical framework of IS sourcing has been developed. The development of the framework may be viewed as a preliminary step of theory development. That is, working definitions of the constructs that manifest the framework have been developed, and the relationships between these constructs have been explicated by hypotheses. On the other hand, Germany and the US have been selected as two alternative social groups on the national level. There are two reasons for the choice of countries. First, the researcher brings in the perspective of a native German, who has grown up, been educated, and experienced working in Germany. Moreover, he has also experienced working for companies in the US (Milwaukee) and Canada (Toronto) for a limited time of six months, during internships, and maintains a cooperative relationship with staff members of the MIS group at the University of Houston, Texas, where he also stayed for a three months visiting scholarship. Accordingly, the researcher speaks fluent (business) English and has personally experienced some of the cultural differences between the two countries. Both are important prerequisites for conducting cross-cultural research. The second reason for choosing the US as a comparative study object is related to the origin of most of the theoretical concepts used to build the mid-range theoretical framework. The theoretical lenses applied to study IS outsourcing primarily stem from US-based research. Moreover, the majority of empirical research on the topic has been conducted by Anglo-American researchers. Although the selected theories have been recognized by German researchers and tend to find a growing rate of acceptance, they have rarely been tested empirically in Germany. Therefore, it would be interesting to know, how the explanatory and predictive power of the theoretical relationships compare between Germany and the US (see also Cheng, et al., 2001; Hofstede, 1994).

There is, however, one note of caution on the approach by Lytle et al. (1995). It appears to be obvious that, as soon as the cultural dimensions have been identified and their impact on the already existing concepts and relationships of the mid-range theoretical framework on IS sourcing been spelled out, these concepts themselves become part of the mid-range theoretical framework. Therefore, the cultural dimensions may be viewed as complementary to the concepts of the mid-range theoretical framework rather than as independent external forces. This integrative character of the concept of culture has been recognized by Kroeber and Kluckhohn (1963, p. 367 - italics original) early on:

> "Culture is not a mystical 'force' acting at a distance. *Concretely*, it is created by individual organisms and by organisms acting as a group. It is internalized in individuals and also becomes part of the environment through the medium of other individuals and of cultural products. (...) Culture is an intervening variable between human 'organism' and 'environment'."

Consequently, cultural dimensions can contribute to the explanatory power of the mid-range theoretical framework, rather than just explaining differences in its explanatory power across different cultural groups. The question is, however, which of the many cultural dimensions, that have been identified in previous research, to consider as complementary concepts.

2.4.2 Selection of Cultural Dimensions

The task of selecting cultural dimensions from the existing pool of constructs, again, raises the question for the appropriate selection criteria. Lytle et al. (1995, p. 193) have suggested two complementary ways of selecting cultural dimensions: an inductive way and a deductive way.

Inductively, those cultural dimensions would be taken into account that were found to differ between the selected cultural groups in former cross-cultural studies – in this case Germany and the US. On the other hand, the *deductive* way would suggest to only consider those dimensions that obviously impact the mid-range theoretical framework on IS sourcing. This way appears to be the more difficult and theoretically important task. In fact, even if cultural dimensions have been separated based on induction, the deductive task remains to be accomplished. For the purpose of this research project, both approaches will be combined. In order to limit the number of potential dimensions, the selection begins with the inductive approach.

2.4.2.1 Inductive Selection

In general, the number of cross-cultural studies that are related to an organizational context and that include both Germany and the US in their analysis appear to be quite limited. One of the reasons may be attributed to the "(...) a-sociological and a-psychological tradition of German business studies" (Kieser, 1990, p. 1577). There are, however, a few large scale comparative cultural studies, conducted by non-Germans, that include both Germany and the US in their analysis (Haire, et al., 1963; 1966; Hampden-Turner and Trompenaars, 1993; Heller, et al., 1981; Hofstede and Bond, 1988; Hofstede, 1980; Trompenaars and Hamden-Turner, 1994).

An early example is that of Haire et al. (1963). They gathered data through a mail survey in 14 different countries from 3,641 managers. On the one hand, they gathered data about manager attitudes toward leadership. On the other hand, they assessed the perceived importance of and satisfaction with different kinds of individual needs.

In another study, Hofstede (1980) explored an extensive data base, provided by IBM, that included the data from a worldwide survey about employee attitudes in 66 countries, conducted between 1967 and 1973. In an initial analysis of this data set, Hofstede (1980) explored cultural patterns in 40 of these countries, including about 116,000 respondents. Later on, he extended the data base to include 64 countries divided into 50 single cultural regions and 3 multicultural regions (Hofstede, 1983a; Hofstede, 1991). By studying only one company worldwide, Hofstede was able to concentrate on national characteristics, since organizational culture was mostly kept constant through the corporate identity of IBM. Hofstede (1980, p. 21) defined culture as "(...) the collective programming of the mind which distinguishes the members of one group from another." In particular, four cultural dimensions emerged from his analysis of the data: The constructs (1) "power distance" and (2) "masculinity versus femininity" were derived through theoretical reflections, while (3) "individualism-collectivism" and (4) "uncertainty avoidance" were extracted by using exploratory factory analysis. In a later analysis of data obtained from a study among students in 23 countries around the world, which was designed by Chinese scholars, a fifth dimension was extracted. This dimension was originally called (5) "Confucian dynamism", and should reflect the long-term versus short-term orientation of a social group (Hofstede, 1991).

A third study is that from Heller and Hilpert (1981). They gathered data from about 1,600 managers at two different management levels within 129 companies in eight different countries. They used questionnaires and qualitative feedback sessions to gather their data. Their objective was to obtain information about decision making processes, participation, and power sharing. Rather than elaborating specific cultural factors, their study was more on successful decision making strategies. In particular, the degree of centralization of decision making has been used to differentiate countries from each other.

The fourth study is that from Tromenaars and Hampden-Turner (1993; 1994). They conducted a field study including about 1,000 intercultural trainee programs, plus an additional study of 30 organizations with locations in 50 different countries. Their overall sample included about 30,000 managers. Overall, their approach of data gathering and analyzing appears to be more qualitative rather than quantitate in nature. It is less clear how the authors extracted the cultural dimensions (although the authors report on the use of factor analysis in the appendix). In particular, they differentiate seven dimensions: (1) universalism versus particularism, (2) individualism versus communitarianism, (3) affective versus neutral cultures, (4) specific versus diffuse orientation, (5) achievement versus ascription orientation, (6) orientation toward time and (7) orientation to nature. Moreover, the perception of (8) firm culture (analytic versus integrative) has been assessed.

From these four cross-cultural studies, that included both Germany and the US in the analysis, the majority of the cultural dimensions are summarized in Table 2-3. In particular, those cultural dimensions have been considered that were found to differ between Germany and the US in at least one study. Whenever, similar dimensions to those that showed different instances in one study were analyzed in another study, the results are also listed. For example, the notion of "participative management" was found to slightly differ between Germany and the US in the study from Haire et al. (1963, 1966), while "power distance", which measures similar aspects, was found to be about equal in Germany and the US in the study from Hofstede (1980, 1983, 1991). Moreover, only those dimensions have been considered that clearly relate to an organization context. For example, the concept "relation to nature" by Trompenaars and Hampden-Turner appears to be too far abstracted from the organizational level. Finally, each of the selected cultural dimensions was mapped with one of the six categories identified by Lytle et. al. (1995), which were introduced earlier (p. 121 f.).

The mapping shows that non of the selected cultural dimensions fits into the categories: (1) definition of self and others, (4) patterns of communication, and (6) patterns of institutional and social systems. They will, therefore, not be taken into account. It has to be noted, however, that some of the institutional differences between Germany and the USA have been addressed in Section 2.3.4.2 (p. 93f.).

Only the dimension *individualism* versus *communitarianism* from Trompenaars and Hamden-Turner (1993, p. 51) fits into the "(2) motivational orientation" category. This dimension is based on the "self-orientation versus collectivity-orientation" concept from Parson and Shils (1951), which has been classified under the "motivational orientation" category by Lytle et al. (1995, p. 180). Individualism, as opposed to communitarianism, reflects (a) how much managers believe that the quality of life depends on individual freedom rather than taking care of each other, (b) how much individuals rather than groups are credited for their performance, and (c) the extent to which faults are the responsibility of individuals rather than groups. Consistently across each of these dimensions, the US sample showed a higher percentage of individualism than Germany.

Table 2-3: Comparison of Cultural Dimensions in USA and Germany (Page 1 from 2)

Category (Lytle et al., 1995)	Cultural Dimension	Study	Germany	USA
(1) Definitions of self and others	–	–	–	–
(2) Motivational orientation	Individualistic versus cummunitarian (Self-orientation vs. collectivity-orientation)	Trompenaars and Hampden-Turner (1994), based on Parson and Shils (1951)	Medium individualism	Relatively high individualism
(3) Relationship between societal members	Individualism versus collectivism	Hofstede (1980, 1983, 1991)	Medium individualism	Highest individualism
	analytical versus integrative (social group) view of the firm	Trompenaars and Hampden-Turner (1994)	Toward integrative view	Toward analytical view
	Social needs	Haire et al. (1963, 1966)	Average importance / quite satisfied	Higher importance / quite satisfied
	Power distance	Hofstede (1980, 1983, 1991)	About the same – quite small	
	Participative management	Haire et al. (1963, 1966)	About the same – toward participation	
	Sharing information from principal to agent	Haire et al. (1963, 1966)	Neutral	Slightly more sharing
	Self rather than external control	Haire et al. (1963, 1966)	About the same – toward self control	
	Centralization of decision making	Heller et. al. (1981)	About the same – toward centralization	
	Particularism versus universalism (focus on rules and regulations)	Trompenaars and Hampden-Turner (1994), based on Parson and Shils (1951)	Toward universalism (slightly less than US)	Toward universalism (slightly more than Germany)
	Capacity for leadership	Haire et al. (1963, 1966)	More limited to minority	Neutral – more democratically distributed

Table 2-3: Comparison of Cultural Dimensions in USA and Germany (Page 2 from 2)

Category (Lytle et al., 1995)	Cultural Dimension	Study	Germany	USA
(4) Patterns of communication	–	–	–	–
(5) Orientation toward time, change, and uncertainty or risk	Uncertainty avoidance	Hofstede (1980, 1983, 1991)	Relatively high to medium	Relatively low
	Security needs	Haire et al. (1963, 1966)	Very important / medium satisfaction	Important / full satisfaction
	Confucian Dynamism (long versus short term orientation)	Hofstede and Bond (1988)	Similar, but slightly more toward long-term orientation	Similar, but slightly less toward long-term orientation
	Time horizon: long- versus short-term	Trompenaars and Hampden-Turner (1994)	Similar, but slightly more toward long-term horizon	Similar, but slightly less toward long-term horizon
(6) patterns of institutions and social systems	–	–	–	–

The majority of cultural dimensions fit into the third category: "(3) relationship between societal members". This category contains dimensions that reflect how individuals in a society interact with each other and perceive their relationships with others.

According to Hofstede (1980), the dimension *individualism versus collectivism* should reflect the degree to which individuals are integrated into groups. Examples of items measuring individualism versus collectivism are: (a) staying with one company is not desirable, (b) larger corporations are not more desirable than smaller ones, (c) a corporation is not responsible for its employees, and (d) interesting work is not as important as earnings. Notably, the US sample showed the highest *individualism* ranking from all countries, while Germany ranked still above the average but significantly lower at the index scale (rank 15 from 50; index 67 as opposed to 91 from the US).

Closely related to this dimension is the *analytical* versus *integrative* dimension from Trompenaars and Hamden-Turner (1993, p. 18). It characterizes the perception of organizational culture. The analytical view reflects the extent to which a firm is perceived as a collection of *tasks*, functions, people, and machines rather than as a *group* of related persons working together, which represents the integrative view.

Overall, Germany shows a higher tendency towards an integrative view of an organization than the US. Interestingly, German managers tend to perceive *social needs* as less important than their US colleagues (Haire, et al., 1963; 1966), while the satisfaction with the social situation appears to be quite high in both countries. It needs to be considered, however, that the term social, as used here, has nothing to do with social behavior in work groups. Social needs have been defined as the desire to develop close friendship and as the opportunity to give help to other people. Moreover, it is not clear if the term friendship is interpreted equally in different countries.

A number of dimensions characterize the leadership style and the relationship between superiors and subordinates within organizations. Overall, Germany and the US appear to be quite similar on these dimensions. *Power distance*, which refers to the extent to which less powerful members of organizations and institutions (like the family) accept and expect that power is distributed unequally, is quite low in both countries (Hofstede, 1980; 1983c; 1991). The working relationships seem to be dominated by *sharing of information* between principals and agents, *participation*, and *self control* of employees, rather than purely external control (Haire, et al., 1963; 1966). These relationships are framed by rules and regulations, to which US managers or employees appear to feel slightly more committed than Germans – reflected by a slightly higher level of *universalism* in the US (Trompenaars and Hamden-Turner, 1994, p. 35).

In spite of the general tendency towards ("higher order") interactive management practices in both countries (Haire et al, 1963, p. 98f.), *centralized decision making* seems to be preferred in both Germany and the US (Heller, et al., 1981). On the other side, the belief that individuals have the *capacity for leadership* appears to be more democratically distributed in the USA, whereas in Germany leadership appears to be reserved for a minority (Haire, et al., 1963; 1966).

The remaining cultural dimensions refer to the fifth category from Lytle et al. (1995), which is the "(5) orientation toward time, change, and uncertainty or risk".

According to Hofstede (1980; 1983c; 1991), *uncertainty avoidance* should indicate the extent to which employees feel uncomfortable in unstructured situations. Unstructured situations are novel, unknown, surprising, and different from usual. Uncertainty avoiding cultures try to minimize the possibility of such situations by strict laws and rules, as well as safety and security measures. Examples of items measuring this dimension on the organizational level are: (a) rule orientation (not breaking company rules), (b) employment stability (intention to stay with the company), and (3) frequency of stress at the workplace. While the US sample ranked relatively low at that dimension (rank 43), Germany ranked somewhat higher (rank 29 from 50).

Consistent with these findings, Haire et al. (1963) found German managers to show a very high *need for security*, reflected by the feeling of safety and assurance in a particular managerial position. Moreover, US managers appear to be very satisfied with the state of security, while Germans appear to be less satisfied.

Finally, Germans appear to be slightly more long-term oriented than US managers. It has to be noted, however, that the *confucian dynamism* concept, adapted by Hofstede and Bond (1988), requires a lot of interpretation to identify the notion of *long- versus short-term orientation* in their definition and measurement of the concept. According to Hofstede and Bond (1988), values associated with long-term orientation are thrift and preservation, while those of short-term orientation are respect for tradition, fulfilling social obligations, and protecting one's face. The approach by Trompenaars and Hamden-Turner (1994) appears to be more straight forward. They measure the time horizon that managers relate to the past, presence, and future. Although both studies, suggest that the time horizon of Germans is somewhat longer than those of US managers, the differences appear to be not too strong. There are, however, two additional studies that indirectly support the view that German organizations may be more long-term oriented.

Based on a review of studies on institutional and contextual differences between countries (U.S.A, U.K., Germany, and Japan) Carr and Tomkins (1998, p. 214) conclude that German and Japanese companies tend to be under less pressure to maximize short-term benefits than US and U.K. firms. Carr and Tomkins (1998, p. 226) examines financial and strategic appraisal techniques in investment decisions of companies within each of the four countries. Their findings revealed that US and U.K. companies heavily rely on financial control systems to guide investment decisions, while German and Japanese companies afford more influence to strategic considerations. Theses findings appear to be consistent with the descriptive findings from a cross-cultural survey conducted by Yoshimori (1995) on the major stakeholder interests that companies seek to satisfy. The management objectives of US and U.K. companies are dominated by shareholder interests, while the priority of German, French, and especially Japanese companies, is to satisfy the interests of all stakeholders and to secure jobs rather than pay high dividends. Thus, the longer-term view of German organizations appears to be partially grounded in weaker influences of external shareholders that foster a short-term orientation.

2.4.2.2 Deductive Selection

After having gone through the inductive process of selecting cultural dimensions, it needs to be examined if the identified dimensions potentially impact the mid-range theoretical framework on IS sourcing.

All of the cultural dimensions that have been used to compare cultural characteristics of Germany and the US refer to the subjective elements of culture. They represent values and norms that are shared among the members of a social group and that when taken together constitute a design for living (Hill, 1997, p. 67; cited by Doney, et al., 1998, p. 607).

Accordingly, it is important to recall what the *behavioral assumptions*, norms, and values were, on which the *mid-range theoretical framework* on IS sourcing is based.

- First, it is believed that the decision to insource or outsource IS functions falls into the responsibility of the highest ranking IS executives of organizations. It is assumed that they evaluate and compare alternative sourcing options. In doing so, they are restrained by their role as managers of the organization for which they work. That is, they act in accordance with the overall strategic objectives and directives of the organization. This view reflects a *boundedly or intendedly rational* actor view of organizational decision makers. It is assumed that their personal attitudes, values, and beliefs are significantly overrided by those of the organization for which they work. Opposed to this purely rationalist view of organizational actors, it has been taken into account, however, that IS managers may be restricted by institutional constraints, that limit their behavioral control over the outsourcing decision. Moreover, it has been considered that both the actual decision about and the evaluative appraisal of IS outsourcing may be influenced by other stakeholders.

- Second, it has been assumed that some economic actors have a strong attitude towards *opportunism*. The potential of another party to behave opportunistically is assumed to be taken into account by IS managers when evaluating and comparing alternative sourcing options. The influencing role of opportunism has explicitly been considered by the inclusion of two antipodes of opportunism, namely comparative advantages in trustworthiness and non-monetary incentives of in-house versus outsourced IS workers.

Overall, the behavioral assumptions are twofold. On the one hand, they refer directly to the motivational forces and interests of the main decision makers, whereas it is assumed that those values are aligned with the overall values of the client-organization for which the IS executives work. On the other hand, they refer to an IS executive‘s perception and belief about the behavior of their subordinates, that do the actual work within an IS function.

Therefore, the question about the influence of cultural dimensions on the mid-range theoretical framework of IS sourcing can be unpacked and specified as follows:

- Can the pre-selected cultural dimensions provide additional information about the value orientation of an organization from the perceptive of an IS executive? And how and why do these organization oriented values impact the IS sourcing decision?

- Can the pre-selected cultural dimensions provide additional information about the value orientation of the IS workers from the perspective of an organization's IS executive? And how and why do these person or group oriented values impact the IS sourcing decision?

In answering question one, three of the cultural dimensions appear to be of relevance. These are the control orientation (based on uncertainty avoidance and security need), the long- versus short-term orientation, and the analytical versus integrative view of an organization. The notion of *control* plays an important role in

IS outsourcing. A number of authors have stressed the danger or risk of loosing control over an IS function through IS outsourcing (e.g., Duncan, 1998; Earl, 1996). The notion of *long- versus short-term orientation* has been suggested to reflect the planning horizon of an organization (Triandis, 1982, p. 156). Foresight and planning play an important role when it comes to an IS sourcing decision since different future scenarios need to be taken into account. Interestingly, the notion of *analytical versus integrative* has already been addressed on the organizational level. It is represented by the *systemic impact* of an IS function.

In answering the second question, two cultural dimensions are apparently related to the behavioral norms and values of IS workers. In particular, different notions of individualism versus collectivism and the long- versus short-term orientation of the IS workers may be of relevance. The aspect of *individualism versus collectivism* appears to be a multi-facetted construct. It helps to understand the working relationships between employees as well as their motivations. The motivational aspects are covered by Trompenaars and Hampden-Turner (1994). In this realm, the construct refers to the extent to which individuals are solely motivated by aspects that help to satisfy their self interest rather than those of the IS group. The relationship aspect refers to the degree to which individuals are integrated into teams of workers (Hofstede, 1980). Moreover, the *integrative versus analytical view* (Trompenaars and Hamden-Turner, 1994) of an organization may be broken down to the level of the IS group. In this realm, the construct recognizes the extent to which IS workers consider the interdependence between their own work and the work of others.

The motivational and relationship aspects of individualism versus collectivism appear to be closely related to the concepts of trust and non-monetary incentives. Interestingly, Ang and Slaughter (1998) have found external IS workers to be more individualistic than in-house IS employees. Moreover, individualistic behavior was found to be negatively related to IS performance. If IS executives recognize these dependencies between the behavior of IS workers and IS performance, individualism versus collectivism can become an important factor in the IS sourcing decision. In this realm, its relationship to the concepts of trust and non-monetary incentives appears to be of special interest. Moreover, the link between the extent to which IS workers have an integrative view in performing an IS function and the systemic impact of an IS function deserves closer examination. Finally, IS workers with a long- versus short-term orientation may be preferred in situations, where planning is important.

On the other hand, all the cultural dimensions that describe leadership issues, i.e., the relationships between superiors and subordinates do not apparently influence any of the values on which the mid-range theoretical framework is based. Moreover, some of these dimensions show similar instances in Germany and the US. Since they appear to neither explain differences in IS sourcing behavior at the organizational nor at the national level, they will be neglected in this research study.

In the following, the impacts of the selected cultural dimensions on IS sourcing will be examined more closely and hypotheses will be developed about their impact on the concepts and relationships of the mid-range theoretical framework of IS sourcing.

2.4.3 Impact of Selected Cultural Dimensions

2.4.3.1 Individualism-Collectivism

The concept of individualism-collectivism is, by far, the most extensively studied cultural dimension in the field of cross-cultural research. The arrival of a number of literature reviews, that synthesize its various conceptualizations, measures, and impacts, highlight the intensity of research on this dimension (e.g., Earley and Gibson, 1998; Hui and Triandis, 1986; Roberts and Wasti, 2002; Schwartz, 1990; Triandis, 1995).

From the numerous advances along the line of inquiry about the concept, the synthesis of Hui and Triandis (1986) appears to be especially fruitful. They take the view that collectivism may best be understood as a multidimensional construct that comprises seven categories (see also Bhawuk and Brislin, 1992, p. 417), including

(a) the people's concern about how their decisions could affect others in their collectivity;

(b) the sharing of material resources;

(c) the sharing of non-material resources, e.g. time, affection or fun, or sacrificing some interesting activities for a member of the collective;

(d) the willingness of people to accept the opinion of others, or, in other words, willingness to conform;

(e) the concern about face saving or gaining the approval of the collective;

(f) the belief in the correspondence of one's own outcomes, both positive and negative, with the outcome of others; and

(g) the feeling of involvement in others' life.

In most research studies, *individualism* has been treated as the opposite of collectivism. That is, individualism-collectivism has been taken as a *bipolar* construct (e.g., Hofstede, 1980). For example, if people are not concerned about how their decisions could affect others in their collectivity, this would be an indication for individualism.

By contrast, some researchers have found it useful to *distinguish* between collectivism and individualism. That is, the polar extremes may be treated as independent constructs (Schwartz, 1990; Triandis, et al., 1986). For the purpose of this research, the focus will be on collectivism, since it obviously contrasts the individualist view of human behavior, on which most economic and strategic thinking is based. The notion of individualism, however, will not be neglected. It appears fruitful to recognize the contrast between both dimensions.

When matching the seven categories of collectivism, identified by Hui and Triandis (1986), with the different aspects of individualism-collectivism, that have been identified within the previously selected cultural dimensions, some interesting overlaps can be observed.

On the one hand, the relational individualism versus collectivism concept from Hofstede (1980) and the motivational individualism versus communitarianism concept from Trompenaars and Hamden-Turner (1994), appear to be related to the willingness of people to accept the opinion of others and to the concern about face saving or gaining the approval of the collective (collectivism categories (d) and (e) in Hui and Triandis, 1986).

On the other hand, the analytical versus integrative view of individuals or work groups (based on Trompenaars and Hamden-Turner, 1994) appears to be closely related to the concern of people about how their decisions could affect others of the collectivity, and to the interdependence of one's outcomes with the outcomes of others (collectivism category (a) and (f) in Hui and Triandis, 1986). The other three collectivism categories (b, c, and g) are not obviously covered by any of the identified cultural dimensions. Accordingly, the broad notion of collectivism will be narrowed down to two specific types of collectivism: *group behavior* and *systemic view.*

Group (collectivist) behavior is defined as the degree to which individuals, i.e., IS workers, orient their actions for the benefit of the group or collective rather than on their own or individual believes.

Systemic (collectivist) view is defined as the degree to which individuals, i.e., IS workers, take into account how work in one area fits in and affects all other work throughout the organization.

The next step is to analyze how these two constructs influence the concepts and relationships of the mid-range theoretical framework. On the one hand, it is necessary to clarify why it may matter that IS workers behave collectivistic rather than individualistic. On the other hand, it has to be analyzed, why and how the propensity of IS workers to behave collectivistic rather than individualistic may be affected by the governance choice (i.e. the insourcing or outsourcing of an IS function). At first, the influence of group-oriented behavior will be analyzed.

Impact of group-oriented behavior (collectivism). First of all, performing an IS function, like the development and maintenance of applications software, often requires exchange relationships and team work between IS workers as well as between IS workers and client users. Especially, if an IS function requires a high amount of firm specific knowledge, social collaboration is needed. The necessity to acquire firm specific knowledge equals a specific investment by the IS workers. It increases their opportunistic propensity and hence the transaction costs and strategic vulnerability of the principal (i.e. the client organization). As outlined previously, however, opportunistic behavior may not be the rule. Instead, IS workers may signal their trustworthiness and may be intrinsically motivated rather than purely extrinsically motivated through monetary incentives. Both trustworthy behavior and non-monetary incentives can lower transaction costs and the strategic vulnerability in situations where performing an IS function requires a high level of team and group work. One could ask further, however, *why* IS workers may be trusted and perceived as being intrinsically motivated.

There are a number of indications that suggest that group (collectivist) behavior is positively related to both trustworthiness and non-monetary incentives. For example, collectivism has been found to be positively related to job satisfaction (Hui, et al., 1995; Kirkman and Shapiro, 2001) and organizational commitment (Kirkman and Shapiro, 2001; Palich, et al., 1995). Moreover, the study from Ang and Slaughter (1998) on IS employment insourcing and outsourcing showed that individualism was strongly negatively correlated with the performance of IS workers as well as with their trustworthiness (see Ang and Slaughter, 1998, p. 653).

It has to be noted, however, that collectivist behavior, and hence the positive impacts of such behavior, critically depend on the working environment. In particular, it depends on whether collectivists are working within their *ingroup* or with *outgroup* members. According to Early (1993) an *ingroup* may be defined "(...) as an aggregate of people sharing similar traits and background characteristics" (see also Triandis, et al., 1988). The ingroup is the social entity in which the collectivistic values and norms of an individual are being developed. The phenomenon of ingroups is inevitably linked to collectivist behavior. People with collectivist orientations emphasize the importance of belonging to a stable, select ingroup. They expect the group to help provide for the welfare of the group members (Hofstede, 1983b; Hofstede, 1980; Hui and Triandis, 1986). In the context of this study, an IS worker may perceive the department or the whole organization for which s/he works as an ingroup.

In reviewing the literature, Earley (1993, p. 322) noted that altruistic behavior is positively related to ingroup behavior, that ingroup members derive a positive self-identity from their group membership, and that ingroup members tend to be more cooperative and cohesive. Moreover, ingroup members are more committed to, satisfied with, and trusting of their teams (*cf.* Thomas, 1999).

On the other side, poor communication has been observed between *different* ingroups (Earley, 1993, p. 322). Chen et al. (2002, p. 289) have argued that "(...) collectivists typically draw the distinction between those they are personally related to (in-groups) and those they are not (out-groups)". According to them, individualists have a greater propensity towards opportunistic behavior in intra-group transactions, and collectivists in inter-group transactions. Moreover, Triandis (1995) observed that individualists are more flexible in moving in and out between multiple loosely affiliated groups based on their individual objectives and needs, while collectivists are more likely to form and stay in few, stable, and closely knit groups that satisfy the needs and objectives of the group. Early (1993, p. 322) found out that individualists perform at the highest level, when they work alone. Working in an ingroup or outgroup context reduces their performance. By contrast, the performance of collectivists is highest when working in an ingroup, as opposed to working alone or in an outgroup.

Overall, these findings suggest that in situations where group work is essential to complete a task, e.g., in performing highly specific IS functions, collectivists may work more efficient – provided that they work within an ingroup setting.

However, how is collectivistic ingroup behavior in performing an IS function affected by its sourcing arrangement? At the first view, the likelihood for collectivistic behavior and the formation of ingroups appears to be higher within in-house as opposed to outsourcing IS arrangements. In collectivistic client organizations, the personnel of external vendors may be perceived as an outgroup. This can severely limit the cooperative work between in-house staff (i.e. users and IS employees) and external personnel. If IS managers recognize a strong ingroup behavior in-house, they may perceive in-house employees to be more trustworthy and to show a higher level of non-monetary incentives.

On the other side, ingroup relationships can also be formed between client and vendor personnel. This is especially likely if both parties enter into a long-term cooperative exchange relationship. Accordingly, it appears to be decisive if the level of group-behavior is perceived to be higher in case of insourcing or outsourcing. This leads to the following two hypotheses:

Hypothesis 21a: The higher the level of *group* (collectivist) oriented behavior of in-house employees as opposed to outsourced workers, the higher is the *trustworthiness* of in-house as opposed to outsourced personnel.

Hypothesis 21b: The higher the level of *group* (collectivist) oriented behavior of in-house employees as opposed to outsourced workers, the higher are the *non-monetary incentives* of in-house as opposed to outsourced personnel.

Impact of systemic (collectivist) behavior. Many of the positive effects of an organization's IS depend on the smooth interplay between different IS components, including the application software, the network infrastructure, and the systems architecture. In accordance, it is necessary to coordinate the work provided in the respective IS functions and to recognize the systemic impact of each of the IS functions. As already outlined previously, comparative advantages of insourcing as opposed to outsourcing in recognizing the systemic impact of an IS function are proposed to lower both an organization's attitude towards outsourcing and the extent to which an IS function is being outsourced.

Up to know, it has been assumed that the coordination of different IS tasks can better be achieved, if all IS functions are equally governed – that is, if they are either totally outsourced or completely insourced. Implicitly, it has been assumed that a certain level of central authority is required that coordinates different IS functions in a way that recognizes the interdependency between work in different areas. Either an in-house group or an external vendor may be superior in leveraging the systemic impact of an IS function.

The flip is, that centralized coordination increases coordination costs. If, however, IS workers recognize the interdependency of their own work with the work of other units, the benefits (strategic, operational, systemic) from integration can be obtained without suffering increasing coordination costs (as part of both transaction costs and production costs). In other words, IS workers that feel responsible not only for their own work, but also for how their work relates to the work of others, may be viewed as *valuable resources*. They typify mature rather than immature IS workers and, for that reason, may be valued higher by an IS executive than those that only take care about their own piece of work.

Consistent with resource-based theory, it may be expected that the extent to which IS workers have a systemic view is taken into account by IS executives when evaluating and comparing alternative sourcing options for the provision of an IS function. Therefore, the following two hypotheses may be put forth:

Hypothesis 22a: The more *systemic* (collectivistic) the view of in-house employees as opposed to outsourced workers in performing an IS function, the less this function will be *outsourced*.

Hypothesis 22b: The more *systemic* (collectivistic) the view of in-house employees as opposed to outsourced workers in performing an IS function, the lower is an IS executive's positive *attitude towards* outsourcing this function.

2.4.3.2 Long-term Versus Short-term Orientation

The notion of long-term orientation is closely related to the systemic view of IS workers. While IS workers with a systemic view consider how their work affects and is affected by others, IS workers with a long-term orientation consider how their work affects *future* actions required to perform an IS function. That is, they consider the longer term implications of their decision and planning effort. In application development and maintenance, such behavior may become very important. An organization's IS, and in particular its application software, may change frequently. It is often essential to anticipate these dynamics during the development and maintenance work. For example, if an organization introduces an ERP package, it is necessary to consider the ability to migrate to a new release in the future. Every significant modification of the programme's source code may hinder a smooth upgrade in the future. Similarly, when developing customized applications, designers and programmers are well advised to consider the "maintainability" and "transformability" of the software in the future. For example, maintainability may be achieved by considering the principle of compatibility, integrity, simplicity, usability, extensibility, stability and familiarity (Swanson, 1999, p. 67). Of course, the same principles apply to the maintenance work. Especially maintenance workers are often confronted with urgent demands from the users, e.g., to fix bugs in a software programme. Any of these corrections can be accomplished with a short-term perspective, i.e. without deep investigations of the real sources of the mistakes and without considering how to avoid similar or related bugs in the future, or, they can be performed with a long-term view, in which IS workers try to find solid and stable solutions for the problem in order to minimize future maintenance efforts.

IS executives may recognize the value of IS workers that employ a long-term rather than short-term view in doing their work. Long-term IS workers may again be viewed as a *valuable resource*. Consistent with resource-based theory the following two hypotheses may be put forth:

Hypothesis 23a: The more *long-term oriented* in-house employees are as opposed to outsourced workers in performing an IS function, the less this function will be *outsourced.*

Hypothesis 23b: The more *long-term oriented* in-house employees are as opposed to outsourced workers in performing an IS function, the lower is an IS executive's positive *attitude towards* outsourcing this function.

2.4.3.3 Directive Control

Directive control is the extent to which an organization has the ability to direct and influence the work within an IS function and its related activities (e.g., control over the choice of hardware, software, tools, methods, standards, staffing, and overall architecture).

Directive control *is not* related to the notion of controlling. While controlling is an actual behavior that causes transaction costs, control is a capability or a potential. It reduces the dependence on another party and allows to reduce the uncertainty and the risks associated with delegating a task to another party.

The notion of control has often been emphasized in relation to the strategic objectives of an organization. Some authors have stressed the risk that outsourcing lowers the ability to control the strategic direction of an IS function (e.g., Duncan, 1996; Earl, 1996). In order to reach the strategic objectives associated with an IS function, the IS strategy needs to be aligned with the organizational strategy (Henderson and Venkatraman, 1993). Sääksjärvi (2002) has found empirical support for the notion that strategic alignment remains to be an important issue in case of IS outsourcing. During the life of an IS outsourcing contract, it needs to be ensured that the IS strategy and the overall firm strategy are compatible with each other.

Whenever, the realization of a certain output requires the combination of different tasks into a coherent whole, a certain level of active direction and goal setting is required. This, however, requires a solid understanding of what is directed. In other words, an organization has to keep a certain level of control over the processes and activities of an IS function in order to direct. These requirements are reflected by the notion of directive control.

Given the importance of *directive control* to achieve the strategic and operational objectives of an IS function, it appears necessary to consider how the directive control is being affected by the sourcing decision. Accordingly, the following hypotheses may be put forth:

Hypothesis 24a: The more an organization believes that it looses the *directive control* over an IS function if it is outsourced rather than provided in-house, the less this function will be *outsourced.*

Hypothesis 24a: The more an organization believes that it looses the directive control over an IS function if it is outsourced rather than provided in-house, the lower is an IS executive's *attitude* towards outsourcing this function.

2.4.4 Extended Mid-range Theoretical Framework on IS Sourcing

In total, five cultural dimensions have been identified that potentially influence the IS sourcing decision. They were derived from former cross-cultural studies and redefined, so that they could be integrated into the mid-range theoretical framework of IS sourcing, as illustrated in Figure 2-13 (p. 133). Please note that the cultural dimensions are marked with an asterisk. A summary of all the hypotheses that are included in the framework is provided in Table 2-4 (p. 128 f.).

Organizational Level. Perceived comparative in-house advantages in the *directive control* over an IS function and in the *systemic impact* of an IS function refer to *organizational consequences* that IS executive attribute to the IS sourcing decision. They are proposed to directly impact the current degree of outsourcing and an IS executive's attitude towards IS outsourcing. The influence of the systemic impact dimension has already been deduced from resource-based theory.

Worker Level. The other three dimensions provide insight into the perceptions and beliefs that IS executives have about the behavioral attitudes of insourced versus outsourced IS workers, and how these perceptions influence the sourcing decision. In particular, three different types of *IS worker attitudes* emerged from the analysis of cultural dimensions. First, the extent to which in-house employees are more *group (collectivist) oriented* than external vendor staff has an indirect impact on the IS sourcing decision by influencing an IS executive's perception of differences in the trustworthiness and the non-monetary incentives between in-house and outsourced IS workers. Second, comparative advantages of in-house IS workers in having a *systemic view* in doing their work are supposed to have a direct impact on both the attitudes of IS managers toward outsourcing and the degree of IS outsourcing. Third, the extent to which in-house IS workers are more *long-term oriented* in performing an IS function is also proposed to directly influence the IS sourcing decision.

Overall, the cultural dimensions *complement* the explanatory and predictive power of the mid-range theoretical framework on IS sourcing. Moreover, they help to understand the impact of *national culture* on the mid-range theoretical framework.

Proposed National Differences. First, considering that German managers appear to be more collectivistic than their US colleagues, the influence of *group-behavior* on trustworthiness and non-monetary incentives may be higher in Germany than in the US. This assumption is consistent with findings from Gomez et al. (2000). Their results revealed that collectivists evaluate ingroup members more generously than individualists would do. Accordingly German managers may be more inclined to appreciate group behavior than their US colleagues. Second, German IS managers may value IS workers with a *systemic view* higher than US executives. Hence, the sourcing decision will more likely be influenced by perceived differences in the integrative view of in-house versus outsourced IS workers in Germany than in the US. Third, the *systemic impact* of an IS function may strongly be considered as a criteria for evaluating and comparing alternative sourcing options in Germany while being less influential in the US. Fourth, considering that German managers appear to be more *long-term oriented* than their US colleagues, they may have a stronger recognition of the long-term versus short-term orientation of IS workers. Therefore, the influence of comparative in-house advantages in the long-term orientation of IS workers may be stronger in Germany than in the USA. Finally, Germans were found to show a higher level of uncertainty avoidance and a higher preference for security. Accordingly, German IS executives may be more interested in keeping the *directive control* over an IS function. Therefore, comparative in-house advantages in the directive control over an IS function will likely be more influential on the sourcing decision in Germany than in the US.

It has to be recognized, however, that these expected national differences critically depend on the reliability and consistency of the results of the large scale cross-cultural studies that have been analyzed previously. Moreover, it has to be recognized that cultural values may change or converge over time.

Therefore, the examination of these expected cultural differences is more exploratory in nature. By no means is this study meant to replicate any of the large scale cross-cultural research studies. Rather this study seeks to adapt and integrate selected cultural dimensions into the mid-range theory of IS sourcing. Thereby, a new perspective is brought in that sheds light on personal perceptions and attitudes, which have rarely been considered in previous research on the IS sourcing decision.

Table 2-4: Summary of Hypotheses (Page 1 from 5)

No.	Hypotheses
1a:	The more *specific* the *human assets* required to perform an IS function are, the higher the comparative transaction cost advantage of insourcing as opposed to outsourcing an IS function.
1b:	The more *specific* the *human assets* required to perform an IS function are, the higher the comparative production cost advantage of insourcing as opposed to outsourcing an IS function.
1c:	The more *specific* the *human assets* required to perform an IS function are, the higher is the advantage of insourcing as opposed to outsourcing in providing a strategically significant IS function.
1d:	The more *specific* the *human assets* required to perform an IS function are, the higher is the strategic significance of an IS function.
1e:	The higher the *human asset specificity* required to perform an IS function, the higher is the advantage of an organization's in-house base of intellectual capital as compared to that of an external vendor.
2a:	The higher the comparative *transaction cost advantage* of insourcing as opposed to outsourcing an IS function, the less it will be outsourced.
2b:	The higher the perceived comparative *transaction cost advantage* of insourcing as opposed to outsourcing an IS function, the more negative is an IS executive's attitude towards outsourcing this IS function.
3a:	The higher the comparative *production cost advantage* of insourcing as opposed to outsourcing an IS function, the less it will be outsourced.
3b:	The higher the perceived comparative *production cost advantage* of insourcing as opposed to outsourcing an IS function, the more negative is an IS executive's attitude towards outsourcing this IS function.
4a:	The higher the *technology driven uncertainty* associated with the provision of an IS function, the higher the comparative transaction cost advantage of insourcing as opposed to outsourcing an IS function.
4b:	The higher the *technology driven uncertainty* associated with the provision of an IS function, the lower the comparative production cost advantage of insourcing as opposed to outsourcing an IS function.

Table 2-4: Summary of Hypotheses (Page 2 from 5)

5a:	The higher the *business driven uncertainty* associated with the provision of an IS function, the higher the comparative transaction cost advantage of insourcing as opposed to outsourcing an IS function.
5b:	The higher the *business driven uncertainty* associated with the provision of an IS function, the higher the comparative production cost advantage of insourcing as opposed to outsourcing an IS function.
6:	The higher the *work load variations* associated with the provision of an IS function, the lower the comparative production cost advantage of insourcing as opposed to outsourcing an IS function.
7a:	The higher the *difficulty in measuring the performance* of an IS function, the more likely it will be outsourced to an external vendor.
7b:	The higher the *difficulty in measuring the performance* of those that do the work in an IS function, the higher the comparative transaction cost advantages of insourcing as opposed to outsourcing an IS function.
8a:	The higher the *trustworthiness* in-house as opposed to outsourced IS workers, the higher is the impact of human asset specificity (H1a) on in-house transaction cost advantages in performing an IS function.
8b:	The higher the *trustworthiness* of in-house as opposed to outsourced IS workers in providing an IS function, the higher is the production cost advantage of the in-house as opposed to outsourced provision of an IS function.
8c:	The higher the *trustworthiness* of in-house as opposed to outsourced IS workers in providing an IS function, the higher is the impact of human asset specificity on in-house advantages in providing a strategically significant IS function (H1c).
8d:	The higher the *trustworthiness* of in-house as opposed to outsourced IS workers in providing an IS function, the higher is the perceived advantage of providing an operationally significant IS function internally rather than outsourcing it to an external service provider.
9a:	The higher the level of *non-monetary incentives* of in-house as opposed to outsourced IS workers, the higher is the impact of human asset specificity (H1a) on in-house transaction cost advantages in performing an IS function.
9b:	The higher the n*on-monetary incentives* of in-house as opposed to outsourced IS workers in providing an IS function, the higher is the production cost advantage of the in-house as opposed to outsourced provision of an IS function.
9c:	The higher the level of *non-monetary incentives* of in-house as opposed to outsourced IS workers, the higher is the impact of human asset specificity on in-house advantages in providing a strategically significant IS function (H1a).

Table 2-4: Summary of Hypotheses (Page 3 from 5)

9d:	The higher the *non-monetary incentives* of in-house as opposed to outsourced IS workers in providing an IS function, the higher is the perceived advantage of providing an operationally significant IS function internally rather than outsourcing it to an external service provider.
9d:	The higher the *non-monetary incentives* of in-house as opposed to outsourced IS workers in providing an IS function, the higher is the perceived in-house advantage in recognizing the systemic impact of an IS function.
10a:	The higher the advantage of insourcing as opposed to outsourcing in providing a *strategically significant* IS function, the less it will be outsourced.
10b:	The higher the perceived comparative advantage of insourcing as opposed to outsourcing in providing a *strategically significant* IS function, the more negative is an IS executive's attitude towards outsourcing this IS function.
11a:	The higher the level of the *strategic contribution* of an IS function, the higher is the impact of comparative advantages in providing a strategically significant IS function on the degree of IS outsourcing (H10a).
11b:	The higher the level of the *strategic contribution* of an IS function, the higher is the impact of comparative advantages in providing a strategically significant IS function on the attitude towards outsourcing this IS function (H10b).
12a:	The higher the advantage of insourcing as opposed to outsourcing in providing a *operationally significant* IS function, the less it will be outsourced.
12b:	The higher the perceived comparative advantage of insourcing as opposed to outsourcing in providing a *operationally significant* IS function, the more negative is an IS executive's attitude towards outsourcing this IS function.
13a:	The higher the level of *operational contribution* of an IS function, the higher is the impact of comparative advantages in providing a strategically significant IS function on the degree of IS outsourcing (H12a).
13b:	The higher the level of *operational contribution* of an IS function, the higher is the impact of comparative advantages in providing a strategically significant IS function on the degree of IS outsourcing (H12a).
14a:	The higher the advantage of insourcing as opposed to outsourcing in recognizing the *systemic impact* of an IS function, the less it will be outsourced.
14b:	The higher the perceived comparative advantage of insourcing as opposed to outsourcing in keeping up the *systemic impact* of an IS function, the more negative is an IS executive's attitude towards outsourcing this IS function.
15a:	The higher the in-house advantages compared to an external vendor in the base of *intellectual capital* required to perform an IS function, the less the IS function will be outsourced.

Table 2-4: Summary of Hypotheses (Page 4 from 5)

15b:	The higher the perceived in-house advantages compared to an external vendor in the base of *intellectual capital* required to perform an IS function, the more negative is an IS executive's attitude towards outsourcing this IS function.
16a:	The higher the in-house advantages compared to an external vendor in the base of *other* (than intellectual) *resources* required to perform an IS function, the less the IS function will be outsourced.
16b:	The higher the perceived in-house advantages compared to an external vendor in the base of *other* (than intellectual) *resources* required to perform an IS function, the more negative is an IS executive's attitude towards outsourcing this IS function.
17a:	The higher the degree of *ownership* in the external service provider(s), the less will an increasing degree of human asset specificity lead to lower in-house as opposed to outsourcing transaction costs in performing an IS function (H1a).
17b:	The higher the degree of *ownership* in the external service provider(s), the less will an increasing degree of human asset specificity lead to in-house advantages in providing a strategically significant IS function (H1c).
18a:	The more negative the overall *attitudes* towards outsourcing an IS function are, the less it will be outsourced.
18b:	The more negative the overall *attitudes* towards outsourcing an IS function are, the lower is the perceived ideal degree of outsourcing.
19a:	The more negative the opinion of *influential others* (subjective norm) towards outsourcing an IS function, the less it will be outsourced.
19b:	The more negative the opinion of *influential others* (subjective norm) towards outsourcing an IS function, the more negative is the overall attitude towards outsourcing this IS function.
20a:	The lower the *perceived behavioral control* over the outsourcing of an IS function, the less it will be outsourced.
20b:	The lower the *perceived behavioral control* over the outsourcing of an IS function, the more negative is the attitude towards outsourcing.
21a:	The higher the level of *group* (collectivist) *oriented behavior* of in-house employees as opposed to outsourced workers, the higher is the trustworthiness of in-house as opposed to outsourced workers.
21b:	The higher the level of *group* (collectivist) *oriented behavior* of in-house employees as opposed to outsourced workers, the higher are the non-monetary incentives of in-house as opposed to outsourced work.

Table 2-4: Summary of Hypotheses (Page 5 from 5)

22a:	The more *integrative* (collectivistic) the *view* of in-house employees as opposed to outsourced workers in performing an IS function, the less this function will be outsourced.
22b:	The more *integrative* (collectivistic) the *view* of in-house employees as opposed to outsourced workers in performing an IS function, the lower is an IS executive's attitude towards outsourcing this function.
23a:	The more *long-term oriented* in-house employees are as opposed to outsourced workers in performing an IS function, the less this function will be outsourced.
23b:	The more *long-term oriented* in-house employees are as opposed to outsourced workers in performing an IS function, the lower is an IS executive's attitude towards outsourcing this function.
24a:	The more an organization believes that it looses the *directive control* over an IS function if it is outsourced rather than provided in-house, the less this function will be outsourced.
24b:	The more an organization believes that it looses the *directive control* over an IS function if it is outsourced rather than provided in-house, the lower is an IS executive's attitude towards outsourcing this function.

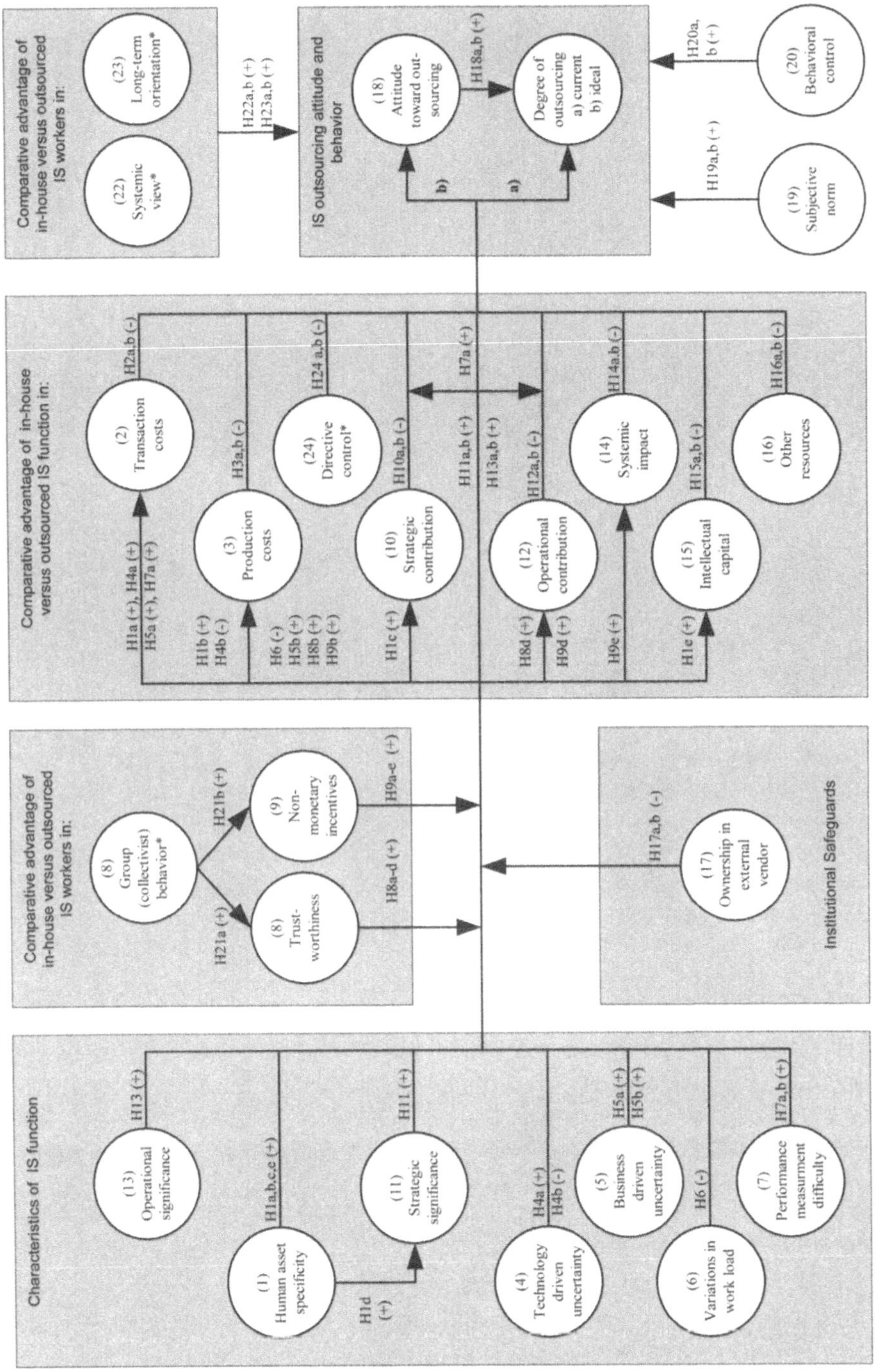

Figure 2-13: Extended Mid-range Theoretical Framework of IS Sourcing (Cultural dimensions marked with *)

3 Empirical Test of Sourcing Model

In this Chapter, the mid-range theoretical framework on IS sourcing will be tested empirically. This requires to transform the theoretical language into an observable language (Fornell, 1989). In other words, the constructs have to be operationalized as measurable variables. In doing so, it is necessary to satisfy both the theoretical and the empirical requirements.

One method that provides a formal structure which allows the matching of theory and data is that of *structural equation modeling* (SEM). This statistical modeling technique provides rules on how to specify a variance type theoretic framework in a way that recognizes the requirements of the statistical procedures that are applied to rigorously estimate and evaluate the parameters of the model.

Structural equation modelling may be viewed as one of the most advanced methods of *theoretical empiricism* (Wold, 1989a). Theoretical empiricism seeks to *unify* two traditionally opposing views of the philosophies of sciences, i.e., ways of acquiring and creating scientific knowledge, namely that of *idealism* or logical empiricism, which places the importance on ideas and reasons, and that of *empiricism*, which emphasizes the determination to learn primarily form experiences (Dagum, 1989, p. 146).

> "Theoretical empiricism represents a harmonic integration between observation-sensation and reason, within a given frame of reference, leading to model specifications possessing properties of rigor, relevance and realism" (Dagum, 1989, p. 119).

Scientific model building has emerged in Econometrics in the 1930s and 1940s. It includes a synthesis of (i) model specification, (ii) model estimation, (iii) model evaluation, and (iv) model application (Wold, 1989a, p. XXXII).

In order to specify a model, extensive "pre-modeling knowledge" is required (see also Dagum, 1989, p. 130; Wold, 1989a, p. XXXII). That is, "(...) before theoretical empiricism is ripe for exploration by a model, it passes through several stages in the theoretical and empirical work" (Wold, 1989a, p. IX).

As outlined previously, research on why organizations insource or outsource their IS function(s) has already reached a very advanced state, reflected by a high theoretical and methodological diversity (see Table 2-1, p. 25). The mid-range theoretical framework on IS sourcing, that has been developed in the previous chapter, builds on this knowledge. Drawing on prior empirical and conceptual work on IS outsourcing, it integrates different theoretical lenses into a coherent whole. The resulting framework serves as an important basis for the model specification. Working definitions of each construct have been provided and the linkages between them have been explicated through hypotheses.

> "Predictor specification is instrumental as a pre-modelling device in the passage from logical empiricism to theoretical empiricism" (Wold, 1989a, p. IX)

The theoretical groundwork simplifies the model building. However, in order to specify and subsequently test the framework, the requirements of the modeling technique have to be considered *a priori*. Therefore, the SEM method will first be introduced. Subsequently, the constructs of the mid-range theoretical framework on IS sourcing will be operationalized. After the development of the measurement instrument, the conduct of the empirical study will be outlined. This includes the data collection and the data analysis. The analysis is separated into the descriptive analysis of the sample data and the more extensive model estimation and evaluation.

3.1 Structural Equation Modeling

Within the last twenty years, structural equation modeling techniques have become increasingly popular among social scientist (Chin, 1998b; Hildebrandt and Homburg, 1998). They allow the rigorous statistical examination of theoretical relationships. Their popularity is essentially attributed to their ability to combine an *econometric* perspective, focusing on prediction, with *psychometric* modelling, which focuses on the measurement of not directly observable (i.e. latent) variables by multiple observables – also called indicators or manifest variables (Chin, 1998b, p. vii; Fornell, 1989, p. 154 f.; Lee, et al., 1997, p. 120). The approach is primarily *confirmatory* in nature. It is generally used to determine whether a pre-specified model is valid, rather than to find a model by exploring the data – although it often includes some exploratory elements in the analysis (Chin, 1998a; Homburg and Dobratz, 1991; 1992).

In particular, two alternative approaches, namely that of *covariance-based* SEM and of *component-based* SEM, also referred to as partial least squares (PLS), can be distinguished (Chin, 1998a). Both modeling approaches can be characterized and compared with each other based on their procedures of model (1) specification, (2) estimation, and (3) evaluation, as well as based on their (4) applicability (Wold, 1989a, p. XXXII). As indicated subsequently, the model specification, evaluation, and applicability are restrained by the alternative statistical procedures used to estimate the model parameters. Nevertheless, it appears useful to first abstract from the estimation procedure and to outline the basic ways of specifying a structural equation model.

3.1.1 Ways of Model Specification

SEM techniques allow the researcher to *simultaneously* test the strength of the relationships between multiple latent variables and the accuracy of the measures of the latent variables (Chin, 1998b; Fornell, 1989; Wold, 1989b, p. XXV).

Structural Model. The relationships between latent variables form the *structural model*, which sometimes is also called inner model (see Figure 3-1). The structural model equals a variance type theoretical framework. Accordingly, the mid-range theoretical framework on IS sourcing, as illustrated in Figure 2-13 (p. 133), can also be treated as a structural model of IS sourcing. For example, comparative in-house production cost advantages are hypothesized to have both a *direct* negative impact on an organization's degree of IS outsourcing (H3a–), and an *indirect* impact by decreasing an IS executive's attitude towards IS outsourcing (H3b–), which is positively related to the actual degree of IS outsourcing (H18+) (see Figure 2-13, p. 133).

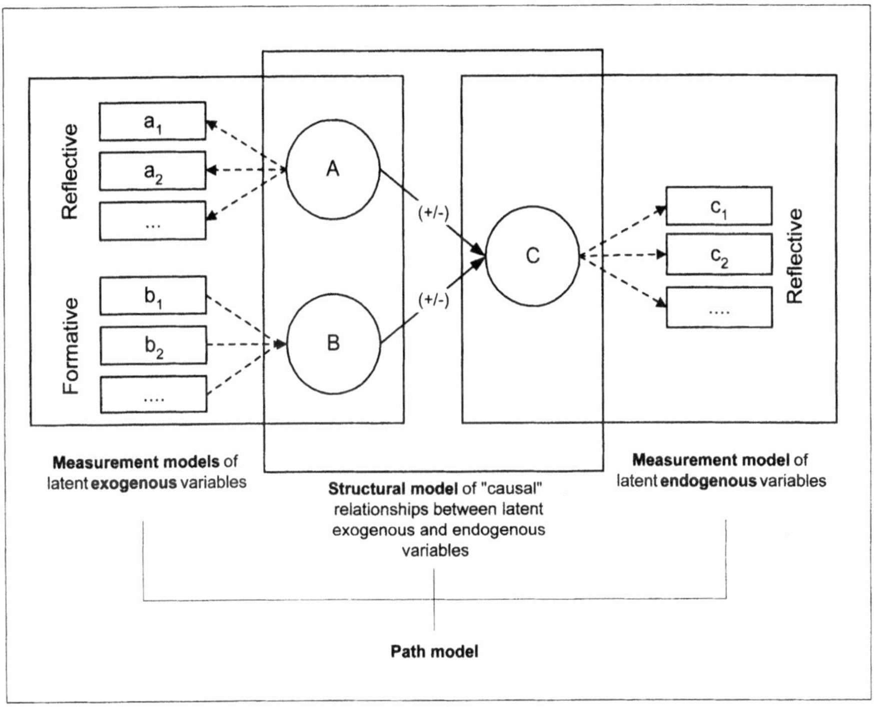

Figure 3-1: Measurement Model, Structural Model and Path Model (based on Backhaus 1998, p. 326, 349)

At that point of time, it is appropriate to note, however, that the proposed directional link between the latent variables is not truly causal in a *theoretical* sense. In fact, Popper (1994/1934) has generally rejected causality as to be "metaphysical". Instead he points out to a simple methodological rule. It suggests that researchers should not stop searching for general laws and comprehensive theoretical systems. This puts the theoretical meaning of the term "causal analysis", which is widely used as a synonym for SEM (Hildebrandt and Homburg, 1998, p. 5), into perspective. From a *methodological* point of view, the term "causal" is less questionable. Here, it simply refers to cause-affect or stimulus-response relationships between variables (Lohmöller, 1989, p. 16-21). This means that the researcher wants to account for the extent to which the variation in one (dependent) variable Y corresponds with the variation of another (independent) variable X.

Measurement Model. In order to empirically examine the structural model, the theoretical constructs need to be measured. That is, the instances of each latent variable have to be determined. Unfortunately, most of the constructs in social sciences are not directly observable. They have a subjective rather than objective character. For example, an IS executive's attitude towards outsourcing can not be observed directly. Attitudes have to be measured indirectly, e.g., by asking different questions. The more questions one is asking, the more complete will be the picture of an IS executive's attitude towards outsourcing. Asking multiple questions allows to account for the potential measurement error ("noise") that is included in the respondent's answers. In other words, if only one measure is used, i.e., one question asked, it is implicitly assumed that the measure is perfect, i.e., without measurement error, which is a rather unrealistic assumption.

Structural equation modelling recognizes the issue of measurement error. It allows to measure one construct with more than one item. Each measure of a construct is called indicator or manifest variable. The sum (or block) of indicators of one construct is called *measurement model* of the construct (see Figure 3-1).

The linkages between the indicators and their constructs are based on *correspondence rules*. Accordingly, one also speaks of correspondence hypotheses, that link indicators with a construct. In general, two different correspondence rules (i.e. measurement modes) may be distinguished (Fornell, 1989, p. 160ff.). On the one hand, the indicators can reflect the construct. In this *reflective* mode, each indicator is an alternative or redundant measure of the construct. That is, the indicators are *interdependent*. They "(...) covary as a consequence of their common content" (Fornell, 1989, p. 161). If the magnitude of one of the measures increases, the magnitude of the other indictors should increase as well (Chin, 1998b, p. Ix; Chin and Newsted, 1999, p. 310). Graphically, this is depicted by having arrows pointing from the construct to its indicators (see Figure 3-1). On the other hand, the measures could be designed in a way so that they form the construct. In this *formative* mode, the indicators are "(...) conceptually independent subdimensions of the concept" (Fornell, 1989, p. 161). That is, the indicators do not need to covary. Each indicator is "(...) defined as a portion of the object or event implied by the focal concept" (Fornell, 1989, p. 161). This is illustrated by drawing arrows from the indicators to their respective latent variable (see Figure 3-1). Covariance-based SEM usually requires a construct to be measured by reflective indicators, while the component-based PLS procedure allows to model both formative and reflective indicators (Chin, 1998c). Finally, the combination of the structural model and the measurement models forms the whole *path model* (see Figure 3-1).

Moderator Effects. Beside the traditional modeling of direct and indirect relationships between latent variables, SEM also allows to test the *moderating influence* of a latent variable on the relationship between two other constructs. For example, in the mid-range theoretical framework on IS sourcing (Figure 2-13, p. 133), comparative in-house advantages in trustworthiness of IS workers have been proposed to strengthen the impact of human asset specificity on in-house transaction cost advantages (H8a+). The general procedure to model moderator effects with continuos variables is the *two-way interaction* procedure (Chin, et al., 1996; Jaccard and Wan, 1996). This is illustrated in Figure 3-2.

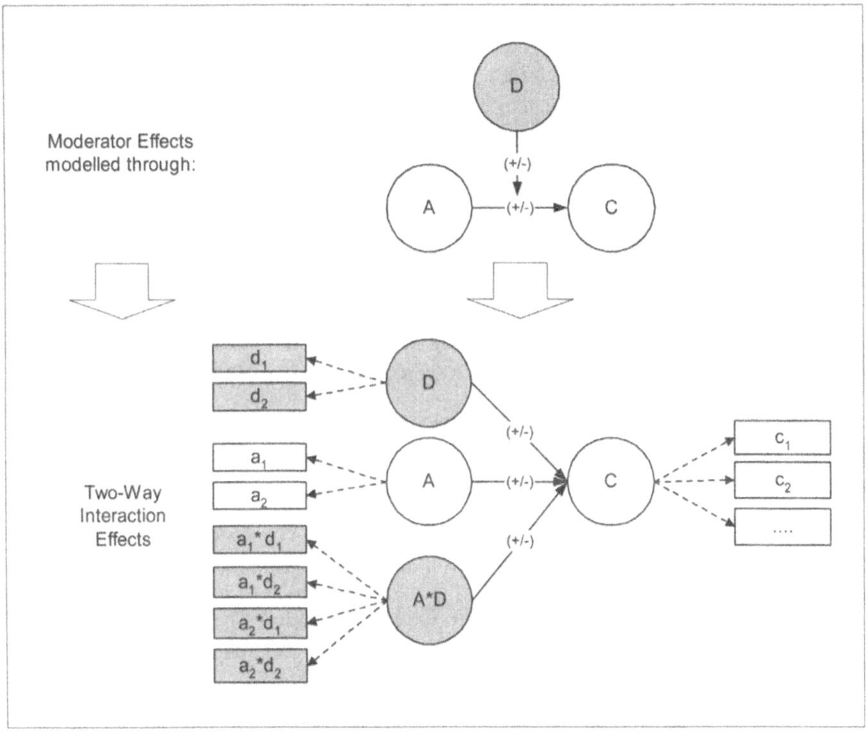

Figure 3-2: Interaction Effects in Structural Equation Modeling
(based on Chin et al., 1996, p. 28; and Jaccard and Wan, 1996, p. 7)

The influence of the moderator D on the relationship between A and C is modelled as a direct impact of the moderator D on the dependent variable C, together with a direct impact of a newly created variable that consists of a *product term* of the moderator variable D with the independent variable A. "Product term" means that all the indicators of variable A are multiplied with all the measures of moderator D. The modelling of two-way interaction effects works both with the covariance-based approach (Jaccard and Wan, 1996) and with PLS (Chin, et al., 1996).

Second-order Constructs. A second interesting feature, that goes beyond the basic model specification in SEM, is that of using *second-order factors*. Second-order factors are aggregates of regularly measured first-order latent variables. They are linked to first-order latent variables just as latent variables are linked to their indicators. Therefore, the same correspondence rules as in case of linking indicators with latent variables need to be considered. That is, the reflective and the formative mode need to be distinguished. Again, the covariance-based procedure only supports the reflective mode. In covariance-based SEM "(...) these second-order factors are not directly connected to any measured items" (Chin, 1998b, p. x). By contrast, second-order factors are directly linked to a set of indicators when using the component-based PLS approach. One approach of modeling second-order constructs in PLS is that of repeated indicators, also known as the hierarchical component model by Wold (*cf.* Chin, et al., 1996, p. 39; Lohmöller, 1989, pp. 130-133; 1982a). In this case, the indicators from all the first-order constructs are taken over by the second-order construct. However, it is also possible to use the estimated component scores of the first-order constructs as indicators of the second-order construct (see 3.1.2 Estimation Procedures). The first-order constructs can either *form* (molar analysis) or *reflect* (molecular analysis) the second-order construct (Chin and Gopal, 1995). Beside their role as *aggregates* of a number of first-order factors, the second-order factors usually *mediate* the impact of a number of exogenous latent variables on one or more endogenous latent variables. They are especially useful within complex models, because they help to simplify the model structure and to better understand the semantic of the constructs (for an example, see Goles, 2001).

Overall, it may be concluded that the basic way of specifying path models is mostly similar between the covariance- and the component-based procedure. In detail, however, there are a number of important differences between both approaches:

(a) *Formative* indicators and formative first-order constructs (in relation to second-order constructs) can only be modelled with the PLS procedure.

(b) The covariance-based procedure explicitly models *error terms* of variables, while PLS implicitly models error terms in equations.

(c) *Second-order constructs* are linked to redundant indicators or construct scores in PLS, whereas they are not directly measured in covariance-based SEM.

These specification differences are grounded in the different estimation procedures of both approaches. This is taken up next.

3.1.2 Estimation Procedures

The covariance-based SEM approach and PLS differ in the *algorithms* used to estimate the main parameters of the model. Two basic types of parameters may be distinguished. First, the *path coefficients* reflect the strength of the relationships of the structural model. Second, the *item loadings* indicate the strength of the link between constructs and measures.

The covariance-based procedure is the more well-known and widely used technique. It has been implemented in various software packages, like LISREL (Jöreskog, 1993), AMOS (Arbuckle, 1999), or EQS (Bentler, 1995). Advanced versions of these software packages have significantly improved the ease of using this technique within the last decade. By contrast, PLS is less common in usage. A likely explanation is the fact that a user friendly Windows-based software package has not been available until recently. Fortunately, this has changed with the availability of PLS-graph, a Windows-based PLS Beta version, developed by Wynne Chin, from the University of Houston, Texas.

Basically, the *covariance-based* SEM algorithm equals a search procedure that seeks to find those "(...) parameters that maximize the Likelihood Function of the model" (Wold, 1989a, p. XXVI). In fitting the data with the specified model, it takes into account the covariances between all indicators of the model. In addition to the main parameters of the model, i.e., the factor loadings and path coefficients, it also estimates the error terms of all observed variables and all dependent latent variables. That is, covariance-based procedures "(...) always seek to recover the full correlation matrix of observed variables" (Fornell, 1989, p. 166). This is the reason, why covariance-based SEM always requires reflective indicators, because

> "(...) SEM techniques such as LISREL attempt to account for the covariances among its measures, the inclusion of formative measures becomes problematic. All items must be reflective to be consistent with the statistical algorithm that assumes that the correlations among indicators for a particular LV [latent variable] are caused by that LV" (Chin, 1998b, p. lx).

Moreover, the covariance-based estimation procedure is based on the assumption that the data points for each indicator follow a multivariate distribution (often normal), and that the observations are independent from each other (Chin, 1998c, p. 301; Chin and Newsted, 1999, p. 309; Wold, 1989a, p. XXIV-V).[15]

In contrast to the parameter oriented covariance-based approach, the *component-based PLS* method is *prediction oriented* (Chin, 1998b; Chin, 1998c; Chin and Newsted, 1999; Lohmöller, 1989; Wold, 1982b; Wold, 1989a). It seeks to predict the variations in all the dependent variables of the model. More specifically, it uses an

---

[15] Notably, however, Monte Carlo simulations (e.g., Bollen, 1989) have shown that the maximum likelihood analysis is robust to certain violations of the normality assumption (Jaccard and Wan, 1996, p. 57).

iterative algorithm of ordinary least square regressions that seeks to minimize the residual variances of the dependent latent variables and all the reflective indicators, that is, all variables where arrows are pointing in (Wold, 1989a, p. XXVI). Consequently, it has also been called "variance-structure" approach (Fornell, 1989, p. 166). Within the iterative test procedure, three categories of parameters may be distinguished. They are estimated in a step wise manner (for a detailed explanation of the PLS algorithm see e.g., Chin, 1999, p. 315 ff.]. The first category (i.e. step) includes the estimation of the indicator *weights* for each latent variable. The weights enable the calculation of *component scores* for each latent variable. The second stage includes the calculation of the path coefficients and the item loadings. The third refers to the estimation of the means and location parameters for indicators and latent variables.

Since PLS does not account for the covariances of all indicators, but only for those variances that have been specified in the model, it is closer to the actual data than the covariance-based procedure. Consequently, it is less likely that the theory "overrides" the data (p. 165), i.e., that the analysis goes "beyond the data" (Fornell, 1989, p. 167).

At the same time, however, there is a problem of consistency at large (Chin and Newsted, 1999, p. 328f.; Wold, 1989a, p. XXV). As outlined previously, PLS allows the calculation of construct scores. These scores are aggregates of the indicator weights, which may include measurement error. They are used to estimate the loadings and path coefficients ("error-in equations approach" Wold, 1989a, p. XVIII). The measurement error in the scores appears to translate into higher estimates for the loadings and lower estimates for the path coefficients. The resulting bias decreases when increasing the number of indicators – which should be accompanied by an increase in sample size (Chin and Newsted, 1999, p. 328f.).

When using the *covariance-based procedure*, the calculation of construct scores is highly problematic since different rotations of the factor solutions could lead to different factor scores (indeterminacy). This, however, is not too dramatic, since the scores are not part of the estimation procedure and therefore do not effect the estimation. Notably, however, the covariance-based approach faces a different problem of consistency at large, in that the consistent estimation of the parameters critically depends on sample size (Wold, 1989a, p. XXVI). In fact, the covariance-based procedure usually requires sample sizes of 200 and higher, while sample size is much less critical in PLS. The latter can produce consistent results with sample sizes as low as 20 (Chin and Newsted, 1999).

Thus, in addition to specification differences, there are differences in both approaches that directly follow from their underlying estimation procedures:

(d) The covariance-based procedure usually requires the data to follow a certain distribution, while PLS is distribution free.

(e) The covariance-based procedure requires the data to stem from independent observations, while PLS does not make assumptions on observation independency.

(f) The covariance-based estimation procedure is parameter oriented, while PLS is prediction oriented.

(g) Both approaches show different problems of consistency at large. The covariance-based procedure critically depends on sample size (usually >200) to achieve consistent parameter estimates. PLS is much less dependent on sample size (usually >30), but produces inconsistent construct scores. While this problem does not really impede the estimation procedure, it can be alleviated by increasing the number of indicators and sample size.

3.1.3 Evaluation Procedures

The objective of the model evaluation is twofold. On the one hand, it is of interest to evaluate how well the *model* (i.e. theory) explains the phenomenon of interest. On the other hand, it is important to know how much the estimated *parameters* of the model can be trusted. Given the different objectives and estimation procedures of the covariance-based and the component-bases SEM approach, their evaluation techniques partly differ as well.

Overall Model Evaluation. As already outlined, the covariance-based algorithm is parameter rather than prediction oriented. Therefore, the explanatory power of the model is evaluated by determining how well the data, i.e., the empirical covariance matrix, fits the model, i.e., the theoretically reproduced covariance matrix based on the evaluated parameters. For this purpose, numerous *global fit indices* have been proposed in the literature (Homburg and Baumgartner, 1985; Jaccard and Wan, 1996, pp. 86ff.).

PLS takes a different approach. Since it is prediction rather than parameter oriented, non-parametric measures are used to evaluate a model (Chin and Newsted, 1999, p. 316). In structural equation models, the causal agency is of a variance theoretic nature (see the difference between variance and process theory, as shown in Section 2.1.3.1, p. 20ff). That is, the phenomenon of interest, e.g., the varying extent to which organizations outsource particular IS functions, is modelled as a dependent variable, whose variation is explained by a number of independent variables. Accordingly, it is of central concern to know the extent to which the model explains the variation of the dependent variable. Satisfying this interest is the primary concern of PLS. The indices taken to assess the amount of explained variance of a dependent variable are the *R-Square* or the Stone-Geiser Q^2-Test. Both indicate the predictive relevance of a model (Chin and Newsted, 1999, p. 317). Of course, R-Square measures could also be achieved through simple regression, however, this would not allow the modelling of latent variables. Moreover, they can be calculated in covariance-based SEM, based on the estimated parameters. However, since the underlying parameter values are estimated based on parameter rather than prediction-oriented estimation procedures, the R-squares differ from those obtained by the PLS algorithm.

Parameter Evaluation. Beside the global measures of the explanatory and predictive power of the model, the parameter values provide insight into the strength of the particular parameter estimates (local measures). In this realm, it is important to test whether the parameter estimates are *statistically significant*, i.e., to determine the level of probability with which the hypotheses that the parameter estimates are not different from zero (Null-hypothesis) can be rejected. This probability is also called *confidence level* (usually 99%, 97,5%, 95% or 90%). Alternatively, one may also speak of the probability that the null-hypotheses is true. In this case one speaks of *critical distances*. They should be limited to probability levels of 1% (p=0,01), 2,5% (p=0,025), 5% (p=0,05), or 10% (p=0,1) (e.g., Mohr, 1991).

In covariance-based SEM, t-values can be calculated based on the standard errors of the parameters (Backhaus, et al., 1996). Knowing both the *t-values* for each parameter and the *degrees of freedom* of the model, the statistical significances can be read from Student-t-Statistics tables. For the convenience of the researcher, these tables usually are already implemented in the respective software programs.

Since the component-based PLS approach is prediction rather than parameter oriented, standard errors, and hence the t-values, are obtained by using non-parametric resampling procedures. Either jackknifing or bootstrapping can be applied for this purpose. As noted by Chin (1998c, p. 320), "(...) the jackknife is viewed as less efficient than bootstrap, because it can be considered a approximation of the bootstrap (Elfron and Tibshirani, 1993)." In order to calculate the standard errors, *bootstrap* produces N sample sets in order to create N estimates of the parameters. The N samples are created by randomly selecting N cases from the given sample – one after another with replacement. Usually the N equals the sample size (Chin, 1998c, p. 320).

Finally, both covariance and component-based approaches allow an in-depth evaluation of the measurement model. The internal consistency of a given block of indicators is examined through selected indices. For example, the composite reliability and the average variance extracted are suggested measures in PLS (Chin and Newsted, 1999, p. 320f.).

Overall, the differences in the ex-post analysis of the parameter estimates mainly refer to the evaluation of the predictive and explanatory power of the entire model:

(h) While covariance-based SEM evaluates a model by testing how well all the observed covariances fit the theoretical covariances reproduced by the estimated parameters (parameter oriented), PLS examines the extent to which the sample variance in the dependent variable(s) of the model is explained by the respective independent variable(s) (prediction oriented).

3.1.4 Applicability

The identified seven main differences (a-h) between the covariance-based procedure and the component-based PLS approach provide the basis for choosing the appropriate modelling technique.

The purpose of this research project is to explain why organizations behave different in the sourcing of their IS functions. A theoretical framework has been developed that seeks to explain the variations in both the attitudes of IS executives towards outsourcing and the current degree of outsourcing the development and the maintenance of software applications. Accordingly, it is of interest to know the amount of *variance* in both variables, that is *explained* by their predictors. This objective is satisfied best by the PLS approach, since it is prediction oriented.

At the same time, however, a complex net of theoretical relationships, that explain the IS sourcing behavior, has been developed. Accordingly, it would be interesting to know the *goodness of fit* between the data and the overall model. This would speak for covariance-based SEM.

Given that both approaches have their merits in satisfying the research objective, the best solution appears to be the use of both approaches in a complementary manner. This, however, can not be decided until the tasks of operationalization and data collection have been accomplished. The PLS approach has clear advantages in specification flexibility (modeling of both formative and reflective indicators), and is facing considerably lower constraints in the requirements for data distribution, independence of observations, and sample size. Therefore, the answer to the question of method choice will not be given until the data analysis (Section 3.5).

3.2 Operationalization of Constructs

Each of the constructs from the mid-range theoretical framework (see Figure 2-13, p. 133) needs to be measured with a block of indicators. Whenever possible, existing measures from prior empirical studies are adopted.

Measures are either formulated as questions, that need to be answered, or as statements, that need to be evaluated by the respondents. All of the indicators are provided with continuos measurement scales. In particular, three different types are applied. Most of the variables are measured on a (positive-to-negative) *five-point Likert scale* ranging from "strongly agree" to "strongly disagree", with "neither agree nor disagree" as a mid-point. In a few questions the respondent is asked to provide *percentages* ranging form 0% to 100%. In two cases, the *semantic differential approach* to measurement is adopted (Osgood, et al., 1957), where each response is located on an evaluative bipolar (negative-to-positive) dimension, using a *seven-point Likert scale*. Whenever possible, blocks of *reflective* indicators are created.

As outlined previously, the *unit of analysis* is the IS function (see Section 2.1.1.1, p. 10). More specifically, it refers to two different IS functions, namely the development of application software and the maintenance of application software. Therefore, the respondents have to answer each question, i.e., evaluate a given statement, *both* for the development *and* for the maintenance of application software.

Independent of the unit of analysis, and following the theoretical structure, as illustrated in Figure 2-13 (p. 133), the indicators can be *semantically differentiated* into *four clusters*:

- The first cluster is represented by those constructs that directly refer to the *behavior in question*: The outsourcing of the two IS functions. Following the logic of the theory of planned behavior, they measure the actual behavior, the attitude towards the behavior, the subjective norm, i.e., attitude of others toward the behavior, the perceived behavioral control over the behavior, and the ideal degree of outsourcing.
- The second category refers to *comparative advantage* constructs at the *organizational level*. They represent believes about different types of comparative advantages in providing an IS function in-house versus outsourcing it to an external vendor.
- The third refers to *comparative advantage* constructs at the *worker level*. Rather than comparing organizations with each other, in-house versus outsourced IS workers are compared with each other on a number of dimensions.
- Finally, contextual variables are measured. They represent different *characteristics of the IS functions*. The particular questions or statements are unrelated to the issue of insourcing or outsourcing.

In the following, the measures of the constructs for each of these four semantic categories will be presented. In each section, tables are provided that show the numbered *abbreviations of the measures* (item numbers), as used in the analysis, the *working definition,* as elaborated in Chapter 2, and shortened versions of the *actual measures*. The entire measurement instrument, in form of a 12-page questionnaire, is presented in Appendix D.1 (English) and D.2 (German version).

3.2.1 Outsourcing Behavior and Attitude Variables

The *degree of IS outsourcing* is one of the two central dependent variables of the theoretical framework. Various operationalizations of the construct have been provided in previous empirical studies on IS outsourcing. Exemplified measures are

- the *approximate percentage* per IS function that is currently outsourced (Apte, et al., 1997; Poppo and Zenger, 1998; Sobol and Apte, 1995), or the *overall degree* of outsourcing with respect to particular IS functions (Loh, 1994; Loh and Venkatraman, 1995);
- the *difference* between the current percentage of an *IS function's budget* allocated for outsourcing and that of three years ago (overall IS outsourcing is measured as the weighted sum of the outsourcing percentages of all IS functions) (Grover, et al., 1994a; Grover, et al., 1994b; Teng, et al., 1995);
- the amount of *change in* outsourcing *IT requirements* of an IS function within the last 3 years (from decreased to increased) (Loh, 1994; Loh and Venkatraman, 1995);
- the percentage of each *IS function's budget currently* allocated for outsourcing (Dibbern and Heinzl, 2001 – based on Teng et al., 1995);
- the degree to which *decision rights or responsibilities* for an IS activity are located at the vendor site (Loh, 1994; Loh and Venkatraman, 1995; Nam, et al., 1996), or the *locus of decisions* concerning IS management and operational control of IS functions (Ang and Straub, 1998);
- the degree to which the vendor *controls the rules and procedures* with respect to one selected IS function (Nam, et al., 1996);
- the degree of *ownership* that the vendor has over the system's hardware and software with respect to one selected IS function (Nam, et al., 1996); and
- the degree of *replacement of in-house IS personnel* through the vendor with respect to one selected IS function (Nam, et al., 1996).

For the purpose of this research, items measuring IS outsourcing should reflect the extent to which the tasks and activities necessary for the provision of an IS function are carried out by one (or more) external service provider(s) with an independent legal form. It is important to note that external vendors with an independent legal form could be connected with the client organization by capital, e.g., they may include a spin-off from the former in-house department. This opens the way to treat *ownership* as a separate construct, as suggested in the theoretical framework. Accordingly, the measure for ownership is the percentage of capital that a client shares with an external vendor, if part or all of an IS function is outsourced (see Table 3-1).

The measures of the *current degree of outsourcing* should be as objective and neutral as possible. One example of such a measure is the percentage of an IS function's *budget* spent on external vendors (Dibbern and Heinzl, 2001; 2002; Teng, et al., 1995). Since the budget for the development and maintenance of an organization's application software is inevitably linked to human rather than physical capital (e.g., hardware or software), alternative measures for budget may refer to the total *person working days* and the *number of people* that are allocated to perform an IS function (see Table 3-1). By contrast, issues such as the location of decision rights or responsibility would not tap into the same underlying construct, since an organization could allocate a major part of its budget to external vendors, but still keep the responsibility for or the main decision rights over an IS function in-house. Moreover, in-house employees do not necessarily need to be replaced by vendor personnel in case of outsourcing. They could be taken over by the external vendor. For descriptive purposes, however, it appears useful to include a measure of the percentage of *former in-house employees working for external vendors* (see Table 3-1).

Attitude towards outsourcing is the second central dependent variable. The attitude construct is one of the most extensively studied concepts in social psychology (Pratkanis, et al., 1989). Moreover, it has been used in various applied fields of social sciences such as MIS – exemplified by IT adoption research (Harrison, et al., 1997; Mathieson, 1991; Taylor and Todd, 1995). Drawing on its definition, as part of the theory of reasoned action and the theory of planned behavior (Ajzen, 1991, p. 188), *attitude towards outsourcing* refers to the overall evaluative appraisal of an IS executive towards having an IS function provided by an external vendor. In measuring the variable, the semantic differential approach has been adopted. Four of the six bipolar dimensions have been adapted from Ajzen and Fishbein (1980, p. 267) and Ajzen and Madden (1986) (bad-good, harmful-beneficial, foolish-wise) as well as from Harrison et al. (1997) (negative-positive).

Subjective norm. Drawing again on the work from Ajzen (1991, p. 195), this variable refers to the normative belief that important referent individuals or groups approve or disapprove the outsourcing of an IS function. In measuring this variable, the bipolar dimensions of the attitude construct have been adapted.

Behavioral Control is operationalized by drawing on the definition from Ajzen (1991, p. 195) and its measurement in former IS studies (Harrison, et al., 1997; Taylor and Todd, 1995). The variable is measured by three items that reflect the extent to which an organization has unlimited power of direction over all necessary activities associated with outsourcing an IS function to an external service provider. Conceptually, the measures are intended to account for hidden external influences, that could limit the decision maker's ability to unrestrictedly decide upon the insourcing or outsourcing of an IS function.

Table 3-1: Outsourcing and Attitude Measures (Page 1 from 2)

Item #	Constructs, Definitions and Indicators
Current Degree of IS Outsourcing (Out) *"IS Outsourcing refers to the extent to which the tasks and activities necessary for the provision of an IS function are carried out by one or more external service providers with an independent legal form."*	
Out1	Average percentage currently allocated to external service providers in terms of the function's total budget.
Out2	(...) in terms of total person working days.
Out3	(...) in terms of total number of people that participate in doing the work.
Ownership in External Service Provider (Owner)	
Propert3	Average share of capital with the service providers (in%).
Transfer of In-house employees (Trans)	
Out5	Approximate percentage of former in-house employees now working for external vendor.
Ideal degree of IS outsourcing (Ideal)	
Ideal	Percentage of IS function that is believed should ideally be spent on external service providers.
Attitude towards Outsourcing (Attitude) *"Attitude towards outsourcing is defined as the overall evaluative appraisal of an IS executive towards having an IS function provided by an external vendor"*	
Attitud1	Overall having an external service provider perform this IS function is bad–good.
Attitud2	(...) is negative–positive
Attitud3	(...) is harmful–beneficial
Attitud5	(...) is foolish–wise
Attitud6	(...) is illogical–logical
Attitud7	(...) is worthless–valuable
Subjective Norm – Opinion of Others (Other) *"Subjective norm refers to the normative belief that important referent individuals or groups approve or disapprove the outsourcing of an IS function"*	
Other1	Persons or groups whose opinion is important to our organization think that outsourcing this particular IS function is bad–good
Other2	(...) is negative–positive
Other3	(...) is harmful–beneficial
Other4	(...) is foolish–wise
Other5	(...) is illogical–logical

Table 3-1: Outsourcing and Attitude Measures (Page 2 from 2)

Item #	Constructs, Definitions and Indicators
Other6	(...) is worthless–valuable
Behavioral Control over Outsourcing Process (BehCoPro) *"Perceived behavioral control is defined as the extent to which an organization has unlimited power of direction over all necessary activities associated with outsourcing an IS function to an external service provider."*	
CoPro1	When it comes to outsourcing this IS function (...) our organization can act unrestrictedly.
CoPro2	(...) there are no impediments to our organization.
CoPro3	(...) our organization has total control over all necessary activities.

3.2.2 Comparative Advantage Variables at the Organizational Level

The notion of "comparative advantage" is closely related to that of "relative advantage" from innovation diffusion theory (Rogers, 1983). In the IS field, it has been used to explain IT adoption behavior (e.g., Agarwal and Prasad, 1997; Chin and Gopal, 1995; Moore and Benbasat, 1991). For example Agarwal and Prasad (1997, p. 562 – italics original) note: "*Relative advantage* captures the extent to which a potential adopter views the innovation as offering an advantage over previous ways of performing the same task." Similarly, the concept of *comparative advantages* in the IS sourcing context may be defined as the extent to which an organization views the in-house provision of an IS function as offering an advantage over outsourcing the same function. Notably, in case of IS sourcing, it is indifferent if outsourcing or insourcing is viewed as offering an advantage. Organizations that currently outsource part or all of an IS function may view insourcing as an innovative organizational alternative, while those that currently insource may view outsourcing as a new way of providing an IS function.

Comparative advantages can be assessed globally, or they can be related to particular evaluative criteria. Within the theoretical framework, a number of evaluative criteria have been deduced from transaction cost theory, resource-based theory, and cross-cultural research. At the organizational level, they refer to the production costs, the transaction costs, the strategic contribution, the operational contribution, and the systemic impact associated with providing an IS function, as well as the directive control over the function. Each of these concepts can be evaluated in favour of insourcing or outsourcing. They refer to the organizational level because the comparison of insourcing versus outsourcing is related to entire organizations or organizational units rather than to characteristics of individual workers that perform an IS function.

Production cost advantage. One would have expected a lot of different measures on production cost differences between organizations, however, surprisingly few studies have operationalized the construct. In the marketing area, Anderson and Weitz (1986) provided measures of economies of scale. However, rather than measuring the actual degree of economies of scale, their measure included alternative sources of economies of scale. For example, one of their questions reads as follows: "Are large providers of marketing services significantly more efficient than small ones because of more intense utilization of personnel and facilities?" (p. 14). In the management field, Walker and Weber (1987) provide a measure for supplier production advantages rather than production cost advantages.

There is, however, one notably exception from the paucity in operationalizing production cost advantages. This is the study from Ang and Straub (1998). They provide a measure for IS outsourcing production cost advantages using five different items that refer to (a) advantages in the *scale and volume* of data processing management and operations, (b) the ability to *reduce hardware costs*, (c) the ability to *reduce software costs*, (d) the ability to *reduce* information systems *personnel costs*, and (e) the question where it is *cheaper* to manage data processing facilities and services.

Drawing on the definition and the measures from Ang and Straub (1998), five items have been developed. They reflect the extent to which the costs, in terms of time, effort, and money included in performing the actual activities necessary to provide an IS function, are lower in-house than when outsourced (see Table 3-2). In recognizing the required theoretical interdependency of the items (reflective mode), five measures have been created based on the following ideas. In application development and maintenance, the costs are inevitably linked to personnel costs. Accordingly, the (a) *efficiency* and the (b) *speed* of working are two redundant measures. At the same time, however, it is more likely that the efficiency and the speed of working increase if an organization can realize (c) *economies of scale,* which allow the efficient allocation of workers to specialized tasks. The consequence are lower overall costs, indicated by lower (d) *prices* for a service and the issue of being (e) *cheaper* (see Table 3-2).

Transaction cost advantage. A similar paucity of measuring production costs can be observed in terms of transaction costs. The few studies that were identified as to provide measures of transaction costs, solely focus on "market transaction costs". They generally neglect in-house transaction costs (e.g., Ang and Straub, 1998; Loh, 1994; Prosser, 1997; Walker and Poppo, 1991). Examples are the difficulty of agreement with the supplier on the allocation of costs due to different types of changes in the task environment (Walker and Poppo, 1991), problems associated with negotiating a contract with an external provider, the necessity to closely and constantly monitor the external provider, and the difficulty to modify contracts with a provider once a contract is signed (Ang and Straub, 1998).

Table 3-2: Measures of Comparative Organizational Level Advantages (Page 1 from 2)

Item #	Constructs, Definitions and Indicators
Production Cost Advantage (Pc) *"Production costs comprise the costs in terms of time, effort and money spent that arise for performing the actual activities necessary to complete the tasks associated with the provision of an IS function."*	
Pc1	Our internal staff works more cost efficiently than an external service provider.
Pc2	Our internal staff works faster than (...).
Pc3	We can realize higher economies of scale internally than (...).
Pc4	In-house performance is cheaper (...).
Pc5	The price that an external service provider charges is higher than (...).
Transaction Cost Advantage (Tc) *"Transaction costs comprise all costs in terms of time, effort and money spent, that arise when delegating tasks of an IS function to one or more agents."*	
Tc1	The costs incurred in negotiating, managing and coordinating are lower within the firm than in case of contracting with an external service provider.
Tc2	More organizational resources would be required externally (...).
Tc3	It would result with more organizational overhead and administrative costs when using an external service provider (...).
Tc4	Less transaction costs are incurred for internal employees (...).
Strategic Contribution Advantage (StratII) *"Strategic contribution is defined as the degree to which a partial IS function contributes to generate a sustained competitive advantage (e.g., through reducing costs, adding new features to differentiate existing products or services, or improving customer service)."*	
Strat2	The contribution of this IS function to achieve a competitive advantage is weakened if it is carried out by an external (...) as opposed to (...) our (...).
Strat4	The ability of this IS function to help our company successfully compete against our competitors is weakened if it is carried out by an external (...)
Strat6	The contribution of this IS function to meet our company's strategic objectives is weakened if it is carried out by an external (...).
Operational Contribution Advantage (OperatII) *"Operational contribution is defined as the degree to which an organization's day-to-day business operations critically depend on the performance of an IS function."*	
Operat2	The contribution of this IS function to support our day-to-day business activities is weakened if its is carried out by an external (...) as opposed to (...).
Operat4	Our firm's ability to carry out this IS function in a way so that our day-to-day business operations are not threatened, is weakened if (...) external (...).
Operat6	Our company is better than a service provider when it comes to limiting delays, project failures, and other poor results for this IS function.

Table 3-2: Measures of Comparative Organizational Level Advantages (Page 2 from 2)

Item #	Constructs, Definitions and Indicators
	Intellectual Capital Advantage (Intell) *"Intellectual capital refers to the knowledge and knowing capability of a social collectivity, such as a group of IS workers performing an IS function."*
Res1	Skill sets for an IS function are better (or worse) within the organization compared to external service provider.
Res2	Capabilities (...) are better (or worse) (...)
Res3	Knowledge set (...) is better (or worse) (...)
Res4	Social competencies (...) are better (or worse) (...)
Res6	Experiences (...) are better (or worse) (...)
	Advantage in Other Resources (ResOther) – [formative mode] *"Other resources represent more objective measures of an organization's IS service capacity including such issues like the staffing level, the financial resources, and the technical equipment"*
Res5	Staffing level
Res7	Financial resources
Res8	Technical equipment
	Systemic Impact Advantage (SystImpa) *"Systemic impact is defined as the extent to which a particular IS function is an integral part within the overall IS function."*
Impact1	The integration of this IS function into the overall IS function is weakened if not performed in-house, but (...)
Impact2	The overall performance of our entire IS function will be greatly affected if (...)
Impact3	The synergetic effects to other IS functions will be threatened if (...)
	Directive Control Advantage (Control) *"Directive control is the extent to which an organization has the ability to direct and influence the work within an IS function and its related activities (e.g., control over the choice of hardware, software, tools, methods, standards, staffing, overall architecture)"*
DecCont1	Our firm loses its control over the direction of the work and its related activities if the IS function is not performed in-house, but (...)
DecCont2	Our organization will have less influence over how the work is to be accomplished if (...)

For the purpose of this study, the measures are required to capture both in-house and outsourcing transaction costs. Therefore, four measures have been developed that reflect the extent to which the costs, in terms of time, effort, and money spent, which arise when *delegating* tasks of an IS function to one or more agents, are lower in-house than when outsourced (see Table 3-2).

Strategic contribution advantage. There are numerous conceptual contributions on the strategic role of IS/IT. However, few studies have operationalized the concept and applied it in quantitative empirical studies. In most of the empirical papers, the strategic role of IS has been assessed by asking for the extent to which IS contributes to achieve various types of strategic objectives. Based on prior literature, Nam (1995, p. 162) has taken 15 different items that refer to different strategic objectives associated with IS/IT. The most popular pair of strategic objectives refers to the two generic types developed by Porter (1985), including the contribution to differentiate the existing products/services from competitors and the contribution to achieve cost advantages in products/services (Dibbern and Heinzl, 2001; Dibbern and Heinzl, 2002; Nam, et al., 1996). In general, however, different strategic objectives do not represent alternatives of the same overall strategy. From a conceptual point of view, they may even contradict each other. Grover et al. (1994b; see also Teng, et al., 1995) have used an alternative way of measurement by distinguishing between three alternative strategic roles of IS/IT (traditional, evolving or integral). For the purpose of this research, however, a continuos measurement scale is preferred. Drawing on Barney's (1991, p. 102) definition of sustained competitive advantage, three items have been developed that reflect the degree to which the contribution of an IS function to generate a sustained competitive advantage can better be achieved in-house rather than through outsourcing. The actual way through which the competitive advantage is achieved, e.g., through reducing costs, adding new features to differentiate existing products or services, or improving customer service, is not of direct interest.

Operational contribution advantage. Drawing on the empirical study from Raghunathan et al. (1999), that developed and tested measures of the "strategic" importance of an organization's current systems portfolio, three items have been developed that measure in-house advantages in an IS function's operational contribution. The measures reflect the degree to which the contribution of an IS function to an organization's day-to-day business operations is weakened if provided by an external vendor rather than in-house.

Intellectual capital advantage. Drawing on the definition from Nahapiet and Ghoshal (1998, p. 245), this variable captures the extent to which the knowledge and knowing capabilities for an IS function are superior in-house as compared to those of an external service provider. The human capabilities necessary to develop and maintain an organization's application software are thought to be reflected by skill sets, capabilities, knowledge sets, and experiences. It may be argued that skill sets and capability refer more to applied intellectual capital, while knowledge and experiences are more general. However, intentionally they appear to tap into the same underlying construct. In order to control for the semantic consistency of the measures, social competencies have been added as a fifth item. It is expected that this measure clearly deviates from the other measures in the reflective mode.

Advantage in other resources. Beside the intellectual capital, there may be other resources that differ between insourcing and outsourcing. These resources represent more objective measures of an organization's IS service capacity. They may include the staffing level, the financial resources, and the technical equipment. These resources do not necessarily covary with each other, e.g., if the financial resources are better in-house, the technical equipment can still be better at the external vendor. Therefore, they form rather than reflect this construct.

Systemic impact advantage. This variable captures the extent to which the overall performance of an organization's IS function, which depends on the smooth interplay of its constituent (sub-)functions, is weakened if an IS (sub-)function is outsourced rather than provided in-house. The notion of systemic impact is related to constructs such as task interdependence or reciprocal interdependence, which have been used to understand how task-technology fit influences IS performance (Goodhue and Thompson, 1995), how relationship issues influence IS outsourcing success (Goles, 2001; Goles and Chin, 2002), and to understand the assignment of tasks to labor-contractors versus employee engineers (Pearce, 1993). In contrast to the concept of interdependence, which captures the extent to which each party completes behaviors, acts, or goals that the other party is dependent on for the completion of their own behaviors, acts, or goals (Pfeffer and Salancik, 1978; Thompson, 1967), the concept of systemic impact captures the variation in the potential impact on the overall system, which may result from the interdependence among parts of the system, i.e., particular IS functions. Three items reflect systemic impact advantages of insourcing versus outsourcing.

Directive control advantage. This variable refers to the extent to which an organization's ability to direct and influence the work within an IS function and its related activities (e.g., control over the choice of hardware, software, tools, methods, standards, staffing, overall architecture) is weakened, if the function is outsourced rather than provided in-house. This variable is assumed to be culturally sensitive, since it is closely related to the concepts of uncertainty avoidance and security need. The concept is not related to a manager's control orientation in terms of monitoring and close coercive leadership styles, which may be manifested in centralized and formalized work structures as well as practices that limit an employee's freedom to exert control (Winter, et al., 1997, p. 9). Directive control refers to an organization's ability to actively determine and influence the task structure and the way of performing an IS function, rather than to control the actual performance of delegated tasks. Two items have been created to reflect the comparative advantages in directive control (scc Table 3-2).

3.2.3 Comparative Advantage Variables at Worker Level

The comparative advantage variables at the worker level reflect an IS executive's perception of differences between the personal attributes of insourced versus outsourced IS workers (*cf.* Ang and Slaughter, 1998; 2001).

Systemic View Advantage. This variable refers to the extent to which in-house IS workers are more likely than personnel from external vendors to take into account how work in one area fits in and affects all other work throughout the organization when performing an IS function. This definition is based on two of the seven categories of the cultural dimension "collectivism" identified by Hui and Triandis (1986). These categories are (a) the people's concern about how their decisions could affect others in their collectivity and (b) the belief in the correspondence of one's own outcomes, both positive and negative, with the outcome of others. In the context of this study, the terms "collecitvity" and "others" refer to the overall organization that is served by an IS function. Three items have been worded in accordance to the construct definition (Table 3-3).

Trustworthiness Advantage. Drawing on the definition of trust from Zaheer and Venkatraman (1994), three items have been developed to measure comparative advantages in trustworthiness. They reflect the extent to which in-house employees can be trusted more than the personnel from external vendors. The trust in IS workers, i.e., trustworthiness, refers to the emotional feeling and cognitive belief that IS workers will act predictably, will fulfill their obligations, and will behave fairly in performing an IS function even if the possibility for opportunism is present.*Non-monetary Incentives Advantage.* This variable captures the extent to which an organization's IS employees are more likely to do quality work without being motivated by incentives that result in monetary benefits for them than personnel from external vendors. Non-monetary incentives of IS workers are closely related to the notion of intrinsic motivation. Intrinsically motivated individuals autonomously realize and accept the correctness and sense of their work and therefore value it for its own sake (Calder and Staw, 1975, p. 599; Steinmann, 1997, p. 589). Provided that the opposite of intrinsic motivation is extrinsic motivation and that the latter is largely attributed to monetary incentives, non-monetary incentives may be viewed as to capture an IS worker's major part of her/his intrinsic motivation. Three items have been developed that reflect comparative advantages in non-monetary incentives (see Table 3-3).

Group Behavior Advantage. This variable is a second variation of the collectivism construct. It refers more to the behavior of individuals in relation to others. It is closely related to two of the seven categories of collectivism, identified by Hui and Trianids (1986). First, and foremost, it refers to the willingness of people to accept the opinion of others and to conform to the group. Second, it reflects the extent to which individuals are concerned about face saving and gaining the approval of the collective.

Table 3-3: Measures of Comparative Worker Advantages (Page 1 from 2)

Item #	Constructs, Definitions and Indicators
	Systemic View Advantage (SysView) *"Systemic (collectivist) view is defined as the degree to which individuals, i.e. IS workers, take into account how work in one area fits in and affects all other work throughout the organization."*
EmplOri1	(...) our own employees tend much more than personnel of external service providers to have a systems view of the organization.
EmplOri2	(...) to have an organization wide perspective of how work in different areas effect one another.
EmplOri3	(...) to consider the task interdependencies in our organization.
EmplOri4	(...) to have an integrated view of the organization.
	Trustworthiness Advantage (Trust) *"Trustworthiness of IS workers refers to the combined emotional feeling and cognitive belief that those that perform an IS function will act predictably, will fulfill their obligations, and will behave fairly in performing an IS function even when the possibility for opportunism is present."*
Trust1	(...) compared to our own employees personnel from an external service provider will tend to behave much more in an ethical manner when doing the actual work.
Trust2	(...) will tend much more to do the job right even when the opportunity to behave opportunistically is present.
Trust3	(...) will tend much more to work in a fair and professional manner independent of your organization's ability and effort to monitor them?
	Non-monetary Incentives Advantage (Incent) *"Non-monetary incentives are all factors that encourage the willingness of the task carriers to do quality work without resulting in a direct monetary benefit for them."*
Incen1	Factoring out performance incentives that result in direct monetary benefits (e.g., extra payments) our firm's employees (...) are much more motivated to do quality work in the particular IS function.
Incen2	(...) much more interested to do quality work in the particular IS function.
Incen3	(...) much more committed to do quality work in the particular IS function
	Group Behavior Advantage (Group) *"Group (collectivist) behavior is defined as the degree to which individuals, i.e. IS workers, orient their actions for the benefit of the group or collective rather than on their own or individual believes."*
Group1	(...) our own employees tend much more than personnel of external service providers to subordinate his or her own goals and thoughts to those of the project team.
Group2	(...) to do what he or she believes is best rather than what the group believes [reversed].

Table 3-3: Measures of Comparative Worker Advantages (Page 2 from 2)

Item #	Constructs, Definitions and Indicators
Group3	(...) to be direct and forthright when dealing with people [reversed].
Group4	(...) to be modest in talking about their own accomplishments.
Group5	(...) to give opinions that will help people save face rather than give a statement of the truth.
Group6	(...) to be willing to downplay his or her beliefs that may conflict with the group in order to maintain consensus.
Group7	(...) to listen and value the general opinion of the group.
Long-term Orientation Advantage (LongWo) *"Long-term orientation refers to the extent to which IS workers employ a long term view in the planning and decision making when doing the work necessary to provide an IS function."*	
LongWo1	Our own employees tend much more (...) to use a long-term horizon when it comes to planning.
LongWo2	(...) to consider the longer term implications of a decision.
LongWo3	(...) to orient their planning on the future rather than on the present.

In the IS sourcing context, it refers to the extent to which in-house IS workers show a higher tendency than external vendor staff in orienting their actions for the benefit of the group or collective rather than on their own or individual believes. Seven items have been developed. The first collectivism item (Group1) has been adapted from Kirkman and Shapiro (2001). The second measure (Group2) is based on Wagner and Moch (1986). It has been reversed coded and reflects individualist rather than collectivist behavior. The next three items have been adapted from Bhawuk and Brislin (1992). The third, again, has been reversed coded and reflects individualism rather than collectivism, while the fourth (Group4) and fifths (Group5) are collectivism measures. Item six has been worded in accordance to the "face savings" collectivism category from Hui and Triandis (1986), introduced earlier. Item seven has been newly developed to reflect collectivist behavior. The inclusion of individualism items enables a reevaluation of the more recently developed view that collectivism and individualism are independent constructs rather than bipolar items (that, when reversed coded, reflect the same underlying construct). They also allow a qualitative check of the answering behavior of the respondents.

Long-term Orientation Advantage. This variable refers to the extent to which in-house IS workers show a higher tendency to employ a long term view in planning and decision making than external vendor staff (based on Trompenaars and Hamden-Turner, 1994). Three items have been developed to measure this construct.

3.2.4 Contextual Variables

Human Asset Specificity. This variable has been conceptualized as a *second-order construct*. Dimensions of human asset specificity are (1) the specificity of business knowledge, (2) the specificity of software knowledge, (3) social collaboration between IS-workers and users/clients, as well as (4) social collaboration within the group of IS workers (see also Figure 2-2, p. 50). Each of the four constructs have been measured with two items.

The *specificity of business knowledge* refers to the extent to which knowledge about unique work practices and business processes is required to perform an IS function. The concept is closely related to asset specificity in terms of knowledge about customer accounts, as elaborated in the marketing literature (Anderson, 1985). Drawing on this conceptualization and informed by items measuring asset specificity in the IS outsourcing literature (Ang and Cummings, 1997; 2002; Aubert, et al., 1996a; Dibbern and Heinzl, 2001; Poppo and Zenger, 1998), two items have been developed to measure this variable. The *specificity of software knowledge* refers to the extent to which performing an IS function requires knowledge about software applications that are especially tailored to the requirements of the client organization. The items measuring this variable are based on previous operationalizations that included the notion of unique technical skills (Ang and Cummings, 1997; Nam, et al., 1996; Walker and Poppo, 1991) and unique IT knowledge (Loh, 1994). Related is also the notion of unique product knowledge, as elaborated in the marketing literature (Anderson, 1985).

The two variables on *social collaboration* refer to the way in which the specific business and software knowledge may be acquired. The concept of collaboration is closely related to the concepts of coordination, cooperation, and integration. According to Pinto (1993, p. 1286), the "(...) lowest common denominator which integrates the four concepts is joint behavior toward some goal of common interest." The notion of social collaboration specifies the *nature* of the relationship between individuals working together to accomplish a specific task. In application development and maintenance, *social collaboration* refers to the extent to which the work within an IS function requires close interpersonal relations and communication between individuals. The relationships between individuals may be classified according to the parties involved in the relationship. One important relationship is that between the IS workers and the users/clients of the IS services. The other class of relationships is that within the group of IS workers, e.g., programmers, analysts, designers. For both types of relationships two measures have been worded in accordance to the definition of social collaboration (see Table 3-4).

The relationships between the four first-order variables and the second-order factor "human asset specificity" are modelled in the *formative* mode. That is, together they form the specificity of human assets.

Measurement Difficulty. Drawing on work in the marketing field (Anderson and Weitz, 1986; Heide and John, 1990) and prior empirical studies on IS outsourcing (Dibbern and Heinzl, 2001; 2002; Poppo and Zenger, 1998), this variable measures the difficulty in evaluating and determining the performance of those that do the work within an IS function. Three items have been worded accordingly.

Environmental Uncertainty. In general, environmental uncertainty refers to unanticipated and unpredictable changes in the circumstances surrounding an exchange (Noordewier, et al., 1990, p. 82). From the IS perspective, two types of environmental uncertainty may be distinguished. On the one hand, it refers to changes in the external environment of the entire organization. These changes are especially represented by technological changes. On the other hand, they refer to business driven changes within the organization.

Table 3-4: Measures of Contextual Variables (Page 1 from 2)

Item #	Constructs, Definitions and Indicators
Specificity of Business Knowledge (SpecBus) *"The specificity of business knowledge refers to the extent to which performing an IS function requires unique knowledge about the work processes in the business units which are to be supported and reflected by an organizations's application software."*	
Spec1	(...) it requires good understanding of business processes that are unique to your organization.
Spec2	(...) it requires knowledge about the special requirements of the business units of your organization.
Specificity of Software Knowledge (SpecTec) *"Specificity of software knowledge refers to the extent to which performing an IS function requires knowledge about the software applications, e.g., its structure, functionality, underlying operational procedure and use, that is unique by being especially tailored to the requirements of the user organization."*	
Spec4	(...) it requires detailed knowledge of software systems developed specifically for your organization.
Spec5	(...) it requires software technical knowledge unique only to your organization.
Social Collaboration between IS Workers and Users/Client (SoNet-IS-Us) *"Socializing collaboration between IS users and clients is defined as the extent to which the work within an IS function requires close interpersonal relations and communication between both groups."*	
SoNet1	(...) it is important to have strong social / interpersonal working relationships between IS workers and user/clients of the system.
SoNet3	(...) it is Important to have strong collegial / collaborative relationships (...).

Table 3-4: Measures of Contextual Variables (Page 2 from 2)

Item #	Constructs, Definitions and Indicators
	Social Collaboration between IS Workers (SoNet-IS) *"Socializing collaboration within the group of IS workers is defined as the extent to which the work within an IS function requires close interpersonal relations and communication between IS workers."*
SoNet2	(...) it is important to have strong social / interpersonal working relationships within the group of IS workers (...).
SoNet4	(...) it is important to have strong collegial / collaborative relationships (...).
	Worker Measurement Difficulty (Meas) *"Measurement difficulty is the extent to which it is difficult to evaluate and determine the performance of those who do the work to complete the tasks within an IS function."*
Meas1	(...) it is difficult to measure their individual contribution to its outcome.
Meas2	(...) we are unable to accurately evaluate their individual input-output relation.
Meas3	(...) it is difficult to keep accurate records related to their performance.
	Environmental Technology Driven Uncertainty (EnvUnc) *"Technology driven uncertainty is the extent to which the required technical skill sets for the completion of tasks within an IS function constantly change due to the technological environment."*
Uncert1	(...) necessary skills constantly change due to the environmental dynamics in technology.
Uncert2	(...) necessary skills require a process of constant learning and adaptation in response to the environmental dynamics in technology.
	Business Driven Uncertainty (BusUnc) *"Business driven uncertainty is the extent to which the required business skill sets for the completion of tasks within an IS function constantly change."*
Uncert3	(...) necessary skills constantly change due to the dynamics in the work and business processes of our organization.
Uncert4	(...) necessary skills require a process of constant learning and adaptation in response to the dynamics in the work and business processes of our organization.
	Variations in Work Load (WorkLoad) *"Variations in work load refers to the frequency with which the amount of work involved in performing a particular IS function changes."*
WoLoad1	The work load involved for this particular IS function tends to constantly change.
WoLoad2	The amount of work associated with this particular IS function varies significantly.

In providing an IS function, it is necessary to adapt to both types of changes. In the literature, the primary focus has been on the frequency of technological change, which increases the difficulty in forecasting future trends and requirements as well as the speed with which the current technology becomes obsolescent (Ang and Cummings, 1997; Dickson and Weaver, 1997; Heide and John, 1990; Nam, et al., 1996; Walker and Weber, 1984; Walker and Weber, 1987). Implicitly, it is assumed that these changes in the environment will affect the way of performing organizational tasks. In providing an organization's IS function, however, it is less the change in technology per se, but more the constantly changing skill sets about the technology that reflect increases in the uncertainty surrounding the completion of an IS function. The notion of changes in skill sets has been recognized in the study from Poppo and Zenger (1998) by one of two items measuring technological uncertainty in the IS outsourcing context. Accordingly, *technology driven uncertainty* is defined as the extent to which the required skill sets for the completion of tasks within an IS function constantly change due to dynamics in the technological environment. Likewise, *business driven uncertainty* is the extent to which the business skill sets required for the completion of tasks within an IS function constantly change. Both variables are measured with two items that are worded accordingly.

Variations in Work Load. Another type of uncertainty refers to variations in work load. This variable is related to the notion of frequency of transactions (Williamson, 1975; 1985) and volume unpredictability. The latter refers to the inability to forecast in an accurate fashion the demands for a particular exchange object (Heide and John, 1990; Heide and Stump, 1995; Walker and Weber, 1984). Drawing on theses conceptualizations, variation in work load is the extent to which the amount of work involved in performing a particular IS function changes frequently. Two items have been developed to measure this variable.

3.3 Data Collection

This study involves a cross-sectional field study via a questionnaire-based mail survey. A questionnaire was developed and administered to companies in the USA and Germany in order to test the previously developed model on IS sourcing. The actual measurement instrument for the survey has already been introduced in the previous section. In the following, background information will be provided on (1) the design of the questionnaire, (2) the sample selection, and (3) the mailing procedure. Moreover, the (4) survey response, that resulted from these procedures, will be described.

(1) Questionnaire Design. In designing the questionnaire, two partially opposing objectives had to be brought in line. On the one hand, the questionnaire had to match the theoretical objectives of the study. On the other hand, it had to be assured that the questionnaire is respondent-friendly, which is critical for achieving a high response rate (Dillman, 1978; 2000).

One of the preconditions to achieve both objectives is the researcher's familiarity with the survey method, as well as with the language and the main concepts used in practice. Therefore, *two pre-studies* on the determinants of IS outsourcing have been conducted.

In the first pre-study a preliminary model on the determinants of IS outsourcing was tested. This model included concepts from transaction cost theory, resource-based theory, and power theory. It was tested via a questionnaire-based mail survey in Germany (Dibbern and Heinzl, 2001; 2002). The findings of this quantitative study motivated the reevaluation and potential extension of the model. For this purpose, an alternative research method was chosen. Face-to-face interviews with 20 IS executives and managers in 11 German organizations – belonging to the same industry as those included in the previous quantitative study – were conducted. The interviews and the subsequent analysis of the qualitative data enabled the critical reflection of the initial theoretical framework and the discovery of a number of hidden relationships (Sieber, 1973). Moreover, they enhanced the researcher's understanding of outsourcing decision practices and provided a more immediate assessment of the practical relevance of the theoretical constructs. Part of the results are documented in Dibbern et. al (2003b).

The combination of the quantitative and qualitative pre-studies, together with a reexamination of the relevant literature, provided the basis for the development of the theoretical framework on IS sourcing, developed in this research project. Moreover, it helped the researcher to operationalize the constructs of the theoretical framework and to elaborate a first version of the measurement instrument in German language.

This preliminary version was reviewed by a faculty member and researcher from the University of Bayreuth in Germany, conversant with both the topic of IS outsourcing and the research design. The resulting revised version was then translated into English by the researcher, and worked over face-to face with a faculty member and researcher at the University of Houston, Texas, who is a native American and experienced in the design of questionnaire surveys. The research model and each of its measures were discussed intensively and reworded to assure that the German meaning of the items is appropriately reflected by the English version. Based on this modified English version, the German wording was adjusted by the researcher. After another round of slight adjustments, based on comments from German faculty members, the German version was pretested in a face-to-face session between the researcher and a senior IS executive in Germany. Overall, the questionnaire was well understood by the IS executive. However, the test person suggested to delete a few questions that appeared to be redundant, i.e., too similar in wording, and made suggestions for the rewording of a few items. After discussions with faculty members in the US and Germany, the respective adjustments were made in both the German and the English version. The finalized German version was then translated by a native American, who works as an English lecturer in Germany. Together with the US researcher, this translation was compared with the English version elaborated earlier. No significant differences could be detected, which increased the confidence in the fit between the English and the German version. The resulting product of this recursive pre-test procedure is the finalized version of the questionnaire – available both in English and German language, as presented in Appendix C and D.

Sample Selection. In accordance with prior studies on IS outsourcing (Ang and Cummings, 1997; Apte, et al., 1997; Aubert, et al., 1996a; Barthélemy and Geyer, 2001; Poppo and Zenger, 1998; Teng, et al., 1995), the highest ranking IS executives of organizations were chosen as the target group to answer the questionnaire. In order to explore potential industry differences in IS sourcing, the sample of organizations was drawn from two opposing Industries: Machinery and Finance. Both Industries differ in their product categories. While the Machinery Industry primarily produces, i.e., manufactures, physical goods, the Finance Industry provides services. The different product categories imply different business processes, which are reflected by different IS requirements. This opens the way to explore differences in the IS sourcing behavior between both industries.

Only companies with more than 500 employees were selected. Both in the USA and in Germany, it was intended to mail the questionnaire to approximately 1000 companies distributed about equally among both Industries.

In Germany, the "Hoppenstedt" directory for company data was used to achieve the desired sample. In the Finance Industry, 406 firms initially matched the required company size of at least 500 employees. They included insurance companies, private banks, and public banks ("Sparkassen" and "Genossenschaftsbanken"), as well as related financial institutions, e.g., insurance brokers. In the Machinery Industry, the initial selection resulted in 552 companies.

In the USA, the required samples were obtained from the company directory "InfoUSA". The initial Finance sample included 676 firms, while the Machinery sample covered 591 companies. Only those SEC-codes were included in the industry samples that approximately matched the corresponding codes (NACE) in Germany. For example the SEC-code "35: Industrial and Commercial Machinery and Computer Equipment" included "357: Computer and Office Equipment", which was excluded from the list of codes.

In both countries, only the head quarters of the companies were considered. Both the German and the US directory service provided the full contact information of the companies and occasionally the names of the respective senior IS executives. To ensure that the names were correct and to obtain the missing names of the highest ranking IS executives, each company in the US and German sample was contacted by telephone. The initial idea of directly contacting the IS executives was given up, since it was impossible, in most of the cases, to speak with the senior IS managers directly. In a number of cases the secretary or other company stakeholders were not allowed to hand out the name of the IT executive. These firms were still considered in the sample. Some companies, however, did not exist any longer, or the companies were subsidiaries of other companies in the data set. This resulted in the deletion of a number of firms from the list. The final list of companies included 400 firms in the

Finance and 516 in the Machinery Industry in Germany as well as 542 Machinery Firms and 672 Financial Institutions in the US.

Mailing procedure. The initial survey package included a questionnaire[16]; a personally addressed cover letter, explaining the purpose of the study; a postage-paid business reply envelope; a postage-paid business reply postcard, used to identify the responding companies; and a small gift in form of a historical stock, that served as an incentive to fill out the questionnaire. In addition, respondents were offered an executive summary of the research results to encourage their participation. Approximately three weeks after the initial mailing, a follow-up mailing was initiated, including all companies that did not return the business reply postcard. This mail included a reminder cover letter, another copy of the questionnaire, a postage-paid business reply envelope, and a postage-paid business reply postcard. The initial and follow-up cover letters in both English and German are presented in Appendix C. The survey packages administered to US companies were mailed from the US. They were prepared in Germany, sent to the University of Houston, Texas, and then sent off from the University post office.

After another four weeks, it was attempted to personally contact the IS executives of those companies that did not return the business reply postcard. A group of students were given instructions on how to contact the desired respondents. In particular, they were instructed to ask for the reasons of non-response and to reply the purpose of the study and the importance of their participation.

Survey Response. Overall, 180 usable questionnaires were returned from the total sample of 2130 companies. This equals a response rate of 8,4%. This relatively low response rate may partly be attributed to the cross-national survey procedure. Based on her literature review, Harzing (2000, p. 244) concludes: "Cross-national mail surveys aiming at industrial population generate very low response rates. If questionnaires are not either preceded or followed by telephone contact, response rates typically vary between 6% and 16%." Although the US survey packages were sent off from the US, and follow-up phone calls conducted in both countries, differences in the response rates between Germany and the US could not be prevented. Indeed, the differences are drastic. As presented in Table 3-5, the overall response rate in the US is 3,4%, as compared to 15,1% in Germany. This may partially be attributed to the fact that the English questionnaires still contained information on their German origin. First, the cover of the questionnaire included both the University of Houston and the University of Bayreuth as survey originators. Second, for reasons of design and printing technique, the questionnaire was printed in the European A4 format.

---

16 In designing the questionnaire, one version was printed with *blue* and the other with *red* colored hatchings and headlines The blue version was used for the Finance Industry, while the red one was used for the Machinery Industry. This allowed to distinguish both Industries. Another option would have been to ask for the industry affiliation in the questionnaire. However, since non-response of particular survey questions could not be ruled out, this way of differentiating industries was not considered a "secure" option.

Table 3-5: Response from the Mail Survey

Sample		USA						Germany						All (USA and Germany)					
		Machinery		**Finance**		**All**		**Machinery**		**Finance**		**All**		**Machinery**		**Finance**		**All**	
Original Sample		**542**	100%	**672**	100%	**1214**	100%	**516**	100%	**400**	100%	**916**	100%	**1058**	100%	**1072**	100%	**2130**	100%
Non-Response (Background from Phone Calls)	Company Policy	24	4,4%	36	5,4%	60	4,9%	54	10,5%	4	1,0%	58	6,3%	78	7,4%	40	3,7%	118	5,5%
	No specific reason	90	16,6%	130	19,3%	220	18,1%	82	15,9%	234	58,5%	316	34,5%	172	16,3%	364	34,0%	536	25,2%
	No time / interest	8	1,5%	27	4,0%	35	2,9%	98	19,0%	16	4,0%	114	12,4%	106	10,0%	43	4,0%	149	7,0%
	Wanted to return	11	2,0%	4	0,6%	15	1,2%	15	2,9%	12	3,0%	27	2,9%	26	2,5%	16	1,5%	42	2,0%
	Request but no response	53	9,8%	51	7,6%	104	8,6%	16	3,1%	23	5,8%	39	4,3%	69	6,5%	74	6,9%	143	6,7%
	Could not be reached	332	61,3%	407	60,6%	739	60,9%	190	36,8%	34	8,5%	224	24,5%	522	49,3%	441	41,1%	963	45,2%
Response		**24**	4,4%	**17**	2,5%	**41**	3,4%	**62**	12,0%	**77**	19,3%	**139**	15,2%	**86**	8,1%	**94**	8,8%	**180**	8,5%

Other potential reasons for the somewhat disappointing response in the US emerged from the follow-up telephone contacts, that were primarily done to motivate people to answer the questionnaire. The phone calls were done from Germany. In many cases, the caller was directed through a line of answering machines until finally – or occasionally – being connected. As seen from Table 3-5, it was impossible in 60,9% of the non-respondent cases (even after three or four attempts) to be directed to the CIO. In the majority of these cases, it was at least possible to leave a message on the voice-mail. In 8,6% of the non-response cases, we were told – either by the CIO or her/his secretary – to send the questionnaire again. For any reason, a large number of CIOs appeared to have never received the questionnaire, although the address was correct. In 1,2% of the cases, their promise to send the questionnaire back was not kept. In 2,9% of the cases, people said that they were too busy or that the topic would not be of interest for them. In 18,1% of the non-responses, no specific reason was provided. There are, however, a number of indications, that time constraints were a very critical factor for non-response. The length and the detail of the questionnaire appeared to be problematic for many CIOs. This view is confirmed by one of the US survey respondents. He wrote us an e-mail on his participation:

> "I found the study interesting but the length of time required to complete the response was probably far too long for the average CIO unless he assigns the work to someone. In reality, any CIO or IT Director gets many requests for survey responses and most of these are probably not completed. In your case, I completed the survey because we are highly outsourced and I am on the global team managing the contract with the vendor. I wish you good results with the survey and if you ever want personal input on one of the largest global outsourcing agreements, just drop me a note." (E-mail from one of the CIO respondents in the US).

Moreover, a lot of CIOs in both Germany and the US complained about being overloaded with questionnaires from all kind of institutions and expressed their disbelief in the value that they can achieve from survey participation (for exploring reasons for non-response, see also Baruch, 1999). Similar results were obtained in the IS outsourcing mail survey by Poppo and Zenger (1998, p. 862). They achieved a response rate of 5% (152 from 3000) in the US, and noted that CIOs were receiving between three and five questionnaires per week. It is also telling, that in response to the increasing number of requests for survey participation, a few CIOs in this study asked for quite significant monetary incentives, that appear to be provided by commercial market research institutes.

The literature on survey responses is very inconsistent in evaluating the impact of the length of questionnaires on the survey response (Dillman, et al., 1993). On the one hand, the length of the questionnaire is taken as a signal for its importance (Heberlein and Baumgartner, 1978). On the other hand, it increases the respondent's cost perceptions in comparison to the expected benefits from participation. As a general rule for questionnaire length, twelve pages have been mentioned, with shorter versions leading to slightly higher response rates (Thoma and Zimmermann, 1996, p. 145). These recommendations, however, do not exclusively stem from surveys with top management. Finally, 4,9% in the US sample told us that their company policy did not allow the participation in any survey.

A similar non-response picture could be achieved in Germany. Most, obviously, however, the number of cases in which it was impossible to personally speak with the highest ranking IT executive, or at least with one of her/his lower level managers, was smaller (45,2% compared to 60,9% in the US).

3.4 Sample Characteristics

Before starting to test the model on IS sourcing across countries, industries, and IS functions, it is worth to present a number of statistics that describe the average characteristics of the respondent organizations. A few of these descriptive items are part of the model on IS sourcing. Most of them, however, were added to the questionnaire. Together, they provide more detailed information on the (1) demographics of the respondents, (2) the outsourcing practices of the respondents, (3) the importance that the respondents attribute to the main decision factors considered in the model of IS sourcing, and (4) more detailed information on two of the variables of the model: transaction costs and trustworthiness of in-house versus outsourced IS workers.

These descriptives will be provided in a differentiated manner, distinguishing between countries (USA versus Germany), industries (Machinery versus Finance) and two IS functions (Application Development versus Maintenance). An overview of the sub-samples and their respective sample sizes is presented in Figure 3-3. When comparing countries with each other, differences between industries and IS functions are ignored, when comparing industries, the specific country and functional characteristics are neglected, and when comparing both IS functions with each other, industry and country differences reside to the background. It should also be noted that not all individual respondents answered all the questions for descriptive purpose. Therefore, the actual number of responses for particular survey items occasionally deviates from the responses as presented in Figure 3-3.

Moreover, it needs to be taken into consideration that due to the low sample size – in particular in the US – the descriptives may not be representative for a larger population. The main purpose of their presentation is to give the reader background information on the sample, that will be used for model testing subsequently.

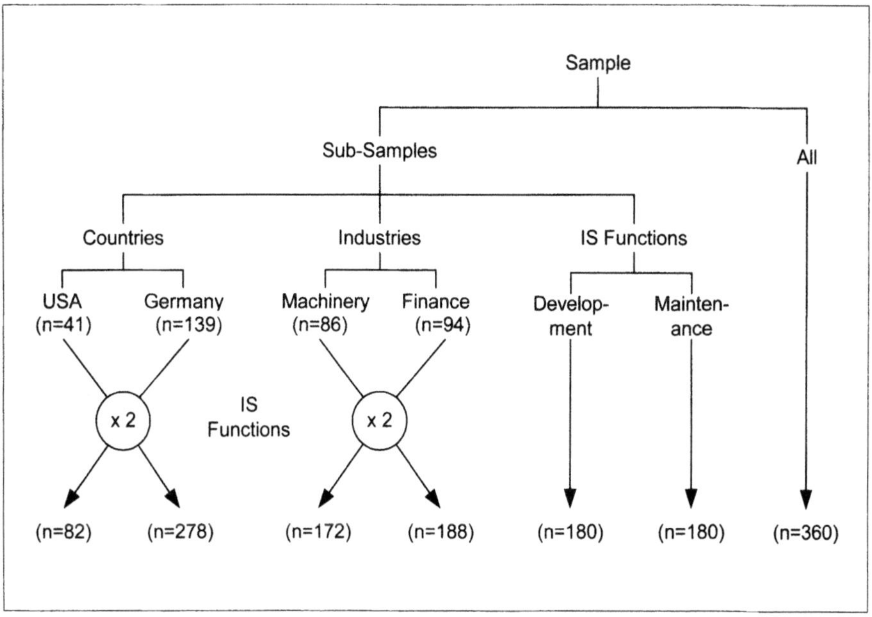

Figure 3-3: Grouping of Sample into Sub-Samples

(1) Demographics. Overall, the CIOs that answered the questionnaire had more than 10 years working experience with their company. Notably, the German respondents have stayed longer with their company than those of the US sample (see Table 3-6). In this realm, it may be noted that in both the US and the German sample about 90% of the respondents returned the postage-paid business reply postcard. All of them requested the executive summary. About 95% of the names of the respondents on the postcard matched the original addressees. This, together with our personal telephone contacts with many CIOs, increases the confidence that the questionnaires where actually answered by the target CIO group.

On average, the organizations in the Machinery Industry are about 50% larger in terms of the number of employees than those in the Finance Industry – both in the US and the German sample. Moreover, the US organizations are about 50% larger than those in the German sample regarding the number of employees. In both the US and in Germany, the Finance Industry is spending more than twice as much money and human resources on IS – relative to the size of the entire organization – than the Machinery Industry. More detailed demographic information is presented in Table 3-6.

Table 3-6: Respondent Demographic Information

Demographics		USA				Germany				USA and Germany			
		Machinery		Finance		Machinery		Finance		Machinery		Finance	
		n	Mean	n	Mean	n	Mean	n	Mean	n	Mean	n	Mean
CIO Company Membership (in Years)		24	9,8	15	11,5	61	13,6	74	17,8	85	12,5	89	16,7
Number of Employees in	Entire Organization	22	5119,1	16	2953,5	58	3474,6	67	1951,7	80	3926,8	83	2144,8
	Entire IS Function	24	226,5	16	259,9	61	51,9	73	118,0	85	101,2	89	143,5
	Applications Development	23	178,7	16	65,8	59	16,4	73	38,5	82	61,9	89	43,4
	Applications Maintenance	23	51,5	16	42,8	59	13,1	72	39,2	82	23,9	88	39,9
No. of IS Employees as Percentage from Entire Organization		21	1,7%	15	9,7%	58	1,5%	66	6,1%	79	1,5%	81	6,8%
IS Budget as Percentage from Total Sales (Machinery), i.e. Assets (Finance)		24	2,4%	13	5,1%	56	2,1%	48	6,6%	80	2,2%	61	5,4%
Total Sales, i.e. Assets of Organization (in Mio. EUR)		22	806,1	13	1595,5	55	483,5	56	6417,3	77	575,7	69	5508,8

(2) Outsourcing Practices. In both the Machinery and the Finance Industry, the US is spending less resources on the outsourcing of application development and maintenance than Germany (see Table 3-7). Overall, the degree of outsourcing is surprisingly low in the US sample. In a previous cross-cultural survey by Apte et al. (1997), including 48 US organizations, the average percentage spent on outsourcing was 33,3% in software development and 14,6% in software maintenance. On the other hand, the average degree of outsourcing is relatively large in Germany. In a previous cross-cultural survey by Barthélemy and Geyer (2001), including 99 German companies, the average degree of outsourcing application development was 20,9%. By comparison, the average percentage of the IS budget spent on the outsourcing of the development of software applications is about twice as high in this study (41,6% – see Table 3-8, 2nd column).

In particular, in the Finance Industry in Germany, the degree of outsourcing both functions is relatively high (see Table 3-7). This phenomenon may partly be attributed to institutional characteristics of the German sample. From the Finance sample in Germany, 43% of the respondents are so called "Sparkassen" (20% are private banks, 35% insurance institutions, and 2% other public banks). These special financial institutes make up the majority of the Banking Industry in Germany. They serve the public welfare ("gemeinnützige Kreditinsitute"), and most of them are public law ("öffentlich-rechtlich") institutions (Grill and Perczynski, 1992). Their common institutional frame has enhanced collaboration and facilities sharing among them. Within each federal state in Germany, associated data centers ("Verbundrechenzentren") – usually called "Sparkassen Informatik" – have emerged. They provide

IS services for the associated "Sparkassen". Each "Sparkasse" can choose whether to make use of these associated institutions or not. The "Sparkassen Informatik" organizations have specialized on the IS/IT requirements of "Sparkassen", and appear to be an attractive alternative to the internal provision of IS services or to other external IS/IT vendors.

Table 3-7: Sourcing Behavior in Different Industries within Countries

Variable		USA				Germany			
		Machinery		Finance		Machinery		Finance	
		n	Mean	n	Mean	n	Mean	n	Mean
Current Budget Spent on Outsourcing	Development	24	17,5%	17	18,6%	62	30,4%	77	50,6%
	Maintenance	24	18,5%	17	15,8%	62	28,9%	77	46,6%
Person Working Days Allocated to External Vendor	Development	24	16,2%	17	16,3%	55	28,9%	72	47,5%
	Maintenance	24	14,5%	17	13,8%	53	26,1%	72	42,8%
No. of People Working for External Vendor	Development	24	19,7%	17	15,1%	57	27,1%	72	47,7%
	Maintenance	24	17,3%	17	14,5%	57	29,6%	72	45,2%
Ideal Expenditure for Outsourcing	Development	24	26,9%	17	24,2%	59	34,2%	67	50,2%
	Maintenance	23	16,6%	17	27,1%	58	39,4%	67	49,6%
Expected Change in Outsourcing Expenditure (in 1 Year)	Development	24	7,9%	17	-0,3%	56	-0,7%	71	3,9%
	Maintenance	21	1,4%	15	4,3%	54	4,1%	71	6,3%
No. of Employees Transferred to External Vendor	Development	23	10,0%	16	3,6%	58	4,7%	69	9,0%
	Maintenance	22	6,4%	16	6,6%	57	3,1%	69	9,5%
Capital Share in External Vendor	Development	17	15,7%	14	6,4%	50	6,8%	59	14,0%
	Maintenance	17	14,6%	14	4,9%	50	6,9%	59	14,3%
No. of Contracts in Last 5 Years		24	8,5	17	14,6	61	6,2	71	13,3
No. of Decisions Against Outsourcing in Last 5 Years		24	1,9	17	2,4	59	5,2	70	0,1

The collaboration between the "Sparkassen" could also explain the higher amount of capital sharing with external vendors in the German Finance Industry compared to the US sample. Somewhat surprising is the relatively high amount of capital shares in the US Machinery Industry. Although this phenomenon could again be attributed to the small sample size in the US, capital shares in external vendors do not appear to be a special feature of German organizations any longer, as shown by Heinzl (1993a) in the early 90s (see Table 3-8).

Another exception of the German Finance Industry is the marginal level of decisions against outsourcing within the last five years (see Table 3-7). Obviously, nearly every sourcing decision resulted in an outsourcing contract since, on average, 13 contracts have been completed within the last 5 years, but nearly no decisions (0,1) been made against outsourcing. By contrast, the Machinery Industry in Germany shows the highest level of decisions against outsourcing. Relatively low, across all subsamples, is the percentage of former in-house employees working for the client's vendor(s) in case of outsourcing. On average, less than 10% of the vendor staff, working for the client organization, stems from the respective client. This indicates that in-house employees either resist to be employed by an external vendor, or they are transferred to the vendor, but are assigned to other customer accounts either immediately or after a transitional period.

Table 3-8: Sourcing Behavior in Different Industries and Countries

Variable		USA versus Germany				USA and Germany			
		USA		Germany		Machinery		Finance	
		n	Mean	n	Mean	n	Mean	n	Mean
Current Budget Spent on Outsourcing	Development	41	18,0%	139	41,6%	86	26,8%	94	44,8%
	Maintenance	41	17,4%	139	38,7%	86	26,0%	94	41,1%
Person Working Days Allocated to External Vendor	Development	41	16,2%	127	39,5%	79	25,0%	89	41,6%
	Maintenance	41	14,2%	125	35,7%	77	22,5%	89	37,3%
No. of People Working for External Vendor	Development	41	17,8%	129	38,6%	81	24,9%	89	41,4%
	Maintenance	41	16,1%	129	38,3%	81	26,0%	89	39,3%
Ideal Expenditure for Outsourcing	Development	41	25,8%	126	42,7%	83	32,1%	84	44,9%
	Maintenance	40	21,1%	125	44,8%	81	32,9%	84	45,0%
Expected Change in Outsourcing Expenditure (in 1 Year)	Development	41	4,5%	127	1,9%	80	1,9%	88	3,1%
	Maintenance	36	2,6%	125	5,3%	75	3,3%	86	5,9%
No. of Employees Transferred to External Vendor	Development	39	7,4%	127	7,0%	81	6,2%	85	8,0%
	Maintenance	38	6,5%	126	6,6%	79	4,0%	85	9,0%
Capital Share in External Vendor	Development	31	11,5%	109	10,7%	67	9,1%	73	12,5%
	Maintenance	31	10,2%	109	10,9%	67	8,9%	73	12,5%
No. of Contracts in Last 5 Years		41	11,0	132	10,0	85	6,9	88	13,5
No. of Decisions Against Outsourcing in Last 5 Years		41	2,1	129	2,4	83	4,2	87	0,5

On average, there is no large deviation between the average current degree of outsourcing and the degree of outsourcing that the CIOs belief would be ideal for them. Moreover, the highest amount of change in the degree of outsourcing is believed to occur in the maintenance of software applications. Both across and within industries and countries, the degree of outsourcing of the maintenance of software applications is believed to increase slightly between 1,4% and 6,3% on average. The expected level of change in the outsourcing of the development of software applications ranges from +7,9% in the US to -0,7% in the German Machinery sample (see Table 3-7, 3-8). In general, these are lower growth rates in the outsourcing of application development than reported in earlier studies on IS outsourcing. For example, in a scientific survey conducted by Grover et al. (1994a, p. 41) in 1992, which included 188 US companies, the portion of the IS budget, spent on the outsourcing of the development and maintenance of applications, increased by 30% within a three years period.

(3) Importance of Decision Factors. From the variables included in the model on IS sourcing, 12 factors represent perceived comparative advantages of insourcing versus outsourcing IS functions at the organization and the worker level. From a practical point of view, these variables may be viewed as IS sourcing decision criteria. It therefore appears to be of interest to know, how the CIO respondents would rate the importance of taking each of these factors into account, when deciding upon the insourcing or outsourcing of the development and maintenance of software applications. The importance of each factor was rated on a negative-to-positive scale from "-2 = absolutely unimportant" to "+2 = absolutely important".

Overall Importance. The findings for the entire sample, including both IS functions (n= 2 x 180), are presented in Figure 3-4.

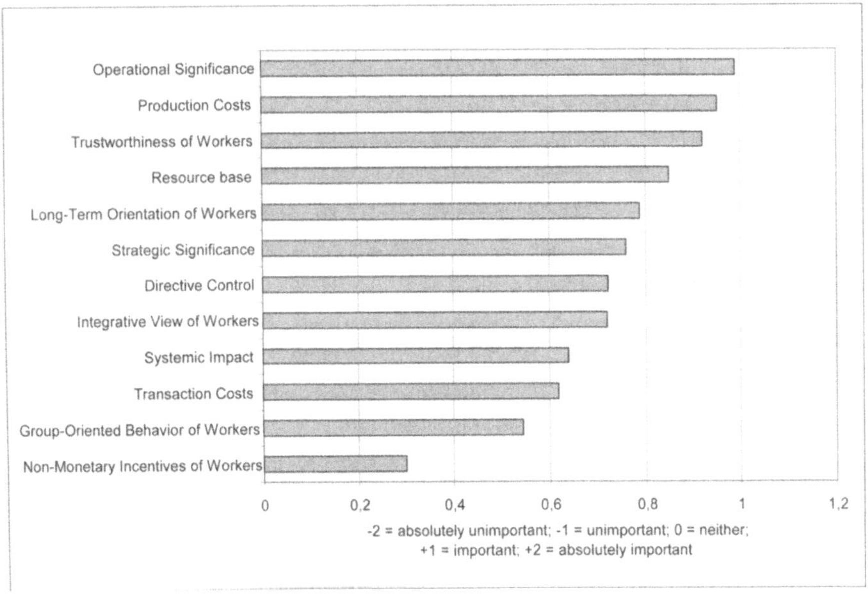

Figure 3-4: Overall Importance of Decision Factors

Overall, all of the means of the 12 factors are higher than zero. This indicates that, on average, non of them tends to be unimportant when deciding upon the sourcing of the development and maintenance of software applications. The operative significance of an IS function is rated as the most important decision criteria, followed by production costs. Interestingly, personal attributes, like the trustworthiness and the long-term orientation of IS workers, appear to be relatively important decision criteria. At the same time, however, the behavior of IS workers in work groups and their intrinsic motivation, reflected by non-monetary incentives, show the lowest level of importance.

In the following, the importance factors are broken down into three pairs of subsamples: USA versus Germany, Finance versus Machinery Industry, and Application Development versus Maintenance.

USA versus Germany. A comparison of the US with the German sample shows that the differences in the importance that CIOs attribute to the decision factors are not very large (see Figure 3-5). Most obviously, managers of the German sample especially take the operational significance of an IS function into account when evaluating and comparing alternative sourcing options. In both countries, production costs are rated as very important, compared to other factors. From the worker oriented factors, the evaluation of the long-term orientation of IS workers is taken into account more strongly in Germany than in the US.

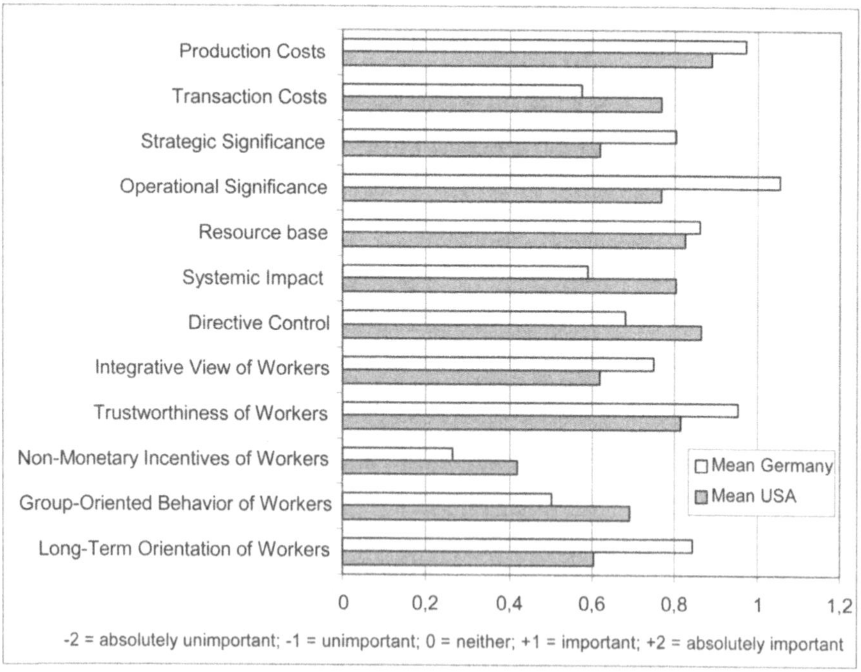

Figure 3-5: Importance of Decision Factors: USA versus Germany

Machinery versus Finance. A comparison of the industry means also shows quite a homogenous picture (see Figure 3-6). The only differences, that stand out, are those in the evaluation of the importance of the operational significance and the trustworthiness of IS workers. The development and maintenance of software applications appear to be more critical for the day-to-day business operations in the Finance than in the Machinery Industry. Paralleling this trend, the trustworthiness of IS workers plays a more important role in the Finance Industry. Interestingly, the consideration of the strategic importance of an IS function is more strongly taken into account in the Machinery than in the Finance Industry.

Machinery versus Finance. A comparison of the industry means also shows quite a homogenous picture (see Figure 3-6). The only differences, that stand out, are those in the evaluation of the importance of the operational significance and the trustworthiness of IS workers. The development and maintenance of software applications appear to be more critical for the day-to-day business operations in the Finance than in the Machinery Industry. Paralleling this trend, the trustworthiness of IS workers plays a more important role in the Finance Industry. Interestingly, the consideration of the strategic importance of an IS function is more strongly taken into account in the Machinery than in the Finance Industry.

Figure 3-6: Importance of Decision Factors: Finance versus Machinery

Development versus Maintenance. A comparison of the importance of the decision criteria, attributed to each of the two IS functions, reveals that production costs are given more emphasis when deciding upon the sourcing of the development as compared to the maintenance of software applications. In addition, the directive control over an IS function appears to be a more important factor when it comes to decide upon the right sourcing of the development as opposed to the maintenance work.

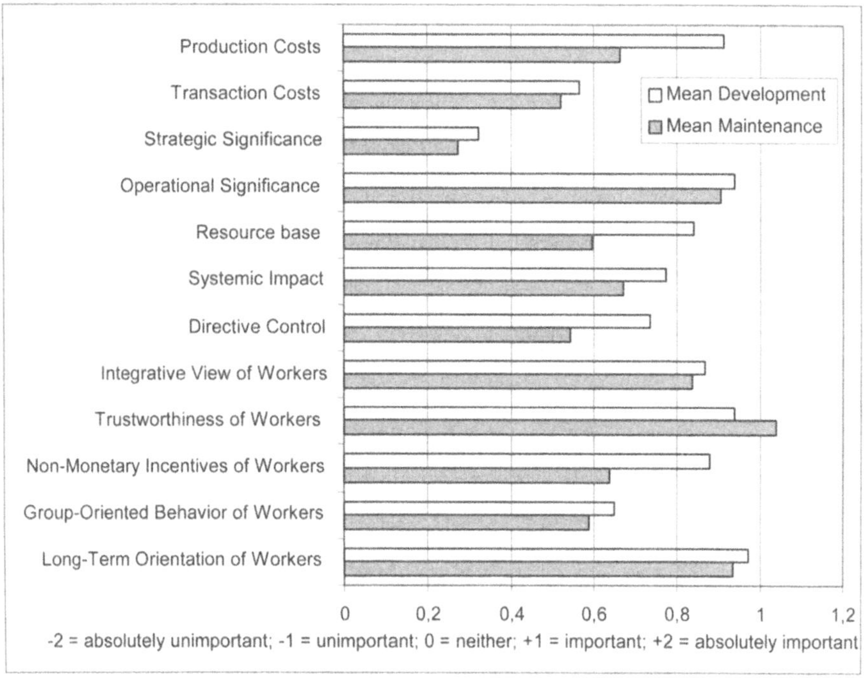

Figure 3-7: Importance of Decision Factors: Development versus Maintenance

This is not surprising, since development work usually is the more creative part of both functions and requires a higher level of involvement of various parties (Swanson and Beath, 1989). Taking an active part in the development is often more important than in the maintenance of software applications because failures in development can lead to difficulties in the maintenance work, but not necessarily vice-versa. Moreover, it is notable that the trustworthiness and long-term orientation of IS workers play an important role in evaluating the insourcing versus outsourcing of both functions. In addition, it is interesting to see that non-monetary incentives of IS workers, which showed a relatives low importance in the previous sub-samples, are rated as quite important when it comes to the sourcing of the development of software applications.

Finally, it is notable that across all of the sub-samples, transaction costs play a medium role when it comes to an IS sourcing decision, while the trustworthiness of IS workers is given a relatively high importance. As outlined in the theory part, there is a close link between transaction costs and trustworthiness. Indeed, if IS workers can be fully trusted, transaction costs are significantly lowered. IS executives, may implicitly be aware of this trade-off. Since it is generally quite difficult to anticipate and quantify transaction costs, they may place a higher emphasize on the trustworthiness of IS workers. One may even go so far as to see the trustworthiness of IS workers as a substitute decision criteria of transactions costs when it comes to evaluating alternative sourcing options. In order to more closely examine this trade-off, however, more detailed information on transaction costs and trust were collected in the survey.

(4) Transaction Costs and Trust. Transaction costs have also been referred to as "hidden costs of IT outsourcing" (Barthélemy, 2001). They appear to be underestimated in many outsourcing decisions (Lacity and Willcocks, 2003). Poppo and Lacity (2002) have found evidence for the fact that organizations that experienced outsourcing are more aware of transaction costs than unexperienced organizations.

In previous research, transaction costs have mostly been treated as market transaction costs. In-house transaction costs have largely been neglected. In order to evaluate and compare alternative sourcing arrangements based on transaction costs, however, both the level of in-house and outsourcing transaction costs needs to be considered. Table 3-9 provides an overview of both potential in-house and outsourcing transaction costs.

As suggested in the literature, five phases of transactions can generally be distinguished (Albach, 1988b, p. 1160; Picot, 1982, p. 270; Windsperger, 1983, p. 896). These are (1) the initiation, (2) the agreement, (3) the control and relationship management, (4) the adaptation, and (5) the cancellation (see Section 2.3.1.1, p. 45ff). Within each of these phases, one or more activities have been identified and assigned to both in-house and outsourcing transactions. Most of the typical outsourcing transactions are paralleled by respective in-house transactions and vice-versa. There are, however, two activities in the agreement phase that do not find an analog in an in-house setting. When outsourcing an IS function, both negotiations with the external vendor as well as agreements with employee representatives, and occasionally with unions, need to be settled (see also p. 98ff.). Moreover, internal firm resources need to be transferred to the external vendor or otherwise dissolved, if no longer needed. These activities usually do not equally occur in-house.

The approach of measuring transaction costs has been illuminated by the study from Prosser (1997, p. 154). He measured the transaction costs involved in cooperations between software producing companies in Austria as the percentage of total sales of each software company spent on the initiation and maintenance of cooperations with other software producers.

Analogically, the in-house and outsourcing transaction costs associated with performing an IS function are measured as the percentage from total costs, involved in performing the respective IS function that is attributed to either in-house or outsourcing transactions. A five-point measurement scale has been developed that includes five alternative intervals of percentages, ranging from "0 to 0,5% of total costs" to "more than 2% of total costs". In the latter option, the respondent was given the opportunity to key in the exact percentage rate (see Appendix D.1, p. 3 of the questionnaire).

Table 3-9: In-house versus Outsourcing Transaction Costs

Phases	**Outsourcing Transaction Costs**	**In-house Transaction Costs**
Initiation	Searching and selecting external service provider.	Searching and identifying appropriate employees.
Agreement	Negotiating with employee representatives and unions.	---
	Initial negotiating and creating of contract with service provider.	Defining task structures and delegating employees to tasks.
	Dissolution and transfer of firm resources (employees, hardware, software) that possibly are no longer necessary within the organization after outsourcing.	---
Control and Relationship Management	Establishing and imparting rules, principles and procedures for getting along with each other in your organization.	Establishing and imparting rules, principles and procedures for coexisting in your organization.
	Monitoring service provider performance.	Monitoring employee performance.
	Enforcing and motivating service provider performance.	Enforcing and motivating employee performance.
	Coordinating external workers (eventually multiple service providers).	Coordinating employees.
	Organizational justification and approval of prices that the service provider charges.	Justifying and accounting of costs with management and internal departments.
Adaptation	Modifying and renegotiating contracts with service provider.	Adjusting individual job descriptions and work/ departmental structures.
Cancellation	Contract cancellation.	Dissolution of employee contracts.

The findings of both the relative in-house and outsourcing transaction costs are presented in Table 3-10. The results are surprisingly consistent among all sub-samples. Independent of the industry, the country, or the IS function, the sum of the means of the *outsourcing transaction costs* ranges from 12,8% to 13,8% of total costs.

On the other side, the sum of all *in-house transaction costs* ranges from 8,4% to 9,5% of total costs. That is, consistent across all sub-samples, the transaction costs associated with the development and maintenance of software applications make up about 4% more of total costs than when kept in-house. Or, to put it differently, outsourcing transaction costs are about 31-35% higher than in-house transaction costs.

In order to control for the consistency of these differences between in-house and outsourcing transaction costs, three additional questions have been included in the survey. They directly ask for the percentage of outsourcing and in-house transaction costs from total costs and for the percentage to which both types of costs differ. The findings show that, on average, outsourcing transaction costs range from 13,7% to 19,1% of total costs, while in-house transaction costs range from 11% to 12,4% of total costs. Moreover, in-house transaction costs, on average, are between 25 to 31,9% lower than outsourcing transaction costs. This means, that outsourcing transaction costs, make up about 4% *more* of total costs than in-house transaction costs. These percentages closely correspondent with the aggregated figures calculated earlier.

Overall, these findings confirm the view that transaction costs make up quite a significant part of the overall costs involved in providing an IS function, and that in-house transaction costs are lower than those that arise from outsourcing.

In addition, the extent to which IS executives *trust* in-house and outsourced IS workers has been assessed. On the one hand, the respondents were asked to state the percentage to which they trust in-house and outsourced IS workers. On the other hand, they were asked to provide the rate of percentage to which the trustworthiness of in-house and outsourced workers differs. The findings are very consistent among all sub-samples. On average, in-house workers are trusted between 82,6% and 87,2%, while outsourced workers are trusted between 67,5% and 70%. Moreover, in-house workers are trusted about 21,8% to 29% more than external work forces.

Overall, these percentage figures signal a certain level of correspondence between in-house advantages in transaction costs and a higher level of trustworthiness of in-house workers. Further conclusions on the relationship between trust and transaction costs, however, can not be drawn based on the descriptive findings.

The hypothetical relationships between variables will be examined in the course of testing the IS sourcing model. This is taken up next.

Table 3-10: Transaction Costs and Trust in Percentages

	Variables	Industry		Country		IS Function		All
		Machinery	Finance	USA	Germany	Development	Maintenance	
Outsourcing Transaction Costs (% from Total Costs)	Searching and selecting external service provider	1,5%	1,4%	1,5%	1,4%	1,5%	1,4%	1,5%
	Negotiating with employee representatives and unions	0,5%	0,5%	0,6%	0,5%	0,5%	0,5%	0,5%
	Initial negotiating and creating of contract with service provider	1,4%	1,5%	1,1%	1,5%	1,5%	1,3%	1,4%
	Dissolution and transfer of firm resources	1,5%	2,2%	1,6%	2,0%	1,8%	2,0%	1,9%
	Modifying and renegotiating contracts with service provider	0,8%	0,9%	0,8%	0,9%	0,9%	0,8%	0,9%
	Establishing and imparting rules, principles and procedures	1,3%	1,5%	1,1%	1,5%	1,4%	1,5%	1,4%
	Monitoring service provider performance	1,9%	1,4%	1,9%	1,6%	1,7%	1,6%	1,6%
	Enforcing and motivating service provider performance	0,7%	0,8%	0,8%	0,7%	0,8%	0,7%	0,7%
	Coordinating external workers or multiple service providers	1,2%	1,1%	1,4%	1,1%	1,3%	1,0%	1,2%
	Organizational justification and approval of prices	0,7%	0,8%	1,0%	0,7%	0,8%	0,8%	0,8%
	Contract cancellation	1,5%	1,0%	2,1%	1,0%	1,2%	1,3%	1,3%
	Total	**13,0%**	**13,1%**	**13,8%**	**12,8%**	**13,4%**	**12,8%**	**13,1%**
In-house Transaction Costs (% from Total Costs)	Searching and identifying appropriate employees	1,0%	1,2%	0,9%	1,1%	1,2%	1,0%	1,1%
	Defining task structures and delegating employees to tasks	1,0%	0,9%	1,3%	0,8%	1,0%	0,9%	0,9%
	Adjusting individual job descriptions and structures	0,6%	0,8%	1,0%	0,6%	0,7%	0,6%	0,7%
	Establishing and imparting rules, principles and procedures	0,8%	0,9%	0,7%	0,9%	0,9%	0,8%	0,9%
	Monitoring employee performance	1,1%	0,9%	1,4%	0,9%	1,0%	1,0%	1,0%
	Enforcing and motivating employee performance	1,2%	1,0%	1,3%	1,0%	1,1%	1,1%	1,1%
	Coordinating employees	1,4%	1,1%	1,5%	1,1%	1,2%	1,2%	1,2%
	Justifying and accounting of costs	0,6%	0,8%	0,8%	0,7%	0,8%	0,7%	0,8%
	Dissolution of employee contracts	0,9%	1,3%	0,6%	1,3%	1,1%	1,2%	1,1%
	Total	**8,4%**	**9,0%**	**9,5%**	**8,5%**	**9,0%**	**8,5%**	**8,7%**
Overall TC	Percentage of outsourcing TC from all costs	17,1%	13,7%	19,1%	14,2%	16,2%	14,5%	15,3%
	Percentage of in-house TC from all costs	11,0%	12,3%	11,6%	11,7%	12,4%	10,9%	11,7%
	Percentage to which in-house TC are lower than outsourced TC	27,4%	29,2%	33,0%	27,0%	25,0%	31,9%	28,4%
Trust	Percentage to which in-house workers are more trustworthy	21,9%	24,8%	29,0%	21,8%	22,3%	24,7%	23,5%
	Percentage of trust in in-house workers	83,4%	83,9%	87,2%	82,6%	82,8%	84,5%	83,7%
	Percentage of trust in outsourced workers	67,6%	68,9%	70,0%	67,7%	69,0%	67,5%	68,3%

3.5 Model Estimation and Evaluation

After having provided an overview of the sample characteristics, the model on IS sourcing, as developed in Chapter 2, will be tested across countries (Germany versus USA), industries (Finance versus Machinery), and IS functions (Application Development versus Maintenance). As outlined previously, the statistical method of structural equation modeling (SEM) will be utilized to analyze the data. In Section 3.5.2, the comparison of the covariance-based and the component-based SEM approach revealed that using both approaches would provide the most complete assessment of the validity of the model. There are, however, a number of limitations that suggest to only go with PLS.

First of all, the majority of the sample sizes of the country, industry, and functional sub-samples, as presented in Figure 3-3 (p. 169), fall below the minimum recommendation of 200 cases for covariance-based SEM. Second, in the course of operationalization, the measures of one construct (other resources) and one second-order construct (human asset specificity) have been specified in the formative mode. This mode is only supported by PLS. Third, the observations are not truly independent since both questions on the development and on the maintenance of software applications were answered by the same person. Fourth, the model as presented in Figure 2-13 (p. 133) is a complex model and is untested. The PLS estimation technique is more simple and faster in calculating the parameter estimates and therefore has procedural advantages over the covariance-based method. Consequently, PLS Graph version 3.0 was selected to test the model.

In the following, the results of the analysis of the *full model* will be presented. Although the parameters of the measurement and structural model were estimated and evaluated simultaneously, the results for both are presented separately.

3.5.1 Measurement Model

Two basic types of validity tests are performed in order to check whether the indicators of each construct measure what they are supposed to measure. These are the tests for convergent and discriminant validity.

- The first, *convergent validity*, "(...) is the degree to which two or more attempts to measure the same concepts are in agreement (Bagozzi, 1982, p. 468 – cited by Homburg and Giering, 1996, p. 117). A widespread synonym is the *reliability* or *internal consistency* of the measurement. Technically spoken, it is defined as the ratio of true score variance to observed score variance. The higher the percentage of the variance explained in the observed score that is attributable to the trait being measured, the higher is the reliability (Schnell, et al., 1995, p. 141). In general, it should be determined both at the individual indicator level and at a given construct level (Homburg and Baumgartner, 1985).

- *Indicator reliability* indicates the percentage of variation that is explained by the underlying factor of a given indicator, rather than by its measurement error (Peter, 1981, p. 65; Peter and Churchill, 1986, p. 4; cited by Homburg and Giering, 1996, p. 116). In the *reflective* mode of measurement, the individual item reliability can be examined by looking at the *item loadings* of each construct. As a rule of thump, the item loadings should be higher than 0,6, indicating that each measure is approximately accounting for more than 50 percent of the variance of the latent variable (Bagozzi and Yi, 1988; Chin, 1998b, p. xiii). In addition to the item loadings, PLS provides the *weights*, with which the indicators are related to a construct. In the *reflective* mode of measurement, the weights should be distributed about equally across the indicators of a given construct, indicating that each item is approximately accounting for the same amount of variance of the underlying construct. In the *formative* mode, the loadings reside to the background. Here it is suggested to focus on the weights of each indicator since they express the strength with which each indicator forms a given construct (Chin, 1998c). Moreover, the weights provide information about the predictive power of each indicator in relation to the dependent variable(s) that is (are) associated with the construct.

- *Construct reliability* indicates the consistency of the measurement of a block of indictors for a given construct. It captures the extent to which the variation in a construct is explained by the combined variation of its indicators, rather than by measurement error. Two alternative indices are (1) the *composite reliability* (CR) and (2) the *average variance extracted* (AVE). They are calculated by using the following formulas,

$$(1) \qquad CR = \frac{(\Sigma\lambda_i)^2}{(\Sigma\lambda_i)^2 + \Sigma_i \, var(\varepsilon_i)}$$

$$(2) \qquad AVE = \frac{\Sigma\lambda_i^2}{\Sigma\lambda_i^2 + \Sigma_i \, var(\varepsilon_i)}$$

where λ_i are the parameter estimates for the indicator loadings of a construct and $var(\varepsilon_i) = 1 - \lambda_i^2$ represents the measurement error (Chin, 1998c, p. 320-321). For the composite reliability, the recommended scores should be 0,6 and higher, whereas the threshold value for the average variance extracted is 0,5 (Bagozzi and Yi, 1988). For example, an AVE value that is greater than 0,5 means that at least 50% of the variance in the indicators of a construct can be accounted for (Chin, 1998c, p. 321).

- The second local fit index is the *discriminant validity*. It captures the extent to which items appear to measure the construct of interest and not relate to any other construct (Bagozzi and Phillips, 1982, p. 469; Chin, 1997, p. 354; Schnell, et al., 1995, p. 148). In PLS the discriminant validity can either be assured by examining if the AVEs are greater than the square of the correlations among the latent variable scores, or by examining the cross loadings. The latter are obtained by correlating the component scores of each latent variable with both their respective block of indicators and all other items that are included in the model (Chin, 1998c, p. 321).

Both the convergent and the discriminant validity have been assessed for each sub-sample. The loadings and weights (*item reliability*) of each indicator are presented in Table 3-11.

All the estimated parameters are significant at the 0,01 level, except for those that are marked with lower levels of significance (0,05 level: ***; 0,025 level: **; 0,1 level: *) and those that are non significant (n/s). Moving across the rows reveals that nearly all loadings are significant at the 0,01 level and above the recommended 0,7 parameter value. One exception is indicator Pc4 in the US sample. However, since the other four indicators of the construct "comparative production cost advantage" (PC) are above the threshold, the item was not deleted. The same is true for the comparative trustworthiness construct (Trust), where occasionally the loadings are slightly below 0,7.

Deletions of indicators were necessary in only two cases. First, the indicators of the construct "comparative advantages in group (collectivist) behavior" (Group) showed some inconsistencies. The items Group2 and Group3, that reflect individualist rather than collectivist behavior, showed very low or even negative loadings (in spite of recognizing their reversed coding scheme). These findings are in accordance with results from cross-cultural studies, that suggested individualism and collectivism to be different constructs rather than bipolar dimensions of the same underlying construct (e.g., Triandis, et al., 1986).

In addition, item 5 loaded relatively low and hence was deleted. It reflected the notion of face saving which has been suggested to be a separate feature of collectivism by Hui and Triandis (1986). The other four indicators were kept, although some of them are still below the threshold of 0,7. This was done in order to keep as much of the variation in the construct as possible. Overall, the reliability test of this construct increases the confidence in the rigor with which respondents answered the questionnaire. Each of the semantic differences that were outlined in the literature have shown up in the item loadings of group (collectivist) behavior. In this realm, it may also be noted that whenever indicators were removed, this occurred simultaneously for all sub-samples in order to maintain the comparability among the groups.

Table 3-11: Item Reliability (Page 1 from 2)

Variable		Country				Industry				IS Function			
		USA		Germany		Finance		Machinery		Development		Maintenance	
		Weight	Load	Weight	Load	Weight	Load	Weight	Load	Weight	Load	Weight	Load
Out	Out1	0,35	0,95	0,37	0,95	0,35	0,97	0,38	0,92	0,37	0,95	0,35	0,95
	Out2	0,35	0,98	0,36	0,92	0,35	0,97	0,35	0,90	0,34	0,93	0,37	0,95
	Out3	0,35	0,94	0,36	0,93	0,35	0,95	0,38	0,93	0,37	0,94	0,35	0,93
PC	Pc1	0,30	0,86	0,28	0,83	0,28	0,85	0,28	0,81	0,28	0,83	0,28	0,84
	Pc2	0,25	0,71	0,21	0,67	0,21	0,65	0,21	0,71	0,22	0,70	0,21	0,66
	Pc3	0,27	0,80	0,27	0,75	0,27	0,76	0,27	0,79	0,25	0,76	0,30	0,78
	Pc4	0,20	0,54	0,26	0,79	0,24	0,78	0,27	0,72	0,26	0,76	0,24	0,73
	Pc5	0,30	0,84	0,25	0,85	0,27	0,85	0,25	0,85	0,26	0,85	0,26	0,85
TC	Tc1	0,36	0,80	0,33	0,82	0,37	0,83	0,28	0,78	0,34	0,82	0,32	0,80
	Tc2	0,24	0,69	0,31	0,84	0,25	0,79	0,31	0,82	0,25	0,79	0,31	0,81
	Tc3	0,34	0,83	0,30	0,82	0,32	0,81	0,30	0,85	0,33	0,86	0,30	0,80
	Tc4	0,34	0,77	0,30	0,76	0,32	0,76	0,35	0,80	0,31	0,77	0,33	0,78
StratII	Strat2	0,34	0,93	0,39	0,93	0,35	0,94	0,38	0,92	0,38	0,93	0,35	0,93
	Strat4	0,34	0,95	0,35	0,93	0,37	0,94	0,34	0,95	0,35	0,95	0,36	0,94
	Strat6	0,37	0,95	0,33	0,94	0,33	0,95	0,35	0,95	0,33	0,94	0,36	0,95
StratI	Strat1	0,26	0,80	0,35	0,78	0,30	0,71	0,33	0,82	0,32	0,75	0,32	0,76
	Strat3	0,51	0,91	0,46	0,88	0,45	0,87	0,49	0,90	0,54	0,90	0,46	0,88
	Strat5	0,38	0,85	0,36	0,88	0,44	0,89	0,33	0,87	0,32	0,84	0,40	0,89
OperaII	Operat2	0,34	0,87	0,37	0,90	0,36	0,89	0,36	0,91	0,37	0,91	0,35	0,89
	Operat4	0,35	0,90	0,36	0,90	0,37	0,92	0,34	0,89	0,35	0,91	0,37	0,91
	Operat6	0,45	0,88	0,43	0,81	0,41	0,83	0,44	0,84	0,42	0,84	0,43	0,84
OperatI	Operat1	0,44	0,71	0,45	0,84	0,50	0,86	0,34	0,77	0,55	0,89	0,30	0,74
	Operat3	0,52	0,77	0,33	0,84	0,30	0,75	0,54	0,91	0,39	0,84	0,45	0,85
	Operat5	0,37	0,78	0,44	0,80	0,44	0,79	0,33	0,77	0,26	0,69	0,47	0,83
Intell	Res1	0,35	0,86	0,41	0,82	0,35	0,79	0,43	0,85	0,37	0,78	0,34	0,83
	Res2	0,21	0,88	0,36	0,79	0,36	0,83	0,27	0,80	0,37	0,81	0,31	0,84
	Res3	0,34	0,87	0,26	0,76	0,27	0,79	0,34	0,83	0,31	0,76	0,31	0,86
	Res6	0,25	0,88	0,25	0,70	0,28	0,75	0,19	0,74	0,25	0,71	0,25	0,80
Res-Other [Form]	Res7	0,58**	0,87	0,26 n/s	0,71	0,24 n/s	0,62	0,40 n/s	0,34	0,20 n/s	0,67	0,10 n/s	0,59
	Res8	0,51 n/s	0,81	0,74	0,94	0,70	0,90	0,73 n/s	0,78	0,73***	0,94	0,78	0,93
	Res5	0,13 n/s	0,64	0,23 n/s	0,54	0,35**	0,65	0,70*	0,81	0,29 n/s	0,65	0,34*	0,63
SysImp	Impact1	0,38	0,92	0,38	0,89	0,37	0,90	0,40	0,91	0,36	0,90	0,40	0,91
	Impact2	0,34	0,91	0,39	0,88	0,38	0,89	0,37	0,90	0,38	0,90	0,37	0,90
	Impact3	0,37	0,93	0,37	0,87	0,37	0,89	0,35	0,88	0,37	0,90	0,35	0,88
Control	DecCont1	0,46	0,85	0,79	0,97	0,79	0,97	0,58	0,92	0,71	0,94	0,66	0,95
	DecCont2	0,65	0,93	0,29	0,79	0,30	0,77	0,51	0,90	0,41	0,81	0,43	0,87
Trust	Trust1	0,42	0,84	0,22	0,65	0,12	0,60	0,46	0,82	0,20	0,67	0,23	0,67
	Trust2	0,25	0,76	0,51	0,81	0,61	0,88	0,25	0,71	0,34	0,76	0,69	0,92
	Trust3	0,50	0,91	0,56	0,81	0,49	0,82	0,53	0,84	0,67	0,92	0,32	0,69
Incent	Incen1	0,34	0,91	0,40	0,87	0,39	0,87	0,35	0,89	0,37	0,90	0,36	0,87
	Incen2	0,37	0,97	0,38	0,92	0,41	0,92	0,35	0,95	0,37	0,94	0,39	0,94
	Incen3	0,35	0,96	0,33	0,92	0,32	0,91	0,37	0,95	0,34	0,94	0,34	0,93
Group	Group1	0,40	0,62	0,52	0,80	0,46	0,75	0,49	0,78	0,47	0,76	0,51	0,78
	Group4	0,52	0,67	0,23	0,50	0,41	0,63	0,31	0,56	0,34	0,58	0,37	0,60
	Group6	0,07	0,41*	0,28	0,56	0,16	0,50	0,26	0,57	0,19	0,53	0,18	0,48
	Group7	0,53	0,72	0,43	0,75	0,45	0,70	0,42	0,75	0,46	0,75	0,43	0,70
Sys-View	EmplOri1	0,31	0,79	0,21	0,75	0,22	0,71	0,25	0,80	0,23	0,76	0,22	0,74
	EmplOri2	0,28	0,84	0,35	0,88	0,35	0,85	0,35	0,91	0,34	0,88	0,36	0,88
	EmplOri3	0,30	0,89	0,29	0,83	0,32	0,86	0,24	0,85	0,27	0,84	0,31	0,86
	EmplOri4	0,29	0,88	0,32	0,89	0,31	0,89	0,31	0,89	0,34	0,89	0,29	0,89

Table 3-11: Item Reliability (Page 2 from 2)

Variable		Country				Industry				IS Function			
		USA		Germany		Finance		Machinery		Development		Maintenance	
		Weight	Load	Weight	Load	Weight	Load	Weight	Load	Weight	Load	Weight	Load
Long-Wo	LongWo1	0,36	0,96	0,44	0,91	0,38	0,90	0,37	0,89	0,35	0,89	0,44	0,93
	LongWo2	0,36	0,98	0,43	0,89	0,47	0,92	0,25	0,87	0,37	0,91	0,43	0,92
	LongWo3	0,32	0,95	0,29	0,76	0,29	0,79	0,50	0,90	0,41	0,87	0,26	0,77
SpeBus	Spec1	0,58	0,93	0,55	0,93	0,58	0,93	0,53	0,94	0,57	0,94	0,55	0,92
	Spec2	0,51	0,91	0,52	0,93	0,51	0,91	0,53	0,94	0,50	0,92	0,54	0,92
Spec-Tec	Spec4	0,56	0,85	0,69	0,89	0,61	0,82	0,67	0,92	0,59	0,86	0,68	0,88
	Spec5	0,60	0,88	0,49	0,77	0,61	0,82	0,46	0,82	0,58	0,85	0,51	0,78
SoNet-IS-US	SoNet1	0,55	0,94	0,61	0,86	0,63	0,87	0,56	0,91	0,58	0,85	0,61	0,91
	SoNet3	0,52	0,93	0,57	0,84	0,55	0,82	0,55	0,91	0,59	0,86	0,52	0,87
SoNet IS	SoNet2	0,60	0,92	0,56	0,91	0,56	0,92	0,55	0,92	0,56	0,91	0,55	0,93
	SoNet4	0,51	0,89	0,54	0,91	0,53	0,91	0,54	0,91	0,54	0,90	0,53	0,92
2nd Order Spec-Hum	SoNet1	0,23	0,74	0,21	0,72	0,22	0,72	0,22	0,76	0,23	0,70	0,22	0,79
	SoNet2	0,24	0,77	0,24	0,79	0,25	0,79	0,23	0,80	0,28	0,81	0,21	0,80
	SoNet3	0,19	0,70	0,20	0,67	0,17	0,63	0,21	0,75	0,22	0,72	0,18	0,67
	SoNet4	0,17	0,66	0,25	0,76	0,24	0,74	0,23	0,78	0,27	0,78	0,21	0,76
	Spec1	0,21	0,72	0,19	0,66	0,20	0,65	0,16	0,65	0,14	0,51	0,19	0,70
	Spec2	0,16	0,64	0,19	0,62	0,19	0,58	0,16	0,64	0,13	0,44	0,18	0,68
	Spec4	0,13	0,49	0,15	0,47	0,16	0,44	0,13	0,54	0,14	0,43	0,15	0,53
	Spec5	0,16	0,53	0,10	0,34	0,14	0,43	0,10	0,37	0,14	0,42	0,10	0,40
Meas	Meas3	0,55	0,96	0,66	0,93	0,59	0,94	1,20	0,94	0,60	0,92	0,64	0,95
	Meas2	0,50	0,95	0,45	0,85	0,49	0,91	0,42	0,31	0,50	0,89	0,44	0,88
Env-Unc	Uncert1	0,46	0,81	0,34	0,85	0,64	0,96	0,11	0,63	0,49	0,87	0,37	0,86
	Uncert2	0,68	0,92	0,74	0,97	0,43	0,90	0,94	0,99	0,63	0,92	0,71	0,96
Bus-Unc	Uncert3	0,53	0,90	0,35	0,88	0,05	0,78	0,66	0,95	0,50	0,89	0,03	0,77
	Uncert4	0,57	0,92	0,71	0,97	0,96	0,99	0,42	0,88	0,60	0,93	0,98	0,99
Wo-Load	WoLoad1	0,75	0,98	0,23	0,85	0,07	0,70	0,65	0,97	0,31	0,88	0,89	0,99
	WoLoad2	0,32	0,85	0,81	0,99	1,05	0,99	0,40	0,91	0,75	0,98	0,14	0,81
Owner	Propert3	1,00	1,00	1,00	1,00	1,00	1,00	1,00	1,00	1,00	1,00	1,00	1,00
Atti-tude	Attitud2	0,23	0,90	0,25	0,87	0,25	0,88	0,25	0,90	0,25	0,89	0,24	0,89
	Attitud3	0,23	0,88	0,23	0,88	0,22	0,88	0,23	0,88	0,22	0,86	0,23	0,89
	Attitud5	0,21	0,92	0,24	0,88	0,24	0,87	0,23	0,92	0,23	0,88	0,23	0,91
	Attitud6	0,22	0,95	0,24	0,86	0,24	0,87	0,22	0,90	0,24	0,89	0,22	0,89
	Attitud7	0,21	0,92	0,20	0,84	0,21	0,87	0,20	0,86	0,20	0,87	0,21	0,86
Beha-Contr	CoPro1	0,33	0,87	0,40	0,90	0,36	0,87	0,32	0,89	0,35	0,88	0,40	0,90
	CoPro2	0,34	0,94	0,30	0,89	0,30	0,91	0,30	0,89	0,27	0,89	0,36	0,92
	CoPro3	0,44	0,88	0,43	0,89	0,47	0,89	0,50	0,91	0,49	0,91	0,36	0,85
Sub-Norm	Other1	0,17	0,94	0,19	0,91	0,18	0,93	0,20	0,92	0,19	0,92	0,18	0,93
	Other2	0,17	0,93	0,18	0,92	0,18	0,93	0,18	0,92	0,18	0,92	0,18	0,93
	Other3	0,17	0,94	0,20	0,92	0,19	0,93	0,18	0,91	0,18	0,91	0,18	0,93
	Other4	0,19	0,97	0,18	0,88	0,18	0,90	0,18	0,92	0,18	0,89	0,18	0,93
	Other5	0,18	0,96	0,18	0,88	0,18	0,89	0,19	0,92	0,19	0,90	0,17	0,92
	Other6	0,19	0,89	0,18	0,89	0,19	0,90	0,18	0,88	0,18	0,88	0,18	0,91
Ideal	Ideal	1,00	1,00	1,00	1,00	1,00	1,00	1,00	1,00	1,00	1,00	1,00	1,00

The second construct that showed some instability across all sub-samples was that of "performance measurement difficulty" (Meas). Item one (Meas1) was deleted since it showed very low or even negative signs in some of the sub-samples. In the Machinery Industry sample, Meas2 is still loading below the recommended value. However, since the loadings of all other samples were reasonably high, the item was kept for reasons of consistency across the samples.

Moreover, there are two cases that deserve special mentioning. First, a closer examination of Table 3-11 reveals that the indicators of the *second-order* construct "human asset specificity" (SpecHum) show a relatively low item reliability. However, this is of no concern since this construct is an aggregate of all the first-order constructs, and it is not necessary that those repeated indicators load high on the second-order construct. Second, there is one construct that was specified in the *formative* mode of measurement. It is the construct "other resources" (Other). In the formative mode, the focus is on the weights rather than loadings. For example, the findings reveal that in the US sample, only "comparative advantages in financial resources" (Res7) significantly form the construct, whereas in Germany, "comparative advantages in technical resources" (Res8) are significant. That is, in the US, only financial resources are important potential predictors for the degree of and attitude towards outsourcing, whereas in Germany the focus is on technical resources.

A few measurement instabilities can also be observed when looking at the *construct reliability*, as presented in Table 3-12. In only one instance, the *AVE* falls below the recommended 0,7 level. This is the construct "measurement difficulty" (Meas) in the Machinery sample. Moreover, the *composite reliability* does not reach the recommended 0,5 level in two cases. First, the composite reliability of the construct "comparative advantages in group behavior" (Group) falls below the threshold across all sub-samples. Second, the construct "measurement difficulty" is again slightly off in the Machinery sample.

Finally, the *discriminant validity* of the construct items was assured by looking at the cross-loadings. In Appendix E, the cross loadings for each sub-sample are presented. Each sub-sample has its own table, resulting in six different tables – each of them with four pages. The loadings on their respective constructs are shadowed. Moving across the rows reveals that each item loads higher on its respective construct than on any other construct, implying discriminant validity in each sub-sample.[17]

[17] There is only one single exception. In the US sample Group 6 is not loading higher than items from two other constructs (Incent* and LongWo*).

Table 3-12: Construct Reliability

Variable	Country				Industry				IS Function			
	USA		Germany		Finance		Machinery		Development		Maintenance	
	AVE	CR	AVE	CR	AVE	CR	AVE	CR	AVE	CR	AVE	CR
Out	0,97	0,91	0,95	0,87	0,98	0,93	0,94	0,84	0,96	0,88	0,96	0,89
PC	0,87	0,58	0,89	0,61	0,89	0,61	0,89	0,61	0,89	0,61	0,88	0,60
TC	0,86	0,60	0,88	0,66	0,87	0,63	0,89	0,66	0,88	0,66	0,87	0,63
StratII	0,96	0,90	0,95	0,88	0,96	0,89	0,96	0,88	0,96	0,88	0,96	0,89
StratI	0,89	0,73	0,88	0,72	0,87	0,69	0,90	0,75	0,87	0,69	0,88	0,71
OperatII	0,91	0,78	0,90	0,76	0,91	0,78	0,91	0,78	0,92	0,79	0,91	0,77
OperatI	0,80	0,57	0,87	0,68	0,84	0,64	0,86	0,67	0,85	0,66	0,85	0,65
Intell	0,93	0,76	0,85	0,59	0,87	0,63	0,88	0,65	0,85	0,58	0,90	0,69
ResOther	0,82	0,61	0,78	0,56	0,78	0,54	0,70	0,46	0,80	0,58	0,77	0,54
SystImpa	0,94	0,85	0,91	0,78	0,92	0,80	0,92	0,80	0,93	0,81	0,92	0,80
Control	0,89	0,79	0,88	0,78	0,87	0,77	0,91	0,83	0,87	0,78	0,90	0,83
Trust	0,88	0,70	0,80	0,58	0,82	0,60	0,84	0,63	0,83	0,62	0,81	0,59
Incent	0,96	0,90	0,93	0,82	0,93	0,81	0,95	0,87	0,95	0,86	0,94	0,83
Group	0,70	0,38	0,75	0,44	0,74	0,43	0,76	0,45	0,76	0,44	0,74	0,42
SysView	0,91	0,72	0,90	0,70	0,90	0,69	0,92	0,74	0,91	0,72	0,91	0,71
LongWo	0,97	0,93	0,89	0,73	0,91	0,76	0,92	0,79	0,92	0,79	0,91	0,76
SpecBus	0,92	0,85	0,93	0,87	0,91	0,84	0,94	0,89	0,93	0,87	0,92	0,85
SpecTec	0,86	0,75	0,82	0,70	0,80	0,67	0,86	0,76	0,84	0,73	0,82	0,69
SoNetIS-	0,93	0,87	0,84	0,73	0,83	0,72	0,90	0,82	0,85	0,74	0,88	0,79
SocNetIS	0,90	0,82	0,91	0,83	0,91	0,84	0,91	0,84	0,90	0,82	0,92	0,86
SpecHum	0,86	0,44	0,84	0,42	0,84	0,40	0,87	0,46	0,82	0,39	0,87	0,46
Meas	0,95	0,91	0,89	0,80	0,92	0,85	0,61	0,49	0,90	0,82	0,91	0,84
EnvUnc	0,86	0,75	0,91	0,83	0,93	0,87	0,81	0,69	0,89	0,80	0,91	0,83
BusUnc	0,91	0,83	0,92	0,86	0,89	0,80	0,91	0,84	0,91	0,83	0,88	0,79
WoLoad	0,91	0,84	0,92	0,85	0,85	0,75	0,94	0,89	0,93	0,87	0,90	0,82
Attitude	0,96	0,83	0,94	0,75	0,94	0,76	0,95	0,80	0,94	0,77	0,95	0,79
BehavCon	0,93	0,81	0,92	0,80	0,92	0,79	0,93	0,81	0,92	0,80	0,92	0,79
SubNorm	0,98	0,88	0,96	0,81	0,97	0,83	0,97	0,83	0,96	0,82	0,97	0,85
Owner	1,00	1,00	1,00	1,00	1,00	1,00	1,00	1,00	1,00	1,00	1,00	1,00
Ideal	1,00	1,00	1,00	1,00	1,00	1,00	1,00	1,00	1,00	1,00	1,00	1,00

3.5.2 Structural Model

The preceding section provided confidence that the constructs are measured appropriately. The next step is to test the explanatory and predictive power of the model on IS sourcing. More specifically, the strength of the overall model and the validity of the particular hypotheses will be examined for each of the six sub-samples.

3.5.2.1 Overall Model Evaluation

First of all, the *squared multiple correlation* (R^2) of each dependent variable of the model will be examined. The R-square provides evidence about the percentage of variance that is explained by one or more independent variables (i.e. predictors) that are hypothesized to impact the respective dependent variable. The model has two central dependent variables: (1) the current degree of outsourcing and (2) the attitude towards outsourcing. It is intended to explain as much of the variance of these two variables as possible.

In covariance-based SEM it is suggested that the R^2 of the central dependent variables of a model should approximately reach values of 0,4 or higher, indicating that approximately 40% of their variation can be accounted for (Homburg and Baumgartner, 1985, p. 364). For all other dependent variables that the researcher is interested in, without being of central concern, it is suggested to take note of the R-squares, but not to consider them as critical for the predictive merit of the model (Homburg and Baumgartner, 1985, p. 364). As shown in Table 3-13, the R-squares of the current degree of outsourcing (Outs) meets the threshold value, with two exceptions. In the Machinery and the Maintenance sub-sample, the values are slightly below 0,4. By contrast, all the R-squares are reasonably high regarding the attitude towards outsourcing (Attitude). It is also interesting to note that the R^2 of the ideal degree of outsourcing is nearly as high as that of the current degree of outsourcing, although it is *only* predicted by the attitude construct.

A closer examination of Table 3-13 also reveals that the highest predictive power of the model is achieved in the US sample. Not only the R-square of the attitude towards outsourcing is higher in the US than that in Germany and in all other sub-samples, but also that of a number of other constructs, e.g., comparative in-house advantages in production costs (PCosts: R^2=0,37) and in the operative contribution of an IS function (OperatII: R^2=0,46), as well as in non-monetary incentives of IS workers (Incent: R^2=0,54).

Table 3-13: Squared Multiple Correlations of Dependent Variables

Variable		Country		Industry		IS Function	
		USA	Germany	Finance	Machinery	Development	Maintenance
		R^2	R^2	R^2	R^2	R^2	R^2
Outsourcing Behavior & Attitude	**Outs**	**0,44**	**0,40**	**0,48**	**0,38**	**0,44**	**0,37**
	Attitude	**0,75**	**0,55**	**0,62**	**0,59**	**0,62**	**0,63**
	Ideal	0,38	0,39	0,46	0,34	0,41	0,40
Comparative Advantages: (a) Organization Level	PCost	0,37	0,21	0,35	0,23	0,30	0,27
	TCost	0,25	0,20	0,23	0,19	0,22	0,12
	StrateII	0,28	0,16	0,26	0,16	0,24	0,17
	OperaII	0,46	0,15	0,24	0,24	0,22	0,23
	Intel	0,02	0,12	0,17	0,03	0,08	0,12
	SysImpac	0,17	0,10	0,15	0,16	0,15	0,14
(b) Worker Level	Trust	0,01	0,04	0,02	0,00	0,01	0,01
	Incent	0,54	0,13	0,24	0,12	0,17	0,17
Functional Characteristics	StrateI	0,09	0,16	0,16	0,21	0,08	0,21
	SpecHum (2nd order)	1,00	1,00	1,00	1,00	1,00	1,00

3.5.2.2 Hypotheses Testing

The next step is to examine the strength of the hypothesized relationships between the variables of the model on IS sourcing (see Figure 2-13, p. 133). A first impression about the strength of the relationships can be obtained by looking at the magnitude of the standardized parameter estimates between constructs. These *path coefficients* can be interpreted similar to regression coefficients. They indicate the extent to which a marginal increase in the independent variable is followed by a positive or negative variation in the dependent variable. In order to gain confidence in the robustness of the strength of the theoretical relationships, tests of significance were conducted. In accordance with the assessment of the significance of the item loadings and weights, the levels of significance of the structural paths were obtained using the bootstrap routine (see also Section 3.1.3).

With reference to the structure of the model on IS sourcing (see Figure 2-13, p. 133), three types of relationships can be distinguished. First, the strength of the *direct* impact of the predictors of the degree of outsourcing and of the attitude towards outsourcing will be assessed. Second, the hypothesized *indirect* impacts on the degree of and attitude towards outsourcing will be examined. Third, the effects of the moderators on some of the preceding relationships will be analyzed. Although, all three types of relationships were tested simultaneously, the results of the parameter estimation and evaluation are presented subsequently.

(1) Test of Direct Impacts on Outsourcing Behavior and Attitude.

An overview of the path coefficients and the respective levels of significance for the direct impacts on the IS sourcing decision is presented in Table 3-14.

The first two constructs, comparative in-house advantages in transaction costs and in productions costs, were derived from *transaction cost theory*. They were hypothesized to be negatively related to both the degree of outsourcing and the attitude towards outsourcing. Consistent across all sub-samples, no support could be found for the negative impact of in-house advantages in *transaction costs*, contradicting H2a and H2b. In the US sample, however, there is one notable exception from non significant path coefficients. Contrary to H2a, a high magnitude of perceived in-house transaction cost advantages was found to be positively rather than negatively related to the extent to which the development and maintenance of software applications is outsourced in US organizations. More encouraging are the findings for the hypothesized impacts of comparative advantages in *production costs* (H3a and H3b). They could widely be supported. Only two relationships were not significant. In the US sample and in the sample that exclusively referred to Maintenance work, no impact of comparative in-house production cost advantages on the current degree of outsourcing could be ascertained.

The next set of predictor variables includes constructs derived from *resource-based theory*. They comprise comparative advantages of insourcing as opposed to outsourcing in the strategic, operational, and systemic impact achieved from the development and maintenance of software applications, as well as comparative in-house advantages in the base of intellectual capital and other resources required to perform both IS functions. All of these independent variables are proposed to negatively impact both the extent to which a company outsources these functions and an IS executive's attitude towards outsourcing. Moreover, difficulties in measuring the performance of those that develop and maintain application software are expected to be positively related to the degree of outsourcing (H7a).

Overall, the findings from the analysis of these relationships are less consistent across the sub-samples than those from the impacts of perceived cost differences. First of all, it is obvious that H7a is supported across all sub-samples, except for the US sample. Week support could be found for the impact of the evaluation of an IS function's *strategic contribution* on the current degree of outsourcing (H10a). Only in the Finance Industry, a significant impact could be ascertained, confirming the expected directional link. All other path coefficients are insignificant or of minor magnitudes. A similar picture was obtained regarding the impact on the attitude towards outsourcing (H10b). Both in the Finance and in the Maintenance sample H10b was supported moderately. That is, as expected, comparative in-house advantages in generating a strategic advantage through an IS function, were found to decrease the attitude towards outsourcing that function in these two samples.

Table 3-14: Test of Impacts on Attitudes towards and Degree of Outsourcing

Independent Variable	Hypothesis	Dependent Variable	Country		Industry		IS Function	
			USA	Germany	Finance	Machinery	Development	Maintenance
TC	H2a (-)	Out	0,26**	-0,022	0,045	-0,083	0,034	-0,061
	H2b (-)	Attitude	0,105	0,009	0,033	-0,009	-0,011	0,034
PC	H3a (-)	Out	-0,228	-0,124*	-0,169*	-0,302****	-0,241****	-0,061
	H3b (-)	Attitude	-0,318***	-0,289****	-0,332****	-0,239****	-0,201****	-0,319****
Meas	H7a (+)	Out	0,031	0,141****	0,271****	0,128*	0,163***	0,167***
SratII	H10a (-)	Out	-0,260	-0,013*	-0,184*	0,019	-0,013	-0,084
	H10b (-)	Attitude	-0,184	-0,061	-0,127*	0,045	-0,002	-0,123*
OperatII	H12a (-)	Out	-0,286	-0,040	-0,043	-0,112	-0,102	-0,076
	H12b (-)	Attitude	0,130	0,013	0,020	-0,066	-0,104	0,099
SysImpact	H14a (-)	Out	0,135	-0,186****	0,030	-0,118	-0,156*	-0,093
	H14b (-)	Attitude	-0,038	-0,097***	0,000	-0,123*	-0,039	-0,105
Intell	H15a (-)	Out	0,163	0,038	-0,054	0,236****	0,020	0,134*
	H15b (-)	Attitude	0,004	-0,143***	-0,080	-0,142****	-0,052	-0,152***
ResOther	H16a (-)	Out	0,212	-0,053	-0,090	-0,042	-0,072	0,066
	H16b (-)	Attitude	-0,082	-0,015	-0,109*	-0,005	0,008	-0,067
Control	H24a (-)	Out	-0,107	0,029	-0,108**	0,1*	0,054	-0,024
	H24b (-)	Attitude	-0,05	-0,115***	-0,095*	-0,097*	-0,126	-0,033
SysView	H22a (-)	Out	0,234**	-0,241****	-0,186***	-0,063	-0,121	-0,23****
	H22b (-)	Attitude	-0,106	-0,007	-0,066	0,064	-0,057**	-0,027
LongWo	H23a (-)	Out	-0,021	0,048	0,118*	0,048	0,125**	0,047
	H23b (-)	Attitude	0,060	0,165****	0,134*	0,093*	0,138**	0,117*
SubNorm	H19a (+)	Out	-0,018	0,146****	0,121*	0,089	0,209****	0,051
	H19b (+)	Attitude	0,601****	0,428****	0,453****	0,48****	0,468****	0,496****
BehavContr	H20a (+)	Out	-0,119	-0,171****	-0,21****	-0,018	-0,111****	-0,139**
	H20b (+)	Attitude	0,196****	0,037	-0,001	0,169****	-0,084*	0,094*
Attitude	H18a (+)	Out	0,283	0,168***	0,085	0,237***	0,112	0,269**
	H18b (+)	Ideal	0,613****	0,623****	0,677****	0,582****	0,639****	0,636****

Moreover, the analysis revealed no support for hypotheses H12a and H12b. This is in stark contrast to the descriptive findings, where the consideration of the *operational significance* of an IS function was, on average, rated as the most important factor by IS executives when it comes to deciding upon the sourcing of the development and maintenance of software applications.

H14a and H14b could partially be supported. In particular, in the German sample, the negative impact of in-house advantages in recognizing the *systemic impact* of an

IS function on the outsourcing of the development or maintenance of software applications could be confirmed. Moreover, as expected, German organizations appear to be more inclined to recognize the systemic impact of an IS function than US companies, where no significant impact could be found. Furthermore, the findings reveal partial support for H14a in the Application Development sample and for H14b in the Machinery Industry.

Some unexpected findings emerged from the analysis of the impact of in-house advantages in the *base of intellectual capital,* required to perform an IS function, on the governance choice. Consistent with H15b, in-house advantages in intellectual capital were found to damage the attitude towards outsourcing in the Machinery Industry and in Application Maintenance. Contrary to H15a, however, there was a positive rather than negative impact on the current degree of outsourcing.

Moreover, national differences appeared to play a role, in that only the German sample showed the expected negative impact of superior in-house intellectual capital on the attitude towards outsourcing, confirming H15b. Furthermore, hardly any impact could be ascertained for the directional link between comparative advantages in *other resources* and the IS sourcing decision. Only in the Finance Industry, a minor impact on the attitude towards outsourcing could be ascertained. Looking at Table 3-11 (p. 184) reveals that from the three types of other resources, only differences in "technical equipment" and – to a lower extent – differences in the "staffing level" between the in-house and outsourced provision of the Development and Maintenance of Applications contribute to confirm this impact.

The next three comparative advantage variables were derived from the review of *cultural dimensions*. Partial support was found for the notion that the perception of loosing the *directive control* over an IS function, if outsourced to an external service provider, will damage the attitude towards outsourcing (H24b) and lead to a lower level of outsourcing (H24a). H24b could be partially confirmed in the German and in both Industry samples, whereas H24a could be ascertained only in the Industry Samples. The support for both hypotheses, however, is on a low level. Moreover, the observed national differences partially support the view that German organizations tend to be more concerned about keeping control over their IS functions.

More significant findings were found for the impact of perceived comparative in-house advantages in the *systemic view* of IS workers on the current degree of IS outsourcing (H22a). On the national group level, there is a stark difference in the direction of that link. While the findings for H22a are consistent with the proposed negative impact in the German sample, the US sample shows exactly the opposite impact: in the US, advantages in the systemic view of in-house IS workers are positively rather than negatively related to the extent to which an IS function is outsourced. The other significant path coefficients in the Finance and Maintenance sample confirm the expected directional link of H22a. Moreover, no meaningful paths could be found to validate the effect of that construct on the attitude towards outsourcing for all sub-samples (H22b).

The second culturally sensitive variable is that of comparative advantages in the *long-term orientation* of IS workers. The impacts of this construct are surprising. Contrary to H23a and H23b, the impacts of differences in the long-term orientation between in-house and outsourced IS workers on the current degree of outsourcing and the attitude towards outsourcing, were found to be positive rather than negative in all cases were significant path coefficients could be detected. Again, there are differences on the national level. While the recognition of the long-versus short term orientation of IS workers does not play a role for the IS sourcing decision in the US, it appears to be taken into consideration in Germany.

Finally, the relationships that were exclusively derived from the *theory of planned behavior* are analyzed. First, it was posited that the *opinion of others* (*subjective norm*) influences both the extent to which a particular IS function is outsourced (H19a) and the attitude towards outsourcing (H19b). The findings reveal moderate support for the first of these relationships in the German sample, in Application Development, and in the Finance Industry. By contrast, strong support across all subsamples was found for the notion that the evaluative appraisal of others will influence the attitude towards outsourcing, validating H19b. This highlights the influential role of other stakeholders in shaping an IS executive's evaluative appraisal of alternative sourcing options.

Second, the magnitude of the *perceived control* that an organization has over the outsourcing of the development and maintenance work was posited to be positively related to the current degree of outsourcing (H20a). Moreover, it is expected to influence an IS executive's attitude towards outsourcing (H20b). The findings for these relationships brought to light an interesting trade-off. Contrary to H20a, perceived behavioral control had a significant negative rather than positive impact on the current degree of outsourcing in four of the sub-samples. In other words, the lower the perceived control over outsourcing an IS function, the more it was found to be outsourced in these groups. On the other hand, in those two sub-samples (US and Machinery Industry), where no significant relationships could be detected, perceived behavioral control served as a strong predictor of the attitude towards outsourcing the development and maintenance work, validating H22b. Moreover, H22b was weakly supported in the two functional sub-samples. This again indicates differences between managerial perceptions and organizational realities.

Third, the impacts of *attitudes* towards outsourcing on the current degree and the ideal degree of outsourcing was examined. The findings show partial support for the proposed relationship between attitude and degree of outsourcing in the German sample, the Machinery Industry, and the Maintenance of Software Applications (H18a). Moreover, very strong support for all sub-samples was found for the impact of attitudes on the ideal degree of outsourcing, confirming H18b.

(2) Test of Indirect Impacts

Having examined the direct effects on the degree of and attitude towards outsourcing, the next step is to analyze the indirect impacts. These relationships seek to explain the variation in those dimensions that directly impact the sourcing decision. In particular, they help to understand why organizational level variables, like production costs or the strategic contribution of an IS function, appear to differ between the in-house and outsourced provision of IS services.

Two groups of predictor variables may be distinguished. The first group comprises *contextual* variables that characterize an organization's perceptions of the requirements and various forces that challenge the appropriate provision of an IS function. These dimensions were primarily derived from transaction cost theory, but also relate to causal agencies derived from resource-based theory. The second group includes different types of perceived comparative advantages in the personal attributes of in-house versus outsourced IS workers.

At first, the impact of the contextual variables will be examined, starting with the analysis of the effect of *human asset specificity*. This variable has been specified as a second-order construct. It is formed by four different first-order constructs, namely the specificity of business knowledge, the specificity of technological (i.e. software) knowledge, the extent of social collaboration between IS workers and user (i.e. clients), and the extent of social collaboration within the group of IS workers. Table 3-15 (1st four rows) shows that each of these first-order constructs is significantly related to the second-order factor in each of the six sub-samples. It is instructive to note, however, that the impact of the specificity of technological knowledge shows the lowest magnitude in the path coefficient, whereas the extent of social collaboration among IS workers shows the strongest link. These differences in the formative strength of the relationships should be kept in mind when looking at the impacts of human asset specificity on the dependent variables. They do not only indicate the extent to which each of the first-order constructs forms the second-order construct, but also provide information on the contribution of each of the first-order constructs to the predictive power of human asset specificity. That is, the specificity of software knowledge is less influential in explaining differences in cost-benefit differences between insourcing and outsourcing than the other three variables.

A high level of human asset specificity is proposed to indirectly influence the IS sourcing decision in five different ways. The first two effects reflect the logic of transaction cost theory. It is expected that the specificity of the human assets required to perform an IS function increases in-house advantages in both transaction costs (H1a) and production costs (H1b). The other three impacts reflect the reasoning of resource-based theory. It is hypothesized that the magnitude of human asset specificity increases in-house advantages in securing the strategic contribution of an IS function (H1c), that it escalates in-house advantages in the intellectual capital required to perform an IS function (H1e), and that it raises the likelihood that an IS function is in fact rated as a strategic asset (H1d).

Overall, solid support could be found for the notion that human asset specificity explains a significant part of the differences in the comparative advantages between insourcing and outsourcing across all sub-samples. Only in the US sample and in the Machinery sample no significant impact on differences in transaction costs could be ascertained, partially falsifying H1a. Moreover, it is has to be noted that the other path coefficients for that link are not very high and show a relatively low level of significance – except for the Finance Industry, where the impact of human asset specificity on relative advantages in transaction costs appears to be more substantial.

Table 3-15: Test of Impacts on Comparative Advantage Constructs

Independent Variable	Hypothesis	Dependent Variable	Country		Industry		IS Function	
			USA	Germany	Finance	Machinery	Development	Maintenance
SpecBus	Formative 2nd order Relations	SpecHum	0,341****	0,346****	0,353****	0,304****	0,251****	0,345****
SpecTec			0,251****	0,206****	0,24****	0,201****	0,236****	0,211****
SoNet-IS-Us			0,398****	0,349****	0,33****	0,393****	0,39****	0,349****
SoNet-IS			0,364****	0,442****	0,443****	0,413****	0,492****	0,393****
SpecHum	H1a (+)	TC	0,105	0,098*	0,208***	0,028	0,122*	0,141*
	H1b (+)	PC	0,238****	0,226****	0,294****	0,158****	0,21****	0,311****
	H1c (+)	StratII	0,186*	0,168****	0,222****	0,192****	0,212****	0,194****
	H1d (+)	StratI	0,306****	0,403****	0,397****	0,456****	0,289****	0,46****
	H1e (+)	IntelI	0,144*	0,342****	0,409****	0,187***	0,277****	0,348****
EnvUnc	H4a (+)	TC	0,328***	-0,016	0,006	0,133	0,126	-0,013
	H4b (-)	PC	0,070	-0,111**	-0,102	-0,16**	-0,041	-0,103*
BusUnc	H5a (+)	TC	-0,147	0,088	0,068	0,005	0,055	0,031
	H5a (-)	PC	-0,238*	0,041	-0,011	0,081	0,083	-0,097
WoLoad	H6a (-)	PC	-0,049	-0,111***	-0,177****	-0,013	-0,166***	0,052
Meas	H7b (+)	TC	0,122	-0,069	-0,058	-0,016	-0,047	-0,047
Trust	H8b(+)	PC	0,254****	0,157***	0,188****	0,041	0,133**	0,126**
	H8d (+)	OperatII	-0,003	0,17****	0,105*	0,060	0,02	0,029
Incent	H9b (+)	PC	0,46****	0,291****	0,313****	0,389****	0,368****	0,315****
	H9d (+)	OperatII	0,681****	0,292****	0,445****	0,502****	0,466****	0,467****
	H9e (+)	SysImpact	0,415****	0,317****	0,383****	0,401****	0,381****	0,371****
Group	H21a (+)	Trust	-0,119	0,198****	0,134**	0,001	-0,083	0,074
	H21b (+)	Incent	0,738****	0,367****	0,49****	0,339****	0,407****	0,409****

The next four contextual variables were also derived from transaction cost theory. They relate to different types of uncertainty surrounding the completion of IS tasks. First, the analysis found little empirical support for the notion that a high level of technology driven *environmental uncertainty* will increase in-house transaction cost advantages (H4a). Only in the US sample, this relationship could be confirmed. Moreover, it was proposed that a higher magnitude of environmental uncertainty will negatively effect IS managers' perceptions of in-house production cost advantages (H4b). This hypothesis was partially accepted in the German sample, the Machinery Industry, and in Application Maintenance. Second, the examination of the effects of *business uncertainty* revealed no significant positive impact on comparative in-house advantages in transaction costs, falsifying H5a. Similarly, business uncertainty hardly had an impact on production cost differences. Only in the US sample, H5b was accepted. Third, *variations in work* load were found to damage in-house production cost advantages in the German sample, the Finance Industry, and in the Development of Software Applications, validating H6 for these groups. Finally, no support could be found for the impact of *difficulties in measuring the performance* of IS workers on relative in-house advantages in transaction costs, rejecting H7b. Moreover, this finding provides clarification for the competing hypotheses associated with measurement difficulty. Rather than negatively impacting the degree of outsourcing by increasing transaction costs, there is a positive link between measurement difficulty and the degree of IS outsourcing, reflecting resource-based reasoning, as ascertained previously (H7a).

Having assessed the impact of the contextual factors, the focus shifts to the predictive power of the comparative advantage constructs at the worker level. First of all, the *trustworthiness* of in-house versus outsourced IS workers was found to be a significant predictor of comparative advantages in production costs for all sub-samples, except for the Machinery Industry. This widely supports H8b. Less consistent are the results regarding its impact on relative advantages in the operational contribution of an IS function. H8d could only be confirmed in the German sample and – to a minor extent – in the Finance Industry.

The second worker level variable is that of comparative in-house advantages in *non-monetary incentives* of IS workers. This variable is meant to reflect the intrinsic motivation of IS workers. It is proposed to increase the decision maker's belief of in-house production cost advantages (H9b), as well as the belief that the operational contribution of an IS function (H9d) and its systemic impact (H9e) would be threatened, if outsourced to an external service provider. The findings indicate relatively strong support for all three hypotheses across the sub-samples. Notably, the US sample shows the highest magnitude in the path coefficients among the groups. Especially, the perception of operational advantages in providing an IS function in-house appear to be substantially effected by the awareness of comparative in-house advantages in non-monetary incentives.

The last variable refers to comparative advantages in *group (collectivist) behavior* of in-house versus outsourced IS workers. This construct is assumed to positively impact the perception of both in-house advantages in the trustworthiness (H21a) and in the intrinsic motivation (H21b) of IS workers. In particular, in the German sample, H21a was found to be significant, validating the view that strong group behavior increases the trustworthiness of IS workers. The same link could be ascertained in the Finance Industry, whereas it was not accepted in the other sub-samples. More consistent results were found for the impact of group behavior on non-monetary incentives (H21b). In fact, H21b was strongly supported across all sub-samples, with the US sample showing an exceptionally strong relationship between both variables.

(3) Test of Moderator Effects.

Finally, there are two types of moderator effects.

- The first refers to influences on the relationship between human asset specificity and comparative in-house advantages in transaction costs and in the strategic contribution of an IS function. Three moderators are proposed to influence these two relationships. The first two are perceived comparative in-house advantages in the trustworthiness of IS workers (Trust: H8a and H8bc) and perceived advantages in non-monetary incentives of in-house as opposed to outsourced IS workers (Incent: H9a and H9c). Both are proposed to strengthen the relationship between human asset specificity and the two comparative advantage constructs. The third refers to the share of capital that a client organization has with the external vendor in case of outsourcing (ownership). Ownership is supposed to safeguard against the risks of IS outsourcing and hence decreases the impact of human asset specificity on both in-house advantages in transaction costs (H17a) and the strategic leverage of an IS function (H17b).
- The second type of interaction effects includes two moderators: the strategic impact of an IS function and its operational significance. The former is proposed to strengthen the relationship between in-house advantages in the strategic contribution of an IS function and both the current degree of outsourcing (H11a) as well as the attitude towards outsourcing (H11b). The latter, operational significance, is assumed to increase the impact of comparative advantages in operational contribution on the sourcing decision (H13a and H13b).

As introduced in Section 3.1.1 (p. 137), the moderator impacts are modelled as two-way interaction effects. That is, product terms were generated between the moderators and the independent variables of those relationships that are proposed to be influenced. The calculation of product terms requires standardized data. Instead of standardizing all the case values within each of the six sub-samples and multiplying the respective indicators with each other, the *construct scores* were used as substitutes for the data points of each block of indicators. Since the component scores produced by PLS graph version 3.0 are already available in standardized form, no extra transformations were necessary. To ensure that the scores served as reasonable substitutes for the original item values, each model was first run without the interaction effects. The output was then compared with that including the original indicators. Only very minor deviations could be found in the magnitude of the path coefficients and their respective significance levels. Having satisfied concerns regarding the use of the component scores as substitutes for the original blocks of indicators, the product terms were calculated using SPSS version 10. Then the product terms were added to the full component score model and linked to the respective dependent variables of the moderated relationships.

Table 3-16: Test of Moderator Impacts

Independent Variable	Hypothesis	Dependent Variable	Country		Industry		IS Function	
			USA	Germany	Finance	Machinery	Development	Maintenance
Trust	H8a	TC	0,125*	0,121**	0,074	0,071	0,091	0,092
Trust*SpecHum	H8a*	TC	0,006	0,011	0,118	0,173	0,084	0,032
Trust	H8c	StratII	0,154**	0,038	-0,081	0,048	-0,035	0,003
Trust*SpecHum	H8c*	StratII	0,087	-0,121	-0,154	0,104	0,185	-0,070
Incent	H9a	TC	0,362****	0,256****	0,243****	0,279****	0,272****	0,191***
Incent*SpecHum	H9a*	TC	-0,111	0,177****	0,075	0,124	0,085	0,127
Incent	H9c	StratII	0,401****	0,248****	0,372****	0,297****	0,334****	0,326****
Incent*SpecHum	H9c*	StratII	-0,223**	-0,022	-0,045	0,038	-0,006	0,013
Owner	H17a	TC	0,016	-0,143***	-0,154****	-0,040	-0,17****	-0,038
Owner*SpecHum	H17a*	TC	0,001	-0,119	0,096	-0,177	-0,032	-0,006
Owner	H17b	StratII	-0,011	-0,21****	-0,202**	-0,053	-0,229***	-0,074
Owner*SpecHum	H17b*	StratII	-0,040	-0,171	-0,186	-0,085	-0,123	-0,034
StratI	H11a	Out	0,344***	0,132**	0,104	0,189****	0,231****	0,104
StratI*StratII	H11a*	Out	0,311*	-0,009	-0,090	0,271***	-0,073	0,084
StratI	H11b	Attitude	0,053	0,103**	0,079	0,043	-0,091*	0,154***
StratI*StratII	H11b*	Attitude	0,205*	-0,009	0,008	-0,028	-0,037	0,058
OperatI	H13a	Out	-0,319**	0,043	0,006	-0,156****	-0,100	0,085
OperatI*OperatII	H13a*	Out	0,042	0,015	0,075	-0,136*	0,082	0,019
OperatI	H13b	Attitude	-0,120	-0,022	-0,035	0,009	0,019	-0,013
OperatI*OperatII	H13b*	Attitude	-0,136	0,038	-0,015	0,004	0,063	-0,027

The results of the test procedure are presented in Table 3-16. The findings revealed that the two-way interaction of trust and human asset specificity (Trust*SpecHum) was not significant, which implies that the effect of human asset specificity on comparative advantages in transaction costs and on relative advantages in the strategic contribution of an IS function is independent of the *trustworthiness* of insourced versus outsourced IS workers, rejecting H8a and H8c. However, a significant impact could be detected for the direct impact of in-house advantages in the trustworthiness of IS workers on in-house transaction cost advantages in both the US and the German Sample. Moreover, a direct impact on in-house advantages in generating strategic benefits through an IS function could be ascertained in the US sample.

Somewhat more encouraging are the findings for the moderator effect of comparative advantages in *non-monetary incentives*. This variable was found to significantly moderate the relationship between human asset specificity and in-house transaction cost advantages in Germany, indicated by a significant path coefficient of 0,177 at the 0,01 level for the impact of the product term (Incent*SpecHum). Since no significant relationship for that link could be detected in any other sub-sample, the moderating influence of advantages in the intrinsic motivation of in-house versus outsourced IS workers appears to be a special German feature. By contrast, only in the US sample, non-monetary incentives were found to moderate the relationship between human asset specificity and in-house advantages in the strategic contribution. Other than expected, however, comparative advantages in non-monetary incentives were found to decrease rather than increase the strength of that relationship. Overall, both types of moderator impacts appear to be strongly driven by national characteristics. By contrast, strong support across all sub-samples could be found for the *direct* impact of in-house advantages in non-monetary incentive of IS workers on both in-house advantages in transaction costs and in the strategic contribution of an IS function.

Furthermore, no support could be found for the moderating influence of the degree of asset *ownership* on the impact of human asset specificity (H13a,b). In this realm, it is notable, however, that the bootstrap procedure failed to calculate the standard deviations, and hence the levels of significance, for that particular link. The reason appears to be grounded in missing data. The amount of missing data for the ownership dimension was particularly high for both the US and the German sample. The relatively large number of missing values seems to damage the evaluation procedure. Therefore, the interaction effects of the ownership dimension were deleted from the model when executing the bootstrap routine for the full model. The strength and directional link for the relationship between the product term Owner*SpecHum and the constructs TC as well as StratII in the German sample as well as in the Finance Industry and in Application Development, however, gives raise for the supposition that this relationship deserves further examination. Moreover, it is interesting to see that the magnitude of the share of capital in the external vendor *decreases* both in-house advantages in transaction costs and in the strategic contribution of an IS function in the German sample, the Finance Industry, and in Application Development.

Finally, the examination of the moderator effects of the strategic and operational factors reveal some interesting findings. The moderating impact of the strategic significance of an IS function on the relationship between comparative in-house advantages in the strategic contribution of an IS function and the degree of outsourcing could partially be supported. Both in the US and in the Machinery sample the interaction effect of StratI*StratII was found to be significant, implying that organizations will only consider the strategic contribution of an IS function in the sourcing decision, if indeed the function is strategic. Furthermore, the moderating impact on the attitude towards outsourcing could only be supported in the US sample, indicated by a path coefficient of 0,205, that was significant at the 0,1 level.

Furthermore, the analysis of the direct impacts of the moderators reveals that strategically significant IS functions are more often outsourced and associated with positive attitudes towards outsourcing than non-strategic functions. Only in the Application Development sub-sample, a higher level of strategic importance of an IS function appears to be negatively related to the attitude towards outsourcing.

Finally, except for the Machinery sample, no support could be found for the moderating impacts of the operative significance of an IS function. Moreover, a direct negative impact on the degree of outsourcing was ascertained in the US and Machinery sample.

3.6 Overview

In this chapter, the mid-range theory on IS sourcing, developed in the previous chapter, was transformed into a structural equation model and tested using the Partial Least Squares (PLS) approach. To empirically test the model, information was gathered from 180 Finance and Machinery organizations in the USA and Germany. Overall, the empirical findings provided solid support for the proposed model. The explained variances for the two dependent variables are encouraging. They exceed the threshold of 40% in nearly all sub-samples. Closer examinations of the path coefficients revealed strong support for a few hypotheses across all sub-samples, while for the majority of hypotheses mixed support could be ascertained across the groups. This indicates that there is a core pattern of relationships, that explains the IS sourcing behavior of organizations, which is complemented by a set of context dependent relationships. The context is reflected by the IS function that is being examined, as well as by the industry affiliation and the country of origin of the study subjects. The interpretation of these commonalities and differences between the groups is taken up in the next chapter.

4 Discussion of Model Findings

Having presented the findings of the model testing, the next step is to interpret the findings. First, the smallest common denominator from the survey results for the six sub-samples will be extracted. This will crystallize out those findings that appear to be most generalizable for a larger population. Second, the group results will be examined more closely. In particular, differences in the IS sourcing behavior between countries (Germany versus USA), industries (Finance versus Machinery), and IS functions (Application Development versus Maintenance) will be pointed out and interpreted. Third, the major theoretical contributions will be summarized. Fourth, practical implications from the study results will be presented. Fifth, the theoretical and methodological limitations of this study will be identified and, finally, avenues for future research will be suggested.

4.1 Commonalities between Groups

When comparing the findings from the model testing across the six sub-samples, there are a number of commonalities. Moving across the rows of Table 3-14, Table 3-15, and Table 3-16, reveals that some of the path coefficients are significant for *all* of the sub-samples, while others are *consistently* non-significant. The net of hypotheses that was strongly supported for all sub-samples is illustrated in Figure 4-1. For each of these relationships, both the maximum (max) and the minimum (min) values of the path coefficients from the model testing across the six sub-samples are added to the respective paths.

First of all, the ideal degree of outsourcing was found to be strongly predicted by the *attitude towards outsourcing* in all of the groups (H18b). Following the logic of the theory of planned of behavior (TPB), the *ideal degree of outsourcing* may be viewed as a substitute of intentions at the organizational level. Similarly, Cordano and Hanson Frieze (2000, p. 634) – in a rare example of applying the TPB to explain organizational behavior (pollution reduction preferences) – replaced managers' intentions by asking for their preferences, i.e., what behavior they would like to perform. This subtle modification recognizes the fact that IS managers may not be in the position to make organizational decisions on their own. Overall, the findings appear to justify this modification. Apparently, there are some discrepancies between the optimal sourcing behavior in the eyes of the highest ranking IS executives and the actual sourcing practices of their organization.

Moreover, there are two variables that were found to influence the IS managers' attitude towards outsourcing across all sub-samples. These are perceived differences in *production costs* between insourcing and outsourcing (H3b) and the *subjective norm* (opinion of others) regarding the outsourcing of the development and maintenance of software applications (H19b). Both findings are in line with the empirical literature on IS outsourcing. Ang and Straub (1998) found comparative advantages in production costs to be a strong predictor of outsourcing in the US Banking Industry. Moreover, there are a number of other studies that support the contention that the expectation to save costs is the most common driver of IS outsourcing decisions (Apte, et al., 1997; Clark, et al., 1995; Lacity and Willcocks, 1998; McLellan, et al., 1995).

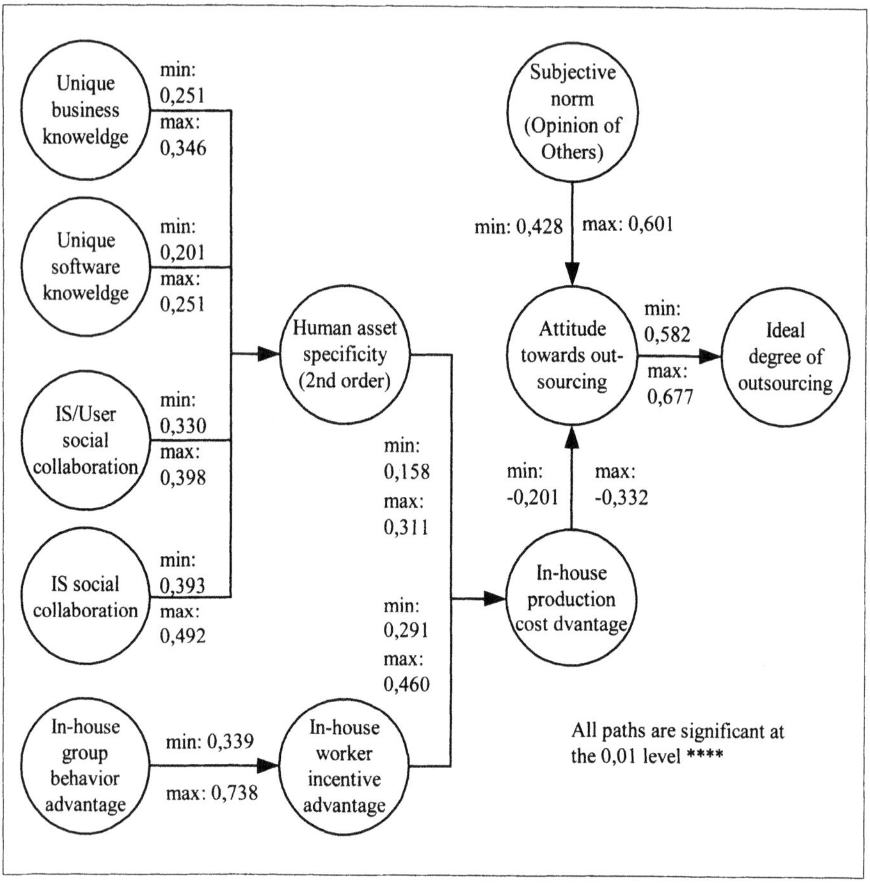

Figure 4-1: Significant Paths Coefficients in All Sub-Samples

The findings of the strong impact of the evaluative appraisal of others on an IS executive's attitude towards outsourcing support the view that IS sourcing is a participative and often political decision, where various stakeholders are involved in the process of finding the right sourcing strategy. For example, some studies report on the influential role of external consultants in the IS sourcing decision (Huber, 1993; Lacity and Hirschheim, 1993a; Lacity and Willcocks, 1997), and of different stakeholder groups within the organization – including the users, business unit managers, and senior executives (Hirschheim and Lacity, 1998; 2000). On the other hand, the strong impact of the opinion of others indicates that imitative behavior (Hu, et al.,

1997; Lacity and Hirschheim, 1993b; 1995; Loh and Venkatraman, 1992b) and the (hidden) impetus to strive for conformity (Ang and Cummings, 1997) may still play a significant role in explaining current sourcing practices.

While the deeper exploration of the influential role of others on the sourcing decision has not been the focus of this study, the sources of differences in production costs between insourcing and outsourcing have been addressed explicitly. Consistent across all sub-samples, both the specificity of the human assets required to perform an IS function and the motivational forces of in-house versus outsourced workers were found to be strong predictors of differences in production costs. When the work required to perform an IS function involves a high amount of *human asset specificity*, insourcing appears to be the more efficient governance mode (H1b). More specifically, human asset specificity was found to be significantly formed by four characteristics of the development and maintenance work. The first two are termed *attributes* of human asset specificity. They refer to the knowledge required to perform each of the IS functions. Consistent across all sub-samples, the analysis showed that knowledge about unique business processes of an organization is the more critical attribute in determining the specificity of human assets than knowledge about custom tailored application software. Second, two types of *process characteristics* contribute to explain differences in the amount of human asset specificity. The findings revealed that both social collaboration between users and IS worker as well as social collaboration within the group of IS workers strongly relate to the second-order construct and hence contribute considerably to explain cost differences between insourcing and outsourcing. In particular, when social interaction within the entire group of IS workers is essential to exchange knowledge required to develop and maintain software applications, insourcing appears to be the more cost efficient organizational arrangement.

Beside the character of the work required to perform an IS function, however, the attributes of the actual workers were found to be critical in explaining production cost differences between insourcing and outsourcing. In particular, *motivational forces* of IS workers that go beyond monetary incentives appear to be an important antecedent of cost differences (H9b). While there are various factors that can stipulate the *intrinsic motivation* of IS workers, group behavior was found to be a very strong predictor of *non-monetary incentives (*H21b). *Group behavior* expresses the extent to which workers orient their actions for the benefit of the group or collective rather than on their own or individual believes. Such a behavior is believed to stipulate good working relationships between those that are involved in developing and maintaining software applications and, hence, has a positive influence on the intrinsic motivation of IS workers.

Overall, the background information on the factors that explain production cost differences between insourcing and outsourcing contribute to better understand the production and cost function of providing IS services. In previous IS research, the notion of user participation and social interaction has been recognized as an important factor in the IS development work (Hirschheim, et al., 1991; 1996; Newman and

Robey, 1992; Nygaard, 1986; Robey and Newman, 1996). However, the direct impact of these "soft input factors" on the costs of developing and maintaining software applications, as part of an organizational IS, has rarely been explicated.

In this realm, it is notable that beside their impact on production cost differences between insourcing and outsourcing, human asset specificity and relative advantages in non-monetary also significantly contribute to explain variations in other criteria of the IS sourcing decision across *all* sub-samples. First, a higher degree of *human asset specificity* was found to significantly increase in-house advantages in the strategic contribution of an IS function and in the base of intellectual capital required to perform an IS function across all sub-samples. Moreover, it was found to be positively related to the strategic significance of an IS function in each group. Second, comparative advantages in *non-monetary incentives* were found to damage the competitiveness of IS outsourcing with regard to transaction costs, the operational contribution of an IS function, its strategic contribution, and its systemic impact.

It is important to note, however, that these other comparative advantage constructs did *neither* consistently impact the attitude towards outsourcing nor the current degree of outsourcing across *all* sub-samples. Indeed, a few of these proposed impacts were found to be insignificant in all sub-samples. A first point that is striking out, is the lack of correlation between comparative advantages in *transaction costs* and the *attitude* towards outsourcing. Other than predicted, managers were apparently not cognizant of the need to factor in transaction costs when comparing alternative sourcing arrangements for the development and maintenance of software applications. This finding may partially be explained by the hidden character of transaction costs (Barthélemy, 2001; Dibbern, et al., 2003b). Second, comparative advantages in the *operational contribution* of an IS function neither had an impact on the current degree of outsourcing, nor on the attitude towards outsourcing. These findings strongly contradict the descriptive findings, where (on average) IS executives rated the operational significance of an IS function as the most important factor to consider, when it comes to an IS sourcing decision (see Figure 3-4, p. 173). Third, comparative advantages in other resources did not appear to have an impact on the current degree of outsourcing. Moreover, neither business uncertainty nor measurement difficulty lead to the perception of in-house advantages in transaction costs. And, finally, the moderating impacts of comparative advantages in the trustworthiness of IS workers, of the ownership dimension, and of the operative significance of an IS function could not be ascertained in any of the sub-samples.

A number of these partially significant and absolutely insignificant paths will be examined more closely in the subsequent sections. They provide a more differentiated picture of the IS sourcing behavior of organizations.

4.2 Group Differences

Moving across the rows of each of the groups (country, industry, and IS function) of Table 3-14, Table 3-15, and Table 3-16 reveals a number of obvious differences in the parameter values and the levels of significance for the hypothesized relationships. These differences will be explored next.

4.2.1 Germany versus USA

In comparing the model on IS sourcing between the USA and Germany, five variables were proposed to be culturally sensitive. They are directly related to cultural dimensions that were found to differ between the USA and Germany in previous cross-cultural studies. Accordingly, their influence on other variables and relationships of the model was expected to differ between the German and the US sample (see Section 2.4.4, p. 126 f.).

Systemic impact. First of all, the findings revealed that – as expected – German and US organizations differ in the extent to which the systemic impact of an IS function influences the sourcing decision (H14a,b). While perceived in-house advantages in the systemic impact of an IS function appear to damage both the extent to which an IS function is outsourced and the attitude towards outsourcing in Germany, the relationship was found to be insignificant and even in the opposite direction in the US. Apparently, in the USA, the smooth interplay between different IS functions is not felt to be severely affected if partial IS functions are performed by different companies, whereas in Germany it matters greatly if IS workers belong to the same or to different groups. These obvious discrepancies between Germany and the US may be explained by the fact that German managers have more of an integrative view of the organization, where the firm is viewed as a *group* of related persons working together, whereas US managers appear to favor an analytical view, where the firm is viewed as a collection of tasks, functions, people, and machines, that can be changed and exchanged more flexible, without leading to severe consequences for the overall firm performance (Hampden-Turner and Trompenaars, 1993, p. 18).

Systemic View. Closely related to the different importance that German and US managers attribute to the systemic impact of an IS function are the observed discrepancies in how managers in both countries factor in variations in the systemic view of in-house versus outsourced workers when deciding upon the sourcing of the application development and maintenance work (H22a). While in Germany, a higher level of perceived advantages of in-house IS workers in considering how work in one area fits in and affects all other work throughout the organization was found to significantly decrease the extent to which an IS function is outsourced, the effect is directly the opposite in the US. Different explanations can be provided for these opposing results. First, employees that do not solely concentrate on their particular piece of work, but how their work relates to the work of others, may indeed be seen as a disadvantage in the US. This interpretation, however, would be more likely if in-house advantages in the systemic view of IS workers were also positively related to an IS executive's attitude towards outsourcing – which is not the case. Given the cross-sectional nature of this research, a second interpretation appears to be more promising. This research supports the view that organizations rarely outsource entire IS functions. In most of the cases, IS functions are partially outsourced. This means that organizations keep at least a few of their IS employees in-house. Consequently, it may further be argued that in case of outsourcing, in-house workers in the US will be given the responsibility for the coordination and integration of various distributed tasks into a coherent whole. This would mean that US firms clearly separate the roles of in-house versus outsourced workers, which is in accordance with the more analytical view of the firm in the US. Accordingly, in-house workers may be viewed as superior in having a systemic view, while at the same time the major part of the work may be carried out by external vendor staff. Such a separation of tasks into those that require an integrative view and those that do not, may not work as well in Germany. In Germany, IS workers may generally have more of an integrative view in doing their work, due to their higher tendency to behave collectivistic. Therefore, IS managers in Germany may generally value such behavior quite high and consider it as an important criteria when deciding upon the right sourcing arrangement.

Long-term Orientation. Partial support can be found for the notion that the impact of perceived comparative in-house advantages in the long-term orientation of IS workers on the attitude towards outsourcing is stronger in Germany than in the US (H23b). Indeed, only in the German sample, a significant path coefficient for that relationship could be ascertained. Surprisingly, however, that link is in the opposite direction. There is a positive rather than negative relationship between more long-term oriented in-house employees and the attitude towards outsourcing. Provided that an organization currently outsources a major part of an IS function, one potential explanation for this phenomenon could be that only few in-house IS workers need to have – or can afford to have – a long term orientation in their planning and decision making during the development and maintenance work. Most of the IS workers may be busy coping with urgent user requests. That is, even if they would wish to orient their actions more towards the future rather than the presence, business pressures may not allow them to do so. Organizations that wish to partially change this situation may think that outsourcing can overcome these problems by introducing new charging mechanisms, where users directly feel the costs for their service requests. This may enhance their esteem for long-term planning activities. On the other side, organizations that currently experience outsourcing may find outsourced workers to lack a long-term orientation. However, this interpretation would be more likely if the findings would have indicated a positive relationships between in-house advantages in worker long-term orientation and the current degree of outsourcing in Germany.

Group (collectivist) behavior. Partial support could also be found for the expected national differences in the impact of comparative in-house advantages in-group behavior. As predicted, German IS executives appear to place a higher level of confidence in those IS workers that orient their actions for the benefit of the group or collective rather than on their own or individual believes (H21a). By contrast, differences in group behavior do not affect the trustworthiness of IS workers in the US. In spite of these perceptual differences, the wider implications of differences in the trustworthiness of IS workers on other comparative advantage constructs were found to be quite similar in the US and German sample. In both countries, comparative advantages in the trustworthiness of in-house employees slightly escalated the perceived in-house advantages in transaction costs (H8a) and significantly increased the perception of in-house production cost advantages (H8b). On the other side, only in Germany, a positive impact on in-house advantages in the *operational contribution* could be ascertained (H8d), whereas only in the US, a positive impact on the *strategic contribution* could be confirmed (H8c). This means that in Germany, the focus is on the operational risks of IS outsourcing, while in the US, managers emphasize the strategic risks.

Moreover, both in the USA and in Germany, perceived comparative advantages in *non-monetary incentives* (intrinsic motivation) of in-house versus outsourced workers are relatively strong predictors of the evaluative appraisal of a number of other, more immediate decision criteria that help to determine differences in the costs and benefits of insourcing versus outsourcing. Interestingly, the impact on theses dimensions appears to be even stronger in the US than in Germany (H9a-e).

Moderator effects of non-monetary incentives. Meaningful national differences could be observed in the moderating effect of variations in the intrinsic motivation of in-house versus outsourced IS workers. In Germany, non-monetary incentives significantly *increased* the impact of human asset specificity on in-house advantages in *transaction costs (H9a*)*, while in the US sample, they significantly *decreased* the relationship between human asset specificity and in-house advantages in the *strategic contribution* of an IS function (H9c*). The first of these relationships is in accordance with the expected directional link. Moreover, the observation that this link is insignificant in the US could be explained by the fact that US workers generally appear to be more individualistic. Therefore, opportunistic behavior of some agents may generally be expected in the US, irrespective of the organizational belonging of the IS workers. This may be very different in Germany, where IS managers are more inclined to draw a strict line between those IS workers that belong to a select ingroup (e.g., an in-house IS department) and those that belong to an outgroup (e.g., external vendor staff). Therefore, the perceptual differences of the risk of opportunistic behavior between in-house and outsourced workers may be higher in Germany. Accordingly, the influential role of those factors that decrease the perception of opportunistic behavior, like the perception of non-monetary incentives of IS workers, may be stronger.

As already outlined, the second moderator effect of non-monetary incentive advantages could only be ascertained in the US (H9c*). Obviously, the strategic risks and benefits, resulting from the delegation of highly specific IS functions to external vendors, are independent of variations in the motivational forces of IS workers in Germany, whereas they appear to be significantly influenced in the US. Other than expected, however, the link between asset specificity and strategic in-house advantages in the US is weakened rather than strengthened by perceived in-house advantages in the motivation of IS workers. At the same time, however, motivational advantages of in-house IS workers were found to increase in-house advantages in generating strategic benefits through an IS function (H9c). This leads to the conclusion that motivational influences override the impact of human asset specificity on in-house advantages in the strategic contribution of an IS function. Considering that a high magnitude of human asset specificity is meant to increase the opportunistic propensity of the external vendor, US managers appear to neglect the threat of opportunism compared to the benefits that more motivated IS workers have on the strategic contribution of an IS function.

Directive Control. Furthermore, the findings partially support the view that German managers are more inclined to recognize the directive control over an IS function, when it comes to decide upon the sourcing of IS functions. While the proposed negative impact on the attitude towards outsourcing was ascertained in the German sample, no meaningful path coefficient could be detected for that relationship in the US (H24b). This supports the view that German IS managers seek to avoid uncertain situations and prefer to keep control over the direction of work.

Finally, there are a number of additional differences between Germany and the US, that are worth mentioning. First, it is obvious that *ownership* of vendor assets through capital shares decreases in-house advantages in transaction costs and lowers the strategic risks of IS outsourcing in Germany, whereas similar institutional safeguard effects cannot be observed in the US sample (H17a,b). Moreover, although the interaction effects associated with ownership were found to be insignificant in Germany, the path coefficients are in accordance with the proposed directional link, and they are encouragingly high (H17a*,b*). This, at least partially, adds to the notion of a higher propensity towards (legitimized) control in Germany as compared to the US.

Second, the moderating effect of the strategic significance of an IS function was supported in the US, while it was found to be insignificant in Germany (H11a,b). This again, adds to the notion that US organizations appear to recognize the strategic consequences of the sourcing decision more severely than German ones. As predicted, US organizations are more inclined to consider how alternative sourcing arrangements affect the strategic contribution of an IS function if indeed the IS function is strategic. If it is not strategic at all, then strategic considerations become increasingly irrelevant for the sourcing decision.

Moreover, IS functions that are critical for an organization's day-to-day business operations are less outsourced in the US, whereas no impact of the operational contribution of an IS function could be ascertained in Germany.

Finally, there is one more difference that deserves to be discussed. While *transaction costs* appear to be totally ignored in evaluating and comparing an organization's current IS sourcing arrangement in Germany, a significant relationship of the impact of in-house advantages in transaction costs on the current degree of outsourcing could be ascertained in the US (H2a). Notably, however, that impact was found to be positive rather than negative. That is, the lower the in-house transaction cost advantages, the less an IS function is being outsourced, or, in other words, high outsourcing transaction costs are positively related to the degree of outsourcing. This finding – the surprising it may appear at the first view – may be traced back to the cross-sectional nature of this research. It can not be ruled out that there is a mismatch between the perceptions about the current sourcing arrangement for an IS function and the present-day sourcing practices. Although the outsourcing of the application development and maintenance work is associated with higher transaction costs, US managers do not consider transaction costs as an important criteria when evaluating and comparing alternative sourcing options. They are either not aware of transaction cost differences between insourcing and outsourcing or simply ignore them.

Although these findings are in line with empirical studies that advocate the view that transaction costs are "hidden costs", which are mostly ignored by organizations, prior to experiencing alternative sourcing options (Barthélemy, 2001; Poppo and Lacity, 2002), these findings are in partial contradiction with those from Ang and Straub (1998) in the US Banking Industry. They found support for a negative impact of market transaction costs on the extent to which data processing facilities are outsourced. There are, however, two potential reasons for these contradictions. First, Ang and Straub did not particularly study the outsourcing of the application development and maintenance work. Second, their measure of transaction costs was not comparative in nature. That is, they only asked for the level of transaction costs with an external vendor and not for the relation between in-house and outsourcing transaction costs.

In Germany, a similar mismatch can be observed regarding the impact of *behavioral control over IS outsourcing* on the current degree of outsourcing (H20a). Other than expected, a lower level of behavioral control over the decision to outsource an IS function was associated with a higher rather than lower level of outsourcing. Interestingly, the same reversed link, albeit in a different organizational context, could also be found in the study from Cordano and Frieze Hanson (2000, p. 637). From their point of view, this finding may be explained by the limited power of managers, which hinders them to act in accordance with their beliefs. This likely leads to resignation or frustration. Moreover, these findings add to the notion that German firms are more constrained by various internal and external regulatory forces that severely limit the decision maker's ability to act in accordance with her/his personal beliefs.

4.2.2 Machinery versus Finance Industry

Before starting to look at the industry differences in the IS sourcing behavior of organizations, it is worth to outline a number of general differences in the use of IT between the Finance and the Machinery Industry.

- *IS Budget.* As outlined previously, the Finance Industry is spending significantly more money on IS (relative to firm size) than the Machinery Industry (see Table 3-6, p. 170). This phenomenon can partially be attributed to the subsequent structural differences between both industries.
- *Information Intensity.* On average, the actual work of the employees in the Finance Industry is more information intensive (Glazer, 1993; Lassig, et al., 2003). That is, a higher percentage of the actual work places requires information processing capabilities. By contrast, in the Machinery Industry, a considerable part of the actual work is still blue collar. The majority of the information processing capabilities are required in business functions like finance, accounting, marketing, procurement, as well as organization and (production) planning (Mertens, 1995). Moreover, a considerable part of the applied information technology is embedded in the production processes. These embedded systems (e.g., robot and machinery street control systems) are mostly managed by the particular production units. That is, they are not necessarily connected to an organization's overall IS.
- *Business Processes.* These differences are mainly caused by the fundamentally different work processes of both industry types. The core work processes in Finance are administrative and service oriented. They are often highly customized and show a low level of standardization. Therefore, they significantly vary from organization to organization. Such unique business processes are often reflected by unique IS. By contrast, the information intensive business processes in the Machinery Industry are more standardized.
- *Standard Software.* Due to the higher level of standardization in the business processes of the Machinery Industry (i.e. Manufacturing in general), the IT Industry has developed standard software packages that cover the basic information processing capabilities of organizations. In particular, ERP-packages more and more substitute the formerly custom developed applications.[18] This is one of the major differences from the Finance Industry, where such standard ERP-systems are still mostly absent (Chylla, 2003; Mertens and Lohmann, 2000). Most of the financial institutions develop their own applications. Only recently, there are tendencies towards selectively adopting and integrating certain standard software compo-

[18] Moreover, standard computer aided design (CAD) tools are well established. It should be kept in mind, however, that these are average tendencies. Moreover, there are still ares in which standard software is less established, e.g., in the area of product data management (PDM).

nents, e.g., particular ERP-modules, in areas that do not belong to their core business processes (Voigtländer, 2003). One exception are the so called "Sparkassen", that make up a major part of the banking landscape in Germany. They have pooled their interests by establishing so called "Sparkassen Informatik" organizations within each federal state that provide standard applications for their customers (see also p. 202f).

Due to these substantial differences in the use of IT between the Finance and the Machinery Industry, it is no surprise that the IS sourcing practices somewhat deviate between production and service oriented organizations.

Strategic and Operational Impact. First of all, IS executives in the *Finance* Industry appear to be more cognizant of the need to factor in the strategic contribution of an IS function, when deciding upon its insourcing or outsourcing. This is indicated by modest support for Hypotheses 10a and 10b. Moreover, in the Finance Industry, strategic aspects appear to be considered independent of the strength of the strategic impact of an IS function, as indicated by the insignificant moderator effects of Hypotheses 11a and 11b. By contrast, managers in the *Machinery* Industry are more inclined to consider the strategic implications of an IS function in case of outsourcing. This is indicated by a positive relationship between the strategic significance of an IS function and the degree to which it is being outsourced (H11a). At the same time, however, IS functions are less outsourced in this industry if they are especially critical for an organization's day-to day business operations (H13a). As already outlined, firms in the Machinery Industry increasingly make use of standard ERP-packages. Organizations that effectively deploy these packages can gain a strategic advantage over their competitors (Pereira, 1999). The deployment of these integrated systems, however, often requires the help of external vendors (Dibbern, et al., 2002). This may explain why Machinery organizations that see their IS functions as strategic show a higher level of outsourcing. At the same time, however, wrong specifications or misuse in one of the modules of these integrated ERP systems can severely affect the overall system and hence the business operations of the overall company (Davenport, 2000). Therefore, organizations in which the *operational* consequences of the development and maintenance work are especially high may prefer insourcing.

Intellectual Capital. One interesting trade-off can be observed in the *Machinery* Industry regarding the impact of perceived differences between insourcing and outsourcing in the intellectual capital required to perform an IS function. Consistent with H15b, perceived comparative in-house advantages in the base of knowledge resources appear to damage an IS executive's *attitude* towards outsourcing. At the same time, however, a positive rather than negative impact on the *current degree* of outsourcing can be ascertained (H15a). This phenomenon may again be explained by the increasing use of standard software applications in the Machinery Industry. Before a company can utilize an ERP package, the software must first be configured in accordance with the company's individual organizational processes and structures (Appelrath and Ritter, 2000; Krcmar, 1997; Markus and Tanis, 2000). This requires both technical knowledge about the functionality of the ERP software and knowledge about the organizational requirements. External service providers have recognized that they can realize specialization advantages in acquiring the necessary technical (i.e. software) knowledge. By contrast, the clients still have advantages in the required business knowledge (Beath and Walker, 1998; Dibbern, et al., 2002). Organizations that have outsourced major parts of the application development and maintenance work may realize that the more critical knowledge component in deploying an ERP package is the business knowledge, in which their in-house IS employees show advantages. This view is consistent with the observed significant impact of human asset specificity on in-house advantages in the intellectual capital required to perform an IS function (H1e). In this realm, it is also instructive to note that the strength of the impact of human asset specificity on in-house advantages in the base of intellectual capital is substantially lower in the Machinery Industry. This indicates that firm specific knowledge required to develop (i.e. deploy) and maintain application software is less influential in the Machinery than in the Finance Industry.

Environmental Uncertainty. Moreover, it is interesting to note that hypotheses H4b could be ascertained in the *Machinery* Industry. This indicates that in case of high environmental uncertainty – due to dynamics in the IT Industry – outsourcing is seen to be more advantageous in terms of production costs. This adds to the notion that external vendors are seen as superior in acquiring the technological knowledge that is required to develop (i.e. deploy) and maintain an organization's application software.

Work Load Variations. Instead of environmental forces, IS executives in the *Finance* Industry see internal production cost advantages to be damaged by a high variation of the work load associated with performing both functions. Obviously, they believe that outsourcing allows them to react more flexible to high deviations in the development and maintenance work. This could partially be explained by the higher diversity of the applications landscape in the Finance Industry. Heterogeneous systems are often associated with hybrid IS organizations, in which each business unit has its own custom-made information sub-system (Brown, 1997). In coping with their individual IS requirements, business units may perceive outsourcing as the more flexible governance solution. By contrast, an increasing number of organizations in the *Machinery* Industry has begun to substitute their heterogeneous systems by streamlined ERP-systems. Paralleling this movement towards a monolithic software solution, mechanical engineering organizations likely consolidate their outsourcing arrangements. Examples of such practices have been observed in the qualitative pre-study in the German Manufacturing Industry (Dibbern, et al., 2003b).

Systemic view. It is also interesting to note that perceived in-house advantages in the systemic view of IS workers were found to be negatively related to the current degree of outsourcing in the Finance Industry, whereas no significant relationship could be ascertained in the Machinery Industry. One way to interpret this difference, again, refers to the different use of standard software applications in both industries.

In the *Machinery* Industry, the increasing use of ERP-packages may have lowered the differences between in-house and outsourced workers in understanding how work in different areas effects one another. ERP standard software usually reflects the standard business processes of industries or business types (Mertens and Lohmann, 2000). These business processes reflect best practice knowledge, which can easily be acquired by external vendor staff (Beath and Walker, 1998). As soon as external workers understand the software architecture of an ERP system (i.e. how the different modules of the ERP software affect each other) and the business architecture, on which these modules are based, they are able to understand the task interdependencies of the client organization. Therefore, the systemic view capabilities of IS workers become more unified and hence less influential on the IS sourcing decision in the Machinery Industry.

Trustworthiness. Another striking difference is the way in which trustworthiness of IS workers is considered in both industries. While the extent to which in-house workers are more trustworthy than outsourced workers significantly increases in-house production cost advantages (H8b) and perceived comparative in-house advantages in the operational contribution of an IS function (H8d) in the Finance Industry, no impact could be detected in the Machinery Industry. Moreover, comparative in-house advantages in the trustworthiness of IS workers are affected by corresponding in-house advantages in the group-behavior of IS employees in the Finance Industry (H21a), whereas collectivistic behavior has no significant impact on trust in the Machinery Industry. The notion that trusted workers perform at a higher level has already been ascertained by Ang and Slaughter (1998). Obviously, the working context plays a role for this phenomenon. In the Machinery Industry a higher level of IS standardization may have lowered the uncertainty about the IS work and, hence, may have lowered the propensity towards trusted workers.

Perceived Behavioral Control. Furthermore, there are industry differences in the consequences that the perceived control over IS outsourcing has on the sourcing decision. While, consistent with Hypothesis 20b, perceived control over outsourcing an IS function to an external vendor increases the positive attitudes towards outsourcing in the Machinery Industry, no such impact can be ascertained in the Finance Industry. On the other side, perceived behavioral control, other than expected, is negatively rather than positively related to the current degree of outsourcing in the Finance Industry (H20a). These industry differences indicate that IS sourcing decisions in the Finance Industry are significantly influenced by external forces, that are not under the control of organizations. This view is consistent with the findings from Ang and Slaughter (1997) in the US Banking Industry. They found support for the notion that institutional pressures impact the sourcing decision of banks. By contrast, the sourcing decision in the Machinery Industry appears to be less influenced by external forces.

Impact of Attitudes. This view is also supported by the different impacts of managerial attitudes on the current degree of outsourcing. Only in the Machinery Industry, the attitudes of IS executives towards the outsourcing of an IS function are reflected by the current sourcing practices of their organization. This further strengthens the impression that IS managers in the Machinery Industry have more control over the sourcing decision than their colleagues in the Finance Industry.

Ownership. Finally, organizations in the Finance Industry appear to be more inclined to safeguard against potential outsourcing risks through special capital sharing arrangements with external vendors. In the Finance Industry, equity shares with an external service provider appear to decrease in-house advantages in transaction costs (H17a). Moreover, they seem to lower the strategic risks associated with IS outsourcing (H17b) (see Table 3-16, p. 198). Beside these benefits of capital shares, however, the potential darker side of such arrangements may not be overseen. The practice of capital sharing may freeze the ability of IS executives to flexibly change the current IS sourcing arrangement in response to perceptual changes about the advantages and disadvantages of insourcing versus outsourcing an IS function. Such a limited adaptability of the current sourcing arrangement may be particularly high in outsourcing arrangements where the practice of capital sharing is institutionalized. One example where ownership arrangements are institutionalized can be found in the German Banking Industry. As already outlined previously, a considerable portion of the German Finance sample is made up by so called "Sparkassen". Many of the these Sparkassen are served by related "Sparkassen Informatik" organizations. The latter are specialized IS service providers that are jointly owned by their clients (i.e. the "Sparkassen"). These "conglomerates" may be seen as institutionalized IS outsourcing arrangements that considerably decrease the flexibility of Sparkassen to change their current sourcing arrangements. Apparently, however, the benefits of these special types of facilities sharing, are widely believed to outweigh the decrease in organizational flexibility.

4.2.3 Application Development versus Maintenance

Finally, group differences between the development and maintenance of software applications will be examined more closely.

Production costs. The first discrepancy between both IS functions refers to the perceived impact of production costs on the governance choice. As expected, perceived in-house advantages in the production costs involved in *developing* software applications are associated with both a lower level of outsourcing and negative attitudes towards outsourcing (H3a,b). Contrastingly, perceived in-house production cost advantages in the *maintenance* work do not have a significant impact on the current degree of outsourcing (H3a). Apparently, there is a gap between the expected production cost advantages through insourcing or outsourcing the *maintenance* work and the current extent to which cost savings are achieved. However, how can this discrepancy be explained? One potential explanation could be the limited understanding of organizations about the true drivers of maintenance production costs, and how these drivers are affected by alternative sourcing arrangements. This view is partially supported by the literature on the management of the maintenance work. The general tenor is that there is a dearth of research on the management and organization of software maintenance, which parallels the negative image and low recognition of maintenance work in practice. In most organizations, maintenance is merely seen as a cost burden (Swanson and Beath, 1989; 1990). Although a number of researchers have begun to study the determinants of maintenance productivity (Banker and Slaughter, 1997; Banker, et al., 1991) and performance (Banker, et al., 1998), as well as the drivers of maintenance costs (Banker, et al., 1993) and effort (Swanson, 1999), there is still limited knowledge about the production and cost function of the maintenance work.

When looking at the drivers of perceived production cost differences between insourcing and outsourcing, in this study, there are two interesting differences between the maintenance and the development work. In-house advantages in the production costs of the development work are significantly damaged if the *work load* for that function *varies* substantially (H6a). Apparently, outsourcing is seen as the more cost efficient organizational mode to adapt to major deviations in the amount of work in software development projects. One reason, why this effect can not be observed for the maintenance work, may be that external vendors cannot that easily be integrated into maintenance projects. The time until an external vendor becomes familiar with the client's pool of software applications may often take too long as to be an efficient alternative to insourcing. On the other side, in-house production cost advantages of the maintenance work are negatively affected by a high amount of perceived *environmental uncertainty* due to dynamics in the IT Industry (H4b). This could partially be explained by an increasing diffusion of maintenance tools that can enhance maintenance productivity (Dishaw and Strong, 1998). Again, external vendors may be seen as having advantages in acquiring the (technical) knowledge that is required to effectively deploy such tools in the maintenance process.

Strategic contribution. In view of the scant regard of maintenance management in research and practice, it is surprising to note that the strategic importance of the *maintenance* work appears to be taken into account by IS executives when evaluating and comparing the options of insourcing versus outsourcing, whereas, at the first view, the decision about the sourcing of the *development* of software applications seems to be independent of strategic considerations. This is indicated by the fact that modest support for Hypotheses 10b could only be ascertained for the maintenance work. Moreover, IS executives tend to believe that the strategic potential of the maintenance work is better exhausted through outsourcing, as indicated by a significant positive impact of the strategic importance of the maintenance function on the attitude towards outsourcing (H11b). The large portion that the maintenance work makes up of the IS budget (Bennet, 1996; Krogstie, 1995; both cited by Brehm, 2001, p. 47), may have sharpened the awareness of IS executives in considering the strategic role of this IS function when it comes to important decisions about its organizational arrangement. Moreover, the ability to pool maintenance projects, and, thereby, realize economies of scale in the maintenance work (Banker and Slaughter, 1997), may be higher in case of outsourcing – in fact, not necessarily because such economies of scale cannot be achieved in-house, but more because it may be politically harder to enforce such pooling strategies in-house than through outsourcing (see also Hirschheim and Lacity, 2002).

Turning over to the *development* of software applications, a closer examination of Table 3-16 (p. 198) reveals that strategic aspects are not totally disregarded for that function. The findings for Hypotheses 11a show that those organizations that perceive their application development work as a strategic asset, spend significantly more money on the outsourcing of that function. This result is consistent with the empirical findings from the multiple case study analysis by McLellan et al. (1995) in the US Banking Industry. Their findings indicate that banks outsourced major parts of their IS function when at the organizational level IS was rated as a core activity. Notably, however, a negative relationship between the strategic impact of the development work and the attitude of IS executives towards outsourcing could be found (H11b). Apparently, the beliefs of IS managers are not fully reflected by the actual sourcing practices of their organization. This gives raise to the supposition that the strategic intentions associated with outsourcing the development of software applications may be overestimated.

Intellectual Capital. Another interesting trade-off between the attitudes of IS executives and the current sourcing practices can be observed regarding the impact of perceived differences between insourcing and outsourcing in the *intellectual capital* required to *maintain* software applications. Consistent with Hypotheses 15b, perceived comparative in-house advantages in the base of knowledge resources appear to damage an IS executive's attitude towards outsourcing. Contrary to Hypothesis 15a, however, organizations appear to outsource maintenance work in situations where the base of intellectual capital required to perform that function is believed to be superior in-house. Apparently, organizations that currently experience outsourcing find their own personnel to have superior experiences, skill sets, and knowledge sets in maintaining application software.

Systemic Impact. Furthermore, there is a difference in how the systemic impact of an IS function is considered in the sourcing decision. While the results show that the *development* work is less outsourced if its impact on the overall performance of an organization's IS is believed to be negativity affected through outsourcing, no such impact could be ascertained for maintenance work (H14a). One way to interpret this finding is that the maintenance work can more easily be outsourced selectively than the development work, without negatively affecting the overall performance of the system. Looking at the individual worker level, however, puts that view into perspective.

Systemic view. Interestingly, in-house advantages in the systemic view of IS workers significantly inhibit organizations from outsourcing the *maintenance* of software applications (H22a). This means that even if organizations do no not consider the organizational link between the maintenance work and other IS functions in their sourcing decision, they may see this issue differently at the actual worker level. It apparently plays a significant role for the current sourcing *situation* if in-house or outsourced workers are perceived as superior in recognizing the interdependencies between their work and the work of others throughout the client organization. Nevertheless, IS executives appear to ignore both types of systemic impact as criteria for their personal evaluative appraisal of insourcing versus outsourcing the maintenance work. This is slightly different with regard to the *development* of software applications, where a weak significant relationship between in-house advantages in the systemic view of IS worker and the attitude towards outsourcing could be ascertained (H22b).

Subjective Norm. Moreover, both for the development and for the maintenance of software applications, external pressures, in terms of the opinion of others, significantly influence the attitudes of IS executives towards outsourcing. The current degree to which the maintenance work is outsourced, however, was found to be independent of the subjective norm.

Attitude. Related to these findings, only the current degree of maintenance outsourcing is significantly affected by the attitudes of IS executives, whereas the current sourcing of the application development work is not reflected by the attitudes of IS executives. Taking both the findings for the impact of subjective norm and the results for the influence of attitudes on the current degree of outsourcing together, implies that the sourcing decision about the *maintenance* work is more robust against the influential opinion of others and, at the same time, is more in line with the actual believes of IS executives. Apparently, the importance of effectively and efficiently managing the maintenance function has not yet been recognized as an important topic by those "opinion leaders" that usually exert a significant influence on the believes of IS executives. IS managers, which may be referred to as organizational "insiders", appear to be more cognizant of its importance.

Ownership. Finally, there is one stark difference that deserves mentioning. The findings reveal relatively strong support for the notion that capital shares with an external vendor decrease in-house transaction cost advantages in *developing* software applications (H17a) and limit the strategic risks associated with outsourcing the development work (H17b). By contrast, no empirical evidence could be found for the impact of asset ownership on an IS executive's beliefs about differences in transaction costs and the strategic contribution of the *maintenance* work in alternative sourcing arrangements. One way to interpret these discrepancies is that organizations do not see the maintenance work as critical enough to justify equity shares with an external vendor.

Overall, both the commonalities and differences in the IS sourcing behavior of organizations across countries, industries application services have important implications for research and practice. These implications will be shown next.

4.3 Theoretical Implications

From a *theory-building* standpoint, this study adopted the view of theoretical pluralism (Groenewegen and Vromen, 1996; Spinner, 1974). Referred to the organizational context, this view is based on the contention that the explanation of organizational phenomena should not be constrained by any single theoretical perspective (*cf.* Ang and Cummings, 1997, p. 251). Rather, to ensure that the sourcing practices of organizations are understood as completely as possible, multiple theoretical lenses have been integrated into a coherent framework. The value of such a multi-theoretical approach is widely supported by this research. Each particular theoretical lens has added its piece of information to improve the understanding of the current sourcing practices of organizations.

The basic idea underlying the theory development was that IS sourcing may best be understood as a general management decision that can be broken down into the basic process elements of decision making, as identified by Simon (1957) and others (for an overview see Witte, 1968, p. 626; 1972, p. 164). If transferring this dynamic view of decision making into a static variance theoretic perspective, an organization's current sourcing behavior may be seen as a decision outcome derived from evaluating, weighting, and aggregating a number of decision criteria. Moreover, it may be argued that the actual instances of these decision criteria are dependent on a set of other variables that indirectly influence the final decision. Viewed in this vein, fruitful parallels to the attitude-behavior structure of individual decision making in social psychology can be drawn. In particular, the theory of planned behavior (TPB) emerged as a useful complementary framework to understand managerial decision making. Although the TPB has traditionally been used as a general framework to understand individual behavior, this research shows that it can significantly enhance the understanding of organizational behavior as well. It is instructive to note that Cordano and Frieze Hanson (2000), who applied the TPB in a different organizational context, came to the same conclusion.

The combination of the theory of planned behavior with the two-level variance theoretic approach deduced from Simon's decision process model (see Figure 2-1, p. 23), provides an overall conceptual umbrella to understand the IS sourcing decision of organizations. Taken alone, however, it tells very little about the actual criteria that decision makers may consider as important when evaluating and comparing alternative sourcing options. The actual decision factors and their determinants were derived from three selected *theories of the firm*. In particular, transaction cost theory, resource-based theory, and incomplete contracts (property rights) theory were considered. Moreover, *cultural dimensions* were integrated into the resulting mid-range theoretical framework on IS sourcing.

In the following, the major implications from the *theory validation* will be presented. For this purpose, the main *implications* from the testing of each theoretical lens will be presented.

Theory of Planned Behavior. The integration of the TPB into the mid-range theory of IS sourcing has provided a number of very valuable insights. First of all, the incorporation of the *attitude* construct as a *mediator* between the comparative advantage constructs and the current degree of outsourcing allowed for a number of meaningful interpretations. While attitudes reflect the overall evaluative appraisal of an organization's IS executive towards outsourcing an IS function, the current degree of outsourcing reflects the actual sourcing practices of an organization. Whenever *mismatches* between the influences on the attitudes and those on the current degree of outsourcing can be ascertained, this gives rise to the supposition that the current sourcing practices are either not governed optimally from the perspective of the CIO, or that IS management is not cognizant of certain important relationships that have a profound impact on the current sourcing situation. In this realm, it is also interesting to note that the attitudes of IS executives were not consistently reflected by an organization's current sourcing behavior, but rather by the ideal degree of outsourcing. The concept of the "ideal degree of outsourcing" was treated as a substitute for *intentions* (Cordano and Frieze Hanson, 2000). Therefore, the findings strongly support the view of the TPB that attitudes are more likely to influence intentions rather than current behavior. This finding could be of general interest for researchers that study organizational phenomena in cross-sectional research settings, because it shows how the explanatory power of variance theoretic frameworks can be increased by considering the trade-off between current organizational behavior and those practices that are seen as ideal or optimal from the stand-point of an organization's main decision makers.

Moreover, there appears to be a theoretically interesting relation between the theory of planned behavior and institutional theory. The concept "subjective norm" from the TPB may be viewed as building a bridge to institutional theory, which is based on the contention that organizational behavior is socially influenced by its environment. It may be argued that organizations are made up by individuals. Hence, it is not an entire organization that passively adapts to environmental forces, but the individuals that together constitute the social network of an organization. The main decision makers within such a social network may be influenced by various internal and external institutional forces. This view is supported by the relatively strong impact that the opinion of others (subjective norm) had on the IS sourcing decision. Moreover, the influential role that "behavioral control" had on the sourcing decision invites a reconsideration of the rational actor view of behavior. It suggests to generally consider factors that account for the bounded rationality of human beings when studying major organizational decisions (see also Cordano and Frieze Hanson, 2000).

Transaction Cost Theory. No less enlightening are the empirical findings from the test of the transaction cost theoretic relationships. This study is one of the rare examples that directly tested the efficiency argument of transaction cost theory by incorporating both transaction costs and production costs in the analysis (see also Ang and Straub, 1998). This approach is in line with Williamson's original contributions.

He emphasized that beside transaction costs, production cost would have to be considered in the governance choice. Moreover, he argued that both types of costs would partially be influenced by the same contextual factors, e.g., asset specificity (Williamson 1981, p. 560, 1985, p. 93, 1990, p. 153).

Based on this conceptualization, this research supports the findings of former empirical studies which showed that organizations rarely recognize transaction costs when evaluating and comparing alternative sourcing options (Barthélemy, 2001; Dibbern, et al., 2003b; Dillmann, 1997; Lacity and Willcocks, 1995). This does not mean that organizations are not aware of transaction costs. Indeed, the descriptive findings have shown that, on average, IS executives believe that the transaction costs associated with the development and maintenance of software applications make up about 8,7% of total costs, if performed *in-house*, and about 13,1% of total costs, if provided by an *external* service provider. This means that most organizations may have realized that transaction costs make up a considerable part of the overall IS costs and they differ between insourcing and outsourcing, but their primary focus is still on *production costs* when determining the value of alternative sourcing options (see also Ang and Straub, 1998).

Second, this research enhances the knowledge about the impact of *contextual factors* on the governance choice. Previous research has mostly examined the direct impact of factors like asset specificity or uncertainty on the governance choice.[19] Although, the empirical support for these impacts was quite encouraging, the actual reasoning for these influences remained untested. This often resulted in a mixture of production and transaction economic arguments in support of these relationships. In trying to overcome these explanatory limitations, and in line with the main structural elements of the IS souring decision derived from Simon's decision process model, this research has treated comparative in-house transaction and production cost advantages as *mediators* between the contextual factors and the sourcing decision. By way of testing theses mediator effects, it soon became apparent that human asset specificity had a stronger and more consistent impact on differences in production costs between insourcing and outsourcing than on transaction cost differences. This means that most of the background economic reasoning of transaction cost theory can be traced back to differences in production costs. Moreover, it is important to note that both transaction and production costs can be lower or higher internally than when using the market. This partially contradicts the view of Williamson (1981, 1985, 1990), who assumed that production costs would generally be lower when using the external market. (For a qualitative empirical assessment of this phenomenon through multiple case studies, see Dibbern, et al., 2003b). This justifies the adjustments of Williamson's graphical representation of the relationship between asset specificity and cost differences between market and hierarchy, as illustrated in Fig-

[19] For an overview of TCE research on vertical integration and make-or-buy in general, see Shelanski and Klein (1995). For an overview of IS outsourcing research that tested "market failure arguments", see Dibbern et al. (2003).

ure 2-3 (p. 52). There is a point, where human asset specificity leads to in-house production cost advantages in developing and maintaining software applications.

Consequently, the *third* important contribution of this study refers to a more advanced understanding of those factors that explain cost differences between insourcing and outsourcing. As already outlined, insourcing is more cost efficient than outsourcing if the software development and maintenance work requires a high amount of specific human assets. In this realm, the way in which *human asset specificity* has been conceptualized deserves special mentioning. Informed by the notion of tacit knowledge (Polanyi, 1958) and the way in which such knowledge can be acquired and transferred (Nonaka, 1994), human asset specificity was treated as a multidimensional construct. On the one hand, it capturers the extent to which different types of knowledge (business and software knowledge), required to develop and maintain application software, are unique. On the other hand, it refers to the process of social collaboration that takes place in order to acquire and exchange these types of knowledge between different groups of stakeholders, that are involved in the development and maintenance work. Both the empirical stability and the predictive power of this multi-facetted approach is very encouraging. Hence, this conceptualization of human asset specificity may serve as a spring board for future research that seeks to rigorously examine the governance of service oriented (knowledge) work. Moreover, it contributes to a more advanced understanding of the production and cost function of IS services.

Furthermore, the empirical findings reinforce the conclusions from Sutcliffe and Zaheer (1998) that *uncertainty* needs to be treated as a multidimensional construct. The results revealed that different types of uncertainty (technological uncertainty, business uncertainty, work load variations, measurement difficulty) have different impacts on production and transaction cost differences between insourcing and outsourcing. For example, partial support could be found for the notion that a high level of environmental uncertainty decreases in-house production cost advantages and hence leads to a higher level of outsourcing. Moreover, work load variation, which are also associated with the notion of the frequency of transactions, appear to decrease in-house production cost advantages. Furthermore, absolutely no support could be found for the notion that measurement difficulty would lead to lower in-house transaction costs. Rather, it is positively related to the degree of outsourcing. These findings invite a reconsideration of the impacts of uncertainty on the governance choice. They partially contradict Williamson's (1975, 1985) original propositions. Again, distinguishing between the impact of uncertainty on both differences in transaction and production costs between alternative governance modes enhances the understanding of its "true" effects.

Related to these considerations is a *fourth* theme that emerged from the analysis of TCT. It refers to the value of including potential *behavioral antipodes of opportunism* in the analysis. Comparative in-house advantages in the *trustworthiness* and in *non-monetary incentives* (intrinsic motivation) of IS workers appear to decrease in-house advantages in transaction and production costs. In particular, motivational factors have rarely been considered in previous research on transaction cost theory. Moreover, they have largely been ignored in IS research. One notable exception is the work from Couger and Colter (1985). They have found support for the notion that a higher level of motivation increases software maintenance productivity. Therefore, stronger consideration of motivational aspects could not only improve the explanatory power of transaction cost theory, but also contribute to understand the cost function of the IS work.

Resource-based Theory. The inclusion of resource-based theoretic arguments into the theoretical framework of IS sourcing recognizes the fact that alternative sourcing arrangements could be associated with severe consequences for the required base of IS resources and the benefits attained from using these resources. This view could partially be confirmed. Although production costs are the dominant rational for the sourcing decision, organizations appear to be cognizant of the importance to consider how the inputs and outputs of the development and maintenance work are affected by alternative sourcing arrangements. From a theorizing point of view, the theoretical overlaps to transaction cost theory are especially interesting. Some of the contextual and behavioral factors that play an important role in predicting transaction and production cost differences between insourcing and outsourcing, also serve as predictors of differences in the resources and organizational impacts associated with the provision of IS functions. First, *human asset specificity* significantly influences in-house advantages in the strategic contribution of an IS function and in the intellectual capital required to perform an IS function. Moreover, the application development and maintenance work is more likely to be perceived as a strategic asset if its provision requires highly specific human assets (see also Dibbern and Heinzl, 2001; 2002). Second, *behavioral differences* of in-house versus outsourced IS workers apparently influence the perception of IS executives about the comparative in-house advantages in the strategic and operational contribution of an IS function, as well as its systemic impact. Consequently, the consideration of behavioral factors, like trust and non-monetary incentives, should be given more emphasis in resource-based theory. They can help to overcome one of the major limitations of the resource-based view: its silence about behavioral assumptions.

Incomplete Contracts Theory. There are few, if any, studies that have empirically tested incomplete contracts theory (ICT). Most of the work on ICT is conceptual an mathematical in nature. One of its major strength is the consideration of both the costs and the benefits in analyzing the issue of asset ownership. Therefore, it is of little surprise that there is a close link between the ICT and the twin theoretical lenses of transaction cost theory and resource base theory. These inter-theoretical linkages are empirically supported by the fact that asset ownership – represented by capital shares with external vendors – decreases in-house advantages in transaction costs and lowers the strategic risks associated with outsourcing. Apparently, capital shares serve as institutional safeguards against high transaction costs and strategic risks associated with IS outsourcing. Interestingly, however, the influential role of asset ownership appears to be independent of asset specificity. That is, the relevance of ownership is not limited to situations where it is difficult to settle "complete contracts" and where the risk of opportunism is conceivably high. This reinforces the view of Holmstrom (1998. p. 92) that special ownership deals are motivated by many other factors than backing up authority. For example, Heinzl (1992; 1993b) has found empirical support for the notion that organizations *spin-off* their IS function for a number of reasons, e.g., in order to increase the controllability of the IS function, to provide a better platform for more advanced charging mechanisms, to improve the motivation and service mentality of IS workers, and to increase the rate of IS innovations.

Cultural Dimensions. Finally, cultural dimensions proved to be relevant in explaining IS sourcing behavior. They did not only significantly enhance the understanding of differences in the IS sourcing behavior between Germany and the USA, but also contributed to understand functional and industry differences. In this realm, it is instructive to note *how* the cultural dimensions were integrated into the mid-range theory of IS sourcing. Instead of taking them as fixed conditions that indirectly influence the relationships of other theoretical lenses, they were "truly" integrated into the framework by treating them as comparative advantage constructs at the organization or at the individual level. Thereby, the cultural dimensions, themselves, became part of the mid-range theory. In this way, researchers can avoid an overreliance on the results of former large scale cross-cultural studies like that of Hofstede (1980) – a practice that has been criticized in IS research more recently (Myers and Tan, 2002).

4.4 Practical Implications

Before starting to delve into the practical implications of this research, it appears useful to provide some background information on why and how research of this type provides fruitful insights for practitioners. According to Lee (1999b, p. 31), there are two (non-exclusive) ways in which practical relevance can be achieved in IS research.[20] The first, which he calls the "instrumental model of practice", is described as follows:

> "A researcher formulates, tests, and validates a theory that specifies independent variables, dependent variables, and the relationships among them. In doing this, the researcher is careful to make sure that, first, the dependent variables represent the outcomes the practitioner is interested in achieving and, second, the independent variables represent factors that not only indeed influence the outcome but also can

[20] It has to be noted that IS research appears to be predominantly seen as *empirical* research by Lee (1999). This neglects the more *constructive* type of IS research, which is concerned with actually building IS. This includes important issues like developing prototypes of particular IS components, designing IS architectures, or establishing principles of IS development (Krcmar, 1999; Lyytinen, 1999).

> be manipulated or changed by the practitioner. A practitioner could then apply the theory by manipulating the independent variables in order to achieve the desired level in the dependent variable" (Lee, 1999b, p. 31).

Following this model of research relevance, the practitioner is seen as "(...) the 'customer' of research", in terms of a consumer or adopter, that can readily apply the research results. In the second way of practical relevance, the practitioner is also treated as a customer, but more in sense of a 'patient', whose behavior is being analyzed and critically reflected. Thereby, potential avenues for improving organizational practices can be pointed out. Accordingly, Lee (1999b, p. 31) concludes,

> "(...) research can be relevant not only in the sense intended by the instrumental model of practice, but also in the sense intended by critical social theory, where false consciousness and inappropriate work relationships are brought to light. (...) Furthermore, a critical-social-theory researcher could even question the sort of relevance delivered by the instrumental model of practice to the extent that an instrumentally produced theory could be used to perpetuate false consciousness and inappropriate work relationships."

In the following, it will be shown that in spite of the fact that this research primarily deploys an instrumental view of practice, it *also* allows to critically point out some abnormalities or false consciousness of organizations in their current sourcing behavior. In particular, the concerns of two different groups of practitioners are addressed: (a) those of *client organizations,* that have to decide upon the insourcing versus outsourcing of their IS functions, and (b) those of the *external vendors,* that are interested in selling their services and satisfying their clients.

(1) Instrumental Model of Practice. The model of IS sourcing comprises two central dependent variables. The first refers to the current degree of outsourcing and the attitude towards outsourcing. Manipulating this pair of variables is particularly important for external vendors, since it is the vendors' business to sell IS services. According to the model of IS sourcing, the degree and attitude towards outsourcing is influenced by a number of comparative advantage variables. They reflect the major decision criteria that client organizations may use to evaluate and compare alternative sourcing options. Hence, it is important for external vendors to know these criteria in order to influence the client's sourcing decision. Of course, client organization should also be well informed about the set of criteria that need to be factored in when evaluating and comparing alternative sourcing options. However, for them, it is even more important to know under which circumstances it is more advantageous to insource rather than outsource an IS function. This concern is addressed by a second set of independent variables that impact the comparative advantage variables. In order to illustrate the practical application of the model, the vendor perspective is taken up first.

(a) Vendor perspective. The empirical findings show that, from the list of decision criteria, perceived differences in *production costs* between insourcing and outsourcing are most influential on the IS sourcing decision. Consequently, vendors predom-

inantly have to prove their ability to lower IS production costs. However, how can this be achieved? The empirical findings indicate that external vendors are very likely to have *production cost disadvantages* if the provision of an IS function requires *firm specific knowledge* about the software and the business processes of the client organization and if the acquisition of this knowledge requires extensive social collaboration with various client stakeholders (H1b).

If external vendors see themselves confronted with massive specific investments, they may pursue two alternative strategies. First, they may try to convince the client of the potential benefits from *standardization*. In cases, in which clients show a highly heterogeneous applications landscape, such an effort may indeed pay out for the client, since the benefits of standardized integrated systems may outweigh the benefits of highly customized "island solutions", which usually require a significant amount of maintenance and systems integration effort. Second, or indeed complementary to the standardization strategy, a vendor may develop specific industry expertise. This could significantly reduce the entry barriers in adapting firm specific knowledge. If vendors lack such industry expertise, one promising strategy could be to build joint-ventures with those clients that show particularly strong IS capabilities within a particular industry, or to take over their entire IS departments.

Moreover, vendors need to make sure that they establish an environment that recognizes the social needs of the IS workers. This is important, because the empirical findings consistently revealed that comparative cost and benefit advantages of insourcing or outsourcing an IS function are inevitably linked to advantages in the intrinsic motivation (non-monetary incentives) of IS workers (H9a-d). That is, if an external vendor takes over the IS personnel from the client, their social preferences need to be carefully examined and satisfied. Moreover, if the vendor integrates own personnel into the client organization, the social collaboration between the vendor staff and the client stakeholders (i.e. users and key IS workers) needs to be supported. That is, social aspects need to be addressed carefully by vendors in order to attract and subsequently satisfy new customer accounts.

While these are issues that appear to be generally important, regardless whether vendors operate in Germany or in the US, whether they provide services in the Machinery or Finance Industry, or whether they offer software maintenance or development services, there are other factors which are culturally, industry, or functionally sensitive. Those factors can be directly inferred from the group discussions. For example, for vendors in *Germany*, it is not sufficient to prove their ability to lower costs (H3a,b) or to bring in superior intellectual capital (H15b), they also have to recognize the systemic impact of the IS function(s) that they provide. That is, they need to make sure that their particular work is well integrated into the overall IS function, so that the performance of the entire IS function is not negatively affected (H14a,b). Concurrently, they have to make sure that their IS staff understands the task interdependency at the client organization, i.e. that they have a systemic view in doing their work (H22a). Moreover, they have to ensure that the client does not believe to loose the directive control over an IS function (H24b). This could be achieved by integrating key client stakeholders into the development and maintenance process, e.g., by establishing key account managers at the client site (Heinzl and Sinß, 1993).

(b) Client perspective. Of course, these are issues that the client has to take into account as well. Indeed, it appears to be fruitful to step into the shoes of an external vendor when considering outsourcing an IS function and to anticipate the vendor's objectives. In particular, clients are well advised to examine the plausibility of the vendor offer and to ask for (and question) the actual tactics and actions the vendor intends to take in order to meet the client's expectations (Hirschheim and Lacity, 2002). This research promotes the view that clients should always evaluate and compare the options of insourcing and outsourcing (Lacity, et al., 1996). For that purpose, a number of dimensions have been identified, which are represented by different comparative advantages constructs. The empirical data shows that minimizing production costs is the most important criteria for the sample of 180 organizations in Germany and the US. This is of little surprise, since IS costs are constantly increasing, while, at the same time, it is very difficult for organizations to determine the benefits achieved from their IS function. It has to be recognized, however, that there is a "natural" trade-off between IS cost savings and IS service excellence, as illustrated by the case studies on IS insourcing by Hirschheim and Lacity (2000). The existence of such a trade-off is substantiated by this research. For example, the empirical findings show that insourcing is more cost efficient if the development and maintenance work requires highly *specific human assets*. At the same time, however, specific human assets provide the basis for the strategic contribution of an IS function (H1d). That is, a higher level of standardization may lead to production cost advantages through outsourcing, but the flip side is that the strategic potential of an IS function will likely decrease. This trade-off has to be carefully considered by client organizations.

(2) Critical View of Practice. When looking at the results of the model testing, there are a number of findings that strongly deviate from the expected theoretical linkages. Of course, one may argue that this means that theory is false. However, there are indications that suggest that theory may indeed be ahead of practice. First, it is striking that transaction costs are not considered in the IS sourcing decision (H2b). This would not be of concern if transaction costs would be negligibly small. However, the descriptive findings indicate that transaction costs make up quite a substantial part of overall IS costs. On average, *in-house* transaction costs make up about 8,7% of total costs (~11,7% if directly asked), and *outsourcing* transaction costs approximately account for 13,1% (~15,3% if directly asked) of total costs (see Table 3-10, p. 180). Moreover, across all sub-samples, outsourcing transaction costs were believed to be about 28,4% higher than in-house transaction costs, if directly asked. This means that transaction cost differences between insourcing and outsourcing the development and maintenance work may indeed be underestimated by organizations.

A second concern is related to the fact that, except for US organizations, firms were more likely to outsource the application development and maintenance work when they had difficulties in evaluating the performance of the IS workers. If firms outsource IS functions that they cannot control, they face the risk to enter into an unreflective dependent relationship with external service providers. Previous research has strongly suggested to avoid these situations. In order to ensure quality work, Ang and Slaughter (2002, p. 147) suggest to negotiate and implement specific outcome measures at the beginning of the contract with an external service provider. Cross (1995) and Willcocks et al. (1996) even advocate the view that organizations should prepare for outsourcing by implementing effective measurement instruments to evaluate the internal IS service before considering outsourcing.

A third concern is heading into the same direction. Except for the US and the Machinery Industry sample, organizations were found to increasingly outsource the development and maintenance work, when they had a low level of control over the outsourcing decision. Moreover, the opinion of others appeared to play a substantial role on the IS sourcing decision. While organizations can benefit from the experiences of other stakeholders, e.g., other firms in their industry or consultants, they should not become overly dependent on their opinion. Organizations are well advised to rigorously examine alternative sourcing options by using a set of criteria that reflect their overall IS objectives. If organizations are not in control over the outsourcing decision, it is very likely that they will loose control over the resulting outsourcing contract.

Of course, it is not sufficient to point out these potential abnormal behaviors and to let the practitioner alone with solving (or ignoring) them. Research has to take an active role in addressing these issues. Potential avenues for such an endeavor will be outlined in Section 4.6. First, however, it is necessary to point out the major limitations of this research.

4.5 Study Limitations

Although the findings of this study have emerged from a well grounded research procedure, there are several things that should be kept in mind. First, this research has focused on explaining the sourcing behavior of organizations with respect to only two particular *IS functions*: the development and the maintenance of software applications. When deciding upon the insourcing versus outsourcing of other IS functions, e.g. data center operations, or even other business functions, e.g. accounting or logistics, some different or additional factors may need to be considered.

Second, in validating the model on IS sourcing, only the *perspective of* an organization's highest ranking *IS executive* has been considered. No attempt was made to empirically identify the person or group of persons that decide upon the insourcing or outsourcing of IS functions. Although the design of the study allowed to examine the extent to which the sourcing behavior of an organization is reflected by the beliefs and evaluative appraisal of its IS executive, the influence of other stakeholders, e.g. the chief executive officer or managers of the business functions, was not explicitly considered. Moreover, from a methodological point of view, the reliance on self-reported data may introduce a common response bias across constructs.

Third, the *cross-sectional nature* of this research only allowed to provide a snapshot of current sourcing practices. This certainly limits the ability to draw causal inferences.

Fourth, the *sample sizes* for the groups were not too high. This can lead to two consequences. On the one hand, empirical findings from small samples with low response rates *may not be representative* for a larger population. In particular in the US sample, it can not be ruled out that the responding organizations represent a minority. Compared to other studies in the US, the average degree of outsourcing was relatively small. Hence, companies that insourced may have felt especially attracted by this study. On the other hand, *statistical power* can be affected by small sample size (Baroudi and Orlikowski, 1989; Cohen, 1977). In particular, the sample size in the US may not have been sufficient to detect all significant relationships. It is striking out that a number of path coefficients were insignificant in the US, although they showed a relatively high magnitude. For example, the strength of the relationship between in-house advantages in the strategic contribution of an IS function and the current degree of outsourcing was relatively high (0,260), but not significant. Contrastingly, in sub-samples with higher sample sizes, path coefficients with comparable magnitudes were all significant, while at the same time, the explained variance of the degree of outsourcing did not considerably differ between the groups. Therefore, some of the insignificant findings for the US sample need to be treated with special caution. Moreover, the findings for the interaction effects have to be treated with caution for all sub-samples. The issue of statistical power is particularly critical when testing interaction effects, since each product term increases measurement error and model complexity (Chin, et al., 1996). Accordingly, those interaction effects that showed reasonably high, but still insignificant, path coefficients, should not discourage researchers from further investigations (e.g., the impact of the product term of "trustworthiness" and "human asset specificity", H8a,c).

4.6 Future Research

While these limitations must be kept in mind, when considering the findings, the pioneering character of this study should not be overseen. It is one of the first attempts to integrate multiple theoretical concepts that contribute to explain the IS sourcing phenomenon. Moreover, it is the only comparative empirical study, to date, that recognizes industry, country, and functional differences in the IS sourcing behavior of organizations. Both the study limitations and the enhancements on the theoretical and methodological front provide avenues for *future research*.

First, the findings of this study need to be *replicated* across other settings and across time in order to enhance the extent of generalizability of the findings. The validity tests of the construct measures were very promising. However, researchers that want to replicate the full model, are well advised to take care of the response rate. In particular, if researchers intend to gather data from IS executives, the *length of the questionnaire* appears to be critical. A few constructs whose impact found little support in this study may be deleted. Moreover, the descriptive part can be reduced. Thereby, researchers may end up with eight instead of twelve questionnaire pages. Moreover, researchers do not necessarily have to conduct questionnaire surveys. They can also use *other* empirical research *methods*, like case studies, to examine the theoretical framework.

Promising areas for replication are *other industries* and countries. Researchers that want to compare different industries, may be well advised to anticipate some of the industry differences and to consider them in the model of IS sourcing. For example, this research has shown that the rate of diffusion of ERP-software packages appears to have a profound impact on the sourcing decision. Therefore, researchers may differentiate ERP-adopters from non-adopters or they may treat the rate of adoption as a separate variable in terms of an overriding contingency.

Researchers that wish to include *other IS functions* should take into account the character of the unit of analysis. Both the development and the maintenance of software applications can be characterized as labor intensive knowledge work. If IS functions are examined where physical and technical assets play a more dominant role, e.g., data center operations, many of the construct definitions and measures would need to be adjusted. Another interesting unit of analysis could be the study of *business process outsourcing*. It opens a new perspective to look at the phenomenon of IS sourcing. Almost every business process is supported by IS. Therefore, most decisions about the sourcing of other business functions (e.g., logistics) will inevitably affect the sourcing of IS functions. The study of interdependencies between the sourcing of IS functions and business processes provides an interesting research opportunity.

Second, researchers may consider to examine the model on IS sourcing from *other perspectives* than that of the IS executive. It would be interesting to see how business unit managers or external vendors would evaluate the constructs of this model on IS sourcing. Researchers that want to study multiple stakeholder perspectives within organizations will benefit from research by Hirschheim and Lacity (2000; 2002). Those that are interested in studying client-vendor differences should take a closer look at the work from Goles (2001).

Third, the static nature of this research may be complemented by a *longitudinal* study. Of course, demanding longitudinal research is easier said than done. It requires a long breath by the researcher and a very profound understanding of IS outsourcing prior to entering into such an endeavor. It appears promising to pick out a few variables *ex ante* and to observe how and why they change over time. For example, it could be examined how changes in the sourcing situation of an organization correspondents with variations in other variables, like IS costs, different types of IS impacts, individual behaviors and attitudes of different stakeholders, and asset specificity, over multiple periods. For such a longitudinal research plan, case studies with a selection of companies may be considered. They allow to take into account emergent influences that the researcher is not aware of when starting the research project. Moreover, it may be much easier to convince a few senior IS executives of the benefits from their participation, than an anonymous group of respondents, as it usually is the case in large scale surveys.

Fourth, there are a number of research opportunities that can not be directly inferred from the study limitations. They refer to more fundamental changes in IS outsourcing research. While research on IS outsourcing has been a relatively new and unexplored phenomenon in the early 90s, it is now entering into a phase of *consolidation*. This is indicated by the arrival of research studies that try to synthesize previous research and to establish a solid theoretical foundation to explain the phenomenon. By no means should this mean that no additional empirical and conceptual research is required to understand the phenomenon. Indeed, research that follows suit is well advised to follow in the footsteps of other preexisting research and to make use of the concepts that have already been established.

In parallel, however, researchers may enter into a *new generation of prescriptive research*, that not only seeks to understand what practice is doing, but to actively shape and support their behavior. More critical social research may be one way towards that end (Klein, 2002). However, it should be complemented by a constructivist research approaches. This implies to actually develop tools that support and, thereby, improve the sourcing practices of organizations. For example, the results of this research may serve as a basis to develop a decision support system for the IS sourcing decision. Moreover, tools may be developed that help to manage an ongoing outsourcing relationship, e.g., controlling systems that allow to monitor the life cycle of an IS outsourcing relationship. Some organizations have already implemented balanced score cards to control their IS function. Such systems could be extended to allow for a comparison of in-house and outsourced IS services, based on a number of prefixes.

Furthermore, while these are tools that primarily address the requirements of client organizations, the vendor business may not be overseen. External vendors are facing the challenge of being more cost efficient than clients, while at the same time providing excellent services. One approach that helps to overcome this trade-off has been suggested by Böhmann et al. (2003) more recently. They call it "modular service architecture". In short, this means that vendors develop reusable service components that can be put together flexibly. The recombination of service components allows to offer customized services without loosing the potential to realize economies of scale. Although this concept has been developed for application services that can be delivered over the internet (application service provision), it may usefully be adapted for other IS services.

Finally, IS outsourcing researchers may take a more active role in transferring IS outsourcing knowledge into neighboring disciplines, e.g. management, finance, marketing, or law (see also Hirschheim, 2003). Given the cross-functional nature of IS, there are manifold opportunities for collaborative research projects. Hopefully, this research has contributed to provide a solid basis for taking up these research opportunities.

5 Conclusion

The objective of this research was to find answers to the question why organizations behave so different in IS sourcing. More specifically, the sourcing of two IS functions was addressed: the development and maintenance of software applications. In order to understand the reasons and wider implications of the sourcing decision of these two IS functions, a multi-theoretical framework was developed. It considered the economic, strategic, and social dimension of the IS sourcing decision by integrating concepts from transaction cost theory, resource-based theory, incomplete contracts theory, the theory of planned behavior, and cross-cultural research into a coherent whole. The framework was specified in a research model and empirically tested based on the sourcing decisions of 180 Finance and Machinery organizations in the USA and Germany.

The sourcing of IS functions was treated as a complex decision problem. The behavior of organizations was analyzed form the perspective of their highest ranking IS executives. This group was meant to be most inclined in the sourcing decision and to be best informed about an organization's IS strategy as well as its requirements and infrastructure. Moreover, it was assumed that the sourcing decision is influenced by multiple dimensions that should explain both an IS executive's attitude towards outsourcing and the current degree of outsourcing. The empirical findings have widely supported this view.

There is a consistent pattern of relationships that shapes an IS executive's attitude towards outsourcing an IS function, independent of an organization's country of origin, its industry affiliation, and whether the development or the maintenance of software applications is being examined. In particular, the perception of differences in production costs between the in-house and outsourced provision of both IS functions and the influential opinion of other stakeholders were found to have a profound impact. Moreover, the individual characteristics of an organization's IS functions were found to consistently explain differences in production costs. If the provision of an IS function requires firm specific knowledge that can only be acquired and transferred by a process of social interaction, insourcing is more production cost efficient. Moreover, it is decisive for the sourcing decision whether in-house or outsourced personnel is believed to be more intrinsically motivated and group-oriented. These findings suggest that the social dimension, which has largely been neglected in previous research on the determinants of IS sourcing, should be given more emphasis in the sourcing decision.

Another remarkable finding is that transaction costs were largely neglected in the IS sourcing decision. This is alarming in so far as the descriptive results have shown that transaction costs make up about 10% of the overall costs of the application development and maintenance work and that at the same time they are, on average,

30% higher in case of outsourcing. Accordingly, transaction costs are likely to be underestimated by organizations when evaluating and comparing alternative sourcing options.

Beside these general patterns, however, that appear to be true independent of country, industry and functional differences, the empirical results suggest that there are a number of complementary context-dependent factors that have a profound impact on IS sourcing. This is particularly true for factors other than costs, including the organizational impacts (strategic, operational, systemic) that result from the provision of an IS function. Moreover, other personal attributes of the IS professionals may differ between in-house and outsourced personnel, including their long-term versus short term orientation, their systemic view and their trustworthiness.

When *contrasting* the model findings for the *US sample with* those for the *German one*, the first surprising finding was that German companies – with on average 40% – are outsourcing their application development and maintenance work more than twice as much than US firms. These differences can partially be attributed to differences in the sourcing decision factors between both countries. As expected, a number of culturally sensitive factors play an important role. It is striking out that individual characteristics of the IS professionals, indicated by their long- versus short-term orientation, their systemic view and their group-oriented behavior were found to be more influential on the sourcing decision in Germany than in the USA. Moreover, German IS executives are more inclined to consider how their control over the direction of work in an IS function and the systemic impact of an function is being affected through selective outsourcing. In addition the tendency to use capital shares with an external vendor to decrease the risk of high transaction costs and the loss of strategic opportunities is higher in Germany than in the US. Obviously, capital shares in the US are less motivated by the desire for security. Notably, however, strategic considerations are recognized in the US, while largely neglected in Germany.

Beside these cultural differences, the *industry differences* suggest that an organization's general IS requirements and architecture have an impact on its sourcing behavior. In the Finance Industry, the percentage of information intensive service processes is naturally higher. Its business processes are often supported by customized software applications. Hence, the percentage of standard software packages, that cover substantial parts of the IS requirements, are less common than in production intensive industries, like the Machinery Industry. The level of IS uniqueness increases an organization's potential to differentiate itself through its IS function. Therefore, it is not too surprising that differences between insourcing and outsourcing in leveraging the strategic potential of an IS function were found to have a significant impact on the sourcing decision in the Finance Industry, while mostly ignored in the Machinery Industry. By contrast, the operational consequences are given more emphasis in the Machinery Industry. This could be explained by the fact that integrated IS are more dispersed in the Machinery Industry. An organization's business operations can severely be affected, if one of its components, e.g. a particular application, is not provided properly. While the focus on the operational impact of an IS function appears to match with the IS architecture in the Machinery Industry, it has to be critically noted that advantages in the intellectual capital of external vendors are largely overestimated in the Machinery Industry. While such misconception can not be observed in the Finance Industry, it is striking out that capital shares are more widely used in this industry. In the Finance Industry they were found to serve as safeguards against high transaction costs and the loss of strategic opportunities. However, at the same time, it cannot be ruled out that these practices limit the decision flexibility, e.g. the ability to change from one service provider to another one. In this realm, it is also telling that IS executives in the Finance Industry were found have a relatively low impact on the sourcing decision compared to their colleagues in the Machinery Industry.

Finally, the research findings indicate that the determinants of IS outsourcing partially deviate between the *development and maintenance* of software applications. There is some evidence that, in spite of the fact that perceived differences in production costs between insourcing and outsourcing strongly impact the maintenance sourcing decision, those cost differences are often inaccurately estimated. This could be an indicator for insufficient knowledge about the true cost drivers of the maintenance work. Moreover, there is reason tho believe that the necessary resources for the maintenance work are not evaluated properly. Obviously, an IS executive's attitude toward outsourcing the maintenance work is influenced by perceived advantages of external vendors in their base of knowledge and capabilities. However, at the same time, a higher level of outsourcing is related to deficits rather than advantages in the base of intellectual capital. In spite of these obvious misconceptions regarding the maintenance of software applications, it is remarkable that strategic aspects are considered when evaluating and comparing alternative sourcing options for the maintenance work, while largely ignored in application development. Moreover, IS executives are found to have a higher level of impact on the maintenance sourcing decision. This indicates that the importance of the maintenance work has been recognized by IS managers, however, additional effort is required to better understand the maintenance production function. Otherwise, differences in cost and performance between in-house versus outsourced software maintenance cannot be estimated correctly.

In summarizing the results of this study, it may be concluded that the IS sourcing decision requires the consideration of multiple criteria. Both the individual characteristics of the IS functions, including the attributes of those that do the work within an IS function, and the environment, in which an organization is embedded, need to be carefully examined in order to rigorously evaluate and compare alternative sourcing options.

External vendors are well advised to sensibly react to the context-dependent requirement of their customers. In order to offer IS services that match their client needs, they may segment their potential customers into groups and desegregate their service portfolio into compatible components that can easily be adapted to a customer's existing IS architecture. This may allow them to realize economies of scale, while maintaining the flexibility to react to idiosyncratic customer demands. Moreover, the social dimension of the IS work may not be overseen by IS service providers when offering and providing their services.

Client organizations should always follow a multidimensional approach that recognizes the interdependence between particular IS functions, when evaluating and comparing alternative sourcing options. They should develop a good understanding of the requirements, cost drivers and organizational impacts of an IS function before starting to compare their current sourcing arrangement with alternative ones.

Appendix

Appendix A: Literature Sources on Information Systems Outsourcing

The following table provides an overview of the major Anglo-American and German publication outlets, in which articles have been published on the determinants of and reasons for IS outsourcing. A number of additional Journals such as the 'Academy of Management Journal (AMJ)', 'Academy of Management Review (AMR)', 'Administrative Science Quarterly (ASQ)', and 'Die Betriebswirtschaft (DBW)' were scanned as well. However, no papers on the topic of interest could be found in these sources. A complete overview of IS outsourcing papers that are written in English language is provided in the literature review by Dibbern et al. (2004). This review does not only include articles on the determinants of IS outsourcing, but also on the building and managing of outsourcing relationships and success factors of outsourcing.

Table Appendix-A-1: IS Outsourcing Publication Outlets (Page 1 from 2)

IS Journals	**Management Journals**
Accounting, Management and Information Technologies (AMIT – now called Information & Organization)	Betriebswirtschaftliche Forschung und Praxis (BFuP)
Communications of the Association for Computing Machinery (CACM)	Decision Sciences (DS)
European Journal of Information Systems (EJIS)	Management Science (MS)
Journal of Information Technology (JIT)	Organization Science (OS)
Journal of Management Information Systems (JMIS)	Strategic Management Journal (SMJ)
Information & Management (I&M)	Zeitschrift für Betriebswirtschaft (ZfB)
Information Systems Journal (ISJ)	
Information Systems Research (ISR)	
Management Information Systems Quarterly (MISQ)	
WIRTSCHAFTSINFORMATIK (WI)	

Table Appendix-A-1: IS Outsourcing Publication Outlets (Page 2 from 2)

IS Conferences	**Applied Management Journals**
International Conference of Information Systems (ICIS)	California Management Review (CMR)
Hawaii International Conference on System Sciences (HICSS)	Harvard Business Review (HBR)
	Information Management & Consulting (IM – now called Information, Management & Consulting)
	Sloan Management Review (SLR)

Appendix B: Research Approaches

Galliers (1991), in an analysis of IS research, differentiated between approaches and methods. Approaches are a generic or overarching way of going about research, while methods are more narrowly focused techniques for observing and analyzing events. Two general approaches to categorize the literature are an empirical and non-empirical approach. In our framework, *empirical* research may be defined as that based upon some type of empirical data, in its broadest sense (i.e. data emanating from one or more of the five human senses). It is the process of generating knowledge through various types of sensory perceptions of observed events. This encompasses (1) positivist, (2) descriptive, and (3) interpretive methods. In contrast to empirical research, *non-empirical* research is not based on specific data; it is more abstract and intangible. It is the process of generating knowledge through conceptual or quantitative analytical reasoning, "uncontaminated" by observed events. Non-empirical research may be divided into (4) conceptual and (5) mathematical approaches.

(1) Empirical: Positivist. These are "(…) studies (that) are premised on the existence of a priori fixed [hypothetical-deductive] relationships within phenomena which are typically investigated through structured instrumentation" (Orlikowski and Baroudi, 1991, p. 5). Landry and Banville (1992) note four requirements of positivist research: (1) use of controlled observations; (2) use of controlled deductions; (3) striving for replicability; and (4) desire for generalizability. Positivism typically involves the application of nomothetic methods which include experimental methods (laboratory and field experiments) and non-experimental methods such as field studies and surveys. According to Burrell and Morgan (1979, p.6) they are "(...) epitomized in the approach and methods employed in the natural sciences, which focus upon the process of testing hypotheses in accordance with the canons of scientific rigor."

(2) Empirical: Descriptive. These are studies with "(…) no theoretical grounding or interpretation of the phenomenon; rather they present what they (the researchers) believed to be straightforward 'objective', 'factual' accounts of events to illustrate some issue of interest (...)" (Orlikowski and Baroudi, 1991, p. 5). These are typically descriptive case studies which intent to "tell a story" and often have a normative component to them.

(3) Empirical: Interpretive. These are studies that seek to understand the deeper structure of a phenomenon through different approaches such as trying to understand the meaning an act has for the actor himself, trying to understand the observed world reflected by written or spoken text, or trying to understand the meanings that a particular behavior signifies to the subjects (Lee, 1991). According to Orlikowski and Baroudi (1991), in interpretive studies researchers do not impose their outsiders' *a priori* understanding of the situation. Instead, they adopt a non-deterministic perspective where the intent of the research is to increase understanding of the phe-

nomenon, and the phenomenon of interest is studied in its natural setting from the perspective of the participants. In interpretive research idiographic methods are used. These methods are often case studies and action research, and place "(...) considerable stress upon getting close to one's subject and exploring its detailed background and life-history" (Burrell and Morgan, 1979, p. 6).

(4) Non-Empirical: Conceptual. These are frameworks and arguments that sort out unstructured thoughts and concepts which circumscribe the phenomenon under study. Two different types of conceptual papers may be distinguished. The first group tries to develop frameworks that primarily serve as a basis for research by synthesizing existing knowledge and developing new concepts. The major aim of the second group is to provide guidelines for management on how to solve a particular problem or how to act in a particular situation. According to Alavi (1989), such conceptual research is typically illustrative in nature and involves opinions and examples based on the authors' experiences. The purpose of the research is to give advice and guidelines for practice, often in the form of rules and recommendations, steps and procedures to be followed, hints and warnings.

(5) Non-Empirical: Mathematical. Such studies involve mathematical models and analyses that are based on a set of restrictive assumptions about the nature of the world, and the rationality of the actors involved. The calculation of rationality is often based on minimizing costs or maximizing profits by changing certain parameters while holding others constant (ceteris paribus restrictions). These studies are typically highly analytical (*cf.* Whang, 1992).

Appendix C: Cover Letters

C.1 Initial Cover Letter in English

C.T. Bauer College of Business · DISC · Houston, Texas 77204-6021

C.T. Bauer College of Business
Department of Decision and Information Sciences
University of Houston
Houston, Texas 77204-6021

telephone: (713) 743-4692
fax: (713) 743-4693
email: rudy@uh.edu
web: disc-nt.cba.uh.edu

«MrMs1» «First_Name» «Last_Name»
Head of IT/IS
«Company_Name»
«Address»
«City», «State» «M_5_Digit_Zip_Code»-«Zip__4»

«Date»

Study on Information Systems Insourcing versus Outsourcing

Dear «MrMs2» «Last_Name»:

As globalization and the digital age are exerting an increasing influence on organizations, information systems (IS) are becoming more critical for organizational success. Paralleling this rise in the significance of IS, is a growing reliance on the practice of outsourcing to meet the organization's IS needs. While some organizations have been quick to adopt outsourcing, others have been slow to consider this IS sourcing option. Still others have evaluated outsourcing but adopted insourcing instead.

Recognizing the prominent role the decision to outsource or insource IS functions plays in today's organizations, the Information Systems Research Center (ISRC) of the University of Houston, USA along with the German National Research Foundation (DFG) – in cooperation with the University of Bayreuth, Germany – is sponsoring a cooperative research project.

The objective of our study is to explain why some organizations choose to outsource particular IS functions while others prefer to insource them. In particular, we shall concentrate on the «Industry_Type» looking at the different approaches used in deciding on insourcing or outsourcing of the "development of software applications" as well as the "maintenance of software applications" and elaborating those factors that are especially important for a sourcing decision.

To this end we would like to ask you to fill out the enclosed questionnaire and to send it back to us using the postage-paid envelope provided. In return for filling out the questionnaire, we will send you a summary report of our findings based on the responses of 1200 Chief Information Officers of companies in the «Industry_Type» in both the USA and Germany. The study results should allow you to compare your own approach with the overall industry in both the USA and Germany. In addition you'll receive a well grounded analysis and practical implications from an independent third party. As a gesture of appreciation for completing the questionnaire, we have enclosed a small and interesting gift for you. It is a historical stock. We trust you will enjoy the gift.

All of your answers will be treated anonymously and strictly confidentially. We would like to thank you in advance for your cooperation and greatly appreciate your time.

Yours sincerely,

Rudy Hirschheim
Tennoco/Chase Chair and
Professor of Information Systems

Wynne Chin
Bauer Faculty Fellow and
Associate Professor of Information Systems

C.2 Follow-up Cover Letter in English

C.T. Bauer College of Business · DISC · Houston, Texas 77204-6021

C.T. Bauer College of Business
Department of Decision and Information Sciences
University of Houston
Houston, Texas 77204-6282
telephone: (713) 743-4692
fax: (713) 743-4693
email: rudy@uh.edu
web: www.cba.uh.edu

«MrMs_1»«First_Name» «Last_Name»
Head of IT / IS
«Company_Name»
«Street__PO»
«City», «State», «M_5_Digit_Zip_Code»-«Zip__4»

«Date»

Study on Information Systems Insourcing versus Outsourcing

Dear «MrMs2» «Last_Name»:

About four weeks ago we sent you a questionnaire that asked your personal evaluation of your organization's practices on the question of insourcing versus outsourcing the development and maintenance of software applications. To the best of our knowledge, we have not heard back from you. However, for those that already responded but did not fill out the reply postcard, we would appreciate you sending the attached postcard at your convenience. Again, we very much appreciate your participation in this research project.

An initial analysis of the answers that we have received so far reveals some very interesting results. We discovered that companies in the «Industry_Type» adopt very different sourcing practices, but that there tends to be a coherent pattern in the factors explaining these different organizational practices. An executive summary of our study results will be sent to you if you fill out the questionnaire in the enclosed postage-paid return envelope as well as the attached return postcard.

Your support will help us understand the nature of IS sourcing practices in the «Industry_Type» and to compare them with the practices in Germany. We are also looking at a second Industry in both countries. We would therefore respectfully request that you take about 30 minutes of your time and fill out the enclosed questionnaire. Your responses are of utmost importance to our survey.

The study is designed to address all companies, irrespective of whether your organization currently insources or outsources part or all of its applications software development and maintenance. Additionally, all answers will be treated anonymously and strictly confidentially.

Lastly, we would like to thank you in advance and greatly appreciate your time.

Yours sincerely,

Rudy Hirschheim
Tennoco/Chase Chair and
Professor of Information Systems

Wynne Chin
Bauer Faculty Fellow and
Associate Professor of Information Systems

C.3 Initial Cover Letter in German

Universität Bayreuth · BWL VII · Wirtschaftsinformatik · 95440 Bayreuth

«Anrede_1»
«TITEL»«VORNAME» «NAME»
«FIRMA1»
«STRASSE»
«PLZ» «ORT»

Lehrstuhl für
Betriebswirtschaftslehre VII
Wirtschaftsinformatik

Universitätsstraße 30
D-95440 Bayreuth

Telefon 0921/55-2807
Telefax 0921/55-2216

E-Mail
wi@uni-bayreuth.de

Internet
wi.oec.uni-bayreuth.de

«Datum»

Untersuchung der Eigenerstellung oder des Fremdbezugs der IV

Sehr geehrt«Anrede_2» «TITEL»«NAME»,

mit der zunehmenden Globalisierung und Digitalisierung trägt die Informationsverarbeitung (IV) verstärkt zum Unternehmenserfolg bei. Um den steigenden IV-Bedürfnissen gerecht zu werden, bauen Organisationen vermehrt auf den Fremdbezug bzw. das Outsourcing von IV-Leistungen. Während sich allerdings einige Unternehmen recht schnell für den Fremdbezug entschieden haben, zögern andere, diese Option wahrzunehmen. Wieder andere haben eine Bewertung des Fremdbezugs vorgenommen, sich aber für die Eigenerstellung entschieden.

Die Deutsche Forschungsgemeinschaft (DFG) hat die Wichtigkeit und Tragweite der Frage der Eigenerstellung oder des Fremdbezugs der IV erkannt und fördert zusammen mit dem Information Systems Research Center (ISRC) an der University of Houston, USA, ein Gemeinschaftsprojekt der Universität Bayreuth und der University of Houston.

Wir wollen mit Hilfe der Studie erklären, warum einige Unternehmen sich für den Fremdbezug bestimmter IV-Funktionen entscheiden, während andere die Eigenerstellung vorziehen. Dabei konzentrieren wir uns zunächst auf Organisationen des «Branche», um deren Praktiken bei der Entscheidung über die Eigenerstellung oder den Fremdbezug der Gestaltung und Wartung von Anwendungssoftware zu verstehen und die für eine optimale Entscheidung besonders wichtigen Faktoren herauszuarbeiten.

Zu diesem Zweck bitten wir Sie, den beiliegenden Fragebogen auszufüllen und im beigefügten Freiumschlag an uns zurückzusenden. Wenn Sie den Fragebogen beantworten, erhalten Sie von uns die Auswertung der Ergebnisse der Studie. Neben Ihnen erhalten die Leiter der Informationsverarbeitung von 1200 anderen Unternehmen des «Branche» in Deutschland und den USA diesen Fragebogen. Die Ergebnisse der Studie ermöglichen es Ihnen, Ihr Vorgehen mit der gesamten Branche in Deutschland und den USA zu vergleichen. Zudem erhalten Sie eine fundierte Analyse und Handlungsempfehlungen aus unabhängiger Hand. Als kleines Dankeschön im Voraus haben wir ein interessantes Geschenk für Sie beigelegt. Es handelt sich um eine historische Sammleraktie. Wir hoffen, dass Ihnen das Geschenk gefällt.

Alle von Ihnen gemachten Angaben werden anonym und streng vertraulich behandelt. Wir möchten Ihnen bereits im Voraus unseren persönlichen Dank für Ihre Unterstützung aussprechen und wissen die von Ihnen zur Verfügung gestellte Zeit sehr zu schätzen.

Mit freundlichen Grüßen,

Prof. Dr. Armin Heinzl Dipl. Kfm. Jens Dibbern

C.4 Follow-up Cover Letter in German

Universität Bayreuth · BWL VII · Wirtschaftsinformatik · 95440 Bayreuth

Lehrstuhl für
Betriebswirtschaftslehre VII
Wirtschaftsinformatik

Universitätsstraße 30
D-95440 Bayreuth

Telefon 0921 55-2807
Mobil 0179 2998400
Telefax 0921 55-2216

E-Mail
wi@uni-bayreuth.de

Internet
wi.oec.uni-bayreuth.de

«ANREDE_1»
«TITEL»«VORNAME» «NACHNAME»
«FIRMA1»
«STRASSE»
«PLZ» «ORT»

«Datum»

Untersuchung der Eigenerstellung oder des Fremdbezugs der IV

Sehr «geehrt» «ANREDE_2» «TITEL»«NACHNAME»,

vor ungefähr drei Wochen haben wir Ihnen einen Fragebogen zugesandt, mit dessen Hilfe wir Ihre persönliche Einschätzung zur Frage der Eigenerstellung oder des Fremdbezugs der Gestaltung und Wartung von Anwendungssoftware erheben wollen.

Erste Auswertungen der bisherigen Antworten deuten bereits auf sehr interessante Ergebnisse hin. Wir haben festgestellt, dass Unternehmen im «Branche» zwar völlig unterschiedliche Praktiken bei der Frage des Outsourcing von Funktionen der Informationsverarbeitung (IV) aufweisen, dass sich aber ein kohärentes Muster bei den Faktoren abzeichnet, welche die jeweils gewählte Organisationsform erklären. Insofern möchten wir mit diesem Schreiben verstärkt Ihr Interesse zur Teilnahme an unserer Studie wecken.

Ihre Unterstützung würde uns der einzigartigen Möglichkeit näher bringen, speziell auf den «Branche» in Deutschland zugeschnittene aussagekräftige Ergebnisse zu erzielen und diese den Praktiken in den USA sowie einer Vergleichsbranche in beiden Ländern gegenüberzustellen.

Wir bitten Sie daher, sich ca. 30 Minuten Ihrer Zeit zu nehmen und den nochmals beigefügten Fragebogen auszufüllen. Ihre Antwort ist für unsere Untersuchung von großer Bedeutung.

Unsere Studie ist so angelegt, dass sie alle Unternehmen anspricht, unabhängig davon, ob sie Aufgaben der Gestaltung und der Wartung von Anwendungssoftware ganz oder teilweise eigen oder fremd beziehen und wie hoch ihr Erfahrungsgrad mit beiden Alternativen ist.

Alle von Ihnen gemachten Angaben werden anonym und streng vertraulich behandelt. Wir möchten Ihnen auch im Namen der Deutschen Forschungsgemeinschaft und unserer Kooperationspartner an der University of Houston, Texas, im Voraus unseren persönlichen Dank für Ihre Unterstützung aussprechen und wissen die von Ihnen zur Verfügung gestellte Zeit sehr zu schätzen. Bei Rückfragen können Sie uns jederzeit kontaktieren.

Mit freundlichen Grüßen,

Prof. Dr. Armin Heinzl Dipl.-Kfm. Jens Dibbern

Appendix D: Questionnaires

D.1 Questionnaire in English

UNIVERSITY of HOUSTON

UNIVERSITÄT BAYREUTH

Insourcing versus Outsourcing the Development and Maintenance of Application Software

Confidential Questionnaire for Chief Information Officer

General Instructions

Most questions are related to two different Information Systems (IS) functions:

A) Applications development is generally understood to refer to ...

... the definition, design, and implementation of customized software as well as ...

... the analysis, selection, and tailoring of standardized software packages (e.g. SAP R/3).

B) Applications maintenance includes ...

... all corrective, adaptive, and perfective (i.e., optimizing) modifications of application software that do not include any functional enhancements.

The term **"organization"** refers to the corporation or company that YOU belong to and for whose IS services management and coordination YOU show responsibility.

The term **"external service provider"** refers to a company or corporation, that represents an independent legal entity (e.g. an inc.) including subsidiaries of your organization that perform IS services.

There are no right or wrong answers; we are simply interested in your opinion. It is very important for us that you answer **all** the questions as we need statistical averages for scientific accuracy.

All of your answers will be treated anonymously and strictly confidentially!

Thank you for your help!

C. T. Bauer College of Business
Department of Decision and Information Sciences
Professor Rudy Hirschheim
Professor Wynne Chin

University of Bayreuth, Germany
Department of Information Systems
Professor Armin Heinzl
Research Associate Jens Dibbern

Sponsored by the
Information Systems Research Center
ISRC

Sponsored by the
German National Science Foundation
DFG

Information Systems Insourcing versus Outsourcing

Confidential Questionnaire for Chief Information Officer

1) Current Degree of Outsourcing IS Functions

The **degree of IS outsourcing** is defined as the extent to which the tasks and activities necessary for the provision of an IS function are carried out by one or more external service providers with an independent legal form.

Please try to **distinguish** between **applications development** and **applications maintenance** as described in the previous page even if you do not treat them separately in your organization.

Also please note that **external service providers** can represent independent legal corporations that your organization is connected by capital (e.g. joint-venture, spin-off of former in-house IS department).

Please fill in percentages!	Applications development	Applications maintenance
For each of the two IS functions, please estimate the **average percentage currently allocated to external service providers** in terms of ...		
... **the function's total budget.**	___%	___%
... **total person working days.**	___%	___%
... **total number of people** that participate in doing the work.	___%	___%
If you currently have some tasks and activities that are carried out by **personnel from an external service provider, approximately** what **percentage** of these workers were **former employees of your organization?**	___%	___%

2) Evaluation of Advantages of In-house versus Outsourced IS Functions

Production Costs

+2 = strongly agree   +1 = agree   0 = neither agree nor disagree   -1 = disagree   -2 = strongly disagree

In doing the actual work required for each of the IS functions, ...	Applications development +2 +1 0 -1 -2	Applications maintenance +2 +1 0 -1 -2
... our internal staff works more cost efficiently than an external service provider.	□□□□□	□□□□□
... our internal staff works faster than personnel from an external service provider.	□□□□□	□□□□□
... we can realize higher economies of scale internally than an external service provider.	□□□□□	□□□□□
... the price that an external service provider charges is higher than our internal costs.	□□□□□	□□□□□
... in-house performance is cheaper than outsourcing.	□□□□□	□□□□□

This set of questions pertain to your opinions concerning the transaction costs.

Transaction costs are all costs other than the actual production costs that arise when **delegating tasks** of an IS function to a third party (i.e. the actual workers).

Transaction costs

+2 = strongly agree   +1 = agree   0 = neither agree nor disagree   -1 = disagree   -2 = strongly disagree

When delegating (i.e. transferring) tasks of the particular IS function ...	Applications development +2 +1 0 -1 -2	Applications maintenance +2 +1 0 -1 -2
... the costs incurred in negotiating, managing and coordinating are lower within the firm than in case of contracting with an external service provider.	□□□□□	□□□□□

Information Systems Insourcing versus Outsourcing

Confidential Questionnaire for Chief Information Officer

Transaction costs (Continued)

+2 = strongly agree +1 = agree 0 = neither agree nor disagree -1 = disagree -2 = strongly disagree

	Applications development	Applications maintenance
When delegating (i.e. transferring) tasks of the particular IS function ...	+2 +1 0 -1 -2	+2 +1 0 -1 -2
... more organizational resources would be required with an external service provider than when done in house.	☐☐☐☐☐	☐☐☐☐☐
... it would result in more organizational overheads and administrative costs when using an external service provider than within the company.	☐☐☐☐☐	☐☐☐☐☐
... less transaction costs are incurred for internal employees than when using an external service provider.	☐☐☐☐☐	☐☐☐☐☐

Below are different types of activities that cause **transaction costs** for your organization **in case of outsourcing.** These are additional costs that can arise from outsourcing, but are not included in the price that an external service provider charges.

Outsourcing Transaction Costs

1 = 0 - 0.5% of total costs 2 = 0.5 - 1.0% 3 = 1.0 - 1.5% 4 = 1.5 - 2.0% 5 = more than 2.0% - please fill in number!

	Applications development	Applications maintenance
What **percentage of all costs** involved in this particular IS function would you **estimate** are related to each of the following **transaction costs** (in terms of time, effort, and money) **if** it is **outsourced?**	1 2 3 4 5	1 2 3 4 5
Searching and selecting external service provider.	☐☐☐☐ ___%	☐☐☐☐ ___%
Negotiating with employee representatives and unions.	☐☐☐☐ ___%	☐☐☐☐ ___%
Initial negotiating and creating of contract with service provider.	☐☐☐☐ ___%	☐☐☐☐ ___%
Dissolution and transfer of firm resources (employees, hardware, software) that possibly are no longer necessary within the organization after having outsourced.	☐☐☐☐ ___%	☐☐☐☐ ___%
Modifying and renegotiating contracts with service provider.	☐☐☐☐ ___%	☐☐☐☐ ___%
Establishing and imparting rules, principles and procedures for getting along with each other in your organization.	☐☐☐☐ ___%	☐☐☐☐ ___%
Monitoring service provider performance.	☐☐☐☐ ___%	☐☐☐☐ ___%
Enforcing and motivating service provider performance.	☐☐☐☐ ___%	☐☐☐☐ ___%
Coordinating external workers (eventually multiple service providers).	☐☐☐☐ ___%	☐☐☐☐ ___%
Organizational justification and approval of prices that the service provider charges.	☐☐☐☐ ___%	☐☐☐☐ ___%
Contract cancellation.	☐☐☐☐ ___%	☐☐☐☐ ___%

Below are different types of activities that cause **transaction costs** for your organization **in case of staying in-house**.

What **percentage of all costs** involved in this particular IS function would you **estimate** are related to each of the following **transaction costs** (in terms of time, effort, and money) **if** it is **performed in-house**?

In-house Transaction Costs

1 = 0 - 0.5% of total costs 2 = 0.5 - 1.0% 3 = 1.0 - 1.5% 4 = 1.5 - 2.0% 5 = more than 2.0% - please fill in number!

	Applications development	Applications maintenance
	1 2 3 4 5	1 2 3 4 5
Searching and identifying appropriate employees.	☐☐☐☐ ___%	☐☐☐☐ ___%
Defining task structures and delegating employees to tasks.	☐☐☐☐ ___%	☐☐☐☐ ___%

3

Information Systems Insourcing versus Outsourcing

Confidential Questionnaire for Chief Information Officer

In-house Transaction Costs (Continued)

1 = 0 - 0.5% of total costs 2 = 0.5 - 1.0% 3 = 1.0 - 1.5% 4 = 1.5 - 2.0% 5 = more than 2.0% - please fill in number!

	Applications development 1 2 3 4 5	Applications maintenance 1 2 3 4 5
Adjusting individual job descriptions and work/departmental structures.	☐☐☐☐ ___ %	☐☐☐☐ ___ %
Establishing and imparting rules, principles and procedures for coexisting in your organization.	☐☐☐☐ ___ %	☐☐☐☐ ___ %
Monitoring employee performance.	☐☐☐☐ ___ %	☐☐☐☐ ___ %
Enforcing and motivating employee performance.	☐☐☐☐ ___ %	☐☐☐☐ ___ %
Coordinating employees.	☐☐☐☐ ___ %	☐☐☐☐ ___ %
Justifying and accounting of costs with management and internal departments.	☐☐☐☐ ___ %	☐☐☐☐ ___ %
Dissolution of employee contracts.	☐☐☐☐ ___ %	☐☐☐☐ ___ %

Having gone through both outsourcing and in-house transaction costs, please answer the following questions:

Overall Transaction Costs

Please fill in percentages!

	Applications development	Applications maintenance
What **percentage of all costs** associated with providing each of the IS functions would you estimate are **related to transaction costs** ...		
... when you go with an external service provider?	___ %	___ %
... when you stay in-house?	___ %	___ %

Please check one box and fill in number if applicable!

	Applications development	Applications maintenance
How much **more (or less)** do you believe your **transaction costs** associated with each IS function are **if you go with an external service provider** compared to staying in-house?		
More than staying in-house.	☐ by ___ %	☐ by ___ %
About the same amount of transaction costs.	☐	☐
Less than staying in-house.	☐ by ___ %	☐ by ___ %

Strategic Significance

+2 = strongly agree +1 = agree 0 = neither agree nor disagree -1 = disagree -2 = strongly disagree

	Applications development +2 +1 0 -1 -2	Applications maintenance +2 +1 0 -1 -2
This IS function plays a central role in our organization to achieve a competitive advantage.	☐☐☐☐☐	☐☐☐☐☐
The contribution of this IS function to achieve a competitive advantage is weakened if it is carried out by an external service provider as opposed to our organization.	☐☐☐☐☐	☐☐☐☐☐
This IS function is critical in helping our company to successfully compete against our competitors.	☐☐☐☐☐	☐☐☐☐☐
The ability of this IS function to help our company successfully compete against our competitors is weakened if it is carried out by an external service provider as opposed to our organization.	☐☐☐☐☐	☐☐☐☐☐
This IS function is vital for meeting our company's strategic objectives.	☐☐☐☐☐	☐☐☐☐☐
The contribution of this IS function to meet our company's strategic objectives is weakened if it is carried out by an external service provider as opposed to our organization.	☐☐☐☐☐	☐☐☐☐☐

Information Systems Insourcing versus Outsourcing

Confidential Questionnaire for Chief Information Officer

Operational Significance

+2 = strongly agree +1 = agree 0 = neither agree nor disagree -1 = disagree -2 = strongly disagree

	Applications development +2 +1 0 -1 -2	Applications maintenance +2 +1 0 -1 -2
If our firm's ability to do this IS function weakens, our day-to-day business activities will suffer considerably.	☐☐☐☐☐	☐☐☐☐☐
The contribution of this IS function to support our day-to-day business activities is weakened if it is carried out by an external service provider as opposed to our organization.	☐☐☐☐☐	☐☐☐☐☐
Our company's day-to-day business operations heavily rely on our ability to carry out this IS function well.	☐☐☐☐☐	☐☐☐☐☐
Our firm's ability to carry out this IS function in a way so that our day-to-day business operations are not threatened, is weakened if done by an external service provider as opposed to our organization.	☐☐☐☐☐	☐☐☐☐☐
Delays, project failures, and other poor results for this IS function will cause major problems in our general ability to perform our daily business.	☐☐☐☐☐	☐☐☐☐☐
Our company is better than a service provider when it comes to limiting the preceding problems.	☐☐☐☐☐	☐☐☐☐☐

Resource Base

+2 = in-house much better +1 = better 0 = about the same -1 = worse -2 = in-house much worse

Please evaluate how much **better or worse** the following **resources** are for this particular IS function **within your organization** compared to those of an **external service provider**:	Applications development +2 +1 0 -1 -2	Applications maintenance +2 +1 0 -1 -2
Skill set	☐☐☐☐☐	☐☐☐☐☐
Capabilities	☐☐☐☐☐	☐☐☐☐☐
Knowledge set	☐☐☐☐☐	☐☐☐☐☐
Social competency	☐☐☐☐☐	☐☐☐☐☐
Staffing level	☐☐☐☐☐	☐☐☐☐☐
Experience	☐☐☐☐☐	☐☐☐☐☐
Financial resources	☐☐☐☐☐	☐☐☐☐☐
Technical equipment	☐☐☐☐☐	☐☐☐☐☐
Overall resources	☐☐☐☐☐	☐☐☐☐☐

Impact on Overall System

+2 = strongly agree +1 = agree 0 = neither agree nor disagree -1 = disagree -2 = strongly disagree

If this IS function is not performed in-house but by an external service provider ...	Applications development +2 +1 0 -1 -2	Applications maintenance +2 +1 0 -1 -2
... the integration of this IS function into the overall IS function of our organization is weakened.	☐☐☐☐☐	☐☐☐☐☐
... the overall performance of our entire IS function will be greatly affected.	☐☐☐☐☐	☐☐☐☐☐
... the synergetic effects to other IS functions will be threatened.	☐☐☐☐☐	☐☐☐☐☐

Organization Wide Employee Orientation

+2 = strongly agree +1 = agree 0 = neither agree nor disagree -1 = disagree -2 = strongly disagree

In doing the actual work required for each of the IS functions **our own employees tend much more than personnel of external service providers to ...**	Applications development +2 +1 0 -1 -2	Applications maintenance +2 +1 0 -1 -2
... have a systems view of the organization.	☐☐☐☐☐	☐☐☐☐☐

5

Information Systems Insourcing versus Outsourcing

Confidential Questionnaire for Chief Information Officer

Organization Wide Employee Orientation (Continued)

+2 = strongly agree +1 = agree 0 = neither agree nor disagree -1 = disagree -2 = strongly disagree

In doing the actual work required for each of the IS functions **our own employees tend much more than personnel of external service providers to ...**	Applications development +2 +1 0 -1 -2	Applications maintenance +2 +1 0 -1 -2
... have an organization wide perspective of how work in different areas effect one another.	☐☐☐☐☐	☐☐☐☐☐
... consider the task interdependencies in our organization.	☐☐☐☐☐	☐☐☐☐☐
... have an integrated view of the organization.	☐☐☐☐☐	☐☐☐☐☐

Decision Control

+2 = strongly agree +1 = agree 0 = neither agree nor disagree -1 = disagree -2 = strongly disagree

If this IS function is not performed in-house but by an external service provider ...	Applications development +2 +1 0 -1 -2	Applications maintenance +2 +1 0 -1 -2
... our firm loses its control over the direction of the work and its related activities.	☐☐☐☐☐	☐☐☐☐☐
... our organization will have less influence over how the work is to be accomplished.	☐☐☐☐☐	☐☐☐☐☐

Trust in Worker

+2 = a lot more +1 = more 0 = about the same -1 = less -2 = a lot less

In doing the actual work required for each of the IS functions **how much more or less** do you in general **feel and believe** that the **personnel of an external service provider** compared to your own employees will ...	Applications development +2 +1 0 -1 -2	Applications maintenance +2 +1 0 -1 -2
... behave in an ethical manner when doing the actual work.	☐☐☐☐☐	☐☐☐☐☐
... do the job right even when the opportunity to behave opportunistically is present.	☐☐☐☐☐	☐☐☐☐☐
... work in a fair and professional manner independent of your organization's ability and effort to monitor them?	☐☐☐☐☐	☐☐☐☐☐

Please check one box and fill in number if applicable!

How much more or less **(in percentage)** do you **trust your own employees** compared to personnel from an external service provider in performing the particular IS function?	Applications development	Applications maintenance
More than an external service provider.	☐ by ____ %	☐ by ____ %
About the same.	☐	☐
Less than an external service provider.	☐ by ____ %	☐ by ____ %

Please fill in percentages!

How much **(in percentage)** do you **trust your employees** in doing their work ?	____ %	____ %
How much **(in percentage)** do you **trust external service providers** in doing their work?	____ %	____ %

Non-monetary Incentives

+2 = strongly agree +1 = agree 0 = neither agree nor disagree -1 = disagree -2 = strongly disagree

Factoring out performance incentives that result in direct monetary benefits (e.g. extra payments), our firm's employees compared to the personnel of external sercice providers are ...	Applications development +2 +1 0 -1 -2	Applications maintenance +2 +1 0 -1 -2
... much more motivated to do quality work in the particular IS function.	☐☐☐☐☐	☐☐☐☐☐

Non-monetary Incentives

+2 = strongly agree +1 = agree 0 = neither agree nor disagree -1 = disagree -2 = strongly disagree

Factoring out performance incentives that result in direct monetary benefits (e.g. extra payments), our firm's employees compared to the personnel of external vendors are ...	Applications development +2 +1 0 -1 -2	Applications maintenance +2 +1 0 -1 -2
... much more interested to do quality work in the particular IS function.	□□□□□	□□□□□
... much more committed to do quality work in the particular IS function.	□□□□□	□□□□□

Group Behavior

+2 = strongly agree +1 = agree 0 = neither agree nor disagree -1 = disagree -2 = strongly disagree

In doing the actual work in each of the IS functions it often requires interactions and exchanges with other colleagues and employees in your organization. **To what extend do you agree that your own employees compared to workers from an external service provider show a higher tendency to ...**	Applications development +2 +1 0 -1 -2	Applications maintenance +2 +1 0 -1 -2
... subordinate his or her own goals and thoughts to those of the project team.	□□□□□	□□□□□
... do what he or she believes is best rather than what the group believes.	□□□□□	□□□□□
... be direct and forthright when dealing with people.	□□□□□	□□□□□
... be modest in talking about their own accomplishments.	□□□□□	□□□□□
... give opinions that will help people save face rather than give a statement of the truth.	□□□□□	□□□□□
... be willing to downplay his or her beliefs that may conflict with the group in order to maintain consensus.	□□□□□	□□□□□
... listen and value the general opinion of the group.	□□□□□	□□□□□

Long-term Orientation of Workers

+2 = strongly agree +1 = agree 0 = neither agree nor disagree -1 = disagree -2 = strongly disagree

In doing the actual work required for each of the IS functions our own employees tend much more than personnel of external service providers to ...	Applications development +2 +1 0 -1 -2	Applications maintenance +2 +1 0 -1 -2
... use a long-term horizon when it comes to planning.	□□□□□	□□□□□
... consider the longer term implications of a decision.	□□□□□	□□□□□
... orient their planning on the future rather than on the present.	□□□□□	□□□□□

Organization Long-term Orientation

+2 = strongly agree +1 = agree 0 = neither agree nor disagree -1 = disagree -2 = strongly disagree

Our organization tends to ...	+2 +1 0 -1 -2
... use a long-term horizon when it comes to planning our IS function.	□□□□□
... consider the longer term implications of our IS decisions.	□□□□□
... orient its IS planning towards the future as opposed to just the present.	□□□□□

Overall Advantage

+2 = strongly agree +1 = agree 0 = neither agree nor disagree -1 = disagree -2 = strongly disagree

	Applications development +2 +1 0 -1 -2	Applications maintenance +2 +1 0 -1 -2
In general, it is more advantageous to outsource this IS function than to do it in-house.	□□□□□	□□□□□
The overall costs for this IS function are lower when it is outsourced.	□□□□□	□□□□□
Overall, the benefits are greater when outsourcing this IS function than to do it in-house.	□□□□□	□□□□□

Attitude towards Outsourcing

Please give your opinion!

Overall, having an external service provider perform this IS function is ...

Applications development	-3	-2	-1	0	+1	+2	+3		Applications maintenance	-3	-2	-1	0	+1	+2	+3	
... bad	☐	☐	☐	☐	☐	☐	☐	good	... bad	☐	☐	☐	☐	☐	☐	☐	good
... negative	☐	☐	☐	☐	☐	☐	☐	positive	... negative	☐	☐	☐	☐	☐	☐	☐	positive
... harmful	☐	☐	☐	☐	☐	☐	☐	beneficial	... harmful	☐	☐	☐	☐	☐	☐	☐	beneficial
... more expensive	☐	☐	☐	☐	☐	☐	☐	cheaper	... more expensive	☐	☐	☐	☐	☐	☐	☐	cheaper
... foolish	☐	☐	☐	☐	☐	☐	☐	wise	... foolish	☐	☐	☐	☐	☐	☐	☐	wise
... illogical	☐	☐	☐	☐	☐	☐	☐	logical	... illogical	☐	☐	☐	☐	☐	☐	☐	logical
... worthless	☐	☐	☐	☐	☐	☐	☐	valuable	... worthless	☐	☐	☐	☐	☐	☐	☐	valuable

3) Importance of Factors

-2 = absolutely unimportant -1 = unimportant 0 = neither unimportant nor important +1 = important +2 = absolutely important

How important is it for your organization to take into account the **following factors when deciding** whether to perform tasks of this particular IS function **in-house or** to **outsource** them to an external service provider?	Applications development -2 -1 0 +1 +2	Applications maintenance -2 -1 0 +1 +2
Production costs - which are all costs that arise for performing the actual activities necessary to complete the tasks associated with the provision of an IS function.	☐☐☐☐☐	☐☐☐☐☐
Transaction costs - which are all costs other than the actual production costs that arise when delegating tasks of the IS function to a third party.	☐☐☐☐☐	☐☐☐☐☐
Strategic significance - which is the degree of the IS function's contribution to generate a competitive advantage.	☐☐☐☐☐	☐☐☐☐☐
Operational significance - which is the degree to which the IS function is an integral part of the day-to-day business operations of the organization.	☐☐☐☐☐	☐☐☐☐☐
Resource base - which is the extent to which the resources necessary in providing the IS function meet the requirements and standards of the business.	☐☐☐☐☐	☐☐☐☐☐
Impact on overall system - which is the extent to which the particular IS function is an integral part within the overall IS function.	☐☐☐☐☐	☐☐☐☐☐
Decision control - which is the extent to which your organization has control over the direction of the work within an IS function and its related activities (e.g. control over choice of hardware, software, tools, methods, standards, staffing).	☐☐☐☐☐	☐☐☐☐☐
Organization wide worker orientation - which is defined as the degree to which those working on the IS function have an integrated view of the organization.	☐☐☐☐☐	☐☐☐☐☐
Trust in worker - which is the combined emotional feeling and cognitive belief that those working on the IS function will act predictably, will fulfill their obligations, and will behave fairly in performing an IS function even when the possibility for opportunism is present.	☐☐☐☐☐	☐☐☐☐☐
Non-monetary incentives - which are all factors that encourage the willingness of the task carriers to do quality work without resulting in a direct monetary benefit for them.	☐☐☐☐☐	☐☐☐☐☐
Group behavior - which is defined as the degree to which individuals orient their action for the benefit of the group or collective rather than for their own or individual preferences.	☐☐☐☐☐	☐☐☐☐☐

Information Systems Insourcing versus Outsourcing

Confidential Questionnaire for Chief Information Officer

(Continued)

-2 = absolutely unimportant -1 = unimportant 0 = neither unimportant nor important +1 = important +2 = absolutely important

How important is it for your organization to take into account the **following factors when deciding** whether to perform tasks of this particular IS function **in-house or** to **outsource** them to an external service provider?	Applications development -2 -1 0 +1 +2	Applications maintenance -2 -1 0 +1 +2
Long-term orientation of workers - which is the degree to which the workers employ a long term view in the planning and decision making of the particular IS function.	☐☐☐☐☐	☐☐☐☐☐

4) Characteristics of IS Functions

Firm Specificity of Knowledge

+2 = strongly agree +1 = agree 0 = neither agree nor disagree -1 = disagree -2 = strongly disagree

In doing the actual work for each of the IS functions in your organization, it requires ...	Applications development +2 +1 0 -1 -2	Applications maintenance +2 +1 0 -1 -2
... good understanding of business processes that are unique to your organization.	☐☐☐☐☐	☐☐☐☐☐
... knowledge about the special requirements of the business units of your organization.	☐☐☐☐☐	☐☐☐☐☐
... knowledge that was gained through the task setting in your organization and cannot easily be written down or articulated.	☐☐☐☐☐	☐☐☐☐☐
... detailed knowledge of software systems developed specifically for your organization.	☐☐☐☐☐	☐☐☐☐☐
... software technical knowledge unique only to your organization.	☐☐☐☐☐	☐☐☐☐☐
... knowledge that is unique to your company.	☐☐☐☐☐	☐☐☐☐☐

Knowledge Transfer

Please give your opinion!

How do you rate the process of **transferring your firm specific knowledge to external service providers** to ensure that the IS function is performed adequately?

Applications development	-3 -2 -1 0 +1 +2 +3		Applications maintenance	-3 -2 -1 0 +1 +2 +3	
very hard	☐☐☐☐☐☐☐	very easy	very hard	☐☐☐☐☐☐☐	very easy
very difficult	☐☐☐☐☐☐☐	very simple	very difficult	☐☐☐☐☐☐☐	very simple
very slow	☐☐☐☐☐☐☐	very fast	very slow	☐☐☐☐☐☐☐	very fast

Social Networks

+2 = strongly agree +1 = agree 0 = neither agree nor disagree -1 = disagree -2 = strongly disagree

In doing the actual work for each of the IS functions, it is important to have **strong social / interpersonal working relationships ...**	Applications development +2 +1 0 -1 -2	Applications maintenance +2 +1 0 -1 -2
... between IS workers and users/clients of the system.	☐☐☐☐☐	☐☐☐☐☐
... within the group of IS workers.	☐☐☐☐☐	☐☐☐☐☐
In doing the actual work for each of the IS functions, it is important to have **strong collegial / collaborative relationships ...**	+2 +1 0 -1 -2	+2 +1 0 -1 -2
... between IS workers and users/clients of the system.	☐☐☐☐☐	☐☐☐☐☐
... within the group of IS workers.	☐☐☐☐☐	☐☐☐☐☐

Information Systems Insourcing versus Outsourcing

Confidential Questionnaire for Chief Information Officer

Measurement Difficulty

+2 = strongly agree +1 = agree 0 = neither agree nor disagree -1 = disagree -2 = strongly disagree

In respect to the people who do the actual work within each IS function ...	Applications development +2 +1 0 -1 -2	Applications maintenance +2 +1 0 -1 -2
... it is difficult to measure their individual contribution to its outcome.	□□□□□	□□□□□
... we are unable to accurately evaluate their individual input-output relation.	□□□□□	□□□□□
... it is difficult to keep accurate records related to their performance.	□□□□□	□□□□□

Uncertainty in Task Performance

+2 = strongly agree +1 = agree 0 = neither agree nor disagree -1 = disagree -2 = strongly disagree

The skills necessary to do each of the IS functions ...	Applications development +2 +1 0 -1 -2	Applications maintenance +2 +1 0 -1 -2
... constantly change due to the environmental dynamics in technology.	□□□□□	□□□□□
... require a process of constant learning and adaptation in response to the environmental dynamics in technology.	□□□□□	□□□□□
... constantly change due to the dynamics in the work and business processes of our organization.	□□□□□	□□□□□
... require a process of constant learning and adaptation in response to the dynamics in the work and business processes of our organization.	□□□□□	□□□□□
Overall, the requirements to perform each of the IS functions ...	+2 +1 0 -1 -2	+2 +1 0 -1 -2
... constantly change.	□□□□□	□□□□□
... require a process of constant learning and adaptation.	□□□□□	□□□□□
... are uncertain.	□□□□□	□□□□□

Work Load Uncertainty

+2 = strongly agree +1 = agree 0 = neither agree nor disagree -1 = disagree -2 = strongly disagree

	Applications development	Applications maintenance
The work load involved for this particular IS function tends to constantly change.	□□□□□	□□□□□
The amount of work associated with this particular IS function varies significantly.	□□□□□	□□□□□

5) IS Outsourcing Decision Making and Implementation

-2 = extremely low -1 = low 0 = average +1 = high +2 = extremely high

Overall, how do you rate your organization's ... →	... experience ... → -2 -1 0 +1 +2	... expertise ... → -2 -1 0 +1 +2	... effort ... -2 -1 0 +1 +2
... in making an **IS outsourcing decision?**	□□□□□	□□□□□	□□□□□
... in arranging an **IS outsourcing contract?**	□□□□□	□□□□□	□□□□□

Please fill in a number!

How many **IS outsourcing contracts** would you estimate your organization has made in the **last five years?**	____ (e.g. 4)
How many of your **IS outsourcing decisions** would you estimate **did not result in a completed contract** within the **last five years?**	____ (e.g. 5)

10

Control over Outsourcing Process

+2 = strongly agree +1 = agree 0 = neither agree nor disagree -1 = disagree -2 = strongly disagree

When it comes to outsourcing this IS function to an external service provider ...	Applications development +2 +1 0 -1 -2	Applications maintenance +2 +1 0 -1 -2
... our organization can act unrestrictedly.	☐☐☐☐☐	☐☐☐☐☐
... there are no impediments to our organization.	☐☐☐☐☐	☐☐☐☐☐
... our organization has total control over all necessary activities.	☐☐☐☐☐	☐☐☐☐☐

Opinion of Others

Please give your opinion!

Persons or groups whose opinion is important to our organization think that outsourcing this particular IS function is ...

Applications development	-3 -2 -1 0 +1 +2 +3		Applications maintenance	-3 -2 -1 0 +1 +2 +3	
... bad	☐☐☐☐☐☐☐	good	... bad	☐☐☐☐☐☐☐	good
... negative	☐☐☐☐☐☐☐	positive	... negative	☐☐☐☐☐☐☐	positive
... harmful	☐☐☐☐☐☐☐	beneficial	... harmful	☐☐☐☐☐☐☐	beneficial
... foolish	☐☐☐☐☐☐☐	wise	... foolish	☐☐☐☐☐☐☐	wise
... illogical	☐☐☐☐☐☐☐	logical	... illogical	☐☐☐☐☐☐☐	logical
... worthless	☐☐☐☐☐☐☐	valuable	... worthless	☐☐☐☐☐☐☐	valuable

Process of Outsourcing

Please give your opinion!

Overall, the process of outsourcing this IS function to an external service provider is ...

Applications development	-3 -2 -1 0 +1 +2 +3		Applications maintenance	-3 -2 -1 0 +1 +2 +3	
... very hard	☐☐☐☐☐☐☐	very easy	... very hard	☐☐☐☐☐☐☐	very easy
... very difficult	☐☐☐☐☐☐☐	very simple	... very difficult	☐☐☐☐☐☐☐	very simple
... very slow	☐☐☐☐☐☐☐	very fast	... very slow	☐☐☐☐☐☐☐	very fast

6) Additional Questions on IS Outsourcing Behavior

Ideal Degree of Outsourcing

Please fill in percentages!

	Applications development	Applications maintenance
What **percentage** of this IS function do you **ideally** believe should be spent on **external service providers?**	____ %	____ %

Future Degree of Outsourcing

Please check one box and fill in number if applicable!

How much more or less of this IS function do you **expect will approximately be spent on external** service providers in **one year?**	Applications development	Applications maintenance
More than currently.	☐ by ____ %	☐ by ____ %
About the same.	☐	☐
Less than currently.	☐ by ____ %	☐ by ____ %

Information Systems Insourcing versus Outsourcing

Confidential Questionnaire for Chief Information Officer

Degree of Property Rights in External Service Provider	Applications development	Applications maintenance
+2 = very high +1 = high 0 = medium -1 = low -2 = very low		
For that portion of the work within each of the IS functions that is done by one or more external service providers:	+2 +1 0 -1 -2	+2 +1 0 -1 -2
How high would you rate your organization's authority in directing the management of the service providers?	□□□□□	□□□□□
How high would you rate your organization's impact on decisions regarding the allocation of the service providers' human and physical resources?	□□□□□	□□□□□
What share of capital does your organization have with the service providers on average?	____ %	____ %

7) General Questions

We would like to point out that anonymity of your responses is guaranteed.		
How many years have you been working in this organization?		____ Years
Please estimate your organization's number of employees ...	... overall?	____ Persons
	... in your entire IS function?	____ Persons
	... in applications development?	____ Persons
	... in applications maintenance?	____ Persons
Please indicate your organization's total sales!		____ Mio. $
Please indicate your organization's total IS budget as percentage of total sales!		____ %
Please estimate the percentage of your organization's total IS budget spent on ...	... applications development!	____ %
	... applications maintenance!	____ %

In order to preserve your anonymity but match your answers with a possible one page follow-up, please provide the following information.

Month / day of your birthday	□□ □□	and last three digits of your social security number	□□□

These two sets are specific to you, but cannot be tracked back to you. When combined they will create a unique key to connect your current and future responses.

Thanks a lot for your cooperation!

Please send the questionnaire back to us using the enclosed postage-paid envelope!

In addition we would like to ask you to return the enclosed postage-paid post card to us. Please fill in your name and address and mark the appropriate box if you are interested in receiving an executive summary!

University of Houston, C. T. Bauer College of Business, Department of Decision and Information Sciences, Prof. Wynne W. Chin
334 Melcher Hall, Room 280D, Houston, Texas, 77204-6021, U.S.A.
Phone: (713) 743-4728 E-mail: wchin@uh.edu Internet: disc-nt.cba.uh.edu

D.2 Questionnaire in German

UNIVERSITÄT BAYREUTH

UNIVERSITY of HOUSTON

Eigenerstellung oder Fremdbezug von Aufgaben der Gestaltung und Wartung von Anwendungssoftware

Vertraulicher Fragebogen für den Leiter der Informationsverarbeitung

Allgemeine Hinweise zu den Fragen

Die meisten Fragen beziehen sich auf zwei unterschiedliche Funktionen der Informationsverarbeitung (IV):

A) Die Gestaltung von Anwendungssoftware ...

... umfasst die Definition, den Entwurf und die Implementierung von Individualsoftware sowie ...

... die Analyse, Auswahl und Anpassung von Standardsoftwarepaketen (z.B. SAP R/3).

B) Die Wartung von Anwendungssoftware ...

... umfasst alle Maßnahmen der Fehlerbereinigung und Perfektionierung von Anwendungssoftware, die keine funktionalen Neuerungen beinhalten.

Der Begriff **"Organisation"** bezieht sich auf das Unternehmen, den Konzern oder die Holding, der Sie angehören, und für dessen Management und Koordination der Informationsverarbeitung Sie die Verantwortung tragen.

Der Begriff **"Externer Dienstleister"** bezieht sich auf Unternehmen mit selbstständiger Rechtsform (z.B. AG oder GmbH), eingeschlossen Tochter- oder Beteiligungsunternehmen Ihrer Organisation, die Leistungen der Informationsverarbeitung erbringen.

Es gibt keine richtigen oder falschen Antworten. Wir sind lediglich an Ihrer persönlichen Meinung interessiert. Es ist sehr wichtig für uns, dass Sie **alle** Fragen beantworten, da wir für eine saubere wissenschaftliche Analyse statistische Durchschnitte benötigen.

Ihre Antworten werden anonym und streng vertraulich behandelt!

Vielen Dank für Ihre Unterstützung!

Rechts- und Wirtschaftswissenschaftliche Fakultät
Lehrstuhl für Wirtschaftsinformatik

Prof. Dr. Armin Heinzl
Dipl.-Kfm. Jens Dibbern

C. T. Bauer College of Business
Department of Decision and Information Sciences

Prof. Dr. Rudolph Hirschheim
Prof. Dr. Wynne Chin

Gefördert durch die
Deutsche Forschungsgemeinschaft
DFG

Eigenerstellung oder Fremdbezug von IV-Funktionen

Vertraulicher Fragebogen für den Leiter der Informationsverarbeitung

1) Gegenwärtiger Grad des Outsourcing von IV-Funktionen

Der Grad des Outsourcing bzw. des Fremdbezugs bemisst, in welchem Umfang die mit einer IV-Funktion verbundenen Aufgaben und Tätigkeiten von einem oder mehreren externen Dienstleistern mit eigenständiger Rechtsform erbracht werden.

Bitte versuchen Sie auch dann, wenn Sie die Aufgaben der **Gestaltung und Wartung von Anwendungssoftware** organisatorisch gleich behandeln, eine **Unterscheidung** vorzunehmen.

Zudem bitten wir Sie, zu beachten, dass der Begriff **"externer Dienstleister"** sowohl unverbundene Unternehmen, an denen Ihre Organisation keine Kapitalbeteiligung hält, beinhaltet als auch verbundene Unternehmen, z.B. Joint-Ventures oder ehemalige interne Abteilungen, die Sie ausgegründet haben.

Bitte tragen Sie Prozentwerte ein!	Anwendungs-gestaltung	Anwendungs-wartung
Bitte **schätzen** Sie für jede der beiden IV-Funktionen den **durchschnittlichen gegenwärtigen prozentualen Anteil** (von 0 bis 100 %) **des Fremdbezugs** bzw. des Outsourcing bezogen auf ...		
... das **Gesamtbudget** der IV-Funktion.	____ %	____ %
... die **Gesamtheit der verrechneten Manntage** der IV-Funktion.	____ %	____ %
... die **gesamte Anzahl von Personen**, die an der Arbeitsverrichtung mitwirken.	____ %	____ %
Für den Fall, dass Aufgaben und Tätigkeiten der IV-Funktion von Mitarbeitern eines externen Dienstleisters ausgeübt werden, bitte **schätzen** Sie **wieviele dieser Personen (in Prozent) ehemalige Mitarbeiter Ihrer Organisation sind.**	____ %	____ %

2) Beurteilung der Vorteile interner gegenüber externer Leistungserstellung

Produktionskosten

+2 = trifft voll zu +1 = trifft zu 0 = teils - teils -1 = trifft weniger zu -2 = trifft gar nicht zu

	Anwendungs-gestaltung	Anwendungs-wartung
Bezogen auf die Verrichtung der eigentlichen Tätigkeiten, die für die jeweilige IV-Funktion notwendig sind, ...	+2 +1 0 -1 -2	+2 +1 0 -1 -2
... arbeitet unser internes Personal kosteneffizienter als ein externer Dienstleister.	☐☐☐☐☐	☐☐☐☐☐
... arbeiten unsere internen Mitarbeiter schneller als das Personal externer Dienstleister.	☐☐☐☐☐	☐☐☐☐☐
... können wir intern höhere Skalenerträge erzielen als ein externer Dienstleister.	☐☐☐☐☐	☐☐☐☐☐
... fällt der Preis, den externe Dienstleister verlangen, höher aus als unsere internen Kosten der Leistungserstellung.	☐☐☐☐☐	☐☐☐☐☐
... ist die interne Leistungserstellung kostengünstiger als der Fremdbezug.	☐☐☐☐☐	☐☐☐☐☐

Bitte geben Sie bei den folgenden Fragen Ihre Einschätzung über die Höhe der Transaktionskosten ab!

Transaktionskosten sind alle anderen Kosten außer den Kosten der eigentlichen Leistungserstellung, die mit den Tätigkeiten verbunden sind, die im Rahmen der **Delegation von Aufgaben** einer IV-Funktion an Aufgabenträger entstehen.

Transaktionskosten

+2 = trifft voll zu +1 = trifft zu 0 = teils - teils -1 = trifft weniger zu -2 = trifft gar nicht zu

	Anwendungs-gestaltung	Anwendungs-wartung
Bei der Delegation von Aufgaben der jeweiligen IV-Funktion ...	+2 +1 0 -1 -2	+2 +1 0 -1 -2
... fallen bei interner Leistungserstellung geringere Verhandlungs-, Management- und Koordinationskosten an als beim Fremdbezug.	☐☐☐☐☐	☐☐☐☐☐

Eigenerstellung oder Fremdbezug von IV-Funktionen

Vertraulicher Fragebogen für den Leiter der Informationsverarbeitung

Transaktionskosten (Fortsetzung)

+2 = trifft voll zu +1 = trifft zu 0 = teils - teils -1 = trifft weniger zu -2 = trifft gar nicht zu

Bei der Delegation von Aufgaben der jeweiligen IV-Funktion ...	Anwendungsgestaltung +2 +1 0 -1 -2	Anwendungswartung +2 +1 0 -1 -2
... werden beim Fremdbezug mehr organisatorische Ressourcen benötigt als bei interner Erstellung.	□□□□□	□□□□□
... fallen beim Fremdbezug höhere organisatorische Gemeinkosten und Verwaltungskosten an als bei interner Verrichtung.	□□□□□	□□□□□
... fallen bei eigenen Mitarbeitern weniger Transaktionskosten an als beim Fremdbezug.	□□□□□	□□□□□

Nachfolgend sind eine Reihe von Tätigkeiten aufgeführt, die für Ihre Organisation **Transaktionskosten beim Fremdbezug** verursachen, also zusätzliche Kosten, die durch den Fremdbezug entstehen können, aber NICHT im Preis enthalten sind, den der externe Dienstleister in Rechung stellt.

Transaktionskosten beim Fremdbezug

1 = 0 - 0,5% der Gesamtkosten 2 = 0,5 - 1,0% 3 = 1,0 - 1,5% 4 = 1,5 - 2,0% 5 = mehr als 2,0% - bitte Zahl eintragen!

Wie hoch **schätzen Sie den prozentualen Anteil der Transaktionskosten** (im Sinne von Zeit, Anstrengungen, Ausgaben) **an den Gesamtkosten** der jeweiligen IV-Funktion ein, **wenn sie fremd bezogen** wird?	Anwendungsgestaltung 1 2 3 4 5	Anwendungswartung 1 2 3 4 5
Suche und Auswahl geeigneter Dienstleister.	□□□□ ___%	□□□□ ___%
Verhandlung mit Arbeitnehmervertretern und Gewerkschaften.	□□□□ ___%	□□□□ ___%
Erstmalige Vertragsverhandlung und -gestaltung mit Dienstleistern.	□□□□ ___%	□□□□ ___%
Freisetzung und Transfer von Unternehmensressourcen (Mitarbeiter, Hardware, Software), die nach dem Outsourcing möglicherweise nicht länger intern benötigt werden.	□□□□ ___%	□□□□ ___%
Vertragsanpassungen und Neuverhandlungen mit Dienstleistern.	□□□□ ___%	□□□□ ___%
Einführung und Vermittlung von Regeln, Grundsätzen und Standardprozeduren für das tägliche Miteinander in Ihrer Organisation.	□□□□ ___%	□□□□ ___%
Überwachung der Leistung von Dienstleistern.	□□□□ ___%	□□□□ ___%
Leistungseinforderung und -motivation.	□□□□ ___%	□□□□ ___%
Koordination der externen Aufgabenträger (evt. bei verschiedenen Dienstleistern).	□□□□ ___%	□□□□ ___%
Interne Rechtfertigung und Genehmigung der Preise, die der Dienstleister berechnet.	□□□□ ___%	□□□□ ___%
Auflösung von Verträgen.	□□□□ ___%	□□□□ ___%

Nachfolgend sind nun eine Reihe von Tätigkeiten aufgeführt, die für Ihre Organisation **Transaktionskosten bei der Eigenerstellung** verursachen.

Wie hoch **schätzen Sie den prozentualen Anteil der Transaktionskosten** (im Sinne von Zeit, Anstrengungen, Ausgaben) **an den Gesamtkosten** der jeweiligen IV-Funktion ein, **wenn sie von internen Mitarbeitern** ausgeübt wird?

Transaktionskosten bei der Eigenerstellung

1 = 0 - 0,5% der Gesamtkosten 2 = 0,5 - 1,0% 3 = 1,0 - 1,5% 4 = 1,5 - 2,0% 5 = mehr als 2,0% - bitte Zahl eintragen!

	Anwendungsgestaltung 1 2 3 4 5	Anwendungswartung 1 2 3 4 5
Suche und Auswahl von geeigneten Mitarbeitern.	□□□□ ___%	□□□□ ___%
Festlegung von Aufgabenstrukturen und Zuordnung von Aufgaben an Mitarbeiter.	□□□□ ___%	□□□□ ___%

Eigenerstellung oder Fremdbezug von IV-Funktionen

Vertraulicher Fragebogen für den Leiter der Informationsverarbeitung

Transaktionskosten bei der Eigenerstellung (Fortsetzung)

1 = 0 - 0,5% der Gesamtkosten 2 = 0,5 - 1,0% 3 = 1,0 - 1,5% 4 = 1,5 - 2,0% 5 = mehr als 2,0% - bitte Zahl eintragen!

	Anwendungsgestaltung 1 2 3 4 5	Anwendungswartung 1 2 3 4 5
Anpassung von Stellenbeschreibungen sowie Arbeits- und Abteilungsstrukturen.	☐☐☐☐ ___ %	☐☐☐☐ ___ %
Einführung und Vermittlung von Regeln, Grundsätzen und Standardprozeduren für das tägliche Miteinander in Ihrer Organisation.	☐☐☐☐ ___ %	☐☐☐☐ ___ %
Überwachung der Mitarbeiterleistungen.	☐☐☐☐ ___ %	☐☐☐☐ ___ %
Leistungseinforderung und -motivation.	☐☐☐☐ ___ %	☐☐☐☐ ___ %
Koordination der Mitarbeiter.	☐☐☐☐ ___ %	☐☐☐☐ ___ %
Rechtfertigung und Verrechnung von Kosten gegenüber dem Management und internen Abteilungen.	☐☐☐☐ ___ %	☐☐☐☐ ___ %
Mitarbeiterfreisetzung.	☐☐☐☐ ___ %	☐☐☐☐ ___ %

Nachdem Sie die Höhe der Transaktionskosten sowohl bei der Eigenerstellung als auch beim Fremdbezug beurteilt haben, nehmen Sie bitte folgende Gesamtwertungen vor:

Transaktionskosten insgesamt

Bitte tragen Sie Prozentwerte ein!

Bitte schätzen Sie, wieviel Prozent der Gesamtkosten, die im Rahmen der jeweiligen IV-Funktion anfallen, den Transaktionskosten zuzuschreiben sind ...	Anwendungsgestaltung	Anwendungswartung
... im Falle des Fremdbezugs.	___ %	___ %
... im Falle der Eigenerstellung.	___ %	___ %

Bitte kreuzen Sie eine der drei Optionen an und tragen Sie ggf. einen Prozentwert ein!

Bitte **schätzen Sie**, um wieviel Prozent die **Transaktionskosten beim Fremdbezug höher (oder niedriger)** ausfallen als bei der Eigenerstellung:	Anwendungsgestaltung	Anwendungswartung
Höher als bei der Eigenerstellung.	☐ um ___ %	☐ um ___ %
Ungefähr **gleich** hohe Transaktionskosten.	☐	☐
Niedriger als bei der Eigenerstellung.	☐ um ___ %	☐ um ___ %

Strategische Bedeutung

+2 = trifft voll zu +1 = trifft zu 0 = teils - teils -1 = trifft weniger zu -2 = trifft gar nicht zu

	Anwendungsgestaltung +2 +1 0 -1 -2	Anwendungswartung +2 +1 0 -1 -2
Diese IV-Funktion spielt für unsere Organisation eine zentrale Rolle, um Wettbewerbsvorteile gegenüber Konkurrenten zu erzielen.	☐☐☐☐☐	☐☐☐☐☐
Der zentrale Beitrag dieser IV-Funktion für das Erzielen von Wettbewerbsvorteilen wird geschwächt, wenn sie nicht eigenerstellt, sondern fremdbezogen wird.	☐☐☐☐☐	☐☐☐☐☐
Diese IV-Funktion stellt für unsere Organisation eine kritische Größe dar, da sie einen Beitrag zum erfolgreichen Bestehen gegenüber unseren Wettbewerbern leistet.	☐☐☐☐☐	☐☐☐☐☐
Die Fähigkeit dieser IV-Funktion, einen Beitrag zum erfolgreichen Bestehen gegenüber unseren Wettbewerbern zu leisten, wird geschwächt, wenn sie nicht eigenerstellt, sondern fremdbezogen wird.	☐☐☐☐☐	☐☐☐☐☐
Diese IV-Funktion trägt entscheidend dazu bei, dass unsere Organisation ihre strategischen Ziele erreicht.	☐☐☐☐☐	☐☐☐☐☐
Der entscheidende Beitrag dieser IV-Funktion für das Erreichen der strategischen Ziele unserer Organisation wird geschwächt, wenn sie nicht eigenerstellt, sondern fremdbezogen wird.	☐☐☐☐☐	☐☐☐☐☐

Eigenerstellung oder Fremdbezug von IV-Funktionen

Vertraulicher Fragebogen für den Leiter der Informationsverarbeitung

Operative Bedeutung

+2 = trifft voll zu +1 = trifft zu 0 = teils - teils -1 = trifft weniger zu -2 = trifft gar nicht zu

	Anwendungsgestaltung +2 +1 0 -1 -2	Anwendungswartung +2 +1 0 -1 -2
Unser täglicher Geschäftsbetrieb leidet erheblich darunter, falls die Fähigkeit unserer Organisation geschwächt wird, diese IV-Funktion angemessen auszuüben.	□□□□□	□□□□□
Der Beitrag dieser IV-Funktion zur Unterstützung unseres täglichen Geschäftsbetriebs wird geschwächt, wenn sie nicht eigenerstellt, sondern fremdbezogen wird.	□□□□□	□□□□□
Das Funktionieren unseres täglichen Geschäftsbetriebs hängt maßgeblich von der Fähigkeit ab, die Aufgaben in dieser IV-Funktion zu erfüllen.	□□□□□	□□□□□
Die Fähigkeit, die Aufgaben in dieser IV-Funktion so zu erfüllen, dass das Funktionieren unseres täglichen Geschäftsbetriebs nicht gefährdet wird, wird geschwächt, wenn die Funktion nicht eigenerstellt, sondern fremdbezogen wird.	□□□□□	□□□□□
Verzögerungen, Fehlschläge und andere schlechte Leistungen in dieser IV-Funktion erschweren die Aufrechterhaltung unseres täglichen Geschäftsbetriebs erheblich.	□□□□□	□□□□□
Unsere Organisation ist externen Dienstleistern überlegen, wenn es darum geht, derartige Probleme zu vermeiden.	□□□□□	□□□□□

Ressourcen

+2 = in-house viel besser +1 = besser 0 = ungefähr gleich -1 = schlechter -2 = in-house viel schlechter

Bitte **beurteilen Sie** für die jeweilige IV-Funktion, um wieviel besser (oder schlechter) die folgenden **Ressourcen innerhalb Ihrer Organisation gegenüber denen externer Dienstleister sind:**	Anwendungsgestaltung +2 +1 0 -1 -2	Anwendungswartung +2 +1 0 -1 -2
Fachkenntnisse	□□□□□	□□□□□
Fähigkeiten	□□□□□	□□□□□
Wissen	□□□□□	□□□□□
Sozialkompetenzen	□□□□□	□□□□□
Personalstand	□□□□□	□□□□□
Erfahrungen	□□□□□	□□□□□
Finanzielle Ressourcen	□□□□□	□□□□□
Technische Ausstattung	□□□□□	□□□□□
Gesamtheit aller Ressourcen	□□□□□	□□□□□

Einfluss auf das Gesamtsystem

+2 = trifft voll zu +1 = trifft zu 0 = teils - teils -1 = trifft weniger zu -2 = trifft gar nicht zu

Wenn diese IV-Funktion nicht eigenerstellt, sondern fremdbezogen wird ...	Anwendungsgestaltung +2 +1 0 -1 -2	Anwendungswartung +2 +1 0 -1 -2
... wird die Integration dieser IV-Funktion in die Gesamtfunktion der IV unserer Organisation erschwert.	□□□□□	□□□□□
... wird die Gesamtleistung der IV unserer Organisation nachhaltig beeinträchtigt.	□□□□□	□□□□□
... werden die Synergieeffekte zu anderen IV-Funktionen gefährdet.	□□□□□	□□□□□

Generelle Orientierung am Gesamtsystem

+2 = trifft voll zu +1 = trifft zu 0 = teils - teils -1 = trifft weniger zu -2 = trifft gar nicht zu

Bei der Verrichtung der Arbeiten in der jeweiligen IV-Funktion tendieren unsere Mitarbeiter in stärkerem Maße als externe Dienstleister ...	Anwendungsgestaltung +2 +1 0 -1 -2	Anwendungswartung +2 +1 0 -1 -2
... dazu, die Organisation als Ganzes zu sehen.	□□□□□	□□□□□

Generelle Orientierung am Gesamtsystem (Fortsetzung)

+2 = trifft voll zu +1 = trifft zu 0 = teils - teils -1 = trifft weniger zu -2 = trifft gar nicht zu

Bei der Verrichtung der Arbeiten in der jeweiligen IV-Funktion tendieren unsere Mitarbeiter in stärkerem Maße als externe Dienstleister ...	Anwendungsgestaltung +2 +1 0 -1 -2	Anwendungswartung +2 +1 0 -1 -2
... zu einer Gesamtperspektive, in der die gegenseitige Beeinflussung der Arbeiten in verschiedenen Bereichen Berücksichtigung findet.	☐☐☐☐☐	☐☐☐☐☐
... dazu, die Aufgabeninterdependenzen in unserer Organisation zu berücksichtigen.	☐☐☐☐☐	☐☐☐☐☐
... insgesamt gesehen zu einer integrierten Sichtweise auf die Organisation.	☐☐☐☐☐	☐☐☐☐☐

Entscheidungskontrolle

+2 = trifft voll zu +1 = trifft zu 0 = teils - teils -1 = trifft weniger zu -2 = trifft gar nicht zu

Wenn diese IV-Funktion nicht eigenerstellt, sondern fremdbezogen wird ...	Anwendungsgestaltung +2 +1 0 -1 -2	Anwendungswartung +2 +1 0 -1 -2
... verliert unsere Organisation die Kontrolle über die inhaltliche Ausrichtung der mit dieser IV-Funktion verbundenen Tätigkeiten.	☐☐☐☐☐	☐☐☐☐☐
... wird unsere Organisation weniger Einfluss auf die Art und Weise der Arbeitsverrichtung haben.	☐☐☐☐☐	☐☐☐☐☐

Vertrauen in Aufgabenträger

+2 = viel mehr +1 = mehr 0 = ungefähr gleich -1 = weniger -2 = viel weniger

Bitte **beurteilen Sie** für die jeweilige IV-Funktion, **wieviel mehr oder weniger Sie bei Ihren eigenen Mitarbeitern** im Vergleich zum Personal externer Dienstleister den **Glauben und das Gefühl** haben, dass sie ...	Anwendungsgestaltung +2 +1 0 -1 -2	Anwendungswartung +2 +1 0 -1 -2
... sich bei der Leistungserstellung ethischen Grundsätzen entsprechend verhalten.	☐☐☐☐☐	☐☐☐☐☐
... die Aufgaben auch dann richtig auszuführen, wenn die Möglichkeit besteht, sich opportunistisch zu verhalten.	☐☐☐☐☐	☐☐☐☐☐
... die Leistungen aufrichtig und professionell erbringen - unabhängig von den Fähigkeiten und Anstrengungen Ihrer Organisation, sie zu überwachen.	☐☐☐☐☐	☐☐☐☐☐

Bitte kreuzen Sie eine der drei Optionen an und tragen Sie ggf. einen Prozentwert ein!

Wieviel Prozent mehr oder weniger **vertrauen Sie Ihren eigenen Mitarbeitern** im Vergleich zum Personal externer Dienstleister bei der Ausübung der jeweiligen IV-Funktion?	Anwendungsgestaltung	Anwendungswartung
Mehr als externen Dienstleistern.	☐ um ____ %	☐ um ____ %
Ungefähr im **gleichen** Maße.	☐	☐
Weniger als externen Dienstleistern.	☐ um ____ %	☐ um ____ %

Bitte tragen Sie Prozentwerte ein!

	Anwendungsgestaltung	Anwendungswartung
Bis zu wieviel **Prozent vertrauen** Sie Ihren **eigenen Mitarbeitern** bei der Leistungserstellung?	____ %	____ %
Bis zu wieviel **Prozent vertrauen** Sie dem **Personal externer Dienstleister** bei der Leistungserstellung?	____ %	____ %

Unentgeltliche Anreize

+2 = trifft voll zu +1 = trifft zu 0 = teils - teils -1 = trifft weniger zu -2 = trifft gar nicht zu

Unter **Nichtberücksichtigung von Anreizen** zur Förderung der Leistungsbereitschaft, die zu direkten **geldwerten Vorteilen** führen (z.B. Zusatzprämien), sind **unsere eigenen Mitarbeiter** gegenüber dem **Personal externer Dienstleister** ...	Anwendungsgestaltung +2 +1 0 -1 -2	Anwendungswartung +2 +1 0 -1 -2
... viel motivierter, hochwertige Arbeit in der IV-Funktion zu verrichten.	☐☐☐☐☐	☐☐☐☐☐

Eigenerstellung oder Fremdbezug von IV-Funktionen

Vertraulicher Fragebogen für den Leiter der Informationsverarbeitung

Unentgeltliche Anreize (Fortsetzung)

+2 = trifft voll zu   +1 = trifft zu   0 = teils - teils   -1 = trifft weniger zu   -2 = trifft gar nicht zu

Unter **Nichtberücksichtigung von** solchen **Anreizen** zur Förderung der Leistungsbereitschaft, die zu direkten **geldwerten Vorteilen** führen (z.B. Zusatzprämien), sind **unsere eigenen Mitarbeiter** gegenüber dem **Personal externer Dienstleister** ...	Anwendungsgestaltung +2 +1 0 -1 -2	Anwendungswartung +2 +1 0 -1 -2
... viel interessierter, hochwertige Arbeit in der IV-Funktion zu verrichten.	☐☐☐☐☐	☐☐☐☐☐
... viel engagierter, hochwertige Arbeit in der IV-Funktion zu verrichten.	☐☐☐☐☐	☐☐☐☐☐

Gruppenverhalten

+2 = trifft voll zu   +1 = trifft zu   0 = teils - teils   -1 = trifft weniger zu   -2 = trifft gar nicht zu

Die Verrichtung der Arbeiten in der jeweiligen IV-Funktion verlangt oftmals die Interaktion und den Austausch mit Kollegen und anderen Mitarbeitern in Ihrer Organisation. **Inwiefern trifft es zu, dass Ihre eigenen Mitarbeiter in stärkerem Maße als das Personal externer Dienstleister dazu neigen, ...**	Anwendungsgestaltung +2 +1 0 -1 -2	Anwendungswartung +2 +1 0 -1 -2
... ihre eigenen Ziele und Vorstellungen denen des Teams unterzuordnen.	☐☐☐☐☐	☐☐☐☐☐
... das zu tun, was sie für am besten halten und weniger das, was die Gruppe will.	☐☐☐☐☐	☐☐☐☐☐
... im Umgang mit anderen direkt und "geradeheraus" zu sein.	☐☐☐☐☐	☐☐☐☐☐
... bescheiden zu sein, wenn sie über ihre eigenen Leistungen sprechen.	☐☐☐☐☐	☐☐☐☐☐
... anstatt die Wahrheit auszusprechen, ihre Meinung in einer Art und Weise kund zu tun, die es anderen Personen erlaubt, ihr Gesicht zu wahren.	☐☐☐☐☐	☐☐☐☐☐
... bereit zu sein, die eigenen Vorstellungen, die möglicherweise im Konflikt mit der Gruppe stehen, herunterzuspielen, um den Konsens in der Gruppe nicht zu gefährden.	☐☐☐☐☐	☐☐☐☐☐
... die allgemeine Meinung der Gruppe wertzuschätzen und ihr Gehör zu schenken.	☐☐☐☐☐	☐☐☐☐☐

Langzeitorientierung der Aufgabenträger

+2 = trifft voll zu   +1 = trifft zu   0 = teils - teils   -1 = trifft weniger zu   -2 = trifft gar nicht zu

Bei der Verrichtung der Arbeiten in der jeweiligen IV-Funktion tendieren unsere Mitarbeiter in stärkerem Maße als externe Dienstleister dazu, ...	Anwendungsgestaltung +2 +1 0 -1 -2	Anwendungswartung +2 +1 0 -1 -2
... die Planung langfristig auszurichten.	☐☐☐☐☐	☐☐☐☐☐
... die langfristigen Auswirkungen einer Entscheidung zu berücksichtigen.	☐☐☐☐☐	☐☐☐☐☐
... die Planung eher an der Zukunft als an der Gegenwart zu orientieren.	☐☐☐☐☐	☐☐☐☐☐

Langzeitorientierung der Organisation

+2 = trifft voll zu   +1 = trifft zu   0 = teils - teils   -1 = trifft weniger zu   -2 = trifft gar nicht zu

Unsere Organisation tendiert dazu, ...	+2 +1 0 -1 -2
... die Planung der IV langfristig auszurichten.	☐☐☐☐☐
... die langfristigen Auswirkungen einer IV-Entscheidung zu berücksichtigen.	☐☐☐☐☐
... die IV-Planung eher an der Zukunft als an der Gegenwart zu orientieren.	☐☐☐☐☐

Gesamtbeurteilung

+2 = trifft voll zu   +1 = trifft zu   0 = teils - teils   -1 = trifft weniger zu   -2 = trifft gar nicht zu

	Anwendungsgestaltung +2 +1 0 -1 -2	Anwendungswartung +2 +1 0 -1 -2
Die Gesamtkosten für diese IV-Funktion sind geringer, wenn sie fremdbezogen wird.	☐☐☐☐☐	☐☐☐☐☐
Insgesamt gesehen ist es vorteilhafter, diese IV-Funktion fremd zu beziehen.	☐☐☐☐☐	☐☐☐☐☐
Der Nutzen für unsere Organisation ist größer, wenn wir diese IV-Funktion fremdbeziehen.	☐☐☐☐☐	☐☐☐☐☐

Eigenerstellung oder Fremdbezug von IV-Funktionen

Vertraulicher Fragebogen für den Leiter der Informationsverarbeitung

Einstellung gegenüber dem Outsourcing

Bitte geben Sie Ihre Einschätzung ab!

Insgesamt gesehen ist der Fremdbezug dieser IV-Funktion für unsere Organisation ...

	Anwendungsgestaltung -3 -2 -1 0 +1 +2 +3			Anwendungswartung -3 -2 -1 0 +1 +2 +3	
... schlecht	☐☐☐☐☐☐☐	gut	... schlecht	☐☐☐☐☐☐☐	gut
... negativ	☐☐☐☐☐☐☐	positiv	... negativ	☐☐☐☐☐☐☐	positiv
... schädlich	☐☐☐☐☐☐☐	förderlich	... schädlich	☐☐☐☐☐☐☐	förderlich
... teurer	☐☐☐☐☐☐☐	billiger	... teurer	☐☐☐☐☐☐☐	billiger
... töricht	☐☐☐☐☐☐☐	weise	... töricht	☐☐☐☐☐☐☐	weise
... unlogisch	☐☐☐☐☐☐☐	logisch	... unlogisch	☐☐☐☐☐☐☐	logisch
... wertlos	☐☐☐☐☐☐☐	wertvoll	... wertlos	☐☐☐☐☐☐☐	wertvoll

3) Wichtigkeit der einzelnen Faktoren

-2 = absolut unwichtig -1 = unwichtig 0 = teils - teils +1 = sehr wichtig +2 = äußerst wichtig

Für **wie wichtig** halten Sie es, die **folgenden Faktoren** zu berücksichtigen, wenn eine **Entscheidung** darüber getroffen wird, ob Aufgaben in einer IV-Funktion **eigenerstellt oder fremdbezogen** werden sollen?	Anwendungsgestaltung -2 -1 0 +1 +2	Anwendungswartung -2 -1 0 +1 +2
Produktionskosten: Die Kosten, die für die eigentliche Leistungserstellung der IV-Funktion anfallen.	☐☐☐☐☐	☐☐☐☐☐
Transaktionskosten: Alle Kosten außer den Kosten der eigentlichen Leistungserstellung der IV-Funktion, die im Rahmen der Delegation von Aufgaben entstehen.	☐☐☐☐☐	☐☐☐☐☐
Strategische Bedeutung: Der Beitrag der IV-Funktion zur Erzeugung von Wettbewerbsvorteilen gegenüber Konkurrenten.	☐☐☐☐☐	☐☐☐☐☐
Operative Bedeutung: Die Unerlässlichkeit der IV-Funktion für das Funktionieren des täglichen Geschäftsbetriebs Ihrer Organisation.	☐☐☐☐☐	☐☐☐☐☐
Ressourcen: Eignung der Ressourcen der IV-Funktion zur Befriedigung der Bedürfnisse und Standards des Geschäftsbetriebs.	☐☐☐☐☐	☐☐☐☐☐
Einfluss auf das Gesamtsystem: Das Ausmaß, inwieweit eine einzelne IV-Funktion einen integralen Bestandteil der Gesamtfunktion der Informationsverarbeitung darstellt.	☐☐☐☐☐	☐☐☐☐☐
Entscheidungskontrolle: Das Ausmaß der Kontrolle über die inhaltliche Ausrichtung der mit einer IV-Funktion verbundenen Tätigkeiten (z.B. Kontrolle über die Wahl von Hardware, Software, Werkzeugen, Methoden, Standards, Personal).	☐☐☐☐☐	☐☐☐☐☐
Generelle Orientierung am Gesamtsystem: Das Ausmaß, inwieweit die Aufgabenträger der IV-Funktion eine integrierte Sichtweise auf die Gesamtorganisation pflegen.	☐☐☐☐☐	☐☐☐☐☐
Vertrauen in Aufgabenträger: Der Glaube und das Gefühl, dass die Aufgabenträger bei der Ausübung einer IV-Funktion in einer berechenbaren Art und Weise handeln, ihren Verpflichtungen nachkommen und sich selbst dann aufrichtig verhalten, wenn die Möglichkeit des opportunistischen Verhaltens besteht.	☐☐☐☐☐	☐☐☐☐☐
Unentgeltliche Anreize: Alle Faktoren, die fördernd auf die Leistungsbereitschaft der Aufgabenträger einer IV-Funktion wirken, ohne dass sie mit einem direkten geldwerten Vorteil verbunden sind.	☐☐☐☐☐	☐☐☐☐☐
Gruppenverhalten: Das Ausmaß, inwieweit einzelne Personen in einer IV-Funktion nicht ihren eigenen oder individuellen Vorstellungen entsprechend handeln, sondern zum Vorteil der Gruppe oder des Kollektivs.	☐☐☐☐☐	☐☐☐☐☐

Eigenerstellung oder Fremdbezug von IV-Funktionen

Vertraulicher Fragebogen für den Leiter der Informationsverarbeitung

(Fortsetzung)

-2 = absolut unwichtig -1 = unwichtig 0 = teils - teils +1 = sehr wichtig +2 = äußerst wichtig

	Anwendungs-gestaltung	Anwendungs-wartung
Für **wie wichtig** halten Sie es, die **folgenden Faktoren** zu berücksichtigen, wenn eine **Entscheidung** darüber getroffen wird, ob Aufgaben in einer IV-Funktion **eigenerstellt oder fremdbezogen** werden sollen?	-2 -1 0 +1 +2	-2 -1 0 +1 +2
Langzeitorientierung der Aufgabenträger: Das Ausmaß, inwieweit Aufgabenträger in einer IV-Funktion ihre aufgabenbezogenen Planungen und Entscheidungen langfristig ausrichten.	☐☐☐☐☐	☐☐☐☐☐

4) Eigenschaften der IV-Funktionen

Spezifität des Humankapitals

+2 = trifft voll zu +1 = trifft zu 0 = teils - teils -1 = trifft weniger zu -2 = trifft gar nicht zu

	Anwendungs-gestaltung	Anwendungs-wartung
Die Verrichtung der eigentlichen Arbeiten in der jeweiligen IV-Funktion verlangt ...	+2 +1 0 -1 -2	+2 +1 0 -1 -2
... ein gutes Verständnis über die besonderen Geschäftsprozesse in Ihrer Organisation.	☐☐☐☐☐	☐☐☐☐☐
... Wissen über die speziellen Anforderungen der Fachabteilungen Ihrer Organisation.	☐☐☐☐☐	☐☐☐☐☐
... Wissen, das durch die Aufgabenstellung in Ihrer Organisation erlangt wird und sich nicht einfach dokumentieren oder niederschreiben lässt.	☐☐☐☐☐	☐☐☐☐☐
... detailliertes Wissen über Softwaresysteme, die speziell auf die Bedürfnisse Ihrer Organisation zugeschnitten sind.	☐☐☐☐☐	☐☐☐☐☐
... softwaretechnisches Wissen, das einzigartig für Ihre Organisation ist.	☐☐☐☐☐	☐☐☐☐☐
... Wissen, das einzigartig für Ihre Organisation ist.	☐☐☐☐☐	☐☐☐☐☐

Wissenstransfer

Bitte geben Sie Ihre Einschätzung ab!

Wie schätzen Sie den Prozess der Übertragung des für Ihre Organisation **spezifischen Wissens an externe Dienstleister** ein, um eine aufgabengerechte Leistungserstellung der jeweiligen IV-Funktion zu gewährleisten?

Anwendungsgestaltung			Anwendungswartung		
	-3 -2 -1 0 +1 +2 +3			-3 -2 -1 0 +1 +2 +3	
sehr mühsam	☐☐☐☐☐☐☐	sehr einfach	sehr mühsam	☐☐☐☐☐☐☐	sehr einfach
sehr schwierig	☐☐☐☐☐☐☐	sehr leicht	sehr schwierig	☐☐☐☐☐☐☐	sehr leicht
sehr langwierig	☐☐☐☐☐☐☐	sehr kurz	sehr langwierig	☐☐☐☐☐☐☐	sehr kurz

Soziale Netzwerke

+2 = trifft voll zu +1 = trifft zu 0 = teils - teils -1 = trifft weniger zu -2 = trifft gar nicht zu

	Anwendungs-gestaltung	Anwendungs-wartung
Bei der Verrichtung der eigentlichen Arbeiten in der jeweiligen IV-Funktion Ihrer Organisation ist es wichtig, **ausgeprägte soziale / interpersonale Arbeitsbeziehungen ...**	+2 +1 0 -1 -2	+2 +1 0 -1 -2
... zwischen Aufgabenträgern in der IV und Anwendern / Auftraggebern zu pflegen.	☐☐☐☐☐	☐☐☐☐☐
... innerhalb der Gruppe von IV-Aufgabenträgern zu pflegen.	☐☐☐☐☐	☐☐☐☐☐
Bei der Verrichtung der eigentlichen Arbeiten in der jeweiligen IV-Funktion Ihrer Organisation ist es wichtig, **eine ausgeprägte kollegiale Zusammenarbeit ...**	+2 +1 0 -1 -2	+2 +1 0 -1 -2
... zwischen Aufgabenträgern in der IV und Anwendern / Auftraggebern zu pflegen.	☐☐☐☐☐	☐☐☐☐☐
... innerhalb der Gruppe von IV-Aufgabenträgern zu pflegen.	☐☐☐☐☐	☐☐☐☐☐

Eigenerstellung oder Fremdbezug von IV-Funktionen

Vertraulicher Fragebogen für den Leiter der Informationsverarbeitung

Schwierigkeit der Leistungsmessung

+2 = trifft voll zu +1 = trifft zu 0 = teils - teils -1 = trifft weniger zu -2 = trifft gar nicht zu

	Anwendungs-gestaltung	Anwendungs-wartung
Bezogen auf diejenigen Aufgabenträger, welche die eigentlichen Arbeiten in der IV-Funktion verrichten, ...	+2 +1 0 -1 -2	+2 +1 0 -1 -2
... ist es schwierig, ihren jeweiligen Ergebnisbeitrags zu messen.	□□□□□	□□□□□
... sind wir nicht in der Lage, die Verhältnismäßigkeit zwischen ihrer individuell eingebrachten Arbeit und der erzielten Leistung zu beurteilen.	□□□□□	□□□□□
... ist es schwierig, einen genauen Nachweis über ihre jeweilige Leistung zu führen.	□□□□□	□□□□□

Unsicherheiten bei der Leistungserstellung

+2 = trifft voll zu +1 = trifft zu 0 = teils - teils -1 = trifft weniger zu -2 = trifft gar nicht zu

	Anwendungs-gestaltung	Anwendungs-wartung
Die notwendigen Fertigkeiten zur Aufgabenerfüllung in der jeweiligen IV-Funktion ...	+2 +1 0 -1 -2	+2 +1 0 -1 -2
... unterliegen aufgrund der technologischen Umweltdynamik einem ständigen Wandel.	□□□□□	□□□□□
... erfordern als Folge der technologischen Umweltdynamik einen ständigen Lern- und Anpassungsprozess.	□□□□□	□□□□□
... unterliegen aufgrund der Dynamik in den Arbeits- und Geschäftsprozessen der Organisation einem ständigen Wandel.	□□□□□	□□□□□
... erfordern als Folge der Dynamik in den Arbeits- und Geschäftsprozessen der Organisation einen ständigen Lern- und Anpassungsprozess.	□□□□□	□□□□□
Die Anforderungen an die Aufgabenerfüllung in der jeweiligen IV-Funktion ...	+2 +1 0 -1 -2	+2 +1 0 -1 -2
... unterliegen einem ständigen Wandel.	□□□□□	□□□□□
... erfordern einen ständigen Lernprozess.	□□□□□	□□□□□
... sind unsicher.	□□□□□	□□□□□

Unsicherheiten im Arbeitsaufkommen

+2 = trifft voll zu +1 = trifft zu 0 = teils - teils -1 = trifft weniger zu -2 = trifft gar nicht zu

	Anwendungs-gestaltung	Anwendungs-wartung
Der Arbeitsanfall ändert sich bei dieser IV-Funktion sehr oft.	□□□□□	□□□□□
Die mit dieser IV-Funktion verbundene Arbeitslast unterliegt starken Schwankungen.	□□□□□	□□□□□

5) IV-Outsourcingentscheidung und -umsetzung

-2 = extrem niedrig -1 = niedrig 0 = mittelmäßig +1 = hoch +2 = extrem hoch

Wie hoch schätzen Sie insgesamt gesehen die ... →	... Erfahrung ... →	... Expertise ... →	... Sorgfalt ...
	-2 -1 0 +1 +2	-2 -1 0 +1 +2	-2 -1 0 +1 +2
... Ihrer Organisation bei einer **IV-Ousourcingentscheidung** ein?	□□□□□	□□□□□	□□□□□
... Ihrer Organisation bei der **Vertragsgestaltung** ein?	□□□□□	□□□□□	□□□□□

Bitte tragen Sie eine Zahl ein!

Bitte schätzen Sie, wie viele **IV-Outsourcingverträge** Ihre Organisation in den **letzten 5 Jahre** abgeschlossen hat!	____ (z.B. 4)
Bitte schätzen Sie, wieviele **IV-Outsourcingentscheidungen** Ihrer Organisation innerhalb der **letzten 5 Jahre NICHT zu einem IV-Outsourcingvertrag** geführt haben!	____ (z.B. 5)

Kontrolle über den Outsourcingprozess

+2 = trifft voll zu +1 = trifft zu 0 = teils - teils -1 = trifft weniger zu -2 = trifft gar nicht zu

Wenn es zum Outsourcing dieser IV-Funktion an einen externen Dienstleister kommt, ...	Anwendungsgestaltung +2 +1 0 -1 -2	Anwendungswartung +2 +1 0 -1 -2
... kann unsere Organisation unbeschränkt agieren.	☐☐☐☐☐	☐☐☐☐☐
... ist unsere Organisation keinerlei Behinderungen ausgesetzt.	☐☐☐☐☐	☐☐☐☐☐
... hat unsere Organisation die völlige Kontrolle über alle notwendigen Handlungen.	☐☐☐☐☐	☐☐☐☐☐

Meinung Anderer

Bitte geben Sie Ihre Einschätzung ab!

Personen oder Personengruppen, deren Meinung für unsere Organisation wichtig ist, halten den Fremdbezug dieser IV-Funktion für ...

Anwendungsgestaltung	-3 -2 -1 0 +1 +2 +3		Anwendungswartung	-3 -2 -1 0 +1 +2 +3	
... schlecht	☐☐☐☐☐☐☐	gut	... schlecht	☐☐☐☐☐☐☐	gut
... negativ	☐☐☐☐☐☐☐	positiv	... negativ	☐☐☐☐☐☐☐	positiv
... schädlich	☐☐☐☐☐☐☐	förderlich	... schädlich	☐☐☐☐☐☐☐	förderlich
... töricht	☐☐☐☐☐☐☐	weise	... töricht	☐☐☐☐☐☐☐	weise
... unlogisch	☐☐☐☐☐☐☐	logisch	... unlogisch	☐☐☐☐☐☐☐	logisch
... wertlos	☐☐☐☐☐☐☐	wertvoll	... wertlos	☐☐☐☐☐☐☐	wertvoll

Outsourcingprozess

Bitte geben Sie Ihre Einschätzung ab!

Für unsere Organisation ist der mit dem Outsourcing dieser IV-Funktion an externe Dienstleister verbundene Prozess ...

Anwendungsgestaltung	-3 -2 -1 0 +1 +2 +3		Anwendungswartung	-3 -2 -1 0 +1 +2 +3	
... sehr mühsam	☐☐☐☐☐☐☐	sehr einfach	... sehr mühsam	☐☐☐☐☐☐☐	sehr einfach
... sehr schwierig	☐☐☐☐☐☐☐	sehr leicht	... sehr schwierig	☐☐☐☐☐☐☐	sehr leicht
... sehr langwierig	☐☐☐☐☐☐☐	sehr rasch	... sehr langwierig	☐☐☐☐☐☐☐	sehr rasch

6) Zusatzfragen zum Outsourcingverhalten

Idealer Grad des Outsourcing

Bitte tragen Sie Prozentwerte ein!

	Anwendungsgestaltung	Anwendungswartung
Wieviel Prozent der Aufgaben und Tätigkeiten dieser IV-Funktion sollte Ihre Organisation **idealerweise** an externe Dienstleister vergeben?	____ %	____ %

Zukünftiger Grad des Outsourcing

Bitte kreuzen Sie eine der drei Optionen an und tragen Sie ggf. einen Prozentwert ein!

Wieviel Prozent dieser IV-Funktion **erwarten Sie**, wird in Ihrer Organisation schätzungsweise **in einem Jahr** für externe Dienstleister ausgegeben werden?	Anwendungsgestaltung	Anwendungswartung
Mehr als zum gegenwärtigen Zeitpunkt.	☐ um ____ %	☐ um ____ %
Ungefähr **gleichbleibend**.	☐	☐
Weniger als zum gegenwärtigen Zeitpunkt.	☐ um ____ %	☐ um ____ %

Eigenerstellung oder Fremdbezug von IV-Funktionen

Vertraulicher Fragebogen für den Leiter der Informationsverarbeitung

Umfang der Verfügungsrechte an externen Dienstleistern

+2 = sehr hoch +1 = hoch 0 = mittelmäßig -1 = niedrig -2 = sehr niedrig

Bitte schätzen Sie für den Anteil der jeweiligen IV-Funktion, der von externen Dienstleistern erbracht wird, ...	Anwendungsgestaltung +2 +1 0 -1 -2	Anwendungswartung +2 +1 0 -1 -2
... wie hoch der Grad der Weisungsbefugnisse Ihrer Organisation gegenüber dem Management des externen Dienstleisters ist.	□□□□□	□□□□□
... wie hoch der Grad des Einflusses Ihrer Organisation auf Entscheidungen über die Allokation von menschlichen und physischen Ressourcen des externen Dienstleisters ist.	□□□□□	□□□□□
... wieviel Prozent des Kapitals der externen Dienstleister Ihre Organisation durchschnittlich hält.	____ %	____ %

7) Allgemeine Fragen

Wir möchten nochmals darauf hinweisen, dass die Anonymität Ihrer Angaben gewährleistet ist.

Wieviele Jahre arbeiten Sie schon in dieser Organisation?		____ Jahre
Wieviele Mitarbeiter beschäftigt Ihre Organisation ...	... insgesamt?	____ Pers.
	... in der gesamten Informationsverarbeitung?	____ Pers.
	... in der Anwendungsgestaltung?	____ Pers.
	... in der Anwendungswartung?	____ Pers.
Wie hoch ist der Umsatz Ihrer gesamten Organisation?		____ Mio. €
Wieviel Prozent des Umsatzes werden in Ihrer Organisation pro Jahr für die gesamte Informationsverarbeitung ausgegeben?		____ %
Wieviel Prozent der Ausgaben für die gesamte Informationsverarbeitung entfallen auf die ...	... Anwendungsgestaltung?	____ %
	... Anwendungswartung?	____ %

Um die Anonymität zu wahren und dennoch Ihre jetzigen Antworten einer eventuellen 1-seitigen Folgeuntersuchung zuordnen zu können, bitten wir Sie um Angabe der folgenden Informationen.

Tag / Monat Ihres Geburtsdatums	□□ □□	Die letzten drei Ziffern Ihres Personalausweises	□□□

Beide Angaben haben für Sie spezifischen Charakter, sind aber für uns unmöglich zurückzuverfolgen. Ihre Kombination dient uns als Schlüssel, um eine Verbindung zwischen Ihren jetzigen und zukünftigen Antworten herzustellen.

Vielen Dank für Ihre Mitarbeit!

Bitte senden Sie den Fragebogen im beiliegenden Freiumschlag an uns zurück!

Zudem bitten wir Sie, die beiliegende Postkarte ebenfalls vollständig ausgefüllt an uns zurückzusenden. Bitte kreuzen Sie an, ob Sie an einer Zusammenfassung der Ergebnisse interessiert sind!

Universität Bayreuth, Lehrstuhl für Wirtschaftsinformatik (BWL VII), Prof. Dr. Armin Heinzl
Universitätsstraße 30, D-95440 Bayreuth
Telefon: +49 (0) 9 21 / 55 28 07 E-Mail: heinzl@uni-bayreuth.de Internet: wi.oec.uni-bayreuth.de

Appendix E: Cross-Loadings

Table Appendix-E-1: Cross-Loadings USA (Page 1 from 4)

Item	Out	PC	TC	StratII	StratI	Oper-atII	Oper-atI	Intell	Behav-Con	Sub-Norm	Work-Load	Spec-Bus	Spec-Tec	SoNet-IS-US
Out1	0,95	0,22	0,02	0,18	0,07	0,28	0,28	0,10	0,02	0,29	0,06	0,09	0,01	0,04
Out2	0,98	0,32	0,13	0,25	0,00	0,34	0,31	0,18	0,01	0,31	0,05	0,03	0,01	0,04
Out3	0,94	0,39	0,07	0,26	0,04	0,42	0,22	0,23	0,01	0,37	0,06	0,14	0,07	0,02
Out4	0,45	0,15	0,17	0,02	0,09	0,02	0,09	0,12	0,20	0,04	0,15	0,01	0,05	0,07
Pc1	0,36	0,86	0,30	0,58	0,39	0,58	0,04	0,52	0,08	0,30	0,08	0,19	0,12	0,09
Pc2	0,14	0,71	0,28	0,46	0,29	0,51	0,14	0,51	0,26	0,21	0,03	0,18	0,27	0,08
Pc3	0,31	0,80	0,41	0,52	0,12	0,56	0,01	0,60	0,07	0,34	0,04	0,24	0,16	0,18
Pc4	0,26	0,54	0,41	0,22	0,27	0,30	0,10	0,12	0,11	0,21	0,06	0,10	0,13	0,43
Pc5	0,16	0,84	0,46	0,42	0,41	0,51	0,18	0,46	0,16	0,30	0,03	0,05	0,04	0,35
TC1	0,11	0,41	0,80	0,39	0,23	0,39	0,13	0,32	0,12	0,26	0,32	0,06	0,01	0,23
TC2	0,17	0,20	0,69	0,17	0,05	0,22	0,12	0,16	0,13	0,21	0,08	0,22	0,08	0,23
TC3	0,07	0,34	0,83	0,20	0,17	0,33	0,10	0,16	0,08	0,30	0,25	0,04	0,10	0,27
TC4	0,30	0,50	0,77	0,35	0,13	0,42	0,19	0,31	0,06	0,20	0,11	0,15	0,12	0,20
Strat1	0,08	0,38	0,17	0,24	0,80	0,17	0,06	0,17	0,06	0,05	0,09	0,11	0,24	0,04
Strat2	0,26	0,50	0,37	0,93	0,14	0,72	0,05	0,56	0,10	0,40	0,02	0,14	0,16	0,11
Strat3	0,07	0,32	0,15	0,32	0,91	0,33	0,25	0,13	0,14	0,16	0,24	0,20	0,25	0,14
Strat4	0,20	0,61	0,29	0,95	0,30	0,70	0,04	0,53	0,08	0,32	0,00	0,20	0,11	0,30
Strat5	0,07	0,34	0,12	0,12	0,85	0,16	0,21	0,03	0,21	0,11	0,33	0,09	0,14	0,29
Strat6	0,22	0,60	0,39	0,96	0,33	0,76	0,04	0,54	0,09	0,32	0,01	0,22	0,16	0,23
Operat1	0,19	0,04	0,20	0,06	0,08	0,20	0,71	0,10	0,05	0,31	0,13	0,04	0,03	0,02
Operat2	0,26	0,48	0,44	0,67	0,27	0,87	0,23	0,37	0,17	0,53	0,13	0,31	0,39	0,16
Operat3	0,27	0,05	0,12	0,08	0,17	0,09	0,77	0,00	0,06	0,24	0,22	0,14	0,21	0,05
Operat4	0,23	0,64	0,37	0,83	0,30	0,90	0,16	0,56	0,07	0,48	0,01	0,17	0,18	0,21
Operat5	0,16	0,22	0,08	0,01	0,27	0,11	0,78	0,15	0,10	0,10	0,18	0,01	0,07	0,11
Operat6	0,43	0,61	0,38	0,55	0,18	0,88	0,10	0,50	0,15	0,60	0,16	0,23	0,13	0,31
Res1	0,17	0,54	0,34	0,57	0,12	0,50	0,15	0,86	0,05	0,41	0,04	0,05	0,21	0,11
Res2	0,11	0,37	0,08	0,40	0,03	0,41	0,07	0,88	0,14	0,24	0,05	0,02	0,16	0,04
Res3	0,23	0,55	0,36	0,46	0,13	0,47	0,13	0,87	0,15	0,23	0,01	0,17	0,20	0,17
Res5	0,09	0,23	0,07	0,31	0,15	0,24	0,01	0,48	0,10	0,15	0,07	0,04	0,20	0,14
Res6	0,08	0,58	0,20	0,51	0,12	0,49	0,04	0,88	0,08	0,17	0,04	0,03	0,03	0,11
Res7	0,11	0,23	0,15	0,15	0,23	0,14	0,09	0,24	0,11	0,22	0,04	0,12	0,18	0,13
Res8	0,09	0,17	0,22	0,36	0,19	0,33	0,03	0,38	0,08	0,11	0,01	0,12	0,24	0,26
Impact1	0,22	0,67	0,31	0,58	0,13	0,62	0,10	0,56	0,16	0,34	0,05	0,11	0,02	0,28
Impact2	0,16	0,49	0,27	0,64	0,17	0,64	0,11	0,45	0,03	0,44	0,04	0,31	0,23	0,17
Impact3	0,14	0,60	0,34	0,68	0,21	0,64	0,00	0,54	0,01	0,41	0,11	0,19	0,09	0,28
EmplOri1	0,09	0,31	0,32	0,32	0,13	0,41	0,19	0,35	0,20	0,28	0,22	0,21	0,20	0,39
EmplOri2	0,03	0,41	0,42	0,23	0,18	0,37	0,17	0,27	0,10	0,28	0,15	0,15	0,24	0,46
EmplOri3	0,11	0,30	0,41	0,35	0,29	0,49	0,01	0,36	0,01	0,36	0,15	0,14	0,35	0,32
EmplOri4	0,08	0,25	0,22	0,39	0,24	0,52	0,05	0,33	0,12	0,28	0,04	0,17	0,38	0,27
DecCont1	0,23	0,29	0,24	0,23	0,05	0,50	0,12	0,18	0,15	0,41	0,20	0,08	0,12	0,01
DecCont2	0,33	0,37	0,22	0,53	0,06	0,60	0,03	0,30	0,17	0,52	0,09	0,17	0,16	0,10

Table Appendix-E-1: Cross-Loadings USA (Page 2 from 4)

Item	Out	PC	TC	StratII	StratI	Oper-atII	Oper-atI	IntelI	Behav-Con	Sub-Norm	Work-Load	Spec-Bus	Spec-Tec	SoNet-IS-US
Trust1	0,02	0,27	0,08	0,19	0,15	0,10	0,11	0,17	0,16	0,06	0,03	0,05	0,01	0,04
Trust2	0,11	0,20	0,09	0,00	0,05	0,05	0,20	0,00	0,15	0,05	0,03	0,10	0,21	0,19
Trust3	0,20	0,27	0,08	0,22	0,13	0,21	0,28	0,01	0,03	0,19	0,10	0,03	0,10	0,06
Incen1	0,27	0,52	0,28	0,43	0,20	0,68	0,13	0,48	0,08	0,49	0,05	0,05	0,00	0,27
Incen2	0,24	0,54	0,33	0,51	0,17	0,71	0,01	0,44	0,16	0,39	0,10	0,18	0,09	0,31
Incen3	0,30	0,63	0,26	0,46	0,26	0,68	0,07	0,48	0,13	0,38	0,03	0,24	0,17	0,28
Group1	0,28	0,45	0,24	0,55	0,05	0,47	0,07	0,35	0,15	0,35	0,01	0,06	0,11	0,11
Group4	0,00	0,37	0,15	0,32	0,23	0,44	0,12	0,24	0,17	0,28	0,03	0,17	0,09	0,25
Group6	0,26	0,00	0,01	0,31	0,03	0,24	0,02	0,07	0,08	0,24	0,06	0,12	0,04	0,15
Group7	0,17	0,31	0,19	0,33	0,26	0,38	0,03	0,24	0,04	0,13	0,15	0,09	0,00	0,28
LongWo1	0,22	0,58	0,34	0,42	0,17	0,53	0,02	0,41	0,01	0,28	0,15	0,12	0,16	0,11
LongWo2	0,18	0,64	0,29	0,52	0,23	0,59	0,03	0,47	0,01	0,26	0,05	0,15	0,20	0,15
LongWo3	0,20	0,51	0,20	0,51	0,25	0,55	0,08	0,37	0,07	0,26	0,02	0,16	0,22	0,12
Attitud2	0,43	0,60	0,34	0,51	0,31	0,67	0,24	0,44	0,10	0,68	0,12	0,29	0,24	0,36
Attitud3	0,36	0,51	0,31	0,51	0,23	0,62	0,23	0,49	0,18	0,66	0,01	0,28	0,32	0,14
Attitud5	0,29	0,50	0,34	0,42	0,21	0,57	0,10	0,38	0,30	0,67	0,11	0,23	0,25	0,24
Attitud6	0,37	0,49	0,35	0,41	0,22	0,58	0,22	0,36	0,21	0,72	0,02	0,24	0,26	0,26
Attitud7	0,34	0,47	0,37	0,41	0,10	0,56	0,16	0,41	0,25	0,67	0,06	0,19	0,18	0,24
Spec1	0,11	0,28	0,13	0,22	0,23	0,27	0,14	0,10	0,01	0,35	0,10	0,93	0,51	0,36
Spec2	0,05	0,08	0,12	0,14	0,07	0,21	0,03	0,06	0,08	0,20	0,06	0,91	0,61	0,24
Spec4	0,12	0,17	0,05	0,09	0,07	0,20	0,14	0,19	0,14	0,21	0,10	0,51	0,85	0,11
Spec5	0,07	0,02	0,11	0,17	0,35	0,24	0,12	0,13	0,04	0,26	0,15	0,54	0,87	0,11
SoNet1	0,06	0,39	0,29	0,27	0,20	0,31	0,11	0,21	0,07	0,25	0,07	0,35	0,17	0,94
SoNet2	0,01	0,28	0,32	0,27	0,30	0,41	0,11	0,13	0,09	0,37	0,18	0,32	0,25	0,63
SoNet3	0,10	0,13	0,26	0,14	0,16	0,18	0,01	0,00	0,02	0,24	0,10	0,26	0,07	0,93
SoNet4	0,04	0,06	0,01	0,15	0,26	0,21	0,08	0,15	0,04	0,35	0,06	0,27	0,19	0,52
Meas2	0,16	0,21	0,01	0,08	0,17	0,09	0,30	0,05	0,25	0,07	0,07	0,01	0,14	0,34
Meas3	0,17	0,26	0,00	0,04	0,07	0,09	0,24	0,08	0,22	0,02	0,16	0,03	0,13	0,25
Uncert1	0,11	0,04	0,24	0,15	0,28	0,01	0,00	0,14	0,02	0,02	0,24	0,21	0,30	0,01
Uncert2	0,19	0,24	0,16	0,13	0,32	0,12	0,06	0,23	0,02	0,02	0,19	0,18	0,28	0,12
Uncert3	0,19	0,17	0,18	0,19	0,34	0,26	0,05	0,07	0,09	0,31	0,53	0,22	0,21	0,14
Uncert4	0,10	0,13	0,22	0,03	0,06	0,03	0,19	0,01	0,04	0,25	0,37	0,25	0,30	0,14
WoLoad1	0,07	0,09	0,29	0,06	0,34	0,15	0,26	0,01	0,16	0,08	0,98	0,03	0,10	0,09
WoLoad2	0,02	0,14	0,14	0,15	0,06	0,03	0,13	0,15	0,14	0,02	0,85	0,22	0,22	0,08
CoPro1	0,02	0,01	0,11	0,16	0,03	0,14	0,11	0,17	0,87	0,01	0,00	0,01	0,05	0,05
CoPro2	0,00	0,07	0,10	0,08	0,07	0,09	0,01	0,15	0,94	0,03	0,16	0,08	0,03	0,05
CoPro3	0,04	0,03	0,00	0,03	0,03	0,16	0,02	0,03	0,88	0,06	0,24	0,05	0,06	0,03
Other1	0,27	0,33	0,34	0,34	0,12	0,55	0,31	0,25	0,06	0,94	0,08	0,24	0,25	0,20
Other2	0,28	0,34	0,31	0,33	0,10	0,54	0,25	0,20	0,10	0,93	0,08	0,28	0,22	0,23
Other3	0,25	0,32	0,20	0,30	0,20	0,55	0,23	0,26	0,02	0,94	0,05	0,32	0,28	0,26
Other4	0,37	0,39	0,33	0,37	0,12	0,61	0,28	0,33	0,07	0,97	0,08	0,30	0,25	0,31
Other5	0,35	0,37	0,32	0,38	0,13	0,64	0,26	0,32	0,05	0,96	0,07	0,30	0,31	0,21
Other6	0,38	0,30	0,24	0,30	0,10	0,52	0,27	0,37	0,11	0,89	0,02	0,27	0,21	0,23
IDEAL	0,58	0,52	0,38	0,49	0,27	0,56	0,17	0,50	0,05	0,46	0,01	0,05	0,13	0,06
Propert3	0,36	0,00	0,09	0,05	0,13	0,14	0,14	0,18	0,28	0,24	0,09	0,07	0,09	0,05

Table Appendix-E-1: Cross-Loadings USA (Page 3 from 4)

Item	Soc-NetIS	Meas	Env-Unc	Bus-Unc	Trust	Incent	Res-Other	Group	Spec-Hum	Syst-Impa	Sys-View	Long-Wo	Own-er	Atti-tude	Ideal	Con-trol
Out1	0,05	0,19	0,18	0,17	0,09	0,21	0,16	0,19	0,00	0,08	0,05	0,18	0,43	0,34	0,50	0,22
Out2	0,05	0,21	0,14	0,18	0,16	0,23	0,13	0,18	0,02	0,19	0,00	0,23	0,32	0,37	0,59	0,30
Out3	0,07	0,09	0,19	0,11	0,09	0,35	0,05	0,26	0,10	0,25	0,00	0,17	0,26	0,42	0,56	0,41
Out4	0,05	0,27	0,06	0,08	0,03	0,07	0,12	0,14	0,07	0,10	0,04	0,16	0,54	0,17	0,20	0,01
Pc1	0,06	0,14	0,18	0,04	0,28	0,52	0,18	0,48	0,16	0,53	0,17	0,64	0,03	0,44	0,55	0,25
Pc2	0,14	0,27	0,14	0,01	0,35	0,48	0,08	0,39	0,21	0,49	0,34	0,48	0,02	0,35	0,31	0,20
Pc3	0,15	0,00	0,10	0,02	0,16	0,41	0,19	0,34	0,25	0,58	0,36	0,50	0,00	0,46	0,46	0,37
Pc4	0,29	0,28	0,04	0,07	0,12	0,32	0,22	0,32	0,29	0,36	0,24	0,22	0,00	0,29	0,30	0,34
Pc5	0,16	0,27	0,13	0,06	0,22	0,50	0,27	0,47	0,21	0,48	0,32	0,42	0,04	0,56	0,34	0,29
TC1	0,17	0,01	0,22	0,40	0,21	0,29	0,11	0,29	0,18	0,31	0,34	0,28	0,02	0,30	0,34	0,15
TC2	0,12	0,01	0,18	0,09	0,04	0,12	0,22	0,02	0,23	0,16	0,20	0,02	0,20	0,30	0,06	0,18
TC3	0,24	0,03	0,20	0,13	0,03	0,23	0,27	0,16	0,24	0,18	0,33	0,13	0,21	0,29	0,26	0,18
TC4	0,07	0,03	0,11	0,03	0,06	0,27	0,02	0,32	0,19	0,36	0,35	0,43	0,11	0,30	0,44	0,28
Strat1	0,04	0,01	0,31	0,11	0,03	0,09	0,23	0,18	0,13	0,17	0,14	0,22	0,15	0,18	0,25	0,09
Strat2	0,16	0,16	0,04	0,09	0,20	0,43	0,30	0,44	0,20	0,63	0,42	0,42	0,06	0,50	0,50	0,54
Strat3	0,35	0,02	0,34	0,23	0,18	0,21	0,20	0,22	0,32	0,21	0,23	0,15	0,10	0,28	0,28	0,11
Strat4	0,25	0,05	0,06	0,02	0,15	0,49	0,30	0,63	0,30	0,63	0,31	0,49	0,00	0,44	0,41	0,41
Strat5	0,32	0,31	0,23	0,18	0,11	0,23	0,23	0,30	0,30	0,07	0,25	0,23	0,10	0,13	0,16	0,13
Strat6	0,26	0,07	0,04	0,12	0,21	0,53	0,28	0,58	0,31	0,70	0,37	0,53	0,07	0,49	0,49	0,36
Operat1	0,19	0,01	0,01	0,19	0,25	0,05	0,06	0,08	0,09	0,21	0,14	0,02	0,04	0,18	0,08	0,13
Operat2	0,27	0,17	0,01	0,08	0,21	0,53	0,29	0,45	0,37	0,51	0,46	0,42	0,15	0,58	0,45	0,61
Operat3	0,06	0,21	0,10	0,01	0,07	0,04	0,00	0,11	0,14	0,07	0,08	0,01	0,10	0,15	0,19	0,04
Operat4	0,27	0,09	0,11	0,00	0,14	0,57	0,28	0,61	0,29	0,73	0,40	0,57	0,11	0,56	0,42	0,45
Operat5	0,03	0,47	0,06	0,13	0,26	0,18	0,03	0,03	0,06	0,03	0,01	0,03	0,17	0,15	0,08	0,02
Operat6	0,37	0,01	0,10	0,28	0,09	0,78	0,19	0,60	0,38	0,58	0,52	0,54	0,10	0,61	0,59	0,58
Res1	0,02	0,04	0,07	0,11	0,13	0,37	0,30	0,35	0,13	0,58	0,34	0,43	0,24	0,47	0,45	0,33
Res2	0,03	0,06	0,28	0,05	0,06	0,42	0,29	0,24	0,03	0,40	0,27	0,29	0,18	0,30	0,35	0,20
Res3	0,03	0,14	0,18	0,05	0,05	0,42	0,35	0,32	0,19	0,44	0,39	0,35	0,02	0,42	0,47	0,22
Res5	0,02	0,19	0,06	0,09	0,18	0,08	0,64	0,16	0,00	0,40	0,27	0,27	0,41	0,18	0,13	0,26
Res6	0,03	0,06	0,31	0,10	0,01	0,51	0,47	0,40	0,06	0,52	0,32	0,43	0,22	0,37	0,42	0,20
Res7	0,13	0,17	0,01	0,00	0,04	0,22	0,87	0,02	0,19	0,26	0,14	0,13	0,24	0,26	0,29	0,10
Res8	0,29	0,02	0,17	0,12	0,12	0,29	0,81	0,17	0,31	0,22	0,40	0,26	0,02	0,25	0,35	0,09
Impact1	0,20	0,17	0,15	0,05	0,24	0,49	0,25	0,45	0,23	0,92	0,37	0,52	0,17	0,42	0,41	0,42
Impact2	0,24	0,13	0,07	0,07	0,20	0,36	0,19	0,38	0,32	0,91	0,30	0,50	0,38	0,48	0,35	0,42
Impact3	0,30	0,01	0,08	0,02	0,21	0,41	0,41	0,47	0,31	0,93	0,44	0,47	0,24	0,50	0,39	0,43
EmplOri1	0,32	0,11	0,06	0,31	0,06	0,31	0,25	0,41	0,40	0,33	0,79	0,37	0,14	0,40	0,14	0,29
EmplOri2	0,38	0,08	0,02	0,15	0,02	0,23	0,21	0,27	0,44	0,30	0,84	0,34	0,00	0,36	0,20	0,24
EmplOri3	0,41	0,10	0,10	0,28	0,03	0,34	0,37	0,40	0,42	0,39	0,89	0,39	0,19	0,38	0,28	0,32
EmplOri4	0,45	0,08	0,13	0,12	0,06	0,34	0,26	0,37	0,42	0,34	0,88	0,40	0,19	0,37	0,22	0,29
DecCont1	0,02	0,19	0,02	0,30	0,24	0,46	0,03	0,34	0,05	0,33	0,25	0,27	0,31	0,36	0,23	0,85
DecCont2	0,14	0,21	0,06	0,08	0,04	0,35	0,24	0,38	0,19	0,47	0,34	0,31	0,11	0,51	0,33	0,93

Table Appendix-E-1: Cross-Loadings USA (Page 4 from 4)

Item	Soc-NetIS	Meas	Env-Unc	Bus-Unc	Trust	Incent	Res-Other	Group	Spec-Hum	Syst-Impa	Sys-View	Long-Wo	Own-er	Atti-tude	Ideal	Con-trol
Trust1	0,01	0,34	0,05	0,22	0,84	0,29	0,05	0,02	0,03	0,19	0,06	0,24	0,12	0,15	0,17	0,07
Trust2	0,03	0,23	0,31	0,12	0,76	0,13	0,12	0,15	0,17	0,11	0,04	0,02	0,11	0,06	0,13	0,05
Trust3	0,06	0,11	0,14	0,25	0,91	0,27	0,11	0,02	0,04	0,26	0,02	0,13	0,13	0,19	0,20	0,20
Incen1	0,26	0,22	0,25	0,17	0,25	0,92	0,23	0,52	0,22	0,43	0,36	0,39	0,03	0,46	0,51	0,43
Incen2	0,29	0,09	0,18	0,20	0,27	0,97	0,27	0,52	0,31	0,45	0,36	0,48	0,07	0,46	0,54	0,43
Incen3	0,28	0,22	0,22	0,18	0,32	0,96	0,31	0,45	0,34	0,43	0,31	0,49	0,08	0,52	0,55	0,40
Group1	0,15	0,08	0,20	0,12	0,00	0,30	0,27	0,62	0,11	0,49	0,31	0,47	0,10	0,36	0,41	0,33
Group4	0,15	0,04	0,00	0,26	0,10	0,39	0,09	0,67	0,24	0,36	0,32	0,38	0,21	0,32	0,12	0,43
Group6	0,00	0,25	0,17	0,20	0,13	0,04	0,06	0,41	0,12	0,06	0,17	0,21	0,07	0,19	0,05	0,34
Group7	0,15	0,23	0,03	0,01	0,16	0,38	0,11	0,72	0,20	0,17	0,25	0,31	0,16	0,11	0,21	0,05
LongWo1	0,02	0,05	0,13	0,25	0,18	0,45	0,22	0,52	0,13	0,48	0,43	0,96	0,18	0,38	0,49	0,32
LongWo2	0,08	0,04	0,01	0,11	0,16	0,50	0,23	0,60	0,19	0,58	0,46	0,98	0,15	0,40	0,48	0,33
LongWo3	0,06	0,06	0,12	0,15	0,15	0,44	0,25	0,49	0,18	0,50	0,37	0,95	0,16	0,35	0,45	0,29
Attitud2	0,33	0,21	0,16	0,10	0,26	0,57	0,26	0,39	0,42	0,53	0,38	0,30	0,08	0,90	0,56	0,49
Attitud3	0,12	0,01	0,10	0,20	0,15	0,58	0,34	0,30	0,27	0,40	0,32	0,36	0,11	0,88	0,64	0,39
Attitud5	0,27	0,00	0,06	0,07	0,09	0,37	0,26	0,36	0,34	0,45	0,43	0,33	0,26	0,92	0,47	0,49
Attitud6	0,29	0,07	0,03	0,22	0,14	0,38	0,25	0,35	0,36	0,46	0,43	0,39	0,18	0,95	0,53	0,47
Attitud7	0,24	0,07	0,12	0,11	0,16	0,38	0,26	0,34	0,30	0,48	0,47	0,41	0,25	0,92	0,53	0,45
Spec1	0,36	0,06	0,18	0,23	0,02	0,12	0,10	0,19	0,72	0,30	0,24	0,15	0,05	0,34	0,08	0,16
Spec2	0,23	0,09	0,23	0,24	0,06	0,19	0,16	0,02	0,64	0,08	0,11	0,11	0,08	0,15	0,02	0,11
Spec4	0,18	0,04	0,20	0,25	0,06	0,11	0,21	0,14	0,50	0,11	0,36	0,19	0,07	0,20	0,09	0,19
Spec5	0,24	0,20	0,37	0,24	0,13	0,05	0,23	0,02	0,53	0,10	0,25	0,15	0,22	0,27	0,14	0,10
SoNet1	0,57	0,37	0,01	0,13	0,01	0,38	0,25	0,30	0,74	0,30	0,43	0,19	0,04	0,29	0,13	0,12
SoNet2	0,92	0,16	0,10	0,21	0,04	0,38	0,25	0,27	0,77	0,36	0,55	0,10	0,08	0,28	0,17	0,14
SoNet3	0,63	0,20	0,17	0,16	0,10	0,17	0,10	0,27	0,70	0,18	0,36	0,06	0,06	0,21	0,02	0,02
SoNet4	0,89	0,09	0,14	0,09	0,02	0,13	0,13	0,09	0,66	0,11	0,27	0,01	0,05	0,21	0,01	0,00
Meas2	0,16	0,95	0,14	0,00	0,19	0,18	0,05	0,10	0,16	0,01	0,00	0,01	0,34	0,05	0,14	0,22
Meas3	0,12	0,96	0,18	0,06	0,29	0,17	0,07	0,00	0,10	0,02	0,00	0,10	0,20	0,10	0,15	0,21
Uncert1	0,06	0,24	0,81	0,37	0,12	0,21	0,18	0,00	0,16	0,04	0,08	0,14	0,23	0,00	0,01	0,11
Uncert2	0,15	0,08	0,92	0,53	0,16	0,19	0,00	0,08	0,23	0,12	0,08	0,03	0,15	0,16	0,02	0,14
Uncert3	0,24	0,07	0,47	0,90	0,16	0,28	0,15	0,23	0,27	0,13	0,26	0,23	0,06	0,21	0,23	0,28
Uncert4	0,07	0,01	0,49	0,92	0,18	0,08	0,05	0,06	0,24	0,04	0,20	0,10	0,12	0,08	0,14	0,07
WoLoad1	0,16	0,08	0,23	0,47	0,10	0,10	0,01	0,12	0,13	0,03	0,16	0,10	0,08	0,03	0,08	0,02
WoLoad2	0,06	0,20	0,22	0,44	0,07	0,03	0,11	0,01	0,18	0,18	0,07	0,00	0,10	0,14	0,15	0,05
CoPro1	0,08	0,18	0,01	0,05	0,01	0,18	0,01	0,13	0,03	0,13	0,10	0,11	0,25	0,17	0,13	0,18
CoPro2	0,07	0,13	0,01	0,09	0,06	0,09	0,02	0,01	0,02	0,09	0,05	0,03	0,27	0,18	0,05	0,08
CoPro3	0,05	0,32	0,01	0,12	0,07	0,10	0,07	0,02	0,01	0,06	0,03	0,01	0,25	0,23	0,02	0,22
Other1	0,39	0,13	0,05	0,28	0,12	0,35	0,20	0,22	0,37	0,40	0,29	0,21	0,21	0,69	0,42	0,54
Other2	0,45	0,08	0,05	0,31	0,14	0,37	0,16	0,24	0,40	0,38	0,25	0,25	0,16	0,66	0,40	0,50
Other3	0,38	0,04	0,03	0,28	0,11	0,39	0,19	0,36	0,42	0,42	0,31	0,26	0,27	0,69	0,38	0,48
Other4	0,34	0,04	0,03	0,29	0,07	0,42	0,18	0,43	0,41	0,42	0,34	0,29	0,21	0,75	0,43	0,51
Other5	0,40	0,09	0,00	0,31	0,10	0,44	0,17	0,41	0,41	0,39	0,41	0,29	0,18	0,71	0,47	0,51
Other6	0,28	0,10	0,11	0,26	0,20	0,44	0,25	0,40	0,34	0,37	0,36	0,26	0,27	0,71	0,48	0,43
IDEAL	0,09	0,15	0,01	0,20	0,20	0,56	0,36	0,34	0,12	0,42	0,25	0,49	0,08	0,60	1,00	0,32
Propert3	0,02	0,28	0,21	0,10	0,04	0,07	0,20	0,02	0,04	0,28	0,16	0,17	1,00	0,19	0,08	0,22

Table Appendix-E-2: Cross-Loadings Germany (Page 1 from 4)

Item	Out	PC	TC	StratII	StratI	Oper-atII	Oper-atI	Intell	Behav-Con	Sub-Norm	Work-Load	Spec-Bus	Spec-Tec	SoNet-IS-US
Out1	0,95	0,39	0,35	0,31	0,01	0,31	0,06	0,27	0,05	0,36	0,08	0,01	0,06	0,09
Out2	0,96	0,41	0,37	0,29	0,00	0,30	0,01	0,22	0,07	0,30	0,03	0,04	0,10	0,12
Out3	0,96	0,39	0,35	0,33	0,00	0,32	0,03	0,24	0,08	0,39	0,06	0,01	0,07	0,09
Out4	0,38	0,17	0,16	0,08	0,04	0,07	0,10	0,04	0,08	0,12	0,13	0,12	0,20	0,05
Pc1	0,35	0,83	0,56	0,39	0,19	0,40	0,15	0,42	0,15	0,26	0,10	0,13	0,12	0,21
Pc2	0,21	0,67	0,42	0,25	0,20	0,30	0,21	0,34	0,03	0,17	0,01	0,03	0,10	0,12
Pc3	0,38	0,76	0,46	0,45	0,26	0,45	0,21	0,44	0,09	0,34	0,03	0,21	0,21	0,15
Pc4	0,38	0,79	0,51	0,33	0,23	0,34	0,18	0,38	0,01	0,27	0,14	0,12	0,09	0,08
Pc5	0,27	0,85	0,57	0,37	0,23	0,42	0,16	0,38	0,05	0,28	0,08	0,15	0,12	0,02
TC1	0,36	0,57	0,82	0,30	0,12	0,32	0,17	0,32	0,13	0,31	0,01	0,05	0,04	0,08
TC2	0,28	0,49	0,84	0,36	0,18	0,35	0,20	0,34	0,16	0,27	0,06	0,10	0,16	0,08
TC3	0,25	0,51	0,82	0,31	0,11	0,32	0,13	0,39	0,04	0,31	0,03	0,07	0,18	0,12
TC4	0,28	0,53	0,77	0,39	0,13	0,43	0,09	0,40	0,03	0,30	0,06	0,04	0,11	0,04
Strat1	0,08	0,32	0,26	0,34	0,78	0,33	0,26	0,33	0,02	0,04	0,05	0,28	0,11	0,21
Strat2	0,34	0,48	0,43	0,93	0,35	0,70	0,18	0,42	0,06	0,38	0,02	0,12	0,08	0,22
Strat3	0,05	0,20	0,09	0,31	0,88	0,23	0,47	0,34	0,01	0,08	0,05	0,25	0,15	0,33
Strat4	0,30	0,42	0,38	0,93	0,39	0,70	0,24	0,37	0,16	0,29	0,00	0,08	0,05	0,12
Strat5	0,03	0,21	0,09	0,33	0,88	0,29	0,43	0,35	0,00	0,04	0,03	0,22	0,09	0,22
Strat6	0,26	0,39	0,36	0,94	0,34	0,71	0,21	0,38	0,19	0,31	0,00	0,10	0,03	0,15
Operat1	0,03	0,21	0,11	0,22	0,42	0,26	0,84	0,24	0,07	0,11	0,14	0,08	0,03	0,13
Operat2	0,26	0,41	0,35	0,70	0,24	0,90	0,22	0,41	0,19	0,26	0,06	0,03	0,05	0,17
Operat3	0,03	0,19	0,12	0,16	0,51	0,22	0,84	0,24	0,03	0,02	0,05	0,07	0,07	0,19
Operat4	0,29	0,40	0,37	0,71	0,25	0,90	0,21	0,41	0,15	0,27	0,03	0,06	0,06	0,15
Operat5	0,08	0,18	0,21	0,17	0,26	0,20	0,80	0,26	0,06	0,07	0,00	0,03	0,06	0,32
Operat6	0,28	0,45	0,41	0,55	0,34	0,81	0,28	0,52	0,25	0,28	0,06	0,05	0,05	0,15
Res1	0,33	0,44	0,39	0,36	0,35	0,42	0,26	0,82	0,02	0,16	0,15	0,15	0,15	0,20
Res2	0,18	0,40	0,33	0,35	0,31	0,46	0,26	0,79	0,04	0,31	0,05	0,07	0,12	0,25
Res3	0,10	0,36	0,34	0,25	0,32	0,33	0,20	0,76	0,02	0,21	0,00	0,08	0,18	0,26
Res5	0,09	0,17	0,09	0,23	0,28	0,30	0,18	0,36	0,03	0,12	0,06	0,15	0,31	0,17
Res6	0,11	0,31	0,30	0,33	0,25	0,38	0,18	0,70	0,02	0,16	0,16	0,12	0,22	0,17
Res7	0,16	0,23	0,26	0,13	0,20	0,14	0,24	0,34	0,17	0,08	0,15	0,06	0,18	0,13
Res8	0,19	0,24	0,19	0,24	0,19	0,26	0,20	0,44	0,00	0,20	0,10	0,00	0,06	0,12
Impact1	0,36	0,52	0,44	0,57	0,24	0,64	0,19	0,48	0,22	0,22	0,01	0,13	0,04	0,11
Impact2	0,41	0,44	0,41	0,60	0,25	0,64	0,27	0,42	0,13	0,28	0,02	0,16	0,13	0,17
Impact3	0,34	0,43	0,38	0,49	0,21	0,57	0,17	0,44	0,13	0,21	0,00	0,13	0,01	0,15
EmplOri1	0,21	0,35	0,38	0,28	0,22	0,35	0,24	0,28	0,18	0,18	0,07	0,16	0,00	0,18
EmplOri2	0,39	0,46	0,43	0,31	0,16	0,36	0,24	0,33	0,11	0,32	0,09	0,12	0,11	0,15
EmplOri3	0,35	0,39	0,36	0,37	0,28	0,35	0,16	0,29	0,20	0,17	0,01	0,25	0,14	0,18
EmplOri4	0,33	0,43	0,39	0,35	0,22	0,38	0,13	0,33	0,14	0,19	0,05	0,18	0,11	0,13
DecCont1	0,22	0,35	0,31	0,54	0,33	0,50	0,16	0,33	0,22	0,28	0,04	0,14	0,13	0,17
DecCont2	0,02	0,15	0,09	0,31	0,18	0,20	0,07	0,13	0,34	0,15	0,07	0,12	0,05	0,10

Table Appendix-E-2: Cross-Loadings Germany (Page 2 from 4)

Item	Out	PC	TC	StratII	StratI	Oper-atII	Oper-atI	IntelI	Behav-Con	Sub-Norm	Work-Load	Spec-Bus	Spec-Tec	SoNet-IS-US
Trust1	0,01	0,04	0,11	0,05	0,05	0,12	0,09	0,12	0,15	0,01	0,06	0,01	0,02	0,12
Trust2	0,00	0,19	0,16	0,15	0,06	0,25	0,04	0,16	0,16	0,09	0,13	0,07	0,07	0,08
Trust3	0,13	0,30	0,24	0,11	0,11	0,22	0,12	0,24	0,04	0,02	0,01	0,11	0,04	0,13
Incen1	0,04	0,28	0,26	0,28	0,07	0,38	0,12	0,21	0,27	0,22	0,08	0,03	0,10	0,01
Incen2	0,14	0,37	0,28	0,27	0,16	0,31	0,08	0,29	0,13	0,17	0,03	0,07	0,04	0,10
Incen3	0,10	0,31	0,20	0,19	0,18	0,27	0,06	0,25	0,09	0,09	0,11	0,01	0,01	0,09
Group1	0,09	0,25	0,27	0,22	0,17	0,31	0,13	0,19	0,21	0,12	0,04	0,02	0,01	0,03
Group4	0,04	0,07	0,04	0,05	0,05	0,11	0,02	0,09	0,05	0,11	0,11	0,02	0,05	0,04
Group6	0,06	0,08	0,06	0,13	0,04	0,19	0,09	0,01	0,03	0,21	0,16	0,02	0,03	0,07
Group7	0,13	0,28	0,22	0,14	0,15	0,25	0,12	0,22	0,18	0,21	0,16	0,07	0,09	0,03
LongWo1	0,19	0,31	0,24	0,35	0,22	0,39	0,11	0,35	0,06	0,27	0,02	0,09	0,07	0,17
LongWo2	0,15	0,29	0,30	0,42	0,23	0,43	0,10	0,35	0,12	0,23	0,01	0,17	0,04	0,22
LongWo3	0,12	0,22	0,27	0,26	0,11	0,33	0,11	0,29	0,12	0,21	0,00	0,10	0,16	0,11
Attitud2	0,42	0,57	0,44	0,45	0,11	0,44	0,15	0,39	0,15	0,55	0,11	0,06	0,07	0,02
Attitud3	0,38	0,44	0,34	0,46	0,11	0,41	0,14	0,37	0,13	0,52	0,09	0,04	0,13	0,01
Attitud5	0,44	0,45	0,39	0,33	0,07	0,32	0,13	0,33	0,05	0,51	0,03	0,03	0,12	0,03
Attitud6	0,40	0,44	0,39	0,27	0,09	0,29	0,14	0,35	0,10	0,53	0,06	0,03	0,11	0,00
Attitud7	0,33	0,41	0,34	0,31	0,08	0,28	0,09	0,33	0,13	0,44	0,03	0,07	0,09	0,03
Spec1	0,02	0,14	0,04	0,06	0,29	0,00	0,06	0,13	0,07	0,02	0,07	0,93	0,38	0,33
Spec2	0,04	0,18	0,11	0,14	0,26	0,10	0,07	0,14	0,09	0,04	0,01	0,93	0,37	0,30
Spec4	0,12	0,19	0,20	0,13	0,11	0,07	0,05	0,19	0,11	0,06	0,01	0,47	0,89	0,13
Spec5	0,01	0,07	0,02	0,06	0,14	0,06	0,06	0,15	0,10	0,10	0,04	0,16	0,77	0,12
SoNet1	0,10	0,09	0,12	0,19	0,28	0,17	0,21	0,26	0,11	0,07	0,00	0,31	0,12	0,86
SoNet2	0,08	0,16	0,14	0,18	0,31	0,16	0,21	0,30	0,07	0,05	0,05	0,34	0,18	0,66
SoNet3	0,07	0,17	0,05	0,11	0,24	0,14	0,24	0,22	0,02	0,01	0,17	0,27	0,14	0,84
SoNet4	0,10	0,29	0,16	0,13	0,38	0,14	0,28	0,33	0,00	0,03	0,14	0,24	0,22	0,66
Meas2	0,14	0,05	0,04	0,08	0,04	0,03	0,04	0,01	0,11	0,07	0,16	0,03	0,06	0,02
Meas3	0,21	0,00	0,01	0,10	0,14	0,01	0,10	0,00	0,16	0,08	0,26	0,07	0,03	0,01
Uncert1	0,04	0,01	0,04	0,05	0,07	0,08	0,13	0,10	0,12	0,00	0,10	0,22	0,09	0,18
Uncert2	0,04	0,00	0,10	0,03	0,13	0,08	0,14	0,08	0,03	0,05	0,02	0,29	0,14	0,22
Uncert3	0,08	0,03	0,05	0,06	0,17	0,04	0,00	0,06	0,12	0,00	0,14	0,26	0,13	0,25
Uncert4	0,05	0,02	0,11	0,01	0,12	0,04	0,04	0,07	0,15	0,02	0,21	0,28	0,12	0,21
WoLoad1	0,07	0,04	0,05	0,04	0,04	0,03	0,02	0,01	0,13	0,08	0,85	0,10	0,05	0,05
WoLoad2	0,05	0,10	0,03	0,02	0,08	0,02	0,09	0,05	0,13	0,07	0,99	0,02	0,05	0,11
CoPro1	0,07	0,09	0,12	0,16	0,00	0,20	0,03	0,08	0,90	0,05	0,11	0,12	0,09	0,00
CoPro2	0,05	0,10	0,14	0,15	0,01	0,24	0,07	0,05	0,89	0,05	0,10	0,11	0,06	0,02
CoPro3	0,07	0,03	0,05	0,08	0,04	0,18	0,08	0,05	0,89	0,16	0,14	0,00	0,17	0,11
Other1	0,35	0,36	0,39	0,41	0,13	0,31	0,15	0,28	0,11	0,92	0,05	0,09	0,09	0,09
Other2	0,33	0,36	0,37	0,36	0,10	0,30	0,11	0,26	0,10	0,93	0,05	0,07	0,07	0,05
Other3	0,34	0,34	0,33	0,36	0,06	0,32	0,07	0,22	0,07	0,92	0,05	0,04	0,08	0,06
Other4	0,32	0,25	0,29	0,26	0,03	0,25	0,06	0,26	0,12	0,89	0,09	0,00	0,08	0,01
Other5	0,31	0,26	0,26	0,25	0,01	0,27	0,01	0,22	0,13	0,88	0,09	0,04	0,02	0,02
Other6	0,34	0,28	0,34	0,27	0,03	0,24	0,08	0,25	0,03	0,89	0,08	0,02	0,13	0,03
IDEAL	0,73	0,56	0,46	0,42	0,18	0,44	0,18	0,40	0,01	0,48	0,03	0,14	0,12	0,14
Propert3	0,32	0,19	0,25	0,17	0,01	0,27	0,05	0,14	0,08	0,03	0,06	0,15	0,11	0,06

Table Appendix-E-2: Cross-Loadings Germany (Page 3 from 4)

Item	Soc-NetIS	Meas	Env-Unc	Bus-Unc	Trust	Incent	Res-Other	Group	Spec-Hum	Syst-Impa	Sys-View	Long-Wo	Own-er	Atti-tude	Ideal	Con-trol
Out1	0,10	0,19	0,03	0,06	0,05	0,07	0,24	0,08	0,08	0,42	0,36	0,17	0,27	0,47	0,74	0,15
Out2	0,08	0,19	0,03	0,06	0,08	0,11	0,14	0,06	0,11	0,42	0,40	0,17	0,34	0,41	0,68	0,19
Out3	0,10	0,20	0,05	0,07	0,09	0,13	0,20	0,18	0,09	0,39	0,38	0,20	0,32	0,43	0,70	0,19
Out4	0,03	0,06	0,10	0,02	0,11	0,17	0,02	0,14	0,11	0,03	0,27	0,11	0,37	0,09	0,28	0,08
Pc1	0,29	0,01	0,07	0,06	0,28	0,29	0,21	0,22	0,27	0,41	0,45	0,26	0,19	0,44	0,45	0,20
Pc2	0,23	0,02	0,03	0,07	0,22	0,28	0,21	0,28	0,18	0,33	0,39	0,11	0,15	0,33	0,31	0,19
Pc3	0,23	0,00	0,07	0,08	0,22	0,25	0,28	0,27	0,27	0,50	0,43	0,37	0,17	0,43	0,46	0,31
Pc4	0,10	0,06	0,04	0,04	0,13	0,27	0,18	0,19	0,13	0,45	0,32	0,21	0,11	0,43	0,49	0,27
Pc5	0,11	0,03	0,07	0,04	0,21	0,27	0,20	0,18	0,13	0,38	0,33	0,29	0,14	0,46	0,47	0,29
TC1	0,14	0,01	0,08	0,09	0,21	0,23	0,16	0,17	0,11	0,34	0,33	0,24	0,18	0,36	0,38	0,14
TC2	0,11	0,02	0,05	0,09	0,20	0,22	0,17	0,25	0,14	0,39	0,42	0,24	0,20	0,37	0,40	0,28
TC3	0,22	0,01	0,09	0,04	0,11	0,21	0,22	0,20	0,20	0,36	0,36	0,29	0,27	0,35	0,32	0,25
TC4	0,09	0,03	0,06	0,08	0,28	0,24	0,20	0,21	0,09	0,41	0,39	0,26	0,17	0,34	0,38	0,22
Strat1	0,25	0,02	0,08	0,16	0,10	0,13	0,21	0,20	0,30	0,21	0,27	0,22	0,07	0,09	0,27	0,33
Strat2	0,21	0,06	0,03	0,03	0,11	0,27	0,22	0,20	0,23	0,59	0,35	0,39	0,17	0,42	0,43	0,43
Strat3	0,37	0,11	0,14	0,09	0,07	0,09	0,20	0,13	0,40	0,23	0,18	0,20	0,04	0,11	0,08	0,23
Strat4	0,12	0,11	0,05	0,00	0,15	0,23	0,29	0,20	0,13	0,60	0,39	0,39	0,15	0,42	0,38	0,54
Strat5	0,32	0,14	0,07	0,14	0,09	0,16	0,24	0,13	0,31	0,24	0,22	0,15	0,00	0,08	0,14	0,24
Strat6	0,15	0,11	0,04	0,05	0,17	0,27	0,23	0,23	0,16	0,57	0,35	0,37	0,16	0,35	0,37	0,49
Operat1	0,16	0,07	0,13	0,03	0,11	0,06	0,22	0,07	0,15	0,22	0,15	0,09	0,00	0,14	0,16	0,04
Operat2	0,14	0,00	0,10	0,04	0,25	0,28	0,22	0,31	0,14	0,60	0,33	0,44	0,24	0,32	0,39	0,40
Operat3	0,22	0,09	0,14	0,05	0,15	0,07	0,18	0,08	0,20	0,14	0,16	0,13	0,13	0,11	0,09	0,14
Operat4	0,15	0,03	0,07	0,04	0,20	0,28	0,25	0,31	0,16	0,59	0,35	0,45	0,20	0,31	0,38	0,39
Operat5	0,29	0,06	0,10	0,01	0,01	0,12	0,21	0,08	0,26	0,22	0,24	0,11	0,03	0,12	0,18	0,20
Operat6	0,14	0,01	0,05	0,03	0,27	0,36	0,29	0,28	0,12	0,64	0,42	0,30	0,26	0,40	0,39	0,38
Res1	0,27	0,03	0,01	0,06	0,18	0,21	0,45	0,14	0,27	0,44	0,34	0,30	0,06	0,39	0,40	0,21
Res2	0,33	0,09	0,05	0,03	0,20	0,17	0,32	0,16	0,28	0,40	0,29	0,31	0,22	0,36	0,29	0,24
Res3	0,29	0,05	0,12	0,11	0,18	0,21	0,36	0,23	0,28	0,31	0,23	0,32	0,00	0,22	0,24	0,22
Res5	0,24	0,05	0,08	0,05	0,09	0,13	0,54	0,20	0,28	0,18	0,10	0,28	0,10	0,14	0,20	0,16
Res6	0,16	0,11	0,16	0,01	0,19	0,29	0,40	0,15	0,22	0,38	0,27	0,29	0,12	0,25	0,27	0,28
Res7	0,19	0,00	0,05	0,03	0,03	0,02	0,71	0,14	0,18	0,20	0,24	0,20	0,07	0,14	0,20	0,04
Res8	0,17	0,05	0,09	0,07	0,02	0,13	0,94	0,17	0,13	0,26	0,15	0,17	0,15	0,22	0,27	0,07
Impact1	0,14	0,10	0,03	0,01	0,20	0,30	0,30	0,20	0,16	0,89	0,46	0,25	0,20	0,42	0,36	0,40
Impact2	0,13	0,08	0,04	0,02	0,18	0,25	0,32	0,22	0,20	0,89	0,44	0,33	0,25	0,40	0,41	0,39
Impact3	0,09	0,09	0,00	0,02	0,23	0,28	0,12	0,16	0,13	0,87	0,41	0,30	0,18	0,39	0,35	0,42
EmplOri1	0,15	0,12	0,21	0,15	0,23	0,32	0,16	0,30	0,18	0,40	0,75	0,42	0,20	0,22	0,31	0,23
EmplOri2	0,17	0,13	0,18	0,08	0,24	0,37	0,15	0,37	0,19	0,41	0,88	0,28	0,20	0,31	0,43	0,25
EmplOri3	0,23	0,01	0,15	0,09	0,27	0,27	0,17	0,22	0,28	0,39	0,83	0,28	0,26	0,23	0,34	0,31
EmplOri4	0,16	0,01	0,19	0,07	0,24	0,31	0,20	0,30	0,20	0,46	0,89	0,35	0,19	0,32	0,35	0,29
DecCont1	0,12	0,03	0,06	0,01	0,13	0,27	0,11	0,26	0,19	0,49	0,36	0,28	0,12	0,40	0,32	0,97
DecCont2	0,11	0,04	0,05	0,10	0,12	0,20	0,03	0,20	0,13	0,22	0,11	0,10	0,10	0,18	0,09	0,79

Table Appendix-E-2: Cross-Loadings Germany (Page 4 from 4)

Item	Soc-NetIS	Meas	Env-Unc	Bus-Unc	Trust	Incent	Res-Other	Group	Spec-Hum	Syst-Impa	Sys-View	Long-Wo	Own-er	Atti-tude	Ideal	Con-trol
Trust1	0,02	0,12	0,14	0,03	0,65	0,27	0,10	0,08	0,03	0,09	0,15	0,11	0,12	0,01	0,01	0,10
Trust2	0,08	0,04	0,10	0,03	0,81	0,30	0,07	0,20	0,10	0,20	0,17	0,10	0,27	0,11	0,05	0,13
Trust3	0,14	0,01	0,17	0,04	0,81	0,27	0,03	0,14	0,15	0,20	0,31	0,27	0,19	0,18	0,16	0,10
Incen1	0,04	0,15	0,00	0,00	0,33	0,88	0,10	0,36	0,03	0,33	0,28	0,18	0,05	0,15	0,11	0,22
Incen2	0,14	0,09	0,04	0,02	0,33	0,92	0,12	0,31	0,13	0,29	0,39	0,33	0,05	0,22	0,29	0,27
Incen3	0,10	0,15	0,02	0,00	0,34	0,92	0,13	0,33	0,08	0,24	0,36	0,24	0,00	0,18	0,20	0,25
Group1	0,05	0,17	0,04	0,03	0,16	0,34	0,15	0,80	0,02	0,23	0,31	0,12	0,02	0,18	0,07	0,27
Group4	0,07	0,07	0,10	0,06	0,03	0,17	0,13	0,50	0,02	0,02	0,11	0,09	0,12	0,02	0,04	0,02
Group6	0,07	0,15	0,07	0,00	0,17	0,13	0,02	0,56	0,06	0,05	0,12	0,20	0,11	0,07	0,12	0,13
Group7	0,03	0,18	0,16	0,07	0,14	0,27	0,23	0,75	0,07	0,18	0,33	0,38	0,10	0,16	0,16	0,20
LongWo1	0,18	0,12	0,15	0,03	0,22	0,21	0,21	0,25	0,18	0,27	0,33	0,91	0,15	0,15	0,29	0,24
LongWo2	0,22	0,03	0,19	0,07	0,15	0,30	0,25	0,30	0,24	0,33	0,39	0,89	0,26	0,18	0,30	0,25
LongWo3	0,09	0,15	0,11	0,07	0,23	0,19	0,15	0,21	0,15	0,27	0,25	0,76	0,32	0,11	0,19	0,15
Attitud2	0,00	0,10	0,04	0,04	0,15	0,22	0,25	0,25	0,03	0,47	0,35	0,18	0,09	0,87	0,57	0,33
Attitud3	0,01	0,07	0,05	0,02	0,11	0,16	0,17	0,24	0,04	0,42	0,28	0,14	0,10	0,88	0,53	0,32
Attitud5	0,06	0,12	0,12	0,09	0,12	0,16	0,18	0,10	0,05	0,37	0,26	0,17	0,11	0,88	0,58	0,34
Attitud6	0,02	0,08	0,12	0,07	0,14	0,17	0,20	0,06	0,04	0,34	0,24	0,13	0,16	0,86	0,58	0,32
Attitud7	0,03	0,11	0,11	0,06	0,15	0,16	0,20	0,16	0,05	0,38	0,27	0,13	0,11	0,84	0,44	0,29
Spec1	0,32	0,09	0,28	0,31	0,07	0,06	0,06	0,03	0,66	0,09	0,21	0,14	0,17	0,00	0,11	0,15
Spec2	0,28	0,02	0,26	0,23	0,10	0,02	0,04	0,01	0,63	0,21	0,17	0,12	0,11	0,08	0,15	0,12
Spec4	0,18	0,07	0,17	0,15	0,11	0,01	0,12	0,01	0,47	0,16	0,17	0,10	0,15	0,11	0,13	0,11
Spec5	0,19	0,11	0,02	0,05	0,03	0,03	0,16	0,06	0,34	0,10	0,00	0,05	0,02	0,09	0,06	0,09
SoNet1	0,65	0,04	0,17	0,17	0,10	0,01	0,15	0,02	0,72	0,18	0,13	0,18	0,05	0,00	0,16	0,13
SoNet2	0,91	0,02	0,15	0,09	0,06	0,01	0,16	0,01	0,79	0,15	0,17	0,14	0,08	0,02	0,13	0,06
SoNet3	0,59	0,04	0,20	0,23	0,14	0,13	0,12	0,04	0,67	0,10	0,19	0,17	0,06	0,01	0,08	0,14
SoNet4	0,91	0,02	0,19	0,14	0,15	0,12	0,25	0,14	0,76	0,10	0,22	0,22	0,04	0,02	0,16	0,17
Meas2	0,02	0,85	0,08	0,09	0,09	0,13	0,05	0,27	0,04	0,11	0,04	0,02	0,21	0,07	0,04	0,10
Meas3	0,02	0,93	0,16	0,23	0,01	0,12	0,05	0,15	0,02	0,07	0,09	0,15	0,19	0,12	0,17	0,01
Uncert1	0,16	0,13	0,85	0,45	0,16	0,01	0,06	0,03	0,23	0,01	0,13	0,16	0,10	0,09	0,12	0,04
Uncert2	0,18	0,14	0,97	0,50	0,16	0,03	0,06	0,10	0,29	0,03	0,23	0,17	0,00	0,09	0,13	0,06
Uncert3	0,16	0,16	0,46	0,88	0,06	0,05	0,03	0,01	0,28	0,01	0,06	0,02	0,08	0,07	0,05	0,06
Uncert4	0,09	0,18	0,50	0,97	0,03	0,04	0,03	0,01	0,23	0,01	0,12	0,04	0,02	0,05	0,05	0,03
WoLoad1	0,05	0,24	0,10	0,28	0,08	0,07	0,03	0,10	0,01	0,02	0,06	0,00	0,20	0,01	0,01	0,09
WoLoad2	0,12	0,24	0,03	0,16	0,04	0,08	0,15	0,16	0,09	0,02	0,02	0,00	0,02	0,09	0,04	0,04
CoPro1	0,03	0,14	0,05	0,09	0,14	0,22	0,02	0,20	0,04	0,19	0,16	0,09	0,01	0,12	0,01	0,25
CoPro2	0,05	0,10	0,11	0,17	0,11	0,10	0,07	0,18	0,00	0,21	0,17	0,12	0,14	0,09	0,01	0,26
CoPro3	0,08	0,16	0,03	0,14	0,10	0,17	0,05	0,17	0,11	0,11	0,16	0,10	0,07	0,13	0,02	0,24
Other1	0,09	0,05	0,02	0,09	0,03	0,13	0,18	0,20	0,12	0,28	0,26	0,29	0,04	0,55	0,42	0,26
Other2	0,06	0,07	0,01	0,03	0,03	0,14	0,20	0,21	0,08	0,27	0,29	0,30	0,08	0,53	0,43	0,25
Other3	0,04	0,01	0,01	0,05	0,04	0,16	0,20	0,21	0,07	0,27	0,22	0,28	0,08	0,57	0,44	0,22
Other4	0,02	0,02	0,06	0,01	0,01	0,17	0,17	0,23	0,01	0,21	0,23	0,21	0,10	0,52	0,42	0,23
Other5	0,02	0,03	0,10	0,03	0,03	0,21	0,15	0,25	0,01	0,23	0,20	0,20	0,04	0,53	0,41	0,29
Other6	0,02	0,00	0,06	0,05	0,02	0,18	0,16	0,19	0,03	0,21	0,23	0,20	0,01	0,53	0,48	0,21
IDEAL	0,16	0,13	0,13	0,05	0,12	0,22	0,30	0,15	0,20	0,42	0,42	0,31	0,28	0,62	1,00	0,28
Propert3	0,07	0,22	0,04	0,02	0,27	0,04	0,15	0,06	0,13	0,24	0,25	0,27	1,00	0,13	0,28	0,07

Table Appendix-E-3: Cross-Loadings Finance Industry (Page 1 from 4)

Item	Out	PC	TC	StratII	StratI	Oper-atII	Oper-atI	Intell	Behav-Con	Sub-Norm	Work-Load	Spec-Bus	Spec-Tec	SoNet-IS-US
Out1	0,97	0,40	0,30	0,49	0,05	0,41	0,09	0,33	0,12	0,38	0,12	0,01	0,11	0,15
Out2	0,99	0,44	0,32	0,45	0,04	0,37	0,08	0,34	0,16	0,38	0,15	0,01	0,10	0,14
Out3	0,97	0,42	0,28	0,49	0,05	0,40	0,05	0,31	0,16	0,42	0,13	0,04	0,07	0,11
Out4	0,41	0,22	0,17	0,16	0,07	0,11	0,12	0,19	0,15	0,07	0,09	0,13	0,25	0,04
Pc1	0,39	0,85	0,60	0,43	0,23	0,47	0,16	0,52	0,16	0,34	0,14	0,17	0,20	0,28
Pc2	0,21	0,65	0,42	0,34	0,22	0,40	0,19	0,48	0,04	0,22	0,06	0,16	0,20	0,23
Pc3	0,35	0,76	0,43	0,51	0,28	0,53	0,18	0,50	0,09	0,36	0,15	0,26	0,25	0,21
Pc4	0,40	0,78	0,53	0,35	0,23	0,34	0,22	0,39	0,03	0,30	0,20	0,19	0,16	0,20
Pc5	0,30	0,85	0,64	0,40	0,23	0,48	0,22	0,50	0,08	0,37	0,17	0,24	0,24	0,14
TC1	0,28	0,62	0,83	0,42	0,22	0,43	0,31	0,47	0,19	0,35	0,07	0,15	0,07	0,18
TC2	0,17	0,41	0,79	0,26	0,10	0,28	0,20	0,29	0,11	0,29	0,03	0,26	0,23	0,13
TC3	0,21	0,52	0,81	0,33	0,11	0,33	0,09	0,33	0,02	0,37	0,12	0,14	0,24	0,25
TC4	0,30	0,53	0,76	0,33	0,03	0,38	0,15	0,42	0,03	0,26	0,18	0,18	0,21	0,14
Strat1	0,08	0,29	0,19	0,26	0,71	0,18	0,17	0,18	0,05	0,01	0,13	0,33	0,13	0,07
Strat2	0,44	0,52	0,44	0,94	0,27	0,77	0,10	0,46	0,05	0,45	0,06	0,16	0,12	0,25
Strat3	0,03	0,24	0,13	0,25	0,87	0,15	0,40	0,31	0,02	0,11	0,10	0,22	0,24	0,23
Strat4	0,48	0,50	0,40	0,94	0,32	0,75	0,17	0,42	0,12	0,44	0,10	0,14	0,16	0,19
Strat5	0,03	0,24	0,07	0,26	0,89	0,15	0,31	0,24	0,05	0,07	0,01	0,32	0,22	0,18
Strat6	0,42	0,46	0,38	0,95	0,27	0,77	0,10	0,43	0,16	0,42	0,08	0,18	0,11	0,19
Operat1	0,09	0,25	0,18	0,18	0,32	0,15	0,86	0,22	0,04	0,13	0,11	0,02	0,06	0,03
Operat2	0,34	0,49	0,38	0,72	0,15	0,89	0,09	0,45	0,27	0,40	0,09	0,14	0,24	0,21
Operat3	0,01	0,19	0,10	0,01	0,43	0,06	0,75	0,13	0,03	0,07	0,06	0,07	0,16	0,04
Operat4	0,35	0,49	0,40	0,80	0,18	0,92	0,14	0,47	0,22	0,42	0,10	0,18	0,19	0,22
Operat5	0,07	0,14	0,28	0,09	0,18	0,14	0,79	0,14	0,07	0,09	0,02	0,01	0,12	0,14
Operat6	0,36	0,52	0,42	0,63	0,16	0,84	0,17	0,55	0,23	0,35	0,02	0,17	0,09	0,24
Res1	0,38	0,51	0,45	0,41	0,23	0,44	0,19	0,79	0,01	0,23	0,23	0,20	0,25	0,15
Res2	0,28	0,48	0,35	0,43	0,26	0,53	0,19	0,83	0,10	0,43	0,13	0,19	0,19	0,29
Res3	0,21	0,49	0,40	0,24	0,24	0,36	0,13	0,79	0,06	0,27	0,13	0,09	0,22	0,27
Res5	0,19	0,25	0,16	0,26	0,22	0,35	0,14	0,35	0,02	0,26	0,05	0,23	0,33	0,23
Res6	0,15	0,45	0,33	0,35	0,23	0,41	0,14	0,75	0,07	0,24	0,08	0,25	0,30	0,20
Res7	0,20	0,29	0,40	0,17	0,19	0,10	0,19	0,26	0,25	0,12	0,19	0,10	0,25	0,21
Res8	0,31	0,36	0,29	0,39	0,22	0,39	0,15	0,43	0,08	0,28	0,11	0,03	0,13	0,15
Impact1	0,40	0,55	0,43	0,67	0,17	0,66	0,15	0,49	0,13	0,28	0,10	0,22	0,06	0,30
Impact2	0,43	0,47	0,39	0,61	0,23	0,63	0,26	0,44	0,07	0,39	0,14	0,20	0,24	0,26
Impact3	0,37	0,49	0,35	0,55	0,09	0,63	0,09	0,50	0,08	0,30	0,14	0,19	0,06	0,29
EmplOri1	0,23	0,35	0,36	0,28	0,20	0,31	0,24	0,41	0,20	0,16	0,15	0,26	0,13	0,16
EmplOri2	0,37	0,51	0,38	0,37	0,21	0,41	0,23	0,41	0,04	0,31	0,02	0,28	0,31	0,27
EmplOri3	0,32	0,51	0,35	0,46	0,31	0,44	0,04	0,40	0,15	0,16	0,12	0,36	0,29	0,22
EmplOri4	0,31	0,45	0,30	0,39	0,21	0,44	0,03	0,42	0,13	0,17	0,10	0,31	0,29	0,15
DecCont1	0,26	0,27	0,24	0,45	0,19	0,44	0,10	0,29	0,28	0,31	0,03	0,20	0,18	0,11
DecCont2	0,04	0,11	0,05	0,25	0,00	0,28	0,06	0,10	0,42	0,21	0,17	0,10	0,02	0,01

Table Appendix-E-3: Cross-Loadings Finance Industry (Page 2 from 4)

Item	Out	PC	TC	StratII	StratI	Oper-atII	Oper-atI	IntelI	Behav-Con	Sub-Norm	Work-Load	Spec-Bus	Spec-Tec	SoNet-IS-US
Trust1	0,01	0,04	0,11	0,08	0,11	0,04	0,01	0,07	0,09	0,08	0,09	0,01	0,03	0,00
Trust2	0,02	0,27	0,19	0,11	0,10	0,28	0,06	0,18	0,13	0,00	0,06	0,04	0,02	0,07
Trust3	0,03	0,29	0,13	0,02	0,08	0,16	0,07	0,31	0,02	0,12	0,06	0,12	0,05	0,10
Incen1	0,10	0,32	0,28	0,38	0,00	0,47	0,02	0,40	0,34	0,25	0,07	0,13	0,02	0,05
Incen2	0,21	0,47	0,34	0,41	0,21	0,45	0,00	0,49	0,13	0,18	0,05	0,30	0,25	0,15
Incen3	0,13	0,35	0,18	0,28	0,20	0,37	0,06	0,45	0,15	0,09	0,19	0,24	0,15	0,12
Group1	0,12	0,30	0,24	0,25	0,06	0,29	0,08	0,16	0,23	0,24	0,14	0,01	0,00	0,04
Group4	0,03	0,14	0,07	0,23	0,08	0,30	0,04	0,15	0,06	0,25	0,05	0,05	0,14	0,02
Group6	0,10	0,03	0,03	0,20	0,01	0,25	0,06	0,09	0,08	0,25	0,16	0,02	0,01	0,01
Group7	0,18	0,36	0,24	0,26	0,24	0,35	0,16	0,38	0,28	0,23	0,08	0,16	0,18	0,01
LongWo1	0,20	0,39	0,32	0,37	0,19	0,45	0,06	0,46	0,06	0,27	0,09	0,21	0,29	0,13
LongWo2	0,17	0,47	0,41	0,45	0,26	0,51	0,10	0,53	0,19	0,30	0,02	0,32	0,26	0,19
LongWo3	0,15	0,30	0,32	0,29	0,09	0,38	0,11	0,40	0,15	0,33	0,07	0,18	0,24	0,10
Attitud2	0,45	0,62	0,42	0,55	0,13	0,54	0,15	0,43	0,12	0,62	0,14	0,17	0,13	0,10
Attitud3	0,38	0,50	0,36	0,54	0,12	0,48	0,16	0,40	0,14	0,60	0,13	0,15	0,18	0,02
Attitud5	0,45	0,50	0,39	0,43	0,11	0,40	0,14	0,37	0,00	0,58	0,05	0,03	0,25	0,14
Attitud6	0,43	0,49	0,43	0,36	0,12	0,36	0,20	0,41	0,08	0,59	0,08	0,04	0,26	0,12
Attitud7	0,38	0,46	0,37	0,44	0,11	0,43	0,06	0,42	0,08	0,50	0,05	0,17	0,19	0,14
Spec1	0,03	0,20	0,17	0,10	0,37	0,13	0,00	0,20	0,09	0,10	0,05	0,93	0,42	0,28
Spec2	0,01	0,27	0,24	0,21	0,25	0,22	0,02	0,23	0,12	0,09	0,00	0,91	0,38	0,25
Spec4	0,15	0,28	0,25	0,20	0,16	0,21	0,10	0,28	0,12	0,19	0,09	0,47	0,82	0,08
Spec5	0,01	0,16	0,13	0,03	0,24	0,10	0,11	0,22	0,06	0,21	0,03	0,25	0,82	0,19
SoNet1	0,17	0,21	0,19	0,25	0,29	0,24	0,14	0,26	0,08	0,18	0,03	0,27	0,14	0,87
SoNet2	0,15	0,27	0,19	0,29	0,34	0,31	0,08	0,34	0,10	0,18	0,09	0,29	0,19	0,71
SoNet3	0,04	0,25	0,19	0,11	0,04	0,19	0,01	0,22	0,04	0,03	0,19	0,22	0,13	0,82
SoNet4	0,10	0,36	0,22	0,24	0,30	0,29	0,16	0,33	0,02	0,12	0,19	0,21	0,18	0,67
Meas2	0,33	0,10	0,07	0,17	0,07	0,06	0,04	0,14	0,15	0,05	0,26	0,02	0,19	0,08
Meas3	0,41	0,09	0,06	0,23	0,06	0,16	0,02	0,08	0,20	0,24	0,30	0,10	0,06	0,10
Uncert1	0,16	0,09	0,03	0,18	0,06	0,20	0,07	0,15	0,08	0,12	0,08	0,16	0,02	0,01
Uncert2	0,15	0,03	0,06	0,11	0,23	0,13	0,12	0,02	0,10	0,20	0,01	0,35	0,22	0,11
Uncert3	0,13	0,02	0,00	0,01	0,13	0,07	0,03	0,02	0,22	0,01	0,06	0,17	0,07	0,11
Uncert4	0,08	0,01	0,11	0,03	0,05	0,07	0,00	0,01	0,24	0,01	0,20	0,27	0,18	0,12
WoLoad1	0,04	0,01	0,05	0,03	0,11	0,01	0,00	0,01	0,10	0,13	0,70	0,01	0,04	0,06
WoLoad2	0,13	0,18	0,11	0,08	0,07	0,07	0,08	0,13	0,15	0,05	1,00	0,03	0,07	0,11
CoPro1	0,07	0,17	0,18	0,21	0,03	0,30	0,01	0,15	0,87	0,12	0,15	0,17	0,07	0,00
CoPro2	0,08	0,16	0,15	0,12	0,01	0,29	0,07	0,12	0,91	0,08	0,11	0,16	0,06	0,02
CoPro3	0,21	0,04	0,03	0,01	0,03	0,16	0,07	0,03	0,89	0,07	0,13	0,01	0,13	0,14
Other1	0,35	0,40	0,41	0,45	0,14	0,38	0,17	0,32	0,08	0,92	0,03	0,14	0,17	0,15
Other2	0,36	0,41	0,40	0,44	0,14	0,40	0,14	0,32	0,08	0,93	0,02	0,12	0,13	0,16
Other3	0,40	0,42	0,39	0,41	0,09	0,41	0,10	0,31	0,02	0,93	0,01	0,13	0,27	0,15
Other4	0,37	0,36	0,35	0,37	0,05	0,37	0,11	0,35	0,14	0,90	0,07	0,09	0,25	0,09
Other5	0,35	0,32	0,29	0,42	0,02	0,43	0,07	0,36	0,17	0,90	0,07	0,01	0,19	0,13
Other6	0,39	0,35	0,38	0,45	0,05	0,43	0,13	0,39	0,07	0,91	0,11	0,09	0,27	0,07
IDEAL	0,74	0,61	0,48	0,58	0,29	0,55	0,21	0,51	0,04	0,55	0,13	0,17	0,30	0,19
Propert3	0,47	0,33	0,27	0,21	0,01	0,27	0,03	0,21	0,02	0,17	0,06	0,03	0,10	0,14

Table Appendix-E-3: Cross-Loadings Finance Industry (Page 3 from 4)

Item	Soc-NetIS	Meas	Env-Unc	Bus-Unc	Trust	Incent	Res-Other	Group	Spec-Hum	Syst-Impa	Sys-View	Long-Wo	Own-er	Atti-tude	Ideal	Con-trol
Out1	0,16	0,40	0,14	0,07	0,00	0,15	0,33	0,15	0,14	0,46	0,38	0,21	0,45	0,46	0,74	0,19
Out2	0,13	0,39	0,17	0,06	0,01	0,15	0,29	0,10	0,12	0,44	0,37	0,17	0,48	0,48	0,73	0,23
Out3	0,13	0,40	0,17	0,11	0,01	0,18	0,35	0,23	0,10	0,44	0,35	0,20	0,48	0,47	0,72	0,23
Out4	0,04	0,13	0,03	0,07	0,04	0,25	0,07	0,17	0,13	0,03	0,29	0,15	0,44	0,11	0,33	0,09
Pc1	0,33	0,13	0,03	0,11	0,26	0,37	0,37	0,32	0,34	0,44	0,49	0,42	0,32	0,51	0,55	0,12
Pc2	0,30	0,03	0,04	0,04	0,23	0,31	0,28	0,34	0,31	0,38	0,49	0,23	0,23	0,37	0,32	0,21
Pc3	0,28	0,09	0,00	0,01	0,33	0,40	0,34	0,31	0,35	0,52	0,48	0,47	0,26	0,44	0,47	0,26
Pc4	0,22	0,06	0,14	0,08	0,15	0,25	0,21	0,20	0,27	0,44	0,37	0,25	0,23	0,41	0,50	0,19
Pc5	0,22	0,08	0,13	0,10	0,25	0,32	0,38	0,24	0,29	0,41	0,35	0,36	0,24	0,56	0,54	0,21
TC1	0,18	0,04	0,04	0,15	0,23	0,34	0,31	0,20	0,21	0,39	0,28	0,35	0,15	0,42	0,39	0,13
TC2	0,08	0,04	0,05	0,11	0,18	0,17	0,20	0,16	0,23	0,30	0,31	0,19	0,16	0,30	0,31	0,20
TC3	0,27	0,06	0,05	0,02	0,04	0,21	0,27	0,17	0,31	0,32	0,36	0,34	0,32	0,37	0,37	0,20
TC4	0,15	0,13	0,00	0,04	0,14	0,22	0,32	0,22	0,23	0,36	0,36	0,37	0,22	0,34	0,45	0,14
Strat1	0,14	0,01	0,15	0,07	0,03	0,16	0,18	0,12	0,23	0,11	0,29	0,17	0,03	0,09	0,32	0,23
Strat2	0,30	0,12	0,15	0,04	0,06	0,40	0,34	0,35	0,30	0,63	0,42	0,44	0,19	0,48	0,55	0,39
Strat3	0,36	0,01	0,07	0,03	0,12	0,09	0,28	0,16	0,37	0,18	0,19	0,19	0,07	0,12	0,20	0,11
Strat4	0,26	0,29	0,19	0,05	0,04	0,35	0,45	0,31	0,27	0,68	0,46	0,40	0,20	0,55	0,56	0,45
Strat5	0,32	0,01	0,13	0,05	0,03	0,13	0,20	0,14	0,36	0,15	0,25	0,18	0,03	0,11	0,22	0,07
Strat6	0,26	0,21	0,13	0,00	0,09	0,37	0,35	0,36	0,27	0,61	0,41	0,40	0,19	0,46	0,54	0,37
Operat1	0,11	0,02	0,09	0,01	0,11	0,06	0,21	0,10	0,07	0,21	0,09	0,12	0,09	0,15	0,18	0,04
Operat2	0,26	0,05	0,19	0,04	0,25	0,39	0,31	0,46	0,30	0,56	0,40	0,47	0,24	0,41	0,54	0,39
Operat3	0,11	0,05	0,01	0,06	0,04	0,09	0,10	0,06	0,12	0,01	0,08	0,04	0,05	0,12	0,13	0,01
Operat4	0,32	0,09	0,19	0,07	0,17	0,42	0,38	0,42	0,33	0,62	0,42	0,48	0,18	0,43	0,52	0,35
Operat5	0,10	0,01	0,11	0,03	0,10	0,03	0,15	0,03	0,12	0,19	0,18	0,06	0,13	0,13	0,19	0,09
Operat6	0,27	0,17	0,11	0,08	0,24	0,46	0,40	0,33	0,28	0,69	0,47	0,43	0,29	0,50	0,41	0,40
Res1	0,23	0,14	0,04	0,06	0,23	0,32	0,45	0,18	0,28	0,49	0,39	0,45	0,13	0,40	0,46	0,20
Res2	0,38	0,15	0,13	0,01	0,21	0,39	0,35	0,29	0,38	0,45	0,40	0,39	0,27	0,42	0,38	0,28
Res3	0,32	0,09	0,11	0,05	0,21	0,41	0,31	0,30	0,32	0,32	0,36	0,43	0,12	0,29	0,37	0,09
Res5	0,31	0,00	0,17	0,12	0,07	0,18	0,65	0,16	0,37	0,20	0,21	0,32	0,16	0,27	0,37	0,15
Res6	0,20	0,05	0,15	0,05	0,21	0,49	0,42	0,24	0,32	0,41	0,40	0,41	0,12	0,35	0,42	0,24
Res7	0,23	0,08	0,09	0,06	0,07	0,00	0,62	0,08	0,26	0,19	0,27	0,18	0,06	0,25	0,30	0,08
Res8	0,25	0,19	0,04	0,02	0,07	0,31	0,90	0,29	0,20	0,35	0,26	0,30	0,25	0,35	0,46	0,06
Impact1	0,35	0,27	0,08	0,10	0,18	0,35	0,33	0,25	0,35	0,90	0,50	0,29	0,23	0,43	0,39	0,40
Impact2	0,25	0,23	0,07	0,08	0,09	0,33	0,43	0,28	0,33	0,89	0,44	0,26	0,21	0,45	0,44	0,32
Impact3	0,23	0,26	0,11	0,17	0,24	0,35	0,20	0,24	0,28	0,89	0,42	0,32	0,11	0,46	0,40	0,35
EmplOri1	0,23	0,06	0,11	0,14	0,17	0,28	0,20	0,33	0,28	0,35	0,71	0,45	0,15	0,22	0,32	0,29
EmplOri2	0,30	0,00	0,06	0,03	0,12	0,39	0,24	0,43	0,40	0,44	0,85	0,33	0,32	0,36	0,44	0,29
EmplOri3	0,35	0,12	0,00	0,01	0,14	0,35	0,32	0,32	0,42	0,45	0,86	0,38	0,30	0,37	0,45	0,36
EmplOri4	0,27	0,10	0,10	0,04	0,14	0,40	0,29	0,45	0,35	0,44	0,89	0,40	0,25	0,34	0,38	0,28
DecCont1	0,11	0,06	0,03	0,01	0,08	0,26	0,11	0,24	0,20	0,43	0,40	0,29	0,13	0,38	0,33	0,97
DecCont2	0,04	0,15	0,08	0,03	0,12	0,23	0,06	0,26	0,05	0,21	0,16	0,12	0,05	0,18	0,06	0,77

Table Appendix-E-3: Cross-Loadings Finance Industry (Page 4 from 4)

Item	Soc-NetIS	Meas	Env-Unc	Bus-Unc	Trust	Incent	Res-Other	Group	Spec-Hum	Syst-Impa	Sys-View	Long-Wo	Own-er	Atti-tude	Ideal	Con-trol
Trust1	0,10	0,16	0,24	0,11	0,60	0,22	0,16	0,04	0,04	0,03	0,12	0,14	0,08	0,05	0,00	0,05
Trust2	0,08	0,10	0,04	0,03	0,88	0,29	0,10	0,12	0,08	0,22	0,12	0,21	0,35	0,10	0,08	0,10
Trust3	0,17	0,03	0,14	0,06	0,82	0,24	0,03	0,12	0,16	0,11	0,16	0,22	0,10	0,11	0,02	0,07
Incen1	0,03	0,05	0,06	0,02	0,27	0,87	0,22	0,48	0,08	0,39	0,26	0,31	0,05	0,20	0,16	0,23
Incen2	0,23	0,05	0,02	0,08	0,30	0,92	0,28	0,41	0,32	0,37	0,48	0,47	0,19	0,25	0,34	0,30
Incen3	0,19	0,10	0,03	0,11	0,30	0,91	0,27	0,45	0,24	0,26	0,43	0,34	0,13	0,19	0,20	0,22
Group1	0,02	0,13	0,03	0,01	0,11	0,37	0,12	0,75	0,00	0,25	0,41	0,22	0,03	0,30	0,12	0,27
Group4	0,10	0,13	0,13	0,04	0,07	0,33	0,23	0,63	0,09	0,17	0,23	0,19	0,08	0,15	0,11	0,10
Group6	0,05	0,17	0,01	0,10	0,12	0,11	0,06	0,50	0,03	0,02	0,06	0,15	0,16	0,12	0,09	0,18
Group7	0,06	0,13	0,12	0,03	0,08	0,37	0,27	0,70	0,13	0,23	0,38	0,40	0,14	0,21	0,28	0,17
LongWo1	0,13	0,12	0,10	0,00	0,27	0,31	0,25	0,27	0,24	0,25	0,38	0,90	0,22	0,22	0,37	0,20
LongWo2	0,23	0,06	0,09	0,02	0,20	0,47	0,42	0,41	0,34	0,37	0,49	0,92	0,23	0,34	0,41	0,30
LongWo3	0,10	0,14	0,03	0,01	0,19	0,31	0,24	0,31	0,20	0,20	0,30	0,79	0,31	0,18	0,25	0,15
Attitud2	0,14	0,18	0,09	0,02	0,12	0,30	0,39	0,40	0,19	0,54	0,41	0,26	0,16	0,88	0,59	0,29
Attitud3	0,05	0,09	0,01	0,05	0,10	0,22	0,35	0,38	0,12	0,45	0,34	0,27	0,16	0,88	0,55	0,27
Attitud5	0,18	0,23	0,16	0,08	0,06	0,14	0,34	0,21	0,20	0,40	0,34	0,27	0,19	0,87	0,62	0,32
Attitud6	0,13	0,21	0,17	0,04	0,09	0,19	0,37	0,13	0,17	0,36	0,30	0,23	0,22	0,87	0,64	0,35
Attitud7	0,18	0,24	0,27	0,09	0,10	0,19	0,29	0,25	0,23	0,42	0,34	0,25	0,19	0,87	0,55	0,32
Spec1	0,31	0,09	0,24	0,26	0,06	0,25	0,11	0,12	0,65	0,16	0,37	0,29	0,09	0,10	0,15	0,18
Spec2	0,18	0,04	0,23	0,24	0,09	0,20	0,13	0,05	0,58	0,26	0,29	0,22	0,03	0,14	0,18	0,15
Spec4	0,10	0,00	0,17	0,20	0,13	0,13	0,22	0,09	0,44	0,24	0,37	0,28	0,13	0,21	0,26	0,14
Spec5	0,22	0,22	0,01	0,09	0,07	0,12	0,22	0,14	0,44	0,02	0,15	0,21	0,04	0,16	0,24	0,10
SoNet1	0,68	0,14	0,00	0,08	0,04	0,09	0,25	0,04	0,72	0,31	0,20	0,17	0,10	0,11	0,23	0,11
SoNet2	0,92	0,10	0,05	0,02	0,08	0,16	0,30	0,07	0,79	0,33	0,32	0,16	0,16	0,15	0,23	0,07
SoNet3	0,58	0,02	0,08	0,13	0,12	0,11	0,14	0,02	0,63	0,22	0,23	0,11	0,14	0,09	0,09	0,03
SoNet4	0,91	0,08	0,03	0,06	0,14	0,14	0,32	0,02	0,74	0,24	0,32	0,18	0,15	0,14	0,22	0,12
Meas2	0,12	0,91	0,22	0,20	0,02	0,07	0,13	0,22	0,03	0,29	0,03	0,04	0,21	0,20	0,22	0,11
Meas3	0,07	0,94	0,22	0,20	0,09	0,06	0,15	0,15	0,02	0,23	0,07	0,16	0,35	0,20	0,32	0,07
Uncert1	0,08	0,24	0,96	0,51	0,13	0,06	0,09	0,01	0,02	0,13	0,03	0,08	0,01	0,15	0,19	0,04
Uncert2	0,02	0,20	0,90	0,52	0,08	0,03	0,01	0,01	0,22	0,03	0,13	0,08	0,15	0,13	0,13	0,06
Uncert3	0,05	0,20	0,52	0,78	0,07	0,09	0,01	0,05	0,14	0,07	0,01	0,03	0,21	0,06	0,11	0,01
Uncert4	0,02	0,22	0,54	1,00	0,06	0,07	0,05	0,00	0,19	0,13	0,06	0,01	0,10	0,04	0,08	0,00
WoLoad1	0,04	0,24	0,08	0,24	0,04	0,13	0,03	0,15	0,03	0,06	0,02	0,01	0,08	0,06	0,08	0,13
WoLoad2	0,14	0,31	0,05	0,20	0,01	0,11	0,13	0,15	0,11	0,13	0,03	0,06	0,05	0,09	0,12	0,08
CoPro1	0,02	0,12	0,07	0,17	0,13	0,31	0,07	0,30	0,05	0,15	0,23	0,21	0,01	0,16	0,05	0,32
CoPro2	0,05	0,13	0,10	0,26	0,06	0,24	0,02	0,25	0,02	0,15	0,20	0,13	0,05	0,10	0,01	0,31
CoPro3	0,12	0,23	0,09	0,22	0,03	0,10	0,07	0,18	0,13	0,00	0,00	0,09	0,01	0,02	0,14	0,30
Other1	0,18	0,13	0,09	0,05	0,10	0,15	0,29	0,32	0,22	0,33	0,21	0,30	0,16	0,59	0,46	0,27
Other2	0,21	0,20	0,12	0,00	0,08	0,15	0,31	0,32	0,22	0,33	0,27	0,33	0,22	0,60	0,49	0,26
Other3	0,16	0,13	0,08	0,04	0,03	0,14	0,29	0,33	0,22	0,33	0,20	0,30	0,22	0,62	0,50	0,20
Other4	0,11	0,15	0,14	0,01	0,05	0,17	0,25	0,34	0,17	0,33	0,22	0,28	0,01	0,62	0,48	0,31
Other5	0,14	0,14	0,25	0,00	0,08	0,23	0,26	0,30	0,15	0,33	0,20	0,27	0,16	0,61	0,48	0,38
Other6	0,10	0,16	0,24	0,04	0,04	0,25	0,32	0,31	0,16	0,32	0,25	0,33	0,14	0,63	0,58	0,30
IDEAL	0,25	0,30	0,18	0,08	0,06	0,26	0,52	0,24	0,31	0,45	0,47	0,40	0,44	0,68	1,00	0,28
Propert3	0,16	0,31	0,07	0,10	0,27	0,14	0,24	0,07	0,16	0,20	0,31	0,28	1,00	0,21	0,44	0,08

Table Appendix-E-4: Cross-Loadings Machinery Industry (Page 1 from 4)

Item	Out	PC	TC	StratII	StratI	Oper-atII	Oper-atI	Intell	Behav-Con	Sub-Norm	Work-Load	Spec-Bus	Spec-Tec	SoNet-IS-US
Out1	0,91	0,38	0,29	0,16	0,07	0,27	0,19	0,11	0,04	0,34	0,02	0,04	0,03	0,09
Out2	0,90	0,38	0,33	0,20	0,15	0,32	0,11	0,06	0,10	0,26	0,13	0,11	0,09	0,16
Out3	0,93	0,41	0,35	0,23	0,15	0,35	0,17	0,15	0,10	0,38	0,05	0,11	0,11	0,17
Out4	0,29	0,07	0,06	0,08	0,08	0,04	0,05	0,27	0,07	0,08	0,05	0,03	0,02	0,01
Pc1	0,37	0,81	0,43	0,46	0,27	0,45	0,10	0,36	0,01	0,25	0,01	0,13	0,07	0,14
Pc2	0,20	0,71	0,39	0,28	0,25	0,31	0,20	0,29	0,14	0,18	0,03	0,03	0,09	0,04
Pc3	0,42	0,79	0,49	0,47	0,28	0,44	0,20	0,46	0,01	0,35	0,04	0,17	0,15	0,17
Pc4	0,39	0,72	0,48	0,31	0,26	0,38	0,13	0,22	0,07	0,28	0,02	0,06	0,02	0,16
Pc5	0,24	0,85	0,48	0,39	0,33	0,43	0,12	0,29	0,08	0,26	0,01	0,03	0,03	0,10
TC1	0,34	0,44	0,78	0,18	0,09	0,19	0,04	0,14	0,04	0,20	0,08	0,06	0,04	0,04
TC2	0,25	0,45	0,81	0,34	0,19	0,32	0,20	0,29	0,18	0,17	0,09	0,03	0,02	0,07
TC3	0,23	0,46	0,85	0,30	0,21	0,36	0,18	0,33	0,05	0,25	0,15	0,00	0,10	0,10
TC4	0,31	0,54	0,81	0,47	0,27	0,51	0,09	0,32	0,04	0,33	0,16	0,05	0,04	0,08
Strat1	0,09	0,40	0,33	0,40	0,82	0,45	0,30	0,42	0,12	0,15	0,08	0,18	0,15	0,30
Strat2	0,27	0,48	0,42	0,92	0,42	0,67	0,23	0,45	0,08	0,40	0,08	0,09	0,10	0,22
Strat3	0,14	0,27	0,15	0,46	0,90	0,46	0,47	0,30	0,05	0,26	0,10	0,29	0,16	0,43
Strat4	0,16	0,47	0,35	0,95	0,48	0,71	0,22	0,40	0,14	0,28	0,09	0,08	0,02	0,25
Strat5	0,09	0,28	0,18	0,39	0,88	0,49	0,47	0,32	0,03	0,20	0,08	0,12	0,04	0,34
Strat6	0,16	0,45	0,37	0,95	0,49	0,72	0,28	0,40	0,15	0,30	0,10	0,06	0,06	0,27
Operat1	0,07	0,09	0,08	0,21	0,41	0,38	0,77	0,19	0,06	0,23	0,00	0,17	0,01	0,18
Operat2	0,27	0,41	0,36	0,73	0,45	0,91	0,38	0,34	0,08	0,35	0,08	0,02	0,04	0,25
Operat3	0,21	0,17	0,19	0,26	0,47	0,38	0,92	0,24	0,05	0,16	0,16	0,10	0,07	0,31
Operat4	0,27	0,46	0,36	0,73	0,43	0,89	0,31	0,43	0,02	0,31	0,07	0,01	0,04	0,22
Operat5	0,12	0,21	0,10	0,15	0,30	0,20	0,76	0,32	0,03	0,04	0,00	0,05	0,00	0,37
Operat6	0,34	0,49	0,41	0,53	0,51	0,84	0,35	0,46	0,20	0,45	0,22	0,01	0,07	0,22
Res1	0,19	0,38	0,33	0,35	0,32	0,38	0,27	0,85	0,05	0,24	0,01	0,07	0,03	0,19
Res2	0,05	0,31	0,21	0,31	0,29	0,38	0,26	0,80	0,03	0,17	0,00	0,07	0,08	0,10
Res3	0,05	0,35	0,29	0,41	0,37	0,40	0,24	0,83	0,06	0,20	0,06	0,11	0,18	0,25
Res5	0,03	0,18	0,01	0,33	0,32	0,32	0,15	0,44	0,09	0,11	0,07	0,05	0,29	0,06
Res6	0,02	0,30	0,23	0,38	0,26	0,38	0,15	0,74	0,07	0,08	0,09	0,04	0,08	0,13
Res7	0,01	0,16	0,05	0,09	0,23	0,19	0,25	0,36	0,04	0,08	0,06	0,03	0,08	0,04
Res8	0,08	0,09	0,10	0,17	0,22	0,19	0,20	0,42	0,05	0,10	0,06	0,02	0,09	0,21
Impact1	0,32	0,60	0,40	0,53	0,36	0,66	0,23	0,50	0,08	0,31	0,09	0,04	0,05	0,09
Impact2	0,35	0,48	0,38	0,68	0,40	0,69	0,29	0,41	0,14	0,31	0,10	0,18	0,07	0,19
Impact3	0,25	0,50	0,40	0,58	0,44	0,58	0,24	0,43	0,11	0,29	0,10	0,09	0,01	0,14
EmplOri1	0,15	0,35	0,40	0,33	0,26	0,43	0,26	0,19	0,17	0,27	0,08	0,08	0,04	0,31
EmplOri2	0,38	0,43	0,48	0,32	0,26	0,40	0,26	0,22	0,09	0,37	0,17	0,03	0,02	0,24
EmplOri3	0,28	0,25	0,39	0,33	0,33	0,38	0,26	0,20	0,14	0,36	0,21	0,10	0,07	0,27
EmplOri4	0,24	0,37	0,45	0,40	0,36	0,43	0,23	0,24	0,14	0,32	0,07	0,04	0,03	0,26
DecCont1	0,15	0,42	0,36	0,50	0,39	0,55	0,25	0,30	0,12	0,31	0,10	0,07	0,10	0,17
DecCont2	0,14	0,32	0,18	0,48	0,29	0,31	0,20	0,26	0,16	0,27	0,08	0,16	0,16	0,22

Table Appendix-E-4: Cross-Loadings Machinery Industry (Page 2 from 4)

Item	Out	PC	TC	StratII	StratI	Oper-atII	Oper-atI	IntelI	Behav-Con	Sub-Norm	Work-Load	Spec-Bus	Spec-Tec	SoNet-IS-US
Trust1	0,06	0,10	0,09	0,16	0,13	0,09	0,15	0,18	0,21	0,05	0,03	0,00	0,08	0,11
Trust2	0,07	0,06	0,09	0,03	0,11	0,03	0,18	0,02	0,03	0,08	0,13	0,03	0,04	0,10
Trust3	0,14	0,13	0,20	0,06	0,05	0,03	0,23	0,03	0,07	0,01	0,06	0,00	0,14	0,08
Incen1	0,16	0,37	0,27	0,29	0,17	0,48	0,23	0,21	0,10	0,40	0,12	0,04	0,13	0,14
Incen2	0,21	0,39	0,27	0,32	0,14	0,44	0,13	0,20	0,15	0,36	0,03	0,06	0,08	0,22
Incen3	0,29	0,47	0,28	0,32	0,22	0,46	0,19	0,22	0,07	0,36	0,01	0,07	0,02	0,22
Group1	0,24	0,32	0,31	0,37	0,20	0,42	0,08	0,32	0,01	0,20	0,06	0,04	0,07	0,08
Group4	0,02	0,19	0,08	0,09	0,14	0,18	0,01	0,15	0,09	0,17	0,15	0,01	0,02	0,15
Group6	0,15	0,14	0,14	0,19	0,13	0,20	0,06	0,10	0,00	0,22	0,03	0,02	0,01	0,11
Group7	0,06	0,21	0,19	0,09	0,12	0,19	0,02	0,06	0,03	0,12	0,14	0,02	0,02	0,19
LongWo1	0,08	0,36	0,18	0,36	0,32	0,34	0,18	0,27	0,01	0,19	0,07	0,03	0,15	0,19
LongWo2	0,07	0,28	0,15	0,41	0,26	0,38	0,09	0,22	0,03	0,13	0,01	0,01	0,14	0,21
LongWo3	0,12	0,29	0,18	0,40	0,28	0,41	0,17	0,21	0,05	0,10	0,08	0,04	0,11	0,17
Attitud2	0,44	0,55	0,42	0,46	0,30	0,52	0,22	0,38	0,15	0,59	0,10	0,04	0,13	0,16
Attitud3	0,41	0,42	0,31	0,43	0,24	0,46	0,19	0,42	0,14	0,52	0,05	0,01	0,17	0,10
Attitud5	0,41	0,47	0,37	0,37	0,22	0,45	0,14	0,32	0,26	0,58	0,12	0,01	0,07	0,13
Attitud6	0,37	0,45	0,34	0,34	0,23	0,43	0,16	0,30	0,18	0,61	0,03	0,11	0,06	0,11
Attitud7	0,33	0,43	0,33	0,30	0,14	0,32	0,18	0,30	0,24	0,54	0,01	0,03	0,07	0,01
Spec1	0,06	0,12	0,06	0,08	0,22	0,00	0,14	0,06	0,01	0,09	0,15	0,94	0,37	0,38
Spec2	0,10	0,06	0,02	0,08	0,23	0,03	0,11	0,01	0,04	0,07	0,13	0,94	0,41	0,32
Spec4	0,11	0,10	0,10	0,08	0,08	0,02	0,03	0,09	0,13	0,05	0,23	0,49	0,92	0,21
Spec5	0,00	0,00	0,05	0,02	0,18	0,04	0,04	0,09	0,09	0,10	0,04	0,19	0,82	0,12
SoNet1	0,11	0,16	0,13	0,27	0,34	0,26	0,26	0,26	0,05	0,14	0,01	0,36	0,18	0,91
SoNet2	0,13	0,15	0,20	0,21	0,35	0,22	0,30	0,19	0,05	0,19	0,04	0,39	0,26	0,65
SoNet3	0,16	0,13	0,03	0,20	0,42	0,21	0,37	0,13	0,06	0,17	0,04	0,31	0,17	0,91
SoNet4	0,23	0,19	0,11	0,15	0,47	0,17	0,34	0,13	0,00	0,20	0,03	0,29	0,31	0,64
Meas2	0,05	0,05	0,03	0,02	0,01	0,03	0,12	0,13	0,14	0,10	0,05	0,01	0,11	0,12
Meas3	0,00	0,10	0,02	0,03	0,03	0,04	0,03	0,04	0,13	0,04	0,14	0,00	0,14	0,16
Uncert1	0,07	0,06	0,09	0,06	0,08	0,04	0,14	0,10	0,09	0,01	0,16	0,24	0,16	0,15
Uncert2	0,09	0,15	0,12	0,12	0,03	0,17	0,12	0,28	0,08	0,03	0,12	0,16	0,01	0,17
Uncert3	0,05	0,13	0,13	0,12	0,24	0,09	0,06	0,10	0,08	0,13	0,33	0,32	0,20	0,29
Uncert4	0,01	0,03	0,14	0,00	0,16	0,01	0,16	0,09	0,05	0,12	0,32	0,27	0,10	0,22
WoLoad1	0,02	0,04	0,16	0,14	0,15	0,18	0,12	0,04	0,01	0,08	0,97	0,18	0,20	0,03
WoLoad2	0,10	0,02	0,11	0,01	0,02	0,08	0,01	0,01	0,05	0,06	0,92	0,09	0,11	0,00
CoPro1	0,08	0,01	0,07	0,13	0,00	0,10	0,03	0,08	0,89	0,00	0,06	0,03	0,08	0,06
CoPro2	0,06	0,04	0,11	0,14	0,03	0,11	0,04	0,05	0,89	0,03	0,00	0,05	0,06	0,02
CoPro3	0,08	0,05	0,08	0,09	0,03	0,13	0,07	0,01	0,92	0,13	0,07	0,01	0,18	0,05
Other1	0,38	0,36	0,35	0,42	0,27	0,43	0,24	0,25	0,04	0,92	0,10	0,11	0,13	0,18
Other2	0,33	0,36	0,32	0,38	0,22	0,41	0,19	0,19	0,02	0,93	0,10	0,11	0,13	0,15
Other3	0,26	0,28	0,20	0,35	0,22	0,40	0,15	0,18	0,08	0,92	0,03	0,05	0,00	0,15
Other4	0,34	0,28	0,25	0,30	0,19	0,42	0,15	0,24	0,08	0,93	0,11	0,06	0,03	0,18
Other5	0,35	0,33	0,27	0,29	0,27	0,42	0,13	0,19	0,04	0,92	0,09	0,07	0,07	0,15
Other6	0,34	0,28	0,24	0,19	0,17	0,30	0,15	0,21	0,04	0,89	0,01	0,08	0,08	0,13
IDEAL	0,67	0,54	0,40	0,37	0,26	0,47	0,19	0,32	0,07	0,43	0,00	0,08	0,06	0,18
Proport3	0,03	0,06	0,06	0,02	0,00	0,04	0,17	0,14	0,04	0,32	0,13	0,20	0,03	0,02

Table Appendix-E-4: Cross-Loadings Machinery Industry (Page 3 from 4)

Item	Soc-NetIS	Meas	Env-Unc	Bus-Unc	Trust	Incent	Res-Other	Group	Spec-Hum	Syst-Impa	Sys-View	Long-Wo	Own-er	Atti-tude	Ideal	Con-trol
Out1	0,14	0,07	0,11	0,02	0,03	0,16	0,01	0,14	0,11	0,26	0,22	0,05	0,03	0,45	0,65	0,10
Out2	0,16	0,02	0,04	0,02	0,05	0,22	0,05	0,15	0,18	0,35	0,33	0,13	0,07	0,34	0,55	0,15
Out3	0,23	0,07	0,09	0,06	0,08	0,28	0,07	0,23	0,22	0,33	0,34	0,12	0,02	0,41	0,63	0,20
Out4	0,02	0,13	0,06	0,01	0,09	0,04	0,15	0,13	0,01	0,09	0,03	0,07	0,37	0,08	0,08	0,03
Pc1	0,20	0,09	0,14	0,04	0,22	0,37	0,06	0,26	0,19	0,47	0,32	0,35	0,04	0,40	0,43	0,29
Pc2	0,15	0,06	0,19	0,14	0,20	0,37	0,07	0,29	0,08	0,37	0,27	0,20	0,01	0,32	0,32	0,16
Pc3	0,20	0,18	0,04	0,13	0,02	0,26	0,20	0,30	0,23	0,55	0,36	0,31	0,05	0,44	0,48	0,38
Pc4	0,11	0,05	0,02	0,17	0,03	0,35	0,12	0,25	0,12	0,47	0,29	0,20	0,08	0,42	0,47	0,38
Pc5	0,06	0,03	0,14	0,05	0,08	0,37	0,05	0,23	0,07	0,44	0,35	0,29	0,06	0,43	0,38	0,36
TC1	0,09	0,02	0,14	0,18	0,14	0,16	0,02	0,19	0,03	0,23	0,37	0,08	0,10	0,23	0,29	0,14
TC2	0,12	0,08	0,09	0,09	0,11	0,21	0,10	0,22	0,07	0,36	0,42	0,17	0,05	0,38	0,35	0,30
TC3	0,23	0,02	0,13	0,08	0,07	0,27	0,11	0,25	0,15	0,35	0,38	0,13	0,04	0,32	0,26	0,26
TC4	0,10	0,05	0,04	0,11	0,23	0,30	0,04	0,27	0,06	0,46	0,45	0,24	0,09	0,34	0,37	0,28
Strat1	0,31	0,01	0,01	0,24	0,11	0,09	0,26	0,26	0,33	0,37	0,24	0,33	0,04	0,17	0,23	0,28
Strat2	0,20	0,01	0,09	0,12	0,08	0,27	0,31	0,21	0,22	0,62	0,39	0,36	0,02	0,45	0,40	0,48
Strat3	0,45	0,03	0,09	0,15	0,13	0,17	0,24	0,16	0,48	0,40	0,33	0,28	0,00	0,29	0,22	0,36
Strat4	0,16	0,01	0,11	0,03	0,12	0,31	0,27	0,33	0,19	0,61	0,37	0,45	0,02	0,38	0,31	0,51
Strat5	0,38	0,06	0,03	0,22	0,05	0,24	0,27	0,18	0,33	0,40	0,34	0,25	0,04	0,18	0,23	0,34
Strat6	0,20	0,05	0,11	0,08	0,12	0,36	0,32	0,30	0,22	0,65	0,37	0,43	0,02	0,38	0,31	0,53
Operat1	0,24	0,11	0,09	0,07	0,13	0,06	0,15	0,02	0,22	0,25	0,25	0,04	0,15	0,18	0,16	0,11
Operat2	0,20	0,01	0,14	0,01	0,05	0,37	0,30	0,27	0,19	0,65	0,40	0,38	0,02	0,43	0,33	0,45
Operat3	0,31	0,19	0,17	0,12	0,20	0,16	0,15	0,05	0,29	0,28	0,28	0,23	0,23	0,19	0,19	0,24
Operat4	0,15	0,02	0,16	0,03	0,05	0,36	0,27	0,36	0,16	0,67	0,38	0,47	0,07	0,39	0,31	0,40
Operat5	0,32	0,04	0,01	0,06	0,26	0,27	0,08	0,03	0,30	0,15	0,18	0,11	0,01	0,12	0,11	0,27
Operat6	0,20	0,03	0,13	0,16	0,07	0,53	0,18	0,38	0,16	0,59	0,46	0,31	0,03	0,47	0,55	0,42
Res1	0,15	0,12	0,14	0,10	0,15	0,16	0,31	0,17	0,16	0,43	0,26	0,23	0,13	0,41	0,35	0,25
Res2	0,14	0,10	0,21	0,06	0,02	0,15	0,38	0,06	0,09	0,37	0,17	0,20	0,09	0,28	0,24	0,16
Res3	0,18	0,13	0,28	0,12	0,01	0,20	0,51	0,23	0,24	0,41	0,19	0,20	0,15	0,30	0,24	0,34
Res5	0,16	0,02	0,12	0,01	0,13	0,11	0,78	0,28	0,16	0,37	0,16	0,32	0,16	0,13	0,10	0,24
Res6	0,05	0,09	0,33	0,02	0,04	0,25	0,37	0,17	0,07	0,41	0,14	0,23	0,05	0,20	0,14	0,24
Res7	0,12	0,03	0,08	0,01	0,05	0,14	0,35	0,17	0,09	0,23	0,16	0,18	0,06	0,05	0,08	0,05
Res8	0,18	0,04	0,14	0,12	0,16	0,08	0,81	0,11	0,19	0,17	0,17	0,06	0,08	0,10	0,07	0,07
Impact1	0,04	0,02	0,11	0,08	0,14	0,41	0,23	0,29	0,07	0,91	0,43	0,41	0,01	0,46	0,46	0,37
Impact2	0,18	0,07	0,02	0,09	0,10	0,30	0,27	0,28	0,22	0,90	0,43	0,49	0,00	0,43	0,42	0,45
Impact3	0,11	0,09	0,09	0,17	0,11	0,35	0,24	0,28	0,13	0,88	0,44	0,39	0,04	0,41	0,35	0,45
EmplOri1	0,17	0,17	0,20	0,19	0,12	0,38	0,16	0,34	0,21	0,44	0,80	0,34	0,07	0,32	0,25	0,16
EmplOri2	0,23	0,01	0,06	0,11	0,09	0,35	0,12	0,31	0,18	0,39	0,91	0,20	0,08	0,31	0,41	0,16
EmplOri3	0,25	0,04	0,19	0,22	0,15	0,26	0,12	0,24	0,25	0,38	0,85	0,21	0,02	0,20	0,22	0,25
EmplOri4	0,24	0,00	0,09	0,12	0,06	0,30	0,20	0,22	0,22	0,46	0,89	0,28	0,12	0,35	0,30	0,27
DecCont1	0,10	0,10	0,11	0,16	0,20	0,40	0,10	0,29	0,15	0,48	0,26	0,26	0,12	0,41	0,26	0,92
DecCont2	0,21	0,11	0,10	0,19	0,05	0,26	0,26	0,22	0,25	0,36	0,17	0,20	0,16	0,36	0,25	0,90

Table Appendix-E-4: Cross-Loadings Machinery Industry (Page 4 from 4)

Item	Soc-NetIS	Meas	Env-Unc	Bus-Unc	Trust	Incent	Res-Other	Group	Spec-Hum	Syst-Impa	Sys-View	Long-Wo	Own-er	Atti-tude	Ideal	Con-trol
Trust1	0,04	0,08	0,03	0,04	0,82	0,24	0,17	0,00	0,01	0,14	0,07	0,16	0,07	0,08	0,04	0,13
Trust2	0,05	0,11	0,06	0,00	0,71	0,15	0,12	0,04	0,06	0,06	0,07	0,04	0,11	0,03	0,05	0,10
Trust3	0,13	0,08	0,20	0,11	0,85	0,18	0,23	0,03	0,11	0,10	0,13	0,20	0,26	0,08	0,12	0,11
Incen1	0,06	0,06	0,12	0,07	0,25	0,90	0,04	0,33	0,04	0,37	0,38	0,22	0,04	0,32	0,34	0,33
Incen2	0,17	0,03	0,14	0,01	0,20	0,96	0,06	0,34	0,12	0,36	0,34	0,30	0,16	0,39	0,45	0,34
Incen3	0,16	0,03	0,19	0,02	0,22	0,96	0,11	0,30	0,13	0,40	0,34	0,32	0,17	0,45	0,49	0,38
Group1	0,16	0,11	0,10	0,10	0,08	0,29	0,22	0,78	0,10	0,39	0,25	0,26	0,07	0,19	0,26	0,26
Group4	0,15	0,01	0,07	0,05	0,06	0,19	0,05	0,56	0,12	0,13	0,14	0,16	0,21	0,11	0,12	0,17
Group6	0,24	0,15	0,17	0,00	0,04	0,15	0,07	0,56	0,15	0,14	0,24	0,27	0,02	0,11	0,20	0,17
Group7	0,06	0,05	0,09	0,07	0,03	0,25	0,22	0,74	0,09	0,13	0,21	0,28	0,10	0,07	0,01	0,15
LongWo1	0,17	0,10	0,16	0,04	0,15	0,28	0,16	0,38	0,11	0,35	0,27	0,89	0,14	0,14	0,20	0,29
LongWo2	0,14	0,06	0,17	0,11	0,13	0,28	0,07	0,34	0,11	0,39	0,26	0,87	0,02	0,09	0,18	0,19
LongWo3	0,12	0,08	0,14	0,15	0,17	0,26	0,20	0,28	0,15	0,50	0,25	0,90	0,05	0,19	0,25	0,20
Attitud2	0,11	0,03	0,18	0,02	0,13	0,42	0,11	0,17	0,15	0,48	0,34	0,18	0,13	0,90	0,59	0,42
Attitud3	0,08	0,03	0,25	0,00	0,08	0,39	0,12	0,12	0,11	0,39	0,25	0,11	0,12	0,88	0,57	0,40
Attitud5	0,13	0,09	0,20	0,04	0,03	0,37	0,13	0,18	0,13	0,45	0,31	0,15	0,22	0,93	0,52	0,41
Attitud6	0,12	0,09	0,15	0,01	0,05	0,34	0,10	0,16	0,14	0,42	0,31	0,15	0,12	0,90	0,50	0,33
Attitud7	0,05	0,03	0,07	0,03	0,09	0,30	0,18	0,19	0,05	0,43	0,33	0,18	0,17	0,86	0,42	0,32
Spec1	0,34	0,01	0,16	0,36	0,02	0,06	0,04	0,01	0,65	0,11	0,07	0,01	0,18	0,04	0,09	0,14
Spec2	0,36	0,02	0,16	0,25	0,01	0,05	0,03	0,04	0,64	0,10	0,02	0,01	0,20	0,04	0,07	0,09
Spec4	0,29	0,14	0,05	0,20	0,06	0,05	0,18	0,04	0,53	0,08	0,05	0,00	0,12	0,08	0,01	0,12
Spec5	0,24	0,03	0,02	0,08	0,17	0,09	0,24	0,00	0,37	0,03	0,05	0,08	0,12	0,14	0,12	0,12
SoNet1	0,63	0,08	0,15	0,24	0,00	0,17	0,16	0,15	0,76	0,17	0,27	0,20	0,03	0,13	0,18	0,17
SoNet2	0,92	0,01	0,17	0,20	0,12	0,09	0,13	0,08	0,80	0,15	0,23	0,11	0,06	0,11	0,18	0,12
SoNet3	0,64	0,09	0,16	0,27	0,03	0,20	0,19	0,20	0,75	0,11	0,29	0,18	0,02	0,08	0,15	0,20
SoNet4	0,91	0,01	0,19	0,19	0,06	0,16	0,23	0,31	0,78	0,08	0,24	0,18	0,07	0,10	0,19	0,19
Meas2	0,02	0,97	0,04	0,06	0,06	0,04	0,01	0,10	0,07	0,05	0,00	0,02	0,26	0,00	0,04	0,09
Meas3	0,09	0,38	0,19	0,18	0,10	0,06	0,01	0,01	0,13	0,02	0,12	0,13	0,04	0,13	0,08	0,06
Uncert1	0,22	0,01	0,63	0,34	0,10	0,12	0,02	0,04	0,25	0,05	0,09	0,24	0,07	0,09	0,11	0,01
Uncert2	0,19	0,02	1,00	0,44	0,13	0,16	0,17	0,02	0,19	0,10	0,15	0,16	0,11	0,20	0,16	0,12
Uncert3	0,24	0,12	0,37	0,95	0,07	0,11	0,15	0,04	0,35	0,12	0,15	0,12	0,07	0,01	0,12	0,23
Uncert4	0,12	0,12	0,49	0,88	0,07	0,08	0,01	0,08	0,24	0,10	0,18	0,09	0,07	0,03	0,05	0,10
WoLoad1	0,01	0,15	0,13	0,38	0,11	0,06	0,06	0,08	0,09	0,15	0,18	0,06	0,19	0,04	0,01	0,03
WoLoad2	0,00	0,01	0,10	0,27	0,01	0,01	0,07	0,08	0,05	0,03	0,08	0,05	0,02	0,12	0,02	0,01
CoPro1	0,03	0,13	0,07	0,01	0,03	0,11	0,04	0,04	0,03	0,09	0,09	0,00	0,11	0,15	0,09	0,16
CoPro2	0,03	0,04	0,02	0,06	0,08	0,05	0,06	0,02	0,00	0,11	0,07	0,05	0,02	0,15	0,04	0,12
CoPro3	0,05	0,12	0,07	0,09	0,21	0,18	0,10	0,02	0,07	0,13	0,21	0,02	0,03	0,25	0,06	0,14
Other1	0,24	0,06	0,06	0,18	0,10	0,31	0,13	0,15	0,23	0,36	0,37	0,17	0,25	0,60	0,42	0,36
Other2	0,20	0,10	0,06	0,15	0,06	0,33	0,13	0,19	0,20	0,34	0,36	0,18	0,25	0,56	0,40	0,33
Other3	0,15	0,09	0,02	0,14	0,05	0,36	0,15	0,21	0,13	0,32	0,33	0,18	0,30	0,59	0,36	0,34
Other4	0,16	0,10	0,03	0,08	0,01	0,40	0,08	0,30	0,16	0,28	0,35	0,14	0,32	0,58	0,40	0,29
Other5	0,23	0,14	0,01	0,08	0,03	0,42	0,10	0,35	0,19	0,30	0,39	0,12	0,26	0,59	0,42	0,26
Other6	0,19	0,09	0,04	0,09	0,05	0,36	0,01	0,23	0,17	0,27	0,33	0,04	0,37	0,56	0,39	0,21
IDEAL	0,20	0,08	0,17	0,10	0,07	0,45	0,09	0,22	0,17	0,46	0,35	0,25	0,13	0,58	1,00	0,28
Propert3	0,07	0,31	0,11	0,07	0,20	0,10	0,14	0,02	0,02	0,01	0,05	0,02	1,00	0,17	0,13	0,15

Table Appendix-E-5: Cross-Loadings Application Development (Page 1 from 4)

Item	Out	PC	TC	StratII	StratI	Oper-atII	Oper-atI	IntelI	Behav-Con	Sub-Norm	Work-Load	Spec-Bus	Spec-Tec	SoNet-IS-US
Out1	0,95	0,41	0,28	0,36	0,03	0,41	0,18	0,24	0,02	0,44	0,09	0,02	0,06	0,15
Out2	0,95	0,42	0,32	0,35	0,03	0,40	0,15	0,21	0,03	0,38	0,08	0,02	0,08	0,17
Out3	0,96	0,45	0,30	0,36	0,01	0,40	0,15	0,25	0,06	0,47	0,11	0,04	0,08	0,15
Out4	0,31	0,16	0,10	0,07	0,02	0,09	0,02	0,04	0,07	0,17	0,06	0,14	0,14	0,08
Pc1	0,40	0,83	0,47	0,44	0,26	0,45	0,16	0,46	0,09	0,26	0,14	0,07	0,07	0,24
Pc2	0,22	0,70	0,42	0,39	0,30	0,43	0,29	0,46	0,00	0,21	0,03	0,07	0,18	0,12
Pc3	0,39	0,76	0,40	0,51	0,20	0,52	0,27	0,45	0,10	0,34	0,10	0,17	0,18	0,16
Pc4	0,42	0,76	0,48	0,35	0,31	0,39	0,23	0,32	0,03	0,26	0,17	0,10	0,03	0,26
Pc5	0,30	0,85	0,54	0,40	0,32	0,48	0,19	0,40	0,07	0,30	0,17	0,15	0,09	0,16
TC1	0,30	0,52	0,82	0,26	0,06	0,29	0,18	0,27	0,13	0,23	0,03	0,06	0,02	0,14
TC2	0,12	0,39	0,79	0,26	0,10	0,26	0,23	0,20	0,16	0,12	0,09	0,08	0,07	0,06
TC3	0,21	0,48	0,86	0,31	0,10	0,33	0,19	0,25	0,05	0,28	0,07	0,04	0,20	0,15
TC4	0,33	0,50	0,77	0,36	0,09	0,42	0,12	0,31	0,05	0,22	0,09	0,00	0,10	0,13
Strat1	0,03	0,38	0,21	0,29	0,75	0,29	0,35	0,26	0,02	0,03	0,11	0,05	0,06	0,11
Strat2	0,39	0,53	0,39	0,93	0,24	0,72	0,19	0,40	0,07	0,43	0,06	0,09	0,13	0,25
Strat3	0,01	0,27	0,06	0,26	0,90	0,22	0,45	0,26	0,04	0,10	0,05	0,07	0,20	0,24
Strat4	0,33	0,52	0,31	0,95	0,32	0,74	0,16	0,35	0,13	0,32	0,06	0,07	0,14	0,19
Strat5	0,07	0,26	0,01	0,19	0,84	0,22	0,43	0,23	0,14	0,02	0,05	0,04	0,07	0,13
Strat6	0,31	0,46	0,32	0,95	0,29	0,73	0,17	0,34	0,17	0,33	0,05	0,07	0,10	0,22
Operat1	0,18	0,29	0,19	0,21	0,41	0,30	0,89	0,21	0,08	0,17	0,07	0,03	0,08	0,00
Operat2	0,38	0,47	0,32	0,72	0,23	0,91	0,30	0,33	0,16	0,38	0,05	0,03	0,19	0,21
Operat3	0,11	0,22	0,15	0,11	0,51	0,24	0,84	0,18	0,05	0,07	0,01	0,02	0,13	0,11
Operat4	0,36	0,48	0,33	0,76	0,23	0,91	0,24	0,38	0,13	0,35	0,09	0,09	0,17	0,22
Operat5	0,08	0,15	0,21	0,09	0,29	0,15	0,69	0,20	0,07	0,11	0,06	0,05	0,08	0,21
Operat6	0,37	0,57	0,42	0,59	0,29	0,84	0,25	0,51	0,19	0,41	0,02	0,11	0,07	0,25
Res1	0,27	0,44	0,31	0,30	0,24	0,34	0,23	0,78	0,00	0,15	0,20	0,01	0,07	0,11
Res2	0,20	0,43	0,20	0,35	0,28	0,45	0,23	0,81	0,02	0,26	0,06	0,03	0,13	0,17
Res3	0,16	0,38	0,24	0,20	0,21	0,28	0,13	0,76	0,00	0,16	0,00	0,00	0,18	0,26
Res5	0,10	0,16	0,01	0,26	0,30	0,32	0,15	0,41	0,10	0,16	0,08	0,11	0,32	0,09
Res6	0,08	0,35	0,23	0,32	0,17	0,35	0,10	0,71	0,03	0,13	0,09	0,08	0,18	0,15
Res7	0,12	0,25	0,28	0,15	0,26	0,16	0,24	0,34	0,16	0,05	0,08	0,07	0,17	0,12
Res8	0,20	0,28	0,16	0,26	0,22	0,27	0,20	0,42	0,00	0,11	0,05	0,01	0,16	0,14
Impact1	0,37	0,56	0,36	0,58	0,24	0,63	0,21	0,48	0,06	0,24	0,06	0,12	0,06	0,21
Impact2	0,44	0,47	0,37	0,63	0,23	0,67	0,25	0,38	0,08	0,37	0,06	0,16	0,16	0,21
Impact3	0,37	0,51	0,31	0,61	0,25	0,63	0,17	0,43	0,11	0,29	0,06	0,16	0,04	0,25
EmplOri1	0,21	0,42	0,43	0,32	0,16	0,38	0,24	0,28	0,20	0,20	0,06	0,19	0,12	0,19
EmplOri2	0,38	0,50	0,42	0,34	0,15	0,44	0,23	0,29	0,09	0,34	0,05	0,13	0,22	0,28
EmplOri3	0,29	0,42	0,38	0,36	0,20	0,42	0,15	0,26	0,16	0,23	0,00	0,27	0,28	0,23
EmplOri4	0,32	0,46	0,35	0,39	0,17	0,46	0,13	0,31	0,17	0,25	0,05	0,22	0,29	0,22
DecCont1	0,22	0,31	0,27	0,48	0,18	0,51	0,20	0,28	0,13	0,35	0,03	0,07	0,14	0,11
DecCont2	0,10	0,17	0,08	0,33	0,04	0,27	0,00	0,09	0,32	0,26	0,00	0,07	0,03	0,04

Table Appendix-E-5: Cross-Loadings Application Development (Page 2 from 4)

Item	Out	PC	TC	StratII	StratI	Oper-atII	Oper-atI	Intell	Behav-Con	Sub-Norm	Work-Load	Spec-Bus	Spec-Tec	SoNet-IS-US
Trust1	0,07	0,06	0,09	0,01	0,04	0,05	0,00	0,07	0,19	0,05	0,01	0,00	0,05	0,04
Trust2	0,06	0,14	0,12	0,02	0,04	0,09	0,03	0,09	0,10	0,00	0,06	0,01	0,00	0,02
Trust3	0,02	0,29	0,22	0,09	0,09	0,17	0,16	0,16	0,04	0,04	0,03	0,09	0,00	0,00
Incen1	0,15	0,39	0,31	0,35	0,08	0,47	0,15	0,34	0,21	0,34	0,01	0,05	0,00	0,12
Incen2	0,20	0,44	0,33	0,36	0,15	0,43	0,11	0,37	0,13	0,32	0,01	0,08	0,13	0,19
Incen3	0,20	0,43	0,26	0,31	0,19	0,41	0,10	0,35	0,07	0,24	0,04	0,07	0,10	0,17
Group1	0,14	0,39	0,32	0,37	0,18	0,42	0,19	0,30	0,10	0,21	0,06	0,03	0,08	0,08
Group4	0,00	0,20	0,12	0,18	0,15	0,21	0,00	0,15	0,06	0,21	0,09	0,02	0,10	0,05
Group6	0,08	0,06	0,03	0,19	0,02	0,22	0,03	0,00	0,08	0,22	0,08	0,03	0,03	0,10
Group7	0,14	0,30	0,18	0,22	0,16	0,32	0,18	0,25	0,18	0,18	0,06	0,07	0,12	0,09
LongWo1	0,19	0,40	0,23	0,35	0,16	0,40	0,16	0,37	0,08	0,27	0,03	0,01	0,06	0,18
LongWo2	0,15	0,42	0,29	0,45	0,16	0,48	0,15	0,40	0,14	0,25	0,03	0,08	0,07	0,20
LongWo3	0,19	0,32	0,26	0,43	0,16	0,49	0,18	0,37	0,15	0,29	0,08	0,08	0,20	0,14
Attitud2	0,46	0,57	0,35	0,55	0,23	0,58	0,24	0,37	0,12	0,62	0,17	0,12	0,13	0,16
Attitud3	0,38	0,43	0,24	0,50	0,21	0,50	0,22	0,33	0,09	0,52	0,14	0,09	0,18	0,07
Attitud5	0,44	0,46	0,36	0,42	0,19	0,47	0,16	0,28	0,11	0,58	0,10	0,00	0,18	0,18
Attitud6	0,47	0,45	0,34	0,36	0,19	0,43	0,21	0,29	0,11	0,62	0,07	0,04	0,14	0,13
Attitud7	0,35	0,43	0,32	0,35	0,14	0,40	0,17	0,28	0,15	0,51	0,10	0,10	0,14	0,09
Spec1	0,03	0,12	0,00	0,03	0,06	0,04	0,03	0,01	0,03	0,09	0,01	0,94	0,37	0,21
Spec2	0,04	0,15	0,11	0,13	0,02	0,13	0,00	0,04	0,08	0,13	0,02	0,92	0,34	0,16
Spec4	0,09	0,13	0,13	0,16	0,05	0,16	0,06	0,15	0,15	0,08	0,01	0,46	0,86	0,06
Spec5	0,03	0,10	0,06	0,06	0,21	0,11	0,14	0,15	0,08	0,20	0,02	0,19	0,85	0,16
SoNet1	0,16	0,16	0,13	0,25	0,21	0,25	0,08	0,23	0,08	0,17	0,03	0,16	0,09	0,85
SoNet2	0,19	0,25	0,24	0,27	0,26	0,29	0,18	0,31	0,07	0,26	0,02	0,23	0,20	0,66
SoNet3	0,12	0,25	0,13	0,15	0,14	0,19	0,09	0,15	0,02	0,17	0,12	0,18	0,13	0,86
SoNet4	0,20	0,31	0,17	0,22	0,33	0,24	0,24	0,21	0,00	0,19	0,12	0,12	0,22	0,65
Meas2	0,21	0,01	0,03	0,07	0,00	0,01	0,02	0,01	0,12	0,00	0,16	0,03	0,01	0,09
Meas3	0,25	0,08	0,01	0,16	0,04	0,13	0,04	0,04	0,09	0,17	0,22	0,02	0,06	0,13
Uncert1	0,13	0,04	0,11	0,00	0,05	0,06	0,09	0,05	0,15	0,04	0,19	0,10	0,02	0,03
Uncert2	0,16	0,03	0,14	0,11	0,12	0,12	0,14	0,12	0,10	0,12	0,04	0,20	0,10	0,07
Uncert3	0,05	0,13	0,10	0,07	0,17	0,07	0,01	0,11	0,11	0,09	0,22	0,14	0,07	0,15
Uncert4	0,03	0,06	0,18	0,03	0,01	0,01	0,08	0,04	0,18	0,08	0,22	0,14	0,08	0,11
WoLoad1	0,10	0,07	0,12	0,01	0,04	0,01	0,07	0,04	0,08	0,06	0,88	0,02	0,07	0,05
WoLoad2	0,09	0,18	0,04	0,08	0,12	0,06	0,05	0,08	0,05	0,02	0,98	0,02	0,05	0,09
CoPro1	0,03	0,08	0,12	0,16	0,05	0,18	0,03	0,05	0,88	0,01	0,09	0,11	0,11	0,03
CoPro2	0,03	0,07	0,14	0,14	0,04	0,19	0,07	0,02	0,89	0,03	0,03	0,11	0,06	0,02
CoPro3	0,05	0,03	0,07	0,07	0,09	0,13	0,11	0,04	0,91	0,10	0,04	0,02	0,17	0,10
Other1	0,42	0,35	0,29	0,40	0,08	0,39	0,23	0,22	0,02	0,92	0,04	0,15	0,12	0,19
Other2	0,39	0,34	0,29	0,39	0,05	0,40	0,16	0,18	0,03	0,93	0,04	0,16	0,13	0,21
Other3	0,40	0,31	0,21	0,37	0,08	0,39	0,12	0,17	0,01	0,92	0,00	0,14	0,17	0,19
Other4	0,42	0,32	0,23	0,32	0,03	0,40	0,11	0,26	0,07	0,90	0,04	0,05	0,12	0,17
Other5	0,43	0,32	0,22	0,34	0,01	0,43	0,10	0,21	0,09	0,91	0,03	0,04	0,13	0,19
Other6	0,41	0,27	0,25	0,28	0,04	0,35	0,12	0,23	0,03	0,89	0,04	0,10	0,20	0,16
IDEAL	0,71	0,60	0,40	0,47	0,20	0,53	0,26	0,36	0,00	0,52	0,09	0,08	0,09	0,20
Propert3	0,29	0,19	0,25	0,18	0,03	0,22	0,19	0,05	0,00	0,01	0,02	0,11	0,12	0,02

Table Appendix-E-5: Cross-Loadings Application Development (Page 3 from 4)

Item	Soc-NetIS	Meas	Env-Unc	Bus-Unc	Trust	Incent	Res-Other	Group	Spec-Hum	Syst-Impa	Sys-View	Long-Wo	Own-er	Atti-tude	Ideal	Con-trol
Out1	0,19	0,26	0,16	0,05	0,05	0,16	0,21	0,13	0,17	0,42	0,33	0,21	0,27	0,48	0,70	0,16
Out2	0,21	0,24	0,14	0,03	0,01	0,19	0,17	0,10	0,20	0,44	0,36	0,19	0,30	0,44	0,67	0,20
Out3	0,22	0,24	0,16	0,04	0,01	0,23	0,21	0,20	0,18	0,42	0,35	0,18	0,27	0,46	0,69	0,21
Out4	0,08	0,08	0,03	0,00	0,12	0,14	0,00	0,14	0,13	0,00	0,16	0,11	0,38	0,14	0,22	0,02
Pc1	0,28	0,03	0,04	0,12	0,26	0,39	0,22	0,35	0,26	0,44	0,43	0,39	0,19	0,44	0,51	0,17
Pc2	0,27	0,04	0,05	0,02	0,22	0,40	0,22	0,39	0,24	0,40	0,42	0,26	0,15	0,36	0,36	0,20
Pc3	0,22	0,02	0,04	0,10	0,18	0,34	0,26	0,33	0,25	0,54	0,47	0,45	0,15	0,39	0,46	0,30
Pc4	0,26	0,07	0,02	0,12	0,10	0,30	0,23	0,22	0,26	0,44	0,37	0,22	0,07	0,41	0,51	0,22
Pc5	0,18	0,05	0,03	0,03	0,21	0,35	0,25	0,28	0,21	0,41	0,40	0,31	0,17	0,50	0,51	0,26
TC1	0,15	0,01	0,15	0,21	0,24	0,28	0,16	0,22	0,14	0,30	0,33	0,26	0,21	0,31	0,35	0,10
TC2	0,13	0,02	0,13	0,14	0,20	0,24	0,11	0,21	0,12	0,28	0,36	0,13	0,16	0,26	0,24	0,20
TC3	0,27	0,03	0,14	0,13	0,06	0,27	0,20	0,21	0,25	0,30	0,41	0,25	0,27	0,32	0,29	0,22
TC4	0,17	0,04	0,05	0,03	0,16	0,25	0,10	0,25	0,16	0,36	0,41	0,28	0,16	0,31	0,38	0,22
Strat1	0,18	0,01	0,08	0,04	0,09	0,09	0,21	0,18	0,16	0,19	0,21	0,18	0,03	0,17	0,25	0,15
Strat2	0,29	0,05	0,06	0,03	0,06	0,35	0,24	0,32	0,30	0,64	0,41	0,42	0,17	0,50	0,48	0,43
Strat3	0,32	0,01	0,08	0,06	0,01	0,11	0,25	0,19	0,32	0,25	0,15	0,16	0,02	0,23	0,17	0,12
Strat4	0,20	0,17	0,07	0,01	0,06	0,33	0,31	0,36	0,22	0,65	0,39	0,44	0,18	0,49	0,44	0,47
Strat5	0,30	0,04	0,08	0,10	0,04	0,19	0,29	0,16	0,20	0,22	0,15	0,11	0,02	0,12	0,10	0,01
Strat6	0,27	0,16	0,07	0,03	0,07	0,36	0,28	0,39	0,26	0,62	0,37	0,45	0,15	0,42	0,40	0,44
Operat1	0,15	0,03	0,11	0,05	0,14	0,14	0,24	0,15	0,10	0,26	0,16	0,16	0,11	0,24	0,23	0,10
Operat2	0,24	0,09	0,14	0,01	0,11	0,38	0,28	0,40	0,25	0,60	0,41	0,44	0,18	0,47	0,47	0,43
Operat3	0,24	0,02	0,12	0,02	0,08	0,03	0,18	0,15	0,19	0,14	0,18	0,16	0,23	0,18	0,20	0,11
Operat4	0,25	0,05	0,11	0,03	0,10	0,37	0,28	0,46	0,27	0,63	0,42	0,53	0,18	0,43	0,45	0,40
Operat5	0,20	0,05	0,10	0,07	0,05	0,14	0,14	0,10	0,21	0,13	0,21	0,14	0,16	0,12	0,21	0,16
Operat6	0,28	0,08	0,05	0,10	0,19	0,50	0,28	0,36	0,28	0,66	0,49	0,41	0,21	0,53	0,48	0,42
Res1	0,21	0,00	0,06	0,14	0,18	0,25	0,37	0,18	0,16	0,39	0,27	0,34	0,03	0,33	0,33	0,14
Res2	0,25	0,05	0,13	0,03	0,11	0,30	0,37	0,23	0,23	0,41	0,27	0,34	0,17	0,32	0,31	0,21
Res3	0,25	0,04	0,14	0,07	0,07	0,30	0,34	0,31	0,27	0,27	0,21	0,28	0,04	0,20	0,22	0,19
Res5	0,22	0,08	0,12	0,06	0,09	0,16	0,64	0,21	0,25	0,25	0,12	0,28	0,00	0,15	0,22	0,15
Res6	0,17	0,05	0,13	0,01	0,10	0,36	0,44	0,22	0,21	0,36	0,29	0,34	0,05	0,21	0,23	0,17
Res7	0,23	0,07	0,06	0,01	0,04	0,06	0,67	0,14	0,21	0,19	0,27	0,13	0,01	0,15	0,23	0,01
Res8	0,23	0,06	0,09	0,07	0,11	0,16	0,94	0,25	0,20	0,21	0,21	0,21	0,10	0,17	0,28	0,01
Impact1	0,25	0,15	0,02	0,04	0,11	0,37	0,26	0,30	0,25	0,90	0,52	0,39	0,15	0,42	0,40	0,36
Impact2	0,25	0,12	0,01	0,05	0,04	0,30	0,27	0,28	0,29	0,90	0,47	0,40	0,13	0,45	0,47	0,34
Impact3	0,26	0,12	0,04	0,01	0,14	0,36	0,19	0,28	0,28	0,90	0,51	0,38	0,10	0,45	0,43	0,40
EmplOri1	0,21	0,07	0,24	0,19	0,19	0,31	0,15	0,37	0,25	0,45	0,76	0,41	0,09	0,29	0,31	0,25
EmplOri2	0,33	0,04	0,11	0,06	0,12	0,37	0,19	0,37	0,35	0,47	0,88	0,26	0,16	0,37	0,42	0,24
EmplOri3	0,34	0,00	0,11	0,07	0,18	0,30	0,22	0,32	0,39	0,46	0,84	0,31	0,19	0,29	0,37	0,30
EmplOri4	0,31	0,01	0,17	0,09	0,12	0,33	0,25	0,40	0,36	0,49	0,89	0,38	0,13	0,41	0,39	0,29
DecCont1	0,11	0,03	0,03	0,08	0,13	0,30	0,06	0,30	0,15	0,44	0,35	0,30	0,04	0,44	0,34	0,94
DecCont2	0,06	0,04	0,05	0,05	0,09	0,18	0,02	0,27	0,07	0,24	0,16	0,18	0,06	0,27	0,14	0,81

Table Appendix-E-5: Cross-Loadings Application Development (Page 4 from 4)

Item	Soc-NetIS	Meas	Env-Unc	Bus-Unc	Trust	Incent	Res-Other	Group	Spec-Hum	Syst-Impa	Sys-View	Long-Wo	Own-er	Atti-tude	Ideal	Con-trol
Trust1	0,06	0,07	0,21	0,08	0,67	0,25	0,17	0,06	0,03	0,04	0,09	0,21	0,04	0,02	0,03	0,10
Trust2	0,03	0,03	0,11	0,05	0,75	0,20	0,04	0,06	0,02	0,08	0,10	0,07	0,21	0,06	0,01	0,06
Trust3	0,07	0,09	0,16	0,12	0,92	0,25	0,10	0,08	0,06	0,11	0,18	0,24	0,22	0,14	0,11	0,13
Incen1	0,12	0,04	0,07	0,05	0,27	0,90	0,13	0,38	0,12	0,37	0,30	0,25	0,05	0,32	0,23	0,27
Incen2	0,25	0,02	0,02	0,08	0,24	0,94	0,17	0,37	0,24	0,37	0,41	0,33	0,00	0,32	0,32	0,28
Incen3	0,20	0,02	0,07	0,07	0,28	0,94	0,19	0,38	0,20	0,32	0,37	0,29	0,02	0,35	0,29	0,24
Group1	0,11	0,13	0,00	0,05	0,11	0,32	0,22	0,76	0,10	0,33	0,37	0,24	0,01	0,25	0,14	0,34
Group4	0,11	0,02	0,13	0,03	0,03	0,25	0,15	0,58	0,09	0,14	0,18	0,20	0,14	0,09	0,04	0,14
Group6	0,08	0,14	0,10	0,05	0,07	0,13	0,06	0,53	0,06	0,09	0,19	0,23	0,10	0,12	0,12	0,20
Group7	0,04	0,05	0,13	0,04	0,07	0,32	0,23	0,75	0,10	0,21	0,35	0,37	0,14	0,18	0,23	0,15
LongWo1	0,10	0,11	0,20	0,09	0,25	0,24	0,21	0,33	0,14	0,32	0,33	0,89	0,11	0,22	0,33	0,28
LongWo2	0,14	0,04	0,16	0,10	0,17	0,34	0,24	0,41	0,18	0,41	0,41	0,91	0,14	0,27	0,34	0,28
LongWo3	0,15	0,21	0,11	0,09	0,20	0,26	0,23	0,32	0,20	0,43	0,32	0,87	0,23	0,29	0,33	0,21
Attitud2	0,18	0,24	0,09	0,02	0,10	0,40	0,22	0,31	0,21	0,53	0,42	0,27	0,13	0,89	0,61	0,40
Attitud3	0,10	0,11	0,00	0,07	0,10	0,29	0,16	0,26	0,14	0,41	0,31	0,22	0,16	0,86	0,55	0,37
Attitud5	0,23	0,19	0,08	0,00	0,06	0,27	0,17	0,18	0,23	0,41	0,38	0,30	0,11	0,89	0,56	0,39
Attitud6	0,17	0,20	0,10	0,06	0,10	0,28	0,18	0,13	0,18	0,37	0,32	0,26	0,15	0,89	0,60	0,35
Attitud7	0,16	0,23	0,11	0,02	0,13	0,31	0,12	0,23	0,17	0,42	0,37	0,24	0,10	0,87	0,48	0,34
Spec1	0,21	0,01	0,17	0,16	0,05	0,06	0,02	0,03	0,51	0,12	0,21	0,06	0,12	0,05	0,06	0,07
Spec2	0,14	0,01	0,15	0,12	0,07	0,08	0,06	0,02	0,44	0,20	0,22	0,06	0,08	0,11	0,11	0,07
Spec4	0,18	0,10	0,13	0,07	0,08	0,08	0,19	0,09	0,43	0,15	0,31	0,13	0,18	0,09	0,07	0,10
Spec5	0,22	0,03	0,00	0,06	0,10	0,06	0,23	0,12	0,42	0,02	0,15	0,09	0,02	0,21	0,09	0,09
SoNet1	0,62	0,12	0,01	0,09	0,02	0,11	0,11	0,08	0,70	0,24	0,23	0,18	0,01	0,09	0,20	0,08
SoNet2	0,91	0,08	0,00	0,14	0,04	0,19	0,22	0,07	0,81	0,32	0,34	0,12	0,06	0,16	0,24	0,09
SoNet3	0,63	0,09	0,06	0,15	0,02	0,19	0,16	0,11	0,72	0,19	0,24	0,15	0,03	0,15	0,14	0,08
SoNet4	0,90	0,04	0,04	0,12	0,05	0,17	0,28	0,15	0,78	0,19	0,30	0,14	0,05	0,18	0,23	0,10
Meas2	0,09	0,89	0,15	0,10	0,02	0,07	0,04	0,16	0,07	0,12	0,05	0,02	0,17	0,16	0,09	0,12
Meas3	0,04	0,92	0,24	0,21	0,08	0,01	0,10	0,07	0,09	0,14	0,01	0,21	0,16	0,23	0,26	0,03
Uncert1	0,01	0,22	0,87	0,41	0,18	0,04	0,06	0,03	0,01	0,02	0,11	0,19	0,02	0,05	0,12	0,04
Uncert2	0,04	0,17	0,92	0,46	0,15	0,06	0,09	0,03	0,12	0,02	0,20	0,13	0,04	0,10	0,16	0,09
Uncert3	0,20	0,18	0,41	0,89	0,13	0,12	0,06	0,05	0,21	0,04	0,09	0,11	0,09	0,04	0,06	0,09
Uncert4	0,08	0,15	0,47	0,93	0,08	0,02	0,01	0,03	0,13	0,03	0,11	0,08	0,04	0,03	0,01	0,04
WoLoad1	0,02	0,19	0,18	0,27	0,01	0,03	0,01	0,04	0,00	0,04	0,02	0,04	0,09	0,04	0,03	0,05
WoLoad2	0,08	0,21	0,09	0,22	0,01	0,01	0,10	0,04	0,09	0,07	0,01	0,05	0,06	0,16	0,11	0,01
CoPro1	0,03	0,11	0,13	0,14	0,08	0,21	0,00	0,18	0,03	0,11	0,19	0,15	0,05	0,10	0,03	0,19
CoPro2	0,03	0,02	0,17	0,16	0,05	0,08	0,06	0,14	0,01	0,12	0,18	0,15	0,03	0,08	0,01	0,22
CoPro3	0,09	0,14	0,08	0,14	0,12	0,11	0,09	0,14	0,13	0,04	0,13	0,09	0,01	0,15	0,02	0,19
Other1	0,26	0,11	0,04	0,14	0,02	0,25	0,11	0,20	0,27	0,31	0,27	0,29	0,05	0,60	0,47	0,33
Other2	0,27	0,13	0,07	0,08	0,06	0,24	0,13	0,24	0,29	0,31	0,29	0,31	0,04	0,57	0,47	0,33
Other3	0,21	0,07	0,03	0,12	0,03	0,26	0,12	0,26	0,25	0,33	0,25	0,30	0,06	0,60	0,45	0,30
Other4	0,18	0,11	0,10	0,05	0,02	0,33	0,14	0,33	0,20	0,31	0,27	0,28	0,15	0,58	0,45	0,33
Other5	0,23	0,06	0,16	0,05	0,04	0,35	0,12	0,31	0,23	0,30	0,30	0,25	0,01	0,62	0,49	0,35
Other6	0,18	0,08	0,13	0,06	0,03	0,34	0,12	0,27	0,22	0,28	0,30	0,22	0,09	0,59	0,50	0,30
IDEAL	0,26	0,20	0,16	0,02	0,07	0,31	0,32	0,21	0,25	0,48	0,44	0,38	0,28	0,64	1,00	0,30
Propert3	0,06	0,19	0,01	0,07	0,23	0,02	0,08	0,05	0,09	0,14	0,17	0,18	1,00	0,15	0,28	0,01

Table Appendix-E-6: Cross-Loadings Application Maintenance (Page 1 from 4)

Item	Out	PC	TC	StratII	StratI	Oper-atII	Oper-atI	Intell	Behav-Con	Sub-Norm	Work-Load	Spec-Bus	Spec-Tec	SoNet-IS-US
Out1	0,95	0,36	0,35	0,33	0,08	0,32	0,01	0,22	0,06	0,35	0,05	0,04	0,12	0,12
Out2	0,97	0,39	0,37	0,32	0,08	0,32	0,04	0,21	0,06	0,33	0,12	0,11	0,15	0,15
Out3	0,96	0,37	0,34	0,38	0,10	0,37	0,01	0,23	0,04	0,38	0,11	0,09	0,13	0,13
Out4	0,43	0,15	0,06	0,05	0,00	0,01	0,13	0,00	0,16	0,00	0,04	0,07	0,14	0,03
Pc1	0,33	0,84	0,55	0,46	0,25	0,46	0,12	0,43	0,09	0,32	0,07	0,24	0,21	0,18
Pc2	0,19	0,66	0,41	0,23	0,23	0,27	0,11	0,30	0,08	0,19	0,07	0,12	0,12	0,18
Pc3	0,39	0,79	0,53	0,48	0,34	0,47	0,08	0,51	0,00	0,39	0,13	0,30	0,24	0,24
Pc4	0,34	0,73	0,51	0,30	0,21	0,31	0,14	0,30	0,07	0,31	0,03	0,15	0,11	0,10
Pc5	0,23	0,85	0,58	0,39	0,26	0,43	0,18	0,39	0,09	0,33	0,08	0,14	0,14	0,09
TC1	0,33	0,56	0,80	0,36	0,16	0,36	0,18	0,37	0,12	0,36	0,10	0,00	0,07	0,08
TC2	0,29	0,48	0,81	0,34	0,14	0,35	0,16	0,38	0,14	0,36	0,00	0,11	0,20	0,13
TC3	0,25	0,51	0,80	0,31	0,16	0,36	0,03	0,41	0,01	0,38	0,05	0,09	0,15	0,21
TC4	0,29	0,58	0,78	0,44	0,19	0,47	0,09	0,43	0,02	0,38	0,10	0,11	0,15	0,09
Strat1	0,11	0,34	0,25	0,33	0,76	0,31	0,17	0,36	0,06	0,15	0,07	0,32	0,20	0,19
Strat2	0,34	0,48	0,45	0,93	0,41	0,72	0,14	0,52	0,06	0,42	0,12	0,14	0,10	0,21
Strat3	0,06	0,25	0,14	0,40	0,88	0,35	0,48	0,37	0,04	0,20	0,12	0,31	0,19	0,37
Strat4	0,34	0,46	0,42	0,94	0,45	0,72	0,23	0,49	0,14	0,39	0,15	0,11	0,05	0,24
Strat5	0,07	0,27	0,14	0,40	0,89	0,37	0,45	0,36	0,02	0,21	0,14	0,30	0,16	0,32
Strat6	0,33	0,46	0,42	0,96	0,41	0,76	0,19	0,51	0,14	0,41	0,14	0,13	0,07	0,23
Operat1	0,07	0,05	0,06	0,17	0,37	0,19	0,74	0,19	0,00	0,16	0,05	0,14	0,01	0,22
Operat2	0,28	0,44	0,44	0,72	0,33	0,89	0,14	0,47	0,19	0,40	0,09	0,14	0,10	0,25
Operat3	0,03	0,12	0,11	0,16	0,47	0,16	0,85	0,17	0,03	0,11	0,04	0,21	0,09	0,27
Operat4	0,30	0,47	0,45	0,77	0,35	0,91	0,17	0,52	0,12	0,41	0,13	0,11	0,07	0,24
Operat5	0,05	0,20	0,17	0,15	0,28	0,17	0,83	0,24	0,02	0,00	0,00	0,04	0,04	0,32
Operat6	0,33	0,44	0,40	0,58	0,38	0,84	0,23	0,51	0,25	0,40	0,24	0,08	0,04	0,22
Res1	0,25	0,43	0,46	0,46	0,38	0,45	0,23	0,83	0,08	0,25	0,02	0,31	0,22	0,23
Res2	0,19	0,37	0,39	0,43	0,32	0,48	0,20	0,84	0,13	0,35	0,05	0,16	0,16	0,25
Res3	0,15	0,46	0,45	0,45	0,39	0,50	0,22	0,86	0,14	0,33	0,08	0,23	0,22	0,27
Res5	0,10	0,26	0,16	0,34	0,32	0,33	0,15	0,38	0,00	0,18	0,05	0,21	0,31	0,22
Res6	0,15	0,41	0,35	0,43	0,31	0,46	0,16	0,80	0,05	0,22	0,18	0,18	0,21	0,19
Res7	0,12	0,20	0,22	0,12	0,19	0,13	0,19	0,27	0,14	0,17	0,09	0,10	0,18	0,15
Res8	0,14	0,20	0,26	0,33	0,21	0,34	0,12	0,43	0,04	0,30	0,01	0,08	0,07	0,23
Impact1	0,37	0,59	0,48	0,63	0,27	0,69	0,13	0,51	0,16	0,37	0,11	0,15	0,07	0,19
Impact2	0,40	0,48	0,43	0,64	0,33	0,67	0,23	0,46	0,13	0,38	0,12	0,23	0,17	0,25
Impact3	0,30	0,47	0,45	0,52	0,22	0,60	0,11	0,51	0,08	0,32	0,07	0,14	0,03	0,20
EmplOri1	0,21	0,28	0,32	0,28	0,25	0,37	0,23	0,33	0,17	0,26	0,24	0,15	0,02	0,28
EmplOri2	0,42	0,45	0,45	0,35	0,24	0,39	0,19	0,35	0,03	0,39	0,20	0,14	0,11	0,24
EmplOri3	0,34	0,38	0,37	0,43	0,39	0,41	0,12	0,37	0,12	0,30	0,15	0,19	0,09	0,25
EmplOri4	0,30	0,38	0,38	0,39	0,29	0,43	0,06	0,37	0,09	0,27	0,05	0,11	0,06	0,17
DecCont1	0,26	0,38	0,32	0,46	0,35	0,49	0,12	0,32	0,27	0,31	0,16	0,17	0,15	0,16
DecCont2	0,08	0,26	0,14	0,38	0,27	0,32	0,15	0,26	0,27	0,24	0,04	0,15	0,15	0,16

Table Appendix-E-6: Cross-Loadings Application Maintenance (Page 2 from 4)

Item	Out	PC	TC	StratII	StratI	Oper-atII	Oper-atI	Intell	Behav-Con	Sub-Norm	Work-Load	Spec-Bus	Spec-Tec	SoNet-IS-US
Trust1	0,03	0,07	0,07	0,05	0,10	0,04	0,18	0,16	0,10	0,05	0,07	0,03	0,00	0,05
Trust2	0,01	0,20	0,13	0,11	0,08	0,19	0,10	0,11	0,05	0,06	0,07	0,03	0,04	0,03
Trust3	0,06	0,14	0,11	0,02	0,03	0,03	0,14	0,13	0,00	0,08	0,04	0,06	0,08	0,02
Incen1	0,06	0,30	0,22	0,32	0,12	0,45	0,11	0,27	0,21	0,28	0,15	0,01	0,11	0,07
Incen2	0,19	0,43	0,26	0,36	0,18	0,45	0,05	0,32	0,15	0,22	0,11	0,09	0,02	0,17
Incen3	0,16	0,38	0,19	0,29	0,23	0,41	0,06	0,32	0,13	0,20	0,14	0,06	0,02	0,17
Group1	0,14	0,22	0,21	0,24	0,14	0,27	0,03	0,17	0,12	0,19	0,10	0,01	0,03	0,04
Group4	0,04	0,14	0,04	0,14	0,09	0,25	0,03	0,14	0,11	0,19	0,13	0,07	0,07	0,09
Group6	0,18	0,11	0,07	0,20	0,07	0,24	0,11	0,00	0,01	0,27	0,15	0,02	0,02	0,01
Group7	0,13	0,28	0,25	0,15	0,18	0,24	0,01	0,22	0,10	0,20	0,20	0,07	0,05	0,09
LongWo1	0,20	0,36	0,29	0,36	0,23	0,42	0,02	0,38	0,01	0,25	0,05	0,14	0,13	0,13
LongWo2	0,16	0,35	0,30	0,41	0,26	0,44	0,01	0,39	0,03	0,23	0,09	0,20	0,08	0,19
LongWo3	0,13	0,28	0,26	0,24	0,14	0,30	0,04	0,27	0,05	0,20	0,11	0,13	0,16	0,13
Attitud2	0,44	0,61	0,51	0,47	0,18	0,48	0,10	0,42	0,15	0,61	0,03	0,13	0,15	0,12
Attitud3	0,41	0,50	0,44	0,49	0,15	0,46	0,12	0,46	0,21	0,62	0,04	0,13	0,19	0,06
Attitud5	0,45	0,51	0,42	0,39	0,15	0,38	0,08	0,39	0,14	0,60	0,11	0,08	0,17	0,11
Attitud6	0,38	0,49	0,47	0,36	0,17	0,38	0,10	0,40	0,17	0,60	0,07	0,16	0,20	0,13
Attitud7	0,37	0,46	0,41	0,40	0,14	0,36	0,06	0,39	0,19	0,55	0,11	0,17	0,14	0,09
Spec1	0,07	0,24	0,07	0,12	0,36	0,09	0,14	0,26	0,05	0,11	0,21	0,92	0,44	0,40
Spec2	0,08	0,23	0,11	0,13	0,31	0,14	0,16	0,24	0,07	0,07	0,08	0,92	0,48	0,37
Spec4	0,17	0,26	0,23	0,12	0,17	0,08	0,08	0,24	0,08	0,14	0,08	0,53	0,88	0,22
Spec5	0,03	0,07	0,05	0,01	0,19	0,03	0,01	0,17	0,06	0,15	0,05	0,26	0,78	0,15
SoNet1	0,16	0,22	0,20	0,26	0,34	0,26	0,30	0,29	0,06	0,17	0,14	0,44	0,23	0,91
SoNet2	0,10	0,20	0,14	0,22	0,36	0,25	0,21	0,24	0,08	0,12	0,02	0,42	0,23	0,68
SoNet3	0,07	0,14	0,07	0,16	0,30	0,21	0,30	0,21	0,01	0,05	0,05	0,30	0,18	0,87
SoNet4	0,11	0,26	0,15	0,17	0,41	0,21	0,26	0,25	0,01	0,14	0,01	0,34	0,26	0,66
Meas2	0,18	0,06	0,07	0,13	0,06	0,04	0,05	0,05	0,16	0,02	0,03	0,02	0,11	0,11
Meas3	0,27	0,11	0,04	0,12	0,05	0,01	0,03	0,02	0,23	0,06	0,18	0,10	0,01	0,13
Uncert1	0,11	0,06	0,01	0,16	0,01	0,19	0,11	0,18	0,02	0,07	0,04	0,21	0,15	0,12
Uncert2	0,08	0,12	0,02	0,15	0,06	0,17	0,12	0,14	0,08	0,06	0,01	0,22	0,14	0,15
Uncert3	0,05	0,01	0,01	0,04	0,13	0,03	0,04	0,05	0,02	0,05	0,26	0,27	0,20	0,22
Uncert4	0,03	0,07	0,06	0,02	0,09	0,06	0,10	0,09	0,03	0,07	0,32	0,29	0,20	0,20
WoLoad1	0,10	0,11	0,08	0,16	0,15	0,19	0,01	0,10	0,03	0,18	1,00	0,16	0,07	0,07
WoLoad2	0,05	0,00	0,04	0,01	0,01	0,08	0,04	0,05	0,06	0,13	0,81	0,11	0,09	0,02
CoPro1	0,02	0,09	0,12	0,18	0,03	0,21	0,03	0,17	0,90	0,09	0,06	0,08	0,05	0,02
CoPro2	0,02	0,06	0,12	0,12	0,01	0,21	0,03	0,15	0,92	0,09	0,03	0,09	0,06	0,02
CoPro3	0,10	0,02	0,02	0,02	0,02	0,17	0,01	0,00	0,85	0,14	0,00	0,01	0,13	0,09
Other1	0,34	0,41	0,50	0,46	0,25	0,44	0,13	0,34	0,11	0,93	0,13	0,11	0,19	0,16
Other2	0,36	0,43	0,47	0,42	0,24	0,42	0,11	0,31	0,07	0,94	0,17	0,09	0,14	0,12
Other3	0,33	0,40	0,43	0,40	0,20	0,44	0,09	0,30	0,12	0,93	0,15	0,08	0,12	0,14
Other4	0,32	0,32	0,40	0,35	0,17	0,40	0,10	0,31	0,15	0,93	0,18	0,10	0,17	0,13
Other5	0,32	0,32	0,38	0,36	0,18	0,43	0,03	0,31	0,13	0,92	0,21	0,08	0,15	0,12
Other6	0,37	0,36	0,41	0,37	0,20	0,40	0,12	0,34	0,09	0,92	0,15	0,08	0,17	0,07
IDEAL	0,74	0,54	0,50	0,49	0,27	0,50	0,08	0,46	0,03	0,50	0,12	0,18	0,21	0,19
Propert3	0,35	0,11	0,11	0,06	0,02	0,13	0,05	0,05	0,01	0,05	0,17	0,12	0,02	0,10

Table Appendix-E-6: Cross-Loadings Application Maintenance (Page 3 from 4)

Item	Soc-NetIS	Meas	Env-Unc	Bus-Unc	Trust	Incent	Res-Other	Group	Spec-Hum	Syst-Impa	Sys-View	Long-Wo	Own-er	Atti-tude	Ideal	Con-trol
Out1	0,11	0,24	0,09	0,01	0,00	0,12	0,19	0,14	0,12	0,37	0,35	0,15	0,31	0,46	0,74	0,16
Out2	0,09	0,26	0,08	0,01	0,02	0,15	0,09	0,13	0,15	0,40	0,40	0,18	0,35	0,43	0,71	0,21
Out3	0,12	0,24	0,12	0,06	0,01	0,18	0,17	0,24	0,15	0,40	0,38	0,22	0,33	0,46	0,72	0,23
Out4	0,05	0,15	0,08	0,04	0,03	0,14	0,08	0,14	0,02	0,03	0,21	0,15	0,44	0,08	0,28	0,04
Pc1	0,25	0,09	0,08	0,04	0,20	0,34	0,21	0,24	0,29	0,46	0,38	0,35	0,10	0,47	0,45	0,24
Pc2	0,21	0,16	0,06	0,09	0,21	0,30	0,15	0,23	0,21	0,35	0,36	0,17	0,08	0,32	0,29	0,18
Pc3	0,28	0,05	0,02	0,02	0,14	0,29	0,31	0,28	0,35	0,53	0,41	0,38	0,11	0,51	0,50	0,33
Pc4	0,08	0,02	0,10	0,06	0,09	0,30	0,15	0,22	0,15	0,44	0,28	0,21	0,09	0,42	0,43	0,34
Pc5	0,12	0,07	0,18	0,12	0,12	0,34	0,19	0,19	0,16	0,43	0,29	0,34	0,03	0,50	0,41	0,31
TC1	0,12	0,00	0,02	0,08	0,12	0,21	0,17	0,17	0,09	0,36	0,34	0,22	0,08	0,39	0,37	0,17
TC2	0,07	0,06	0,01	0,05	0,08	0,13	0,23	0,16	0,16	0,39	0,37	0,22	0,07	0,45	0,40	0,28
TC3	0,23	0,04	0,01	0,04	0,04	0,19	0,24	0,21	0,22	0,39	0,34	0,26	0,06	0,41	0,38	0,23
TC4	0,08	0,09	0,01	0,10	0,21	0,27	0,24	0,22	0,13	0,47	0,41	0,33	0,15	0,39	0,44	0,21
Strat1	0,22	0,00	0,07	0,12	0,09	0,15	0,25	0,20	0,31	0,23	0,27	0,23	0,08	0,12	0,29	0,30
Strat2	0,21	0,10	0,12	0,01	0,08	0,31	0,35	0,23	0,23	0,61	0,39	0,37	0,05	0,44	0,48	0,42
Strat3	0,45	0,04	0,07	0,05	0,05	0,16	0,24	0,13	0,45	0,28	0,28	0,20	0,08	0,17	0,17	0,28
Strat4	0,20	0,16	0,20	0,07	0,06	0,32	0,39	0,27	0,21	0,64	0,43	0,39	0,04	0,45	0,43	0,48
Strat5	0,36	0,02	0,01	0,09	0,07	0,19	0,25	0,18	0,39	0,26	0,34	0,20	0,02	0,15	0,24	0,31
Strat6	0,19	0,13	0,15	0,01	0,10	0,36	0,33	0,27	0,21	0,64	0,42	0,37	0,07	0,44	0,48	0,44
Operat1	0,20	0,06	0,10	0,07	0,14	0,02	0,16	0,02	0,20	0,17	0,14	0,02	0,11	0,05	0,06	0,03
Operat2	0,23	0,00	0,16	0,06	0,19	0,36	0,31	0,30	0,25	0,63	0,41	0,43	0,12	0,39	0,44	0,42
Operat3	0,18	0,02	0,12	0,13	0,13	0,07	0,10	0,05	0,26	0,08	0,14	0,06	0,01	0,09	0,05	0,13
Operat4	0,23	0,00	0,17	0,05	0,11	0,39	0,36	0,31	0,23	0,67	0,39	0,45	0,07	0,39	0,42	0,38
Operat5	0,23	0,02	0,09	0,04	0,10	0,11	0,14	0,02	0,23	0,18	0,14	0,01	0,04	0,10	0,08	0,16
Operat6	0,20	0,06	0,17	0,04	0,11	0,48	0,35	0,36	0,17	0,63	0,44	0,33	0,13	0,44	0,45	0,41
Res1	0,18	0,03	0,05	0,07	0,17	0,23	0,43	0,19	0,31	0,48	0,36	0,31	0,02	0,42	0,41	0,29
Res2	0,32	0,11	0,11	0,08	0,11	0,24	0,34	0,15	0,30	0,42	0,34	0,30	0,07	0,38	0,34	0,25
Res3	0,26	0,02	0,16	0,13	0,10	0,29	0,45	0,22	0,32	0,47	0,38	0,39	0,03	0,39	0,41	0,23
Res5	0,25	0,01	0,08	0,07	0,03	0,14	0,63	0,22	0,32	0,29	0,24	0,33	0,00	0,21	0,24	0,22
Res6	0,10	0,06	0,26	0,00	0,14	0,36	0,42	0,20	0,21	0,47	0,29	0,34	0,03	0,35	0,38	0,33
Res7	0,14	0,00	0,03	0,03	0,03	0,07	0,59	0,10	0,18	0,23	0,18	0,24	0,01	0,18	0,19	0,05
Res8	0,21	0,09	0,03	0,07	0,00	0,22	0,93	0,16	0,21	0,34	0,26	0,20	0,12	0,32	0,33	0,13
Impact1	0,16	0,19	0,15	0,07	0,17	0,38	0,36	0,25	0,19	0,91	0,42	0,29	0,08	0,48	0,42	0,42
Impact2	0,18	0,08	0,04	0,02	0,14	0,30	0,41	0,27	0,28	0,90	0,44	0,35	0,12	0,46	0,42	0,43
Impact3	0,10	0,11	0,10	0,02	0,17	0,31	0,26	0,23	0,16	0,88	0,37	0,33	0,05	0,45	0,35	0,39
EmplOri1	0,19	0,00	0,05	0,18	0,09	0,33	0,27	0,29	0,22	0,34	0,75	0,40	0,15	0,27	0,29	0,21
EmplOri2	0,20	0,01	0,03	0,11	0,06	0,34	0,22	0,34	0,23	0,39	0,88	0,32	0,16	0,35	0,46	0,22
EmplOri3	0,25	0,04	0,03	0,13	0,10	0,29	0,28	0,23	0,27	0,38	0,86	0,30	0,14	0,32	0,37	0,31
EmplOri4	0,19	0,06	0,05	0,03	0,07	0,34	0,27	0,27	0,19	0,43	0,89	0,32	0,08	0,32	0,34	0,26
DecCont1	0,09	0,06	0,12	0,02	0,15	0,35	0,15	0,24	0,18	0,48	0,33	0,24	0,00	0,36	0,29	0,95
DecCont2	0,17	0,09	0,10	0,07	0,08	0,30	0,16	0,22	0,20	0,33	0,17	0,12	0,14	0,28	0,16	0,87

Table Appendix-E-6: Cross-Loadings Application Maintenance (Page 4 from 4)

Item	Soc-NetIS	Meas	Env-Unc	Bus-Unc	Trust	Incent	Res-Other	Group	Spec-Hum	Syst-Impa	Sys-View	Long-Wo	Own-er	Atti-tude	Ideal	Con-trol
Trust1	0,09	0,17	0,07	0,07	0,67	0,22	0,06	0,00	0,03	0,08	0,06	0,03	0,09	0,00	0,01	0,06
Trust2	0,02	0,11	0,01	0,04	0,92	0,23	0,04	0,10	0,01	0,18	0,06	0,07	0,26	0,05	0,01	0,15
Trust3	0,03	0,04	0,19	0,10	0,69	0,16	0,03	0,02	######	0,11	0,11	0,17	0,12	0,05	0,01	0,06
Incen1	0,02	0,01	0,11	0,03	0,27	0,87	0,18	0,41	0,01	0,35	0,31	0,25	0,02	0,19	0,20	0,31
Incen2	0,15	0,01	0,10	0,06	0,23	0,94	0,21	0,37	0,16	0,35	0,37	0,42	0,04	0,31	0,42	0,35
Incen3	0,15	0,01	0,11	0,04	0,21	0,94	0,22	0,35	0,14	0,32	0,37	0,34	0,06	0,28	0,33	0,35
Group1	0,05	0,14	0,07	0,10	0,10	0,34	0,16	0,78	0,03	0,27	0,27	0,20	0,07	0,21	0,17	0,20
Group4	0,15	0,02	0,10	0,01	0,01	0,25	0,07	0,60	0,13	0,16	0,20	0,17	0,15	0,17	0,16	0,14
Group6	0,10	0,14	0,03	0,03	0,03	0,12	0,04	0,48	0,05	0,08	0,11	0,19	0,09	0,13	0,16	0,17
Group7	0,07	0,10	0,10	0,02	0,03	0,29	0,23	0,70	0,10	0,16	0,26	0,34	0,09	0,13	0,13	0,16
LongWo1	0,18	0,09	0,05	0,06	0,10	0,31	0,25	0,30	0,19	0,31	0,35	0,93	0,04	0,21	0,32	0,20
LongWo2	0,22	0,05	0,07	0,01	0,08	0,38	0,29	0,34	0,24	0,38	0,38	0,92	0,16	0,23	0,33	0,20
LongWo3	0,07	0,08	0,05	0,05	0,10	0,28	0,19	0,26	0,15	0,25	0,26	0,77	0,19	0,11	0,19	0,14
Attitud2	0,09	0,12	0,15	0,04	0,08	0,30	0,31	0,28	0,15	0,51	0,37	0,20	0,05	0,89	0,57	0,31
Attitud3	0,04	0,05	0,15	0,00	0,05	0,30	0,28	0,28	0,12	0,45	0,32	0,20	0,04	0,89	0,57	0,29
Attitud5	0,11	0,12	0,22	0,11	0,00	0,23	0,30	0,20	0,15	0,45	0,31	0,16	0,06	0,91	0,60	0,33
Attitud6	0,10	0,06	0,17	0,04	0,03	0,24	0,29	0,16	0,18	0,44	0,33	0,18	0,00	0,89	0,59	0,34
Attitud7	0,09	0,06	0,16	0,03	0,07	0,19	0,34	0,21	0,15	0,44	0,34	0,22	0,04	0,86	0,49	0,32
Spec1	0,39	0,08	0,21	0,32	0,03	0,08	0,15	0,08	0,70	0,16	0,21	0,20	0,15	0,13	0,17	0,19
Spec2	0,36	0,05	0,22	0,22	0,03	0,03	0,12	0,02	0,69	0,20	0,10	0,14	0,08	0,14	0,17	0,14
Spec4	0,21	0,03	0,17	0,24	0,01	0,01	0,14	0,04	0,53	0,18	0,13	0,13	0,09	0,20	0,20	0,14
Spec5	0,24	0,14	0,07	0,08	0,11	0,03	0,18	0,01	0,40	0,04	0,01	0,09	0,06	0,11	0,15	0,13
SoNet1	0,69	0,20	0,11	0,15	0,01	0,13	0,31	0,09	0,79	0,27	0,22	0,18	0,09	0,16	0,23	0,18
SoNet2	0,93	0,08	0,09	0,02	0,08	0,06	0,23	0,08	0,80	0,18	0,21	0,15	0,05	0,11	0,18	0,07
SoNet3	0,59	0,03	0,17	0,20	0,01	0,14	0,15	0,08	0,67	0,14	0,27	0,12	0,08	0,03	0,09	0,12
SoNet4	0,92	0,11	0,14	0,07	0,01	0,13	0,27	0,16	0,76	0,13	0,25	0,20	0,03	0,07	0,17	0,18
Meas2	0,06	0,88	0,14	0,07	0,13	0,03	0,09	0,17	0,03	0,16	0,09	0,05	0,29	0,06	0,13	0,09
Meas3	0,12	0,95	0,20	0,17	0,08	0,02	0,05	0,10	0,06	0,11	0,01	0,10	0,22	0,10	0,19	0,06
Uncert1	0,09	0,19	0,86	0,36	0,07	0,15	0,03	0,05	0,18	0,11	0,02	0,05	0,02	0,16	0,20	0,11
Uncert2	0,12	0,17	0,96	0,49	0,07	0,09	0,05	0,01	0,21	0,10	0,08	0,06	0,03	0,19	0,15	0,12
Uncert3	0,09	0,12	0,45	0,77	0,01	0,07	0,08	0,05	0,24	0,01	0,06	0,00	0,06	0,04	0,06	0,12
Uncert4	0,04	0,14	0,48	1,00	0,02	0,05	0,03	0,04	0,23	0,04	0,13	0,01	0,01	0,05	0,03	0,04
WoLoad1	0,02	0,12	0,00	0,32	0,05	0,15	0,03	0,20	0,10	0,13	0,19	0,09	0,18	0,09	0,13	0,12
WoLoad2	0,06	0,20	0,03	0,23	0,00	0,10	0,12	0,20	0,03	0,01	0,06	0,04	0,04	0,00	0,02	0,11
CoPro1	0,01	0,14	0,08	0,01	0,06	0,20	0,04	0,19	0,03	0,12	0,12	0,04	0,05	0,19	0,08	0,29
CoPro2	0,06	0,17	0,02	0,08	0,04	0,10	0,01	0,11	0,01	0,14	0,09	0,00	0,05	0,17	0,04	0,22
CoPro3	0,10	0,28	0,03	0,01	0,05	0,16	0,00	0,08	0,09	0,11	0,08	0,02	0,04	0,15	0,05	0,29
Other1	0,17	0,00	0,02	0,11	0,01	0,19	0,32	0,26	0,20	0,41	0,35	0,25	0,07	0,63	0,44	0,32
Other2	0,15	0,06	0,03	0,09	0,00	0,22	0,32	0,26	0,16	0,39	0,38	0,28	0,01	0,61	0,46	0,28
Other3	0,11	0,02	0,04	0,09	0,05	0,24	0,30	0,27	0,14	0,37	0,32	0,26	0,04	0,63	0,46	0,26
Other4	0,09	0,00	0,10	0,07	0,04	0,24	0,25	0,30	0,15	0,34	0,33	0,20	0,11	0,64	0,45	0,29
Other5	0,15	0,00	0,10	0,05	0,03	0,29	0,27	0,32	0,16	0,38	0,34	0,22	0,04	0,60	0,45	0,33
Other6	0,12	0,07	0,12	0,00	0,06	0,25	0,27	0,27	0,13	0,34	0,32	0,24	0,05	0,63	0,52	0,24
IDEAL	0,19	0,18	0,18	0,03	0,01	0,35	0,36	0,23	0,25	0,44	0,43	0,33	0,20	0,64	1,00	0,26
Propert3	0,04	0,27	0,02	0,01	0,23	0,00	0,10	0,03	0,10	0,09	0,16	0,14	1,00	0,04	0,20	0,06

List of Figures

List of Tables

Literature

Adams, D.A., Nelson, R.R. and Todd, P.A. "Perceived Usefulness, Ease of Use, and Usage of Information Technology: A Replication," *MIS Quarterly* (16:2), 1992, pp. 227-247.

Agarwal, R. "Individual Acceptance of Information Technologies," in *Framing the Domain of IT Management: Projecting the Future ... Through the Past*, Pinnaflex, Cincinnati, 2000, pp. 85-104.

Agarwal, R. and Prasad, J. "The Role of Innovation Characteristics and Perceived Voluntariness in the Acceptance of Information Technology," *Decision Sciences* (28:3), 1997, pp. 557-582.

Ajzen, I. "From Intentions to Actions: A Theory of Planned Behavior," in *Action-Control: From Cognition to Behavior*, J. Kuhl and J. Beckmann (Eds.), Springer, Heidelberg, 1985, pp. 11-39.

Ajzen, I. "Attitude Structure and Behavior," in *Attitude Structure and Function*, A. R. Pratkanis, S. J. Breckler and A. G. Greenwald (Eds.), Lawrence Erlbaum, Hillsdale, NJ, 1989, pp. 241-274.

Ajzen, I. "The Theory of Planned Behavior," *Organizational Behavior and Human Decision Processes* (50), 1991, pp. 179-211.

Ajzen, I. and Fishbein, M. *Understanding Attitudes and Predicting Social Behavior*, Prentice Hall, Englewood Cliffs, NY, 1980.

Ajzen, I. and Madden, T.J. "Prediction of Goal-Directed Behavior from Attitudinal and Normative Variables," *Journal of Experimental Social Psychology* (22), 1986, pp. 453-474.

Alavi, M., Carlson, P. and Brooke, G. "The Ecology of MIS Research: A Twenty Year Status Review," *Proceedings of the 10th International Conference on Information Systems*, 1989, pp. 363-375.

Albach, H. "The Nature of the Firm – A Production -Theoretical Viewpoint," *Zeitschrift für die gesamte Staatswissenschaft – Journal of Institutional and Theoretical Economics* (137), 1981, pp. 717-722.

Albach, H. "Editorial," *Zeitschrift für Betriebswirtschaft* (58), 1988a, pp. 3-10.

Albach, H. "Kosten, Transaktionen und externe Effekte im betrieblichen Rechnungswesen," *Zeitschrift für Betriebswirtschaft* (58), 1988b, pp. 1143-1170.

Albach, H. "Eine allgemeine Theorie der Unternehmung," *Zeitschrift für Betriebswirtschaft* (69:4), 1999, pp. 411-427.

Albach, H. *Allgemeine Betriebswirtschaftslehre: Einführung*, Gabler Verlag, Wiesbaden, 2000a.

Albach, H. "In Memory of Erich Gutenberg," in *Theory of the Firm: Erich Gutenberg's Foundations and Further Developments*, H. Albach, K. K. L. Brockhoff, E. Eymann, P. Jungen, M. Steven and A. Luhmer (Eds.), Springer, Berlin et al., 2000b, pp. 3-39.

Alchian, A.A. and Demsetz, H. "Production, Information Costs, and Economic Organization," *American Economic Review* (62:5), 1972, pp. 777-795.

Amit, R. and Schoemaker, P.J.H. "Strategic Assets and Organizational Rent," *Strategic Management Journal* (14:1), 1993, pp. 33-46.

Andelfinger, U. *Diskursive Anforderungsanalyse*, Frankfurt/M., 1997.

Anderson, E. "The Salesperson as Outside Agent or Employee: A Transaction Cost Analysis," *Marketing Science* (4:3), 1985, pp. 234-254.

Anderson, E. and Weitz, B.A. "Make-or-Buy Decisions: Vertical Integration and Marketing Productivity," *Sloan Management Review* (27:3), 1986, pp. 3-19.

Ang, S. and Cummings, L.L. "Strategic Response to Institutional Influences on Information Systems Outsourcing," *Organization Science* (8:3), 1997, pp. 235-256.

Ang, S. and Slaughter, S.A. "Work Outcomes and Job Design for Contract versus Permanent Information Systems Professionals on Software Development Teams," *MIS Quarterly* (25:3), 2001, pp. 321-350.

Ang, S. and Slaughter, S.A. "Organizational Psychology and Performance in IS Employment Outsourcing and Insourcing," *Proceedings of the 31 International Conference on System Sciences*, Hawaii, 1998, pp. 635-643.

Ang, S. and Slaughter, S.A. "A Taxonomy of Employment Insourcing and Outsourcing Strategies in Information Systems," in *Information Systems Outsourcing: Enduring Themes, Emergent Patterns and Future Directions*, R. A. Hirschheim, A. Heinzl and J. Dibbern (Eds.), Springer-Verlag, Berlin et al., 2002, pp. 130-152.

Ang, S. and Straub, D.W. "Production and Transaction Economies and IS Outsourcing: A Study of the U.S. Banking Industry," *MIS Quarterly* (22:4), 1998, pp. 535-552.

Appelrath, H.-J. and Ritter, J. *R/3-Einführung: Methoden und Werkzeuge*, Series: SAP Kompetent, Springer, Berlin et al., 2000.

Applegate, L. and Montealegre, R. "Eastman Kodak Organization: Managing Information Systems Through Strategic Alliances," Harvard Business School Case 9-192-030, Boston, Massachusetts, 1991.

Apte, U.M., Sobol, M.G., Hanaoka, S., Shimada, T., Saarinen, T., Salmela, T. and Vepsalainen, A.P.J. "IS Outsourcing Practices in the USA, Japan and Finland: A Comparative Study," *Journal of Information Technology* (12), 1997, pp. 289-304.

Arbuckle, J. *AMOS User's Guide, Version 4.0*, Chicago, 1999.

Argyres, N.S. and Liebeskind, J.P. "Contractual Commitment, Bargaining and Governance Inseparability: Incorporating History into Transaction Cost Theory," *Academy of Management Review* (24:1), 1999, pp. 49-63.

Arnett, K.P. and Jones, M.C. "Firms that Choose Outsourcing: A Profile," *Information & Management* (26), 1994, pp. 179-188.

Arrow, K.J. "The Organization of Economic Activity," in *The Analysis Evaluation and of Public Expenditure: The PPB System*, J. E. Committee (Ed.), 91st Congress, 1st Session, 1969, pp. 59-73.

Arrow, K.J. "Methodological Individualism and Social Knowledge," *The American Economic Review* (84:2), 1994, pp. 1-9.

Aubert, B.A., Patry, M. and Rivard, S. "Development of Measures to Assess Dimensions of IS Operation Transactions," *Omega, International Journal of Management Sciences* (24:6), 1996a, pp. 661-680.

Aubert, B.A., Patry, M. and Rivard, S. "Assessing the Risk of IT Outsourcing," *Proceedings of the 31st Annual Hawaii International Conference on System Sciences*, 1998, pp. 685-691.

Aubert, B.A., Rivard, S. and Patry, M. "A Transaction Cost Approach to Outsourcing Behavior: Some Empirical Evidence," *Information & Management* (30:2), 1996b, pp. 51-64.

Bacharach, S.B. "Organizational Theories: Some Criteria for Evaluation," *Academy of Management Review* (14:4), 1989, pp. 496-515.

Backhaus, K., Erichson, B., Plinke, W. and Weiber, R. *Multivariate Analysemethoden: eine anwendungsorientierte Einführung; mit 205 Tabellen*, Series: Springer Lehrbuch, Springer, Berlin et al., 1996.

Bagozzi, R.P. and Phillips, L. "Representing and Testing Organizational Theories: A Holistic Construal," *Administrative Science Quarterly* (27:September), 1982, pp. 459-489.

Bagozzi, R.P. and Yi, Y. "On the Evaluation of Structural Equation Models," *Journal of the Academy of Marketing Science* (16), 1988, pp. 74-94.

Baier, A. "Trust and Antitrust," *Ethics* (96:2), 1986, pp. 231-260.

Bain, J.S. *Barriers to New Competition*, Harvard University Press, Cambridge, Mass., 1956.

Bain, J.S. *Industrial Organization*, New York-London-Sydney, 1968.

Bain, J.S. "The Comparative Stability of Market Structures," in *Essays on Price Theory and Industrial Organization*, J. S. Bain (Ed.), Boston, 1972, pp. 166-174.

Balzert, H. *Lehrbuch der Software-Technik: Software-Entwicklung*, Spektrum Akademischer Verlag, Heidelberg, Berlin, 2001.

Banker, R.D., Davis, G.B. and Slaughter, S.A. "Software Development Practices, Software Complexity, and Software Maintenance Performance: A Field Study," *Management Science* (44:4), 1998, pp. 433-450.

Banker, R.D. and Slaughter, S.A. "A Field Study of Scale Economies in Software Maintenance," *Management Science* (43:12), 1997, pp. 1709-1725.

Banker, R.D., Srikant, M.D. and Kemerer, C.F. "A Model to Evaluate Variables Impacting the Productivity of Software Maintenance Projects," *Management Science* (37:1), 1991, pp. 1-18.

Banker, R.D., Srikant, M.D., Kemerer, C.F. and Zweig, D. "Software Complexity and Maintenance Costs," *Communication of the ACM* (36:11), 1993, pp. 81-94.

Bansler, J. and Havn, E. "Information Systems Development with Generic Systems," *European Conference of Information Systems*, Breukelen, The Netherlands, 1994, pp. 707-718.

Barney, J.B. "Firm Resources and Sustained Competitive Advantage," *Journal of Management* (17:1), 1991, pp. 99-120.

Barney, J.B. "How a Firm's Capabilities Affect Boundary Decisions," *Sloan Management Review* (Spring), 1999, pp. 137-145.

Baroudi, J.J. and Orlikowski, W.J. "The Problem of Statistical Power in MIS Research," *MIS Quarterly* (13:1), 1989, pp. 87-106.

Barthélemy, J. "The Hidden Costs of IT Outsourcing," *Sloan Management Review* (Spring), 2001, pp. 60-69.

Barthélemy, J. and Geyer, D. "IT Outsourcing: Evidence from France and Germany," *European Management Journal* (19:2), 2001, pp. 195-202.

Baruch, Y. "Response Rate in Academic Studies – A Comparative Analysis," *Human Relations* (52:4), 1999, pp. 421-438.

Baumol, W.J., Panzer, J.C. and Willig, R.D. "[Contestable Markets] and the Theory of Industry Structure," *American Economic Review*, 1988, pp. 809-822.

Beath, C.M. and Walker, G. "Outsourcing of Application Software: A Knowledge Management Perspective," *Proceedings of the 31st Annual International Conference on System Sciences*, Hawaii, 1998, pp. 666-674.

Bennet, K. "Software Evolution: Past Present and Future," *Information and Software Technology* (38:11), 1996, pp. 673-680.

Bentler, P.M. *EQS: Structural Equation Program Manual*, Encino, 1995.

Berle, A.A. and Means, G. *The Modern Corporation and Private Property*, Commerce Clearing House, New York, 1932.

Beyah, G. and Gallivan, M.J. "Knowledge Management as a Framework for Understanding Public Sector Outsourcing," *Proceedings of the 34th Annual Hawaii International Conference on System Sciences*, Hawaii, 2001.

Bharadwaj, A.S. "A Resource-Based Perspective on Information Technology Capabilities and Firm Performance: An Empirical Investigation," *MIS Quarterly* (24:1), 2000, pp. 169-196.

Bhattacherjee, A. "The Effect of Incentives and Control on Intraorganizational Information Technology Usage: A Principle-Agent Model," Dissertation, University of Houston, available at UMI, 1996.

Bhawuk, D.P.S. and Brislin, R. "The Measurement of Intercultural Sensitivity Using the Concept of Individualism and Collectivism," *International Journal of Intercultural Relations* (16), 1992, pp. 413-416.

Blau, P. *Exchange and Power in Social Life*, Wiley, New York, 1964.

Blois, K.J. "Trust in Business to Business Relationships: An Evaluation of Its Status," *Journal of Management Studies* (36:2), 1999, pp. 197-214.

Boehm, B.W. "Improving Software Productivity," *IEEE Computer* (Sept.), 1987, pp. 43-57.

Böhmann, T., Junginger, M. and Krcmar, H. "Modular Service Architectures: A Concept and Method from Engineering IT Services," *Proceedings of the 36th Hawaii International Conference on System Sciences*, 2003.

Boisot, M. *Knowledge Assets: Securing Competitive Advantage in the Information Economy*, Oxford University Press, Oxford, 1998.

Bollen, K.A. *Structural Equations With Latent Variables*, Wiley, New York, 1989.

Brehm, L. "Postimplementierungsphase von ERP-Systemen in Unternehmen: Organisatorische Gestaltung und kritische Erfolgsfaktoren," Dissertation, Universität Bayreuth, Lehrstuhl für Wirtschaftsinformatik, 2001.

Brehm, L., Heinzl, A. and Markus, M.L. "Tailoring ERP Systems: A Spectrum of Choices and their Implications," *34th Hawaii International Conference on System Sciences*, Hawaii, USA, 2001, pp. 1-9.

Brim, O.G.J., Glass, D.C., Lavin, D.E. and Goodman, N. "Personalty and Decision Processes," Studies in the Social Psychology of Thinking., Stanford Cal., 1962.

Brockhoff, K. "R&D Co-operation between Firms – A Perceived Transaction Cost Perspective," *Management Science* (38), 1992, pp. 514-524.

Brown, C. "Examining the Emergence of Hybrid IS Governance Solutions: Evidence from a Single Case," *Information Systems Research* (8:1), 1997, pp. 69-94.

Brynjolfsson, E. "The Productivity Paradox of Information Technology," *Communications of the ACM* (36:12), 1993, pp. 67-77.

Buhl, H.U. and Wirth, A. "Outsourcing von Informationsverarbeitungsleistungen unter Risikoaspekten," in *Informatique: Rightsourcing, Outsourcing*, D. Berchtold and J. Hess (Eds.), Schriftenreihe der Schweiz. Gesellschaft für Verwaltungswissenschaften SGVW, Vol. 28, Bern, 1995, pp. 126-150.

Bühner, R. and Tuschke, A. "Outsourcing," *DBW* (57:1), 1997, pp. 20-30.

Burr, W. "Fundierung von Leistungstiefenentscheidungen auf der Basis modifizierter Transaktionskostenansätze," *Zeitschrift für betriebswirtschaftliche Forschung* (55:März), 2003, pp. 112-135.

Burrell, G. and Morgan, G. *Sociological Paradigms and Organizational Analysis*, London, 1979.

Calder, B.J. and Staw, B.M. "The Self-perception of Intrinsic and Extrinsic Motivation," *Journal of Personality and Social Psychology* (31), 1975, pp. 599-605.

Carr, C. and Tomkins, C. "Context, Culture and the Role of the Finance Function in Strategic Decisions. A Comparative Analysis of Britain, Germany, the U.S.A. and Japan," *Management Accounting Research* (9), 1998, pp. 213-239.

Chalos, P. and Sung, J. "Outsourcing Decisions and Managerial Incentives," *Decision Sciences* (29:4), 1998, pp. 901-919.

Chatterjee, S. and Wernerfelt, B. "The Link Between Resources and Type of Diversification: Theory and Evidence," *Strategic Management Journal* (12), 1991, pp. 33-48.

Checkland, P. "Systems Thinking," in *Rethinking Management Information Systems: An Interdisciplinary Perspective*, W. J. Currie and B. Galliers (Eds.), Oxford University Press, Oxford, 1999, pp. 45-56.

Checkland, P. and Holwell, S. *Information, Systems and Information Systems: Making Sense of the Field*, Wiley, Chichester, UK, 1998.

Checkland, P. and Scholes, J. *Soft Systems Methodology in Action*, Wiley, Chichester, 1990.

Chen, C.C., Peng, M.W. and Saparito, P.A. "Individualism, Collectivism, and Opportunism: A Cultural Perspective on Transaction Cost Economics," *Journal of Management* (28:4), 2002, pp. 567-583.

Cheng, T.-k., Sculli, D. and Chan, F.S.-f. "Relationship Dominance – Rethinking Management Theories from the Perspective of Methodological Individualism," *Journal of Managerial Psychology* (16:2), 2001, pp. 97-105.

Cheon, M.J. "Outsourcing of Information Systems Functions: A Contingency Model," Dissertation, University of South Carolina, 1992.

Cheon, M.J., Grover, V. and Teng, J.T.C. "Theoretical Perspectives on the Outsourcing of Information Systems," *Journal of Information Technology* (10), 1995, pp. 209-210.

Chiles, T.H. and McMackin, J.F. "Integrating variable risk preferences, trust, and transaction cost economics," *Academy of Management Review* (21:1), 1996, pp. 73-99.

Chin, W.W. "Advancing the Theory of Adaptive Structuration: The Development of a Scale to Measure Faithfulness of Appropriation," *Information Systems Research* (8:4), 1997, pp. 342-367.

Chin, W.W. "Exploratory Structural Equation Modeling," Structural Equation Modeling in IS Research: ISWorld Net Virtual Meeting Center at Temple University, http://interact.cis.temple.edu/~vmc, Access 2001-03-04, 1998a, Last Update 1998-06-25 1998a.

Chin, W.W. "Issues and Opinion on Structural Equation Modeling," *MIS Quarterly* (22:1), 1998b, pp. VII-XVI.

Chin, W.W. "The Partial Least Squares Approach for Structural Equation Modeling," in *Modern Methods for Business Research*, G. A. Marcoulides (Ed.), Lawrence Erlbaum Associates, Hillsdale, 1998c, pp. 295-336.

Chin, W.W. and Gopal, A. "Adoption Intention in GSS: Relative Importance of Beliefs," *The DATA BASE for Advances in Information Systems* (26:2), 1995, pp. 42-63.

Chin, W.W., Marcolin, B.L. and Newsted, P.R. "A Partial Least Squares Latent Variable Modeling Approach for Measuring Interaction Effects: Results from a Monte Carlo Simulation Study and Voice Mail Emotion/Adoption Study," *Proceedings of the 17th International Conference on Information Systems*, Cleveland, Ohio, 1996, pp. 21-41.

Chin, W.W. and Newsted, P.R. "Structural Equation Modeling: Analysis with Small Samples Using Partial Least Squares," in *Statistical Strategies for Small Sample Research*, R. Hoyle (Ed.), Sage Publications, 1999, pp. 307-341.

Chin, W.W. and Todd, P.A. "On the use, usefulness, and ease of use of structural equation modeling in MIS research: A note of caution," *MIS Quarterly* (19:2), 1995, pp. 237-246.

Chmielewicz, K. "Codetermination," in *Handbook of German Business Management*, Vol. 2, C. E. Poeschel Verlag, Stuttgart, 1990, pp. 412-438.

Chylla, P. "Der Wandel von der Konzern-DV zum etablierten Outsourcing-Dienstleister," *WIRTSCHAFTSINFORMATIK* (45:2), 2003, pp. 177-180.

Clark, T.D., Jr., Zmud, R.W. and McCray, G.E. "The Outsourcing of Information Services: Transforming the Nature of Business in the Information Industry," *Journal of Information Technology* (10), 1995, pp. 221-237.

Clemons, E.K. and Row, M.C. "Sustaining IT Advantage: The Role of Structural Differences," *MIS Quarterly* (15:3), 1991, pp. 275-292.

Coase, R.H. "The Nature of the Firm," *Economica* (4:November), 1937, pp. 386-405.

Cohen, J. *Statistical Power Analysis for the Behavioral Sciences*, Academic Press, New York, 1977.

Coleman, J.S. "Social Capital in the Creation of Human Capital," *American Journal of Sociology* (94), 1988, pp. 95-120.

Collis, D.J. and Montgomery, C.A. "Wettbewerbsstärke durch hervorragende Ressourcen," *Harvard Business Manager* (2), 1996, pp. 47-57.

Commons, J.R. "Institutional Economics," *The American Economic Review* (12), 1931, pp. 648-657.

Conner, K.R. "A Historical Comparison of Resource-Based Theory and Five Schools of Thought Within Industrial Organization Economics: Do We Have a New Theory of the Firm?," *Journal of Management* (17:1), 1991, pp. 121-154.

Cordano, M. and Frieze Hanson, I. "Pollution Reduction Preferences of U.S. Environmental Managers: Applying Ajzen's Theory of Planned Behavior," *Academy of Management Review* (43:4), 2000, pp. 627-641.

Couger, J.D. and Colter, M.A. *Maintenance Programming: Improved Productivity Through Motivation*, Prentice Hall, Englewood Cliffs, NJ, 1985.

Cournot, A. *Recherches sur les principles mathèmatiques de la thèorie des richesses*, Paris, 1938.

Cronk, J. and Sharp, J. "A Framework for Deciding What to Outsoure in Information Technology," *Journal of Information Technology* (10), 1995, pp. 259-267.

Cross, J. "IT Outsourcing: British Petroleum," *Harvard Business Review* (May-June), 1995, pp. 94-102.

Currie, W.L. "Using Multiple Suppliers to Mitigate the Risk of IT Outsourcing at ICI and Wessex Water," *Journal of Information Technology* (13), 1998, pp. 169-180.

Currie, W.L. and Willcocks, L.P. "Analyzing Four Types of IT Sourcing Decisions in the Context of Scale, Client/Supplier Interdependency and Risk Mitigation," *Information Systems Journal* (Autumn), 1998, pp. 119-143.

Cyert, R.M. and March, J.G. *A Behavioral Theory of the Firm*, Prentice-Hall, Englewood Cliffs, N.J., 1963.

Dagum, C. "Scientific Model Building: Principles, Methods, and History," in *Theoretical Empiricism: A General Rationale for Scientific Model-Building*, H. Wold (Ed.), Paragon House, New York, 1989, pp. 113-152.

Davenport, T.H. *Mission Critical: Realizing the Promise of Enterprise Systems*, Harvard Business School Press, Boston, 2000.

Davis, F.D., Bagozzi, R.P. and Warshaw, P.R. "User Acceptance of Computer Technology: A Comparison of Two Theoretical Models," *Management Science* (35:8), 1989, pp. 892-1003.

Davis, G.B. and Olson, M.H. *Management Information Systems Conceptual Foundations, Structure, and Development*, McGraw-Hill Series in Management Information Systems, New York et al., 1985.

De Looff, L.A. "Information Systems Outsourcing Decision Making: A Framework, Organizational Theories and Case Studies," *Journal of Information Technology* (10), 1995, pp. 281-297.

De Marco, T. and Lister, T. *Peopleware*, Dorset House Publishing, New York, 1987.

Deci, E.L., Koestner, R. and Ryan, M. "A Meta-analytic Review of Experiments examining the Effects of Extrinsic Rewards on Intrinsic Motivation," *Psychological Bulletin* (125), 1999, pp. 627-668.

Demsetz, H. "Toward a Theory of Property Rights," *American Economic Review* (LVII:May), 1967, pp. 347-359.

Demsetz, H. "The Theory of the Firm Revisited," *Journal of Law, Economics and Organization* (4), 1988, pp. 141-161.

Demsetz, H. "The Theory of the Firm Revisited," in *The Nature of the Firm – Origins, Evolutions, and Development*, O. E. Williamson and S. G. Winter (Eds.), New York, Oxford, 1991, pp. 159-178.

Dibbern, J., Brehm, L. and Heinzl, A. "Rethinking ERP-Outsourcing Decisions for Leveraging Technological and Preserving Business Knowledge," *Proceedings of the 35th Annual Hawai'i International Conference on System Sciences*, Big Island, Hawaii, 2002.

Dibbern, J., Goles, T., Hirschheim, R.A. and Jayatilaka, B. "Information Systems Outsourcing: A Survey and Analysis of the Literature," *The DATA BASE for Advances in Information Systems* (forthcoming), 2004.

Dibbern, J., Güttler, W. and Heinzl, A. "Die Theorie der Unternehmung als Erklärungsansatz für das selektive Outsourcing der Informationsverarbeitung," *Zeitschrift für Betriebswirtschaft (ZfB)* (71:6), 2001, pp. 675-699.

Dibbern, J. and Heinzl, A. "Outsourcing der Informationsverarbeitung in mittelständischen Unternehmen: Teil 1: Eine deskriptive Studie," *BF/M Spiegel* (2), 1999, pp. 6-8.

Dibbern, J. and Heinzl, A. "Outsourcing der Informationsverarbeitung im Mittelstand: Test eines multitheoretischen Kausalmodells," *WIRTSCHAFTSINFORMATIK* (43:4), 2001, pp. 339-350.

Dibbern, J. and Heinzl, A. "Outsourcing of Information Systems in Small and Medium Sized Enterprises: A Test of Multi-Theoretical Model," in *Information Systems Outsourcing: Enduring Themes, Emergent Patterns and Future Directions*, R. A. Hirschheim, A. Heinzl and J. Dibbern (Eds.), Springer-Verlag, Berlin et al., 2002, pp. 77-99.

Dibbern, J., Heinzl, A. and Leibbrandt, S. "Interpretation des Souricng der Informationsverarbeitung: Hintergründe und Grenzen ökonomischer Einflussgrössen," *WIRTSCHAFTSINFORMATIK* 45(5), 2003b, pp. 533-540.

Dickson, P.H. and Weaver, K.M. "Environmental determinants and individual-level moderators of alliance use," *Academy of Management Journal* (40:2), 1997, pp. 404-425.

Dierickx, I., Cool, K. and Barney, J.B. Eds."Asset Stock Accumulation and Sustainability of Competitive Advantage; Comment; Reply," *Management Science* (35:12), 1989, pp. 1504-1514.

Dillman, D.A. *Mail and Telephone Surveys: The Total Design Method*, John Wiley & Sons, New York, 1978.

Dillman, D.A. *Mail and Telephone Surveys: The Tailored Design Method*, John Wiley & Sons, New York, 2000.

Dillman, D.A., Sinclair, M.D. and Clark, J.R. "Effects of Questionnaire Length, Respondent-Friendly Design, and a Difficult Question on Response Rates for Occupant-Addresses Census Mail Surveys," *Public Opinion Quarterly* (57), 1993, pp. 289-304.

Dillmann, L. "Die zunehmende Fremdvergabe pharmazeutischer Produktionsentwicklungsaufgaben an Contract Research Organizations," *Schmalenbachs Zeitschrift für betriebswirtschaftliche Forschung* (49), 1997, pp. 1047-1065.

DiMaggio, P.J. and Powell, W.W. "The Iron Cage Revised: Institutional Isomorphism and Collective Rationality in Organizational Fields," *American Sociological Review* (48:April), 1983, pp. 147-160.

DiRomualdo, A. and Gurbaxani, V. "Strategic Intent for IT Outsourcing," *Sloan Management Review* (Summer), 1998, pp. 67-80.

Dishaw, M.T. and Strong, D.M. "Supporting Software Maintenance With Software Engineering Tools: A Computer Task-Technology Fit Analysis," *The Journal of Systems and Software* (44), 1998, pp. 107-120.

Doney, P.M., Cannon, J.P. and Mullen, M.R. "Understanding the Influence of National Culture on the Development of Trust," *Academy of Management Review* (23:3), 1998, pp. 601-620.

Dowes, G.W. and Mohr, L.B. "Towards a Theory of Innovation," *Administration and Society* (10:4), 1979, pp. 379-408.

Dubin, R. "Theory Building in Applied Areas," in *Handbook of Industrial and Organizational Psychology*, M. D. Dunette (Ed.), Chicago, 1976, pp. 17-40.

Duncan, N.B. "Beyond Opportunism: A Resource-based View of Outsourcing Risk," *Proceedings of the 31st Annual Hawaii International Conference on System Sciences*, 1998, pp. 675-684.

Earl, M.J. "The Risks of Outsourcing IT," *Sloan Management Review* (37:3), 1996, pp. 26-32.

Earley, P.C. "East meets West meets Mideast: Further explorations of collectivistic and individualistic work groups," *Academy of Management Journal* (36:2), 1993, pp. 319-348.

Earley, P.C. and Gibson, C.B. "Taking Stock in Our Progress on Individualism-Collectivism: 100 Years of Solidarity and Community," *Journal of Management* (24:3), 1998, pp. 265-304.

Eisenberger, R. and Cameron, J. "Determinantal Effects of Reward: Reality or Myths?," *American Psychologist* (51), 1996, pp. 1153-1166.

Elfron, B. and Tibshirani, R.J. *An Introduction to the Bootstrap*, Series: Monographs on Statistics and Applied Probability, No. 57, Chapman & Hill, New York, 1993.

Elitzur, R. and Wensley, A. "Game Theory as a Tool for Understanding Information Services Outsourcing," *Journal of Information Technology* (12), 1997, pp. 45-60.

Emerson, R.M. "Power-Dependence Relations," *American Sociological Review* (27), 1962, pp. 31-41.

England, G.W. "Japanese and American Management: Theory Z and Beyond," *Journal of International Business Studies* (14), 1983, pp. 131-141.

Fichman, R.G. "Information Technology Diffusion: A Review of Empirical Research," *Proceedings of the 13th International Conference of Information Systems*, Dallas, TX, 1992, pp. 195-206.

Fichman, R.G. "The Diffusion and Assimilation of Information Technology Innovations," in *Framing the Domain of IT Management: Projecting the Future ... Through the Past*, R. W. Zmud (Ed.), Pinnaflex, Cincinnati, Ohio, 2000, pp. 105-127.

Fishbein, M. and Ajzen, I. *Belief, Attitude, Intention and Behavior: An Introduction to Theory and Research*, Addison-Wesley, Reading, Mass., 1975.

Fornell, C. "The Blending of Theoretical Empirical Knowledge in Structural Equations with Unobservables," in *Theoretical Empiricism: A General Rationale for Scientific Model-Building*, H. Wold (Ed.), Paragon House, New York, 1989, pp. 153-174.

Foss, N.J. "Theories of the Firm: Contractual and Competence Perspectives," *Journal of Evolutionary Economics* (3), 1993, pp. 127-144.

Foss, N.J. "'Coase vs Hayek': Authority and Firm Boundaries in the Knowledge Economy," *63. Tagung des Verbandes für Hochschullehrer*, Freiburg, 2000.

Foss, N.J., Knudsen, C. and Montgomery, C.A. "An Exploration of Common Ground: Integrating Evolutionary and Strategic Theories of the Firm," in *Resource-based and evolutionary theories of the firm: towards a synthesis*, C. A. Montgomery (Ed.), Kluwer Academic Publishers, Norwell, Massachusetts, 1995, pp. 1-17.

Fowler, A. and Jeffs, B. "Examining Information Systems Outsourcing: A Case Study from the United Kingdom," *Journal of Information Technology* (13), 1998, pp. 111-126.

Frey, B.S. and Osterloh, M. "Sanktionen oder Seelenmassage? Motivationale Grundlagen der Unternehmensführung," *DBW* (57:3), 1997, pp. 307-321.

Friedewald, M., Rombach, H.D., Stahl, P., Broy, M., Hartkopf, S., Kimpeler, S., Kohler, K., Wucher, R. and Zoche, P. "Softwareentwicklung in Deutschland: Eine Bestandsaufnahme," *Informatik Spektrum* (24:2), 2001, pp. 81-90.

Fudenberg, D. and Tirole, J. "Noncooperative Game Theory for Industrial Organization," in *Handbook of Industrial Organizations*, R. Schmalensee and R. D. Willig (Eds.), Vol.1, New York, Oxford, Tokyo, 1990, pp. 259-327.

Galliers, R. "Choosing Information Systems Research Approaches," in *Information Systems Research: Contemporary Approaches and Emergent Traditions*, H. E. Nissen, H. K. Klein and R. A. Hirschheim (Eds.), North-Holland, Amsterdam, 1991, pp. 327-345.

Ghoshal, S. and Insead, P.M. "Bad for Practice: A Critique of the Transaction Cost Theory," *Academy of Management Review* (21:1), 1996, pp. 13-47.

Glazer, R. "Measuring the Value of Information: The Information-Intensive Organization," *IBM Systems Journal* (32:1), 1993, pp. 99-110.

Goles, T. "The Impact of the Client/Vendor Relationship on Outsourcing Success," Dissertation, University of Houston, Department of Decision and Information Sciences, 2001.

Goles, T. and Chin, W.W. "Relational Exchange Theory and IS Outsourcing: Developing a Scale to Measure Relationship Factors," in *Information Systems Outsourcing*, R. A. Hirschheim, A. Heinzl and J. Dibbern (Eds.), Springer-Verlag, Berlin et al., 2002, pp. 221-250.

Gomez, C., Kirkman, B., L. and Shapiro, D., L. "The Impact of Collectivism and In-Group/ Out-Group Membership on the Evaluation Generosity of Team Members," *Academy of Management Journal* (43:6), 2000, pp. 1097-1106.

Goo, J., Kishore, R. and Rao, H.R. "A Content-Analytic Longitudinal Study of the Drivers for Information Technology and Systems Outsourcing," *Proceedings of the 21st International Conference on Information Systems*, Brisbaine, Australia, 2000, pp. 601-611.

Goodhue, D.L. and Thompson, R.L. "Task-Technology Fit and Individual Performance," *MIS Quarterly* (19:2), 1995, pp. 213-236.

Ghoshal, S. and Moran, P. "Bad for Practice: A Critique of the Transaction Cost Theory," *Academy of Management Review* (21:1), 1996, pp. 13-47.

Grant, R.M. "The Resource-Based Theory of Competitive Advantage: Implications for Strategy Formulation," *California Management Review* (33:3), 1991, pp. 114-135.

Grill, W. and Perczynski, H. *Wirtschaftslehre des Kreditwesens*, Verlag Dr. May Gehlen, Bad Homburg, 1992.

Groenewegen, J. and Vromen, J.J. "A Case for Theoretical Pluralism," in *Transaction Cost Economics and Beyond*, J. Groenewegen (Ed.), Kluwer Academic Publishers, Boston, Dordrecht, London, 1996, pp. 365-380.

Grossmann, S. and Hart, O. "The Costs and Benefits of Ownership: A Theory of Vertical and Lateral Integration," *Journal of Political Economy* (94), 1986, pp. 671-719.

Grover, V., Cheon, M.J. and Teng, J.T.C. "A Descriptive Study on the Outsourcing of Information Systems Functions," *Information & Management* (27:1), 1994a, pp. 33-44.

Grover, V., Cheon, M.J. and Teng, J.T.C. "An Evaluation of the Impact of Corporate Strategy and the Role of Information Technology on IS Functional Outsourcing," *European Journal of Information Systems* (3:3), 1994b, pp. 179-190.

Grover, V., Cheon, M.J. and Teng, J.T.C. "The Effect of Service Quality and Partnership on the Outsourcing of Information Systems Functions," *Journal of Management Information Systems* (12:4), 1996, pp. 89-116.

Gutenberg, E. *Die Unternehmung als Gegenstand betriebswirtschaftlicher Theorie*, Berlin et al., 1929.

Gutenberg, E. *Grundlagen der Betriebswirtschaftslehre: Die Produktion*, 1st edition 1951; 24th edition 1983, Berlin et al., 1951/1983.

Gutenberg, E. *Grundlagen der Betriebswirtschaftslehre: Der Absatz*, 1st edition 1955; 17th edition 1984, Berlin et al., 1955/1984.

Gutenberg, E. *Grundlagen der Betriebswirtschaftslehre: Die Finanzen*, 1st edition 1969; 8th edition 1980, Berlin et al., 1969/1980.

Güth, W. and Kliemt, H. "Intrinsische Motivation: Ausnahme oder Regel?," *DBW* (57), 1997, pp. 585-586.

Haire, M., Ghiselli, E.E. and Porter, L.W. "Cultural Patterns in the Role of the Manager," *Industrial Relations* (2), 1963, pp. 95-117.

Haire, M., Ghiselli, E.E. and Porter, L.W. *Managerial Thinking: An International Study*, John Wiley & Sons, New York, 1966.

Hall, R. "A Framework Linking Intangible Resources and Capabilities to Sustained Competitive Advantage," *Strategic Management Journal* (14:8), 1993, pp. 607-618.

Hammes, M. and Poser, G. "Die Messung von Transaktionskosten," *Das Wirtschaftsstudium* (11), 1992, pp. 885-889.

Hampden-Turner, C. and Trompenaars, A. *The Seven Cultures of Capitalism: Value Systems for Creating Wealth in the United States, Japan, Germany, France, Britain, Sweden, and the Netherlands*, Doubleday, New York u. a., 1993.

Hancox, M. and Hackney, R. "Information Technology Outsourcing: Conceptualizing Practice in the Public and Private Sector," *Proceedings of the 32nd Annual Hawaii International Conference on System Sciences*, 1999.

Harrison, D.A., Mykytyn, P.P. and Riemenschneider, C.K. "Executive Decision About Adoption of Information Technology in Small Business: Theory and Empirical Tests," *Information Systems Research* (8:2), 1997, pp. 171-195.

Hart, O. "An Economist's View of Authority," *Rationality and Society* (8), 1996, pp. 371-386.

Hart, O. and Moore, J. "Property Rights and the Nature of the Firm," *Journal of Political Economy* (98), 1990, pp. 1119-1158.

Harzing, A.-W. "Cross-National Industrial Mail Surveys: Why Do Response Rates Differ Between Countries?," *Industrial Marketing Management* (29:243-254), 2000.

Hayek, F.A. "The Use of Knowledge in Society," *American Economic Review* (35), 1945, pp. 519-530.

Hayek, F.A. "Individualism: True and False," in *The Essence of Hayek*, C. Nishiyama and K. R. Leube (Eds.), Hoover Institution Press, Stanford, California, 1948, pp. 131-159.

Heberlein, T.A. and Baumgartner, R. "Factors Affecting Response Rates to Mailed Questionnaires: A Quantitative Analysis of the Published Literature," *American Sociological Review* (43), 1978, pp. 447-462.

Heide, J.B. and John, G. "Alliances in Industrial Purchasing: The Determinants of Joint Action in Buyer-Supplier Relationships," *Journal of Marketing Research* (27:1), 1990, pp. 24-36.

Heide, J.B. and Stump, R.L. "Performance implications of buyer-supplier relationships in industrial markets: A transaction cost explanation," *Journal of Business Research* (32:1), 1995, pp. 57-66.

Heinrich, L.J. "Zur Frage "Eigenfertigung oder Fremdbezug" bei der Informationsverarbeitung," *Schmalenbachs Zeitschrift für betriebswirtschaftliche Forschung* (10/11), 1969, pp. 676-688.

Heinrich, L.J. *Systemplanung: Planung und Realisierung von Informatik-Projekten*, R. Oldenbourg Verlag, München, Wien, 1996.

Heinrich, L.J. *Informationsmanagement – Planung, Überwachung und Steuerung der Informationsinfrastruktur*, München, Wien, 1998.

Heinzl, A. "Die Ausgliederung der betrieblichen Datenverarbeitung," *Information Management* (4), 1992, pp. 28-40.

Heinzl, A. *Die Ausgliederung der betrieblichen Datenverarbeitung: eine empirische Analyse der Motive, Formen und Wirkungen*, Poeschel, Stuttgart, 1993a.

Heinzl, A. "Outsourcing the Information Systems Function Within the Company: An Empirical Survey," *International Conference of Outsourcing of Information Services*, University of Twente, The Netherlands, 1993b.

Heinzl, A. *Die Evolution der betrieblichen DV-Abteilung: eine lebenszyklustheoretische Analyse*, Physica, Heidelberg, 1996.

Heinzl, A. and Sinß, M. "Kooperationen zur zwischenbetrieblichen Entwicklung von Anwendungssystemen," *Information Management* (2), 1993, pp. 60-67.

Heinzl, A. and Stoffel, K. "Formen, Motive und Risiken der Auslagerung der betrieblichen Datenverarbeitung," *DV-Management* (4), 1991, pp. 161-173.

Heinzl, A. and Uhrig, M. "DV-Management durch externe Dienstleistungsanbieter: Zur Notwendigkeit von Informatikpartnern," *DV-Management* (4), 1991, pp. 190-199.

Heinzl, A. and Weber, J. *Alternative Organisationskonzepte der betrieblichen Datenverarbeitung*, Poeschel, Stuttgart, 1993.

Heisekanen, A., Newman, M. and Similä, J. "Software Contracting: A Process Model Approach," *International Conference on Information Systems*, 1996, pp. 51-62.

Heller, F.A., Wilpert, B., Docherty, P., Fourcade, J.M., Fokking, P., Mays, R., Roig, B., Weinshall, T. and Hooft, W. *Competence and Power in Managerial Decision-Making: A Study of Senior Levels of Organization in Eight Countries*, Wiley, New York, 1981.

Henderson, J. and Venkatraman, N. "Strategic Alignment: Leveraging Information Technology for Transforming Organizations," *IBM Systems Journal* (32:1), 1993, pp. 4-16.

Hickson, D., Hinigs, C.R., Lee, C.A., Schneck, R.E. and Pennings, J.M. "A Strategic Contingencies Theory of Intraorganizational Power," *Administrative Science Quarterly* (16:June), 1971, pp. 216-279.

Hildebrandt, L. and Homburg, C. "Editorial Preface," in *Die Kausalanalyse*, Schäffer-Poeschel Verlag, Stuttgart, 1998, pp. 5-6.

Hill, C.W.L. *International Business: Competing in the Global Market*, Irwin, Chicago, 1997.

Hill, C.W.L. "Cooperation, Opportunism, and the Invisible Hand: Implications for Transaction Cost Theory," *Academy of Management Review* (15:3), 1990, pp. 500-513.

Hirschheim, R., Klein, H.K. and Newman, M. "Information Systems Development as Social Action: Theoretical Perspective and Practice," *Omega, International Journal of Management Sciences* (19), 1991, pp. 587-608.

Hirschheim, R.A. "Backsourcing: An Emerging Trend?," Infoserver, http://www.infoserver.com/sep1998/html/academic.html, Access, 1998, Last Update September 1998.

Hirschheim, R.A. "Perspectives on Information Systems Outsourcing," *WIRTSCHAFTSINFORMATIK* (45:2), 2003, pp. 111-114.

Hirschheim, R.A. and Dibbern, J. "Information Systems Outsourcing: An Introduction," in *Information Systems Outsourcing: Enduring Themes, Emergent Patterns and Future Directions*, R. A. Hirschheim, A. Heinzl and J. Dibbern (Eds.), Springer-Verlag, Berlin et al., 2002, pp. 3-23.

Hirschheim, R.A., Klein, H.K. and Lyytinen, K. "Exploring the Intellectual Structures of Information Systems Development: A Social Action Theoretic Analysis," *Accounting, Management and Information Technologies* (6:1/2), 1996, pp. 1-64.

Hirschheim, R.A. and Lacity, M.C. "Reducing Information Systems Costs through Insourcing: Experiences from the Field," *Proceedings of the 31st Annual Hawaii International Conference on System Sciences*, Hawaii, 1998, pp. 644-653.

Hirschheim, R.A. and Lacity, M.C. "The Myths and Realities of Information Technology Insourcing," *Communications of the ACM* (43:2), 2000, pp. 99-107.

Hirschheim, R.A. and Lacity, M.C. "Four Stories of Informations Systems Insourcing," in *Information Systems Outsourcing: Enduring Themes, Emergent Patterns and Future Directions*, R. A. Hirschheim, A. Heinzl and J. Dibbern (Eds.), Springer-Verlag, Berlin et al., 2002, pp. 348-392.

Hodgson, G.M. "Corporate Culture and the Nature of the Firm," in *Transaction Cost Economics and Beyond*, J. Groenewegen (Ed.), Kluwer Academics Publications, Boston, Dordrecht, London, 1996, pp. 249-270.

Hofstede, G.H. *Culture's Consequences, International Differences in Work-Related Values*, Sage Publications, Beverly Hills, 1980.

Hofstede, G.H. "National Culture in Four Dimensions," *International Studies of Management and Organization* (13:2), 1983a, pp. 46-74.

Hofstede, G.H. "National Cultures in Four Dimensions," *International Studies of Management and Organization* (13), 1983b, pp. 75-89.

Hofstede, G.H. "The Cultural Relativity of Organizational Practices and Theories," *Journal of International Business Studies* (Fall 1983), 1983c, pp. 75-89.

Hofstede, G.H. *Cultures and Organizations: Software of the Mind*, McGraw-Hill, London et al., 1991.

Hofstede, G.H. "Cultural Constraints in Management Theories," *Academy of Management Executive* (7), 1993, pp. 81-94.

Hofstede, G.H. "Management Scientists are Human," *Management Science* (40:1), 1994, pp. 4-13.

Hofstede, G.H. and Bond, M.H. "The Confusian Connection: From Cultural Roots to Economic Growth," *Organizational Dynamics*), 1988, pp. 5-21.

Hofstede, G.H., Neuijen, B., Ohayv, D.D. and Sanders, G. "Measuring Organizational Cultures: A Qualitative and Quantitative Study Across Twenty Cases," *Administrative Science Quarterly* (35:2), 1990, pp. 286-316.

Holmstrom, B. "The Firm as a Subeconomy," *Journal of Law, Economics and Organization* (15), 1999, pp. 74-102.

Holmstrom, B. and Roberts, J. "The Boundaries of the Firm Revisited," *Journal of Economic Perspectives* (12), 1998, pp. 73-94.

Holmstrom, B. and Tirole, J. "The Theory of the Firm," in *Handbook of Industrial Organization*, R. Schmalensee and R. D. Willig (Eds.), North-Holland, Amsterdam, 1989, pp. 61-133.

Homburg, C. and Baumgartner, H. "Beurteilug von Kausalmodellen: Bestandsaufnahme und Anwendungsfelder," *Marketing ZFP* (17:3), 1985, pp. 162-176.

Homburg, C. and Dobratz, A. "Iterative Modellselektion in der Kausalanalyse," *Zeitschrift für betriebswirtschaftliche Forschung* (43:3), 1991, pp. 213-237.

Homburg, C. and Dobratz, A. "Covariance Structure Analysis via Specification Searches," *Statistical Papers* (32:2), 1992, pp. 119-142.

Homburg, C. and Giering, A. "Konzeptualisierung und Operationalisierung komplexer Konstrukte – Ein Leitfaden für die Marketingforschung," *Marketing ZFP* (18:1), 1996, pp. 5-24.

Hu, Q., Saunders, C. and Gebelt, M. "Research Report: Diffusion of Information Systems Outsourcing: A Reevaluation of Influence Sources," *Information Systems Research* (8:3), 1997, pp. 288-301.

Huber, R.L. "How Continental Bank Outsourced its 'Crown Jewels'," *Harvard Business Review* (71:1), 1993, pp. 121-129.

Hui, C.H. and Triandis, H.C. "Individualism-collectivism: A Study of Cross-Cultural Research," *Journal of Cross-Cultural Psychology* (17), 1986, pp. 222-248.

Hui, C.H., Yee, C. and Eastman, K.L. "The Relationship between Individualism-Collectivism and Job Satisfaction," *Applied Psychology: An International Review* (44), 1995, pp. 276-282.

IDC "European Outsourcing Markets and Trends, 1996-2002," by M. Lucacs, No. P04E, International Data Corporation, 1998.

IDC "U.S. and Worldwide Outsourcing Markets and Trends, 1998-2003," by C. Murphy, S. Ker and S. Chen, No. 19322, International Data Corporation, 1999.

Igbaria, M., Guimaraes, T. and Davis, G.B. "Testing the determinants of microcomputer usage via a structural equation model," *Journal of Management Information Systems* (11:4), 1995, pp. 87-114.

Iivari, J. and Hirschheim, R. "Analyzing Information Systems Development: A Comparison and Analysis of eight IS Development Approaches," *Information Systems* (21:7), 1996, pp. 551-575.

Iivari, J., Hirschheim, R. and Klein, H.K. "Towards More Professional Information Systems Development: ISD AS Knowledge Work," *Proceedings of the 9th European Conference on Information Systems*, Bled, Slovenia, 2001.

Ives, B. and Learmonth, G.P. "The Information System as a Competitive Weapon," *Communications of the ACM* (27:12), 1984, pp. 1193-1201.

Jaccard, J. and Wan, C.K. *LISREL Approaches to Interaction Effects in Multiple Regression*, Series: Quantitative Applications in the Social Sciences, Sage Publications, Thousands Oaks et al., 1996.

Jensen, M.C. and Meckling, W.H. "Theory of the Firm: Managerial Behavior, Agency Costs and Ownership Structure," *Journal of Financial Economics* (3), 1976, pp. 305-360.

Jensen, O. *Key-Account-Management: Gestaltung – Determinanten – Erfolgsauswirkungen*, Deutscher Universitäts-Verlag, Wiesbaden, 2001.

Jöreskog, K.G. *LISREL 8 – User's Reference Guide*, Chicago, 1993.

Joshi, A.W. and Stump, R.L. "The Contingent Effect of Specific Investments on Joint Action in Manufacturer-Supplier Relationships: An Empirical Test of the Moderating Role of Reciprocal Asset Investments, Uncertainty, and Trust," *Journal of the Academy of Marketing Science* (27:3), 1999, pp. 291-305.

Jurison, J. "The Role of Risk and Return in Information Technology Outsourcing Decisions," *Journal of Information Technology* (10), 1995, pp. 239-247.

Kaas, K. "Marketing und neue Institutionenlehre," Arbeitspapier 1, Forschungsprojekt Marketing und ökonomische Theorie, Frankfurt am Main, 1992.

Keen, P.G.W. "Transforming Intellectual Property into Intellectual Capital: Competing in the Trust Economy," in *Capital For Our Time: The Economic, Legal and Management Challenges of Intellectual Capital*, N. Imparato (Ed.), Hoover Institutions Press, Stanford, 1999, pp. 3-35.

Keller, E. *Management in Fremden Kulturen*, Haupt, Bern, Stuttgart, 1982.

Kern, T. "The Gestalt of an Information Technology Outsourcing Relationship: an Exploratory Analysis," *Proceedings of the 18th International Conference on Information Systems*, Atlanta, Georgia, 1997.

Kieser, A. "Organizational Culture," in *Handbook of German Business Management*, E. Grochla and E. Gaugler (Eds.), C. E. Poeschel Verlag, Stuttgart, 1990, pp. 1575-1581.

Kilmann, R.H. "The Costs of Organization Structure: Dispelling the Myths of Independent Divisions and Organization-Wide Decision Making," *Accounting, Organization and Society* (8:4), 1983, pp. 341-357.

King, J.L. "Centralized versus Decentralized Computing: Organizational Considerations and Management Options," *Computing Surveys* (15:4), 1983, pp. 319-349.

Kirkman, B., L. and Shapiro, D., L. "The Impact of Cultural Values on Job Satisfaction and Organizational Commitment in Self-Managing Work-Teams: The Mediating Role of Employee Resistance," *Academy of Management Journal* (44), 2001, pp. 557-569.

Kirsch, W. "Über den Sinn der empirischen Forschung in der angewandten Betriebswirtschaftslehre," in *Der praktische Nutzen der empirischen Forschung*, E. Witte (Ed.), Tübingen, 1981, pp. 189-226.

Klein, H.K. "On the Theoretical Foundations of Current Outsourcing Research," in *Information Systems Outsourcing: Enduring Themes, Emergent Patterns*, R. A. Hirschheim, A. Heinzl and J. Dibbern (Eds.), Springer, Berlin et al., 2002, pp. 24-44.

Klepper, R. "The Management of Partnering Development in I/S Outsourcing," *Journal of Information Technology* (10), 1995, pp. 249-258.

Knolmayer, G. "Der Fremdbezug von Information-Center-Leistungen," *Information Management* (1), 1994a, pp. 54-60.

Knolmayer, G. "Zur Berücksichtigung von Transaktions- und Koordinationskosten in Entscheidungsmodellen für Make-or-Buy-Probleme," *BFuP* (4), 1994b, pp. 316-331.

Knolmayer, G. "Cybermediaries Supporting the Management of Independent Workers: A Case Study of Extended Outsourcing Relationships," in *Information Systems Outsourcing: Enduring Themes, Emergent Patterns and Future Directions*, R. A. Hirschheim, A. Heinzl and J. Dibbern (Eds.), Springer-Verlag, Berlin et al., 2002, pp. 432-448.

Knudsen, C. "Theories of the Firm, Strategic Management, and Leadership," in *Resource-Based and Evolutionary Theories of the Firm: Towards a Synthesis*, C. A. Montgomery (Ed.), Boston, Dordrecht, London, 1995, pp. 179-217.

Koffka, N. "Arbeitsrecht," in *Outsourcing in Banken und Sparkassen: Strategien, Rechtsgrundlagen, Praxisbeispiele*, D. Sparkassenverlag (Ed.), Deutscher Sparkassen Verlag, Stuttgart, 1997, pp. 121-152.

Kosiol, E. *Grundlagen und Methode der Organisationsforschung*, Duncker & Humblot, Berlin, 1959.

Krcmar, H. *Informationsmanagement*, Springer, Berlin u. a., 1997.

Krcmar, H.C. "Einige Anmerkungen zu 'Von Leitbildern, Moden und Langfristzielen der Wirtschaftsinformatik' von Prof. Dr. Arno Rolf," *WIRTSCHAFTSINFORMATIK* (41:2), 1999, pp. 186-187.

Kreps, D., Wilson, R., Milgrom, P. and Robertsm, J. "Rational Cooperation in the Finitely Repeated Prisoner's Dilemma," *Journal of Economic Theory* (27), 1982, pp. 245-252.

Krieger, D.J. *Einführung in die Allgemeine Systemtheorie*, München, 1996.

Kroeber, A.L. and Kluckhohn, C. *Culture – A Critical Review of concepts and Definitions*, Vintage Books – A Division of Random House (originally published in 1952 as Vl XLVII–No. 1 of the Papers of the Peabody Museum of American Archaeology and Ethnology, Harvard University), New York, 1963.

Krogstie, J. "On the Distinction between Functional Development and Maintenance," *Software Maintenance: Research and Practice* (7:6), 1995, pp. 383-403.

Kubitschek, C. and Meckl, R. "Die ökonomischen Aspekte des Wissensmanagements – Anreize und Instrumente zur Entwicklung und Offenlegung von Wissen," *Zeitschrift für betriebswirtschaftliche Forschung* (52:Dezember), 2000, pp. 742-761.

Kuchinke, P.K. "Leadership and Culture: Work-Related Values and Leadership Styles Among One Company's U.S. and German Telecommunication Employees," *Human Resource Development Quarterly* (10:2), 1999, pp. 135-154.

Lacity, M.C. and Hirschheim, R.A. *Information Systems Outsourcing: Myths, Metaphors, and Realities*, Wiley, Chichester, New York, 1993a.

Lacity, M.C. and Hirschheim, R.A. "The Information Systems Outsourcing Bandwagon," *Sloan Management Review* (35:1), 1993b, pp. 73-86.

Lacity, M.C. and Hirschheim, R.A. *Beyond the information systems outsourcing bandwagon: the insourcing response*, Wiley, Chichester; New York, 1995.

Lacity, M.C., Hirschheim, R.A. and Willcocks, L.P. "Realizing Outsourcing Expectations: Incredible Promise, Credible Outcomes," *Journal of Information Systems Management* (11:4), 1994, pp. 7-18.

Lacity, M.C. and Willcocks, L. "IT Sourcing Reflections: Lessons for Customers and Suppliers," *WIRTSCHAFTSINFORMATIK* (45:2), 2003, pp. 115-125.

Lacity, M.C. and Willcocks, L.P. "Interpreting Information Technology Sourcing Decisions from a Transaction Cost Perspective: Findings and Critique," *Accounting, Management and Information Technologies* (5:3/4), 1995, pp. 203-244.

Lacity, M.C. and Willcocks, L.P. "Information Systems Sourcing: Examining the Privatization Option in USA Public Administration," *Information Systems Journal* (7), 1997, pp. 83-108.

Lacity, M.C. and Willcocks, L.P. "An empirical investigation of information technology sourcing practices: Lessons from experience," *MIS Quarterly* (22:3), 1998, pp. 363-408.

Lacity, M.C., Willcocks, L.P. and Feeny, D.F. "IT Outsourcing: Maximize Flexibility and Control," *Harvard Business Review* (May-June), 1995, pp. 84-93.

Lacity, M.C., Willcocks, L.P. and Feeny, D.F. "The Value of Selective IT Sourcing," *Sloan Management Review* (37:3), 1996, pp. 13-25.

Landry, M. and Banville, C. "A Disciplined Metodological Pluralism for MIS Research," *Accounting, Management and Information Technologies* (2:2), 1992, pp. 77-97.

Langlois, R.N. "Capabilities and Coherence in Firms and Markets," in *Resource-Based and Evolutionary Theories of the Firm: Towards a Synthesis*, C. A. Montgomery (Ed.), Boston, Dordrecht, London, 1995, pp. 71-100.

Lassig, P., Lamberti, H.-J. and Jochum, C. "Scouring- und beidseitige Due-Diligence-Prozesse im Rahmen der Lieferantenauswahl beim Infrastrukturoutsourcing," *WIRTSCHAFTSINFORMATIK* (45:2), 2003, pp. 147-156.

Lee, A.S. "Integrating Positivist and Interpretive Approaches to Organizational Research," *Organization Science* (2:4), 1991, pp. 342-365.

Lee, A.S. "Researching MIS," in *Rethinking Management Information Systems: An Interdisciplinary Perspective*, W. L. Currie and B. Galliers (Eds.), Oxford University Press, New York, 1999a, pp. 7-27.

Lee, A.S. "Rigor and relevance in MIS research: Beyond the approach of positivism alone," *MIS Quarterly* (23:1), 1999b, pp. 29-33.

Lee, B., Barua, A. and Whinston, A.B. "Discovery and Representation of Causal Relationships in MIS Research: A Methodological Framework," *MIS Quarterly* (21:1), 1997, pp. 109-136.

Lee, J.-N., Huynh, M.Q., Chi-wai, K.R. and Pi, S.-M. "The Evolution of Outsourcing Research: What is the Next Issue?," *Proceedings of the 33rd Annual Hawaii International Conference on System Sciences*, 2000.

Lee, J.-N. and Kim, Y.-G. "Effect of Partnership Quality on IS Outsourcing Success: Conceptual Framework and Empirical Validation," *Journal of Management Information Systems* (15:4), 1999, pp. 29-61.

Loh, L. "An Organizational-Economic Blueprint for Information Technology Outsourcing: Concepts and Evidence," *Proceedings of the 15th International Conference on Information Systems*, Vancouver, Canada, 1994, pp. 73-89.

Loh, L. and Venkatraman, N. "Determinants of Information Technology Outsourcing: A Cross-Sectional Analysis," *Journal of Management Information Systems* (9:1), 1992a, pp. 7-24.

Loh, L. and Venkatraman, N. "Diffusion of Information Technology Outsourcing: Influence Sources and the Kodak Effect," *Information Systems Research* (3:4), 1992b, pp. 334-358.

Loh, L. and Venkatraman, N. "An Empirical Study of Information Technology Outsourcing: Benefits, Risks, and Performance Implications," *Proceedings of the 16th International Conference on Information Systems*, Amsterdam, The Netherlands, 1995, pp. 277-288.

Lohmöller, J.-B. *Latent Variable Path Modeling with Partial Least Squares*, Physica-Verlag, Heidelberg, 1989.

Luhmann, N. *Soziale Systeme*, Frankfurt am Main, 1994.

Lytle, A.L., Brett, J.M., Barsness, Z.I., Tinsley, C.H. and Maddy, J. "A Paradigm for Confirmatory Cross-Cultural Research in Organizational Behavior," in *Research in Organizational Behavior*, B. M. Staw and L. L. Cummings (Eds.), JAI Press, Vol. 17, Greenwich, CT, 1995, pp. 167-214.

Lyytinen, K. "Empirical research in information systems: On the relevance of practice in thinking of IS research," *MIS Quarterly* (23:1), 1999, pp. 25-27.

Lyytinen, K. and Hirschheim, R.A. "Information Systems Failures: A Survey and Classification of the Empirical Literature," *Oxford Surveys in Information Technology* (4), 1987, pp. 257-309.

Madden, T.J., Scholder Ellen, P. and Ajzen, I. "A Comparison of the Theory of Planned Behavior and the Theory of Reasoned Action," *Personality and Social Psychology Bulletin* (18:1), 1992, pp. 3-9.

Markus, M.L. and Robey, D. "Information Technology and Organizational Change: Causal Structure in Theory and Research," *Management Science* (34:5), 1988, pp. 583-598.

Markus, M.L. and Tanis, C. "The Enterprise Systems Experience – From Adoption to Success," in *Framing the Domains of IT Research: Glimpsing the Future Through the Past*, R. W. Zmud (Ed.), Pinnaflex Educational Resources, Inc., Cincinnati, OH, 2000, pp. 173-207.

Marshall, A. *Principles of Economics*, (New Ed., Macmillan, 1949), London, 1890.

Mason, E.S. *The Corporation in Modern Society*, Harvard University Press, Cambridge, MA, 1959.

Mason, R.O. and Mitroff, I.I. "A Program for Research on Management Information Systems," *Management Science* (19:5), 1973, pp. 475-487.

Mata, F.J., Fuerst, W.L. and Barney, J.B. "Information Technology and Sustained Competitive Advantage: A Resource-Based Analysis," *MIS Quarterly* (19:4), 1995, pp. 487-505.

Mathieson, K. "Predicting User Intentions: Comparing the Technology Acceptance Model with the Theory of Planned Behavior," *Information Systems Research* (2:3), 1991, pp. 173-191.

Matiaske, W. and Mellewigt, T. "Motive, Erfolge und Risiken des Outsourcings – Befunde und Defizite der empirischen Outsourcing-Forschung," *Zeitschrift für Betriebswirtschaft* (72:6), 2002, pp. 641-659.

McFarlan, F.W. "Information Technology Changes the Way You Compete," *Harvard Business Review* (May-June), 1985, pp. 98-103.

McFarlan, F.W. and McKenney, J. *Corporate Information Systems Management*, Richard D. Irwin, Homewood, IL, 1983.

McFarlan, F.W. and Nolan, R.L. "How to Manage an IT Outsourcing Alliance," *Sloan Management Review* (36:2), 1995, pp. 9-23.

McLellan, K.L., Marcolin, B.L. and Beamish, P.W. "Financial and Strategic Motivations Behind IS Outsourcing," *Journal of Information Technology* (10), 1995, pp. 299-321.

Mertens, P. *Integrierte Informationsverarbeitung 1: Administrations- und Dispositionssysteme in der Industrie*, Gabler Verlag, Wiesbaden, 1995.

Mertens, P. and Knolmayer, G. *Organisation der Informationsverarbeitung: Grundlagen – Aufbau – Arbeitsteilung*, Wiesbaden, 1998.

Mertens, P. and Lohmann, M. "Branche oder Betriebstyp als Klassifikationskriterien für die Standarsoftware der Zukunft?," Bayerischer Forschungsverbund Wirtschaftsinformatik (FORWIN), 2000.

Mertens, P. and Plattflaut, E. "Informationstechnik als strategische Waffe," *Information Management* (2), 1986, pp. 6-17.

Meyer, J.W. and Rowan, B. "Institutionalized Organizations; Formal Structures as Myth and Ceremony," *American Journal of Sociology* (83:2), 1977, pp. 340-363.

Milgrom, P. and Rorbertsm, J. "The Economics of Modern Manufacturing: Technology, Strategy and Organization," *The American Economic Review* (80:511-528), 1990.

Milgrom, P. and Rorbertsm, J. "Complimentarities and Fit: Strategy, Structure and Organizational Change in Manufacturing," *Journal of Accounting and Economics* (19), 1995, pp. 179-208.

Mintzberg, H., Raisinghani, D. and Theorèt, A. "The Structure of 'Unstructured' Decision Processes," *Administrative Science Quarterly* (21), 1976, pp. 246-275.

Mohr, L.B. *Explaining Organizational Behavior: The Limits and Possibilities of Theory and Research*, Jossey-Bass Publishers, San Francisco, Washington, London, 1982.

Mohr, L.B. *Understanding Significance Testing*, Series: Quantitative Applications in the Social Sciences, Sage Publications, Newbury Park, CA, 1991.

Montgomery, C.A. "Corporate Diversification," *Journal of Economic Perspectives* (8:3), 1994, pp. 163-178.

Moore, G.C. and Benbasat, I. "Development of an Instrument to Measure the Perceptions of Adopting an Information Technology Innovation," *Information Systems Research* (2:3), 1991, pp. 192-222.

Myers, M.D. and Tan, F.B. "Beyond Models of National Culture in Information Systems Research," *Journal of Global Information Management* (Jan-Mar), 2002, pp. 24-32.

Nahapiet, J. and Ghoshal, S. "Social Capital, Intellectual Capital, and the Organizational Advantage," *Academy of Management Review* (23:2), 1998, pp. 242-266.

Nam, K. "Three Essays on Information Systems Outsourcing," Ph. D. Dissertation, State University of New York at Buffalo, School of Management, 1995.

Nam, K., Rajagopalan, S., Rao, H.R. and Chaudhury, A. "A Two-Level Investigation of Information Systems Outsourcing," *Communications of the ACM* (39:7), 1996, pp. 36-44.

Nash, J.F. "The Bargaining Problem," *Econometrica* (18), 1950, pp. 155-162.

Nash, J.F. "Two-Person Cooperative Games," *Econometrica* (21), 1953, pp. 128-140.

Nelson, P., Richmond, W. and Seidmann, A. "Two dimensions of software acquisition," *Communications of the ACM* (39:7), 1996, pp. 29-35.

Nelson, R.R. "Educational Needs as Perceived by IS and End-User Personnel: A Survey of Knowledge and Skill Requirements," *MIS Quarterly* (15:4), 1991a, pp. 503-525.

Nelson, R.R. "Why Do Firms Differ, and How Does It Matter?," *Strategic Management Journal*), 1991b, pp. 61-74.

Nelson, R.R. and Winter, S.G. *An Evolutionary Theory of Economic Change*, Belknap Press of Harvard University Press, Cambridge, Mass., 1982.

Newman, M. and Robey, D. "A Social Process Model of User-Analyst Relationships," *MIS Quarterly* (16), 1992, pp. 249-266.

Nonaka, I. "Dynamic Theory of Organizational Knowledge Creation," *Organization Science* (5:1), 1994, pp. 14-37.

Noorderhaven, N.G. "Opportunism and Trust in Transaction Cost Economics," in *Transaction Cost Economics and Beyond*, J. Groenewegen (Ed.), Kluwer Academic Publishers, Boston, Dordrecht, London, 1996, pp. 105-128.

Noordewier, T.G., John, G. and Nevin, J.R. "Performance Outcomes of Purchasing Arrangements in Industrial Buyer-Vendor Relationships," *Journal of Marketing* (54:4), 1990, pp. 80-93.

Nygaard, K. "Program Development as a Social Activity," in *Information Processing 86, Proc. IFIP 10th World Computer Congress*, H.-J. Kugler (Ed.), Amsterdam, 1986, pp. 189-198.

OECD "Information Technolgy Outlook: 2000," Paris, 2000.

Oliver, C. "Strategic Responses to Institutional Processes," *Academy of Management Review* (16:1), 1991, pp. 145-179.

Olson, J.M. and Zana, M.P. "Attitudes and Attitud Change," *Annual Review of Psychology* (44), 1993, pp. 117-154.

Orlikowski, W.J. and Baroudi, J.J. "Studying Information Technology in Organizations: Research Approaches and Assumptions," *Information Systems Research* (2:1), 1991, pp. 1-28.

Osgood, C.E., Suci, G.J. and Tannenmann, P.H. *The Measurement of Meaning*, University of Ilinois Press, Urbana, IL, 1957.

Osterloh, M. and Frey, B.S. "Motivation, Knowledge Transfer, and Organizational Forms," *Organization Science* (11:5), 2000, pp. 538-550.

Ouchi, W. "Markets, Bureaucracies and Clans," *Administrative Science Quarterly* (25), 1980, pp. 129-142.

Palich, L.E., Hom, P.W. and Griffeth, R.W. "Managing in the International Context: Testing the Cultural Generality of Sources of Commitment to Multinational Enterprises," *Journal of Management* (21), 1995, pp. 671-690.

Palvia, P.C. "A Dialectic View of Information Systems Outsourcing: Pros and Cons," *Information & Management* (29), 1995, pp. 265-275.

Parson, T. and Shils, E.A. *Towards a General Theory of Action*, Harvard University Press, Cambridge, Mass., 1951.

Parsons, G.L. "Information Technology: A New Competitive Weapon," *Sloan Management Review* (25:1), 1984, pp. 3-14.

Pearce, J.L. "Toward an Organizational Behavior of Contract Laborers: Their Psychological Involvement and Effect on Employee Co-Workers," *Academy of Management Journal* (36:5), 1993, pp. 1082-1096.

Penrose, E.T. *The Theory of the Growth of the Firm*, Blackwell, New York, 1959.

Pereira, R.E. "Resource View Theory Analysis of SAP as a Source of Competitive Advantage," *The DATA BASE for Advances in Information Systems* (30:1), 1999, pp. 38-46.

Peter, J. "Reliability: A Review of Psychometric Basics and Recent Marketing Practices," *Journal of Marketing Research* (16:February), 1981, pp. 6-17.

Peter, J. and Churchill, G. "Relationships Among Research Design Choices and Psychometric Properties of Rating Scales: A Meta-Analysis," *Journal of Marketing Research* (23:February), 1986, pp. 1-10.

Pfeffer, J. *Power in Organizations*, Pitman Pub., Marshfield, Mass., 1981.

Pfeffer, J. and Salancik, G.R. *The External Control of Organizations: A Resource Dependence Perspective*, Harper & Row, New York, 1978.

Picot, A. "Transaktionskostentheorie der Organisation," *Beiträge zur Unternehmensführung und Organisation*, Universität Hannover, 1981.

Picot, A. "Transaktionskostenansatz in der Organisationstheorie: Stand der Diskussion und Aussagewert," *DBW* (42), 1992, pp. 267-284.

Picot, A. and Dietl, H. "Transaktionskostentheorie," *WiSt* (19), 1990, pp. 178-184.

Picot, A. and Maier, M. "Analyse- und Gestaltungskonzepte für das Outsourcing," *Information Management* (4), 1992, pp. 14-27.

Pinto, M.B., Pinto, J.K. and Prescott, J.E. "Antecedents and Consequences of Project Team Cross-functional Cooperation," *Management Science* (39:10), 1993, pp. 1281-1297.

Polanyi, M. *Personal Knowledge: Towards a Post-Critical Philosophy*, University of Chicago Press, Chicago, 1966 (1958).

Popper, K.R. *Logik der Forschung*, Mohr, Tübingen, 1994/1934.

Poppo, L. and Lacity, M.C. "The Normative Value of Transaction Cost Economics: What Managers Have Learned About TCE Principles in the IT Context," in *Information Systems Outsourcing: Emergent Themes, Enduring Patterns and Future Directions*, R. A. Hirschheim, A. Heinzl and J. Dibbern (Eds.), Springer-Verlag, Berlin et al., 2002, pp. 253-276.

Poppo, L. and Zenger, T. "Testing Alternative Theories of the Firm: Transaction Cost, Knowledge-Based, and Measurement Explanations for Make-or-Buy Decisions in Information Services," *Strategic Management Journal* (19), 1998, pp. 853-877.

Porter, M.E. *Competitive Strategy: Techniques for Analyzing Industries and Competitors*, Free Press, New York, 1980.

Porter, M.E. *Competitive Advantage: Creating and Sustaining Superior Performance*, Free Press; Collier Macmillan, New York, London, 1985.

Porter, M.E. and Millar, V. "How Information Gives You Competitive Advantage," *Harvard Business Review* (65:4), 1985, pp. 149-160.

Powell, T.C. and Dent-Micallef, A. "Information Technology as Competitive Advantage: The Role of Human, Business, and Technology Resources," *Strategic Management Journal* (18:5), 1997, pp. 375-405.

Pratkanis, A.R., Breckler, S.J. and Greenwald, A.G. *Attitude Structure and Function*, Lawrence Erlbaum, Hillsdale, New Jersey, 1989.

Prosser, A. "Kooperation in der Softwarebranche aus Sicht der Transaktionskostenökonomie," in *Wirtschaftsinformatik: Ergebnisse Empirischer Forschung*, O. Grün and L. Heinrich, J. (Eds.), Springer, Wien, New York, 1997, pp. 149-162.

Quinn, J.B. and Hilmer, F.G. "Strategic Outsourcing," *Sloan Management Review* (35:4), 1994, pp. 43-55.

Raghunathan, B., Raghunathan, T.S. and Tu, Q. "Dimensionality of the Strategic Grid Framework: The Construct and its Measurement," *Information Systems Research* (10:4), 1999, pp. 343-355.

Rapoport, A. *Allgemeine Systemtheorie*, Darmstadt, 1988.

Reponen, T. "Outsourcing or Insourcing?," *Proceedings of the 14 International Conference on Information Systems*, Orlando, Florida, 1993, pp. 103-113.

Richardi, R. "Labour Right," in *Handbook of German Business Management*, Vol. 2, C. E. Poeschel Verlag, Stuttgart, 1990, pp. 1278-1290.

Richter, R. and Bindseil, U. "Neue Institutionenökonomik," *WiSt* (3), 1995, pp. 132-140.

Rindfleisch, A. and Heide, J.B. "Transaction Cost Analysis: Past, Present, and Future Applications," *Journal of Marketing* (61:4), 1997, pp. 30-54.

Roberts, C. and Wasti, S.A. "Organizational Individualism and Collectivism: Theoretical Development and an Empirical Test of a Measure," *Journal of Management* (28:4), 2002, pp. 544-566.

Robey, D. and Newman, M. "Sequential Patterns in Information Systems Development: An Application of a Social Process Model," *ACM Transactions on Information Systems* (14:1), 1996, pp. 30-63.

Rogers, E.M. *Diffusion of Innovations*, The Free Press, New York, 1983.

Ross, J.W., Beath, C.M. and Goodhue, D.L. "Develop long-term competitiveness through IT assets," *Sloan Management Review* (38:1), 1996, pp. 31-42.

Rubenstein, A.A. and Haberstroh, C.J. *Some Theories of Organization*, Irwin, Homewood, IL, 1965.

Rumelt, R.P. "Towards a Strategic Theory of the Firm," in *Competitive Strategic Management*, B. Lamb (Ed.), Prentice Hall, Englewood Cliffs, NY, 1984, pp. 556-570.

Rumelt, R.P., Schendel, D. and Teece, D.J. "Strategic Management and Economics," *Strategic Management Journal* (12), 1991, pp. 5-29.

Sääksjärvi, M. "Success of Outsourcing and Strategic Alignment as Predictors of IS Effectiveness," in *Information Systems Outsourcing: Enduring Themes, Emergent Patterns and Future Directions*, R. A. Hirschheim, A. Heinzl and J. Dibbern (Eds.), Springer-Verlag, Berlin et al., 2002, pp. 311-328.

Sabherwal, R. "The Role of Trust in Outsourced IS Development Projects," *Communications of the ACM* (42:2), 1999.

Sambamurthy, V. "Business Strategy in Hypercompetitive Environments: Rethinking the Logic of IT Differentiation," in *Framing the Domain of IT Management: Projecting the Future ...Through the Past*, R. W. Zmud (Ed.), Pinnaflex, Cincinnati, Ohio, 2000, pp. 245-261.

Sauer, C. "Deciding the Future for IS Failures: Not the Choice You Might Think," in *Rethinking Management Information Systems: An Interdisciplinary Perspective*, W. J. Currie and B. Galliers (Eds.), Oxford University Press, New York, 1999, pp. 279-309.

Saunders, C., Gebelt, M. and Hu, Q. "Achieving Success in Information Systems Outsourcing," *California Management Review* (39:2), 1997, pp. 63-79.

Schmidt, F.A. and Seger, F. "Arbeitnehmermitbestimmung, Allokation von Entscheidungsrechten und Shareholder Value," *Zeitschrift für Betriebswirtschaft* (68), 1998, pp. 453-473.

Schmidt, R.H. "Erich Gutenberg and the Theory of the Firm," in *Theory of the Firm: Erich Gutenberg's Foundations and Further Developments*, H. Albach, K. K. L. Brockhoff, E. Eymann, P. Jungen, M. Steven and A. Luhmer (Eds.), Springer, Berlin et al., 2000, pp. 3-39.

Schneider, D. "Die Unhaltbarkeit des Transaktionskostenansatzes für die "Markt oder Unternehmung"-Diskussion," *Zeitschrift für Betriebswirtschaft* (55), 1985, pp. 1237-1254.

Schneider, D. "Unternehmerfunktion oder Transaktionskostenökonomie als Grundlage für die Erklärung von Institutionen?," *Zeitschrift für Betriebswirtschaft* (61), 1991, pp. 371-377.

Schneider, D. *Betriebswirtschaftslehre Band 1: Grundlagen*, Oldenbourg, München, Wien, 1995.

Schneider, D. *Betriebswirtschaftslehre, Band 3: Grundlagen*, Oldenbourg, München, Wien, 1997.

Schnell, R., Hill, P.B. and Esser, E. *Methoden der empirischen Sozialforschung*, München, Wien, 1995.

Schott, E. *Markt und Geschäftsbeziehung beim Outsourcing*, Deutscher Universitäts-Verlag, Wiesbaden, 1997.

Schumpeter, J.A. *The Theory of Economic Development*, Harvard University Press, Cambridge (1st edition in German in 1911), 1934.

Schumpeter, J.A. "How the Economic System Generates Evolution," in *Business Cycles*, McGraw-Hill, New York, London, 1939, pp. 59-86.

Schuster, B., Brandstätter, V. and Frey, D. "Wie das Schöne im Menschen bewahren – und dennoch durch Anreize motivitieren?," *DBW* (57:4), 1997, pp. 581-584.

Schwartz, S. "Individualism-collectivism: Critique and Proposed Refinements," *Journal of Cross-Cultural Psychology* (21), 1990, pp. 139-157.

Segars, A.H. and Grover, V. "Re-examining perceived ease of use and usefulness: A confirmatory factor analysis," *MIS Quarterly* (17:4), 1993, pp. 517-525.

Seth, A. and Thomas, H. "Theories of the Firm: Implications for Strategy Research," *Journal of Management Studies* (31:2), 1994, pp. 165-191.

Shelanski, H.A. and Klein, P.G. "Empirical Research in Transaction Cost Economics: A Review and Assessment," *Journal of Law, Economics, & Organization* (11:2), 1995, pp. 335-361.

Sieber, S. "The Integration of Fieldwork and Survey Methods," *American Journal of Sociology* (78), 1973, pp. 1335-1359.

Silverman, B.S. "Technological Resources and the Direction of Corporate Diversification: Toward an Integration of the Resource-Based View and Transaction Cost Economics," *Management Science* (45), 1999, pp. 1109-1124.

Simon, H.A. *Administrative behavior: a study of decision-making processes in administrative organization*, Macmillan, New York, 1947.

Simon, H.A. *Models of Man: Social and Rational*, Wiley, New York, 1957.

Simon, H.A. "Theories of Decision-Making in Economics and Behavioral Science," *American Economic Review* (49), 1959, pp. 253-283.

Simon, H.A. *The New Science of Management Decision*, Harper, New York, 1960.

Simon, H.A. *Administrative Behavior*, New York, London, 1965.

Slaughter, S.A. and Ang, S. "Employment Outsourcing in Information Systems," *Communications of the ACM* (39:7), 1996, pp. 47-54.

Smith, M.A., Mitra, S.A. and Narasimhan, S. "Information Systems Outsourcing: A Study of Pre-Event Firm Characteristics," *Journal of Management Information Systems* (15:2), 1998, pp. 61-93.

Sneed, H.M. *Software Management*, Verlagsgesellschaft Rudolf Müller GmbH, Köln, 1987.

Sobol, M.G. and Apte, U.M. "Domestic and Global Outsourcing Practices of America`s most Effective IS Users," *Journal of Information Technology* (10), 1995, pp. 269-280.

Spence, M. "Competitive and Optimal Responses To Signals," *Journal of Economic Theory* (7), 1976, pp. 298-315.

Spinner, H.F. *Pluralismus als Erkenntnismodell*, Suhrkamp Verlag, Frankfurt, 1974.

Sprott, D. "Componentizing the Enterprise Application Packages," *Communication of the ACM* (4), 2000, pp. 63-69.

Sridhar, S.S. and Balachandran, B.V. "Incomplete Information, Task Assignment, and Managerial Control Systems," *Management Science* (43:6), 1997, pp. 764-778.

Steinmann, H. "Zwei Anmerkungen zu den motivationalen Grundlagen der Unternehmensführung," *DBW* (57:4), 1997, pp. 587-590.

Straub, D.W., Limayem, M. and Karahanna-Evaristo, E. "Measuring System Usage: Implications for IS Theory Testing," *Management Science* (41:8), 1995, pp. 1328-1342.

Stünzner, L. *Systemtheorie und betriebswirtschaftliche Organisationsforschung*, Berlin, 1996.

Sutcliffe, K.M. and Zaheer, A. "Uncertainty in the transaction environment: An empirical test," *Strategic Management Journal* (19:1), 1998, pp. 1-23.

Sutton, R.I. and Staw, B.M. "What theory is not," *Administrative Science Quarterly* (40:3), 1995, pp. 371-384.

Swanson, E.B. "The Dimensions of Maintenance," *Proceedings of the 2nd International Conference on Software Engineering*, San Francisco, California, 1976, pp. 492-497.

Swanson, E.B. "IS 'Maintainability': Should it Reduce the Maintenance Effort?," *The DATA BASE for Advances in Information Systems* (30:1), 1999, pp. 65-76.

Swanson, E.B. and Beath, C.M. *Maintaining Information Systems in Organizations*, Wiley, Chichester, England, 1989.

Swanson, E.B. and Beath, C.M. "Departmentalization in Software Development and Maintenance," *Communications of the ACM* (33:6), 1990, pp. 658-667.

Taylor, S. and Todd, P.A. "Understanding information technology usage: A test of competing models," *Information Systems Research* (6:2), 1995, pp. 144-176.

Teng, J.T.C., Cheon, M.J. and Grover, V. "Decisions to Outsource Information Systems Functions: Testing a Strategy-Theoretic Discrepancy Model," *Decision Sciences* (26:1), 1995, pp. 75-103.

Thoma, M. and Zimmermann, M. "Zum Einfluß der Befragungstechnik auf den Rücklauf bei schriftlichen Umfragen – Experimentelle Befunde zur 'Total-Design-Methode'," *ZUMA-Nachrichten* (39:20), 1996, pp. 141-159.

Thomas, D.C. "Cultural Diversity and Work Group Effectiveness: An Experimental Study," *Journal of Cross-Cultural Psychology* (30), 1999, pp. 242-263.

Thompson, J.D. *Organizations in Action*, McGraw-Hill, New York, 1967.

Tietzel, M. "Die Ökonomie der Property Rights: Ein Überblick," *Zeitschrift für Wirtschaftspolitik* (30), 1981, pp. 207-243.

Todd, P.A. and Benbasat, I. "The Impact of Information Technology on Decision Making: A Cognitive Perspective," in *Framing the Domain of IT Management: Projecting the Future ...Through the Past*, R. W. Zmud (Ed.), Pinnaflex, Cincinnati, Ohio, 2000, pp. 1-14.

Triandis, H.C. "Dimensions of Cultural Variations as Parameters of Organizational Theories," *International Studies of Management and Organization* (12:4), 1982, pp. 139-169.

Triandis, H.C. *Individualism and Collectivism*, Westview, Boulder, CO, 1995.

Triandis, H.C., Bontempo, R., Betancourt, H., Bond, M.H., Leung, K., Brenes, A., Georgas, J., Hui, C.H., Martin, G., Setiadi, B., Sinha, J.B.P., Verma, J., Spangenberg, J., Touzard, H. and De Montmollin, G. "The Measurement of Ethic Aspects of Individualism and Collectivism Across Cultures," *Australian Journal of Psychology* (38), 1986, pp. 257-267.

Triandis, H.C., Bontempo, R., Villareal, M., Asai, M. and Lucca, N. "Individualism and Collectivism: Cross-Cultural Perspective on Self-ingroup Relationships," *Journal of Personality and Social Psychology* (54), 1988, pp. 323-338.

Trompenaars, A. and Hamden-Turner, C. *Riding the Waves of Culture: Understanding Diversity in Global Business*, Irwin Professional Pub., Burr Ridge, Ill., 1994.

Tsang, E.W.K. "Transaction Cost and Resource-based Explanations of Joint Ventures: A Comparison and Synthesis," *Organization Studies* (21:1), 2000, pp. 215-242.

Tushman, M. "A Political Approach to Organizations: A Review and Rationale," *Academy of Management Review* (2:2), 1977, pp. 206-216.

Van De Ven, A.H. "Nothing Is Quite So Practical as a Good Theory," *Academy of Management Review* (14:4), 1989, pp. 486-489.

Venkatraman, N. "Beyond Outsourcing: Managing IT Resources as a Value Center," *Sloan Management Review* (38:3), 1997, pp. 51-64.

Vitalari, N.P. "Knowledge as a Basis for Expertise in Systems Analysis: An Empirical Study," *MIS Quarterly* (9:3), 1985, pp. 221-241.

Voigtländer, D. "Industrialisierung im Bankgeschäft: Outsourcing und Standardsoftware," *WIRTSCHAFTSINFORMATIK* (45:2), 2003, pp. 143-146.

Wagner, J.A., III "Studies of Individualism-Collectivism: Effects on Cooperation in Groups," *Academy of Management Journal* (38:1), 1995, pp. 152-172.

Wagner, J.A., III and Moch, M.K. "Individualism-Collectivism: Concept and Measure," *Group and Organization Studies* (11), 1986, pp. 280-303.

Walker, G. and Poppo, L. "Profit Centers, Single-Source Suppliers, and Transaction Costs," *Administrative Science Quarterly* (36), 1991, pp. 66-87.

Walker, G. and Weber, D. "A Transaction Cost Approach to Make-or-Buy Decisions," *Administrative Science Quarterly* (29:September), 1984, pp. 373-391.

Walker, G. and Weber, D. "Supplier Competition, Uncertainty, and Make-or-Buy Decisions," *Academy of Management Journal* (30:3), 1987, pp. 589-596.

Wang, E.T.G., Barron, T. and Seidmann, A. "Contracting Structures for Custom Software Development: The Impacts of Informational Rents and Uncertainty on Internal Development and Outsourcing," *Management Science* (43:12), 1997, pp. 1726-1744.

Weber, M. *The Theory of Social and Economic Organization*, Free Press, Glencoe, Ill, 1947.

Wernerfelt, B. "A Resource-based View of the Firm," *Strategic Management Journal* (5), 1984, pp. 171-180.

Whang, S. "Contracting for Software Development," *Management Science* (38:3), 1992, pp. 307-324.

Willcocks, L.P. and Fitzgerald, G. "Market as opportunity? Case studies in outsourcing information technology and services," *Journal of Strategic Information Systems* (2:3), 1993, pp. 223-242.

Willcocks, L.P., Fitzgerald, G. and Feeny, D. "Outsourcing IT: The Strategic Implications," *Long Range Planning* (28:5), 1995a, pp. 59-70.

Willcocks, L.P., Fitzgerald, G. and Lacity, M.C. "To Outsource IT Or Not? Recent Research on Economics and Evaluation Practice," *European Journal of Information Systems* (5:3), 1996, pp. 143-160.

Willcocks, L.P. and Kern, T. "IT Outsourcing as Strategic Partnering: The Case of the UK Inland Revenue," *European Journal of Information Systems* (7:1), 1998, pp. 29-45.

Willcocks, L.P., Lacity, M.C. and Fitzgerald, G. "Information technology outsourcing in Europe and the USA: Assessment issues," *International Journal of Information Management* (15:5), 1995b, pp. 333-351.

Willcocks, L.P. and Lester, S. "Information Technology and Organizational Performance: Beyond the IT Productivity Paradox," in *Strategic Information Systems: Challenges and Strategies in Managing Information Systems*, R. D. Galliers, D. E. Leidner and B. S. H. Baker (Eds.), Butterworth-Heinemann, Oxford et al., 2000, pp. 551-572.

Williamson, O.E. *Markets and Hierarchies, Analysis and Antitrust Implications: A Study in the Economics of Internal Organization*, Free Press, New York, 1975.

Williamson, O.E. "Transaction Cost Economics: The Governance of Contractual Relations," *Journal of Law and Economics* (22:October), 1979, pp. 233-261.

Williamson, O.E. "The Economics of Organization: The Transaction Cost Approach," *American Journal of Sociology* (87:3), 1981a, pp. 548-577.

Williamson, O.E. "On the Nature of the Firm: Some Recent Developments," *Zeitschrift für die gesamte Staatswissenschaft – Journal of Institutional and Theoretical Economics* (137), 1981b, pp. 675-680.

Williamson, O.E. *The Economic Institutions of Capitalism: Firms, Markets, Relational Contracting*, Free Press, Collier Macmillan, New York, London, 1985.

Williamson, O.E. "Transaction Cost Economics," in *Handbook of Industrial Organization*, R. Schmalensee and R. D. Willig (Eds.), Amsterdam, New York, Oxford, Tokyo, 1990, pp. 135-182.

Williamson, O.E. "Strategizing, Economizing, and Economic Organization," *Strategic Management Journal* (12), 1991, pp. 75-94.

Williamson, O.E. "Markets, Hierarchies, and the Modern Corporation: An Unfolding Perspective," *Journal of Economic Behavior and Organization* (17), 1992, pp. 335-352.

Windsperger, J.v. "Transaktionskosten in der Theorie der Firma," *ZfB* (53:9), 1983, pp. 889-903.

Winter, R.P., Sarros, J.C. and Tanewski, G.A. "Reframing Manager`s Control Orientations and Practices: A Proposed Organizational Learning Framework," *The International Journal of Organizational Analysis* (5:1), 1997, pp. 9-24.

Winter, S.G. "On Coase, Competence and Corporation," *Journal of Law, Economics and Organization* (4), 1988, pp. 163-180.

Witt, P. *Corporate Governance-Systems im Wettbewerb*, DUV, 2002.

Witte, E. "Phasen-Theorem und Organisation komplexer Entscheidungsverläufe," *Zeitschrift für betriebswirtschaftliche Forschung* (20), 1968, pp. 625-647.

Witte, E. "Field Research on Complex Decision-Making Processes – The Phase Theorem," *International Studies of Management and Organization* (2), 1972, pp. 156-182.

Witte, E. "Decision Theory," in *Handbook of German Business Management*, E. Grochla and E. Gaugler (Eds.), C. E. Poeschel Verlag, Stuttgart, 1990, pp. 703-712.

Wold, H. "Soft Modeling; The Basic Design and Some Extensions," in *Systems under Indirect Observation: Causality, Structure, Prediction*, K. G. Jöreskog and H. Wold (Eds.), North-Holland, Amsterdam, 1982a, pp. 1-54.

Wold, H. "Systems Under Indirect Observations Using PLS," in *A Second Generation of Multivariate Analysis*, C. Fornell (Ed.), Praeger, New York, 1982b, pp. 325-347.

Wold, H. "Introduction to the Second Generation of Multivariate Analysis," in *Theoretical Empiricism: A General Rationale for Scientific Model-Building*, H. Wold (Ed.), Paragon House, New York, 1989a, pp. vii-xl.

Wold, H. *Theoretical Empiricism: A General Rationale for Scientific Model-Building*, Paragon House, New York, 1989b.

Yoshimori, M. "Who's Company is it? The Concept of the Corporation in Japan and the West," *Long Range Planning* (28), 1995, pp. 33-44.

Zaheer, A. and Venkatraman, N. "Determinants of Electronic Integration in the Insurance Industry: An Empirical Test," *Management Science* (40:5), 1994, pp. 549-566.

Druck: betz-druck GmbH, D-64291 Darmstadt
Verarbeitung: Buchbinderei Schäffer, D-67269 Grünstadt

GPSR Compliance

The European Union's (EU) General Product Safety Regulation (GPSR) is a set of rules that requires consumer products to be safe and our obligations to ensure this.

If you have any concerns about our products, you can contact us on ProductSafety@springernature.com

In case Publisher is established outside the EU, the EU authorized representative is:

Springer Nature Customer Service Center GmbH
Europaplatz 3
69115 Heidelberg, Germany

Batch number: 10725973

Printed by Printforce, the Netherlands